Wines and Spirits of the World

Familiar types of European wine bottles.

Top shelf (from left to right): the brown bottle of Rhine wines; the green bottle of Mosels; Chianti flask; amphora-shaped green Verdicchio bottle.

Second shelf (from left to right): standard Burgundy bottle; standard Bordeaux bottle; tall French Anjou rosé bottle.

Bottom shelf: in the background three Champagne bottles, the jeroboam, the magnum and the single bottle size.

In the foreground: typical wicker-bound Madeira flask; two Portuguese Vinho Verde flasks; an antique style Wood Port bottle and a standard Vintage Port bottle.

Frontispiece

Wines and Spirits of the World

Editor: Alec H. Gold

Assistant Editor: Mabel Blattner

Colour Photographs by Percy Hennell

Maps: Edward Blattner

FOLLETT PUBLISHING COMPANY: *Chicago*

© Copyright 1972

Virtue & Company Limited
London and Coulsdon
First edition 1968
Second edition (fully revised) 1972
Library of Congress Catalog Card Number: 71-177450
ISBN 0 695-80316-6

Printed in Great Britain by Billing & Sons Limited, Guildford and London

Publishers Note

Our intention in this book has been to give in one single volume a comprehensive, factual and detailed account of the wines and spirits of the world. To do this we have been fortunate in securing as contributors members of the Wine and Spirit Trade, all of whom are experts in their own specialised field. Their authoritative advice has been invaluable in compiling this complete guide on the subject of Wine and Spirits under the editorship of Mr. Alec H. Gold, a past Chairman of the Wine and Spirit Association of Great Britain.

Acknowledgements

The Publishers would like to thank, in addition to the contributors, all those who have given valuable assistance in the production of this book.

For additional colour photographs:
Dorland Advertising
Anthony Saunders-Davis

for line drawings:
Edward Blattner and James Hart

for black and white photographs:
Australian News and Information Bureau
Camera Press
Claude-François, Landon
Cyprus Trade Tourist Centre
Fox Photos
Gilbey Twiss
A. Gold
S. F. Hallgarten
Hungarian Information Office
Keystone Press
Nazeing Glass Works

Novosti Press
G. B. Palau
Pictorial Press
Press und Informationsamt der Bundesregierung
Swiss Tourist Office
Whitefriars Glass
Embassy of the Socialist Federal Republic of Yugoslavia

for invaluable editorial assistance and advice:
D. J. C. Peppercorn, M.W.

Contents

			Page
	WINE	*Alec H. Gold (*Past Chairman of Gilbeys Ltd.*)	1
Part 1	FRANCE		9
	Bordeaux	D. J. C. Peppercorn, M.W. (*Peter Dominic Ltd.*)	13
	Burgundy	D. J. C. Peppercorn, M.W.	77
	Champagne	V. L. Seyd (*Mentzendorff & Co. Ltd.*)	116
	Rhône	P. A. Hallgarten, Ph.D, F.R.I.C. (*S. F. & O. Hallgarten*)	138
	Loire	S. P. E. Simon, M.W. (*L. Rosenheim & Sons Ltd.*)	168
	Alsace	S. F. Hallgarten (*S. F. & O. Hallgarten*)	195
	Lesser-known Wines	G. Asher (*Asher Storey & Co. Ltd.*)	211
	GERMANY	S. F. Hallgarten (*S. F. & O. Hallgarten*) & P. A. Hallgarten, Ph.D, F.R.I.C.	221
		New German Wine Law	701
	LUXEMBOURG	S. F. Hallgarten	333
	ITALY	Dr. B. Roncarati	341
	SPAIN		361
	Sherry	M. Gonzalez (*Gonzalez Byass & Co. Ltd.*)	361
	Table Wines	C. E. Whitfield, M.W. (*Stowells of Chelsea Ltd.*)	379
	PORTUGAL		389
	Port Wine	G. F. Robertson (*Croft & Co. Ltd.*)	391
	Table Wines	G. F. Robertson	413

		Page
SWITZERLAND	R. W. Hooper (*Peter Dominic Ltd.*)	421
AUSTRIA	A. S. Hogg (*Peter Dominic Ltd.*)	427
HUNGARY	F. May (*F. & E. May Ltd.*)	431
YUGOSLAVIA	R. M. Scott (*Hellmers & Sons Ltd.*)	437
RUMANIA	A. S. Hogg	441
BULGARIA	A. S. Hogg	445
GREECE	A. S. Hogg	449
CYPRUS	A. Hughes (*Brown, Gore & Welch Ltd.*)	453
ISRAEL	S. F. Hallgarten (*S. F. & O. Hallgarten*)	461
U.S.S.R.	A. S. Hogg	465
U.S.A.	*See page x*	
CANADA	W. J. R. Goldie	469
CHILE	A. S. Hogg	473
TUNISIA	D. J. C. Peppercorn, M.W.	477
SOUTH AFRICA	H. M. E. Flockemann (*Gilbey-Santhagens (Pty.) Ltd.*)	481
AUSTRALIA	⋆J. F. Burgoyne (*P. B. Burgoyne & Co. Ltd.*)	497
MADEIRA	⋆A. J. B. Rutherford (*Rutherford, Osborne & Perkins Ltd.*)	513
VERMOUTH	⋆G. U. Salvi (*House of Seagram Ltd.*)	517
BRITISH WINES	D. Roberts (*Vine Products Ltd.*)	527
THE SERVING OF WINE	⋆J. K. Peppercorn (*United Vintners Ltd.*)	533
WINE TASTING	R. W. Hooper	541

⋆ Past Chairmen of Wine & Spirit Association of Great Britain

			Page
	SPIRITS	*Alec H. Gold (*Past Chairman of Gilbeys Ltd.*)	547
Part 2	Brandy (Cognac)	*Hon. F. F. Hennessy (*International Distillers & Vintners Ltd.*)	553
	(Armagnac)	E. Penning–Rowsell	
	Scotch Whisky	A. K. Watson (*Charles Mackinlay & Co. Ltd.*)	564
	Irish Whiskey	A. C. Crichton (*Irish Distillers Ltd.*)	581
	Canadian Whisky	J. S. Napier (*Gilbey (Canada) Ltd.*)	587
	American Whiskey	J. E. Bierworth (*National Distillers & Chemical Corporation*)	591
	Australian Whisky	*Alec H. Gold	595
	Gin	M. B. Henderson (*John Haig & Co. Ltd.*)	597
	Dutch Geneva	*M. Gordon Clark (*Matthew Clark & Sons Ltd.*)	605
	Vodka	R. A. Gold (*International Distillers & Vintners Ltd.*)	609
	Rum	G. B. Palau (*House of Seagram Ltd.*)	613
	Liqueurs, Bitters and Aperitifs	S. P. E. Simon, M.W. (*L. Rosenheim & Sons Ltd.*)	621
	U.S.A.	A C. McNally (*Heublein Inc:*)	631
	Cocktails, Punches and Cups	P. R. Brennan	653
	BEERS AND CIDERS	A. R. Motion (*Allied Breweries Ltd.*)	669
	APPENDICES		677
	British Drinking Glasses	J. W. Chance (*J. W. Chance Ltd.*)	679
	A Cellar of One's Own	D. J. C. Peppercorn, M.W.	693
	GLOSSARY		713
	INDEX		725

* Past Chairmen of Wine & Spirits Association of Great Britain

x

Colour Plates

European wine bottles   *Frontispiece*

Decanting   *Facing p. 32*

The Vintage at Château Yquem   *Facing p. 33*

Initiation Ceremony at St. Émilion   *Facing p. 64*

Château Ausone   *Facing p. 65*

Handling grapes at Château Pichon-Longueville
Baron   *Facing p. 128*

Écoulage and fermentation   *Facing p. 129*

Grape picking at Meursault   *Facing p. 160*

Hospice de Beaune   *Facing p. 160*

Vineyards at Moulin-à-Vent   *Facing p. 161*

Early wine bottles   *Facing p. 208*

Champagne cellars   *Following p. 208*

Assorted drinking glasses   *Following p. 208*

Well-known grape varieties   *Facing p. 209*

Hallgarten cellars   *Facing p. 256*

German wine bottles and glasses   *Facing p. 257*

The Mosel   *Facing p. 288*

Noble Rot   *Facing p. 289*

Alfresco lunch with Chianti   *Facing p. 352*

Types of Sherry   *Facing p. 353*

Port   *Facing p. 384*

Douro vineyard workers   *Facing p. 385*

Loading wine   *Facing p. 385*

Gin distillery   *Facing p. 590*

Cooperage   *Following p. 590*

Making a spirit-tight barrel by firing   *Following p. 590*

All-night checking of furnace in distillery   *Following p. 590*

Whisky—Mash Tun   *Facing p. 591*

      Still House   *Facing p. 591*

      Bottling   *Facing p. 591*

Brandy distillery   *Facing p. 606*

Making glass bottles   *Following p. 606*

Cognac stored in casks   *Following p. 606*

Bottling Chianti   *Following p. 606*

Cellars at Château Loudenne   *Following p. 606*

Grape picking at Château Loudenne   *Following p. 606*

Beachcomber Bar, Mayfair Hotel   *Following p. 606*

4th Hussar Bar, Washington Hotel   *Facing p. 607*

Black and White Illustrations

Château Loudenne	*Facing p. 96*
Examining grapes at Puligny-Montrachet	*Facing p. 96*
Château de Chasselas	*Following p. 96*
Grape gathering at Château Loudenne	*Following p. 96*
Vineyard cellar at Puligny-Montrachet	*Following p. 96*
An official of the Order of Chevaliers du Tastevin at a wine tasting ceremony	*Following p. 96*
Bottling	*Following p. 96*
Labelling of bottles	*Following p. 96*
"Remuage"	*Following p. 96*
Disgorgement	*Following p. 96*
Vine in blossom	*Following p. 96*
Protection against frost	*Following p. 96*
Vineyard sites at St. Goarshausen	*Facing p. 97*
Sculptured caskheads	*Facing p. 224*
Grape picking on the Rhine	*Following p. 224*

The oldest vine in the Palatinate   *Following p. 224*

Grape cakes   *Following p. 224*

Old style bottling   *Following p. 224*

Modern wine press house   *Following p. 224*

An old wine press   *Following p. 224*

Vintage time at Casale Monferrato, Piedmont   *Following p. 224*

Typical baskets and carts of Piedmont   *Following p. 224*

Nailed boots used in "treading" grapes   *Following p. 224*

Pressing of grape pulp for Sherry making   *Following p. 224*

"Must" in the early stages of Sherry making   *Following p. 224*

Sherry taster and assistant   *Following p. 224*

Weighing Sherry butt   *Facing p. 225*

Wine store in Madrid   *Facing p. 225*

The Douro Valley   *Facing p. 416*

Vintage time in Portugal   *Following p. 416*

Cooperage at Oporto   *Following p. 416*

Highest vineyards in Europe   *Following p. 416*

Vintage time in Switzerland   *Following p. 416*

Sampling wine in a Hungarian cellar   *Following p. 416*

Labelling Tokay wines   *Following p. 416*

Vintage time in Yugoslavia   *Following p. 416*

View of Yugoslav vineyard   *Following p. 416*

Grape picking in Moldavia, U.S.S.R.   *Following p. 416*

Wine tasting hall in Yalta   *Following p. 416*

Vintage time in Cyprus   *Following p. 416*

Vineyard in Southern Australia   *Following p. 416*

Grape picking in South Africa   *Facing p. 417*

"Nosing" Cognac at Hennessy's   *Facing p. 638*

Cognac cellars of Maison Otard   *Facing p. 638*

Overhauling the wine press   *Following p. 638*

Coopers' tools   *Following p. 638*

Taking the specific gravity of Whisky   *Following p. 638*

Testing Whisky for strength and purity *Following p. 638*

Cutting sugar cane for Rum   *Following p. 638*

Pulverising ingredients for Liqueur making   *Following p. 638*

Ingredients for Liqueur making   *Following p. 638*

Experimental fermentation in a modern brewery   *Following p. 638*

Mixing yeast   *Following p. 638*

Glass—Modern Swedish crystal   *Following p. 638*

    Basic traditional shape   *Following p. 638*

    Fine-stemmed glasses   *Following p. 638*

    Hand-made wine service in lead crystal   *Facing p. 639*

    Paris suite   *Facing p. 639*

    Hand-cut wine service   *Facing p. 639*

    Paris Pullman suite   *Facing p. 639*

Maps

France	*Page 10*
Bordeaux	*Page 12*
Médoc	*Page 36*
Graves, Sauternes	*Page 48*
Fronsac, Pomerol, St. Émilion	*Page 54*
Entre Deux Mers	*Page 74*
Burgundy	*Page 78*
Chablis	*Page 90*
Côte de Nuits	*Page 92*
Côte de Beaune	*Page 100*
Mâconnais, Beaujolais	*Page 108*
Champagne	*Page 116*
Côtes du Rhône	*Page 138*
Loire	*Page 168*
Alsace	*Page 196*
Germany	*Page 222*

Palatinate   *Page 248*

Rheinhessen   *Page 256*

Nahe, Mittel Rhein   *Page 264*

Rheingau   *Page 270*

Mosel, Saar-Ruwer   *Page 288*

Baden, Württemberg, Franconia   *Page 316*

Italy   *Page 342*

Jerez   *Page 360*

Spain   *Page 382*

Douro Valley   *Page 390*

Portugal   *Page 412*

Switzerland   *Page 422*

Austria   *Page 426*

Yugoslavia   *Page 438*

South Africa   *Page 480*

Australia   *Page 498*

Cognac   *Page 554*

Armagnac   *Page 556*

Eastern United States   *Page 634*

California   *Page 644*

Wines

WINE

"Wine cheers the sad, revives the old, inspires the young, makes weariness forget his toil, and fear her danger, opens a new world when this, the present, palls." (Byron)

WHAT IS WINE?

Wine is a romance. It is not the mystery which in the past deterred many would-be consumers for fear of displaying ignorance. The real mystery is the process of nature which converts the juice of the grape into wine.

In many countries wines are an agricultural crop grown either on a commercial scale or on small allotments just as an Englishman would grow his own vegetables. In such countries, wine is drunk every day, as regularly as an Englishman would drink beer.

In its simplest form, the production of wine is an entirely natural process. The sun produces sugar in the grape; on the skins of a ripe grape are millions of little yeast cells (which show as "bloom"). When the skin is broken, these yeasts dive into the sugar in the juice and start fermentation; the ferments die and there you have wine.

There are various minerals and phosphates in wine derived from the varying soil of different countries, and even of neighbouring vineyards, which impart to wine its different characteristics, but basically all wine is the same.

The vintage (or harvest) takes place every year, the time varying according to the country, and often the quantity and quality will vary from year to year influenced by the weather.

The vine flourishes in most countries, wherever there is sufficient sunshine to ripen the grapes. More and more countries are now offering their wines on the British market, so great has the interest in wine become.

The making of wine is centuries old and is frequently referred to in the Bible. The Romans introduced the vine into England, but the wine they drank was imported, either from France (Gaul) or Germany. Apart from one or two small private enterprises the making of wine from grapes grown in England is impracticable owing to our uncertain climate, although up to three hundred years ago a vineyard existed on the site of Olympia which supplied wine to the taverns of Kensington.

Whilst the basic principle of wine production sounds simple, nevertheless before it reaches the consumer wine has to be looked after with great care and cellar management, both at its birthplace and after it has crossed the sea. It is an art as well as a business. Like human beings, wine is susceptible to indisposition in early life, but by the time it reaches the consumer it will have been looked after at all stages by the shipper and bottler.

In the making of wine, the colour is contained in the skin of the grape. Grape juice, whether of red or white grapes, is an amber colour. When the skins are crushed, the colour mingles with the juice and the longer the skins are left in contact with the juice, the deeper the colour of a red wine becomes.

It is, therefore, possible to produce white wine from red grapes if the skins are separated from the juice immediately.

It used to be argued that the best machine for extracting the colour was the sole of the human foot, which is flexible enough to squeeze the colour from the skins without crushing the pips, which impart bitterness to the wine. This method, though harmless, since the subsequent fermentation removes any impurities from the wine, is now virtually obsolete.

WINE IN THE U.K. For a long time in the United Kingdom, wine, owing mainly to high Customs Duties levied by the Government, was drunk only by a privileged minority, but since the reduction of Duties, mainly on Table (or Beverage) Wines, in 1949, consumption has increased enormously and spread through all classes of society.

With this increase in the number of consumers, the spread of knowledge of wine among those whose task it is to purvey the goods to the public becomes all the more important.

Prior to 1927, there were for many years two rates of Customs Duty on wine, those below 30° Sikes bearing a lower rate than those above. In this period, Tarragona and Lisbon Wines (sweet fortified wines at 29°) enjoyed great popularity, but the Budget of 1927 altered the dividing line of strength between Table and Dessert Wines to 25° and the imports of these two wines were virtually killed at one stroke.

Then, in 1949, the Duty on Table Wines was reduced by 12s. per gallon, with the result that consumption rose from 3½ to 14 million gallons per annum today.

France, of course, had a long start with her Table Wines, especially when Bordeaux and district was part of England, and Claret (or *Clairet*, meaning clear wine) was shipped to England in exchange for wool.

Apart from the interruption of the Napoleonic Wars (though the Duke of Wellington seems to have continued to enjoy his

Claret) and later World Wars, France has continued to command the biggest share of the market in Great Britain.

With such an increasing number of countries exporting their wines to this country and with so great a choice, would-be consumers should be encouraged to try a selection until they find their own preference. Wine-drinking is a subject of absorbing interest, but it should be guided by personal judgement on what one likes rather than by snobbery of what one thinks one ought to like.

FASHIONS IN WINE

Fashions in wine and drinking habits have changed over the years. These changes have often been brought about by the fiscal policy of Governments or by scarcity caused by war.

In the eighteenth and nineteenth centuries, wine-drinking took place mainly with or after meals. After dinner Port would be drunk, often in large quantities, though in the nineteenth century, sometimes, Claret would be consumed both with and after dinner, older vintages being served with dessert.

Prior to the First World War, apart from some drinking of Sherry and Bitters before lunch, nothing was served before meals. For a dinner-party called for 8 p.m., the guests would arrive at a quarter to eight and there ensued the *mauvais quart d'heure* with no drinking or smoking.

After the war, the cocktail habit spread from the United States, to be followed by Sherry parties and then Wine and Cheese parties. Sherry, which had gone out of fashion in the 1900s, is now very much back in the picture as there are so many types, varying between very dry and sweet, that it has become an all-purpose wine which can be drunk at any time of day, either before or after a meal.

Marsala, which was popular in army messes as an alternative to Port after dinner, seems to have lost popularity, and where now is the "Port and Lemon" once so popular with the ladies, particularly in bars?

4

ENJOYMENT OF WINE

For the full enjoyment of wine, the eye, the nose and the palate all come into play: the eye to appreciate the colour; the nose to savour the aroma, and the palate for enjoyment of the taste. Thus wine should be drunk at leisure, when full enjoyment can be derived by all the senses. Fine wines should be sipped rather than gulped, although some of the cheaper varieties may be quaffed.

The eye and the nose are also important at the table, when the bottle is first opened, to ensure the wine is in perfect condition. Sometimes the wine may be cloudy through having become chilled or have thrown a deposit after some time in bottle, and this is where the eye comes into play. The nose is important to detect "corkiness". This is a musty smell, usually easy to detect. In spite of the most stringent precautions by both cork and wine merchants and intensive research, it is impossible to detect a cork so affected before use. The cause is unknown and its incidence haphazard, but luckily it is comparatively rare. Curiously, it occurs less frequently in the stronger or fortified wines. It is quite harmless, but it does spoil a bottle of wine so affected. This drill should always be carried out, whatever wine is being drunk, to ensure that neither you nor your guests are disappointed. Glasses should never be more than three-quarters filled, to allow the aroma to be savoured.

In the drinking of wine, some thought should be given to the food which accompanies it. There are a number of useful hints published on this, but a recommendation to drink white wine with fish need not preclude the enjoyment of a bottle of Claret with a fried sole.

Vintage charts are published as a guide to the best years in various districts, but, again, they need not be slavishly followed, as there is usually some good wine produced each year and not all wines bear, or need bear, the date of their birth. The charts, however, do help to indicate the more notable years, particularly in Claret.

Many travellers abroad nowadays find delightful wines which

never reach the British market. No merchant can possibly stock everything, and often these wines taste better in their birthplace than in the colder British climate, and many are too delicate, or not sufficiently well made, to stand the journey, subject as they would be to severe changes of temperature en route.

WINE NAMES   The nomenclature of wines is an interesting though somewhat controversial subject. Some anglicised words have become generic, but the use of geographical names of one country by another remains a matter of debate. Examples of anglicised words are Claret, Hock, Burgundy and Sherry. A recent British Court judgement on Sherry states that there is no Sherry other than that produced in Jerez. The expressions British Sherry, South African Sherry, Cyprus Sherry, Australian Sherry, and Empire Sherry, however, are allowed to be used because they had been in use for a lengthy period without objection. On the other hand Chablis and Sauternes, which are French place-names, are sometimes used by other countries to denote a type of wine, but, if clearly labelled, this does not deceive the consumer.

Up to the end of the nineteenth century one could find Port from Portugal, Spain and even France, but the word Port is now protected by Treaty and is reserved on the British market for wine from the limited area of the valley of the Douro in Portugal.

Similarly, by a recent decision of the British Courts, the name Champagne can now only be used for wine from the district so defined by the French Government.

Some countries use merely the names of types of grapes to describe their wines (for example Riesling), even though these names had their origin in another country.

No valid objection can be raised against this, for many vines have been exported from their original birthplace.

6

In the 1870s, the vines of Europe were attacked by the virulent disease phylloxera, a parasite which destroyed the roots of the vine. Despite lavish expenditure on treatments no cure was found and vineyards almost everywhere were devastated.

Eventually it was discovered that the roots of American vines, having survived an earlier attack, were now immune to the disease, so throughout Europe the original types of vine were grafted on to American roots though retaining their identity. For some time fears were expressed that the finest wines could never again be produced, but many magnificent vintages since have proved these fears groundless. Once again, the New World was called in to redress the balance of the Old.

PROPER USE
OF WINE

It is perhaps appropriate to sound a note of caution on the use, or rather misuse, of wine. Whilst ever seeking to broaden the consumption of wine, the wine trade of this country has consistently deplored any over-indulgence. Drunkenness is a social evil and can do harm not only to the individual but to the community and not least to the wine trade itself.

Taken in moderation, wine is a wonderful gift. It is a tonic not only to the body but to the spirit, and can make a success of the dullest party. An old monkish Latin doggerel runs:

"*Qui bene bibit, bene dormit*
Qui bene dormit cogitat non malum.
Qui cogitat non malum, nunquam peccat.
Qui nunquam peccat, salvandum est.
Ergo, qui bene bibit, salvandum est."

which being translated means:

"He sleepeth well who wisely drinks.
Who sleepeth well no evil thinks.
Who thinks no evil never sins.
Who sinneth not salvation wins.
Therefore who drinketh well
He shall be saved from Hell."

FRANCE

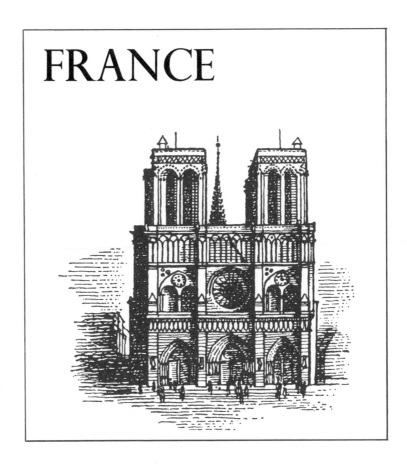

"Omnia Gallia in tres partes divisa est"

So wrote Julius Caesar and, although he was not referring solely to France or to wine-producing districts, the same phrase may be used to describe the wine districts of France today.

France may be divided roughly into three main parts for wine purposes, namely West, North-east and South.

FRANCE

Calvados

Paris

CHAMPAGNE

ALSACE

Chablis

LOIRE

Anjou

Muscadet

Touraine

Pouilly

Côte de Nuits
Côte de Beaune

BURGUNDY

JURA

Maconnais
Beaujolais

COGNAC

Côte Rôtie

BORDEAUX

Hermitage

Médoc

Pomerol
St.Emilion

Côtes du RHONE

Graves

Sauternes

Châteauneuf
du Pape

Tavel

PROVENCE

Armagnac

LANGUEDOC

The Western district stretches from the border of Spain north to the valley of the Loire. This includes the whole of the Bordeaux district, the River Loire and, of course, the spirit-producing districts of Cognac and Armagnac. Although not wine-producing, the apple-orchards of Normandy, the home of Calvados, also lie within this zone.

The North-eastern district includes Burgundy, Champagne, the Jura, Alsace and the upper part of the Rhône Valley.

The Southern district lies along the Mediterranean coast between Spain and Italy, embracing the southern part of the Rhône Valley.

Each of these main districts is dealt with in subsequent chapters, describing the principal wines produced in each.

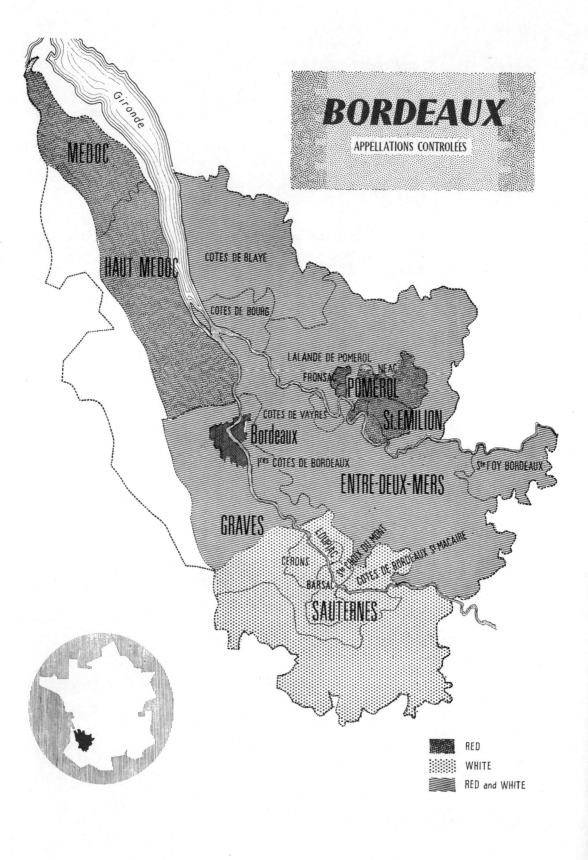

BORDEAUX

Bordeaux must certainly be the most complex of the great wine districts of France, or indeed of the world. The reason is not hard to find. It produces more fine wines than any other area, is large and varied geographically, and a great many of its wines are sold under the names of individual properties, in addition to the district name.

GEOGRAPHY

Geographically the vineyards of Bordeaux are clustered about the great rivers Garonne and Dordogne which then join together to form the mighty Gironde. The large triangular piece of land between the rivers is the Entre-deux-Mers. The city of Bordeaux itself lies on the Garonne. It has a population of a little over a quarter of a million and is the commercial centre of the region and its port. It is the greatest wine city in France and the whole wine trade of the region converges on it. From here one goes north into the Médoc for some fifty miles, south through Graves and into Sauternes for over thirty miles, and east to Libourne and St. Émilion, some twenty-five miles away.

Such a description goes some way to explaining the differences of climate which play such an important part in the great variations to be found in the wines of the region in any one year, but little to conjure up a picture of the city and region itself. The

13

different regions must wait for their respective sections, but this is the place for a brief word about the city.

Bordeaux is an immensely busy, bustling place. There are miles of docks on both sides of the river, and the traffic can justly claim to be about as bad as anywhere else you can think of. Parking is always a headache. There are fine wide streets converging on the theatre, an architectural gem built only a few years before the Revolution. In ancient and often shabby houses along the *quais* and in the narrow old streets leading off them are the offices and cellars of the great Bordeaux merchants, or *négociants* to give them their French name.

The structure of the wine trade here is fairly simple, at least in theory. There is the grower, the *courtier* or broker, and the *négociant*. The *courtier* knows and visits many hundreds of proprietors. He keeps them in touch with what is happening on the market and will have a fairly good idea as to what their wines will fetch. Then he goes to the *négociant* with his offers and his samples, where in turn his intimate knowledge of the way the growers are thinking, their willingness or reluctance to sell, are invaluable to the *négociant*.

Until quite recently even the greatest châteaux in Bordeaux were largely dependent on the *négociants* for the marketing of their wines, and the success or failure of a vintage in the early stages depended on the judgment of these merchants. Now the fame of the great wines is such that much depends on the reactions of their overseas markets in America, Scandinavia and England.

The *négociant's* most important function is and always has been the marketing of lesser known *bourgeois* growths and district or "generic" wines. The name of a great firm is often the customer's principal guarantee that the wine he is buying, whose name he has never heard of, is a good sound wine of good value. The most important firms in this respect are Calvet, Cruse, Eschenauer, Barton and Guestier, Sichel & Co., Mahler-Besse, Delor, Dourthe, Cordier, de Luze and Schroder & Schyler. In addition J. P. Moueix and Alexis Lichine are important firms specialising in château bottled wines and with a big business in America. Many changes are going on in the Bordeaux trade, foreshadowed perhaps by W. & A. Gilbey when they bought Château Loudenne in 1875 and proceeded to equip this beautiful spot in the Médoc as their base for the export of Bordeaux wines direct to England. Today this has been expanded, there is a French company, Domaines de Loudenne, and the firm acts as the *négociant* for the many firms of the International Distillers and Vintners Group such as Justerini & Brooks, Peter Dominic and Gilbey Vintners as well as exporting to the U.S.A. and many other markets.

Now Barton & Guestier are controlled by the giant Canadian distillers, Seagrams; Eschenauer belongs to the Liverpool shipping firm of Holt; John Harveys have bought Delor; while Sichels are, and indeed always have been, an English company. The many English connections can come as no surprise to anyone conscious of the close relationship which has existed between this country and the city of Bordeaux since the twelfth century. But Bordeaux has acted as a magnet to the merchants of many other countries, as the Dutch Mahler-Besse and the Danish Schyler bear witness.

In these days of large groups in the wine trade, the names of the Bordeaux shippers are no longer the only guarantee of quality and reliability for the public. Even companies which belong to organisations whose main *raison d'être* is brewing beer, today usually take a great deal of time and trouble in selecting their wines and employ men who are specialists in this field. Thus names like Grants of St. James's, Kinlochs, Stowells and Liggins are today well respected and have to some extent at least taken their place beside the old-established Wine Merchants such as Harveys, Christophers, Berrys, Averys and Skinner and Rook.

If we now leave Bordeaux and drive north into the Médoc or south to Graves and Sauternes, or east to the Entre-deux-Mers with Pomerol and St. Émilion beyond it, we come to the vineyards themselves where the story begins.

Unlike Burgundy, where the great wines are all produced from one grape, in Bordeaux there are a number of distinct varieties of vine, both for red and white grapes, and their distribution in a vineyard has much to do with the variety of wine to be found in the region. For red wine the principal varieties are: The Cabernet, of which there are two kinds, Cabernet Sauvignon and Cabernet Franc. The Cabernet Sauvignon is the classic vine for the production of red wine and is responsible for the particular characteristics of wine such as Mouton-Rothschild and Latour, where the proportion planted is very high. The Cabernet Franc has the advantage over its cousin of more abundant production. Next to the Cabernet, the most important grape in Bordeaux is now the Merlot with its advantage of plentiful production and early ripening. It has steadily been gaining ground in recent years, particularly in St. Émilion and Pomerol. It is, however, very susceptible to rot and the consequences of too great a reliance on this vine were to be seen in St. Émilion in 1963. Lastly, there are two vines of declining importance, the Malbec and the Petit Verdot. While no vineyards have ever been wholly planted with these vines, a small percentage of them in a vineyard has been found beneficial when blended in with the production from the Cabernet and Merlot.

As far as white wines are concerned, there are three vines: the Sémillon, which is the most widely planted vine in white wine districts; the Sauvignon, which produces a wine of more elegance than the Sémillon, but matures later and produces less. It is an indispensable component of any important vineyard. Finally, there is the Muscadelle. This is the least important of the white wine vines and the proportion planted is small.

The importance of this variety of vines is not difficult to appreciate. Obviously different soils produce different wines, but equally the same or very similar soils will produce a different result if their vineyards are planted in different proportions. For instance, a vineyard planted with 80 per cent Sauvignon, 10 per cent Merlot, 5 per cent Malbec and 5 per cent Petit Verdot will produce a wine with a different character to a vineyard planted with 50 per cent Merlot, 40 per cent Cabernet and 10 per cent

Malbec, and the proportions to be found from vineyard to vineyard, both within the same district and from one district to another, vary tremendously. This is why, in recent years, the wines from St. Émilion have matured more rapidly than those from the Médoc, leaving aside the differences of soil which have always tended towards producing more forward wines in the St. Émilion area. In the Médoc, although there has been a movement towards the more extensive planting of Merlot, the most important vine remains the Cabernet Sauvignon, while in St. Émilion the most widely planted vine is now the Merlot.

It should also be remarked that the considerable extent of the Bordeaux vineyards and their separation by the Gironde, the Garonne and Dordogne make for significant climatic variations especially as to rainfall, so that it is possible to have a successful year in St. Émilion but a mediocre one in the Médoc in the same year. This is one of many reasons why vintage charts should be treated with extreme caution.

VINTAGE

The next stage at which the quality of the wine may be influenced is during its vinification. The grapes are picked between the second half of September and early October. The red grapes are de-stalked and the already partially pulped Must is run off into fermentation vats. Here much will depend on the period during which the fermenting Must remains in contact with the skins from which it derives its colour as well as important acids. If the Must is run off too early the resulting wine will be near to a *Rosé*. If, on the other hand, the Must remains vatted with the skins for too long a period, the resulting wine may have too much acidity and will, therefore, be excessively astringent and slow to develop. This is not something which can be judged by rule of thumb, every year is different depending on the composition of the grapes, so that it is never possible to take a simple decision, as is often supposed, of making lighter wines for more rapid consumption. The balance of the wine has to be considered each year according to the proportions of sugars, acids and water in the Must. The great advance which modern controlled vinification has made is to try to ensure that excessively tannic wines which cannot be drunk or enjoyed for many years are eliminated, so that in years when there is the threat of excessive tannin, a reasonably well-balanced wine can be made which, while being full-bodied and long lasting, can be drunk with pleasure even if not at its best, within a reasonable period of time. From this point of view the 1961 vintage will be watched with great interest. Had it not been for modern methods, this would certainly have been a vintage like 1928, 1937 or 1945. There seems, however, to be every hope that it will prove a much better balanced wine than were the majority of wines produced in these years.

MATURING Once the wine has been made it is kept in casks, holding approximately 48 gallons. For the first year of its life the cask remains with its bung-hole upper-most, so that the wine lost through evaporation and from being absorbed into the new wood of the cask may be frequently and easily made good. Generally, when the wine is about a year old, the cask is tightly bunged up and placed on three-quarter bung, so that the hole is well covered with wine, even if a slight ullage appears in the cask. The period of rapid development is now completed and one of slower maturation, leading up to the time when the wine is ready to bottle, has now begun.

The red wines of Bordeaux are usually bottled at some time between eighteen months (for the small growths of Bourg or St. Émilion) and three years (for only a few great wines like Lafite and Latour these days) of age. But this, of course, also depends on the nature of the vintage. A wine of the 1960 vintage would have been bottled after a shorter period than that of 1961, the wines of 1960 being a good deal lighter than those of 1961. For white wines there is an important difference between dry wines and sweet wines. Dry wines are now usually bottled when about a year old, to preserve their freshness and to prevent maderisation. Sweet wines, on the other hand, being more robust are usually in wood for a similar period to red wines. Yquem, for example, is always kept in cask for three years, but this again is exceptional.

Bordeaux wines are either château bottled, bottled in Bordeaux by a *négociant*, or shipped to England in cask and bottled here by the importer. More and more wines are now being château bottled. This, of course, has the advantage of guaranteeing complete authenticity, and of disturbing the wine as little as possible during the vital change in its life from cask into bottle, but is only really possible or advisable for the more substantial châteaux. Nearly all the wines of lesser growths are removed by the *négociants* into their own cellars when they are about nine months old. This is for a variety of reasons; the merchant may feel that the proprietor is excellent at making his wine but not so good at looking after it in cask, his cellars may be unsatisfactory or too small to keep more than one year's crop in. Once in the *négociant's* cellars, the integrity of the *négociant* as well as his competence become of great importance. There are cases of fraud and wines are stretched, that is, the quantity of a particular wine is increased by the simple expedient of blending another wine of a similar character with it, usually a cheaper one for obvious reasons. This is where it is important to know who can be trusted; all the names mentioned earlier can be thoroughly relied upon in this respect. Where a wine is bottled in England two factors have to be considered: the competence of the English merchant in looking after and bottling the wine, and his judgment in buying from a reliable source. Again, this means knowing and relying on a good wine merchant.

APPELLATIONS

There is one other matter which must be mentioned at this stage: *Appellation Contrôlée*. Although the French laws of *Appellation Contrôlée* have no legal standing in this country, it is by no means certain that this will always be so, and in any case all wines imported in bottle inevitably come under these regulations. The object of these laws is as much to protect certain names and limit the amount of wine that can be sold under them as to indicate the origins of a wine, as the name would imply. For example, each individual *appellation*, such as Sauternes or Margaux, has a regulation as to quantity, so many gallons of wine per acre only are entitled to the *appellation*; if more than this is made it has to be sold under a lesser name such as Bordeaux

Supérieur and, of course, commands a lower price, although there may be no difference in the two wines. Again, the way the laws work in individual cases may seem confusing. No white wine produced in the Médoc, for example, is entitled to the Médoc *appellation*, it may only be called Bordeaux Supérieur. The same applies to the white wines of St. Émilion. In Graves there are two categories of white wine, Graves and Graves Supérieur, but only one for red wines, Graves. Château Ville-georges at Moulis has some vineyards enjoying the Moulis *appellation*, some which are Listrac and others still which are Margaux. The net result is that the wine of the château being a blend of all these elements can only use the inferior *appellation* Haut Médoc which is, so to speak, the lowest common denominator. But as these brief remarks may have suggested, this is far too complex a subject to embark upon here.

SERVING

By the time a bottle of Bordeaux wine arrives upon the shelf of an off-licence or the dispense of a restaurant, a great deal of skill, experience and care has gone into ensuring that within its class it is the best. Nothing that happens now can improve upon what is in the bottle, but unhappily much can and does occur to undo these patient years of care on the part of grower, *négociant* and wine merchant.

Fortunately in most cases the storage of a wine in an off-licence or a restaurant is but a transitory affair. Nevertheless, even a few weeks of storage at unsuitable or violently fluctuating temperatures can do irreparable harm. Heat and light are the great enemies of wine, so that the bright modern display units under powerful lights are hardly an ideal place to store wine for any length of time, although, of course, admirable for display purposes. The important thing here is that if a bottle is not sold it should not be allowed to remain indefinitely exposed to such adverse conditions.

When it comes to serving Bordeaux wines, whether in a restaurant or in the home, the question of temperature is of considerable importance. The wines of the Médoc with their tendency, particularly if not fully mature, to astringency, have a special need to be served at the temperature of a warm room in winter, In summer temperatures the task is of course simpler. Here the important thing is not to carry out the transformation too rapidly for red wines. The ice bucket is all right for white wines, although a refrigerator is probably preferable, but the hot-water tap is pure murder for any decent red wine, and because glass is such a poor conductor of heat, several hours in a warm room are usually necessary to achieve the desired result.

On the subject of decanting it will suffice here to say that Bordeaux red wines of any age nearly always benefit from being decanted, particularly as they frequently throw a deposit after three or four years in bottle. Two hours for a big, robust, fairly young wine, one hour for lighter or older wines, half an hour for anything really old or anything you are uncertain about, is a good general rule which experience of the behaviour of individual wines will render more exact. The proper function of the wine cradle is to bring the bottle from its bin to the place where it is to be uncorked and decanted. If a wine has no sediment there is no possible point in serving it in a wine basket; if it has a sediment this will soon be roused if the wine is served from a basket, and the second half of the bottle may be cloudy.

What faults is a Bordeaux wine likely to display in bottle? The most popular fallacy is the "corked" bottle, something every novice longs to detect, especially before a suitable audience. In fact the corked bottle is, mercifully, a remarkably rare occurrence even amongst old bottles. When it does occur it is an unmistakable tainting of the wine and will get worse the longer the wine is exposed to the air. The corked bottle which improves after it is opened is the one which was a figment of the oversusceptible imagination to start with. If a red wine has been badly looked after in cask either by the *négociant* or the English wine merchant, it may suffer from a degree of volatile acidity which will make it unpleasant to drink. Fortunately, this is rare, but to confuse matters certain vintages such as 1947 and 1957 have early in their careers displayed a degree of acidity which could be easily mistaken for this malady. Should this occur there is one sure test. If the wine is fatally affected it will continue to deteriorate. On the other hand, if the wine is merely passing through a difficult stage, a little patience will soon be rewarded with a drinkable wine.

It is fashionable these days to give long and complex lists of what food can or should accompany any particular wine. The exercise is largely self-defeating because the thing becomes so cumbersome and long-winded that nobody could possibly remember at the end of it what he was supposed to do. It is much nearer to the truth to say that, with a few exceptions, most wines will go with most foods, but that they will be shown to better advantage when drunk with some foods than with others. As far as the red wines of Bordeaux are concerned, they are an ideal accompaniment to a very wide range of meat or game and it is largely a question of selecting the right vintage so that one drinks a big wine or a light wine; or of one's particular preference as between the Médocs, St. Émilions, Pomerols and Graves rather than any hard-and-fast rule that St. Émilion should be drunk with this dish or Margaux with that dish. As far as white wines are concerned, it again depends on taste. The fine, dry white Graves are an admirable accompaniment to oysters or to most hors-d'oeuvres. In Bordeaux they are very keen on drinking Sauternes with *pâté de foie gras*, rather a powerful combination for the taste of most English people. It should also be remembered that red wine always goes better with cheese than white wine, that a light Claret can be drunk with salmon or with lobster when it is cooked with a cheese sauce, and that while Sauternes, Barsac and St. Croix du Mont are admirable with puddings and desserts, they are killed by any chocolate flavoured dish.

EVALUATION
OF VINTAGES

No introductory survey to the wines of Bordeaux would be complete without some mention of the vexed question of the evaluation of vintages. It is the opinion of the writer that much confusion and harm is done by failing to differentiate between different styles of wine. The vintages of Bordeaux red wines can broadly be divided into two categories: slow maturing wines and quick maturing wines. Red wines generally mature slowly because they have a high tannin content, but it can also happen, as with the 1957s, that although the wines are not very full-bodied they have rather a high degree of acidity and therefore take some time to mellow. Slow maturing wines in their early years tend to be rough and astringent, when mature they are full-bodied and usually develop a fine flavour. If, however, as sometimes happens, the balance between tannin on one hand and fruit and sugar on the other fails to achieve equilibrium, the wine may remain hard and ungrateful throughout its life. Thus slow maturing wines are not always the best wines, and sometimes a long wait for a wine to reach maturity is not adequately rewarded. On the other hand, it is a fallacy to suppose that quick maturing vintages are short-lived. Perhaps the most famous example of a quick maturing vintage which has lived long is the now legendary 1900 vintage. Wines are generally quick maturing because they are what is called in the trade "well balanced". In other words, there is an almost ideal equilibrium between the wine's various elements which very early on in its life makes it agreeable to drink. But once having achieved such an equilibrium, wines often go on for many, many years without deteriorating. The table below gives the writer's personal evaluation of vintages since the war; the marks awarded have the following significance:

1 Poor average standard.
2 Mediocre, but some worth while-wines.
3 A reasonable proportion of useful, average quality wines, but needs careful selection.
4 Classic wines in need of selection and not quite of the highest class.
5 Very fine all-round vintage.
6 Very exceptional vintage.

It will be seen that allowance has been made for the fact that one of the difficulties of evaluating vintages is to decide on what is the overall impression of a particular year. In all but the most outstanding years, there is usually a certain proportion of unsatisfactory or indifferent wines, and sometimes in a poor year there are a handful of quite respectable, drinkable wines. These factors have to be taken into account when evaluating a vintage and must also be borne in mind when attempting to sell the wine of a year with a poor reputation to a customer. On this score it is usually safe to say that because of the resistance to vintages with an indifferent reputation, the selections made by good wine merchants in this country of such years are generally to be trusted, since the wine merchant knows they will not be easy to sell merely on reputation.

Quick Maturing		*Slow Maturing*	
1969	4	1961	6
1968	2	1959	5
1967	4	1957	4
1965	1	1956	1
1964	5	1955	5
1963	1	1952	5
1962	5	1949	5
1960	3	1948	3
1958	3	1947	5
1954	2	1945	6
1953	6		
1951	1		
1950	4		

MÉDOC

The Médoc is at once the largest and most important red wine district of Bordeaux. For many English Claret lovers Médoc is practically synonymous with Claret, for although it is the most recently planted of the great red wine districts, it assumed a pre-eminence in the nineteenth century which has left its mark. When an official classification was made in 1855 for the Paris Exhibition, Haut Brion in the Graves was the only red wine in Bordeaux that was accorded a place with the wines of the Médoc, and the English wine trade, always inclined to conservatism, has tended to enshrine this Médoc ascendancy when connoisseurs in other lands allowed at least an equal footing to the great wines of Pomerol, St. Émilion and Graves.

This seems as good a place as any to say something on the subject of classification. The object of a classification is to provide the public with some guide as to the relative standing of the many individual wines that are produced. When it is realised that there are sixty-one classified great growths in the Médoc alone, and several hundred lesser wines classified as *bourgeois* growths, both the necessity for providing a guide and the difficulty in deciding what to put in and what to omit are immediately apparent. The 1855 classification is remarkable for the fact that, in spite of all the changes both in the ownership of châteaux and of the composition of their vineyards over the last hundred years, it remains a very good guide. But, as with any such list which has never been revised, it now has certain serious drawbacks as a practical guide, for while it includes all the finest growths, it omits some very worthy ones, and includes some with rather tenuous claims today, including one which for some years has produced no wine at all under its own name. If the wine-drinking public is to be provided with a practical guide instead of an historical document, a revised and simplified list is essential, and there must be provision for its periodic revision. When all this has been said it must be realised that any classification can only be regarded and must only be used as a form book. As with race-horses the best breed will not always produce the winner, and an outsider can sometimes steal the show.

CLASSIFICATION

Here is the classification of 1855, followed by the proposal sponsored by the *l'Institut National des Appellation d'Origine* in 1961—not as yet adopted.

1855 CLASSIFICATION

1st Growths (*1ers Crus*)	*Communes*
Château Lafite-Rothschild	Pauillac
Margaux	Margaux
Latour	Pauillac
Haut-Brion	Pessac (Graves)

2nd Growths (*2es Crus*)

Château Mouton Rothschild	Pauillac
Rausan-Ségla	Margaux
Rauzan-Gassies	Margaux
Léoville-Las-Cases	St. Julien
Léoville-Poyferré	St. Julien
Léoville-Barton	St. Julien
Durfort-Vivens	Margaux
Gruaud Larose	St. Julien
Lascombes	Margaux
Brane-Cantenac	Cantenac (Margaux)
Pichon-Longueville (Baron)	Pauillac
Pichon-Longueville (Comtesse Lalande)	Pauillac
Ducru-Beaucaillou	St. Julien
Cos-d'Estournel	St. Estèphe
Montrose	St. Estèphe

3rd Growths (*3es Crus*)

Château Kirwan	Cantenac (Margaux)
Issan	Cantenac (Margaux)
Lagrange	St. Julien
Langoa	St. Julien
Giscours	Labarde (Margaux)
Malescot-St. Exupéry	Margaux
Cantenac-Brown	Cantenac (Margaux)
Boyd-Cantenac	Margaux
Palmer	Cantenac (Margaux)
La Lagune	Ludon
Desmirail	Margaux
Calon-Ségur	St. Estèphe
Ferrière	Margaux
Marquis d'Alesme-Becker	Margaux

4th Growths (*4es Crus*)

Château St. Pierre-Sevaistre	St. Julien
St. Pierre-Bontemps	St. Julien
Talbot	St. Julien

Château Branaire-Ducru	St. Julien
Duhart-Milon	Pauillac
Pouget	Cantenac (Margaux)
La Tour-Carnet	St. Laurent
Rochet	St. Estèphe
Beychevelle	St. Julien
Le Prieure-Lichine	Cantenac (Margaux)
Marquis-de-Terme	Margaux

5th Growths (*5es Crus*)

Château Pontet-Canet	Pauillac
Batailley	Pauillac
Haut-Batailley	Pauillac
Grand Puy Lacoste	Pauillac
Grand Puy Ducasse	Pauillac
Lynch-Bages	Pauillac
Lynch-Moussas	Pauillac
Dauzac	Labarde (Margaux)
Mouton d'Armailhacq	Pauillac (Margaux)
Le Tertre	Arsac
Haut-Bages-Liberal	Pauillac
Pedesclaux	Pauillac
Belgrave	St. Laurent
Camensac	St. Laurent
Cos-Labory	St. Estèphe
Clerc-Milon	Pauillac
Croizet-Bages	Pauillac
Cantemerle	Macau

I.N.A.O. CLASSIFICATION OF 1961

Premiers Grands Crus Classes Exceptionnels:

Château Lafite-Rothschild	Pauillac
Latour	Pauillac
Margaux	Margaux
Mouton-Rothschild	Pauillac

Premiers Grands Crus Classes:

Château Beychevelle	St. Julien

Château Brane-Cantenac	Margaux
Calon Ségur	St. Estèphe
Cantemerle	Haut-Médoc
Cos d'Estournel	St. Estèphe
Ducru-Beaucaillou	St. Julien
Gruaud Larose	St. Julien
Lascombes	Margaux
Léoville Barton	St. Julien
Léoville-Las-Cases	St. Julien
Léoville Poyferré	St. Julien
Lynch-Bages	Pauillac
Malescot-St. Exupéry	Margaux
Montrose	St. Estèphe
Palmer	Margaux
Pichon-Longueville (Baron de Pichon)	Pauillac
Pichon-Longueville (Comtesse de Lalande)	Pauillac
Pontet-Canet	Pauillac
Rauzan-Gassies	Margaux
Rausan-Ségla	Margaux
Talbot	St. Julien

Grands crus classes:

Château Batailley	Pauillac
Bel-Air-Marquis d'Aligre	Margaux
Boyd-Cantenac	Margaux
Branaire-Ducru	St. Julien
Cantenac-Brown	Margaux
Chasse-Spleen	Moulis
Cos-Labory	St. Estèphe
Duhart-Milon	Pauillac
Dutruch-Grand-Poujeaux	Moulis
Giscours	Margaux
Gloria	St. Julien
Grand Puy Ducasse	Pauillac
Grand Puy Lacoste	Pauillac
Gressier-Grand-Poujeaux	Moulis
Haut-Batailley	Pauillac

28

Château d'Issan	Margaux
Kirwan	Margaux
La Begorce	Margaux
La Lagune	Haut-Médoc
Lanessan	Haut-Médoc
Langoa-Barton	St. Julien
La Tour-de-Mons	Margaux
Le Prieure-Lichine	Margaux
Marquis de Terme	Margaux
Meyney	St. Estèphe
Mouton Baron Philippe	Pauillac
de Pez	St. Estèphe
Phélan-Ségur	St. Estèphe
Poujeaux	Moulis
Siran	Margaux

In addition to these classifications dealing solely with the Médoc, Alexis Lichine has proposed a more radical solution, a classification embracing on one list the wines of all the great red wine districts. It is a bold concept in that it attempts to compare the wines of widely differing districts. This is at once its attraction and its weakness, for although there is sufficient similarity between the wines of the Médoc and of Graves to permit some useful comparison, as was in fact admitted in 1855 by the inclusion of Haut Brion, the wines of St. Émilion and Pomerol are so different as to make a direct comparison difficult and indeed misleading. As far as the Médoc is concerned it is the present writer's personal opinion that the net has been cast a little too widely. For the sake of interest and comparison the Lichine classification is given below.

ALEXIS LICHINE CLASSIFICATION

Crus Hors Classes (Outstanding Growths)

MÉDOC

Château Lafite-Rothschild	Pauillac
Latour	Pauillac

Château Margaux	Margaux
Haut-Brion	Pessac (Graves)
Mouton-Rothschild	Pauillac

ST. ÉMILION

Château Cheval Blanc
Ausone

POMEROL

Château Petrus

Crus Exceptionnels (Exceptional Growths)

MÉDOC

Château Beychevelle	St. Julien
Brane-Cantenac	Cantenac-Margaux
Calon-Ségur	St. Estèphe
Cantemerle	Macau
Cos d'Estournel	St. Estèphe
Ducru-Beaucaillou	St. Julien
Gruaud-Larose	St. Julien
Lascombes	Margaux
Léoville-Barton	St. Julien
Léoville-Las-Cases	St. Julien
Léoville Poyferré	St. Julien
Lynch-Bages	Pauillac
Montrose	St. Estèphe
Palmer	Cantenac-Margaux
Pichon-Longueville	Pauillac
Pichon-Longueville (Comtesse de Lalande)	Pauillac
Rausan-Ségla	Margaux

ST. ÉMILION

Château Belair
      Canon
      Figeac
Château Gaffelière-Naudes

POMEROL

Château La Conseillante
      Vieux-Château-Certan
      l'Evangile

GRAVES

Domaine de Chevalier	Léognan
Château La Mission-Haut-Brion	Pessac

Grands Crus (Great Growths)

MÉDOC

Château Branaire-Ducru	St. Julien
Duhart-Milon	St. Julien
Durfort	Margaux
Giscours	Margaux
Grand Puy Lacoste	Pauillac
d'Issan	Cantenac-Margaux
La Lagune	Ludon
Malescot-St. Exupéry	Margaux
Mouton Baron Philippe	Pauillac
Pontet Canet	Pauillac
Château Prieure-Lichine	Cantenac-Margaux
Rauzan-Gassies	Margaux
Talbot	St. Julien

ST. ÉMILION

Château Clos Fourtet
      Magdelaine
      Pavie

POMEROL

Château Certan de May
      Lafleur
      Lafleur-Petrus
      Petit-Village
      Trotanoy

GRAVES

Château Haut Bailly   Léognan
      Pape-Clément   Pessac

Crus Supérieurs (Superior Growths)

MÉDOC

Château Batailley	Pauillac
Chasse Spleen	Moulis
Ferrière	Margaux
Gloria	St. Julien-Beychevelle
Grand Puy Ducasse	Pauillac
Haut Batailley	Pauillac
Kirwan	Cantenac-Margaux
Langoa Barton	St. Julien
Marquis d'Alesme-Becker	Margaux
La Tour-de-Mons	Saussons-Margaux
Marquis-de-Terme	Margaux

ST. ÉMILION

Château l'Angelus
      Beauséjour-Duffau-Lagarosse
      Beauséjour-Fagouet
      Canon La Gaffelière
      Croque Michotte
      Cure-Bon-la-Madelaine
      Larcis Ducasse
      Ripeau
      Trottevieille
      Villemaurine

Decanting magnums of old Claret. On the right an interesting early French wine jug.

The vintage at Château Yquem. The grapes are the selected ones with "Noble Rot".

POMEROL

Château Beauregard
        Certan-Giraud
Clos de l'Église-Clinet
Clos l'Eglise
Château Lagrange
        La Pointe
        Latour-Pomerol
        Nénin

GRAVES

Château Carbonnieux	Léognan
Malartic-Lagravière	Léognan
Smith-Haut-Lafitte	Martillac
La Tour-Haut-Brion	Talence
La Tour-Martillac	Martillac

Bons Crus (Good Growths)

MÉDOC

Château Angludet	Margaux
Château Bel-Air-Marquis d'Aligre	Soussans-Margaux
Belgrave	St. Laurent
Boyd-Cantenac	Cantenac-Margaux
Capbern	St. Estèphe
Clerc-Milon-Mondon	Pauillac
Cos Labory	St. Estèphe
Croizet-Bages	Pauillac
Dutruch-Lambert	Moulis
Fourcas-Dupré	Listrac
Fourcas-Hostein	Listrac
Cru Gressier-Grand-Poujeaux	Moulis
Château Haut-Bages-Liberal	Pauillac
Lagrange	St. Julien

Lanessan	Cussac
Lynch-Moussas	Pauillac
Les Ormes-de-Pez	St. Estèphe
Paveil	Soussans-Margaux
de Pez	St. Estèphe
La Tour-Carnet	St. Laurent
Phélan-Ségur	St. Estèphe
Poujeaux-Theil	Moulis
St. Pierre	St. Julien
Siran	Margause

ST. ÉMILION

Château Baleau
    Balestard La Tonnelle
    Cap de Mourlin
    Chatelet
    La Clotte
    Corbin (Giraud)
    Corbin-Michotte
    Coutet
    La Dominique
    Fanroque
    St. Georges Côte Pavie
    Grand-Barrail-Lamarzelle-Figeac
    Grand-Corbin
    Grand-Corbin-Despagne
    Grandes Murailles
Clos des Jacobins
    Soutard
Château La Tour-du-Pin-Figeac-Moueix
    Troplong Mondot

POMEROL

Château La Croix
    La Croix-de-Gay
Château Feytit-Clinet
    La Fleur-Pournet
    Gombaude-Guillot

Château Mazeyres
Rouget
de Sales

GRAVES

Château Bouscaut   Cadaujac
Fieuzal   Léognan

CHARACTERISTICS

In spite of wide variations of style and emphasis all the wines of the Médoc region possess a decided family likeness which gives a unity to the whole area. It is never, however, an easy matter to convey nuances of bouquet and flavour, the best that can be done is to describe some of the most characteristic traits which an intelligent observer may with practice and patience detect. In nearly all good years Médoc wines have in their early years some degree of astringency, but this does not mean that they are full-bodied wines in the sense that Burgundies are. It does mean that ageing in bottle is essential. I remember one case of a *bourgeois* growth of the light 1960 vintage which did not truly begin to reveal itself until it had been two years in bottle. This is typical of the elegant, almost nervous quality of Médoc wines. With age their bouquet grows in subtlety and fragrance, like a beautiful bud slowly unfurling to reveal the full majesty of the flower within.

The charges most often levelled against Médoc wines are that they are sharp and dry. This astringency, so long as it is not excessive, is an essential element in these wines, and the remedy is not to be in too great a hurry to drink good Médoc. Dryness so called is part of the same thing. Except in poor years when official permission has been granted, the wines of Bordeaux, unlike those of Burgundy, may not be chaptalised, so these are completely natural, unadorned and fully fermented wines. In great years they may possess a certain amount of glycerine naturally acquired from the soil which imparts a velvety quality to the wine, and often in old age they acquire a delicious quality which we enthuse over as sweetness, though it is a magical semblance rather than what most people would truly call sweetness. These

Médoc

MEDOC

Soulac

Bégadan

St. Christoly - de Médoc

St. Yzans

Potensac
Ordonnac

Lesparre

St. Germain d'Esteuil

St. Seurin - de Cadourne

Vertheuil

SAINT ESTÈPHE

Cissac

PAUILLAC

St. SAUVEUR

SAINT JULIEN

St. LAURENT
de Médoc

HAUT MEDOC

CUSSAC

LAMARQUE

LISTRAC

ARCINS

MOULIS

SOUSSANS

AVENSAN

MARGAUX

CANTENAC

Castelnau

LABARDE

MACAU

ARSAC

LUDON

le Pian - Medoc

Parempuyre

Blanquefort

le Taillan

Gironde

Dordogne

Garonne

classic qualities are the result of the judicious mixture of Cabernet and Merlot vines in a soil for the most part very poor, a mixture of gravel, flint and clay, laying on a series of planes and small plateaux which towards the north of the region assume the proportion of ridges and hills.

Generally speaking the wines of the Médoc have a tendency towards softness and lightness in the south and gradually acquire more body and robustness with some loss of delicacy as one goes north. In terms of *appellation contrôlée* the region has two general *appellations*, Haut Médoc, which is the southern portion of the region to a point just north of St. Estèphe, and Médoc, the northern part. But within the Haut Médoc there are six further more specific and highly rated *appellations:* Margaux, St. Julien, Moulis, Listrac, Pauillac and St. Estèphe. We shall deal with each of these in detail and then take some note of the more important communes which lie in the Haut Médoc and Bas Médoc, as the area of the Médoc *appellation* is traditionally known.

Haut Médoc

MARGAUX Some intelligence and good sense not always associated with vinous law-makers has been shown here in that the Margaux *appellation* has been extended to include neighbouring areas producing wines of a very similar style, thus most vineyards in the communes of Arsac and Labarde to the south, and of Cantenac and Soussans to the north now have the right to the great name of Margaux. The wines of this region are characterised by their perfumed delicacy and great breed and elegance, they are not big wines for the most part but have great finesse, and are very clean and fresh on the palate. These are the most feminine wines of the Médoc, the most akin to their cousins across the river in St. Émilion in their soft velvety texture.

CHÂTEAU MARGAUX itself has had its ups and downs and in the last generation has not been the most consistent of the first growths, yet at its best it is incomparable for its refinement and distinction and there is evidence that it is now firmly on the upward path once more.

There is an imposing array of classified growths in the region. The most notable are:

RAUSAN-SÉGLA and RAUZAN-GASSIES: Two but rather different wines, with a tendency to be rather robust and stubborn at first. Have both had a lean patch recently.

LASCOMBES: The reconstituted vineyard is making steady progress, a flowery full-flavoured wine of breed.

DURFORT-VIVENS: Just starting out on a new life with a new proprietor. This vineyard is in the best part of Margaux and the wine should be worth watching in the future.

PALMER: Rich and fairly full-bodied, of second growth standard today and generally considered among the best wines of the region.

BRANE-CANTENAC: A Margaux of the Palmer type but rather lighter.

GISCOURS: A very graceful perfumed wine at its best, but not as consistent as one could wish.

MALESCOT-ST.- EXUPÉRY: On the light side, but a wine of finesse and distinction.

ISSAN: After a recent change in ownership this famous old property should re-establish its reputation.

PRIEURE-LICHINE: The wine has greatly improved of late, and is very fruity and elegant.

FERRIERE: The very small quantity of fine wine is carefully made. A wine of character.

MARQUIS-DE-TERME: maintains a consistent standard. A wine of finesse.

LE TERTRE: Came under new management in the early 1960s. Since 1964 has been producing wines of real breed and distinction.

In addition to these classified growths it should be noted that BEL-AIR-MARQUIS D'ALIGRE, LA TOUR-DE-MONS and SIRAN are now generally regarded as being of classed growth quality, and are consistently producing wines of finesse and breed.

Amongst the other *cru bourgeois* the following are sometimes seen in this country and are worthy of note:

ANGLUDET, PAVEIL DE LUZE, LA BEGORCE, L'ABBÉ-GORSSE, LA BEGORCE-ZÉDE, PONTAC-LYNCH, MARTINENS.

ST. JULIEN

This *appellation* is limited to the confines of the commune of this name. The wines produced here are particularly fine, having more body and vinosity than those of Margaux, but more finesse and suppleness than those of Pauillac. Generic wines sold under this name are to be viewed with some suspicion as a high proportion of the wine produced is sold under the name of individual châteaux, and apart from poor years the quantity of genuine St. Julien for sale under the generic *appellation* is not large and is never cheap.

There is a formidable array of classified growths here, nearly all making high quality wines:

LEOVILLE-LAS-CASES, LEOVILLE POYFERRÉ, LEOVILLE-BARTON.

These three are often considered to be the best of the second growths. Las-Cases, a wine of great character and breed, is usually the best of the three, and sometimes the Barton is better than the Poyferré, sometimes vice versa.

DUCRU-BEAUCAILLOU: The quality and reputation of this château has steadily grown in recent years. Today it is often a close rival to Léoville-Las-Cases as the best St. Julien. A wine of great elegance, it tends to be more generous than the Léovilles.

GRUAUD-LAROSE: maintains a high quality, with rather more body than Ducru but with less finesse.

BEYCHEVELLE: At its best this wine is of second growth quality. There has been some inconsistency in recent years but there are now signs of better things.

LANGOA-BARTON and TALBOT: Two good consistent wines of character without being quite in the first flight.

BRANAIRE-DUCRU: Big, full-bodied, robust wine which has made great strides in recent years.

LAGRANGE: A consistent wine of average quality.

In addition to these GLORIA is today considered to be of classified growth quality, the wine is rich and fine. CHÂTEAU DU GLANA is another *cru bourgeois* which is quite often seen in this country.

MOULIS

This is in fact a rather misleading *appellation* as all the best growths are around the village of Grand Poujeaux. The importance of this region has greatly increased in recent years as the sterling quality of many of its wines was recognised.

The wines are rich and powerful with some finesse and a very distinctive flavour and style.

There are no classified growths in the region, but it is generally agreed that four wines are today of sufficient standing to merit inclusion in any new classification. They are:

CHASSE SPLEEN: a wine of considerable finesse and breed.
POUJEAUX-THEIL: a wine of power and consistency.

40

DUTRUCH–GRAND–POUJEAUX
GRESSIER–GRAND–POUJEAUX
} distinctive wines which combine richness and vinosity with finesse.

Mention should also be made here of VILLEGEORGES, for although the château buildings are in Avensan and the *appellation* is Haut Médoc, the most important parts of the vineyard are in Moulis and the wine closely resembles those of this region. It is very full-bodied and powerful and not far behind the four wines mentioned above in quality.

Bourgeois growths worth looking out for are:

CLOSERIE–GRAND–POUJEAUX, MOULIN–À–VENT, MAUCAILLOU, POMEYS, BRILLETTE, DUPLESSIS, TESTERON, MOULIS and BOUQUEYRAN.

LISTRAC

The district adjoins that of Moulis. The wines are consistent and fine without quite the richness or power of Moulis, and the best growths are just a little less fine than the best of Moulis. The best growths are:

FOURCAS–HOSTEIN, FOURCAS–DUPRÉ, FONREAUD, LESTAGE, SEMEILLAN, PIERRE BIBIAN and VEYRIN.

It should also be noted that the Cave Co-operative here, which sells under the name of Ch. Grand Listrac, is of outstanding quality for a Co-operative with one of the best reputations in the whole Médoc.

PAUILLAC

The largest wine producing commune in the Médoc. The great Pauillacs have a regal quality unsurpassed among Bordeaux wines. The bouquet is powerful but elegant and distinctive, and the wines possess a marvellous rich velvety quality without a trace of coarseness. They can be very long-lived and the variety of character is considerable.

LAFITE: At its best the greatest Médoc, or indeed red Bordeaux of all. A remarkable combination of power with grace, richness with finesse and breed, and a bouquet of unforgettable distinction and beauty.

LATOUR: A more masculine wine than Lafite, with a tremendous colour, inclined to be slow to develop but very consistent even in poor years.

MOUTON-ROTHSCHILD: More akin to Latour although a neighbour of Lafite. A rich wine of great vinosity which develops more quickly than Latour. It is one of the mysteries of the 1855 Classification that this wine was not placed with the first growths.

MIS EN BOUTEILLES AU CHÂTEAU

CHATEAU LAFITE-ROTHSCHILD
1961
DÉPOSÉ
APPELLATION PAUILLAC CONTRÔLÉE

It must be pointed out that MOUTON CADET is a branded wine which does not come from either Mouton Rothschild or Mouton Baron Philippe. This wine, which is the most successful brand of Claret in the world, began life with off vintage Mouton Rothschild, but the wine was so successful that Baron de Rothschild was soon compelled to turn it into a blended wine which nevertheless maintains a consistent and excellent standard for a wine of this type.

PICHON-LONGUEVILLE: There are two châteaux of this name usually differentiated as Baron and Lalande or Countess Lalande. Although once forming one property, these are two quite distinct wines. The Baron is a fine robust wine with classic Pauillac characteristics. Lalande, on the other hand, has rather more finesse, and it is interesting to note that a third of the vineyard lies in St. Julien.

DUHART-MILON: A long-lived wine which is on the way back. Has less body than some Pauillacs.

PONTET-CANET: The property of the house of Cruse. A consistent wine which is one of the few classified growths never château-bottled.

LYNCH-BAGES: Has achieved a great reputation for consistency and quality in recent years. Should now be placed with the second growths.

GRAND PUY DUCASSE: A big, robust, very typical Pauillac.

GRAND PUY LACOSTE: Has made progress and enjoys a fine reputation for consistency.

MOUTON BARON PHILIPPE (formerly known as Mouton d'Armailhacq): Although inevitably overshadowed by its illustrious neighbour with the same suffix, enjoys a fine reputation in its own right.

BATAILLEY: Not so full-bodied as some, except in the best years; has shown great consistency for some time. A wine of quality.

HAUT BATAILLEY: Formerly part of Batailley. Now the vineyard has matured, excellent wine is being made rivalling its sister-château.

LYNCH MOUSSAS: A small property, the wine is attractive and reliable.

CROIZET-BAGES: A big wine, generous and fleshy.

CLERC-MILON-MONDON: A wine of average quality.

In addition to this remarkable array of classified growths there are a number of excellent *bourgeois* wines to be found:
LA COURONNE, COLOMBIER-MONPELOU, HAUT-BAGES-MONPELOU, BELLEVUE-ST. LAMBERT, BELLEGRAVE, HAUT-BAGES-AVÉROUS, FONBADET, LA TOUR MILON, ROLLAND, PIBRAN, DUROC-MILON.

The Co-operative enjoys a good reputation and is one of the largest in the Médoc. The wine is sold as La Rose Pauillac.

ST. ESTÈPHE

This is an exception to the general rule about Médoc wine which we made at the start, for the wines of St. Estèphe, while being big and sturdy, are less full-bodied than those of Pauillac to the south of them. There is sometimes a tendency to hardness at first, but generally the wines are more fruity than those of Pauillac. The area is especially strong in good *bourgeois* wines.

The following classified growths enjoy a universal reputation:

MONTROSE: Full-bodied and inclined to be stubborn at first. Its reputation has grown considerably in the last decade and many now consider it the best wine in the district.

COS D'ESTOURNEL: A generous wine of great elegance, at its best very fine indeed.

Grand Cru Classé

CALON SEGUR: Now rated as a second growth. A very consistent wine combining the robustness of Montrose and something of the suppleness of Cos d'Estournel.

There are two *bourgeois* wines which are now generally regarded as of classified growth quality: CH. DE PEZ and PHELAN-SEGUR. The Pez in particular well deserves this rating.

Other good *bourgeois* include: MEYNEY, LES ORMES DE PEZ, CAPBERN, MARBUZET, BEAUSITE, BEAUSITE-HAUT-VIGNOBLE, HOUISSANT, LE BOSCQ, POMYS, CANTELOUP, LA TOUR MARBUZET, TRONQUOY-LALANDE, BEAUSEJOUR, MacCARTHY, LEYSSAC, LAFFITTE-CARCASSET and ANDRON-BLANQUET.

There is a large co-operative, with some small proprietors selling their wines vinified here under their château names, while other wine is sold under the name of Marquis de St. Estèphe.

Other Important Communes in the Haut-Médoc

It is usual for châteaux with only the Haut Médoc *appellation* to give the name of their commune as well. This must not be confused with an *appellation*. For example, Ch. LA LAGUNE, LUDON, *Appellation Haut Médoc Contrôlée*. Ludon is *not* an *appellation* in this case.

44

Ludon

The wines here are full-flavoured and soft with some finesse without quite being comparable to Margaux.

LA LAGUNE is a good classified growth whose vineyard has recently been extensively replanted, so that the wine tends to be on the light side at the moment.

Good *bourgeois* growths are: AGASSAC and NEXON-LEMOYNE.

Macau

These wines are rather full and richer than most Margaux, but lack their bouquet and finesse.

CANTEMERLE: An outstanding classified growth which most people would today place with the second growths.

Good *bourgeois* growths are: DES TROIS MOULINS, MAUCAMPS, and PRIBAN.

Cussac

Chiefly notable for its outstanding growth LANESSAN. This vineyard would have been included in the 1855 classification had it not been for the quixotic behaviour of its proprietor. Today it is regarded as of classified growth quality, the wine somewhat resembles a St. Julien but has a distinctive character of its own. La Tour Haut Moulin is a good *bourgeois* growth.

St. Laurent

Once a very important wine-producing commune, it has suffered both from its vulnerability to frost and its loss of *appellation* status as against its neighbour St. Julien. Many good vineyards have gone out of production. The wines have the weight of a St. Julien but tend to be firmer.

There are three classified growths in the district: LA TOUR CARNET, BELGRAVE and CAMENSAC, but while they sometimes produce quite attractive wines they no longer have the reputation they once enjoyed.

| Saint-Sauveur | A commune lying west of Pauillac and north of St. Laurent. The wines are similar to the lesser growths of Pauillac. The most notable growth is LIVERSAN. |

| Cissac | Lies north of Saint-Sauveur and west of St. Estèphe. The wines are not dissimilar to St. Estèphe and the best growths are: DU BREUIL, CISSAC, LA TOUR DU MIRAIL and LAMOTHE. |

| Saint-Seurin-de-Cadourne | This is the last commune in the Haut Médoc. The best wines have the generosity and body of St. Estèphe but without as much bouquet or finesse. They can be very long-lived. The best growths are: BEL-ORME-TRONQUOY-DE-LALANDE, VERDIGNAN, COUFRAN and LESTAGE. |

Bas-Médoc

This region of the northern Médoc used to be much more important fifty years ago, but today the disadvantage of a lesser *appellation* has greatly reduced the area under vine. However, the best vineyards, which are planted on gravelly ridges overlooking the river, produce good wines with plenty of colour and body, although without the bouquet or quite the finesse of similar wines in Haut Médoc. They often stand up in bottle for many years. The best growths, by commune, are as follows:

ST. GERMAIN D'ESTEUIL:	LIVRAN, DU CASTERA.
ORDONNAC-ET-POTENSAC:	POTENSAC, GALLAIS-BELLEVUE, DES BELLES-GRAVES, LASSELLE
ST. YZANS:	LOUDENNE (also makes a good dry white wine)
BÉGADAN:	LAUJAC, LA-TOUR-DE-BY, PATACHE D'AUX, LANDON
ST. CHRISTOLY-DE-MEDOC:	LA TOUR-ST. BONNET, LA TOUR-DU-BREUIL

The last mentioned commune, is, however, even better known

for the wine sold under the name of St. Christoly which has a good reputation.

GRAVES

This is the only district in Bordeaux which produces both red and white wines of quality. It is curious that Graves is often thought of as being a white wine, because in fact the quantity of really fine red wines produced outnumbers that of fine white wine, although taking the whole region nearly three times as much white is produced as red.

All the best red wines are produced in the northern part of the region nearest to Bordeaux, together with a certain quantity of fine white wines, while in the south the large quantities of white wine are made.

The red wines bear some comparison with those of the Médoc. They have a more vivid and powerful bouquet than Médocs, and the wines are robust and full-bodied with a very clean and well-defined flavour. They develop well with age and will live for a similar period to Médocs. The grapes used are the same as in the Médoc.

The best white wines are truly dry but are distinctly fruity with plenty of individual flavour. The more modern methods of vinification now used are producing cleaner, crisper wines without the pronounced earthy taste which many people find disagreeable in white Bordeaux wines. They also have more acidity and so are fresher and less heavy than in former days. Even so, they require some ageing in bottle to produce their best; a seven-year-old Chevalier was in perfect condition with its flavour and finesse completely developed, but without any hint of maderisation, when I drank it recently. For lesser wines four years is probably a sufficient age. The grapes used are Semillon, Sauvignon and Muscadelle. The last is usually eliminated from the finest vineyards and quality producers usually prefer a preponderance of Sauvignon over Semillon.

Graves
Sauternes

le Haillan •
• Eysines

• Merignac

Bordeaux

PESSAC •
• TALENCE
Canejean •

GRADIGNAN

• VILLENAVE-d'ORNON

LEOGNAN •
• CADAUJAC

MARTILLAC •
• St. Médard-d'Eyrans
LABREDE •
• Ayguemorte
Saucats •
• BEAUTIRAN

GRAVES
PORTETS •

St. Morillon •
• St. Selve

Cabanac •
Villagrains
Virelade •

Garonne

St. Michel •
de Rieufret
PODENSAC

Cérons
⊙ CERONS

• ILLATS
Landiras •

Barsac
⊙ BARSAC

Budos •
BOMMES •
• PREIGNAC

SAUTERNES ⊙
SAUTERNES

Léogeats •
FARGUES •
Langon •

St. PIERRE
de MONS

There are not the complications of *appellation* here that there are in the Médoc, only one for red wines, Graves, and two for white wines, Graves and Graves Supérieur. We shall deal with the red and white wines separately by commune.

Red Wines

Only Haut Brion among the red Graves was classified with the Médocs in 1855, but no one has doubted for many years past the merits and distinction of some of the other fine red wines of the district. A classification was made in 1953 which has since been added to. It is as follows:

Château Haut Brion	Pessac
La Mission-Haut-Brion	Pessac
Haut Bailly	Léognan
Domaine de Chevalier	Léognan
Carbonnieux	Léognan
Malartic-Lagravière	Léognan
Fieuzal	Léognan
Pape Clément	Pessac
Latour	Martillac
Latour-Haut-Brion	Talence
Smith-Haut-Lafitte	Martillac
Olivier	Léognan
Bouscaut	Cadaujac

The trouble with this classification is that no attempt is made to graduate the wines, and there are marked variations of quality. It also highlights the problems of Graves in that there are today only a few famous vineyards and a great many struggling or neglected ones, and others which have gone out of production, for apart from the great wines this has been an unfashionable area for red wines in recent years and therefore rather a depressed one. But in fact many of these lesser known wines offer fine value and are worth looking out for.

Pessac

This is now a suburb of Bordeaux. The amount of wine now produced is small, but includes the most illustrious in Graves.

HAUT BRION: One of the great wines of Bordeaux and certainly one of the oldest, it is mentioned in Pepys' Diary—the first Bordeaux wine to be mentioned by name in English literature. It had a bad patch between the wars, but has now regained much of its former prestige. The wine is very powerful, inclined to be hard at first, but when mature is rich and has a powerful sumptuous flavour.

LA MISSION-HAUT-BRION: Occupies a position amongst Graves similar to that of Mouton Rothschild at the time of the 1855 classification. The wine is well ahead of all others except Haut Brion itself, and deserves the position of a first growth. In lesser years it is inclined to be more consistent and finer than Haut Brion. The style is rather different, but it certainly bears comparison with its illustrious neighbour.

PAPE CLÉMENT: This ancient and famous vineyard now has a great reputation and is equivalent to the second growths of the Médoc. The wine is both generous and fine, with more finesse than most Graves.

Léognan

Together with Pessac, this is the best commune for red wines.

HAUT BAILLY: Enjoyed a great reputation in the past which is now being regained. The wine is of second growth (Médoc) standing and is distinctive in style, fleshy and rich.

DOMAINE DE CHEVALIER: Maintains a very high standard, the wine is lighter and has more delicacy than many Graves. It is of second growth (Médoc) quality.

MALARTIC-LAGRAVIÈRE: A big powerful wine, inclined to hardness at first. Fourth/fifth growth (Médoc) standing.

CARBONNIEUX: The wine is on the light side. Quality at the moment corresponds to fourth/fifth growth (Médoc).

FIEUZAL: An elegant, perfumed wine of increasing reputation. Fourth/fifth growth (Médoc) quality.

Other good growths include: LARRIVET HAUT-BRION, LA LOU-VIERE and LE PAPE.

Martillac   There are a number of good wines here, though they have less body and distinctiveness than the best of Pessac and Léognan.

SMITH-HAUT-LAFITTE: Enjoys a good reputation; the wine is usually well balanced and agreeable. It is of fifth growth (Médoc) quality.

LATOUR-MARTILLAC: Of similar reputation and standing to Smith-Haut-Lafitte.

Another good growth in this commune is LA GARDE.

Talence   The only growth of note now in this suburb of Bordeaux is LATOUR HAUT-BRION.

Villenave d'Ornan   There are two excellent growths in this commune: BARET and PONTAC MONPLAISIR.

Cadaujac   The important growth here is BOUSCAUT.

Of the other communes producing red wines the best is probably PORTETS, but few of these wines appear under their own names.

White Wines   A classification for these wines was produced at the same time as for the red wines. It is as follows:

Domaine de Chevalier   Léognan

Château Carbonnieux	Léognan
Olivier	Léognan
Malartic-Lagravière	Léognan
Laville-Haut Brion	Talence
Bouscaut	Cadaujac
Couhins	Villenave d'Ornan
Latour Martillac	Martillac

Pessac   Only a tiny quantity of white wine is made at HAUT BRION. The wine has body and finesse and is really fine.

Talence   At LAVILLE-HAUT BRION a fine quality dry wine is made.

Villenave d'Ornan   There are some fine white wines made here. The finest is COUHINS, a wine of real finesse and distinction, closely followed by PONTAC-MONPLAISIR and then BARET.

Léognan   Some outstanding wines are made here. DOMAINE DE CHEVALIER is probably the finest white Graves of all today; it is light, dry with a very fine flavour and great finesse. MALARTIC-LAGRA-VIÈRE makes only a very small quantity of a very distinctive and fine flavoured wine. CARBONNIEUX has had a good reputation but has been inconsistent of late. A very attractive wine is made at FIEUZAL. OLIVIER, the property of Eschenauer, is a considerable vineyard, and produces a well-known wine. Under new management LA LAUVIÈRE is making a wine of quality.

Cadaujac   At Cadaujac the white BOUSCAUT has long enjoyed a good reputation for a fine long-lasting wine.

The great mass of white wine is, of course, sold in generic blends and not under individual names. It must be emphasised that the wines discussed in detail bear little resemblance to the often rather indifferent generic wines we are used to seeing as Graves, which are often rather sweet. This is a pity because it has done damage to the reputation of the region. In England where *Appellation Contrôlée* is not legally binding, the quality of these generic blends has been a particular casualty.

It is really rather difficult to give any worthwhile guide to the buying of these generic wines, except to say that the reputation and integrity of the best *négociants* and the best English merchants, allied to one's own observations and discrimination, are really the only worthwhile guides that can be adopted. One observation which must be made, however, is that the cheapest wine is not always the best value, and that a little careful comparison of qualities and prices can be very rewarding—don't simply buy the label.

ST. ÉMILION

The vineyards of St. Émilion are the oldest of Bordeaux and probably some of the oldest in France. The country is quite different from the flat vineyards of the Médoc with its great *domaines*. There are vineyards clustered precariously on the hillsides around the ancient and picturesque town of St. Émilion, then the country flattens out until the gravelly plateau of the Graves-St. Émilion, adjoining Pomerol, is reached.

Even the properties themselves are different. Very few indeed attain the size of the great *châteaux* of the Médoc; there are a multiplicity of small properties mostly worked by resident proprietors, and the *châteaux* themselves are often extremely modest houses; there are few imposing mansions here.

The wines of St. Émilion are characterised by their great richness and suppleness. They attain a high degree of alcohol—between 12° and 14° in fine years—so that although they have less tannin than the Médocs, their fine balance combined with the

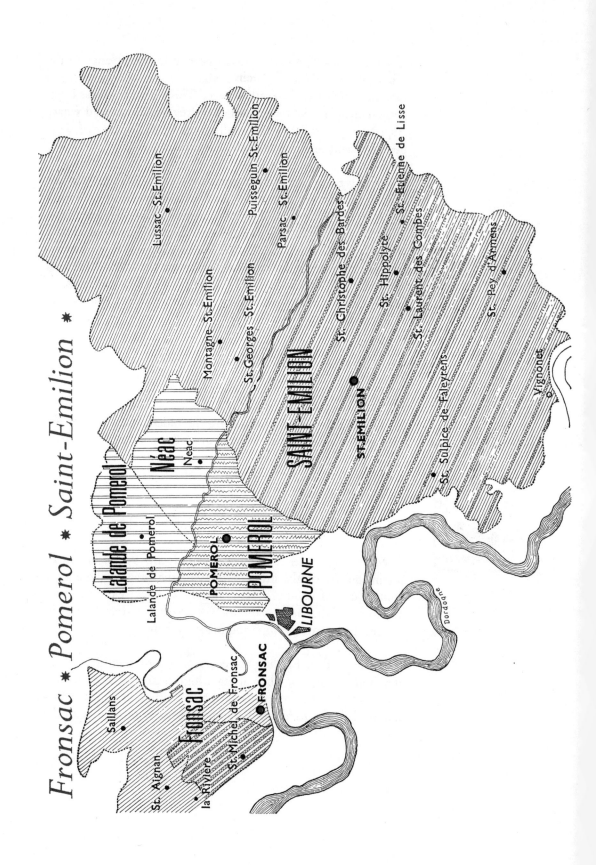

Fronsac * Pomerol * Saint-Emilion *

alcohol enables them to live and flourish for thirty or forty years. It is often the case that in years when some Médoc wines are spoiled by having too much tannin the St. Émilions continue to be fresh and delicious when some of their cousins have become flat and dead. This was very noticeable in a year such as 1928. The attraction of these wines is in their wonderful fruitiness and rich savour, and the complex variety of their flavours. They lack the breed and elegance of the great Médocs, but their own considerable charms go a long way toward making us forget such shortcomings, and for those reared on Burgundy, these wines are certainly the most easily appreciated of the fine Bordeaux. As far as vines are concerned there is a decided tendency for the Merlot to predominate at the expense of the Cabernet (Bouchet in St. Émilion). This movement received considerable impetus from the disastrous frost of February 1956, because the Merlot comes into production more rapidly and is more prolific, and growers were in a hurry to recover their losses.

One of the great difficulties about St. Émilion has always been the number and confusion of its names, there are so many names which are very similar, and there was nothing like the Médoc classification. On the contrary nearly every wine claimed the title of a first growth. Something was done to clarify this muddle by the classification of 1954, which had the additional advantage of making provision for a revision every ten years. This classification is as follows:

Premiers Grands Crus Classes:

    A. Château Ausone
          Cheval Blanc
    B. Château Beauséjour
          Belair
          Canon
     Clos Fourtet
     Château Figeac
          La Gaffelière-Naudes
          Magdelaine
          Pavie
          Trottevieille

Grands Crus Classes:

Château L'Angelus
  Balestard-la-Tonnelle
  Bellevue
  Bergat
  Cadet-Bon
  Cadet-Piola
  Canon-la-Gaffelière
  Cap-de-Mourlin
  Chapelle Madeleine
  Chauvin
  Corbin
  Corbin-Michotte
  Coutet
  Croque-Michotte
  Curé Bon
  Fonplégade
  Fonroque
  Franc Mayne
  Grand-Barrail-Lamarzelle
  Grand-Corbin-Figeac
  Grand Corbin-Despagne
  Grand Mayne
  Grand Pontet
  Grandes Murailles
  Guadet-Saint-Julien
  Jean Faure
Clos des Jacobins
Château La Carte
  La Clotte
  La Clusière
  La Couspaude
  La Dominique
Clos La Madeleine
Château Lamarzelle
  Larcis-Ducasse
  Larmande
  Laroze

Château Lasserre
    La-Tour-du-Pin-Figeac
    La-Tour-Figeac
    Le Chatelet
    Le Couvent
    Le Prieure
    Mauvezin
    Moulin-du-Cadet
    Pavie-Decesse
    Pavie-Macquin
    Pavillon-Cadet
    Petit-Faurie-de-Souchard
    Petit-Faurie-de-Soutard
    Ripeau
    Sansonnet
    Saint-Georges-Côte-Pavie
Clos Saint-Martin
Château Soutard
    Tertre-Daugay
    Trimoulet
    Trois Moulins
    Troplong-Mondot
    Villemaurine
    Yon-Figeac

The disadvantages of this list are obvious, an élite of twelve, but then a mass of sixty-one names all lumped together. A glance at Alexis Lichine's list in the Médoc section will show that opinion about the first twelve is divided, and it would certainly be simpler if there was some intermediary group between the heights of the twelve and the anonymity of the sixty. All that can be said is that an attempt has at last been made to sort out the long prevailing muddle, and a certain standard has been set. It is not without significance that the average yield of the St. Émilion classified growths is half that of the classified growths of the Médoc, so that the large number of St. Émilion growths produce far less wine than the smaller élite of the Médoc. How much longer it will be economically feasible for such a multiplicity of small properties to survive must be a matter of conjecture.

The St. Émilion region is divided by its *appellation contrôlée* into two distinct areas:

First: that part that enjoys the *appellation* St. Émilion. This is restricted to eight communes which lie within the traditional boundaries of St. Émilion. These are: ST. ÉMILION; ST. LAURENT-DES-COMBES; ST. CHRISTOPHE-DES-BARDES; ST. HIPPOLYTE; ST. ETIENNE-DE-LISSE; ST. PEY-D'ARMENS; ST. SULPICE-DE-FALEYRENS, and VIGNONET.

Second: a group of communes which are entitled to add the name of St. Émilion to their own. These are: ST. GEORGES-ST. ÉMILION; MONTAGNE-ST. ÉMILION; LUSSAC-ST. ÉMILION; PUISSEGUIN-ST. ÉMILION; PARSAC-ST. ÉMILION, and SABLES-ST. ÉMILION.

The commune of St. Émilion is of much greater importance than the other seven communes bearing the same *appellation*, and we will deal with this first.

It is usual to divide the commune into two distinct areas, the Côtes St. Émilion and the Graves St. Émilion. Although this is in no way reflected in the *appellation*, it does follow the distinct geographical division which exists in the commune, which in turn is reflected in the character of the wines themselves.

THE CÔTES   Most of the classic St. Émilions come from this part. The hillsides are extremely picturesque and often quite steep, more reminiscent of the Côte d'Or than of Bordeaux.

AUSONE: There was a time when this growth produced great wines and basked in an enviable reputation. For many years now it has proved a great disappointment, but some good judges are now convinced that the tide has turned and the 1962 and 1966 were certainly an improvement.

BELAIR: The adjoining wine to Ausone and shares the same cellars. The wine is elegant but full-flavoured.

MAGDELAINE: On the same slopes as Ausone, the wine has considerable breed and delicacy allied to a full ripe flavour.

GAFFELIÈRE-NAUDES: A wine with a growing reputation. Generous and full-bodied and really fine.

CLOS FOURTET: The vineyard contains more Cabernet (or Bouchet as it is known in St. Émilion) than most St. Émilion today. As a result the wine is rather hard at first and is big and powerful.

CANON: A large property producing a powerful wine.

PAVIE: The largest vineyard among the *Premier Grand Cru.* The wine has improved of late and is supple and rich.

TROTTEVIEILLE: A small vineyard, the wine is full-bodied and powerful, but develops great charm with ageing.

ᴄHÂTEAU MAGDELAINE
1962
Mis en Bouteille au Château
ᴊEAN PIERRE MOUEIX   APPELLATION SAINT-ÉMILION
ᴩRIᴄTAIRES A S⁺ ÉMILION   1ᵉʳ GRAND CRU CLASSÉ CONTRÔLÉE

CANON LA GAFFELIÈRE: A very ripe generous wine.

CURÉ-BON-LA MADELEINE: The wine is fine and distinctive in style.

FONPLÉGADE: A wine of breed and delicacy.

FONROQUE: A big, full-bodied, robust wine.

LA CLOTTE: An elegant, generous, perfumed wine.

LARCIS-DUCASSE: A wine of finesse and delicacy.

LAROZE: A fairly full-bodied wine.

PETIT-FAURIE-DE-SOUCHARD: A wine of elegance with a fragrant individuality.

SOUTARD: The wine has a fine bouquet and is fleshy but elegant.

TROPLONG MONDOT: Is now inclined to be light but has finesse and considerable charm.

In addition to these wines which we have discussed in detail and the other *grand cru* already listed, the following wines are also to be found from time to time on this market and can usually be recommended:

CARDINAL-VILLEMAURINE, CLOS CASTELOT, TAUZINAT-L'HERMITAGE, CLOS LA FIGEAC, LA FLEUR POURRET, LA GRACE DIEU, LA ROSE POURRET, LA TOUR ST. PIERRE, LE BON PASTEUR.

GRAVES-ST. ÉMILION

The wines here have something of the texture of the Pomerols they immediately adjoin, yet are still distinctly St. Émilions in style.

CHEVAL BLANC: Consistently the finest wine in St. Émilion today. It combines great richness and suavity with elegance and a superb bouquet of great charm. It is very supple so that it is often possible to drink it rather early, yet it lives for many years, as vintages like 1926, 1928, and 1929 bear witness.

FIGEAC: A wine which today enjoys a formidable reputation; after Cheval Blanc it is usually one of the best of the *Premier Grand Cru.* The wine is rich and really fine.

CORBIN-DESPAGNE: A generous wine with a fine bouquet.

LA TOUR DU PIN FIGEAC-MOUEIX: A wine with plenty of body but also with breed and finesse.

RIPEAU: A very attractive wine, very supple and rich.

LA DOMINIQUE: The wine is rich and generous.

YON FIGEAC: A meaty, robust wine which also manages to be fairly supple.

This is a much smaller region than the St. Émilion Côtes, hence the much briefer list of wines. In addition to those mentioned and to several other *grand cru*, CORMEY FIGEAC is also quite frequently to be found in this country. The seven remaining communes which enjoy the St. Émilion *appellation* are considerably less important and only boast three *grand cru* from amongst the sixty. These are: LARCIS-DUCASSE in St. Laurent-des-Combes and LE COUVENT and TERTRE DAUGAY both in St. Sulpice de Faleyrans. Apart from these the following unclassified wines are also worth looking out for: DE FERRAND, GROS-CAILLOU, HAUT-LAVALLADE, LA TOUR PUYBLANQUET, MOULIN BELLEGRAVE, PLAISANCE, CLOS PRESSAC and VIEUX-CASTEL-ROBIN. Rather more important are the outlying districts already mentioned; some of these produce wine just as fine as or indeed finer than some made in the seven communes.

Montagne-St. Émilion	A large commune producing two distinct types of wine depending on whether it is made in the vineyards at the top of the hills with its calcareous soil or further down where the soil is a mixture of flint and clay. In the first case the wine can be robust with a very full purple colour, on the latter soil the wine has more delicacy and is lighter and more supple. A few growths are seen here under their own names: CORBIN, BEAUSEJOUR, PARADIS, BELLEVUE, LA BASTIENNE and LA TOUR GILET.
Lussac-St. Émilion	Good full-bodied wines are made on the slopes of Lussac, especially CH. LYONNAT.
Puisseguin-St. Émilion	The wines here are perhaps robuster and rather tougher than those of the preceding communes. Names worth mentioning are: CH. DES LAURETS, TEYSSIER and GUIBEAU-LAFOURVIELLE.
Parsac-St. Émilion	The vineyards are planted on hillsides and the wines are deep-coloured and rich.
St. Georges-St. Émilion	In style and quality these wines are comparable to those of St. Émilion itself. Best known growths are: St. Georges and St. Andre Corbin.

Sables–St. Émilion   It is something of an oddity that these wines are classified as St. Émilion. This small commune near Libourne produces supple wines with some richness which are quick maturing and more reminiscent in style to Pomerols than to St. Émilions.

POMEROL

Although viticulture in Pomerol dates from Roman times and prospered in the Middle Ages, first under the Knights Templars and later under those of St. John of Jerusalem, the emergence of Pomerol in its own right is a rather recent affair. Until well into the nineteenth century indeed Pomerol was regarded merely as an appendage of St. Émilion. The modern reputation of Pomerol may be said to have begun when Château Petrus won a gold medal at the Paris Exhibition of 1878. Of recent years the reputation of Pomerol has risen until it stands as second to none in terms of quality and the meticulous care with which its vineyards are kept and its wines are made.

It is much the smallest of the great red wine districts of Bordeaux and is intensively cultivated. As in St. Émilion few of the properties are very large, and very small ones are the general rule. Indeed, among the principal growths the average yield is nearly 20 per cent less than the average for the *Grand Cru* of St. Émilion. Alone among the great red wine districts there is no official classification, and many varying lists can be found although there is general agreement as to the outstanding growths.

The qualities which make Pomerol one of the great wines are not easy to pin down. It is often said that it is the happy medium between St. Émilion and Médoc, but this is a poor tribute to its originality. The wine is rich and supple but with a quality almost of unctuousness when young. It matures fairly quickly because the wine is so finely balanced, but this superb equilibrium ensures a span of life which is the equal of all but a few St. Émilions. In contrast to St. Émilion it has more breed and refinement of flavour, but how poorly do words encompass the qualities of great wine!

All this needs stressing because outside a small circle the wines of Pomerol, in spite of their reputation, are still far too little known in this country. One of the reasons is that few of the names of its individual growths are at all well known, and because of their popularity in France, Belgium and Holland, and more recently in the U.S.A., the prices for the best growths are high, and Englishmen are loath to pay the same price for a name they do not know as for their beloved BEYCHEVELLE or CALON SEGUR.

PETRUS: Certainly the least known of the great wines of Bordeaux in this country; this is partly explained by the tiny production, on average only 18 *tonneaux* a year, the equivalent of 1,500 cases. This is probably the best wine made on this side of the river and is usually the peer of Cheval Blanc and certainly the equal of the first growths of the Médoc. The wine has great individuality and vinosity, is rich and generous but complex and many-sided in its flavour and nuances. It ages superbly.

VIEUX CHÂTEAU CERTAN: The vineyard adjoins Petrus. This is a great wine, vivid, with great vinosity and ripeness; it ages well.

LA CONSEILLANTE: The vineyard adjoins Cheval Blanc but the wine is very different, full-bodied but inclined to hardness at first. It is very consistent, and is certainly one of the best Pomerols.

TROTANOY: A very fine wine, generous yet with delicacy and elegance.

GAZIN: A fine robust full-bodied wine, delicious when mature, one of the largest vineyards in Pomerol.

PETIT-VILLAGE: A wine with a good reputation, less generous than some but has finesse.

L'EVANGILE: Has a great reputation, a fine, full wine.

LAFLEUR: A wine of great charm with a very distinctive personality.

63

LA FLEUR-PETRUS: A rich, generous wine of breed.

LATOUR-POMEROL: This has a lovely bouquet, a wine combining richness, charm and breed.

CLOS L'ÉGLISE: Lighter than some Pomerols, has a fine flavour.

CERTAN-DEMAY: A wine of fine quality.

BEAUREGARD: A rich, powerful wine of quality.

LE GAY: The wine has plenty of colour and great vinosity, maintains a very fine quality.

NENIN: A fine wine with a good reputation. It is one of the few large vineyards in Pomerol.

CLINET: A robust full-bodied wine which takes a little longer to mature than some.

LA POINTE: Fairly light but has great charm and finesse.

Other growths of note are: CERTAN-GIRAUD, DOMAINE DE L'ÉGLISE, LA CROIX DE GAY, L'ÉGLISE-CLINET, LAGRANGE, ROUGET, LA COMMANDERIE, LA CROIX, MOULINET, PLINCE, DE SALES BOURGNEUF, L'ENCLOS, CLOS RENÉ, MAZEYRES, TAILLEFER, BEL-AIR, FRANC-MAILLET, LA CROIX ST. GEORGES, and LA GRAVE TRIGANT DE BOISSET.

There are two small appendages to Pomerol where the wines are not quite so fine but of similar style.

Néac The wines have plenty of colour and are rich and full-bodied. The following are worthy of note: SIAURAC, BELLES-GRAVES, TEYSSON. (I have also seen this wine which is on the border of Néac and Lalande-de-Pomerol labelled as *appellation* Lalande de Pomerol.)

64

An initiation ceremony in the ruined cloisters at St. Emilion. The initiated will take the title of Commandeur d'Honneur in the Jurade de St. Emilion—an honour bestowed for services rendered to the region and to the vintners.

facing p. 64

Château and vineyards at Ausone (St. Emilion). These vineyards were traditionally founded by a Roman poet, Ausonius, in the fourth century A.D., and have been maintained as such to this day. The Maître du Chai has held his position without a break, father and son, for over 500 years.

Lalande de Pomerol

A generous wine with the style of Pomerol and plenty of finesse. CHATEAU DE BEL-AIR: This is considered to be in a class by itself, rich, fine and long-lived. Other growths of note are: GRAND ORMEAU, DE LA COMMANDERIE, BOURSEAU and DOMAINE DU GRAND ORMEAU.

Other Red Wine Districts

There are three important red wine districts along the eastern side of the Dordogne and Gironde, immediately to the north of Libourne. Going north from Pomerol these are: FRONSAC, BOURG and BLAYE. In addition, just to the east of St. Émilion on the Dordogne is an area which before the days of *appellation* was known simply as St. Émilionais. The centre of this area is the ancient town of Castillon and these wines now have the *appellation* Bordeaux Côtes de Castillon. There are some very pleasant wines in this district which are distinctly better than the run-of-the-mill Bordeaux *rouge*.

FRONSAC

The hilly vineyards of Fronsac cover only a small area in six communes, but are divided by the *appellation* into two regions: CÔTES-CANON-FRONSAC and CÔTES-DE-FRONSAC. There is no *appellation* Fronsac. In the Côtes-Canon-Fronsac there are no fewer than eight *châteaux* which incorporate the name Canon in their name, which makes things rather confusing.

The wines of the Côte Canon are by reputation superior to those of the Côtes-de-Fronsac, but in practice it is hard to discern any worthwhile difference in quality. The best known growths are: CANON (Mme. Edgard Bouché), CANON (ancienne prop. de Mlle de Lange), JUNAYME, JEANDEMAN.

BOURG

In recent years much more has been seen of these wines in England, and deservedly so. There are many good wines offering excellent value. Rather confusingly there are three *appellations* which are used concurrently depending on local custom:

BOURG, BOURGEAIS, and CÔTES-DE-BOURG. These in no way represent either different areas or different qualities.

The district produces a considerable quantity of both red and white wines, but nearly twice as much red as white. The red wines are much more important and I have never seen a bottle of the white in this country. The red wines have plenty of colour, are rich, fruity and soft, the most Burgundian of Bordeaux. The best growths are: CROÛTE-CHARLUS, TAYAC, EYQUEM, ROUSSET, MENDOCE, DE BARBE, ROBERT, DU BOUSQUET, SAUMAN, MACAY.

BLAYE An even larger wine-producing region than Bourg. Again there are three *appellations:* CÔTES DE BLAYE, reserved for white wines, and PREMIERES CÔTES DE BLAYE or BLAYAIS which apply to both red and white wines. As in Bourg the red wines are much more important than the white wines. The reds are supple and quick maturing, but not quite so rich or fine as those of Bourg.

CASTILLON I use this as a general term to cover a group of eight communes adjoining St. Émilion, and producing good full-bodied robust wines resembling St. Émilions. A few growths are now being sold in this country under their own names: BEYNAT, BELCIER, CASTEGENS, TUILLAC and SAVOIE.

CUBZAC An enclave between Fronsac and Bourg on the Paris road. There is one outstanding growth here, CHÂTEAU DE TERREFORT. It is rich and supple, similar to a Bourg in style.

SAUTERNES AND BARSAC

It is one of the ironies of our times that although sweet wines are popular with a large public the great Sauternes and Barsacs languish in a trough of neglect probably unrivalled in their long and proud history. The sad truth is that the public that likes sweet table wines does not usually reckon to pay more than about 75p a bottle for them, while those who can afford to pay £1 and more regard Sauternes as unfashionable, although they are quite prepared to pay £4 to £5 a bottle for a sweet German wine with so low an alcoholic degree as to give it a somewhat tenuous title to the name of wine.

It is Sauternes' proud claim that it is the greatest natural sweet wine in the world. That is to say, it is naturally and fully fermented and the unfermented sugar remains because the yeasts have ceased to function owing to the level of alcohol achieved (anything from 13° to 17° Gay Lussac) and not through the fermentation being artificially arrested. The wine therefore has a natural equilibrium and is capable of living to a great age.

Sauternes achieves its special character not only from the soil and climate, but also from the method of picking. The mild damp autumns of the Gironde encourage the growth of the fungus *Botrytis cinerea* on the skins of the grapes and this results in a state of mild dehydration known as *pourriture noble* or noble rot, thus increasing the concentration of sugar in the grape. This is not unique to Bordeaux, but it occurs here more uniformly and regularly than elsewhere.

The vintage does not usually begin for several weeks after the beginning of the red wine vintage, in about mid-October, and usually lasts well into November. The method is to go through the vineyard several times picking only those grapes in perfect condition for making Sauternes. The grapes used are the same as in Graves—Semillon, Sauvignon and Muscadelle, but here the Semillon is the most important.

And what of the wines themselves? To say that they are sweet is only to state the obvious while giving no hint of the qualities that make them great. First there is that rich and fragrant ripeness, that scent of fruit, then the wonderfully harmonious flavour, the balance of body and strength with fruit and sweetness so there is nothing cloying in the wine. Then among the finest there are those nuances of savour which convey the individual character of each wine in an unexpected array of varieties. But there are so many more adjectives which can be justly applied. One of the most descriptive and true is luscious, for they have an unctuous, peachy, velvety quality which is incomparable. They are also elegant, that is to say, there is nothing heavy or clumsy about them, their superb balance ensures this.

Before going on to speak of the different growths, there is a matter of names to clear up which sometimes causes confusion. The Sauternes region, defined originally by tradition and now by the laws of *appellation contrôlée*, consists of five communes, one of which is Barsac. As the wines of Barsac have traditionally been sold under the name of their own commune, the *appellation* here is now SAUTERNES-BARSAC. Some *châteaux* continue to use the old phraseology Haut-Barsac, but this has no significance today. The same applies to generic wines sold as Haut-Sauternes; this method of indicating a wine of superior quality is now obsolete.

The wines of Sauternes were classified in 1855 at the same time as those of the Médoc. The list is as follows:

1st Great Growth (*Grand 1er Cru*)

Château d'Yquem	Sauternes

1st Growths (*1ers Crus*)

Château La Tour Blanche	Bommes
Lafaurie-Peyraguey	Bommes
Clos Haut-Peyraguey	Bommes
Château Rayne-Vigneau	Bommes
Suduiraut	Preignac
Coutet	Barsac
Climens	Barsac
Guiraud	Sauternes
Rieussec	Fargues
Rabaud-Sigalas	Bommes

Château Rabaud-Promis	Bommes

2nd Growths (*2es Crus*)

Château Myrat	Barsac
Doisy-Dubroca	Barsac
Doisy-Daëne	Barsac
Doisy-Védrines	Barsac
Arche	Sauternes
Arche-Lafaurie	Sauternes
Filhot	Sauternes
Broustet	Barsac
Nairac	Barsac
Caillou	Barsac
Suau	Barsac
de Malle	Preignac
Romer-Lafon	Fargues
Lamothe-Bergey	Sauternes
Lamothe-Espagnet	Sauternes

It is symptomatic of the neglect into which the region has fallen that no one seems to have suggested, of late, that there should be a re-classification. There is some room for revision and certain *bourgeois* growths certainly merit promotion. Because Sauternes, Bommes, Preignac and Fargues are so similar in character, we will deal with them together.

YQUEM: The supreme sweet white wine of France, it has long enjoyed its unique position. The wine usually achieves a high degree both of alcohol (14° to 17°) and of sugar (4° to 7° Baumé) and is meticulously made and aged for three years in cask before bottling. Wines which do not reach the required standard are not sold under the *château* label.

GUIRAUD: The wine is lighter in body and less luscious than some but has great elegance.

FILHOT: A fine wine of breed.

D'ARCHE: A wine with a good reputation

D'ARCHE LAFAURIE: A fairly rich wine of quality.

RAYNE-VIGNEAU: This splendidly situated domaine has produced some of the finest wines in Sauternes, but it does not enjoy quite the reputation today that it once did.

LA TOUR BLANCHE: Less powerful and rich than some, but nevertheless a wine of breed and finesse.

LAFAURIE-PERAGUEY: Now the property of Cordier, this is a very fine wine of good repute.

HAUT-PERAGUEY: Not to be confused with the above wine. The wine is good but different in character.

RABAUD-PROMIS and RABAUD-SIGALAS: After about fifteen years as one property the vineyard is once more divided. A most attractive wine at its best.

SUDUIRAUT: After a period of eclipse between the wars, this is once more one of the great wines of Sauternes. It has a very distinctive savour, and while being pleasantly luscious is extremely elegant, well balanced and fine.

RIEUSSEC: An extremely distinctive wine of great character. This is one of the best wines of the region today.

There are a few *bourgeois* growths which deserve special mention. When found in this country they usually offer exceptional value.

HAUT-BOMMES, D'ARCHE-PUGNEAU, GILETTE, BASTOR-LA-MONTAGNE and DE FARGUES: These are considered to be on a par with the second growths.

BARSAC   The wines of this commune deserve their reputation for producing great wines of the highest quality. The difference between Barsac and the other Sauternes is perhaps a little academic, but is usually described as being less rich in sugar than other Sauternes but with more fruit.

CLIMENS: A great wine which often runs Yquem quite close for quality. The wine is rich and luscious.

COUTET: Almost inseparable from Climens and usually not far behind it in quality. It is very fine, with a decided fragrance and elegance.

DOISY-DAËNE: An outstanding second growth which would probably today be classed as a first growth. The wine has great delicacy and finesse and has richness without any hint of heaviness. The proprietor is one of the outstanding vinificators of the region.

CAILLOU: A very fine wine which deserves to be better known.

There are some outstanding *bourgeois* growths. The following are of second growth standing: PIADA, ROUMIEUX-GOYAUD ROUMIEUX-LACOSTE, ROUMIEUX-BERNADET, DE CARLES.

Among other *bourgeois* growths the following are also worth noting: DUDON, LIOT, COUSTET.

Dry "Sauternes" Something must be said about the so-called dry "Sauternes" which are now made by some properties. I say so-called because strictly speaking these are not Sauternes at all since they lack sufficient sugar and usually the alcohol as well. They are dry wines made in the Sauternes region and entitled only to the *appellation Bordeaux Supérieur*. Here there are two schools of thought. There are those who want to produce a wine retaining as much as possible of the Sauternes character. The result is a rather big, heavy wine with a distinctly earthy flavour, unlikely to please those who like dry white wines. The outstanding wine in this category is YGREG, made at Yquem. A similar type of wine is made at FILHOT. The opposite school of thought believes that the object is to produce a truly dry light wine which will inevitably be of a new and different type. The outstanding wines in this category are made at DOISY-DAËNE and LAFAURIE-PERAGUEY. The Doisy-Daëne is particularly interesting because the vineyard contains some Riesling vines, and the wine has a very distinctive bouquet and savour. It is bottled in the Spring following the vintage.

Other White Wine Districts

After Graves and Sauternes, STE. CROIX-DU-MONT, LOUPIAC, CERONS and PREMIERES CÔTES DE BORDEAUX are the most important districts for quality white wines. Unhappily they are all too seldom seen in England under the names of their best properties, and with the exception of Ste. Croix-du-Mont, not very often even as generic wines. If *appellation contrôlée* laws come to apply in this country these districts must grow in importance, so we shall take a brief look at each in turn.

STE. CROIX-DU-MONT

This district lies just across the river from Sauternes. It produces wine which in style and quality most nearly resembles Sauternes. The control of quality locally is excellent and a reputation for quality has been steadily built up. The wines have not less than 13° of alcohol and in a fine year can achieve 15°, while the degree Baumé is 2° to 4°. Some of the best growths are indeed quite admirable and hard to distinguish from Sauternes.

In England wines from this district are sometimes used in blends sold as Sauternes to keep the price down, and when this is the case the customer has little to complain of. It is when lower quality Première Côtes, often with too much sulphur in them, are used, that quality really suffers. When the wine is sold as a generic in this country it is usually excellent value.

LOUPIAC

This commune immediately adjoins Ste. Croix-du-Mont to the north, and its riverside slopes are a continuation of those of the neighbouring commune. The wines are very similar to those of

Ste. Croix-du-Mont, being only slightly less fine and less rich, but the quality is still admirable. The remarks we have already made about blending apply equally here.

CERONS

These wines are rather a different proposition. The district lies between Graves and Barsac and is a curious mixture of the two. The wine is chiefly notable for its great fruitiness and finesse, so that when vinified dry it is equal to a very good Graves, and when sweet is only slightly less rich than a Barsac. Some wines when made in the dry style also have the right to the *appellation Graves*. In this guise, one can sometimes come across individual growths in this country.

PREMIÈRES CÔTES

This is a long narrow strip along the right bank of the Garonne, which runs from just opposite Bordeaux, down to St. Macaire. The separate *appellations* of Loupiac, Ste. Croix-du-Mont and Côtes de Bordeaux St. Macaire are in fact enclaves within the limits of the Premières Côtes.

Very large quantities of white wine and a fair quantity of red are made here, and this is the principal source for imitation Sauternes. For whereas the average production in Sauternes is only some 650,000 gallons, and 300,000 in Ste. Croix-du-Mont, 22 million gallons of white wine are made in the Premières Côtes.

The sweet wines can be very good, but they are at their best when not too sweet, for there is a tendency to over-improve. One also finds many wines spoiled by the excessive use of sulphur. Although the reputation of the Premières Côtes has been for sweet white wines, some growths are now making dry wines which can be excellent.

ENTRE-DEUX-MERS

There only remains one important region in Bordeaux of which we have not spoken, ENTRE-DEUX-MERS. It is geographically an

73

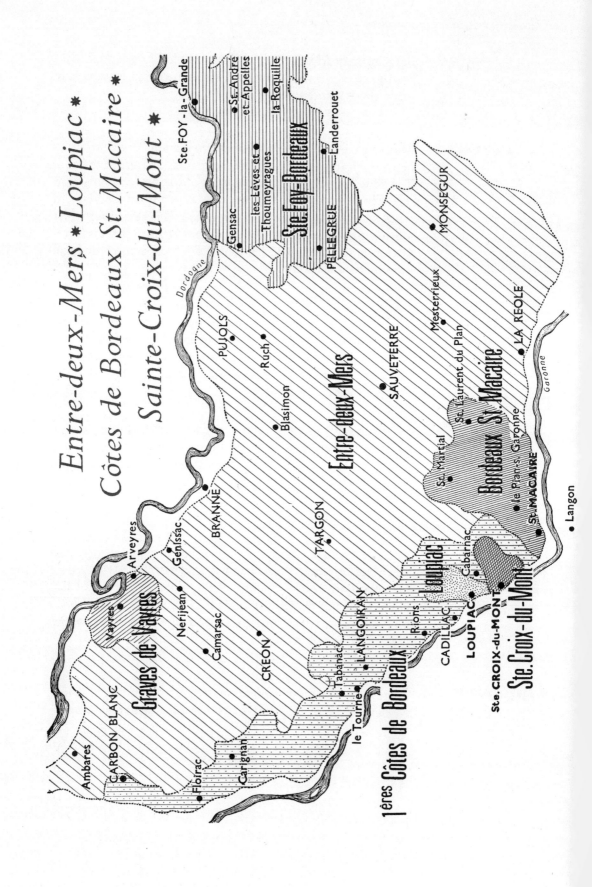

Entre-deux-Mers ✳ Loupiac ✳
Côtes de Bordeaux St. Macaire ✳
Sainte-Croix-du-Mont ✳

Ste.FOY-la-Grande

Dordogne

St.André
et-Appelles

la-Roquille

les-Lèves et-
Thoumeyragues

Landerrouet

Gensac

Ste-Foy-Bordeaux

PELLEGRUE

MONSEGUR

PUJOLS

Ruch

Blasimon

Entre-deux-Mers

SAUVETERRE

Mesterrieux

St.Laurent du Plan

LA RÉOLE

Garonne

St.Martial

Bordeaux St. Macaire

BRANNE

Génissac

Arveyres

TARGON

le Plan-s-Garonne

St.MACAIRE

Langon

Nerijean

Camarsac

Graves de Vayres

Vayres

CRÉON

LANGOIRAN

Tabanac

Rions

CADILLAC

Cabarnac

Loupiac

LOUPIAC

Ste.CROIX-du-MONT

Ste.Croix-du-Mont

CARBON BLANC

Ambares

Floirac

Carignan

le Tourne

1ères Côtes de Bordeaux

enormous area, since it comprises the entire tongue of land between the Garonne and the Dordogne. But in practice a number of places have their own *appellations* and the rest is not so extensively cultivated as some of the more valuable regions of Bordeaux.

The name itself is something of a mystery. As Professor Roger says, one could understand if it were called Entre-Deux-Fleuves (Between the Rivers) rather than Entre-Deux-Mers (Between the Seas).

The white wines of the region (the small production of red is only entitled to be called Bordeaux, or Bordeaux Supérieur) used to be on the sweet side, but there is now a determined policy to make only dry wines, and to plant more Sauvignon vines. In England this change in style has not always been followed, unfortunately, and many English people still seem to expect a medium sweet wine. Although quality varies considerably, at its best the dry wines of Entre-Deux-Mers can be quite fresh and attractive.

There is one other *appellation* which must be mentioned, not because it is especially important, but because its name often leads to confusion. This is GRAVES DE VAYRES. This fairly small *appellation* is an enclave of gravelly soil on the left bank of the Dordogne just below Libourne. The white wines are medium dry to slightly sweet, and the quality is reasonable. But while the wines are certainly superior to those of Entre-Deux-Mers, they must not be confused with those of Graves with which they are hardly comparable.

Reference Books

Bordeaux et Ces Vins by Cocks & Feret, Twelfth Edition 1969 This classic work of reference has at last been thoroughly revised. It remains an indispensable source book for any serious student of the region.

J. R. Roger, *The Wines of Bordeaux*, Andre Deutsch, 1960. This is far away the best book available in English. Although not as encyclopaedic as Cocks & Feret, it is a more than adequate reference book for most purposes and can be warmly recommended. Lichine's *Encyclopaedia of Wines and Spirits* (1967) contains useful thumbnail sketches of most of the leading growths as well as good appendices.

Amongst other useful books which should be mentioned is the Bordeaux section and appendices in the *Wines of France* by Alexis Lichine, Sixth Edition 1964, which is particularly interesting for its tables of average production of a great number of Bordeaux *châteaux*, and Morton Shand's classic *A Book of French Wines* available in a revised edition edited by Cyril Ray and published as a Penguin handbook. The historical sections of the Bordeaux chapter are particularly valuable. *The Wines of Bordeaux* by Edmund Penning-Rowsell, International Wine and Food Society 1969. The first comprehensive book on the subject by an Englishman in modern times. The historical chapters are particularly strong and the writer's opinions are always interesting and sometimes controversial. *Lafite* by Cyril Ray, Peter Davin 1968. A very readable account of the history of this famous château under the Rothschilds.

BURGUNDY

The image of Burgundy is one of good-living writ large. The wines themselves are warm, generous and extrovert, their appeal spontaneous and immediate. Compared with Claret the red wines are more easily appreciated because they lack the tannin and reserve of Bordeaux wines; they are soft, full-flavoured and have great vinosity. The white wines are some of the finest dry wines in the world, ranging from the dry steely wines of Chablis to the rich and almost sweet wine of the great Montrachet vineyard. The rich and gargantuan meals of the region reflect the same personality as the wines, for which they are an ideal accompaniment.

When speaking of Burgundy one must first clearly define the area one is discussing. For, unlike Bordeaux, the vineyards have no focal point in a single great city, nor are they in a single department. But, with the exception of Chablis, the Burgundy vineyards lie along the slopes of a series of hills on the edge of the valley of the river Saône.

First there are the hills of Chablis. These lie north-west of the main Burgundy area towards Paris and to the left of the N.6 as one drives from Paris. Then to the south of Dijon is the most important region in Burgundy, the CÔTE D'OR, itself divided

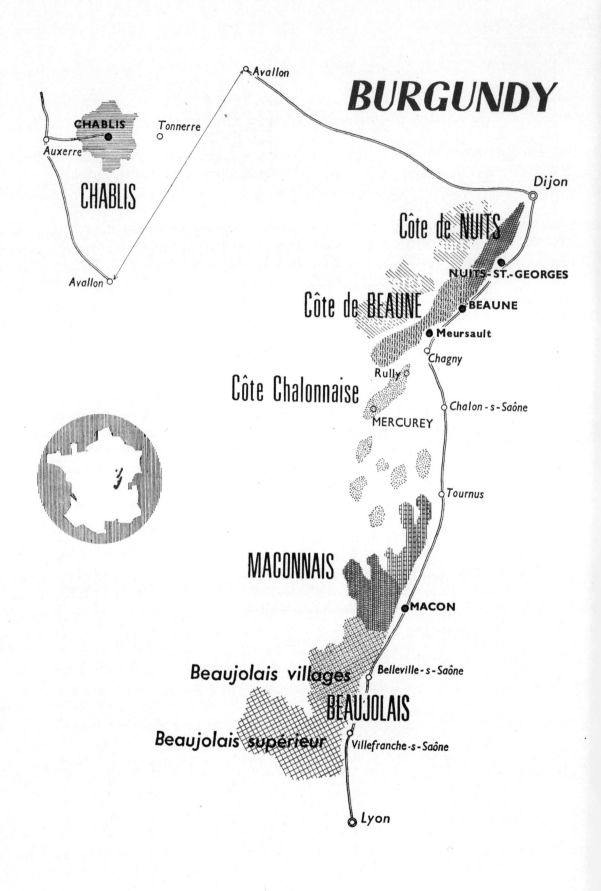

BURGUNDY

CHABLIS

Avallon
Tonnerre
CHABLIS
Auxerre
Avallon

Dijon

Côte de NUITS
NUITS-ST.-GEORGES

Côte de BEAUNE
BEAUNE
Meursault
Chagny

Côte Chalonnaise
Rully
Chalon-s-Saône
MERCUREY

Tournus

MACONNAIS
MACON

Beaujolais villages
Belleville-s-Saône

BEAUJOLAIS

Beaujolais supérieur
Villefranche-s-Saône

Lyon

into the CÔTE DE NUITS and the CÔTE DE BEAUNE. There is then a break in the hills before the Chalonnais, then another gap before the most prolific vineyards of the region are reached, the MACONNAIS and the BEAUJOLAIS. These vineyards are never more than a few miles across but form a very long and narrow ribbon of vineyards from a few miles south of Dijon almost to Lyons, a distance of some 120 miles.

It is natural and inevitable with the vineyards straggling over such a large area that there are several important centres for the trade. In terms of importance if not of geography they are Beaune, Mâcon and Nuits-St. Georges, but there are *négociants* in many other places such as Chablis, Meursault, Santenay and Pontanevaux. This reflects one of the essential characteristics of the region, the way everything is dispersed and fragmented.

Fragmentation begins with the vineyards. Whereas in Bordeaux the great properties nearly all survived the Revolution intact, in Burgundy they were almost irrevocably split up. This was because most of the important properties such as the Clos de Vougeot belonged to the Church, and the attack on Church property was one of the earliest features of the Revolution. Religious houses were dissolved and their property confiscated in 1791. They were then sold not as single entities, as later happened to some Bordeaux *châteaux*, but were split up among peasant proprietors. This has in its turn led to the supremacy of the *négociant* who in Burgundy occupies a far more commanding position than does his counterpart in Bordeaux. For today the greater part of the Burgundy sold both in France and on export markets is under shippers' labels and brands. This is because, with the exception of a few *domaines* who sell their wine in bottle, most proprietors make far too little wine to market it themselves, so they sell their wine to a *négociant* who blends it with the wines of other growers to make a standard Beaune, Nuits-St. Georges or whatever it may be. The position is made more difficult because in the Côte d'Or there are no substantal co-operatives, so there is no standard against which to judge the Pommard or Gevrey Chambertin of one shipper or another, as one can at the co-operatives at Pauillac, St. Estèphe or St. Émilion.

Everything, then, depends on the integrity of the *négociant*, and reputations differ very markedly. Here one must distinguish right away between the commercial wines and the fine wines. The commercial wines are the commune wines, consisting in the Côte d'Or of GEVREY CHAMBERTIN, MOREY ST. DENIS, CHAMBOLLE-MUSIGNY, VOSNE-ROMANÉE, NUITS–ST. GEORGES, ALOXE-CORTON, SAVIGNY–LES–BEAUNE, BEAUNE, POMMARD, VOLNAY, SANTENAY, among the reds, and PULIGNY-MONTRACHET, CHASSAGNE-MONTRACHET and MEURSAULT for the whites. The fine wines are those from individual vineyards or *climats* as they are called in Burgundy. The commercial wines must of necessity be blended and frequently have to be improved. The fine wines sometimes have to be blended if, as in a vineyard like Clos de Vougeot, there are a great number of very small proprietors, but they should be genuine. It is when shippers add Châteauneuf to their Clos Vougeot or their Chambertin that one realises that standards have finally been lowered to a stage bordering on dishonesty and sacrilege. Unhappily this sort of thing does happen; sometimes one comes across compelling evidence, more often it is simply a very strong suspicion based on a knowledge of the true character of the wine. In the Bordeaux chapter I gave a list of the most reputable shippers who export to England. This is not so simple in Burgundy, where some of the biggest operators are suspect but where the small firm is no guarantee of authenticity. However, as it is impossible in practice to set a standard of authenticity which could possibly make any purist happy, for the commercial wines I shall adopt the expedient of naming those *négociants* shipping to England whose wines seem to the author to offer good value for what they are. The cheapest is not always the worst and the most expensive is not, unhappily, always the best. Some may prefer one shipper's style to another and the list is in no way complete or exhaustive.

Firstly, firms meeting the need for sound commune wines: Bouchard Aine, Barton and Guestier, Bichot (sold as Lebegue Bichot in England), Calvet, Geisweiler, Grivelet-Cusset, Marcilly, Pierre Ponnelle, Sichel Frères, Patriarche (the largest firm in Burgundy, but their main business is in branded wines). Secondly, there are the rather smaller firms also producing good commune wines but rather specialising as well in *climats* or vineyard wines: Belin, Bouchard Père et Fils, Chauvenet, Lupé Cholet, J. Drouhin, Faiveley, Hasenklever, Louis Jadot, Louis Latour, Prosper Maufoux, Regnier, Sichel & Co., Doudet-Naudin. In the Beaujolais-Mâconnais region the leading firms are: Thorin, Piat, Mommessin, Aujoux and Faye.

According to individual tastes, the above shippers are safe enough for the everyday wines of the Côte d'Or or for straightforward Beaujolais and Mâconnais wines, although the firms with their headquarters in or around Mâcon are usually to be preferred for the latter. But what about the finer wines? These are more of a problem. One or two shippers do own fine vineyards of their own and produce good wines from them. Louis Latour and Bouchard Père come into this category. Then there are the *domaine* or estate bottled wines. These are nearly always  expensive, but while undoubtedly authentic they are by no means universally excellent. The reason for this is that most of these proprietors are small, producing much less wine than a Bordeaux *château* even where they have holdings in several vineyards. These men are fine viticulturists, but their methods of vinification, while sometimes excellent, do not always measure up to the best modern practice, nor is their keeping and bottling of wines always above reproach. There are nevertheless some magnificent wines which are *domaine* bottled, but it should be emphasised that they represent a tiny percentage of the production of Burgundy.

The mechanics of the market work in much the same way as in Bordeaux. The *négociant* buys from the grower through a *courtier* or broker. But contracts are fairly common, especially in Beaujolais where the larger merchants usually contract with a property to take the entire crop for a number of years. Because of the quantities of wine produced in the Beaujolais and the existence of these agreements, prices have remained remarkably stable in this region. Even in the Côte d'Or the fluctuation of prices has been much less marked in recent years than in Bordeaux. This is partly because the *négociants* are stronger and the growers more numerous and very much smaller, so that they are less able to stand out for a higher price for long should there be any disagreement between *négociant* and grower.

It is, of course, once the wine leaves the grower's cellar and enters the cellars of the merchant that things happen in earnest. Something has already been said about *appellation contrôlée* in the Bordeaux chapter, but the complications and subtleties attached to its application in Burgundy are far worse than anywhere else in France. The reason is not difficult to see. To begin with there are no fewer than 113 separate *appellations* of origin in the whole Burgundy region. These are divided into four categories: general *appellations* such as BOURGOGNE; commune or village *appellations* such as BEAUNE or NUITS-ST. GEORGES in the Côte d'Or; ST. AMOUR or FLEURIE in Beaujolais; *climats* or vineyard *appellations* added to the commune name such as GEVREY-CHAM-BERTIN CLOS ST. JACQUES or POMMARD RUGIENS, and finally the great growths which are allowed to bear the name of the *climat* alone without reference to the commune in which they are situated. CHAMBERTIN, ROMANÉE-CONTI, RICHEBOURG and MON-TRACHET are examples of this.

The difficulty is that a wine with a superior *appellation* may be declassified into a lesser category, so that there are many wines which are entitled to three different *appellations*. While the wine remains in the grower's cellars control is very strict and difficult to evade, but once it arrives in the *négociant's* cellars, where there are wines with perhaps forty or fifty different *appellations*, the task becomes well-nigh impossible. All that can be said is that so many casks enter under certain names and therefore only a corresponding number of casks or cases of wine can leave bearing the same or a defined variation of these names. But it is clearly impossible to say that a cask which leaves the merchant's cellar as Beaune is the same as the one that entered it as Beaune. What can happen is that a cask of genuine Beaune is sold to a country such as England or Holland, where the *appellation* is not enforced, as *vin rouge*, that is to say completely declassified. Then for France or the U.S.A. where the *appellation* is needed, a blend consisting, for example, of the overproduction of a Beaune vine-yard (therefore declassified), some wine from a lesser vineyard in the plain of the same type but of poorer quality and without the Beaune *appellation,* and perhaps some Rhône wine just to give the blend some body, can then be prepared and sold with the Beaune *appellation.* What has happened is a game of musical chairs, the wines that go out are the same as went in, but they have simply exchanged names on the way through. It will also soon be apparent that the possible permutations are enormous.

VINES

It is time now that we left the mysteries of the *négociants'* cellars to explore the vineyards themselves. Another of the contrasts with Bordeaux is that all the fine wines are made from only one grape. In the Côte d'Or this is the Pinot Noir for red wines and the Chardonnay for white wines. It is interesting to note that the Pinot is also one of the grapes used for making Champagne. Because the juice itself is colourless it can be used to make white wine. In Burgundy its colour comes only from the fermentation taking place in the presence of the skins. Much white wine is also made in the Côte d'Or and elsewhere in the Burgundy region from the Aligoté grape. This is more prolific than the Chardonnay and the wine is less fine so that wines made from it cannot bear the name of the place where they are grown, but can only be called Bourgogne Aligoté. The Chardonnay is also used in Chablis and for Pouilly Fuissé. In the Mâconnais and Beaujolais the fine red wines are made from the Gamay, a grape despised in the Côte d'Or where for centuries efforts were made to eradicate it. However, the very different soil of the southern region with its granite sub-soil in contrast to the limestone and clay of the Côte d'Or is ideal for the Gamay, so that here it produces fine wines instead of the common wines it yields further north. A mixture of two-thirds Gamay with one-third Pinot is entitled to the *appellation* BOURGOGNE PASSE TOUT GRAINS.

The climate in Burgundy is continental, that is to say, cold winters but warm summers. On the whole, because of the more reliable summers Burgundy vintages tend to be more consistent than in Bordeaux, but even so, spring frosts and hail often cause serious losses, and wet summers with their consequent trail of disease in the vineyards are not unknown here. The difference between a fine vineyard and an average one is often a matter of situation, protection from frosts and prevailing winds and exposure to the maximum sunshine.

Mention has already been made of the soil when speaking of vines. As all the fine vineyards are situated on hillsides, the pattern of their cultivation is interesting. All the great vineyards are situated about half way up the slopes. Here the soil is neither too acid nor too rich. Higher up the soil becomes thinner and more acid, and often only trees grow on the very tops of the hills. Lower down the soil is richer and the yields are therefore higher and the quality not so fine. Vineyards situated at the very bottom of a hillside are also much more susceptible to frosts.

A great deal has been said and written about vinification in Burgundy. Anyone comparing the deep rich colour of a fine wine of the 1945 or even 1947 vintage with the rather pinkish wines which one often sees today even from very fine properties, can see that a change has taken place. This also applies to white wines. The magnificent golden hue of many great white Burgundies of the past has become a rarity today, and I have tasted wines from some of the greatest vineyards which were so light and delicate that the traditional character of the wine had been reduced to a whisper. One felt that the baby had been thrown out with the bath-water. But such arguments are so often tied up with questions of personal taste. Not everyone wants a white wine which will last for twenty years, and in the past many white wines were badly made and soon oxidised. Some red wines were also coarse and astringent and slow to develop. But one may perhaps be permitted to wonder whether the process of correction has not been carried too far. Certainly many wines have given trouble in bottle in recent years, and some white wines still maderise too quickly.

It should be mentioned here that a certain quantity of *rosé* wines are produced, principally in southern Burgundy, and that a fair quantity of red, *rosé* and white sparkling wines are made, especially in the Chalonnais. The *rosé* wines are not as interesting or as fine as those of Anjou or Tavel, but are dry and fresh and

84

not without merit. The red sparkling wines are probably the best known of the sparkling wines of the region, but the white wines are much better, if less well known.

Apart from the illegal improvement of Burgundy wines by the addition of the wines of other regions, certain improvements are permitted and widely practised. The most important is chaptalisation. This process of adding sugar at the time of the fermentation is much more widely and regularly practised in Burgundy than in Bordeaux. Some connoisseurs today are of the opinion that some of the great wines are over-chaptalised. When red wines have insufficient colour, this can be corrected by warming part of the Must. The colouring matter in the skins is very soluble in warm Must, so that this is quite a simple operation.

Burgundy wines have never been classified in quite the same way as their cousins in Bordeaux. Instead each commune has its own hierarchy, *Grand Cru*, *Premier Cru* and so on, although not every commune can boast of a *Grand Cru*. We shall deal with these *climats* wines under their individual communes.

SERVING

The red and white wines of Burgundy cover such a wide range that they can cope with a great many variations of food. CHABLIS has long enjoyed a great reputation as the perfect accompaniment for shell fish, especially oysters. The charming and delicate wines of POUILLY FUISSÉ are also excellent with many hors-d'oeuvres. The more strongly flavoured wines of CORTON and MEURSAULT are suitable for drinking with fish dishes or with white meat and poultry. The PULIGNY and CHASSAGNE-MONT-RACHETS have a similar function, but their finer wines, culminating in the great MONTRACHET, have considerable body and even richness, so that they can only be served at the beginning of a meal when really fine red wines are to follow. The range of red wines is almost as great. A fresh young BEAUJOLAIS a few months old is delicious served at cellar temperature or even slightly chilled in summer with rather rich spicy dishes which would spoil a more delicate wine. It is also excellent with many traditional Italian dishes and better than most Italian wines. The red wines of the Côte d'Or offer a vast range of various shades of flavour. It is often said that the wines of the Côte de Nuits are heavier than those of the Côte de Beaune. It is more true to say that the difference is one of intensity and depth of flavour, although the red wines of VOLNAY, CHASSAGNE-MONTRACHET and SANTENAY are very noticeably lighter in body as well as being less strongly flavoured. The variations in style are so great that it is impossible to give any precise advice on what goes best with what. Generally speaking these wines go very well with most meat and game dishes, provided that they are not too highly seasoned.

It generally seems to be true that red Burgundies develop a good deal more quickly than they used to. Many good Côte d'Or wines are today drunk after only a year in bottle, that is, when they are only three years old. Many commune wines are today probably at their best at between four and seven years, after which all too many of them begin to decline. But it is still true that the best single vineyard wines are seldom at the height of their powers before they are seven years old. A quite different scale of things applies to Beaujolais. Here some wines are superb when only a few months old. The better wines bearing commune names can be bottled rather later when they are between nine months and a year old, and then need up to a year in bottle to give of their best. Only exceptional single vineyard wines of the best vintages repay keeping more than three or four years.

As with the reds, the keeping properties of white Burgundies vary greatly. Because of their plentiful acidity, wines such as CHABLIS and MEURSAULT can live for many years, but are usually at their best when four to seven years old. The great MONT-RACHET is the exception. The best wines from this exceptional vineyard are often still in their prime when fifteen years old, and are seldom really ready to drink before they are five years old.

VINTAGES Finally a word about Burgundy vintages. One of the interesting points to note here is that the white wines succeed in many years when the reds are poor, and that owing to the greater hazards from frost, good years for white wines in the Côte d'Or are not always followed in Chablis.

1945 A very great year. Production small owing to a late frost. Red wines have developed slowly into outstanding wines only now approaching their best. White wines were rather full-bodied but some were very fine. Now mostly too old. The Chablis crop was destroyed by frost.

1946 A light year, with some good red and white wines, not generally exported to England.

1947 A great year, but owing to the exceptional heat there was a great deal of trouble with the vinification and consequently many failures. Those wines which did succeed have matured into exceptional wines.

1948 As in Bordeaux this vintage suffered from being in between 1947 and 1949. Quality for both red and white was above average. Only a few red wines are now good for drinking.

1949 A very good year which some have preferred to 1947. The red wines have lasted well. The white wines, now mostly too old, were fine, especially successful in Chablis.

1950 A very big crop of light red wines which were not generally exported. White wines were, however, excellent.

1951 A mediocre year all round.

1952 A very good year generally. The red wines have proved slow maturing and lack the charm of the 1953s, the white wines are very fine indeed with superb balance.

1953 A very fine year. The reds had great charm and breed but were not so long-lived as the 1952s. The whites were again exceptionally fine, but very little Chablis was made.

1954 A large crop of very variable quality. Very few wines were exported. A good year for Chablis.

1955 English bottled red wines of this vintage need to be selected with great caution as many suffered malo-lactic fermentation in bottle. Most of the French bottled reds which have been exported are very fine indeed. A very good year for white wines, but very little Chablis was made.

1956 A bad year for red wines. The white wines were, however, quite good especially in Chablis.

1957 A small yield but very successful. The reds are well made and will live, although they lack the charm of the 1955s and 1959s. Whites are good, but Chablis was destroyed by a late frost.

1958 A successful year for white wines; very poor for the reds.

1959 A rare combination of quantity and quality. The reds are very supple and attractive, and have developed better in bottle than many supposed. The best should continue to improve for some time. Some of the white wines were a little heavy, but generally a fine year.

1960 Red wines very poor and not exported. White wines light but good. There is a tendency for them to oxidise early.

1961 A small yield. The red wines have more depth and are more robust than the 1959s, but this is combined with great fruit and breed. Should develop into very fine wines. The whites were perhaps better balanced than the 1959s. A great year in Beaujolais.

1962 Very well constituted wines which, if not as fine as the 1961s, should develop very well.

1963 Some good white wines especially in Chablis, but the reds are unlikely to be exported.

1964 The quality of the reds is somewhat variable, but the best have developed well though sometimes lacking in staying power. The whites are not so well balanced as the 1962s.

1965 A very poor year indeed. Even white wines were below standard, the few successes of 1963 not being repeated.

88

1966 A large crop and good all round quality. Superior to 1964. The best red and white wines should develop and last well.

1967 A very mixed year for quality. Whites much better than reds. Only a few red wines from the Côte de Nuits will be worth ageing.

1968 A few pleasant quick maturing white wines were made. Reds were very poor.

1969 A small crop produced outstanding quality. The red wines may turn out to be the best since 1949; the white are well balanced but a shade heavy.

CHABLIS

These delectable white wines are grown in the hilly vineyards that cluster around the little town of Chablis, just a short detour from Auxerre on the N.6. The wines of Chablis have unhappily been the victims of widespread frauds, and a great deal of very ordinary white wine masquerades under this distinguished name. The only way to be certain that you are indeed drinking Chablis is to buy a *Premier Cru*, which is very little more expensive if English bottled than many an ordinary anonymous Chablis.

The wines of Chablis are divided into four grades: *Grand Cru, Premier Cru, Chablis, Petit Chablis*. They should be pale in colour with a greenish tinge, and are in all but the finest years light in body with a most agreeable blend of acidity and fruit producing a slightly steely crisp impression on the palate. The *Grands Crus* have rather more body than other Chablis and in some ways are not quite so typical as the *Premiers Crus*. Ordinary *Chablis* is also

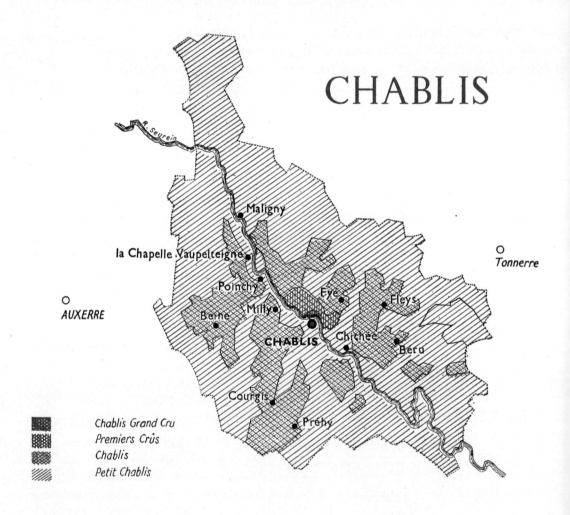

CHABLIS

R. Serein

Maligny

la Chapelle Vaupelteigne

Poinchy

Berne   Milly   Eye   Fleys

CHABLIS   Chichée   Beru

AUXERRE

Tonnerre

Courgis

Préhy

Chablis Grand Cru
Premiers Crûs
Chablis
Petit Chablis

an excellent wine not far behind the *Premiers Crus* in quality, while the *Petit Chablis* wines can also be excellent, though they are seldom to be seen under their own colours. The classified vineyards are as follows:

Grands Crus:

BLANCHOTS	LES PREUSES
BOUGROS	VALMUR
LES CLOS	VAUDÉSIR
GRENOUILLES	

Premiers Crus:

BEAUROY	MONT DE MILIEU
BEUGNON	MONTÉE DE TONNERE
BUTTEAUX	MONTMAIN
CHAPELOT	PIED D'ALOUP
CHÂTAIN	SÉCHET
CÔTE DE FONTENAY	TROEME
CÔTE DE LÉCHET	VAILLON
FOURCHAUME	VAUCOUPIN
LES FORETS	VAULORENT
LES LYS	VAUPINENT
MÉLINOTS	VOSGROS AND VOGIRAS

CÔTE DE NUITS

FIXIN The wines from this most northerly of the communes of the Côte de Nuits are seldom seen in this country. They are similar in character to those of the neighbouring Gevrey Chambertin, being high in alcohol but not so fine.

The outstanding *Premiers Crus* are as follows:

CLOS DE LA PERRIÈRE	LES HERVELETS
CLOS DU CHAPITRE	

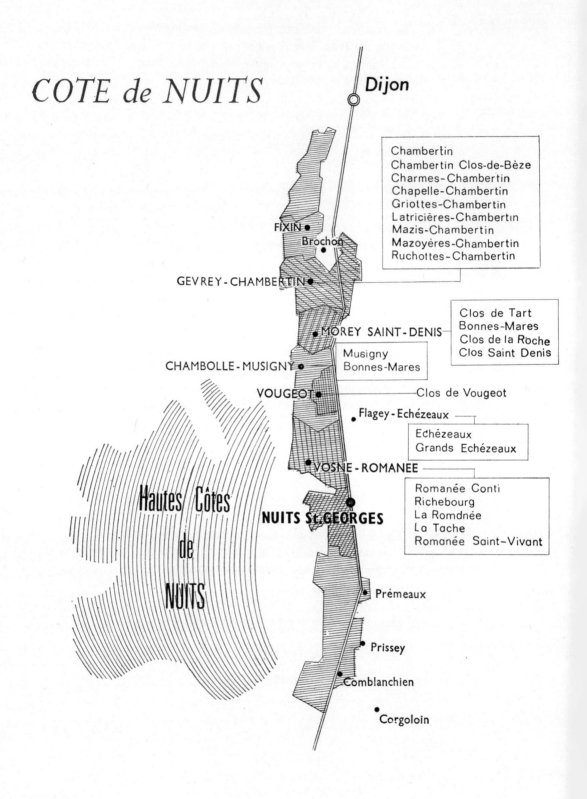

COTE de NUITS

Dijon

Chambertin
Chambertin Clos-de-Bèze
Charmes-Chambertin
Chapelle-Chambertin
Griottes-Chambertin
Latricières-Chambertin
Mazis-Chambertin
Mazoyères-Chambertin
Ruchottes-Chambertin

FIXIN
Brochon

GEVREY-CHAMBERTIN

Clos de Tart
Bonnes-Mares
Clos de la Roche
Clos Saint Denis

MOREY SAINT-DENIS

Musigny
Bonnes-Mares

CHAMBOLLE-MUSIGNY

VOUGEOT — Clos de Vougeot

Flagey-Echézeaux

Echézeaux
Grands Echézeaux

VOSNE-ROMANEE

Romanée Conti
Richebourg
La Romdnée
La Tache
Romanée Saint-Vivant

Hautes Côtes de NUITS

NUITS St.GEORGES

Prémeaux

Prissey

Comblanchien

Corgoloin

These are well worth looking out for, and compare favourably with many wines in Gevrey.

GEVREY-CHAMBERTIN

Like many villages in the Côte d'Or the tiny village of Gevrey basks in the glory of its greatest vineyard by adding its name to its own. The ordinary commune wines of Gevrey are full, robust, and take longer than most Côte d'Or wines to develop.

The two great vineyards here are CHAMBERTIN and CHAMBERTIN CLOS DE BEZE. These are certainly some of the greatest wines of Burgundy, but unhappily there are a number of proprietors and the quality of the wines sold as Chambertin varies tremendously. Of the many wines sold under these names which I have tried, one of the best has been *domaine* bottled by Rousseau, a very good grower in Gevrey. On the other hand the finest bottle of old Chambertin I have ever had came from the private cellar of a *négociant* in Nuits, and was a wine he had bottled himself. All that can be said is that a good deal of care must be taken in selecting reliable and worthy examples of these great vineyards.

The character of the wines themselves shows a wonderful variety of qualities, for they are perhaps the most vigorous and powerful of red Burgundies, yet they excel in finesse and breed.

CHAMBERTIN and CHAMBERTIN CLOS DE BEZE are classed as *têtes de cuvées*. Then come seven vineyards which are something of an anomaly. They are only classified officially as *Premiers Crus*, but have the right to hyphenate their name with that of Chambertin without the commune name. Thus we have CHARMES-CHAMBERTIN but GEVREY-CHAMBERTIN CLOS ST. JACQUES. Given the general rules enunciated in the introduction, most people would assume that the Charmes was a finer wine than the Clos St. Jacques, but this is not necessarily so. Indeed, I have on several occasions found wines from the Clos St. Jacques which were definitely finer than from Charmes-Chambertin, although both were made by the same grower.

The seven vineyards classified as *Premiers Crus* are as follows:

CHARMES–CHAMBERTIN
CHAPELLE–CHAMBERTIN
GRIOTTE–CHAMBERTIN
MAZOYÈRES–CHAMBERTIN
LATRICIÈRES–CHAMBERTIN
MAZIS–CHAMBERTIN
RUCHOTTES–CHAMBERTIN

There are twenty-two other *Premiers Crus* but most of these are seldom to be found individually, that is to say, they are more likely to be blended together and sold as GEVREY-CHAMBERTIN PREMIER CRU. Those most often sold individually are:

CLOS ST. JACQUES, LES VEROILLES and COMBE-AU-MOINE.

MOREY-ST. DENIS

The wines of this commune, which lies between the two famous ones of Gevrey-Chambertin and Chambolle-Musigny, deserve to be better known. The wines are big, robust, sturdy fellows and the great wines can be very long lived. In former days these wines were sold under the names of their two famous neighbours, hence their neglect. For this reason these wines are often very good value.

One curiosity is the name of the commune itself; St. Denis was added to Morey long ago, and the Clos St. Denis is not today regarded as the best wine in the commune, a situation unique in the Côte d'Or.

The great wines here are:

CLOS DE TART
CLOS DE LA ROCHE
CLOS ST. DENIS
BONNES-MARES

The last of these vineyards really belongs to Chambolle, but a tiny part of it, three acres to be precise, against thirty-three acres in Chambolle, lies within the boundaries of Morey.

94

The CLOS DE TART is one of the few important vineyards in Burgundy under the ownership of a single proprietor, the Mâcon firm of Mommessin. Unhappily the wine is now not as consistent as it should be, and does not always achieve the greatness it did in the past. The CLOS DE LA ROCHE is another fine sturdy wine and is today sometimes the best of the great Morey wines. The CLOS ST. DENIS is markedly lighter but has more elegance and finesse, a hint of Bonne-Mares and the wines of Chambolle.

The other famous vineyard here is CLOS DES LAMBRAYS, but this has to hyphenate its name with that of the commune. As with the case of the Clos St. Jacques in Gevrey, the distinction has no very great validity and this vineyard is usually placed alongside those already mentioned for quality.

CHAMBOLLE-MUSIGNY

From here onwards the wines of the Côte de Nuits have more delicacy and finesse, less body and robustness. The wines of Chambolle have a noticeably fine and penetrating bouquet, coupled with great vinosity.

Here is to be found one of the great wines of Burgundy, MUSIGNY, the most feminine and ethereal of them all. At its best it is a wine of supreme delicacy, exquisite bouquet and a wonderful, silky texture. Unfortunately though, there are a number of owners and it is not easy to find worthy examples of this great wine.

BONNES-MARES, which we have already encountered in Morey, is the other great wine of the commune. Curiously it is relatively unknown and unappreciated among the top wines of Burgundy.

The outstanding *Premiers Crus* are LES AMOUREUSES and LES CHARMES. These must have their names hyphenated with that of the commune. These are both delightful and distinctive wines which show the merits of this commune to their best advantage.

Now we come to perhaps the most famous vineyard in Burgundy, if not the best. The great vineyard of CLOS DE VOUGEOT comprises 125 acres entirely enclosed by a great stone wall. The vineyard and the wall, which took two hundred years to build, are the work of the Cistercians, and date back to the twelfth century. Unhappily, the vineyard was split up as a result of the Revolution, re-assembled for a time in the nineteenth century, but now seems irrevocably fragmented again. There are today some seventy owners, and Lichine lists twenty-eight of some substance. The largest parcel was until recently owned by J. Marin, the Shipper in Nuits St. Georges. However this holding has recently been broken up. Among the growers who *domaine* bottle and produce good wine are René Engel and Clair-Dau.

At its best this is one of the great wines of Burgundy, velvety, rich and perfumed. But inevitably there are many unworthy and even fraudulent wines sold under this great name, for unfortunately fame is a great temptation to dishonesty. Another factor is that owing to the great size of the vineyard the style of the wines differs, those at the top of the slope being the finest. Thus, to produce the best balance it is often advisable to blend wines from different parts of the vineyard, a further complication.

It is often supposed that Vougeot and its famous Clos are synonymous, but there are in fact other wines in the commune, and even some *Premiers Crus*. There is the white wine LE CLOS-BLANC, one of the few in the Côte de Nuits, LES CRAS, and CLOS DE LA PERRIÈRE. I came across the last named for the first time quite recently, and found it, rather to my surprise, a wine of real breed, indeed better than many wines from the Clos Vougeot itself.

As the result of various decrees we shall consider under this heading certain wines which in fact lie within the neighbouring commune of FLAGEY-ECHÉZEAUX.

Château Loudenne on the banks of the Gironde estuary at St. Yzans in the Medoc with its rose-pink walls and turreted grey slate roofs surrounded by vineyards. Built in the mid-eighteenth century, Château Loudenne has been owned by W. & A. Gilbey Ltd. since 1875 and is one of the very few properties in France where the Union Jack flies at vintage time.

Very carefully an estate-owner at Puligny-Montrachet parts the vine leaves to examine two fine bunches of his grapes.

Château de Chasselas in the Beaujolais.

following page 96

Grape gathering is a family affair. At Château Loudenne in the Medoc, children help their parents in the vineyards during the vintage. Bin-loads of grapes are shouldered into wagons which will take them to the wine presses.

In a vineyard cellar at Puligny Mont-rachet the estate manager fills a tastevin for his cellarman. The tastevin, or tasting cup, dates from pre-electricity days. Made of silver with reflecting surfaces and shallow, so that the colour and texture of the wine can be observed in a candle-lit cellar, it is a piece o tradition still used today.

following page 96

An official of the Order of Chevaliers du Tastevin at a wine-tasting ceremony. The Chapters of the Vinous Orders of France formed by the growers, shippers and other connoisseurs of wine, meet with grand ceremony for initiation of new members, and membership is considered a great honour. The Chevaliers du Tastevin, Burgundy's famous Order, meet in the castle of Clos de Vougeot, in their ceremonial red robes and tall black hats, with their insignia—the tastevin—the wine taster's silver cup, hanging around their necks.

following page 96

Bottling wine at Château Loudenne in the Medoc. The worker on the left is driving corks into the bottles.

Labelling bottles of wine at Château Loudenne in the Medoc.

following page 96

The "remuage" at Heidsieck & Co., Reims, makers of Dry Monopole Champagne. The "remuage", a stage in the long process of Champagne production, is the daily shaking and twisting of the bottles over a ten to twelve-week period in order to induce the sediment into their necks. Later the necks are frozen and the "plug" of ice containing the sediment removed by the "disgorgement" process.

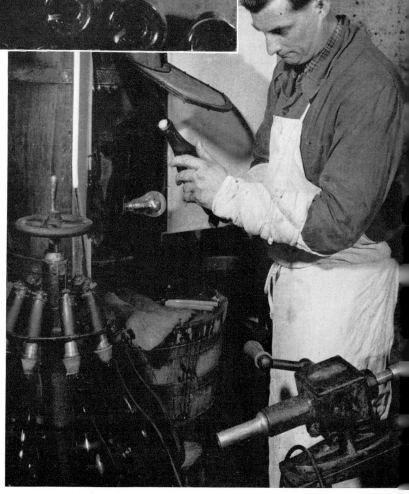

The manual process of removing the frozen sediment from a bottle ("disgorgement") of Dry Monopole Champagne, being carried out by a skilled worker.

following page 9

A vine in blossom (Rudesheim).

Vineyard near Merscheidt in Winkel (Rheingau) showing a simple protection against frost.

following page 96

... wall toward Lagos below the castle

Within the boundaries of Vosne-Romanée are to be found some of the richest treasures in all Burgundy, and the prices fetched by these rare jewels surpass those for any other Burgundy today. Although most of the individual vineyards are small, probably more fine wine is made here than in any other commune of the Côte d'Or. The wines are characterised by their superb bouquet, delicate yet fragrant and penetrating, while the wines themselves are rich but lighter than Clos Vougeot or Chambolle with more finesse and tremendous flavour.

The great *têtes de cuvées* which are sold under their own names without the addition of the commune name, are as follows:

ROMANÉE-CONTI

LA TÂCHE

LA ROMANÉE

RICHEBOURG

ROMANÉE-SAINT-VIVANT

GRANDS-ECHÉZEAUX

ECHÉZEAUX

The most important proprietor of these vineyards is the Domaine de la Romanée-Conti. They own the whole of Romanée-Conti and La Tâche, and parts of Richebourg, Grands-Echézeaux and Echézeaux. All the wines are domaine bottled. The most famous of their vineyards is of course ROMANÉE-CONTI. Until the war the ungrafted French vines were lovingly maintained here, but it proved impossible to give them the necessary care during the war, and the old vines were finally pulled up in 1946. The first wines from the new grafted vines were made in 1952. But if Romanée-Conti is the most famous and expensive of these wines, aided no doubt by the fact that the vineyard is only four and a half acres, for quality it is often closely rivalled by LA TÂCHE and RICHEBOURG, both very great wines. The Echézeaux wines are in the commune of FLAGEY-ECHÉZEAUX, but are for all practical purposes to be classed with the great Vosne-Romanées. They have great finesse but perhaps a little less power than Richebourg. ROMANÉE-ST. VIVANT is the only one of these vineyards not to be represented in the cellars of the Domaine de la Romanée-Conti,

E

so it is not so easy to make a direct comparison. Two of the best
growers here are Marey-Monge and Louis Latour. In 1966 the
Domaine de la Romanée-Conti took over the management
but not the ownership of Marey-Monge's portion of Romanée
St. Vivant.

There are also some very good and well known *Premiers Crus*
and these enjoy a very high reputation. The best known are:
LES MALCONSORTS, LES SUCHOTS, LES BEAUMONTS (or BEAUX-
MONTS), LA GRANDE RUE.

**NUITS-SAINT
GEORGES**

This is the most important town in the Côte de Nuits and also
produces more wine than any other commune on the Côte.
Because of their very similar character, the wines of the neigh-
bourin gcommune of Prémeaux are sold as Nuits-St. Georges.
Nuits itself is a charming little town of narrow twisting streets
and many picturesque houses with a minute river flowing
through its midst crossed by several narrow bridges. This is the
headquarters of many *négociants*, and is second only to Beaune
in importance as a commercial centre for the Côte d'Or.

There are no great wines produced here, but there are plenty of
very good *Premiers Crus*. The wines are robust and full-flavoured
but have less finesse than those of Vosne-Romanée. They develop well in bottle and can often live for many years. The
principal *Premiers Crus* are as follows:

At Nuits: LES ST. GEORGES, LES VAUCRAINS, LES CAILLES,
LES PORRETS, LES PRULIERS, LES RICHEMONNES, LES CRAS,
LES THOREY.

At Prémeaux: CLOS DE LA MARÉCHALE, CLOS ARLOT, CLOS
DES FORÊTS, LES DIDIERS, LES CORVÉES-PAGETS, LES PERDRIX.

The Nuits *négociants*, Lupé Cholet, own a fine property overlooking the town, known as Château Gris. It is meticulously
cared for and the wine is certainly of *Premier Cru* standing.

Nuits also has its own Hospice, although of course a good deal
less famous than that at Beaune. Since 1962 certain parcels of

Premiers Crus have been auctioned yearly for the benefit of the Hospices, but the quantities are small compared with those which have been accumulated by the Hospices de Beaune over the centuries. A tiny quantity of white wine is produced but it is only a curiosity.

CÔTE DE BEAUNE

Here we find very good red wines, but they are not as fine or as long-lived as those on the Côte de Nuits. On the other hand, the white wines are the finest in the whole Burgundy region.

ALOXE-CORTON

RÉCOLTE 1962

ORTON-MARÉCHAUDES
Appellation Corton Contrôlée
du Domaine de Monsieur Tiercé
Propriétaire à Ladoix-Serrigny, Côte-d'Or

Père & Fils, Négociants à Beaune, Côte-d'Or
Mis en bouteilles en Bourgogne

This, the first commune of the Côte de Beaune, produces very fine red wines which mature more slowly than the other wines of the Côte de Beaune, and the first of the great white wines of the Côte. These red wines have an intensity of flavour which steadily develops with age, without quite the richness and body of the Côte de Nuits wines but with more backbone than the other Beaune wines. CORTON-CHARLEMAGNE is one of the most famous white wines of Burgundy, but the quantity produced is tiny, and that made and bottled by Louis Latour and Louis Jadot is usually far superior to that of any other growers. This wine is fine but less rich than Montrachet, not so flowery as a fine Meursault, but has great finesse and elegance and a beautiful balance.

It should be noted in passing that certain vineyards or parts of vineyards lying in the communes of LADOIX-SERRIGNY and PERNAND-VERGELESSES are now classified as Aloxe-Corton.

The two more famous vineyards, CORTON, producing red wines, and CORTON-CHARLEMAGNE, with only white wines, are sold without the commune name. But on a par with the red Corton are CORTON-BRESSANDES, CORTON-CLOS DU ROI and CORTON LES MARÉCHAUDES. Louis Latour makes a very fine wine from an unclassified vineyard known as CORTON CHATEAU GRANCEY which deserves to be classed with the *premiers crus*.

99

COTE de BEAUNE

Comblanchien
Corgoloin

LADOIX-SERRIGNY

Corton
Corton-Charlemagne
Charlemagne

PERNAND-VERGELESSES

ALOXE-CORTON

CHOREY-LES-BEAUNE

SAVIGNY
-LES-BEAUNE

BEAUNE

Hautes Côtes

POMMARD

VOLNAY

de

MONTHELIE

AUXEY-DURESSES

LE MONTRACHET
CHEVALIER-MONTRACHET
BATARD-MONTRACHET
BIENVENUES-BATARD-MONTRACHET
CRIOTS-BATARD-MONTRACHET

SAINT-ROMAIN

BEAUNE

MEURSAULT

PULIGNY-MONTRACHET

SAINT-AUBIN

CHASSAGNE-MONTRACHET

CHAGNY

LE MONTRACHET
BATARD-MONTRACHET
CRIOTS-BATARD-MONTRACHET

DEZIZE-LES-MARANGES

SANTENAY

SAMPIGNY-LES-MARANGES

CHEILLY-LES-MARANGES

RULLY

MERCUREY

Côte Chalonnaise

GIVRY

MONTAGNY

BEAUNE This picturesque old walled town is not only the centre of the Côte which bears its name but the wine capital of the Côte d'Or as well. Practically every important shipper of Burgundy either has an office here, or at least his name on a plate! The great attraction is the famous Hospices founded in 1443 by Nicolas Rollin, for the care of old people. From the beginning people wishing to endow the Hospices have presented it with a vineyard, and the wines from these vineyards are auctioned every November, just after the vintage, for the benefit of the Hospices.

These wines have always been among the finest in the Côte de Beaune and today their more traditional vinification gives them more colour and body than many famous wines from the Côte de Nuits. They are, of course, always expensive, because as they are sold for charity the prices paid are usually well above their strict commercial value, especially as they have achieved a prestige value for restaurants and wine merchants throughout the world. It must be pointed out that the reputation of the merchant whose name appears as bottler on the label is important when buying a Hospices wine, since there is no domaine bottling and all wines bought at the auction have to be taken away and looked after by the purchaser. Unfortunately, there is no control of the quantity of labels which purchasers may obtain. The wines of the Hospices are usually known by the name of the donor, BEAUNE CUVÉE NICOLAS ROLLIN or MEURSAULT GENEVRIÉRES CUVÉE BAUDOT, for example. The list of *Cuvées* is as follows:

Red Wines

Beaune	Guigone de Salins
Beaune	Clos des Avaux
Beaune	Nicolas Rollin
Beaune	Hugues et Louis Bétault
Beaune	Dames Hospitalières
Beaune	Pierre Virely
Beaune	Estienne
Beaune	Brunet
Beaune	Rousseau-Deslandes
Pommard	Dames de la Charité

Pommard	Billardet
Savigny-les-Beaune and Vergelesses	Fouquerand
Savigny-les-Beaune and Vergelesses	Forneret
Savigny-les-Beaune	Arthur Girard
Corton	Charlotte Dumay
Corton	Dr. Peste
Volnay (Santenots)	Jehan de Massol
Volnay (Santenots)	Gauvain
Volnay	Général Muteau
Volnay	Blondeau
Auxey-Duresses	Boillot
Monthélie	Jacques Lebelin
Beaune	Maurice Drouhin

White Wines

Meursault	Loppin
Meursault	Jehan Humblot
Meursault-Genevrières	Baudot
Meursault	Goureau
Meursault-Charmes	Albert Grivault
Meursault-Charmes	de Bahèzre de Lanlay
Corton-Charlemagne	François de Salins
Meursault-Genevrières	Philippe-de-Bon

The wines of Beaune are soft, sometimes full-bodied, and at their best have a silky vinosity which is most attractive, and deservedly makes these wines very popular. There are a good number of excellent *Premiers Crus*, of which the most notable are:

LES MARCONNETS, LES FÈVES, LES BRESSANDES, LES GRÈVES, LES TEURONS, CLOS DES MOUCHES (partly planted with white grapes), CLOS DU ROI, LES CENT-VIGNES, CLOS DE LA MOUSSE, LES VIGNES-FRANCHES, LES AIGROTS, LES AVAUX, LES THEURONS.

A part of the Beaune Grèves vineyard is known as Vigne l'Enfant Jésus. It is a monopole of Bouchard Père et Fils. Many of these vineyards are considerably larger than most of the famous vineyards of the Côte du Nuits or, for that matter, of other communes in the same Côte, and there are more acres of classified vines here than anywhere else on the Côte d'Or. All the names mentioned must be hyphenated with the commune name of Beaune.

SAVIGNY-LES-BEAUNE

The *appellation contrôlée* here is Savigny. These wines have been rather overshadowed by those of Beaune, but they are often excellent value and while not so fine as those of Beaune have many of the same characteristics and are pleasantly perfumed. There are several good *Premiers Crus*: LES MARCONNETS, LES LAVIÈRES, LES GRAVAINS.

POMMARD

There was a time in England when Pommard was the best known Burgundy, and the world-wide demand is still very great. A great deal of wine is produced, but even so this is not sufficient to meet the demand, and these wines have for long been notorious for the degree of fraud which is perpetrated in their name. One also sees here an unfortunate result of the *appellation contrôlée* laws. The Pommard *appellation* is a very valuable one and always fetches a high price, and it is unhappily true that with this assured price some proprietors make very inferior wines, both through over-production and bad vinification. Such wines have to be improved by the *négociants*.

At their best the wines of Pommard are rather firmer than those of Beaune, and keep very well. The best growths have a very fine bouquet, much delicacy and a most distinctive and distinguished flavour. The best *Premiers Crus* are as follows: LES ÉPENOTS (sometimes spelt ÉPENEAUX), LES RUGIENS (divided into BAS and HAUT, but this distinction seldom finds its way on to a label), CLOS DE LA COMMARAINE, LES PETITS-ÉPENOTS, LES ARVELETS.

VOLNAY These wines are decidedly lighter than those of Beaune and Pommard, and mature quickly. However, they are particularly agreeable with a pronounced bouquet of great charm, while the wine itself is soft and well rounded and refreshing to drink. Owing to their great delicacy and finesse, they are sometimes compared with Musigny.

There are a number of very good *Premiers Crus*, but one of the curiosities here is that one of the best known growths, VOLNAY SANTENOTS, is in fact in the adjoining commune of Meursault.

Other outstanding growths are:

CAILLERETS, CHAMPANS, FREMIETS, CHEVRET, CLOS DE CHÊNES, LES ANGLES, CLOS DES DUCS.

MONTHÉLIE One of the least known communes of the Côte d'Or. The wines are very similar to those of Volnay, having much of the same delicacy and charm without quite the same fineness of quality; but they can represent very good value if you can find a wine merchant with the courage to put one on his list.

AUXEY-DURESSES Another little-known commune. Its wines are of similar quality and type as those of Monthélie. It can also boast of a Hospice growth sold as CUVÉE BOILLOT.

MEURSAULT This is the first of the great white wine communes. We have already met a great white wine in Aloxe-Corton, but here white wines reign supreme and 97 per cent of the wines of the commune are white.

Meursault is a small but ancient town, and here many dedicated growers and small *négociants* have their cellars. One of the best is Ropiteau, both a grower and a *négociant*; then there are a number of good growers such as Matrot and the Château de Meursault.

Louis Latour produces an exceptionally good Meursault and the *cuvée* of the Hospices de Beaune are usually very fine if they have been well looked after.

The changes in vinification have affected the white wines as well as the red. In the past these wines were heavier and fuller in flavour, and Meursault often lasted many years in bottle. Today, however, most growers produce a much lighter wine. This suits Meursault better than the Montrachets. The wines are dry and crisp with a very special character which marks them out quite clearly from Corton Charlemagne on the one hand, and the Montrachets on the other. The bouquet is especially characteristic and this tends to be highlighted by bottle age. Because of their dryness and delicacy allied to breed and individuality, these are among the most popular of white Burgundies.

The outstanding growths are: CLOS DES PERRIÈRES, LES PERRIÈRES and LES CHARMES. These are closely followed by: GENEVRIÈRES, BLAGNY, GOUTTE D'OR and LE PORUZOT. The vineyard SANTENOTS is planted with Pinot Noir vines and is sold as Volnay.

**PULIGNY-
MONTRACHET**

Here, as in Meursault, there are a number of important growers, but no cellars because an underground stream makes this impossible. Instead, there are small tightly shuttered stores like miniature Bordeaux *chais* for keeping the precious white wines.

The great treasure here is the famous MONTRACHET vineyard, which the commune of Puligny shares with its neighbour Chassagne. This is the greatest white wine in Burgundy and stands beside Château Yquem as one of the two supreme white wines of France. Unfortunately, the vineyard is divided among a number of proprietors, and not all the wine is of similar excellence. The largest producers are Baron Thenard, Bouchard Père et Fils, Marquis de Laguiche, Domaine de la Romanée-Conti (this portion of the vineyard was until very recently the property of the Comte de Moucheron), Mme Boillereault de Chauvigne, Domaine Jacques Prieur (this wine is sold exclusively by Calvet, *négociants* in Beaune). Montrachet is always an expensive wine, and it is inadvisable to buy any wine not bearing the name of one of the proprietors. Some *négociants* sell a Montrachet under their own label, and while I have occasionally found one which was excellent, many others are poor and of doubtful authenticity.

A true Montrachet well made is a glorious wine never to be forgotten, and nearly every bottle one is privileged to drink leaves an indelible impression on the memory. It is full-bodied and rich yet never truly sweet, it is fresh and velvety with a superb bouquet of great elegance and finesse. The qualities of a great Montrachet only gradually unfurl with age, and in its prime such a wine seems ageless. I have never had the good fortune to drink a bottle which was older than fifteen years, but that was in peak condition, youthful in colour still and beautifully fresh with no hint of the onset of maderisation.

Next to Montrachet comes CHEVALIER-MONTRACHET, then BÂTARD-MONTRACHET. Just to be confusing the *appellation* divides the Bâtard vineyard into three parts: BÂTARD-MONT-RACHET (partly in Puligny and partly in Chassagne), BIENVENUE-BÂTARD-MONTRACHET (wholly in Puligny) and CRIOTS-BÂTARD-MONTRACHET (wholly in Chassagne). Unfortunately, one does not find as many worthy examples of wines from these vineyards as their reputation and price would suggest.

There are several excellent *Premiers Crus* whose names are hyphenated with that of the commune. The best are: LE CAIL-LERET, LES COMBETTES, CHAMP-CANET, LES PUCELLES, CLAVOIL-LONS, LES REFERTS, LES FOLATIÈRES.

CHASSAGNE-MONTRACHET

It comes as something of a shock to learn that 64 per cent of the wines produced in this commune are red, and in England the name is almost exclusively associated with its white wines. As the section on Puligny has shown, it is hardly possible to separate the white wines of these two communes; their most famous vineyards are mostly shared.

Of the vineyards producing white wines which are exclusive to Chassagne, the best are: MORGEOT, ABBAYE DE MORGEOT,

GRANDES-RUCHOTTES, LA MALTROIE (or MALTROYE), CAILLERET.

The red wines are well worth looking out for and are often excellent value. They are soft and easy to drink and are very supple and fruity in flavour. The best of the *Premiers Crus* are: CLOS ST. JEAN, LA BOUDRIOTTE, MORGEOT, ABBAYE DE MORGEOT.

SANTENAY

This is the last important commune of the Côte d'Or. Strangely enough there is a sharp swing back from white wines to red which represent 99 per cent of the wines produced in the commune. These wines are not as widely appreciated as they should be. Like the red wines of Chassagne they are light in both colour and body, but are velvety in texture and have a certain backbone which enables them to age better than one might at first suppose.

There are several *Premiers Crus* which are worth watching out for: LES GRAVIÈRES, CLOS DE TAVANNES, LA MALADIÈRE.

ÔTE DE BEAUNE VILLAGES

This is an *appellation contrôlée* which is used when at least two wines from among sixteen *appellations* are blended together, but wines carrying the *appellations* Pommard, Volnay or Aloxe-Corton can never be transformed into Côte de Beaune Villages.

CÔTE CHALONNAISE

There is a gap in the hills which we have been following from Fixin to Santenay, then there is a further small range before they reach the Mâconnais and Beaujolais to the south. This small area, known either as the Côte Chalonnaise or the Region de Mercurey, contains four communes enjoying their own *appellations*, MERCUREY, GIVRY, RULLY and MONTAGNY. This is really a continuation of the Côte de Beaune, the wines are very similar in style and the Pinot Noir is planted here, not the Gamay.

MACONNAIS
BEAUJOLAIS

MACONNAIS

Viré •

Charbonnières •

Verzé •

Hurigny •

Milly •

Sancé •

Vergisson •   Prisse •

Solutré •

MACON •

Pouilly •

POUILLY-FUISSE •——— Fuissé •   Pouilly-Loche •

Chaintré •   Pouilly-Vinzelles •

JULIENAS •

SAINT-AMOUR •

CHENAS •

MOULIN-A-VENT •

FLEURIE •

CHIROUBLES •   Romanèche-Thorins •

Lancié •

Beaujeu •   MORGON •

Beaujolais villages

COTE DE BROUILLY •   Belleville-s-Saône ○

BROUILLY •   St. Lager •

Odenas •   Charentay •

BEAUJOLAIS

Villefranche-s-Saône ○

Beaujolais supérieur

Mercurey	The best red wines of the district are to be found here. A good quantity of wine is made which is light but fairly rich and has finesse and a very pleasing style about it. These are generous, easy wines with a definite character of their own. A *Premier Cru*, CLOS DU ROI, is sometimes to be found. These wines are usually excellent value.
Givry	The production here is very much smaller than in Mercurey. Again the wine is mostly red and very similar in style to the Mercureys, but rather lighter.
Rully	Here, white wines are in the ascendancy, some 21 per cent are red. This is the centre of the Sparkling wine business. The white wines of Rully are considered especially suitable for converting into sparkling wines by the *Méthode Champenoise*.
Montagny	Only white wines are produced here. These are fairly ordinary, decent unpretentious wines.

MÂCONNAIS

Now we are truly in southern Burgundy. The town of Mâcon itself lies in the south of the region, not far from where the Mâconnais adjoins the Beaujolais, and is the commercial centre of the region. The town lies on the western side of the river Saône, and the cellars of a number of *négociants* are to be found along the banks of this river, which not infrequently floods, especially opposite Mâcon.

The greatest wine of the Mâconnais is the famous white wine, POUILLY FUISSÉ. The grape is the classic Chardonnay, and the wine at its best is vigorous, fairly high in alcohol, often quite rich but dry. This is a most refreshing wine of great charm with a pleasant bouquet. Unfortunately, this popular wine is all too often abused, and everyone has tasted poor, characterless wines under this name, as well as badly kept oxidised wines. Such examples have done some harm to the reputation of what should be a very good wine. Only vigilance and trial and error will discover worthy examples of Pouilly Fuissé, but it is well worth the effort. The area from which Pouilly Fuissé comes is limited to five communes—POUILLY, FUISSÉ, SOLUTRÉ, VERGISSON and CHAINTRÉ. There is a little enclave in the area made by the two communes of POUILLY-LOCHÉ and POUILLY-VINZELLES. These wines can be quite good but are not as fine as Pouilly-Fuissé.

In the rest of the area both red and white wines are to be found. The special *appellation* MÂCON-VILLAGES applies only to white wines, but is seldom seen in this country. Otherwise for both red and white wines the *appellation* is Mâcon Supérieur or Mâcon followed by the name of the commune (MÂCON VIRÉ is an example) and plain MÂCON for the lesser wines. This is the one region of Burgundy where Pinot Noir and Gamay grapes have equal status, while the whites are made from the Chardonay. Rather more than a third of the wines in the Mâcon Supérieur *appellation* are reds, while for the Mâcon *appellation* three-quarters of the wine is white. Some *rosé* wines are also made throughout the area.

These Mâcon wines are not fine wines, but there are large quantities of very agreeable, sound wines, which are soft and pleasantly flavoured and can be bottled and drunk when really young. Mâcon wines should seldom be kept for more than a year in cask, often for less, and once bottled are usually at their best within a year. Bottles bearing elderly vintage slips are not to be sought after!

BEAUJOLAIS

This is the largest and most productive region of Burgundy. The wine is perhaps the most delightful, quick maturing red wine in the world. It is light but extremely fruity and very flavoury, it is soft and easy to drink and yet the young wines keep just a touch of acidity or greenness which makes them so refreshing especially in the summer if served at cellar temperature. These are wines to be quaffed rather than sipped, but their character and flavour ensure that they never pall, so that one bottle succeeds another.

The red wines of Beaujolais are divided in three broad categories. First there are the GROWTH BEAUJOLAIS, sold under one of nine commune names. These begin in the north of the region and follow the range of hills south for some thirty kilometres. Then there is the BEAUJOLAIS VILLAGES area which embraces the whole northern part of the Beaujolais· area and in which the Growth Beaujolais are embedded. Finally, in the south there are the BEAUJOLAIS SUPÉRIEUR and BEAUJOLAIS *appellations*.

The Beaujolais Growths or *Crus* as they are often called, is the name given to the separate *appellations* enjoyed by nine communes in the Beaujolais Villages area. Going from north to south, these are: ST. AMOUR, JULIÉNAS, CHÉNAS, MOULIN À VENT, FLEURIE, CHIROUBLES, MORGON, BROUILLY, and CÔTE DE BROUILLY. Within these communes there are a number of properties which sell their wine under the name of the property in addition to the commune *appellation*, thus: CHÂTEAU BELLEVUE, MORGON.

ST. AMOUR This name is a most fitting description for these delightful wines. They are fleshy and fairly rich in texture, soft and velvety on the palate but not at all heavy. This is combined with a certain distinctive breed and delicacy which sets them apart as wines of quality. In terms of area and production it is one of the four smaller communes. Among the best growths which are likely to be found in England are the CHÂTEAU DE ST. AMOUR and the CLOS DE BILLARDS.

JULIÉNAS A large and important commune. The wines are of similar character to St. Amour but rather fuller. The best growths have a superb silky texture which makes them among the most distinguished wines in Beaujolais. They can both be drunk very young and kept several years in bottle. The best known growths are: CHÂTEAU DE JULIÉNAS, CHÂTEAU D'ENVAUX, LES MOUILLES, CLOS DES POULETTES, LES CAPITANS.

CHÉNAS   This is the smallest of the nine communes. It immediately adjoins Moulin à Vent. The wines have some of the body of Moulin à Vent without quite the breed and savour. The best growths are: DOMAINE DES JOURNETS and LES ROUGEMONTS.

MOULIN À VENT   This is a defined area rather than a commune, and takes its name from the famous windmill. These are big, strongly-flavoured wines of considerable power, and can live for many years in bottle. I have drunk wines twenty years old which have been excellent. It is one of the larger areas of the *Cru* Beaujolais and usually fetches the highest prices. Probably because of its fame, not all wines sold under this name are worthy of this reputation, so if you are disappointed by the Moulin à Vent you have drunk you should try again. The best growths are: CLOS DU MOULIN À VENT, CH. DES JACQUES, CH. DE MOULIN À VENT, LES BRESSES, and MONTPERAY.

FLEURIE   This large commune is perhaps the best known of the Growth Beaujolais in England. The wines are extremely fruity and should be very fresh and delicious. For this, early bottling is essential. This is the epitome of what most people think of as Beaujolais. Among well-known growths which are to be found in England are: CH. DES LABOURONNES, LA CHAPELLE DES BOIS, LA FIERTE and CLOS DE LA ROILETTE.

CHIROUBLES   A small commune, and one of the least known in this country, although the wine is very popular in France. It is one of the lightest of the Growth Beaujolais, but is very fruity and elegant, and one of the most delicious of Beaujolais for really early drinking. It should not be kept for too long once in bottle. Although it appears on remarkably few wine lists in this country, this is a wine well worth looking out for.

MORGON

The first five communes mentioned are clustered fairly closely together in the northern half of the Beaujolais Villages area. Now there is something of a gap before we reach Morgon, just about plumb in the middle of the area. It is a large and important commune with the second largest production in the nine communes. The wines have a reputation for being the most solid and long lived in the district, and some of the wines are even a little heavy for Beaujolais. But at their best these are very pleasing wines with plenty of flavour and meat to make up for what they lack in elegance. The best known growths are: CH. DE PIZAY, CH. DE BELLEVUE, and LE PEZ.

BROUILLY AND CÔTE DE BROUILLY

For reasons best known to the authorities, this commune has been given two quite separate *appellations*. Brouilly, with an area of some 2,000 acres, is the largest in the region, while the Côte with only about 500 acres is the smallest. The wines are only slightly less sturdy than those of Morgon, and are quite rich and really fruity. Like so many of these wines, while some will live and improve in bottle for several years, other wines are delicious when very young. Well-known growths include CH. DE PIERREUX, CH. DE LA CHAISE and CHÂTEAU THIVIN.

BEAUJOLAIS VILLAGES

As has already been explained, the area of the Beaujolais Villages is the northern portion of the Beaujolais area and has the growths or *crus* in its midst. An area of about 4,250 acres produces on average some 2,500,000 gallons of wine, nearly all of which is red. There are, however, sevéral properties making white wine and some of these are now marketed in England. The best known are CH. DE LOYSE, DOMAINE DES DÎMES, CH. DE CHASSELAS and CH. DU CHATELARD.

A wine from this *appellation* should be a Beaujolais of some character and style. A number of wines are sold under the names of individual properties. Wines from this area probably make the best *Beaujolais l'Anée*, that is, wine to be drunk when a few months old.

BEAUJOLAIS SUPÉRIEUR AND BEAUJOLAIS

This is the *appellation* for the vineyards of southern Beaujolais. This covers an area of some 22,800 acres and on average some six and a half million gallons of Beaujolais and 650,000 gallons of Beaujolais Supérieur are produced annually. It should be emphasised, however, that while wines produced in this southern area can never enjoy a more exalted *appellation*, wines from the Beaujolais *Crus* or Beaujolais Villages may always be declassified to Beaujolais Supérieur or Beaujolais.

These are the wines one usually drinks as Beaujolais—if one is lucky! They vary greatly in style but should be fairly light in texture, fresh and fruity. Some are even sold under the names of properties. Unfortunately, some of these wines are sold as rather heavy, full-bodied wines usually by blending with a little Côte du Rhône. This is a great pity, as it smothers these light refreshing wines, and gives the consumer a false idea of what Beaujolais should be like, so that one sometimes finds people objecting to genuine well-made wines when they are given them. The wines of the Côte du Rhône are excellent in their own right and good value as well, but it is a shame to confuse them with their more delicate cousins in Beaujolais.

CHATEAU DE TALANCÉ
BEAUJOLAIS SUPÉRIEUR
Appellation Beaujolais Supérieur Contrôlée
DISTRIBUTEURS EXCLUSIFS
PIAT PÈRE & FILS, NÉGOCIANTS-ÉLEVEURS A MACON, SAONE-ET-LOIRE

Much has been said and written about the adulteration of Beaujolais. However, it should be emphasised that an enormous quantity is produced nearly every year, and a good and discriminating wine merchant should always be able to supply genuine wines, but do not expect it to be the cheapest obtainable under a Beaujolais label.

Reference Books

There are two outstanding books at present available on Burgundy—one is the section in Alexis Lichine's "Wines of

114

France", which is very comprehensive and is in many ways the best section in the book. The other is the book on "The Wines of Burgundy" by Poupon and Forgeot. This book, which hitherto has only appeared in French, is now available for the first time in English and can be obtained from P. Forgeot, Beaune, Côte d'Or, France, for 9.30 Frs. postage paid. This is an extremely comprehensive study and gives up-to-date information on all the *appellation contrôlée* throughout the region as well as information on vines, vinification, areas and quantities of production. The emphasis here is principally on information rather than appreciation; for this the reader must turn back to Lichine.

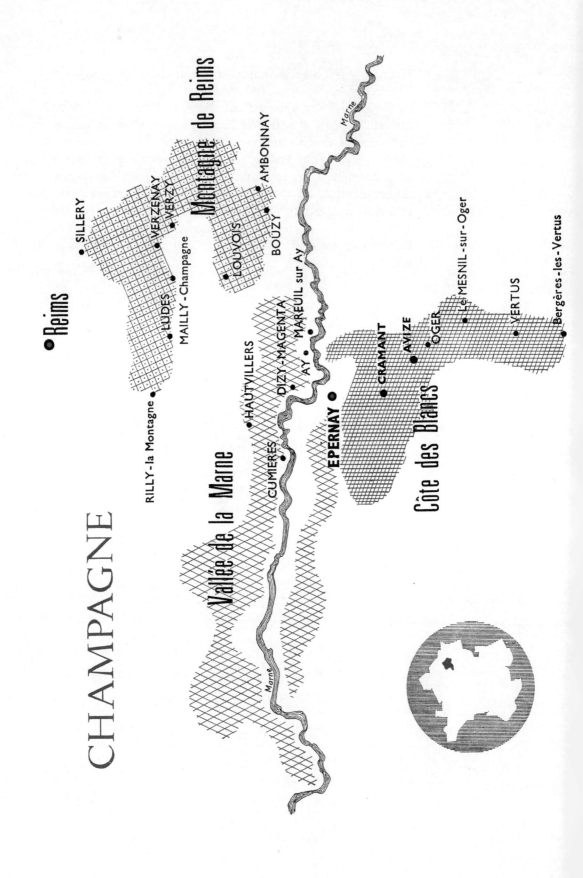

CHAMPAGNE

Montagne de Reims

Vallée de la Marne

Côte des Blancs

Reims

SILLERY

VERZENAY
VERZY

AMBONNAY

LOUVOIS

BOUZY

MAILLY - Champagne

LUDES

MAREUIL sur Ay

AY

RILLY - la Montagne

DIZY-MAGENTA

HAUTVILLERS

CUMIÈRES

EPERNAY

CRAMANT

AVIZE

OGER

Le MESNIL - sur - Oger

VERTUS

Bergères - les - Vertus

Marne

CHAMPAGNE

GEOGRAPHY

The vineyards of the Champagne district are concentrated in a thick belt of limestone and chalk, which is situated some seventy miles east of Paris and dominated by the two important towns of Reims and Épernay.

To the wine-student visiting Reims for the first time, there is little about the city to give an impression of it being the centre of a major wine-producing area. The city centre is dominated by the cathedral and its surrounding buildings, and the rest has become a mixture of the old repaired buildings that remained standing after the First World War and the modern concrete shopping streets that have been constructed in recent years. It is true that signs of an opulent period for the champagne trade are apparent in some of the imposing edifices that were erected at that time, but the establishments of many firms are quietly sheltered in the smaller streets.

Leaving Reims by road in any direction one does not immediately come upon vineyards and it is not until one has followed the road to Épernay for many miles, after climbing what is called the Montagne de Reims and traversing the thick forest along its plateau that all at once a magnificent view comes into sight, with the town of Épernay nestling in the valley, the little village of Hautvillers away on the right, and the whole area covered with vines.

The road from the summit winds down to Épernay. Here, unlike Reims, as one enters the town it is apparent that Champagne production is the industry of major importance. Apart from the proximity of the vines, many famous Champagne Houses are situated in a single street—the Avenue de Champagne—and while some of these remain, on the outside at least, as they were built some eighty to ninety years ago, others have been rebuilt and modernised in the interest of efficiency and to increase their output.

The chalk of this area, when mixed with a light top soil of sand, clay and leaf compost, is, with the temperate climate of the northern part of France, ideal for producing grapes with the perfect balance of acidity, sugar and flavour, for the production of a sparkling wine.

The principal vineyards of Champagne are divided into three parts as follows:

SOUTH OF REIMS (MONTAGNE DE REIMS)
Verzy—Verzenay—Sillery—Ludes
Mailly-Champagne—Rilly—Bouzy—Ambonnay

NORTH OF ÉPERNAY (VALLÉE DE LA MARNE)
Cumières—Hautvillers—Dizy
Mareuil—Ay—Avenay

SOUTH OF ÉPERNAY (CÔTE DES BLANCS)
Avize—Cramant—Le Mesnil
Oger—Vertus

In the early days and before Champagne was a sparkling wine, the products of the parishes or villages of these districts were sold under their own names, and it was not until the Champagne firms were established and made their wines by blending many wines, both red and white together, that the question of quality arose.

It will be apparent that indeed there must be a considerable difference in the quality of wines from different districts, in the same way as in Bordeaux a wine from the vineyards of Château Margaux is accepted as superior to that of a *bourgeois* growth.

Although in Champagne no classification has been made of the different villages as in the case of Médoc, a system, better perhaps because it is flexible, has been formed whereby each parish is given a coefficient of standard of quality, which not only determines the perfection of the wine, but also the price the grapes will fetch at the time of the vintage. This classification was initiated in 1911 and revised in 1920 and 1944 and the C.I.V.C.— *Comité Interprofessionnel des Vins de Champagne*—can modify, if they think fit, the coefficients in accordance with their findings of any vintage.

The coefficients which can be given to any parish are as follows:

Grands Crus—outstanding	100 per cent
Premiers Crus	90-99 per cent
Categories of lower quality	70-89 per cent.

In order to show how this system works, consider the parishes which make up the Department of the Marne, of which 155 contribute 78 per cent of all Champagne produced in any one year.

Of these   12 are *Grands Crus*
               8 are *Premiers Crus*
             135 are of the lower quality categories.

From this it will be seen that a Champagne House has a large choice in its purchases and that a big variation in the quality and the cost of different wines must result.

Some Champagnes made from the *Grands Crus* and *Premiers Crus* coefficient wines and first pressings must be much more expensive than those made from cheaper blends with a high proportion of second pressings, but the result is always noticeable and the connoisseur is prepared to pay the extra few shillings a bottle to enjoy the better product.

As in all industries which prosper, the Champagne industry does not stand still but seeks, at all times, ways and means of increasing output with a reduction in costs.

More and more vines are being planted, some in areas in which it would seem doubtful if the quality that results can justify such action, while methods of mass production and reduction of labour costs are continually being introduced. Nevertheless, Champagne must and always will be an expensive wine, and, in spite of the intense competition from sparkling wines made in other countries all over the world, it seems unlikely that, as the world becomes more and more affluent, the demand for Champagne will do anything but increase.

BRANDS Here we have before us twelve bottles of different brands of Champagne. Even at a casual glance, it is obvious to any observer that while in some ways they resemble each other, they are all different from bottles which are used for other wines.

Let us examine these differences more closely.

We refer to "brands" of Champagne in the same way as we talk about makes of cars, cigars, typewriters, radios and so on.

The first "brand" to be established in Champagne was founded in 1729. Before that date Champagne was sold by the name of the parish from which the wine came, in the same way as Burgundy wines are sold today. For example, Burgundy wines such as Pommard, Nuits St. Georges and Beaune are the products of the parishes of these names, so in that same way before

120

the Champagne houses were formed, the wines were sold under names like Ay, Bouzy, Cramant, Sillery, Verzenay, and so on.

Nor was Champagne always a sparkling wine, for while records show that vines were grown, and wine made, in the province of Champagne some two thousand years ago, it was not until 1688 that the method of producing a second fermentation in bottle was discovered, which resulted in the sparkling wine we enjoy today.

Now all these wines are incorporated in the blends of the different Champagne houses; blends which, because they are a combination of wines from different districts and made from both black and white grapes, very much depend for their quality and character on the skill and knowledge of the blender. Thus the reputation of any firm stands to rise or fall on the deliberations of that most important person—the Master Blender.

In their own locality, the Champagne Houses have established an organisation called the *Syndicat de Grandes Marques*, which comprises twenty-seven firms who are accepted on account of their importance. Other firms are received into membership from time to time as they, so to speak, make the grade.

This is not to be confused with another group of *Grandes Marques* Champagnes which was formed some ten years ago and consists of twelve firms who have been traditionally known in Great Britain and whose wines will be generally found on comprehensive wine lists and price lists. These twelve *Grandes Marques* firms are:

J. Bollinger	Ay
Veuve Cliquot-Ponsardin	Reims
Heidsieck & Co.	Reims
Charles Heidsieck	Reims
Krug & Co.	Reims
Lanson Père et Fils	Reims
Moet & Chandon	Épernay
G. H. Mumm & Co.	Reims
Perrier-Jouet	Épernay

Pol Roger & Co.	Épernay
Pommery & Greno	Reims
Louis Roederer	Reims

This group has done much to help the young man in the trade to understand the intricacies of champagne-making, for they provide courses for students to visit the Champagne area, where each of the twelve firms concerned undertakes to take the students through a particular part of the Champagne process.

Since the beginning of the "brands era", there have been many changes in the Champagne houses, changes brought about by family problems, by wars, by finance, by hard work or the lack of it. As a consequence, some firms have grown and prospered, developing their trade both in France and all the available international markets, of which Great Britain is the most important; while others, through bad management or lack of finance, have been absorbed into the larger organisations or have slowly died to become the ghost names of the past.

To these must be added those houses which, with new capital and abounding energy, are striving with might and main to claim a share of the trade, a trade which, as statistics show, increases year by year, not only in its native France but in Great Britain, the U.S.A., and other markets which are not restricted by import tariffs or financial quotas.

A large market in England is also conducted in the sale of what are termed "B.O.B." wines, standing for Buyers' Own Brands. B.O.B. Champagnes are in effect brands, or the house *marque* of a Wine Merchant. Wines supplied in this manner come from a few specialised firms who concentrate on this type of trade. They hold very large stocks of different *cuvées* and are able to supply wines of different character and at varying prices, according to the quality required and the size and frequency of the orders they receive.

Labels, foils, cork markings, and cases or cartons can all be supplied in accordance with the wishes of the customer. There are several hundred B.O.B. Champagnes available on the British market, the majority being Non-Vintage which are sold at a price rather lower than the brands of the *Grande Marque* firms.

LABELS   Let us now examine closely the labels adorning our Champagne bottles. In every case, the word "Champagne" will be featured, indicating that the wine in the bottle is the sole product of the delimited area of Champagne in France.

From time to time, producers of sparkling wines in other countries have tried to use the name "Champagne" on wines for sale in this country, but all efforts in this direction were finally stopped as a result of the famous "Spanish Champagne Case", so well described in André Simon's book "The History of Champagne".

Regrettably, in other parts of the world this does not apply, and in South Africa, Spain, Australia, the U.S.A. and U.S.S.R., sparkling wines are made and sold with the word "Champagne" on the label.

Originally, Champagne was one of the Provinces of France before the country was divided up into Departments. The name is derived from the Latin *campus* or field, which became *campania* and finally the French *Champagne*. When it was first introduced into England, it was spelt *Champaigne* and wine labels, those charming silver plaques which can be hung on their chains on the necks of decanters, can still be found inscribed in this way.

Secondly, the label will have on it the name of the firm responsible for producing the wine, together with the name of the town or village where the firm is situated. The main Champagne firms are found in Reims, Épernay, and Ay, although there are a few which are resident in other towns.

The label will also have the description of the degree of dryness or sweetness of the wine in the bottle. This is indicated by the words used in the following table:

Brut or Very Dry	$\frac{3}{4}$ to $1\frac{1}{2}$ per cent Liqueuring	
Extra Dry	2 to 3 per cent	,,
Dry or *Sec*	4 per cent	,,
Demi Sec	8 per cent	,,
Doux	10 per cent	,,

In Britain, *demi-sec* wines are often listed and referred to as "rech". In general, the British palate favours dry wines, either "Very Dry", or "Extra Dry", and it is in these wines that the quality of the grapes that are used, and the care in blending and manufacturing, are apparent, for sugar covers up and hides deficiencies which would be noticeable in a more natural wine.

The label will also tell you if the wine is of a vintage year or a non-vintage, while each house may include on its label such features as it thinks will enhance its appearance.

All Champagne bottles are dressed with a foil which covers the neck, cork and retaining wire or *muselet*. This can be made of different materials, usually gold foil or lead, and in a variety of colours with either the name of the firm or some decoration adorning it. While the foil has become traditional to the dress of a Champagne bottle, it also serves a practical purpose, for with sparkling wines a certain space must be left for the compressed gas, and if the foil did not hide it an ugly-looking ullage would result. It also serves to hide the cork top and retaining wire which, uncovered, would give the bottle an untidy appearance.

A necklet with the firm's name or the word "Champagne", or both, is usually attached at the bottom of the foil, although some firms dispense with this extra label and contrive to produce a finished article which looks both tidy and well balanced—it is, of course, all a matter of individual choice. Some operations can be carried out by machines, but foil and necklet are usually applied by hand. This adds considerably to production costs.

CHAMPAGNE BOTTLES

A Champagne bottle is different from other bottles in many ways because its use in the making of Champagne requires certain specific features, and the fact that it is a well-balanced and good-looking bottle is really incidental.

Hold an empty Champagne bottle in the hand and it will be found to be very much heavier than those used for still wines. There is a very good reason for this, since when the second fermentation takes place in the enclosed quarters of the bottle a pressure is built up to approximately six atmospheres.

Before the First World War, Champagne bottles were made by hand, a process which gave only a short life to the "blowers", but since 1936 it has been completely superseded by automatic machinery, with the benefit not only of a humane nature but also of producing a more uniform and much stronger bottle. The hand-blown article, the glass of which obviously varied in thickness, was unreliable and the losses when filled due to bursting under the pressure of the second fermentation were as high as 5 per cent, but today this is reduced to 1 per cent or less by the introduction of the machine-made bottle.

Many people have the idea that because the base of a Champagne bottle is recessed into the bottom of the bottle, to form what is called a "punt", it is done to make the bottle look bigger than it really is. In fact, Champagne bottles are controlled by the French authorities and the legal contents are 77 centilitres or 27 fluid ounces. This is slightly larger than the average still wine's "reputed quart" which measures 26⅔ fluid ounces, but allowance must be made for the air space which is necessary with a sparkling wine. The purpose of the "punt" is to allow bottles to be stacked *sur pointe*, that is, the cork of the upper bottle resting in the recessed bottom or "punt" of the lower one. The reason for this being done is described later in dealing with the making of the wine.

In recent years a change has come over the top of some Champagne bottles in the form of a lip, as used for the attachment of a crown cork similar to those used for mineral waters, Coca Cola and bottled beer. The purpose of this is to replace the first cork and *agraffe*, a sort of steel grip to hold the pressure of the second fermentation in bottle, and it is a practical and less expensive way of doing this.

CROWN AND CHAMPAGNE CORKS

Traditionalists maintain that the use of a crown cork is not as satisfactory as a normal cork and certainly, for those who eye a bottle as a thing of beauty, the top is not improved in appearance. Whether or not the quality of the wine is affected is something which, at the moment, is difficult to determine. Depending on the quality of the cork to be used and the time the wine is kept before its final preparation, a saving of several pennies per bottle can be made using a crown cork, which is undoubtedly attractive to a large producer.

Ask a wine butler to show you his corkscrew and he will invariably produce one supplied by one of the Champagne houses. Since a Champagne cork comes out with a twist of the top, this is certainly surprising, but this ease of extraction has not always been the case and in the early days corks more often than not broke, and had to be removed by a corkscrew. To reduce the inconvenience and annoyance of both the customer and the *sommelier*, the Champagne firms gave away what is known as a Waiter's Knife and the habit continues to the present day, although in 99 per cent of cases they are used to draw the corks of still wines.

Champagne corks are of two kinds: either they are made of stripped cork bark bonded together with glue, or they are made of compressed cork dust or pulverised cork which can be manufactured by machinery with a considerable saving in cost. In both cases, in order that the glue or binding element does not come into contact with, and contaminate, the wine, a disc of best quality cork is glued on to the bottom.

The disc is used to make sure that the wine is in contact with the best cork. Visitors to the Champagne firms are often puzzled by the fact that, in spite of their using automatic bottling plants, corks are always fed into the corking machine by hand

and not through a hopper as is done when bottling still wines. The reason for this is that the end with the clean cork disc must be inserted in the right way, and no machine has yet been devised for doing this.

In order to retain the pressure in the bottle the Champagne cork is very much larger in diameter than the one used normally, and in order to insert it into the bottle it is compressed to approximately half its diameter before it is forced into the bottle neck. A part of the cork is left outside the top of the bottle which provides a platform on which to place a tin cap, the whole being firmly attached to the tip of the bottle by a wire. It also provides a convenient way of removing the cork which, with the added help of the pressure in the bottle, can be extracted by the twisting of the knob.

Nowadays it is rare to experience a "corky" bottle of wine of any sort. It has not been established what produces the musty, corky flavour that sometimes occurs, but undoubtedly it is some disease in the cork which contaminates the wine. There is only one place for the contents of a corky bottle . . . the sink!

Do not think that the wire surrounding the top of the cork is put there for ornamentation, for without it the cork would fly. In some firms, the wire and the tin cap underneath it are still put on by hand, although a machine has now been invented which will carry out this operation.

PRODUCTION   Let us now consider the contents of the bottle: the wine, which, after the cork has been extracted with a pop, foams and sparkles in the glass like a living thing. Champagne is normally a white wine, sometimes pink, but never red, and always sparkling. It is made from two types of grapes, one black and one white. The black grape, of which there are several varieties, is the Pinot Noir, the same grape that produces the fine red Burgundy wines of the Côte d'Or. The white grape is one of the varieties of the Chardonnay. Champagne must come from within the boundaries of the Champagne Viticole, which is the area legally allowed to use the name "Champagne" for the product of its vineyard.

Still white wines are generally made from white grapes, but Champagne, which is not still, is an exception to this rule; the larger proportion of white juice comes from the grapes which appear to have purple or black skins. In fact, the inside of the skin is red, and the greatest care must be taken during the time of pressing to ensure, first, that the fruit is not damaged and, second, that the pressing is carried out at the earliest possible moment in order to prevent a colouring of the juice.

Every man, woman and child is brought in to help with the picking at vintage time, while teams of women are employed to examine each bunch and cut out any bruised or rotten grapes. This is a laborious process which, it would appear, cannot either be avoided or done by machinery and so adds considerably to the cost of production. Picking continues during all hours of daylight and meals are taken in the vineyards, while to relieve the monotony the younger members pass the time to the tune of transistor radios. Because they would interfere with their picking if hung on their fronts, they usually sling them to hang on their backsides, which gives them an odd but nevertheless picturesque appearance.

There is however a champagne, described as *blanc de blancs*, which is made entirely from the juice of white grapes. Such wines are usually lighter in colour and body than those made in the traditional way, but there is no reason why they should be considered superior.

The fact that at present the area of black grape vineyards greatly exceeds that of the white grape areas accounts to some extent for these wines being sold at elevated prices.

Blanc de blancs is a correct description only when applied to Champagne, which is normally made by blending the juice of

128

Top left: Large tubs filled with bunches of grapes are brought on carts from the vineyards of Château Pichon-Longueville Baron and are swung on a hoist into the chai.

Top right: Inside the chai the tubs are tipped into a large wooden trough.

Bottom left: From the trough the grapes are shovelled on to an open grilled table.

Bottom right: The essential process of removing the stalks before pressing (égrappage) is here carried out by hand—the grapes falling through the grill leaving the stalks behind.

facing p. 128

At Château Monbousquet, St. Emilion.

At the top, the process known as "écoulage". This is the cooling of wine which has risen to too high a temperature after a few days fermentation. The wine is run off into open vats and left for a few minutes before pumping back into the large fermentation vats. The illustration below shows the inspection hatch placed in the floor above the vats so that the fermentation can be checked.

black and white grapes, so to describe a normal still white wine as *blanc de blancs*, while factually correct, is quite meaningless.

The selected grapes are put carefully into specially shaped baskets or wooden *caques* and are taken to the nearest press house where they are immediately weighed on a very accurate weighing machine and the amount noted or actually recorded by the purchaser or owner. Press houses are found in all villages in the Champagne area, and not only have these to be kept in perfect condition, in spite of the fact that they are only used for a week or so during the year, but the owners are obliged also to provide accommodation for the workers during the time of the vintage. To combat this cost some firms arrange to do all the pressing at a central press house, usually at their own establishment, bringing in the grapes with a twenty-four-hour service by lorry.

A Champagne press is usually square, sometimes round. It has a flat base and the sides are made of wooden slats reinforced by steel bands. The lid, which can be either in two pieces hinged in the middle, or made of several separate boards, is, after making it completely rigid, lowered on to the grapes either by a power-driven screw or by hydraulic means.

When the press is full the containers for the grapes—either baskets or *caques*—are carefully weighed and the sum of their empty weight deducted from their full weight.

Exactly four tons or four thousand kilos of grapes are put in the press, always from the same area and never mixed from two or more villages or a combination of red and white grapes. As the pressure builds up, the juice runs out of the slits in the side of the press into an inclined trough, and thence into a receiving vat which holds exactly 450 gallons.

The juice from the white grapes is, of course, almost colourless and that from the red grapes only slightly tinged with pink, which diminishes a lot during the period of fermentation and which can be removed later by fining or filtration.

F

This first pressing of 450 gallons is called the *cuvée*. It is the best that the grapes of any one year can produce, and it will contain the most sugar and the least amount of tannin and colouring matter from the skins. It will also cost more than subsequent pressings and is the element most sought after by the leading firms to produce their wine.

After more pressure is applied to the press, more juice will be extracted from the grapes, but the quality will not be as good as that of the *cuvée* and it is used to make wine of a lower quality.

The original 450 gallons of juice, which is now called the Must, ferments violently for anything up to two or three days. The modern method is for this to take place in vast glass-lined or concrete vats, in which great heat is developed as the wine ferments; but some firms prefer to use the traditional principle and rack off the Must into oak casks containing 44-46 gallons, believing that a receptacle of wood, rather than one of glass or cement, is better for maturing a wine, and especially for a wine as fine and delicate as Champagne.

The fermentation gradually slows down and after about two months the wine will be still and clear. It is then run off into fresh containers, leaving the deposit formed by the fermentation in the original casks or vats.

It is at this stage that the most important process in the production of Champagne takes place, namely the assembly or blending of the different wines to make the shipper's or firm's *Cuvée*. This can either be a non-vintage *Cuvée*, that is, a blend of wines from different areas of different years, when it will be the ambition of the blender to make a wine of standard type and quality, or a vintage *Cuvée* which will be characteristic of the particular year.

This blending is the responsibility of the *Chef de Caves* on whose skill the reputation of the firm largely depends, for, as in cooking, it is no good having first-class ingredients without a first-class chef.

When the final deliberation has been made, the different wines are all blended together, usually in the proportion of some one-third white to two-thirds black grapes (although this will vary from year to year), and are thoroughly married in large vats where they are constantly stirred by a rotating mixer.

At this stage an analysis is made to find out if any residual sugar is left in the wine, after which a calculation is made to see how much *liqueur de tirage* must be added. This *liqueur de tirage* consists of the finest cane sugar dissolved in Champagne wine and, according to the amount added, so will the resultant fermentation in the bottle vary in its intensity. If too much is put in, the bottles will burst; too little will produce a wine that is *pétillant* rather than sparkling.

Now the wine is bottled and enclosed by inserting what is known as the first cork which, in order to prevent it blowing out, is held down by an *agraffe* or steel clamp, the ends of which fit under the lip of the bottle which is provided for this purpose. The second fermentation produces carbonic acid gas and a pressure of $5\frac{1}{2}$ to 6 atmospheres. In some firms the first cork has been replaced by the use of a crown cork which not only can be applied mechanically, thus saving labour, but also costs less in the first place. The period that the wine is left in this condition varies from firm to firm and can be from approximately eighteen months to five years, depending upon the style and quality of wine which is being produced.

Each bottle is then well shaken and placed in tilted racks called *pupitres* where a mark is made in whitewash on the base of the punt. It is now necessary to remove the deposit which is caused by the second fermentation which, on account of the addition of the *liqueur de tirage*, now takes place in the bottle.

The removal of the deposit, which forms in a long streak along the bottle side, is done by a laborious process called the *remuage*. This consists of the cellarman giving the bottle a quick shake or twist in each direction and then replacing it in its hole in the *pupitre* one-eighth of a turn further round and with the bottle pointing slightly more vertical. This process is repeated every second day until twenty-four shakings or three complete revolutions have been carried out, by which time the bottle will be nearly vertical and all the deposit will be removed from the glass side, and will be resting on the base of the cork.

In the making of Champagne the *remuage* is the process which is the most expensive and laborious, requiring a number of skilled workmen carrying out a monotonous job in cold and damp cellars. It also requires a vast area for the desks or *pupitres* to be accommodated. Some mechanical devices are now in the experimental stage, but no firm has so far adopted them.

In order to make room for more wine to be dealt with, the bottles are now stacked *sur pointe*, that is, vertically with the cork of one bottle resting in the punt of the bottle beneath. Stacks twenty bottles high can be made in this way, and are stored with the minimum of space until the wine goes to the next operation of removing the deposit or disgorgement.

The common means of doing this is the use of a freezing machine through which the bottle passes, still upside down, so that about two inches of the neck are frozen forming a plug of ice about one-half inch thick in which the dirty deposit is embedded.

The removal of this plug is done by the *degorgeur*, who either removes the crown cork in the normal way or releases the first cork by unclipping the steel clip with a pair of pliers. In both cases, the pressure in the bottle will blow out the plug and the deposit, usually into a cut open cask. At this stage, a certain amount of skill is required to avoid a loss of wine which has been so costly to produce. If the bottle is held vertically the contents flows freely; if held at a certain angle very little is lost.

The *degorgeur*, having done his job carefully, looks through the bottle against a light to see that all traces of deposit have been extracted and hands it to the next operator, who adds the dosage according to the requirement of the market to which the wine is going.

The dosage is made up of cane sugar dissolved in either mature wine or old brandy, the correct name for which is *liqueur d'expedition*. This can, of course, be made in different grades of concentration, so that a percentage of dosage is not always an accurate way of describing the amount of sweetness added.

The final cork bearing the name of the firm on the side, his cork brand on the bottom and giving particulars of the vintage, in the case of a vintage wine, is now applied—this operation being today invariably done by machine.

A tin cap to take the strain of the wire is then placed on top of the cork, and the wire attached and tightened so that the cork is held in against the pressure in the bottle.

Finally the bottle is given a good shake to ensure that *liqueur d'expedition* is well mixed with the wine, and the wine is stored until the bottle is dressed with its foil and labels as required, and finally packed in its case or carton.

To obtain the best quality, there should be two periods of rest or maturing in the making of Champagne. The first is after the wine ferments for the second time in the bottle and can vary from eighteen months to five years, and the second is after the second and final cork has been put in, which can vary from ten years to virtually nil. Firms have different ideas on these two pauses, which are sometimes dictated by the expediency of their business, but immature Champagne tastes "green" and acid, and is more likely to cause indigestion than a matured wine.

Vintage Champagne will continue to improve, if stored in the correct temperature, for about ten years after it has been disgorged, after which time it will gain colour and begin to lose its life and sparkle.

Opinions vary considerably as to the moment when a champagne is at its best. A few show preference for a very old wine and even enjoy one which has become slightly *maderisé* or as we should say "beery".

On average, Champagnes, both vintage and non-vintage, are best drunk between six months (minimum) and six years after their disgorgement but no hard and fast rule can be laid down.

The wines of Champagne have been known and drunk for some two thousand years, but it was not until the seventeenth century that they became famous as sparkling wines. Since then, sparkling wines have been produced in a great number of other wine-producing countries, and in other wine-producing areas of France itself. Some of these are made by the *Méthode Champenoise*, the traditional second fermentation in bottle, while others have been mass-produced by various means. In Germany and Spain, for instance, sparkling wines are made in large quantities by causing a second fermentation to be produced in a large air-tight tank, and then filtering off the resultant sparkling wine by the hundred dozen. Sparkling wine made in this manner can be made in a few days against the several years required by genuine Champagne. A sparkling wine can also be produced simply by adding CO_2 or Carbonic acid gas in the same way as it is added to Coca Cola or Soda water. Nevertheless, in spite of competition from these sources, the quality of Champagne remains unrivalled, and its reputation and popularity in all world markets produces a constantly larger demand as the years go by. The reason for this is to a great extent due to the soil and the climate of the Champagne area of the northern part of France.

WHEN AND HOW
TO DRINK
CHAMPAGNE

To a few unfortunate people sparkling wine of any kind gives no enjoyment and Champagne will be no exception, but to the majority it provides enormous pleasure on a great variety of occasions, since, by its very character, it can be drunk at almost any time of the day or night. To some, eleven o'clock in the morning is the right moment for Champagne to be enjoyed with a friend and accompanied by a dry biscuit. Certainly it can be drunk with any sort of food and at any time that food is consumed from lunch to supper, and, for this purpose, a vintage wine of a little age is certainly more appropriate and pleasant than a freshly prepared non-vintage wine. For celebrations of all and every kind, Champagne contributes greatly to the occasion.

Weddings, anniversaries, receptions and parties owe no small measure of their success to that delightful bubbling liquid.

To those who can afford it, few things are better than a dozen oysters and a tankard of Champagne, although, let it be said, there are few ways of getting rid of your money in such a short time. Some enthusiasts prefer a mixture of half Champagne and half stout in a tankard. This concoction, known as "black velvet", was much appreciated in Victorian times.

Whilst it is said that this is an efficacious pick-me-up for the "morning after", it is perhaps questionable if the Champagne is improved by the stout or the stout by the Champagne.

There is little doubt that those who are convalescing obtain considerable benefit from a morning glass of "fizz" which acts both as a physical and as a morale booster. For this purpose, many firms supply their wine in quarter bottles which can be bought in attractive gift boxes containing six quarters. It should be noted, however, that it is not possible to "make" Champagne (see method of making) in quarter bottles, and therefore it is necessary for each to be decanted from bottles. Under these circumstances, these small bottles should be consumed fairly quickly or they will soon deteriorate. Alternatively, if a bottle or half bottle is too much for a single occasion, it is always possible to attach one of the special closures which are available for this purpose and the wine will still be fresh and lively on the following day—but not longer. Note that it is no use using a cork for this purpose as the pressure will build up and blow it out unless it is carefully tied down with string or wire.

For two people an Imperial pint, holding 20 fluid ozs, is the ideal size, being nicely balanced between a bottle, often too much, and a half bottle, always too little, and this size deserves more popularity than it at present enjoys.

Since Champagne was invented, fashion has produced a number of different styles of glasses from which it should be drunk.

Obviously, the main objective is a glass which shows off to advantage the lovely and delicate colour that Champagne has, and the bubbles working from the bottom of the glass to form a creamy ring round the inside of the rim.

While it must remain a matter of opinion which sort of glass is the best, it is generally accepted that the *flute*, or tall and narrow-bowled, stemmed glass is best. In Victorian days, the flat glass, known as the *coupe* was in vogue, but this has now gone almost completely out of fashion. Failing a special Champagne glass, an ordinary wine glass is perfectly acceptable and indeed infinitely preferable to the *coupe*.

Another Victorian "horror" was the use of the swizzle stick, usually a wooden rod with a stirring wheel at the end which is twirled in a glass of Champagne, producing considerable agitation of the liquid and thereby releasing the gas, and, in consequence, the sparkling effect.

A producer of Champagne, when he was presented with this abomination on one occasion, remarked that in the course of making his wine the most expensive process was putting in the bubbles, and it seemed pretty stupid to remove them with the aid of a piece of wood costing a fraction of a penny!

CHAMPAGNE BOTTLE SIZES		
Quarter bottle	= approx. $6\frac{1}{2}$ fluid ounces	
Half bottle	= ,, 13 ,, ,,	
Imperial pint	= ,, 20 ,, ,,	
Bottle or reputed quart	= ,, 27 ,, ,,	
Magnum	= Two bottles	
Jeroboam	= Double Magnum or four bottles	
Rehoboam	= Triple Magnum or six bottles	
Methuselah	= Quadruple Magnum or eight bottles	
Salmanazar	= Twelve bottles	
Balthazar	= Sixteen bottles	rarely found
Nebuchadnezzar	= Twenty bottles	

"The larger the container the better the wine" applies to all wines, and particularly so to Champagne with certain reservations; for it is only possible to "make" Champagne in certain sizes.

It is normal for Champagne to be made in half-bottles, Imperial pints, bottles and magnums, although a few select firms do make wines in double magnums. For all other sizes, both smaller and larger, it is necessary for the wine to be decanted from bottles, and the passing of the wine through the air has a certain detrimental effect, particularly on the keeping qualities; for this reason quarter bottles and very large sizes should not be kept for any length of time before they are consumed as they are inclined to go flat and lose their sparkle. Quarter bottles are also inclined to deteriorate more quickly than larger sizes on account of the large area of glass in proportion to the quantity of the liquid.

Commercially, the Methuselah is the largest size made by the bottle manufacturers and the twelve, sixteen and twenty bottle sizes are now rarely found, and then as dummy bottles usually, which have been used for special displays or exhibitions.

Opinions vary as to which size of Champagne bottle is the most attractive, but it is generally divided between the bottle and the magnum. Larger sizes appear to become unbalanced with too large a body and too slim a neck.

Côtes du RHÔNE

COTE ROTIE

○ *VIENNE*

Condrieu
● Ampuis
● Condrieu

Château-Grillet

○ *Montélimar*

Rhône

Crozes-Hermitage
Crozes
HERMITAGE
St. Joseph
Tain l'Hermitage
Tournon

Cornas
Cornas
St. Péray
St. Péray
○
VALENCE

Vinsobres

Cairanne
Cairanne ●
Rasteau
● le Rasteau

Chusclan
Chusclan
Laudun ●
ORANGE ○
Laudun

Gigondas
Gigondas ●
Vacqueyras
● Vacqueyras
Courthezon ●
Béaumes de Venise

Lirac
Lirac ●
TAVEL
Tavel ●

CHATEAUNEUF DU PAPE
Chateauneuf-du-Pape

● Bédarrides

● Sorgues

○
Montélimar

Rhône

○
AVIGNON

Laudun   *Red wine*
White wine

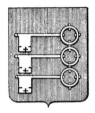

THE RHÔNE

Two great rivers of Europe, the Rhine and the Rhône, flow from one Swiss glacier. The former, flowing north through Switzerland, Germany and Holland, finally disperses in the North Sea producing along its banks in Germany some of the world's finest white wines. The latter, after a short journey through Switzerland, erupts, clean and cold from the west end of the lake of Geneva, into France and after a 500-mile journey pours into the Mediterranean near Marseilles. Along its route through Southern France are produced some of the world's finest red wines and some very good whites in the Côtes-du-Rhône area which takes in six Departments, Rhône, Loire, Drôme, Ardèche, Vaucluse and Gard.

The Côtes-du-Rhône vineyards, which stretch from Vienne to Avignon, are the least frequented vineyards in France, although the great road, the R.N.7 which runs from Paris to the south coast, and cuts straight through the Rhône vineyards, is one of the most widely travelled.

A journey could continue quietly on the R.N.86 through wine villages, stopping every now and again to try a drink and a taste where they are offered, until in the late evening round the bend of the Rhône is seen the mighty hill of Hermitage, which rises above the village of Tain.

On the west side of the river is St. Péray, which lies opposite Valence. Here a most interesting sparkling wine is made from the local wines, but unfortunately production is so small that it is rarely seen outside its own area. St. Péray concludes the northern section of the Rhône vineyards. In the second sector is the Meridional, of which Châteauneuf-du-Pape is the most famous wine centre. The largest town in this area, immortalised by Alphonse Daudet in his "Lettres de mon Moulin", is Avignon, famous for its bridge, and the vast Palais des Papes.

Possibly the other wines of the southern sector of the Rhône are less known, for, more than any other area of France, the growers belong to vast co-operatives who arrange to accept their annual crop of grapes and then, with all the latest scientific aids, make the wine and sell it. Rationalisation of viticulture has become the central feature of post-war Southern France and the smallholder finds it more convenient to become a member of one of these co-operatives whereby his work is confined to cultivation of the vine and the gathering of the crop. He no longer has the worry associated with vinification, keeping the wine and finally negotiating with the buyer for the sale. The co-operative cellars are usually administered by a committee who appoint an acknowledged viniculturalist as manager to supervise the daily cellar routine. The wines in this area are mainly red and *rosé*, although one or two fortified sweet wines such as the Beaumes-de-Venise and Rasteau are also very popular. The wines from the co-operatives are generally no more than *Vins de Café* which are drunk very young, being distributed to the various large cities of France in tankers.

Tavel, on the other side of the Rhône, is where the most famous and fabulous of all dry *Rosé* wines is made, also nearby are Lirac and Chusclan.

CÔTE-RÔTIE The first of the more important Rhône vineyards cling to the hillsides above the villages of Ampuis and stretch into Tupin and Semons. These are the vines of Côte-Rôtie, almost hanging on the steep "sun-roasted" slopes which are stoutly buttressed

140

by stone walls and divided into small terraces, some so tiny that they contain only one or two plants. These retaining walls are known as "Cheys" or "Murgeys", and without them cultivation, already backbreaking, would virtually be impossible. Severity of the slopes makes mechanisation impossible and human labour most arduous. Hard work is the rule the whole year round, much of it with the *bigot* or two-pronged hoe. Often the eroded soil has to be carried back uphill.

But in spite of these difficulties Côte-Rôtie produces one of the oldest, greatest and most aristocratic wines of the Côtes-du-Rhône, more delicate and less "powerful" than those of Châteauneuf-du-Pape. The vineyards run in a green ribbon two miles long, high above the river which by a fortunate bend gives them the advantage of a south-east exposure, and the broiling sun that beats down most of the summer brings them to early harvest. The soil is sandy and stony. Côte-Rôtie has an ancient and noble lineage, and we know from the works of the Latin writers that the Romans knew and loved the wines from these hillsides. It was here that they made their *vinum picatum*, so called because the black picata grape from which it was pressed yielded a slight, but apparent, unmistakable taste of pitch.

Two of the best known slopes of Côte-Rôtie are named CÔTE BRUNE and CÔTE BLONDE, the latter just south of the other. The legend of their names is that centuries ago the *seigneur* of Ampuis had two daughters, a blonde and a brunette, to each of whom he gave one of the vineyards as dowry. The soil, as it happens, matches the names, that of Côte Brune being brownish clay, while the other, being of a silico-calcareous nature, presents a lighter appearance. It is no surprise that from their different soils the blonde and her darker sister draw wines that show marked differences in their qualities. Côte Brune is the more full-bodied, takes time to reach maturity and lasts well. The Blonde is softer, lighter and fruitier, comes of age more quickly and is said to be not so reliable as it ages.

There is however, nothing fierce or fickle in the end product, and the two charming sisters carry their varying qualities to the blending cellars where their virtues are combined in a delectable wine that sometimes comes on the market labelled *Brune et Blonde*. Most of the wine, however, is sold as CÔTE-RÔTIE, although in France some is sold with the individual site name.

By the terms of the control laws introduced in 1940, Côte-Rôtie is produced from two vines—80 per cent Syrah (black) and 20 per cent Viognier (white), and these proportions yield a finely perfumed, full-bodied yet subtle, red wine with a touch of purple in its rich colour and a flavour suggestive of raspberries. One of the admirers (a leading grower) describes it as "a wine of quality, a lord without arrogance or false pretension, but proud of a long past which has opened to it all the most famous cellars".

It keeps well, sometimes requiring twelve years (five of them, as a rule, in the wood) to mature, and it holds its goodness for up to fifteen years, in some cases much longer. Modern red wine techniques, however, tend to bring the wine forward more rapidly, and it is generally bottled two years after vintage.

The official minimum strength is 10 degrees, but the better wines generally exceed these figures according to year and weather. There is also a limitation on output per acre, a restriction which I am sure is easy to comply with on these steep terraced hillsides, where in places the vines prosper only because the granite rock has been smashed with picks to give the vines roothold.

The Syrah grape (known on the Rhône as the Sérine) has a long ancestry, but exactly how long is a matter of distinct difference among French authorities. Some claim that it was brought from Syracuse in Sicily before the dawn of the Christian era; others set it to the credit of the Crusaders who brought it home from the East where it originated in Shiraz, Persia. In support of the Syrah-Syracuse theory it may be noted that the Greeks who took the grape to Provence around 600 B.C. had, over a hundred years earlier, established both colonies and vineyards in Sicily.

142

CONDRIEU Immediately south of the red wine slopes of Côte-Rôtie we come to the smaller areas of CONDRIEU where only the Viognier grape is grown and the yield consequently is white wine. Here too the hillside is steep, calling for numerous retaining walls, and from a distance the terraces resemble a staircase climbing to the sky. The view from the top is fabulous. Work calls for the sweat of the brow, and again the pick is an indispensable tool.

Condrieu is made in various styles, depending on the vintner's choice, the traditional method producing full-bodied dry wines, while modern methods can yield a lighter and slightly sweeter vintage. Some are slightly sparkling, *pétillant* (similar to Moselle and some Portuguese wines), and these are generally drunk during the winter and spring following the harvest. Wine growing is carried out on an individual basis, and growers keep their secrets strictly to themselves as they do in other parts. The wine is supposed to age well, but to lose most of its fruitiness in the process.

Fewer than twenty acres of Condrieu's rocky soil are under these Viognier vines, so the output is limited and most of it is bought by the famous restaurants of Lyon and Vienne, so it is little known in this country.

ÎÂTEAU-GRILLET On the next hillside is a Lilliput among vineyards—CHÂTEAU GRILLET. There are barely three acres of it (with a single proprietor) and even in a good year the yield from the Viognier vines is not more than 3,000 bottles. These normally do not travel far from their locality. Scarcity produces demand, and Château-Grillet is to be found in only three restaurants in the region (at a relatively high price) and in the homes of the proprietor's friends. A small quantity of every vintage is shipped to England and the U.S.A.

The estate is managed in the traditional manner so that the wine is always full-bodied and dry, but with a delicious flower-like bouquet in the most delicate form, reminiscent of violets. During several visits I was able to taste a range of five vintages, and I prefer the wines of lesser years which show more finesse and bouquet to those of magnificent vintages which tend to be too full-bodied and lack elegance—a phenomenon to my mind similar to the Sauvignon grape of Pouilly-Fumé of the Loire. The vineyard (incidentally the smallest to have its own *appellation contrôlée*) shares the granitic soil of its neighbours. Its scarcity and its renown have made it something of a connoisseur's wine, although the recent vintages I have seen in bottle have not been up to reputation—the use of plastic corks seemingly ages the wine much too fast. This has apparently been overcome, as recent vintages are closed with cork. This vintage was full-bodied with a fine flowery flavour (possibly violets) but without appreciable bouquet. Comparison is never perfect but it seems nearest to a Grand Crû Chablis, with more body but less finesse and elegance.

HERMITAGE A journey of thirty miles down the Rhône (during which the appearance of occasional olive groves suggests the approach to the Provençal south) brings the wayfarer to the great vine-clad hill of HERMITAGE that climbs in a sunny amphitheatre of terraces high above the riverside town of Tain. The hill loses hardly a ray of sunshine. A few small chalets dot its slopes, but one sees scarcely a tree—nothing but the grape and the pattern of the retaining walls marching grandly like a gigantic ladder. Some sectors proudly display the owner's name! It is debatable whether the sight is more magnificent at dawn or dusk. It is best viewed from the west bank of the Rhône at Tournon.

The vineyard takes its name from a famous but elusive hermit, for legend is not very precise as to exactly who he was. One story makes him a refugee from the conquering Romans, who fled to the hilltop and there had vines sent down from heaven— vines that ripened in a single night and produced immediate wine. Other legends have it that in the thirteenth century Blanche of Castile, queen and accomplished regent of France, granted the land to Chevalier Caspard de Sterimborough when he returned badly wounded from the Crusades. There he turned hermit, giving his life to the grape and to devotions in the small chapel, dating from Gallo-Roman times, that caps the hill. Alexandre Dumas, visiting Hermitage in 1834, makes the hermit a poor man of the early seventeenth century. From all of which it will be seen that the place was determined to have a hermit. Perhaps it had more than one.

From among a long list of compliments to Hermitage it may be sufficient to recall that George Meredith praised it through one of his characters, and Professor George Saintsbury ("Notes from a Cellar Book") debated whether an 1846 Hermitage or a Romanée-Conti of 1858 was the greatest vintage he had known. Praise indeed! He drank the Hermitage when it was forty years old, and described it as "the manliest French wine I ever drank".

An age-old adage well known along the Côtes-du-Rhône says, "Plant the rugged vine on the slope of the hillside, and the heart of the granite will bleed into your wine". At Hermitage it can bleed red and white, the former from the Syrah grape, and the long-living white from the Rousanne, and above all the Marsanne. About 80 per cent of the wines are red. These have a ruby richness of colour with a suggestion of purple brilliance. They are generous and mellow with a raspberry-like flavour and bouquet; they keep well, and at table, as with most Rhône wines, accompany the traditional dishes that go with Burgundy. The white has a great reputation for longevity, and many gourmets place it among the notable white wines. Certainly in a good year this dry, pleasantly perfumed beverage deserves that rating. Some detect a touch of "gun flint" in its aroma (is this a mythical phenomenon?) and attribute this to the stony nature of the soil. These stones were once on the bed of the Rhône, that is in the far distant prehistoric times during the period when the river was still carving out the great valley through which it now flows.

The white wines should be served well but gently chilled and never iced, which can spoil both the bouquet and flavour. The Hermitage vineyards run for about three miles along the sunny shelf above the Rhône, and are divided into main sections: CROZES-HERMITAGE and L'HERMITAGE. The Crozes-Hermitage vineyards (350 hectares) span eleven communes; l'Hermitage, in the commune of Tain, is barely 120 hectares.

Most of the plots or *quartiers* are small, and the many owners mostly have a few plots scattered throughout the area where variations of slope, sun and soil produce different characteristics for the final blend. This is a necessary step to obtain a uniform product.

The *vignerons* are always proud to tell of how in their grand-fathers' time Hermitage was sometimes used to "stretch" Bordeaux vintages when that area had a lean year. During the same period Burgundy paid a similar compliment to Châteauneuf-du-Pape.

The wines of Crozes are of course less powerful and of less character than l'Hermitage, which has ideal exposure to the sun. The former, although described as "if not brothers then definitely first cousins", is less robust than Hermitage but not more elegant, whereas the latter is very much closer in style and character. Although the vines are the same, vineyard work is less difficult than for l'Hermitage.

SAINT-JOSEPH

On the opposite side of the Rhône above Tournon, twin town-ship of Tain, lie the vineyards of St. Joseph. Its red and white wines were formerly known by the generic term Côtes-du-Rhône, and were largely used for blending with those of other areas, but in 1955 the growers, thanks to improved vinicultural methods, gained *appellation contrôlée* and thus became entitled to market their wine under its own name. This is not dissimilar in principle from a football team gaining promotion from one league to a higher one. The wines, both white and red, are held to have the characteristics (in lesser form) of Côte-Rôtie and Hermitage, and though they are little known outside their locality they have been consistently popular through the ages.

The *appellation* St. Joseph also includes the communes of GLUN, LEMPS, MAUVES, ST. JEAN-DE-MUZELS and VION.

CORNAS   A little way downstream, where the Isère pours its glacial water from the Alps into the Rhône, is the little town of Cornas which has been making red wine from Syrah grape for many centuries. The wine, inclined to be rough at first, requires a few years to tone down to a velvety smoothness, and has a fine raspberry-like bouquet. Its wealth of tannin and mineral salts makes it a prescription among local doctors, and no doubt, like most good red wine used sensibly, it is very great medicine. It is fairly long-lived, and experts accord twenty years at least to the vintage of these outstanding years, 1947 and 1949. A 1955 vintage which I tasted recently had hardly started maturing and would obviously live from fifteen to twenty years. The robust wines of Cornas are exellent for winter drinking in our climate.

SAINT-PÉRAY   Cheek by jowl with Cornas, on the opposite river bank to Valence, overlooked by the ruins of Château de Crusseol in a gorge at the foot of the Cevennes, is St. Péray, interesting for its production of the only real sparkling wine of the Côtes-du-Rhône. There are also still white wines. Both are from the Rousanne and Marsanne vines. More than a hundred years ago the growers (a M. Faure in particular) started experiments in applying Champagne methods, that is, producing a second fermentation in the bottle. Improvements that followed made the product very popular locally, so much so that vintners outside the parish bought ordinary St. Péray and applied the "champanisation" treatment. This resulted in a strict rule being laid down that no St. Péray wine that is made sparkling outside the vineyard area can claim the name. Despite the compliment of imitation this local sparkling wine cannot, of course, rank with Champagne. The ordinary white is a fairly powerful wine with a pleasant aroma. One of its admirers was Richard Wagner, and there still exists a letter from him dated from Bayreuth, December 2nd, 1877, ordering a hundred bottles of St. Péray. He was then composing "Parsifal", and the *vignerons* like to think that the juice of their grapes contributed to that great opera.

The sparkling St. Péray is a good fruity wine a good deal heavier than other sparkling wines. It has a pleasant bouquet and is usually moderately dark for a white wine.

CLAIRETTE DE DIE

Twenty-five miles south-east of Valence around the town of Die in the Drôme valley are the vineyards which produce an excellent sparkling wine usually with a fine muscat flavour.

Two vines are cultivated, Clairette and *Muscat à petits grains* (Muscat d'Alexandre), the wine taking its name from the former, its flavour from the latter. The wine is white, usually dry, with a fine bouquet and always sparkling *méthode champenoise*.

CLAIRETTE DE BELLEGARDE

Strictly outside the Côtes-du-Rhône area the Clairette de Bellegarde (Gard) should be considered beside the Clairette de Die. Bellegarde is 25 miles south-west of Avignon, near the Rhône-Sète Canal—the area of Costières du Gard. The white wine has excellent flavour and relatively long life in bottle.

CHÂTEAUNEUF-DU-PAPE

For more than thirty miles after Valence down by the fast-flowing Rhône the vineyards disappear and the changing landscape goes over to fertile farmland and to fruit growing. There are more olive groves. Cypress trees stand in windbreaks against the seasonal battle with the mistral, and in villages with their Romanesque chapels, hard-pruned plane trees spread a leafy parasol to give shade to the *boule* players in the square. The clear air, the painted countryside, the fantastic light, all proclaim Provence.

The vines return and soon the traveller finds himself in what is by far the most extensive wine-land of the Rhône, with the eight square miles of Châteauneuf-du-Pape its centrepiece.

Strong like the sunshine that brings them to life, the Châteauneuf-du-Pape wines, red and luscious, have attained a world-

148

wide, deserved reputation. The name, evocative of papal associations, is unquestionably an asset, but the vintages stand on their own merit which matches the former magnificence of the papal summer residence overlooking the undulating vineyards. They have a notable place in French vinicultural history for they were the first to have regulations controlling production and guaranteeing place of origin, thus setting a standard that all other great French wine districts have followed. They also have the highest official minimum alcoholic strength, 12·5 per cent. Alphonse Daudet called Châteauneuf-du-Pape the "King of Wines, Wine of Kings". No other Midi wine can match the ruby colour, full bouquet, warm strength and palatal delicacy, a combination founded on the classic art of selection and blending the juices from a choice of thirteen different species of grapes.

Not to be overlooked are the full-bodied dry white wines with their fruit-cup bouquet. They are produced in very small quantities and are a link with the wine formerly used for Mass at the papal palace. Just as the wines are linked across the ages, so too in unbroken tradition are the hardy workers today with ancestors who cultivated the stone-covered red soil to grace the Pope's table.

The village of Châteauneuf-du-Pape, equidistant from Orange and Avignon, sprawls down the gentle hillside dominated from above by the ruins of the Château, which watches over the vines like a general with his widespread army. Deployed amongst the vineyards are the *domaines* with their red roofs, three parts protected from the north wind by rows of cypress and other trees, which dot the countryside and break the endless green lines of vines. Who can be surprised at the quality of the wine produced from such countryside, continually under bombardment from the sun's most beneficent and concentrated rays?

Gently undulating, with slight hillocks and small plains, this small viticultural area of Châteauneuf-du-Pape contains many varied soils, giving us a wonderful variety of fine, perfumed, full-bodied wines. The history of Châteauneuf-du-Pape has been traced back carefully to the twelfth century by Baron le Roy de Boiseaumarie. Monsieur Le Roy, owner of Château Fortia, is the greatest living authority on Châteauneuf-du-Pape and it has been principally through his efforts that this commune has attained its present high reputation; he followed this achievement by similar work with the Côtes-du-Rhône *appellations*. The Rhône *vignerons* have honoured him by erecting a statue in an ornamental garden at St. Cécile-les-Vignes. Shot down as a pilot in the First World War and severely wounded, it was not long after cessation of hostilities that he took the interest of his community to heart and set about formulating a code of viticulture ensuring that quality, not quantity, was sought after by the *vignerons*. The acceptance of control of this area in 1923 preceded the National *Appellation Contrôlée* by twelve years, and since that time the renown of the products of Châteauneuf-du-Pape has gone from strength to strength.

THE VINEYARDS

Julien's work of 1822, "The Topography of all Known Vineyards", places Châteauneuf-Calcernier in the first class, particularly mentioning LA FORTIA, LA NERTHE and others. By 1873, the Châteauneuf vineyards totalled 500 to 600 hectares and were the first in the Vaucluse to be ravaged by the phylloxera devastation. Destruction of the vines was followed by an indiscriminate planting of fruit trees, as the inhabitants attempted to earn money from their poor and arid soil with almonds, cherries and apricots. Success was not overwhelming, but examples are still to be seen at the borders of vine plantations, the quality of the cherries from the region being renowned. Recovery from the disaster did not begin until 1878 and reconstitution of the vineyards was extremely slow. During this period, Commandant Duclos, owner of Château de la Nerthe, set a very high example and the scheme gained momentum, so that, by 1890, the vineyards of Châteauneuf had practically regained their former importance. However, they suffered a slight relapse during the First World War due to the shortage of man power.

It was not until after the end of the First World War that efforts were begun to ensure the quality of the wine made in the region. At that time viniculture was in a state of chaos; many of the wines were sold to other wine-producing districts to bolster production, foreign wines were introduced and hybrid grapes which yield greater quantities of wine per vine than the "pure strains" were indiscriminately planted. Under the leadership of M. le Roy, a group of *vignerons* set out to improve local conditions, M. le Roy, as leader, having the assurance of his colleagues that they would keep to the newly devised and very rigorous regulations.

The original ideas he proposed were:

1. The delimitation of the area of production based on the nature of the soil and its usage, by the association of lavender and thyme. (Where these two plants flourish together it is an excellent indication that the soil is suitable for viticulture).
2. The varieties of grapes allowed (all of noble origin) were to be limited.
3. The method of culture (training and pruning) to be regulated.
4. The minimum alcoholic strength to be 12·5° (Gay-Lussac; percentage by volume).
5. A *triage* (separation of grapes) at the time of harvest to be introduced whereby a minimum of 5 per cent was to be excluded from the *appellation*.
6. Production of *vin rosé* forbidden and any unsound wines to lose the *appellation*.

This syndicate at Châteauneuf-du-Pape which demanded and obtained acceptance of the regulations for wine growing from the Tribunals was the precursor of the *Appellation Contrôlée*, but their principles were not accepted in law until May 1936.

The strict discipline to which the growers agreed has once again assured the high place of honour amongst the finest wines of the world for Châteauneuf-du-Pape.

Reflets de Châteauneuf-du-Pape is a Union of proprietors of
leading estates, and in contrast to the local co-operatives, whose
vins des cafés usually lack distinction, the *Reflets* at Châteauneuf-du-Pape stand by the strictest rules and regulations of the
appellation.

They market only the very finest wines under their very
distinguished seal *Mise en bouteille aux Reflets*, each bottle being
numbered and guaranteed. Endless pain and trouble are put into
the vinification of their wines to ensure that outstanding quality
is obtained. The nine partners (one founder member has retired
from viniculture since its foundation in 1954) vinify and treat
their wines in their own cellars. They have the choice of bottling
them all in their cellars, or of having the best of their *cuvées*
bottled in the *Reflets* cellars; only the latter are entitled to the
Reflets label. The *vignerons* place their products (usually the
têtes de cuvées) before a committee composed of members and
with an outside judge—usually an official of the *Institut National
Appellation d'Origine Contrôlée*; they taste the wines without
grower's label, and judge the quality with an elaborate marking
scheme. The wines must reach a high standard based on colour,
bouquet, alcohol, acidity and, most important of all, balance.
In case of doubt the official has a casting vote, a course of action
rarely, if ever, taken.

The selected wines are bottled with all the care in the world and
are binned in the *Reflets* cellar, each member having his own
separate bins. Conditions in the cellar are perfect—dry sandy
soil with concrete pillars and bins kept at the best temperature
for gentle and smooth maturing. Usually the cellar holds
approximately 100,000 bottles, the red wines being a minimum
of two years old, and the whites one year. The members of the
Reflets are subdivided into two sections; those with single
estates and those who own many small sections of vineyards
widely distributed, with a central cellar in the village. The latter
suffer from the extra work entailed by their subdivided lands,
yet they may benefit, especially when hailstorms occur in small
areas as in 1964. Labour and transport costs are naturally higher,
but separation is a safeguard against spring frosts and summer

hail, neither of which is necessarily widespread over the complete area. The *Reflets* were formed as a means of reducing costs by purchasing communal bottling and labelling machinery; the strict methods adopted by the members have not passed unnoticed and their wines are proudly displayed all over the world. The organisation is recognised as a model *Union des Propriétaires* (Co-operative), and their success has reflected on the Châteauneuf-du-Pape community. A complete range of their wines is available for tasting at their cellars in Châteauneuf-du-Pape village.

THE VINES

Plantations are strictly governed by law, and any deviation from this loses the right to *Appellation Contrôlée*. Yield per hectare (*rendement*), vineyard treatment (irrigation forbidden), (training of vines), methods of vinification are all specified exactly, as well as vine varieties (*Cépages*). For Châteauneuf-du-Pape fewer varieties are permitted than for the Côtes-du-Rhône generic wine.

Appellation Châteauneuf-du-Pape
Principal *Cépages*:

Grenache, Clairette, Syrah, Mourvèdre, Picpoul, Terret noir, Picardan, Cinsault, Roussanne, Bourboulenc.

Accessory *Cépages*:

Counoise, Muscadin, Vaccarèse.

Appellation Côtes-du-Rhone
These are as for Châteauneuf-du-Pape, plus:

Principal *Cépages*:

Viognier, Carignan (Maximum 30%)

Accessory *Cépages*:

Pinot fin de Bourgogne, Mauzac, Pascal blanc, Ugni blanc, Calitor, Gamay noir jus blanc, Cammarèse (according to district).

The major blends for the classical red wine of Châteauneuf-du-Pape are made up of the following major components from four groups, as compiled by Commandant Duclos at the end of the last century.

Group 1 (20%) giving warmth, liqueur and mellowness.

GRENACHE, CINSAULT

Group 2 (30%) giving solidity, durability, colour with a pure refreshing flavour.

MOURVÈDRE, SYRAH, MUSCADIN, VACCARÈSE

Group 3 (40%) giving vinosity, charm, freshness and bouquet.

COUNOISE, PICPOUL

Group 4 (10%) white grapes giving fire and brilliance to the wine.

CLAIRETTE, BOURBOULENC

A more modern scheme of replanting is with vines in proportion:

40–60% Grenache
30–10% Syrah
   20% Cinsault, Mourvèdre, Counoise, Vaccarèse
   10% Clairette, Bourboulenc

On account of phylloxera, pure stock had to be grafted on to roots resistant to the disease, mainly of American origin. Amongst the many varieties available the following were chosen for this purpose as being most suitable for soil and climate conditions of this area. Jacquez, Rupestris du Lot, Riparia Gloire de Montpellier, Solonis, Monticola and others. With new graftings, certain species (Muscadin, Picardin and Terret noir) are tending to disappear as they have low resistance to disease.

The many permitted combinations of grapes in Châteauneuf-du-Pape account for the variation of flavour and quality in a range of wines bearing the same names; each grower will have his particular style which necessarily depends on the distribution of vines in his vineyards. No other wine-producing region of France shows such a large number of vine species (known to Abbé Rozie as early as the eighteenth century), and whereas the Pinot produces the great wines of Burgundy, the Syrah the Hermitage, the Roussette the St. Péray, it took no less than thirteen species to make the classic Châteauneuf-du-Pape, a course no longer followed by modern taste requirements, nine varieties sufficing for present production of Château Fortia.

Châteauneuf-du-Pape *blanc* is generally made only from white grapes, the major *cépages* being Clairette and Grenache *blanc*. Of the two, the Clairette gives the sturdier wine, the Grenache however, a finesse and volatility of fruity aromas not experienced with other wines of comparable alcoholic strength and body. The white wines account for less than 2 per cent of the total production. The method of cultivation is not particularly different from any other district, although special mention must be made of the rapid wear of the ploughshares (and horseshoes) on the stony soil.

The vines planted have always been local growth and are intermixed in proportion, in the vineyards. At harvest time the grapes are hand-sorted (similar to a German *Auslese*) and only the perfect examples are allowed into the Châteauneuf-du-Pape *cuvée*, the remnants producing *Râpé*. The minimum quantity of *râpé* is 5 per cent and is fixed annually by a committee who consider the final condition of the grapes and also any diseases of the vine which might have been prevalent in the region during the summer. In recent years a 15 per cent *râpé* was necessary on some estates.

SOIL AND CLIMATE

Appellation Châteauncuf-du-Pape spreads from Châteauneuf-du-Pape Commune (1,435 ha, 263 growers) across the border of four Communes—Orange in the north (352 ha, 91 growers), Courthézon in the east, (352 ha, 286 growers), Bèdarrides in the south-east (134 ha, 49 growers), and Sorgues in the south (23 ha, 15 growers). Châteauneuf-du-Pape village, which is in the south-west, dominates its sector, in which it is the highest point, although not the highest point of the whole area. The *appellation* area abounds in small plateaux and rising slopes to the hills so that a varied soil structure can be expected, which, coupled with directional plantation and many vine varieties, gives many different qualities of the final product. The stony soils are mainly on the plain, whereas the valleys and slopes are *terre rouge* and sand. The vines grown on stony soil generally produce wine of higher alcoholic content than wines from other soil and this is the great secret of the *vignerons'* art, subtle linking of various *cépages* to give a perfect final product.

The subsoil sediment (from the Helvetian Era) is only found on the surfaces in very few places. The alluvial deposits (from the Pliocene Era) on the plateaux and summit consist of pebbles, usually perfectly rounded, up to the large sizes mainly of quartz and other hard substances of alpine character. Less hard are the felspathic rocks which are completely decomposed slate. Most of the original limestone has been washed away or corroded by centuries of weathering, although a narrow strip is still to be found across the Château Fortia Estate.

The soil and subsoil are extremely permeable and rainwater drains away rapidly from the surface leaving the topsoil dry, a process assisted by the dry, prevailing wind (mistral). This reduces the quantity of fruit borne but immeasurably increases the quality. The continuous warming of the vines round-the-clock by the hot stones (heated by sun during the day and radiating heat at night) must be coupled to the previous phenomena. The quality of the wine does not appear to be determined by the soil type of the vineyard. Analytically it is impossible to find variation of quality with soil by any means, effective ingredients being physical soil type, permeability, tendency to drought, lack of fertilising elements and weathering (extremes of heat and cold). The Rhône climate is completely characterised by the mistral which blows from the north-west. The constancy and violence of this wind obviously affect the vines, which tend to lean north–south from this constant battering force which usually brings unpleasant side-effects after rainfall; the temperature falls and the atmospheric pressure rises. This may stop fermentation during vinification which requires special techniques for re-starting. A certain amount of wind-breaking is achieved by groups of cypress trees, a prominent feature of the landscape.

Rainfall is irregular and tends to be heavy over short periods, the minimal periods being February and July–August, and the maximal during March to May and September to November.

Spring or "mild winter" has two important characteristics, rainy periods and mistral. The wet spell, coupled with frost which may be heavy, is worrying for growers. Summer brings extremely stable weather with dry rainless spells lasting up to two months, and clear, bright blue skies with large temperature increases. Autumn brings a change in weather with heavy, unpleasant thunderstorms and rainy spells which, when short, are followed by excellent weather again, sometimes until the end of October. Winter is a dry season, February sharing with July the distinction of the driest month. Snow is rare, heavy frosts occur occasionally, and this pleasant winter season is high-lighted with clear blue skies.

VINIFICATION OF RHÔNE WINES

White Wines

Immediately after harvesting, the grapes are brought to the press house where the Must or grape-juice is obtained by pressing grapes, stalks and branches, there being no separation of the fruit and tannin-containing materials. The Must is run into sulphured hogsheads and allowed to settle while the unwanted solids from the grapes accumulate at the bottom of the cask. The bright, clean Must is then racked into clean casks, not full to the top, pure yeast added and fermentation allowed to proceed. The cask is sealed with a special glass or plastic bung,

157

to allow the carbon dioxide generated during fermentation to escape freely without any cellar air being drawn into the cask.

The fermentation procedure varies from *vigneron* to *vigneron*, the wine generally being racked away from the lees (the insoluble by-product of fermentation and dead yeasts) into a clean, slightly sulphured cask soon after termination. In exceptional vintages with Musts of high sugar content (giving wines of high alcoholic strength) fermentation may go slowly and with difficulty. The process of racking is repeated several times during the time the wine is kept in cask. Preliminary to bottling, the wine is sometimes "fined" with bentonite sand and/or gelatine, which precipitates any material still suspended in the wine. At the time of writing, most *vignerons* still wait two years before bottling their white wines, but experience has shown that during the second year in cask the wines lose finesse and bouquet, darken appreciably in colour, and maderise, which makes them less palatable for modern style drinking habits. Forward-thinking *vignerons*, certainly those belonging to the *Reflets*, bottle their wine after only one year in cask, to give a product far more appreciated by their clientèle.

Red Wines

Generally, red wines are prepared by fermentation of the Must together with skins, pips and stalks. The grapes, on arrival at the cellars, are crushed between grooved rollers (*foulage*), the mash being pumped into large vats and lightly sulphured. It is at this stage that the more delicate arts of vinification come to force, as this is the best time for blending grapes from different vineyards, and varying wine stock. The partial blend having been made (the final blend is made from several *cuvées* as not all the grapes ripen and are picked at the same time), the mash is allowed to ferment, the temperature being kept, as far as possible, between 20° and 30°C. Higher temperatures give a wine less bouquet and finesse, and also the danger of bacterial infection increases; the optimum temperature for spoilage is over 30°C.

The fermentation must be controlled extremely carefully, and apart from temperature rises, bacterial infection must be avoided. The carbon dioxide gas produced by fermentation bubbles its way to the surface taking the pulp of skins and pips with it, where they are exposed to the air. The layer (the *chapeau*) tends to float on the surface and must be kept from infections which rapidly turn wine to vinegar. Many varied methods are applied to keep the *chapeau* broken up and below the surface; modern vats have submerged grids. Similar results are obtained by pumping from underneath over the top surface. This achieves a cooling effect at the same time. Extreme care is taken during the process, as with all work in cellars during the fermentation period, to avoid excessive concentration of carbon dioxide which can cause asphyxiation of the cellar-man. After the end of fermentation, which may take two weeks or more, this depending entirely upon the individual vintner, the wine remains in the fermentation vat for several days (sometimes weeks or even months) after which it is racked into large wooden vats or individual hogsheads for maturing. The remaining mash from the vat is pressed by hydraulic presses; the wine from this procedure is called *Vin de Presse* and is usually much harsher than the final product, the tannin content being considerably higher. It is used for consumption by the workers and vintners themselves.

Maturing in wood takes from fifteen months upwards, depending upon the harvest, during which time the casks are topped up frequently and racked four times a year (December, February, April and June), preliminary to bottling. This usually takes place after two years, just before harvest time, but can be delayed up to seven years; the wine is fined with a gelatine and may also be filtered. During maturation approximately 10 per cent of the wine is lost in the first year and 5 per cent in the second year. In an extremely hot and dry year, when the grapes are small, fermentation is carried out without stalks and pips, which would increase the tannin content too much. Immediately after their arrival at the cellars, the mass of grapes is pumped or allowed to flow into an extractor machine, which rejects the stalks apart from the skin and Must, a process known as *égrappage*. Fermentation then proceeds as above. In some years it is necessary to adjust the final tannin content to obtain a well-balanced wine. This can only be done by preparing a special *cuvée* with some grapes left on their stalks mixed with those already without stalks (*égrappé*), a procedure which requires expert judgment for success.

Rosé Wines

The production of Rosé wines begins exactly like Red wine production and fermentation is allowed to continue with the grape Must (now partially alcohol) in contact with the skins. It is the alcohol which removes the colouring matters from the skin layers and after twenty-four hours (sometimes longer, depending upon the temperature) the fermenting grape juice has usually attained a pleasant pink colour. When the colour is judged sufficient, the whole mass is passed to the wine press and the partially fermented grape juice separated completely from the skins and residues. From this point, treatment follows the white wine pattern.

TAVEL A few miles away on the other side of the Rhône are the vineyards of Tavel, producing probably the best dry *rosé* of France. The village of about 700 inhabitants perches on a rather steep slope among cypress windbreaks and hillocks of olive groves. While in some parts of the Rhône valley vines are giving way to other crops, the reverse process has operated here, and many acres of former woodland have been added to the land already under the grape, an extension that enables this *rosé* wine to keep pace with the demands from all over the world. Although Tavel wine did not attain the dignity of its own name until the seventeenth century, it had fame long before then. In that time the port of Roquemaure, only a few miles from Tavel and on the opposite bank of the Rhône from Châteauneuf-du-Pape, was extremely busy. It is reported that in one year 12,000 casks of wine were loaded. There is no doubt that in the eighteenth and nineteenth centuries the surrounding communes of ROQUE-MAURE, LIRAC and CHUSCLAN added their wines to those of

Grape pickers in the vineyards at Meursault.

The courtyard of the famous Hospices de Beaune.

facing p. 160

Vineyards at Moulin-à-Vent, Beaujolais.

facing p. 161

Tavel, but they too have their own standing now. Philip le Bel is credited with saying: "There is no good wine except Tavel", and its admirers included Louis XIV, Balzac, Daudet, Brillat-Savarin (the celebrated gastronome), as well as the papal court at Avignon. One may reasonably assume also that it was popular with the medieval troubadours when they brought their music and courts of love over to Provence.

Tavel *Rosé* is made by a judicious blending of several varieties of white and black grapes, grown on stony, red and sandy soil, the lightly pressed berries being left only one night in the vat before the skins are removed from the juice. This is sufficient to give the wine that brilliant pink which is such a delight to the eye. The wine is drunk young and chilled, and goes with almost any food. It is a dry, full-bodied wine of generous bouquet and full flavour. Its pinkness should not give the idea that it is just a pretty wine for the ladies. A good Tavel is usually 12° to 13° (per cent alcohol by volume). Much of the wine is produced on a co-operative basis, and it is shipped to many countries in all continents, especially North America.

LIRAC A close neighbour to Tavel, Lirac also makes a *rosé* as well as a red wine, and a white wine which is little known outside the locality. The village has fewer than 250 inhabitants yet the wine co-operative has 180 members. This does not mean that almost every man, woman and child has a plot of vines. Many of the growers are "outsiders" who own vineyards as a sideline and are glad to share the bounty of this elevated terrace which paradoxically is known as the "plain". The holdings are small, averaging just under an acre and a half, so it naturally follows that most of the wine-making is a joint task. The Comte de Segries is the delightful owner of the most important vineyards, and makes an interesting if somewhat light red wine as well as *rosé*.

Lirac is an excellent example of how vines have to accord to the nature of the soil. Vines are selectively planted—according

G

to experience in the main soil types: stony ground, red gravel, sand and chalk—similar to Tavel. Thus the blending of the plants in the soil may be just as important as the blending of the grapes in the vats, and is another instance of the skill and care required to give balance, bouquet, fragrance and strength to the matured wine.

Much of the land around the village is given over to cereals and fruit and is typically Provençale—cypress trees, pines, hillsides of vines and olive trees. But there are three other places that share Lirac's *appellation*—ST. LAURENT-DES-ARBRES enclosed in the ramparts of its old fortifications, ST. GENIES-DE-COMOLAS, and ROQUEMAURE on the banks of the Rhône.

LAUDUN

Laudun is a city proud of its historic past and its fine wines, acknowledged from ancient times. The vineyards are in fact the oldest in the Gard and stretch across three communes, LAUDUN, ST. VICTOR LA-COSTE and TRESQUES. Red, *rosé* and white wines are made, the latter often showing great finesse.

CAIRANNE

The traveller who follows approximately in the footsteps of Hannibal's elephants over the river and through the old Roman city of Orange (from which King William of Orange took his title) arrives at Cairanne, a neat little village that sits on a small hill in an enormous green belt of vines. Seventy-five per cent of the present-day production is red wine, the remainder being divided between *rosé* (20 per cent) and white (5 per cent). Five main grape varieties are grown, and although a handful of individual vintners still remain, most of the growers belong to the co-operative, which has 250 members. The wines are fine with excellent bouquet, perhaps too powerful for charm and elegance.

RASTEAU

Cairanne's near neighbour Rasteau, apart from its red, *rosé* and golden white, produces a most unusual wine—a partly fortified white. For this, only one type of grape is grown, the Grenache, which draws from the pebbly marl a natural golden wine. During fermentation a small quantity of alcohol is added to the juice which stops this process and prevents the complete transformation of the sugar into alcohol. (cf. Port). Thus the *vin doux naturel* first made in 1934 comes with distinct sweetness and a high degree of alcoholic strength, but only 250,000 litres are made annually. *Vin de liqueur* by regulation may also be made by addition of alcohol to the unfermented grape-juice. Rasteau's local reputation is summed up in the ancient proud claim that it has "the goodness of Pope Boniface, the wit of good King René, the simplicity of St. Francis and the beauty of Queen Johanna", and it is still thought as highly of now that co-operative methods have replaced the former traditional one. The *appellation* decree for Rasteau lays down an unusual special denomination "Rasteau Rancio" for wines which have obtained a peculiar taste (*rancio*) after a long maturing period.

BEAUMES-DE-VENISE	Beaumes-de-Venise, a delightful village of 1,500 people with churches dating back to the eighth-century, nestles on the foothills of the Ventoux range. It is best known for its Muscat, a sweet dessert wine, frequently drunk chilled as an aperitif, but the local co-operative (290 members) also produces a good deal of red wine marketed as CÔTES-DU-RHÔNE and CÔTES-DU-VENTOUX.

The Muscats harvested from only 7 hectares of vineyards are aged in barrels and they acquire a beautiful golden colour to add to their fragrance, strength and sweetness. They are in fact best drunk when reasonably young as the volume of Muscat bouquet diminishes with age. Some of the vines contributing to the yield are more than a hundred years old and are grown on rather infertile sandy soil. Formerly they were cultivated on the supporting walls of the terraces and the fruit was left to become dried almost like raisins before it was gathered. These have now been supplemented by other plants cultivated in the normal manner.

GIGONDAS   Gigondas is a quiet village of some 700 inhabitants proud of its wines and historic associations. Wine and vine are the sole industry already praised by Pliny centuries ago. The vines, producing red (70 per cent), *rosé* (20 per cent) and white wines (10 per cent), are grown on ideally exposed vineyards, the red wines in quality taking second place after Châteauneuf-du-Pape. At harvest time a proportion of the crop is discarded as *râpé*—the quantity determined annually by a commission.

The wines are generous with fine bouquet, rich in flavour and usually high in alcohol, 14-15 per cent in normal, and 17 per cent has been obtained. The wines require a good many years in cask and bottles to show their finer characteristics.

VACQUEYRAS   Vacqueyras, a distinctive village within ancient ramparts, in the shadow of the magnificent Ventoux mountain range, produces mostly red wine with a very small quantity of white.

The Troubadour Raimbaud had already sung the praise of Vacqueyras in the twelfth century, and the Romans had discovered the thermal sulphur sources in the nearby mountains.

The vineyards neighbour those of Gigondas and the wines are made from the same principal grapes. They may not reach the Gigondas quality, but nevertheless "flatter the eye and palate of gourmets". I well remember during the 1959 harvest a notice board at the co-operative cellars proudly stating that a wine of over 18 per cent alcohol had been made.

VINSOBRES   The most northerly vineyards of the Meridional section produce fine characterful wines, the *rosé* similar to other Rhône *rosé*, the red more supple than average. No doubt the climate, less hot than vineyards a few miles further south, helps to make a wine of less alcohol than its neighbours and therefore often more pleasant and with more pronounced bouquet.

VINS DÉLIMITÉS DE QUALITÉ SUPÉRIEURE

V.D.Q.S. is a special *appellation* arranged for local wines rather than the fine wines which are of course covered by *Appellation Contrôlée*. Most V.D.Q.S. growths are in the south and it should be noted that the control exercised in relation to it is similar to *Appellation Contrôlée*.

In the Rhône region there are four such wines:

Côtes du Ventoux   (Vaucluse)
Côtes du Lubéron   (Vaucluse)
Haut Comtat   (Drôme)
Châtillon-en-Diois   (Drôme)

CÔTES DU VENTOUX. A large region around Mont Ventoux which takes in sixty communes growing mainly Grenache, Carignan and Cinsault. An exception is Mazan where a *vin de liqueur* is produced. Red and white wines are 10·5°, whereas the *rosés* can also use the name of the commune which require a minimum strength of 11·5°. Control of viticulture, methods, vines planted, etc., is very rigid and the wines are analysed before they are released for marketing.

CÔTES DU LUBÉRON. Red, white and *rosé* wines, mainly the two latter, are grown around the mountain of Lubéron. Culture of the vine is said to have traditions going back to Roman days. Tradition, soil, climate, choice of vines and methods of viticulture have all helped to promote the quality of these wines. The quality is analogous to the Côtes-du-Rhône wines and they are obviously related. Mainly lighter, they are very fruity—red wines in the northern sector around Apt and Maubec, white and *rosé* wines in the southern region near the Durance river around Lauris and Lourmarin.

HAUT COMTAT. These are wines grown in communes around Nyons. They are usually red and *rosé*. Most growers use the co-operative at Nyons and Vaison-la-Romaine. The former even bottles part of the production. The wines are made from Grenache (50 per cent minimum), Cinsault, Carignan, Mourvèdre and Syrah and have a minimum of 11° alcohol.

CHÂTILLON-EN-DIOIS. Around Châtillon, red and white and *rosé* wines are made, alcoholic strength 10·5° but only 10° for the red. The permitted vines are mainly those of the Maconnais rather than of the Rhône, Gamay (at least 75 per cent), Pinot and Syrah, whereas for the white, Aligoté, Chardonnay are permitted with very small amounts of Melon and Sauvignon. The wines are all made at the co-operative cellars at Die and are sold in bottle only. The vineyards are only 26 hectares and production varies annually, red always predominating.

A SUMMARY

The Rhône is fortunate in having a regular sequence of hot summers and produces fine wines with more frequency than any other of the noted French wine areas. On an average, eight out of ten vintages are very good and of these half are excellent, unfortunately often so good that the wines contain more than 14·2 per cent alcohol which doubles their rate of import duty.

Since the end of World War II only three vintages have disappointed, the most recent being 1963 which produced very light uncharacteristic wines. 1965, in contrast to all other French quality districts, produced excellent wines in the Rhône valley. Normally the red wines are ready for consumption three to four years after the vintage, two years stored in wooden casks and then as long as possible in bottle before drinking. One cannot, however, be dogmatic about this as many wines need much longer in cask, and I remember tasting some from wood seven years after vintage which were then, and only then, ready for bottling.

The white wines of course are bottled much younger and in their youth show great fruitiness and finesse but are, of course, full-bodied and of high alcoholic strength. They would, in my opinion, be better appreciated if bottled much younger, within twelve months of the vintage.

Many fine Rhône wines are shipped to the U.K., the most popular being the ordinary CÔTES-DU-RHÔNE red wines which suit the British palate, pocket and climate admirably. Quality varies enormously, but in general they are excellent value for money. CHÂTEAUNEUF-DU-PAPE, of course, is the best known *vineyard* red Rhône and appears in most restaurant and off-licence wine lists, as does Tavel amongst the *rosé* wines. *Rosé* wines have become very popular recently, the best still being TAVEL for flavour, body and noble colour.

Of the fine growths of the Northern Sector, HERMITAGE and CROZES-HERMITAGE are finding many devotees. Their fine characteristics make them very suitable for our climate and a good proportion of the harvest is for British palates. The fine vintages of CÔTE-ROTIE are obtainable, but the lesser known but equally fine wines of CORNAS, ST. JOSEPH, the white CHÂTEAU GRILLET and the sparkling ST. PÉRAY are only imported by specialist shippers; the sweet fortified wines from the Southern Sector are practically unknown here.

The Rhône has often been unjustifiably treated as inferior to the other regions, but the last few years have seen progress being made in presenting the true picture and value of these wines. The least expensive obtainable will be approximately 12s., the finest 28s., and in this range is represented as fine a collection of red and white wines as can be presented from any other French wine region.

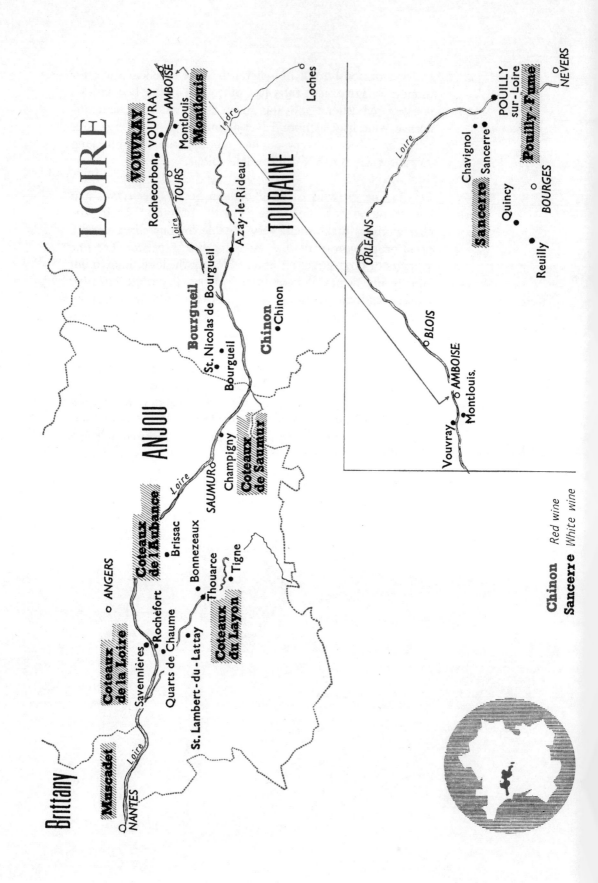

THE LOIRE

The River Loire is linked with the happier part of French history —the few dark episodes of the Hundred Years War only throw into greater relief the general feeling of gaiety and charm.

Here the spoken language seems purest, the women loveliest, the fairy-tale castles most enchanting, the grass and trees greenest, and the wines most appealing and varied.

Much of this variety stems from the geography of this wide and lovely river valley; from its extent—for the distance from one end to the other of its vineyards could almost bridge the gap between Bordeaux and Burgundy; and from its geological structure—mainly limestone and chalk from its upper reaches down to Vouvray, and old sedimentary rocks in the middle and lower reaches. Thus there are red wines, *rosé* wines and white wines ranging from light and crisp to rich and flavoury, sparkling wines and still wines, and those scintillating in-betweens— *pétillant* and *perlant* wines.

MUSCADET

Folk memories linger on, and just as farmers of the North of England recount tales from ancient times of raiders sweeping down on their sheep-stealing forays, so the wine-growers around Nantes have a tradition that their local highlanders—the Bretons—used to obtain their supplies of wines by main force, without having recourse to legitimate channels of commerce. Nor does the parallel end there, for the Bretons play the bagpipes, the difference being that they play the pipes (*Musette* or *Cornemuse*) with the bellows under their arms.

The Bretons were fishermen, and one wonders whether supply and demand resulted from the harmonious linking of Nantes wine with the fish and shell-fish which abound along that coast. The grape which has made the name of Muscadet famous came from Burgundy, where it was known as the Melon de Bourgogne—a relatively large, oval grape, and the least regarded of the Burgundy *cépages* which produced light but less esteemed *ordinaire* wines. In the Loire valley it still produced pristine wine, but from some magic of the soil it now yielded a fresh aroma with a hint of musk.

COTEAUX DE LA LOIRE

The Muscadet district nearest to Brittany lies to the north of the Loire river, namely between this and its tributary, the Indre. The wines have the right to the name MUSCADET DES COTEAUX DE LA LOIRE.

SÈVRE ET MAINE

The other main district lies south of the Loire and has a separate name of MUSCADET DE SÈVRE ET MAINE (sometimes called Muscadet des Coteaux de Sèvre et Maine). These wines generally have a little more staying-power, although most Muscadets are best bottled extremely early (often before Christmas of the year of the vintage) and show their charm to the maximum if drunk within a year of the bottling.

Around and beyond these two main districts are other vineyards where the wines are simply Muscadet, less pretentious but still delicious when drunk fresh and cool.

Apart from the wines which lie outside the Sèvre et Maine and

170

Coteaux de la Loire areas, Muscadet, unqualified, may also originate in these Coteaux areas, for example, in years of surplus production.

In olden times the wines from this region were mainly red and it was only just before the middle of the seventeenth century that the planting of the white grape from Burgundy was begun. The white wines made from it must have been noticeably better than the original red wines, for when frost devastated the vineyards at the beginning of the eighteenth century, and nearly all vines had to be replanted, almost the whole vineyard was replanted with white grapes. Even so, it was not all Muscadet; a large proportion of the vines were the variety known as GROS-PLANT which grows in the Charente region to produce the light acid wines which are distilled into Cognac.

One unusual variation met with in the Muscadet district is known as the *mise sur lie*. This consists of bottling the wine just as it finishes its fermentation (Malo-lactic) and when it still has minute quantities of carbon dioxide gas dissolved in the wine. The lees from this fermentation still lie at the bottom of the cask; if the wine was racked off then into a clean cask, the tingling freshness of the carbon dioxide gas would be lost, so certain growers used to make a speciality of bottling the wines straight from the cask at this early moment and drew attention to the fact by the mention on the label: *mise sur lie*. Such wines, of course, often showed excellent quality and were in considerable demand.

Human nature being what it is, certain other people wanted to get in on the act and, perhaps misunderstanding the phrase, sometimes bottled wines with a certain proportion of lees in them. Although this was not the same as the original technique, it is possible that there may still be something in the idea of "a wine feeding on its lees" and they may have qualities which will not be found in an ordinary star-bright wine.

Scattered along the river between the well-known Noble Vine-yards are others which produce wines highly esteemed in the locality, certainly vastly superior to the *vins ordinaires* or *vins du pays* with which they might otherwise be confused.

To market and reward this quality, while still not classing them with the *appellation contrôlée* wines, they have been granted a label of quality which may only be used by those who have passed a Committee of Inspection and gained the approval of a Tasting Panel.

In the Muscadet district you have the GROSPLANT DU PAYS NANTAIS, more acid than the Muscadet and yet crisp and re-freshing. It is made from a different grape, the Grosplant, which in the Charente further south makes light wines for distillation into Cognac.

Further up the river, approaching the Coteaux de la Loire, lie the COTEAUX D'ANCENIS, producing white wines as well as red and pink ones.

The reds and pinks are made from Cabernet (a Bordeaux grape) and Gamay (the Beaujolais grape) and the whites from the Chenin Blanc as well as the Malvoisie or Pinot Beurot.

It is perhaps this variation of grapes which differentiates these lesser known wines from their better known neighbours.

Nantes may not harbour any transatlantic liners or world-wide mercantile traffic, but it is quite a busy fishing port which also has regular cross-Channel sailings to London, Liverpool and Glasgow, thus it provides a natural outlet for its wine-growing hinterland. So when it was decided that the Vinous Orders of the Loire Valley and other wine-growing districts should meet with grand ceremonial, the ancient walls and towers of Nantes provided an impressive and attractive backdrop. The growers who are members of the Chapters of these Vinous Orders met beneath the walls to enthrone new members in a combined ceremony and the colours of their medieval-style robes glowed and complemented each other—burgundy, claret, yellow, dark-green and blue, and as they walked through the streets in procession, they were supported by young men and girls in traditional costume of the Breton—*Société des Bretvins*—and were accompanied by a skirling of bagpipes. The Gascons, on the other hand, had the traditional pipe and tabour. There is a resonance about the names of these Orders: The *Baillis de Pouilly*, the *Connetables de Guyenne*, the *Jurade de St. Emilion*, the *Chevaliers du Bontemps, du Médoc et des Graves*, the *Compagnons du Beaujolais*, the *Chevaliers du Tastevin*. With dignified ceremonial the wine-growers demonstrated how their roots go back to medieval times and beyond.

ANJOU

The massive towers and walls of old Angers, bare of all crenellations, have a solidity which contrasts with the elegance of the Anjou wines. These have a charm which is seldom found in other pink wines, which tend to be dry. The Anjou wines, however, spread over a gamut of styles, from the palest *vin gris* (where the white wine has only such a slight tinge of pink that it seems to be greyish-pink), on to the deeper-hued full *rosé*. Similarly they range from light wines to the fullness and character of the ANJOU ROSÉ DE CABERNET—a notable grape which, in other districts, makes fine red wine. But no matter what their style within this range of sweetness and colour, the ANJOU ROSÉ have a charm and elegance which delight the eye as well as the nose and palate. They seem to call out for a meal subtly composed in their honour—a table gleaming with white napery and shining silver, bestrewed with half-open rosebuds and asparagus fern; a menu of shrimp cocktail or fresh salmon and strawberries and cream. Yet you do not necessarily have to restrict the menu to lighter foods just for the sake of the colour; these wines will stand up to poultry and the lighter meats and have the great advantage that they can be drunk throughout the meal.

Not all Anjou wines are pink; the Anjou white wines have charm and can be medium-bodied, for they are made from that typical Loire grape Chenin Blanc, otherwise known as Pinot de la Loire. Generally speaking, the higher qualities go under the names (according to their region) of ANJOU-COTEAUX DE LA LOIRE, or ANJOU-SAUMUR, whereas the lighter wines are just called ANJOU.

COTEAUX DU LAYON

The Layon river, a tributary running into the Loire from the south, has some of the finest vineyard sites on the slopes and hillsides along its course. As one goes up the river the wines seem to get fuller and one can sometimes distinguish those special characteristics and styles derived from the soil. The COTEAUX DU LAYON ST. AUBIN have a more steely and very direct style, while those of ROCHEFORT are fuller. Here you can find wines as sweet, fine and rich as fine Sauternes, for the selective picking of only those grapes which are over-ripe and sleepy gives a peaches-and-cream fruitiness and an unctuous flow. This is the *pourriture noble* which produces the finest white wines of Bordeaux, of the Côte d'Or, of the Rhineland, and of Tokay.

The best known of the Chaume wines are the CLOS DE CHAUME and QUARTS DE CHAUME. According to tradition the Lord of the Manor of this area had the right to a quarter of the crop whilst the vignerons who worked the vineyard had the remainder. Legend has it that these Lords of the Manor with their high appreciation of the good things of life always selected the best quarter from which their wines should come, which, in time, became known as the Quarts de Chaume. Further on, the area near ST. LAMBERT DU LATTAY produces a mild wine with creamy fruitiness and reminiscent of the rich wines of Chaume.

There is coal underground at Chaudfonds-sur-Layon and the miners from here and other districts are essential as labour for the grape harvest.

Higher up the valley near Thouarcé a dry wine is made— BONNEZEAUX—esteemed by the few, for it is in short supply.

The wines of SAVENNIÈRES, including COULÉE DU SERRANT in the Coteaux de la Loire, are also appreciated.

SAUMUR

Saumur might be considered the capital of the middle Loire. It has certainly, for many years, been regarded as the centre for all horse-lovers of France, for here was the famous Saumur Riding School where all riding instructors throughout the French cavalry, and indeed the French army as a whole before mechanisation, were trained by the Cadre Noir. This body of officers and non-commissioned officer instructors rivalled the Vienna Riding School for Haute Ecole horsemanship; and their black riding jackets and gleaming boots offset by shining white breeches have been, for years, a feature of the Concours Hippique of Paris. These uniformed centaurs with their Napoleonic cocked hats have attracted horse-lovers from all over the world and one could visit the Musée Hippique and see the skeleton of Flying Fox, a horse famous in French breeding and racing history.

Saumur, as a wine-growing district, makes sparkling wines—mild, flavoury, gay wines, often with the faintest hint of Muscatel. The still white wines of this district also may have this characteristic. They are, however, relatively dry wines as the sweeter ones go under the label ANJOU or COTEAUX DU LAYON.

Not far from Saumur is the famous Abbey of Fontevrault with its curious kitchens and its tombs of the Plantagenet kings, including Richard the Lionheart. Can it have owed its riches and the number of its postulants to the unusual discipline, with monks and nuns ruled by an Abbess?

TOURAINE

Red Wines

The red wines of the Loire grow between Saumur and Vouvray. To the north of the river are the red wines of BOURGUEIL, and to the south of the river, on its tributary, the Vienne, lies the ancient town of Chinon with its three ruined castles and its delicious wines.

BOURGUEIL

Here the wines are a bright purplish colour when young, maturing like a slightly more supple and softer Claret. ST. NICOLAS-DE-BOURGUEIL is the best commune. Its vineyards adjoin those of Bourgueil.

CHINON

The wines of CHINON are light, bright red in colour, with a perfume of strawberries and a drinkable elegance. Chinon is also known as the site of one of the famous châteaux of the Loire which, when illuminated or acting as a backdrop for a *Son et Lumière* presentation, evoke the magnificence of France's historical heredity. These châteaux, strung along the river like pearls, are of a diversity of styles and aims. Some, like Angers, are châteaux-forts—fortresses to withstand the assaults of enemies and time: others, like Chinon, are bijou, romantic fairy-tale castles, built perhaps as love-nests for their favourites by kings of France. This, of course, is the homeland of Rabelais, the medieval French writer who brought such gusto to description of living and drinking.

The three castles of Chinon are now only ruins of their former greatness, but are interesting for their associations with Joan of Arc and Charles VII, Louis XI of France, and Henry II of England.

The next main tributary, upstream, is the Indre with some famous châteaux on it. Loches is more to the south-east, a fortress which does not seem to stand apart from the town like Angers does, but to be part and parcel of it, as if its strength was friendly rather than intimidating. Perhaps it is because the Loire seems to be an amicable river that one repeatedly comes across references to the love-lives of the French kings—Loches is the tomb of Agnès Sorel, a royal favourite.

Nearer to Tours lies AZAY-LE-RIDEAU. The round towers at the corners and candle-snuffer roofs make it an enchanting place, glimpsed between mature trees rather than seen in all its grandeur at once, and mirrored in the waters of the Indre in the harmony which recalls Jean de la Fontaine's poem: *"Eaux, bois et prairies—mère des douces réveries"*.

Near the junction of the Loire and the Cher lies Villandry; its gardens may not have the grandeur or sumptuousness of Versailles, but they are just as typically French; and the patterned *Parterre*, edged and framed with miniature hedges of box, has a charm which must be seen from roof-top level.

Many of the buildings around here are made of Tufa rock which looks something like pumice stone, and the underground galleries from which it has been hewn are now used for growing mushrooms, which is a major industry in these parts.

VOUVRAY

Tours, the capital of Touraine, leads almost automatically to VOUVRAY and MONTLOUIS, which produce excellent white wines, although Montlouis is somewhat overshadowed by its more vigorous and more famous neighbour. The wines of Vouvray seem to have a quality of vigour and sprightliness which expresses itself in their tendency to sparkle, ranging from the fully sparkling VOUVRAY MOUSSEUX, through the semi-sparkling CRÉMANT and PERLANT, to the VOUVRAY PÉTILLANT with its barely stated hint of a sparkle. This is due to the soil: limestone which has been quarried out of the hillsides, yielding building stone and leaving behind it cellars in which the wine can mature. It has also produced a troglodyte existence for some of the inhabitants: why build four walls if one in front of a cave will suffice?

Vouvray also has its châteaux: the Château de Moncontour, known for its sparkling Vouvray, while upstream to the Cher lies another château, mirrored in the water, Chenonceau, bridging the river and framed in its park.

As one ascends the Loire, more châteaux can be seen—Chaumont, associated like Chenonceau with Catherine de Medici and Diane de Poitiers.

VINS DÉLIMITÉS
DE QUALITÉ
SUPÉRIEURE

After passing through the Saumur and Touraine vineyards the apparent gap in the vineyards along the main Loire valley after Blois is in fact filled in with a series of lesser-known V.D.Q.S. vineyards (*Vins Délimités de Qualité Supérieure*). These superior wines each bear the label of quality; the first district is MONT PRÈS CHAMBORD COUR-CHEVERNY, the white wines of which should vary according to the grape from which they are made; Pinot de la Loire is the predominant white grape of the Middle Loire; the Sauvignon is the great vine of the Upper Loire, and Romorantin is a local vine taking its name from the town lying on a tributary of the Cher.

Mont Près Chambord Cour-Cheverny takes its name from the châteaux of Cheverny and Chambord. The latter has, inside its main hall, a unique double-spiral staircase, no doubt ideal for avoiding relatives! It also has the historic coach in which the French Royal Family tried to escape from the Revolution.

But its most striking feature is at roof-top level. Seen from the ground the gables and spires of the central section seem almost fussy; ascend to this level and walk among them and you find yourself in a miniature roof-top city, churches, houses, belfries, a world in miniature constructed no doubt for "little people", for there is a magic touch of genius in the proliferation of imagination.

The VINS DE L'ORLÉANAIS may be red, pink or white and give a considerable variation of styles and qualities over a relatively large vineyard extent.

Half way between Orléans and Pouilly-sur-Loire lie the COTEAUX DU GIENNOIS, or CÔTES DE GIEN, either red wines from the grapes found in the Mâconnais, or white wines from the Sauvignon or Chenin Blanc.

178

BERRY

The earnest seeker after wine would, however, have left the main Loire valley before now and ascended the Cher into the ancient province of Berry to taste the wines of Quincy and Reuilly.

QUINCY AND REUILLY

Here one finds a different grape, the Sauvignon, producing a wine drier and crisper than a Chablis, flintier than a Graves, yet with a perfume and elegance giving it a rightful place on the gourmet's table. From here one can drive through Bourges to Sancerre, where the same grape produces a wine perhaps less severe, perhaps more immediately appealing, but with many of the same qualities—dry and fruity.

SANCERRE

This is a relatively large area containing vineyards interspaced with meadows and fields. The rounded hills and valleys seem to remind one slightly of the area around Chablis. But the whole vineyard is dominated by the little town of Sancerre, perched on its steep hill overlooking the river.

If you were to visit this district early in August, you might well chance to see the popular festival, the *Foire aux Sorciers et aux Birettes*, commemorating an old legend of the struggle between the early Christians and the powers of evil. The newly installed *Birettes d'Honneur*, sitting astride a cask, have to swear an oath: "I will drink the first glass of wine pure, the second without water, and the third the way it comes out of the cask."

NIVERNAISE

Across the river from Sancerre lies the wine-growing district of Pouilly-sur-Loire and in June the Baillis de Pouilly, leaders of the wine-growing community, parade in their medieval robes under a banner bearing the motto: "Water divides us, wine unites us", referring of course to the Loire and their neighbours of Sancerre.

POUILLY-SUR-LOIRE

"All the wines from the valley of this river (the Loire) are delicious, and perhaps none more so than the fragrant Pouilly-Fumé." This tribute from Ambrose Heath is backed by others. Alec Waugh in *In Praise of Wine* cites Pouilly-Fumé as among the best of Loire wines, and P. Morton Shand paid it high compliment in *A Book of French Wines* as extremely fine and delicate in good years.

It is at Pouilly, where the river starts the great westward bend that brings it into the famous Châteaux country, that the first great vineyards of this noble stream make their appearance, and they should not be confused with those of the Burgundy village of the same name that produces Pouilly-Fuissé. The Pouilly-sur-Loire vineyards yield two notable dry white wines, each with the *Appellation Contrôlée* label—the light, evanescent POUILLY-SUR-LOIRE from the Chasselas vine, and the more outstanding POUILLY FUMÉ or BLANC FUMÉ DE POUILLY from the Sauvignon vine.

Although it is well known that the same type of vine can produce different wines according to the soil and climate in which it is grown, this Sauvignon grape yields full dry to medium Graves Supérieures in Bordeaux, and even enters into the making of the fine sweet wines of Sauternes and Barsac, whereas at Pouilly it is completely fermented to give a delicate, light, dry vintage, best drunk when its fresh, lively qualities can be appreciated in full.

The Blanc Fumé grapes of the Sauvignon are small, compact and slightly oblong, and when towards the end of September they turn a yellowish-amber colour their perfume suggests the slightly aromatic nature of the wine. The name Blanc Fumé has given rise to several theories as to its origin. Some people, accepting its literal translation of "white smoke", associate it with the smoky flavour some find in the wine. Others think it may derive from the white, floury powder that appears on the ends of the shoots or from the grey bloom of the grapes towards harvest time. But an equally reasonable explanation is that the soil of the upper Loire valley has imparted a special *fumet* (flavour) to the grape.

Pouilly legends refer to vineyards there before the Roman occupation. This is highly debatable, but there is evidence of wine growing in the third century sufficiently strong to justify Pouilly's claim to have had fifty generations of *vignerons*. During this long run, in which no doubt the viticultural skill and enthusiasm of the monks of the Middle Ages played their customary part, it is presumed that a process of trial and error developed the Sauvignon from semi-wild types. By the late eighteenth century its Blanc Fumé vintages graced Marie Antoinette's dining table and it was subsequently a favourite of Napoleon, but it is not recorded whether he took it with him on his Russian campaign as he did with Chambertin which he vainly hoped to drink in the Kremlin.

Since those days the Sauvignon has been acclimatised in other countries and continents, including South Africa, South America and California.

THE VINTAGE

In Pouilly the *vendange* generally comes in the first half of October (slightly later than in other Loire winefields), by which time the grape has a touch of *pourriture noble* which contributes greatly to the mellowness of Pouilly-Fumé, but this over-ripeness requires to be strictly controlled to prevent too much sugar in the juice which might change the character of the wine. Alcoholic strength ranges from 11 to 15 degrees and the Blanc Fumé bouquet and finesse attain their better qualities when the figure is round about 12 degrees.

The good weather of 1964 brought an earlier-than-usual harvest but also consequential difficulties, with the result that it developed into a race between *pourriture noble* and the vintagers. The grape-pickers had to hold their baskets under the bunches as they cut them, for the grapes were so ripe that at the least touch many of them fell to the ground and burst beyond hope of recovery.

In large measure the grapes, by the time they reached the presses, were so sweet that many *vignerons* found it quite a task to control the fermentation so that the wines possessed the crisp dryness that is so much part of the character of Pouilly-Fumé.

Thus, while the 1964 vintage may seem to be a great one, so far as concerns the ripeness of the grapes, it paradoxically happens that quite a few 1964 Pouilly-Fumés may not keep as well as they generally do, since they lack the acidity that contributes to crispness and staying power. The paradox is that new vines may come to the rescue of the old. When vines are newly planted they do not yield at all during their first three years (or should not), but after that their quality starts to improve. This means that the oldest vines in the vineyard produce the best wine. In 1964 it did not always work out that way with Pouilly-Fumé, since the newly-planted vineyards, lacking over-ripeness, produced wine with a crispness and freshness that made it the best of Pouilly's year.

VINIFICATION A long, slow fermentation makes for quality and produces in good years the dry, fruity flavour and refreshing acidity that are the aim of all Blanc Fumé growers. The first main fermentation turns the sweet juice of the pressed grapes into dry wine and, during this process, the intermittent "glou . . . glou . . ." from cask or vat is a reminder that the microscopic yeasts are still slowly converting the last of the sugar into alcohol. Bubbles of carbon dioxide—a by-product of this reaction—slowly accumulate against the sides of the cask until they suddenly rise to the surface with a gulping eructation.

So long as this continues the wine remains cloudy with minute particles of grape pulp and yeast cells still in suspension. Even so, the young wine can be tasted and at this stage the customary round of visits to cellars begins, enabling a grower to compare

182

his wine with his neighbour's and, by discussing qualities and quantities, try to gain some inkling of what the market prices are likely to be.

Pouilly wines recover quickly from the bottle sickness that affects most vintages and, by spring, make an excellent carafe wine with a slight tinge of green showing through the lemon yellow. They are dry enough to accompany shellfish but yet have sufficient body to suit them to poultry or even red meat. They are becoming increasingly popular both in France and in the many countries to which they are being exported.

In a district like this, with many small growers justly proud of their wines, there are many who have established their own clientèle among wine lovers and Paris restaurants, for whom they bottle their wine and who take up virtually the whole of the crop from that particular vineyard. Thus there are a number of excellent growers who never have any wine available for export unless they have an unusually prolific vintage, for their average production year by year is bespoke in advance.

For the most part, wine growing in the valley of the Loire and its tributaries is on the basis of small holdings and around Pouilly they are smaller than average, approximately two and a half acres, though there are important exceptions of much greater acreage. The smallness of so many holdings is largely due to family inheritance which has led to division and subdivision and, as a result, it is fairly common for growers to have a few rows of vines on one hillside and two or three more on another.

SOIL TYPES

There are three main types of soil. The gravelly soils found around St. Andelain produce the driest wines with the most "gun flint" flavour and nobility of style, while the heavy clay soils (*terres fortes*) yield full-bodied dry wines. In between these two qualities is the wine from the more calcareous soils (*terres blanches*). One seldom encounters these individual styles separately since the scattered nature of most holdings results in their being blended together in the final product.

Pouilly, more than most wine-growing areas, is liable to suffer
from frost, and several disastrous visitations have driven the
growers to improve their methods of cultivation.

In the past, they pruned their vines in the old *taille-genre Bor-
delaise*. This training of the vine consists of forming a stem with
two main branches, each bearing at least two short shoots
(*coques courtes*). As some growers are frosted two years out of
three, they are changing over more and more to the *taille
Guyot*, still with a main stem and two main arms (two *coques
courtes*), one of which carries a long shoot (*verge longue*), and the
other a short spur (*retraite*) which will furnish the *verge* next year,
so that with the *taille Guyot* the fruiting is carried out on alter-
nate arms of the vine. The long *verge* has a better chance of escaping part of the frost, for the upper part of it may escape low-
lying frosts, or alternatively, the lower parts may escape air
frosts. With both systems, the vines are trained on wires; if, in
winter, the long shoot is detached from the wires, it will wave
in the slightest breeze and help to disperse the frost. Other
methods are being tried. The simplest of these depends on the
latest possible timing of the spring cultivation, for it is said that
a carpet of chickweed (*mouron*) or newly turned earth between
the vines attracts the frost. In this area it is not dry cold but white
hoar-frost carried by the damp west wind which seems to cause
the damage, but, even then, the harm is only done when the
sun's rays strike the frost-bitten buds and shoots. So a number of
smoke-producing devices are used, the simplest being steel
drums filled with damp straw in which are burnt canisters
which produce a moisture-combining smoke. On the other
hand, all the time that the cold, dry north wind blows, the
growers sleep secure and do not have to jump out of bed at two
in the morning to attend to their smoke screens.

A more modern form of protection against frost is now being
tested. An experimental infra-red system, lent by the makers,
has been set up and, by means of this, heat-ray lamps fixed to
poles in the vineyard can be switched on whenever heavy frost
threatens. Partial tests during the winter have not yet brought
complete proof, but if spring frosts are successfully combated

it may well end the greatest worry of the Pouilly *vignerons*. It will also be an excellent business for the manufacturers.

Although frost has sometimes severely curtailed production, it has not over the years greatly affected the quality of Pouilly wines. This is shown in an authoritative work, "The Wines and Vineyards of France", by Louis Jacquelin and René Poulain, in which they sum up the quality of various vintages over the last half century or so. For Pouilly their findings are: very great years: 4; great: 6; very good: 4; good: 13; average: 11; mediocre: 5; bad (1925): 1.

PHYLLOXERA   Previous to the phylloxera devastation in the latter half of last century, Pouilly had between 5,000 and 6,000 acres of vineyards, but after that disaster many of them were not replanted and now, in consequence of the laws of *Appellation Contrôlée*, a new vineyard can be created only to replace old vines that have been uprooted.

During many generations it had been the practice to plant vines haphazardly (*en foule*) and to renew them by layering (*provinage*), so that over the years the earth contained a tangled mass of roots. Cultivation had to be by mattock—constant back-breaking work on a stubborn soil, with sudden jarring shocks as the mattock struck some buried vine stem that had probably been layered by the grower's grandfather or great-grandfather.

The clean sweep, after phylloxera, when the land was completely cleared, fumigated and replanted with vines grafted on to American rootstocks, enabled the *vignerons* to lay out their vineyards with the plants neatly arranged in rows between which a horse and plough could pass. Thus a great deal of hard manual labour was cut out. From that stage it was a natural step to increasing mechanisation with tractors and other equipment—more a matter of bank loans than of cultivation methods.

Nevertheless, changes are taking place in the traditional working of the vineyard soil. Earth was piled against the vines in winter to protect the stems against frost and to prevent puddles. Such heavy ridging was undesirable in summer when a level tilth is needed to conserve moisture and reflect the sun's warmth upwards on to the ripening grapes. In the past the mattock or the horse-drawn plough were scarcely powerful enough to do this in two operations, so they were split up into four or five workings (*façons*) of the soil. Heavy tractor-drawn ploughs with mould-boards can now throw up a substantial ridge in one operation.

Another autumn task, apparently contradictory to this ridging, consisted of clearing away the soil from around the graft-point so that suckers and adventitious roots could be cut away. Formerly this was laboriously carried out by mattock after the first ridging and the soil needed to be replaced around the stem after the fibrous roots had withered away. Nowadays the heavier ploughs pile up too much soil for this to be done in the old-fashioned sequence; so the stems are cleaned of suckers and rootlets with mattock and secateur as soon as the leaves have fallen, after which the winter ridging by ploughing can be done in a straightforward manner. Apart from the preparation of new or replacement stakes and pickets the vineyard can then be left until the March pruning.

SAUVIGNON WINES

The main characteristic is that of the Blanc Fumé or Sauvignon grape: some inkling of the different nuances of flavour may be drawn from the following notes which were written in 1964 after a tasting of Sauvignon wines. They included a "stranger" for comparison purposes—a Bordeaux wine made from the same grape.

1962 POUILLY BLANC FUMÉ is young and fresh and crisp with only a hint of the special Fumé characteristic, which will develop more with bottle age.

1961 QUINCY VIN NOBLE: Light, dry and elegant, it has a little less body than the Pouilly Fumés, but is an ideal shellfish wine.

1961 POUILLY BLANC FUMÉ: This is now showing typical Blanc Fumé characteristics, while the bottle age makes it a little milder than the 1962 vintage. It also has a little more body than the Quincy.

1962 POUILLY FUMÉ "La Loge Aux Moines": This wine has a great deal of body, for the 800-year-old vineyard had lain fallow for sixty years and the soil was therefore full of vigour. Moreover, the vines which were replanted over six years ago are now in vigorous production and give the wine a dry fruitiness.

1961 CHÂTEAU DE TRACY (*château* bottled) Pouilly Fumé: The Tracy wines are slower developers than most of the other vineyards at Pouilly and the 1961 Chateau de Tracy (*château* bottled) has pale colour and is still quite firm. It is, however, extremely crisp, with the characteristic Tracy bouquet only just starting to develop.

1960 CHÂTEAU DE TRACY (*château* bottled) Pouilly Fumé: has a much deeper colour and the bouquet has blossomed into suave spiciness overlying the gun-flint aroma.

1959 CHÂTEAU DE TRACY (*château* bottled) Pouilly Fumé has a very suave and full-bodied style and perhaps more alcohol than any subsequent vintage, for the growers had remarked that the grapes of 1959 were the ripest they had seen since the 1921 vintage.

1959 CHÂTEAU CARBONNIEUX (*château* bottled) Graves de Léognan: This was tasted alongside this range of Pouilly Fumés and Quincy wines and was (surprisingly enough) not dissimilar in style, although it was rather more full-bodied, yet dry. The similarity can be explained since the Blanc Fumé grape is used in the production of Château Carbonnieux under the name of Sauvignon. Patches of gravel soil in the Pouilly region might give similar characteristics to the gravel of the Graves.

Many of the vineyards have been cultivated for centuries and two of them—La Loge aux Moines and Château de Tracy—have considerable historical interest, with English and Scottish links.

La Loge aux Moines vineyards date back to about the year 1200 when the site belonged to a religious community at Seyr, nine miles up river from Pouilly. There the monks were noted for the help they gave to the poor, who, when they came to Seyr, used to talk about seeking the charity of the good monks. That was the origin of the place now known as La Charité.

True to tradition the monks had their vineyards, the best of which appear to have been at Pouilly, worked by relays of monks doing ten or fourteen day stints. One winter, severe weather prevented the monastery "relief" getting through and the stranded monks at Pouilly suffered greatly, several dying. To prevent a recurrence of the tragedy it was decided to build near the vineyards a series of lodges or cells. Hence the present name, La Loge aux Moines (The Monks' Lodging), originated.

The vines at La Charité (which never gave a quality wine) have completely disappeared and the last vineyard went out of production over ten years ago and is now lying fallow. The same fate nearly overtook La Loge. It was abandoned last century because the lie of the land prevented cultivation with horse-ploughs and harrows, and hand labour with the mattock was too expensive. In more recent times, however, a courageous *vigneron* replanted part of the old site and, working it with modern mechanical equipment, is getting excellent results.

During the Hundred Years War, La Charité was pillaged by Robert Knolles, an officer in the English army, and at Christmas time 1415 a French lord of the manor, Captain Perrinet-Gressart, took the title of "Captain of La Charité" for the English, probably as a reward for his conduct at the battle of Agincourt, where he took many prisoners whom he held captive at La Charité. In spite of repeated demands from the French king to hand the place back to France, Perrinet-Gressart refused, threatening to call in the English to help him to defend the town.

188

In 1429, soon after her triumph at Orleans, Joan of Arc with a small, badly armed force besieged the place, but failed to take it and her failure virtually ended the glory of her campaign; a year later she was defeated and captured at Compiègne.

In subsequent religious wars La Charité suffered considerably, but even before that, most of the vineyards had been abandoned. Fortunately, while the vines gradually disappeared at La Charité, additional planting was carried out by the *vignerons* at Pouilly and Château de Tracy, the latter one of the outstanding vineyards of the neighbourhood.

The *château* stands on a spur above the river and commands a striking vista. The owners, Count Alain d'Assay and his wife, who was born a d'Estutt de Tracy, reunited by their marriage two branches of the family which had been separated for nearly 500 years. Their distant ancestors were of Scottish origin, the Stutts of Laggan, one of whom, Geoffrey, is recorded as having taken an oath of allegiance to Edward I (Hammer of the Scots) in 1296.

In 1419 four sons of a descendant, Gauthier Stutt, were among the thousands of Scots who fought on the side of France in the Hundred Years War. Some of these were rewarded with French titles and grants of land, among them the eldest of the four brothers, who was made Lord of the Manor of Assay en Berry. When he died without issue, Louis XI (the same that Joan of Arc helped to his crowning) confirmed the gift to another brother, Thomas Stutt. This document, dated 1474, and in the king's own hand, is still in the family archives. In 1566, one of Thomas's grandsons, François, married Françoise Stutt of Bar, who brought in as a dowry the *seigneurie* of Tracy. In more modern times a son of the family married a niece of Isaac Newton, and a daughter became bride of Georges Washington Lafayette, son of the French general who played a big part in the American War of Independence.

No *vigneron* builds a wall round his vineyard unless he believes he has something good inside. That gives a claim to quality to the CLOS DE CHAUMIENNES, lying behind a stone-arched gateway in the middle of the village of Pouilly-sur-Loire. It is the only enclosed one in the neighbourhood. Part of the vineyard that runs down to the river is still planted with Chasselas, but the finest wine comes from the Blanc-Fumé and matures in 130 gallon casks (known as *demi-muids*) ranged round the cellars.

LOCAL RECIPES

Clos des Chaumiennes belongs to the Raveau family. The late proprietor of the Clos de Chaumiennes, M. Raveau, also owned the Restaurant de l'Espérance in Pouilly and his son too is a fine chef, whose reputation extends far beyond the Loire valley. Here is his recipe for *Coquilles St. Jacques au vin de Pouilly* (Scallops in wine):

> For each person take four good pieces of raw *Coquilles St. Jacques* (scallops) and cut each into three scallops. Roll them in flour, fry them to a golden colour in butter, add salt and pepper and remove the pan from the fire as soon as they are cooked (approximately three minutes).
>
> Add to the pan a piece of butter the size of a walnut, a good pinch of finely chopped shallots, Cognac, Madeira, white wine of Pouilly Fumé, a pinch of parsley; blend together with the walnut of butter until smooth and cooked and serve the fish coated with the sauce.

Another local recipe which should be tasted on the spot at the nearby Relais Fleuris is *Coq au Pouilly*:

> Take a fine chicken, weighing three to four pounds, and divide it into eight portions. Gently cook in some butter small portions of bacon and tiny onions. When these are coloured golden brown, remove them and put the pieces of chicken into the butter. When the chicken is coloured, add the bacon and the onions and *flambez* in good Cognac. Sprinkle with flour and moisten with the wine of Pouilly. Add salt, pepper, a clove of garlic, a good *bouquet garni*, a small pinch of nutmeg, and simmer for one and a half to two hours. Serve garnished with *croutons* if you wish.

Ideally this should be enjoyed with the best recent vintage of Pouilly Fumé on a summer evening when their flower-filled garden is a blaze of colour as it drops gently down to the River Loire, meandering through the sandbanks on its way through the vineyards, down to the sea.

Wines of the Loire

AC	— controlled *appellation* wine
VDQS	— superior wine with seal of quality
R	— red wines
W	— white wines
P	— pink or *rosé* wines

The brackets show wines which are not generally found with these *appellations* nowadays.

		R	W	P
AC	Anjou	R	W	
AC	Anjou-Coteaux de la Loire		W	
(AC	Anjou Coteaux de la Loire Rosé de Cabernet			P)
(	Anjou Coteaux du Loir	R	W	P)
	Anjou Coteaux de Saumur	R	W	P)
AC	Anjou Mousseux		W	
(AC	Anjou Rosé			P)
AC	Anjou Rosé de Cabernet			P)
AC	Anjou-Saumur	R	W	P
(AC	Anjou-Saumur Rosé de Cabernet			P)
AC	Blanc Fumé de Pouilly		W	
AC	Bonnezeaux		W	
AC	Bourgueil	R		P)
VDQS	Chateaumeillant	R	W	P
AC	Chinon	R	W	P
VDQS	Coteaux d'Ancenis	R	W	P
AC	Coteaux de l'Aubance		W	
AC	Coteaux de l'Aubance-Rosé de Cabernet			P
AC	Coteaux de la Loire-Rosé de Cabernet			P

(AC	Coteaux de Touraine	R	W	P)
(AC	Coteaux de Touraine Mousseux	R	W	P)
VDQS	Coteaux du Giennois	R	W	P)
AC	Coteaux du Layon		W	
AC	Coteaux du Layon-Chaume		W	
AC	Coteaux du Layon-Rosé de Cabernet			P
AC	Coteaux du Loir	R	W	P
	Coteaux du Loiret			
VDQS	Côtes de Gien	R	W	P
(	Croix de Touraine			)
(	Croix de Touraine Mousseux			)
AC	Coteaux de Saumur	R	W	P
AC	Coteaux de Saumur-Rosé de Cabernet			P
VDQS	Gros-plant du Pays Nantais		W	
AC	Jasnières		W	
AC	Menetou-Salon	R	W	P
VDQS	Mont-près-Chambord Cour-Cheverny		W	
AC	Montlouis		W	
AC	Montlouis Mousseux		W	
AC	Montlouis Pétillant		W	
AC	Muscadet		W	
AC	Muscadet de Sèvre-et-Maine		W	
AC	Muscadet des Coteaux de la Loire		W	
AC	Pouilly-Fumé		W	
AC	Pouilly-sur-Loire		W	
AC	Quarts de Chaume		W	
AC	Quincy		W	
AC	Reuilly		W	
AC	Rosé d'Anjou			P
	Rosé de Cabernet Anjou			P
AC	St. Nicholas-de-Bourgueil	R		
AC	Sancerre	R	W	P
AC	Saumur	R	W	(P)
AC	Saumur-Champigny	R		
AC	Saumur-Mousseux		W	
AC	Saumur Rosé de Cabernet			P
AC	Savennières		W	
AC	Touraine	R	W	P
AC	Touraine-Amboise	R	W	P

AC	Touraine Azay-le-Rideau	R	W	P
AC	Touraine-Mesland	R	W	P
(	Touraine Mousseux			)
(	Touraine Pétillant			)
VDQS	Vins de l'Orléanais	R	W	P
AC	Vouvray		W	
AC	Vouvray Mousseux		W	
AC	Vouvray Pétillant		W	

VIN DE LOIRE In 1969 a new *appellation* was introduced for wines of the Loire valley. It might be likened to the *appellation* Bourgogne covering the whole of Burgundy or Bordeaux covering the whole area of Bordeaux, or perhaps even Vin d'Alsace which is the generic *appellation* for Alsace.

It covers red, white or *rosé* wines and also sparkling wines from the whole region of the Loire valley in which *Appellation Contrôlée* wines are grown. It should help to make the names of Loire wines more widely known and more easily marketed.

ALSACE

The works of Roman historians show that viticulture can be traced back to the first century of the Christian era. It was extended by the Gauls, who transplanted vines from the valleys of the Rhône and the Saône to the left bank of the Rhine. From inscriptions on ancient Roman graves, we learn that inhabitants of the Mediterranean coasts took part in the planting of vines in Alsace.

After the war of 1870, and the annexation by Germany, economic conditions forced the Alsatian wine-growers to make radical changes in the selection of their vine species. German legislation, with its too liberal decrees in respect of the designation of sources and provisions regulating the processes of preparing wine, was not calculated to stimulate the production of high quality wines among Alsatian wine-growers. But in 1918, when Alsace was restored to France, Alsatian wine-growers quickly realised that their only chance of marketing their wines lay in the planting of quality vines.

It has taken many years for Alsace to re-enter the world market, but it is really only during the last decade that Alsace has asserted herself once more as a producer of great wines.

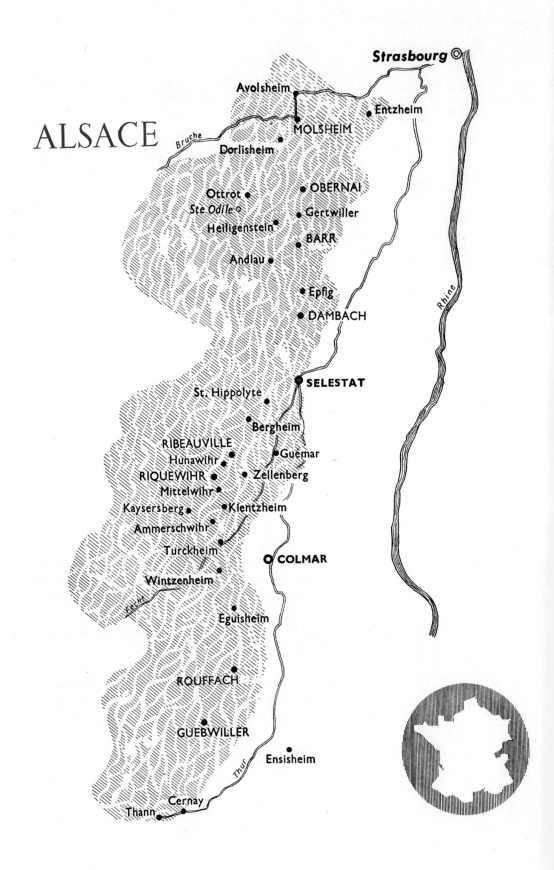

ALSACE

Strasbourg

Avolsheim

Entzheim

Bruche

MOLSHEIM

Dorlisheim

OBERNAI

Ottrot

Ste Odile

Gertwiller

Heiligenstein

BARR

Andlau

Epfig

DAMBACH

Rhine

SELESTAT

St. Hippolyte

Bergheim

RIBEAUVILLE

Guémar

Hunawihr

RIQUEWIHR

Zellenberg

Mittelwihr

Kaysersberg

Kientzheim

Ammerschwihr

Turckheim

COLMAR

Wintzenheim

Fecht

Eguisheim

ROUFFACH

GUEBWILLER

Thur

Ensisheim

Cernay

Thann

The Wines of Alsace—or should I call them "French Rhine Wines"?—both titles are, of course, correct, but when one speaks about Rhine wines, one thinks generally in the first instance of the wines of the German Rhine. But the Alsatian wine district is not further away from the River Rhine than are, for instance, the German Palatinate vineyards, and politically, the districts in which the Alsatian vineyards are situated are the Haut-Rhin and the Bas-Rhin.

GEOGRAPHY

Alsace produces a great variety of wines—red wines, white wines, *rosé* wines, natural and sweetened wines, and these from a great variety of grapes, but, before going into this in detail, let us just say something about Alsatian geography and history, the geological formation of the district, and its climate, for the quality of wines depends upon all these factors.

Alsace is situated between 47° and 49° latitude North, that is, approximately the latitude of Paris, and between 4° and 6° longitude East, that is, approximately 300 miles east of Paris. Its capital, Strasbourg, founded by the Romans, has a very significant name: "The castle commanding the roads". Strasbourg and Alsace are, in fact, situated on the roads going from the Mediterranean towards the North Sea and from the west to the east.

The Alsace plain was obtained by the subsidence of the rift valley which united the Vosges and the Black Forest, and by the deviation of the Rhine which, until then flowing south, wended its way north after the Basle bend.

Today, Alsace extends between the Rhine and Vosges for a width of twenty to twenty-five miles. In the south it rests on the Jura, and in the north it borders the forest of Haguenau: it is also at these two ends that it opens to the west; in the south through the Belfort Gap, in the north by the Saverne Pass.

Alsace is a part of the Rhine valley. The Rhine, which here acts as a natural frontier for 120 miles, runs through an almost uninterrupted forest, between embankments topped by casemates. It does not flow through towns as is the case upstream in Switzerland and downstream in Germany.

The great canal of Alsace, which was begun about 1930 near Basle, would have no value if the frontier in the narrowest sense of the word still persisted.

The Rhine is very actively navigated as far as the great river port of Strasbourg and, similarly, as far as Basle, in spite of a relatively strong current. The Alsace canal should facilitate navigation and permit Switzerland to obtain supplies.

Alsace itself is a sub-region of the Rhine valley, that which is conditioned by the Ill, which runs alongside the Rhine for about ninety miles; it has its source in the last foothills of the Jura mountains, and receives the majority of the Vosges torrents flowing towards the east, converging with the Rhine north of Strasbourg. It is the Ill which divides the Alsatian plain into different parts such as the Harth, the Ried, etc.

The River Ill gives Alsace its name, "Ilsace" or "Elsass"—Alsace. Alsatian wines were always known as the Rhine wines; the German authorities renamed them after 1871 "Elsässer wine" in order to distinguish them from the wines of other districts and to avoid dangerous competition. However, today we meet them as *Vin du Rhin Français* or *Vins d'Alsace*—Alsatian wines.

GEOLOGY

The geological formation of the region is constituted by the chain of the Vosges, from the Belfort Gap to the boundary of the department of Bas-Rhin, with its transverse valleys thus forming a dorsal spine some hundred miles long. The Vosges, flanked by the sub-Vosges hills, fall away to the north to the plain which to the east is bounded by the Rhine.

Some hundreds of thousands of years ago there existed in this plain a great lake. The soil of the former inland lake is composed of various different types, granite, sandy soil, lime soil, loam,

198

alluvial soil and gravel. Owing to their specific properties each of these types of soil has its own particular influence on growth, lifetime and quality of the vine and so, the wine. Later on I shall describe the great variety of vines planted in Alsace. The variety of soil is the reason for the variety of vines, as each vine has its peculiar soil where it flourishes best. The growers receive all necessary advice before planting a vineyard, from the State-owned viticultural institute, especially on which species of vine should be planted.

CLIMATE   Alsace's climate is influenced by the Atlantic winds but the continental influence also makes itself felt. The winters are generally colder and longer than in the rest of France, the summers less temperate. The winds from the west discharge their rain by condensation on the western slopes of the Vosges. As a result, the plain of Alsace, and in particular the northern zone of Colmar, receives hardly more than 30 cubic inches of water. This is the driest region in Central Europe, while St. Die on the other side of the Vosges receives 73 cubic inches and the region immediately to the east of the ridge 90 cubic inches of water.

VINEYARDS   Although there were still 60,000 acres in 1878, there are at present no more than about 27,000 acres in the two Departments of Haut-Rhin and Bas-Rhin. The reasons are manifold.

In 1874 the insect phylloxera invaded Alsace, and as Alsace was part of Germany from then until 1918, the vineyards so affected had, by German law, to be destroyed, and had to be left untouched for many years. Many were never replanted.

There are also political and economic reasons. A most important one is that with the change of nationality the Alsatian grower had to change his market. Under the German régime only cheap, mass-produced wines were wanted—wines with acidity to be turned into sparkling wines, etc.

France produces many ordinary and cheap wines. If the Alsatian wine grower wants to sell his wines in France, he must produce quality wines differing from the quality wines of other French wine-growing districts.

Having to change over from one market to another, to reconstruct vineyards is an expensive hobby, and one can understand why many Alsatian growers started the cultivation of fruit trees and other plants.

The vineyards are situated on the lowest foothills of the Vosges, on the sub-Vosges hills and the entrances to the valleys, thus forming a long, narrow strip, going from Thann in the south in N.N.E. direction for about seventy miles as far as Marlenheim. Certain zones, especially in Bas-Rhin, are given over to both vine-growing and agriculture. The wine region around Colmar is made up of communes devoting themselves exclusively to vine-growing. There are approximately 115 vine-growing communes totalling 9,600 individual properties in Haut-Rhin and 7,800 in Bas-Rhin.

The vine region generally faces east, that is, towards the Alsatian plain, but the best exposures are, of course, south, south-east and south-west.

We have seen that climate and soil are well suited for wine-growing; let us now see what the Alsatians make of their opportunities. When you travel through the vineyards of Alsace, you notice immediately that the vine-dressing system is arranged to facilitate work especially with machines and to give the vine as much sunshine as possible. The height of the vines, which, when fully grown, attain $6\frac{1}{2}$ feet and more (they have been compared with the hop-fields of Kent), may surprise certain people, but it facilitates the working of the ground between the rows and prevents weeds overrunning the vines in rainy years. Finally, the spring frost which every wine-grower dreads each year does less harm three to six feet above the ground than at ground level.

Here perhaps one should mention the fact that Alsatians are bilingual. A German dialect is spoken, except in certain valleys of the Vosges where the French patois is spoken. Towns may be signposted with one name while the inhabitants may call it by the dialect name. See below for the French and local dialect names of some towns and districts.

French	Local Dialect
Alsace	Elsass
Le Bonhomme	Dieboldshausen
Cernay	Sennheim
Château-Salins	Salzburg
Chatenois	Kestenholz
Guebwiller	Gebweiler
Obernai	Oberehnheim
Mulhouse	Muehlhausen
Orbey	Urbeis
Ribeauville	Rappoltsweiler
Riquewihr	Reichenweier
Rouffach	Rufach; Ruffach
Saint-Hippolyte	Sankt Pilt
Sainte-Odile	Odilienberg
Selestat	Schlettstadt
Soultz-les-Bains	Sulzbach

VINE VARIETIES

While Champagne and Bourgogne cultivate two quite distinct vine varieties: Pinot Noir on one side and Chardonnay on the other, Alsace has at times planted a multitude of varieties which have been introduced either by the overlords of that time, seigneurs and ecclesiastical authorities, or by wine-lovers. At present, only some ten or so varieties can be found. These are classified as ordinary grapes or noble grapes. Before listing these kinds it must be emphasised that Alsace, being a border district, is a district of contrast. The majority of the inhabitants—who have had to change their nationality four times since 1870—use two languages, and so we meet some kinds of grapes under two different names. Where a French name exists, it is used for export.

German	*French*
Burger-Elbling	
Knipperle	
Goldriesling	Riesling Doré
Gutedel	Chasselas
Sylvaner, Oesterreicher	
Weiss-Clevner or	Pinot Blanc
Weissburgunder	
Rotclevner	Pinot Noir
Grauer Burgunder ⎱	Pinot Gris-Tokay
Rulaender ⎰	d'Alsace
Riesling	
Muscat	
Traminer or	
Gewürztraminer	

While these vines with many others were still mixed at the beginning of the century, the Alsatian vine-grower has been compelled to graft or plant only pure vines, which has permitted a more rational vinification per variety at the most suitable moment of ripening.

VINIFICATION

One of the most interesting chapters in the study of wine is that of vinification and treatment of wine.

Each district has different soil, different climate, different vines, and aims at different end-products and must, therefore, have different ways of vinification. Whereas, in some districts one waits for the *pourriture noble*, in other districts the grapes are gathered just when they are ripe.

In some districts the wines are bottled after years in cask, in others the wine is bottled in a few months after the harvest. I consider the Alsatian mode of vinification as one of the most interesting ones. The Alsatians have not stood still, they have improved their methods and kept up with the development of science and technique, and are always willing to accept new and better methods.

WINE HARVESTS

Harvesting is undertaken as late as possible; only when the skin of the grape has become very thin and translucent, dotted with little dark spots, and perhaps so late that the grapes are attacked by the *pourriture noble*. Sleepy grapes and grapes with rotting stalks are gathered first, possibly in several gatherings. The healthy remainder is allowed time to reach full maturity (*Edelreife*). What is thus lost in quantity is more than compensated for by improvement in quality.

The grape harvest normally begins at the end of September and continues during October; its beginning is decided by a committee of experts. The grapes are carried on the backs of the harvesters in great wooden *Hottes* in the shape of a truncated cone, to butts standing near a vineyard, or already on the carts which take them from there to the press houses. These long, narrow, four-wheeled carts, eminently suitable for the tortuous mountain roads, carry a single row of high, square buckets having an average capacity of forty-four gallons.

Immediately after arrival in the pressing house, the grapes are first crushed in grape-mills, and then pressed without delay. If the juice is not separated immediately from stalks, the wine may take a taste of tannin, and may become tart and bitter. Some growers strip off the berries from the bunch. Many different kinds of presses are used. In some press houses there are still some of the old wooden presses, which have to be worked by manual labour. Hydraulic presses are also used, and only in the last few years, a new kind of electric press has made its appearance; it works on the principle of an accordion. The press rotates horizontally, the ends moving slowly inwards. It decreases the working time by not less than 80 per cent.

In the vineyards there are plenty of red grapes, but only a little red wine is made—the process is the same as for Bordeaux red wines. Most red grapes—such as the Red Chasselas, the Traminer, the Pinot Noir—are used to make white wines.

The grapes are pressed three times. The Must of the first operation is richer in tannin and acids, and is added to the blend of the next two operations only if the blend is poor in both, and only to such extent as is necessary for the harmony of the wine. Otherwise it is kept separate for use as *vin ordinaire* and for blends of cheaper grade wines.

All growers cleanse the Must from all impurities before its fermentation. The process, called *debourbage* or *Entschleimen*, is very simple. The freshly pressed Must is allowed to stand for some time; it becomes clear by the settling of all solid and flocculent sediments or particles of dirt and other foreign bodies.

By the sulphurisation all bad and wild ferments which effect a quick fermentation—and a quick fermentation is damaging to the quality of the future wine—are killed.

FERMENTATION

After a day or two the clarified Must is separated by draining it off (racking), airing it well, to remove any excess of sulphurous acid, and transferring it then to a warmer fermentation cellar where it is left to ferment with the addition of biologically pure yeast, as a rule originating from the lees of high-class wine produced by the wine-grower himself, or by a Wine Institute. We know for certain that it is due to this treatment of the Must that fermentation can be guided more easily and that Alsatian wines are ready for bottling so soon after the harvest.

The Alsatians prefer a wine with plenty of carbonic acid. They are keen on drinking the Must in the state of fermentation (*le nouveau, Federweisser*). Fermentation lasts from one to three months and even longer. And once the fermentation is finished, many wines are bottled immediately. These are, of course, not for keeping or laying down, but for immediate consumption in Alsace. The better wines are racked in January into slightly sulphured casks, where they may rest for from one month to half a year and are then, as a rule, bottled without any racking after a short rest, after the end of the fermentation. The wines then still contain some carbonic acid in solution which has nothing whatever to do with active fermentation; it is the result and a product of the fermentation which has taken place.

It is the carbonic acid which effects a natural effervescence and which can be found in many Alsatian wines—not only the Sylvaner where everybody expects it.

Not very long ago the general theory of racking wines three times the first year and twice the second year was followed in Alsace. The result was dark-coloured, often brown wines. Today it is common knowledge that the Alsatian wine cannot be treated and looked after like any other wine. Contrary to the great wines of Bordeaux and Burgundy, the Alsatian wines do not gain anything by lying in cask for years. To preserve their exceptional quality and their special character, they must be bottled during the spring after the harvest.

If wines are ready for bottling and for one reason or another cannot be bottled at the right time, the grower or wine-merchant preserves their freshness and avoids any deterioration by racking them from the storage cask into glass-lined vats or tanks. These are actually large bottles without any breathing possibilities whatsoever, and therefore the wine conserves its freshness for years.

Vinification is a difficult job. The vintner has to use all skill and care during the pressing and the treatment of the wine. Unless enough care is taken, the wine may be considered unfit for consumption, and his work in the vineyards, etc., may not only be without reward, but the money he spent may be lost.

TYPES OF WINE   Earlier I dealt with the principal vines cultivated in Alsace. This part will deal with the finished product, the wines of Alsace. I will endeavour to describe the general characteristics of Alsatian wines—that is, as far as it is at all possible to translate a taste into words. On the one hand we have Ordinary Alsatian wines, and on the other, the Great Alsatian wines from noble vine varieties.

ORDINARY WINES

The ordinary Alsatian wines are table wines which the Alsatian consumer takes as an aperitif. First place goes to the Chasselas grape, which gives a light, agreeable, sometimes effervescent wine, with an alcoholic degree of 10 per cent, often with a very low acidity, used also as a cooking wine. Other local varieties: Goldriesling, drunk as a new wine, le Knipperle, Le Burger—in very small quantities as red and *rosé* wines.

Müller-Thurgau grapes, planted in certain communes, give a wine similar to Chasselas—that is, light, with a touch of muscat flavour which makes it appreciated by certain wine-lovers. This wine, a crossing between Riesling and Sylvaner, has often been marketed as Riesling × Sylvaner. It does not appear in the Ordonnance of 1945, but the *comité d'experts* has admitted Müller-Thurgau as Vin d'Alsace (*cépage Courant*). To avoid any misunderstanding, the wine has to be labelled Müller-Thurgau.

Auxerrois Blanc or Pinot Auxerrois is another grape not mentioned in the Ordonnance of 1945. The wine has more alcohol and less acidity than Chasselas, is produced in smaller quantity, and has a much more neutral taste with more body and finesse. It is similar to the Pinot Blanc and is often sold in Alsace as Pinot Blanc, often blended with Pinot Blanc, and Chasselas or Sylvaner, to improve their quality.

KNIPPERLE. The knipperle vine, which was formerly the foundation of the Alsatian wine region, has been largely supplanted by the Chasselas, but on the hillsides it produces a full-bodied wine, which is mellower than the Chasselas.

SYLVANER is a purer species than the foregoing. The wine is more acid, more fruity and often rather effervescent, known locally as *spritzig*; its taste invites one to drink further and it is a very good thirst-quencher. In the Ordonnance of November

206

1945 its name appears not with the ordinary but among the noble wines, but unfortunately many growers, especially in the Bas-Rhin district, use it for mass production. These wines are very often combined in a blend and are then marketed as ZWICKER D'ALSACE, which, frankly speaking, is neither "fish, flesh, fowl, nor good red herring". Some of the Sylvaner, if produced from late gathered grapes, are quality wines.

GREAT WINES

PINOT BLANC is a wine with a neutral flavour and is more full-bodied than Sylvaner. On tasting, its acidity combines harmoniously with its other qualities: tang of the soil and fullness.

LE TOKAY D'ALSACE or LE PINOT GRIS, a good, often slightly pink coloured wine, either dry or conserving a few grammes of sugar, combines with its mellow quality an agreeable and harmonious acidity. It leaves the drinker with a memory of unforgettable purity and its discreet fruity flavour does not diminish with time. The name "Tokay" may be misleading, since many people, when about to drink a "Tokay", will in the first instance think of the full-bodied Hungarian Auslese wines. The Belgian Government has, therefore, prohibited the use of "Tokay" for Alsatian wines. The Alsatians have used it for centuries because this wine had been introduced from Hungary. Pinot Blanc and Gris adapt themselves to many situations. These full-bodied wines are very often used as a basis for blending to give the ordinary wines more fullness.

LE MUSCAT grape, white or red, is very particular with regard to soil, exposure and stock and is slow to ripen. It produces a wine with a very pronounced bouquet (although very spicy). This makes it different from the sweet Muscats of the southern districts. It is very much esteemed by certain wine-lovers. Muscat is very often blended with Pinot and marketed as EDELZWICKER.

RIESLING. The Riesling grape known as "King of Alsace" flourishes in rather dry terrain, half way up gradual slopes which are well sheltered from the wind. Its short cluster bears round grapes with rather thick skins which may in this way remain on the stem for a long time and ripen well although the grape is slow maturing. The wine attains all its qualities only in warm, sunny years. It is then full-bodied, with a high alcoholic content (12° and often more), delicate, and with a very fine aroma. Very agreeable to drink when new, it acquires a remarkable cachet in the bottle. In very good years and in certain exposures it is unquestionably a great wine.

GEWÜRTZTRAMINER. Le Gewürztraminer is a "Traminer" grape with a pink, perfumed skin, cultivated particularly at the foot of hillsides, in rather deep ground. Its pyramidal cluster is formed of tightly packed pink grapes with thick, heavily-perfumed skins. The wine retains this perfume; when new it is both light and alcoholic and not acid.

The Traminer or Gewürztraminer is the best known of Alsatian wines. Its sometimes overpowering fruitiness, like the perfume of a beautiful woman, enchants from the first, especially the non-connoisseur. This perfume, which brings to mind now the Muscat, now the rose, now the violet, is the combined product of the vine, the soil and moderated ageing. Traminer is generally a dry wine, but in good years it may conserve a few grammes of sugar. Its natural mellowness is in harmony with its low acidity and high degree of alcohol.

Riesling, Gewürztraminer and Pinot Gris wines, which are generally dry, may retain a few grammes of unfermented sugar in exceptional years like 1947, 1949 and 1953, and attain high degrees of alcohol.

I will also mention in passing the red wine from the Pinot Noir which in colour is more *rosé* than red, and should be drunk as a *rosé* wine slightly iced. I hope that my suggestion will not raise an outcry—but this exception is necessary for Alsatian red wines. I tried to drink it in the conservative way—*chambré*—it is worth trying, when in Alsace, to know how it tasted like this, but it is not worth importing and paying high duty when the finer French red wines are available at more advantageous prices.

Early account books at Moët & Chandon with early bottles including, on the left, the oldest Champagne bottle in existence.

facing p. 208

The Champagne cellars at Pommery.

following p. 208

An assortment of drinking glasses for Champagne, Hock, Sherry, Port, Brandy, Burgundy, a beer tankard and glass and an early decanter. Also a Champagne, a Mosel and a Claret bottle.

following p. 208

Four well-known grape varieties

Top left: Mourisco, one of the black grape species grown on the Douro for the making of Port.
Top right: Young Riesling grapes growing in the slaty soil on the Mosel.
Bottom left: Pinot Noir grapes growing at Nuits St. Georges, Burgundy.
Bottom right: Pinot Chardonnay grapes growing at Chablis.

facing p. 209

EDELZWICKER, as explained, is a blend of noble wines (among them officially Sylvaner). As a rule the blend consists of Sylvaner and the neutral Pinot Blanc. I have not found a grower who would blend a better wine to sell than Edelzwicker if he can help it. Edelzwicker can be entitled to the denomination *Vin fin d'Alsace* if all other conditions appertaining to this are fulfilled; not so the Zwicker, which is a *vin ordinaire*.

The Alsatians have no difficulty in disposing of all their Riesling, Traminer and Gewürztraminer, the French market being only too willing to take up all production of these. Unfortunately, production at present is still small, as Sylvaner and Chasselas make up more than 60 per cent of the harvest.

Sometimes one meets the name *Gentil*. There exists no legal definition for it. Originally it was used for a Traminer wine, made from a Traminer grape with only a slight Traminer flavour. For some time the Gewürztraminer was known as *gentil aromatique*. Later, *Gentil*, meaning "noble", became the name for round mild wines generally, and is today synonymous with Zwicker in which some noble variety has been used.

VINTAGES Vintages are, of course, important, because some are excellent as the sunshine and rain has assisted with the growing of the grapes, and each vintage is different from the other. On the other hand, the new methods of vinification have given the wine-growers the possibility of treating their wine in such a way that the differences in quality are no longer as great as they used to be in the past. Many growers will always reserve a part of the great and excellent vintages for another year or two in order to assist the next vintages, and by blending even with a small percentage they keep up the average quality, so that the differences in the vintages are no longer as great as they used to be.

Some ten or twenty years ago it was generally accepted that Alsatian wines had to be drunk within two to three years; experience has shown that this theory is incorrect, the vines in

Alsatian vineyards are now older and give their product a longer life. Some of the Rieslings, Traminers and Gewurztraminers especially stand up very well and develop for six, eight and ten years, and are no worse off for the wear. But let it be said, one of the charms of Alsatian wine is its youth; we have seen over the last decade an enormous proportion of good vintage or excellent vintages. 1953, 1959, 1961 and 1964 were excellent, and most of the others were at least good vintages.

APPELLATION CONTRÔLÉE

According to a law of October 3rd, 1962, wines of the quality as laid down in the Statute of November 2nd, 1945, are now entitled to the denomination *Appellation Contrôlée* and a total of 109 Alsatian Communities—of which 52 are situated in the upper Rhine area and 57 in the lower Rhine—are entitled to the *Appellation* "Alsace" or "Vin d'Alsace".

Beginning with vintage 1965, special terms have been laid down regarding pruning of the vineyards, concerning all wines which claim the *Appellation Contrôlée*. These terms are based on the density of the plants, and it is laid down how many buds the vine may have. The decree is based on the various ways of planting the vineyards. For example, in vineyards with a density of 45 to 55 vines per ar the number of buds per vine must not be more than 24.

Although the method may seem complicated, it illustrates the aim of the Alsatian growers to use their *Appellation* only for quality wines. The growers who want to produce merely quantity can only sell their wine as ordinary table wine—*vin ordinaire*, French white wine but without the *Appellation Contrôlée*, "Vin d'Alsace". The decree beginning with the 1965 vintage will result in furthering quality production.

LESSER-KNOWN
WINES OF FRANCE

Excepting the departments bordering the Channel, every part of France produces some sort of wine, and there is greater coherence in the pattern of style and quality than might at first be apparent.

By the Middle Ages, all regions of France were vine-bearing, and they formed five main groupings which remain, even now, as the basic structure of all French viticulture.

Firstly, there is the broad southern strip, seventy miles or so in depth, along the Mediterranean coast from Spain to Italy. Châteauneuf-du-Pape and the associated wines of Tavel, Lirac and Gigondas really belong to it rather than to what we loosely call "Rhône Valley", because they are part of the Languedoc and Provençal scheme of viticulture.

In fact, the "Rhône Valley", our second zone, should stretch only from Lyon down to Valence, but includes the wines from the tributary valleys of the Alps, usually described as Savoy wines.

The third, perhaps the most important, zone is the western, stretching north in a broad sweep across all the low-lying area of France to the west of the *massif central*, from Spain to the valley of the Loire and beyond to the limit of cultivation.

The north-east, the fourth zone, takes in Burgundy, the Jura, Champagne, and all other areas lying east of the Loire and north of the Rhône except Alsace, which is part of the Rhine valley complex and is therefore considered as a fifth and separate zone.

Each of these zones has been determined largely by climatic conditions (for example, the western zone is temperate from the Atlantic; the north-east has a sharper continental contrast of colder winters and hotter summers; the south has the Mediterranean climate of dry summers and mild, wet winters) and this has led to the predominance of one or more principal grape varieties, specially suited to the prevailing climate, which, in turn, has determined the overall character and flavour of all wines in each of these zones. The Pinot grape family, predominating in the north-eastern zone, imposes an unmistakable flavour and pattern of development on all the wines grown there. As a vine variety, it is early (the harvest in Champagne and Burgundy is always earlier than in Bordeaux), its wine comes round quickly, matures early, and is often past its best before a corresponding wine from the western zone, Cabernet, is ready to drink. These western zone wines, from grapes which ripen later, are richer in tannin, usually hard when young, and follow a far wider arc of development in every phase. And in this fashion there is a family bond between all the wines, great or small, of world renown or local repute, in each of the wine zones of France. Nevertheless, in each zone there is a more or less complete range of soil types and sun-exposures, and these, together with variations in methods of viticulture, and of making wine, give rise to a variety of qualities and styles within the broad family likeness.

In the western region, for example, the quality grape is the Cabernet, supported by secondary and related varieties. On chalk (as in parts of Chinon and Bourgueil on the banks of the

Loire) it will give well alcoholised wine with the special aroma of this grape somewhat exaggerated. On sand (as in other parts of Chinon, at St. Nicolas de Bourgueil, at Saumur, and in parts of the Bordelais) it gives a lighter wine, supple and quick to mature, without the same intensity of bouquet. On clay it would be heavier, with deep colour, more body and tannin. The pebble and gravel of Bordeaux bring from this same grape a breed and an equilibrium of qualities unique to these conditions.

Similarly, the white wines of the Sauvignon grape, also of the western zone, can follow a series of mutations related to a parallel range of soil changes (compare Graves with Sancerre).

If we learn to see all French wines as variations within these broad zones, sometimes sharply and sometimes subtly contrasted —for example, to relate naturally Pyrenees, Lot, Dordogne and Bordeaux—there can be no French wine which would be in the least difficult for us to identify, evaluate and relate to other wines. Like a good jigsaw puzzle, every piece is fully inter-locking. There is no French wine district, however small or seemingly remote, which is totally out on a limb.

WESTERN FRANCE

The largest and most important zone is the western, where Bordeaux has a dominating influence. This is not only because of the quality of the wine produced in the Bordelais (the prestige attaching to Bordeaux wines is a recent phenomenon, certainly no older than the eighteenth century when the introduction of ageing in bottle turned the rich tannin content of western zone wines into an advantage from being a disadvantage), but is related to its commercial activity. There is no greater trading centre for wine in France, and it is the main port for exporting French wines to the northern non-wine-producing countries of Europe.

All red wines of the western zone follow the pattern of Bordeaux. That is to say, the grapes ripen slightly later than elsewhere in France, the wines are harsh when young, often combining a high tannin content with a significant acidity. Linked with the tannin is a deep colour and with the acidity a strong character and the possibility of developing subtle flavours and bouquet. In theory, all the red wines of this zone develop slowly, rising to their optimum and gradually descending from their peak in a wide arc; but in fact there will be many exceptions, largely because growers of "little" wines, who must sell them for carafe use soon after the vintage, have to vinify with methods which, though sound in themselves, are often not fully in accordance with local traditions.

On the degree of acceptance by the Bordeaux trade have depended the fortunes of the wines of the hinterland—the Haut Pays of the Dordogne and Lot. During the last century there was a demand for these wines in Bordeaux itself for blending, but this has now been suppressed, and Dordogne and Lot wines are sold under their own names.

Closest to Bordeaux are the wines of the Dordogne: they lie on both sides of the river and centre on the town of Bergerac. The simplest *appellation* is, indeed, BERGERAC, both red and white, and it corresponds roughly to equivalent Bordeaux Rouge and Bordeaux Blanc. The other *appellations* of this district are MONTRAVEL—white wine, usually dry but sometimes sweet; ROSETTE, a white wine, not a *rosé*, usually dry; MONBAZILLAC, on the south side of the Dordogne, a sweet white wine, lighter and less unctuous than Sauternes, but with a more flowery bouquet; and PÉCHARMANT, a brisk red wine from a chalky plateau northeast of the town of Bergerac.

Over the watershed, in the Lot valley, are red wines produced from the Malbec, also known under a number of synonyms, one of the western zone vines with a sweet-perfumed distinguishing smell and taste. The only wine of the Lot with an "official" name is CAHORS, covering a district of the valley some thirty miles along from Cahors itself, stretching westwards to Puy l'Eveque. Once known as the "Black Wine", Cahors still shows a good colour but without the exaggeration of the past. Some

214

growers have a small admixture of white grapes among the Malbec to lighten the wine in colour and style, but others are content to control both by the length of time skins and juice are left together. Some *rosé* wine is produced in the Lot and some white wine, but neither is of very particular interest.

South-east from the Lot are the vineyards of Gaillac, an area intensively cultivated in the Middle Ages, but of less economic importance now. As well as light red, white and *rosé* wines, there are sparkling wines made in the area, notably at LIMOUX.

At the southernmost part of the western zone, in the foothills of the Pyrénées, are the BÉARNAIS wines. JURANÇON, a white wine grown near the town of Pau, is usually slightly sweet, but since the war it has been vinified increasingly as a dry wine. It has a high alcohol level, and a well-developed individual flavour and bouquet which it probably owes to the Manseng vines unique to this area. It lends itself well to shipping long distances, and was one of the first white wines of the area to be exported—it is recorded in Scandinavia at least seven hundred years ago. There are a number of *rosé* wines made—mostly sold as ROSÉ DE BÉARN—but IROULÉGUY is one which usually appears under its own name. Some red is also produced in Irouléguy and considerably more at Madiran.

The whole of the Loire valley, including offshoots like Jasnières on its tributary the Loir, and Quincy and Reuilly, is also well set in the western zone pattern.

NORTHERN AND EASTERN FRANCE

Excepting in the Jura, there is less diversification within the dominating vine family in the north-eastern zone than there is in the west. The Pinot Noir is all-important; the Gamay produces wine of the same type but with less finesse and flavour. Pinot Blanc and Pinot Chardonnay produce the quality white wines; the first producing well-knit wines from tightly bunched grapes, the latter giving soft, occasionally flabby wine, from loosely formed bunches.

Pinot wine has a velvety fragrance; it is richly toned, but always delicate and elegant in style. It is known as a "first season" vine, ripening early, maturing young, degenerating quickly. Burgundy, of course, is the epitome of north-eastern zone wines, but its supremacy was not merely challenged but equalled by the red wines of Champagne until quite recently. In two centuries the demand for sparkling white wine from Champagne has reached such proportions that the still red has been eclipsed, but it persists—especially at Bouzy where a wooded hill-top protects the south-facing slope from north winds. BOUZY is expensive—even on the spot—but has a soft flavour which combines the unmistakable Pinot taste of fine Burgundy with the special chalk-turf bouquet of Champagne.

IRANCY, south of Auxerre, produced a hard, violently flavoured red wine from a vine called the César, alleged to have been brought by the Romans, and which was so rich in tannin and harsh in style that it was completely opposed to the general style of wine of the north-eastern zone and its Pinot grapes. Between the wars, when this fiery, slow maturing wine found little favour, most of the César vines were rooted out and hybrids planted. This policy failed too, and since the last war these have been rooted out in their turn. The area is now planted with Pinot Noir with a proportion of César—never more than a third—and produces a pleasant well-flavoured *rosé*. A small quantity is vinified as red wine, and this is the best of the area. Near Irancy, at St. Bris le Vineux, there have been large-scale plantings of Sauvignon vines, and the wine, which is entitled to no particular *appellation* as yet, has become very popular throughout the area, and in Paris, during the last few years. The rest of the area produces huge quantities of a neutral tasting white wine from Sacy grapes, most of which is exported in tanks to Germany where it serves as the base for making Sekt. East of Burgundy, on a group of hills facing the Côte d'Or across the wide plain of the Saône valley, are the CÔTES DU JURA.

This is still Pinot territory, with sub-varieties peculiar to the Jura, notably Poulsard and Trousseau. Wines of the Jura are sturdy and attractive: they often have a strange background flavour of crushed walnuts. The great curiosity of the region is *vin jaune*, made by leaving the juice of Savagnin grapes in original casks for six years, without racking, topping up, or any of the usual treatments given to wine in cask to ensure its safe keeping. On the surface of the wine appears a fungus growth, kin to the *flor* of Jerez, which catalyses the same changes in the wine to produce a pale golden liquid of austere dryness with a strong flavour, not unlike an unfortified fino sherry. It goes into a special traditional bottle called a *clavelin*, looking like a squared-off version of a Drambuie bottle.

Apart from the *vins jaunes*, which can take the *appellation* CHÂTEAU-CHALON (a commune, not a simple vineyard, by the way) or ARBOIS, depending on origin, the straight table wines of the Jura are at two levels. The simple *appellation* CÔTES DU JURA has a broad application—like Bordeaux Rouge—and within it are the higher *appellations* of ARBOIS and ÉTOILE.

The Jura is famous for *rosé* wines. The reason is that the grapes used to produce them have very few pigment cells. As a result, the juice can macerate with the skins for longer than with most other *rosés*, taking a better balance of tannins and flavouring substances, but nevertheless keeping a fairly light, attractive colour. The palest, as elsewhere in France, are described as *vins gris* (literally, grey wines), particularly light, fresh wines to be consumed young.

The Bourbonnais and Auvergne produce principally ST. POURÇAIN from the Tressalier vine (another name for the Sacy, mentioned above), but usually combined with 50 per cent Pinot Chardonnay or 50 per cent Sauvignon: it is dry but has body and character.

Closer to Clermont-Ferrand is the hill of Châteaugay, where a red wine is produced from the Gamay. It is interesting because the hill is solid chalk and should, in theory, give a wine in which the Gamay flavour is intensified and exaggerated.

It is odd to find that the vine which, in the Beaujolais, gives a clean, direct fruity wine, here shows a strangely spiced almost burnt, taste. CORENT, on the other side of Clermont-Ferrand, now produces almost exclusively *rosé* wine, also from Gamay.

SOUTHERN FRANCE

When considering the wines of the southern strip of France, it is impossible to suppress the old saw that a struggle to survive produces character. The south of France is as much a lotus-land for vines as for human beings, and though it is rare to find a bad wine, it is equally hard to find a distinguished one, which is not to say that they do not exist.

In red wines, the two principal vines (ignoring the hybrids used to produce the tank wines of the Herault) are the Grenache and the Carignan. As a vine, the Grenache is supple, with bunches of large, soft oval grapes, whereas the Carignan, with darker, thicker leaves, has tight-bunched, small, round berries. The wines they produce remain in character: supple in the case of the Grenache: hard and tough in the case of the Carignan. Usually there is a proportion of both, often with some Cinsault, although this is usually reserved for *rosé* wines. White wines are made from the Ugni Blanc and the Clairette.

At Aix-en-Provence there are vineyards producing wine with the *appellation* of PALETTE. The vines are on chalk, and the basic Grenache and Carignan are strongly augmented by the Mourvèdre, an ancient Provençal strain of vine with a more clearly defined aroma than either of them. CHÂTEAU SIMONE, at Palette, is almost entirely Mourvèdre and the bouquet of the wine is unexpectedly striking (again, as the vine is grown on chalk, the primary smell of the grape is intensified).

At BANDOL and CASSIS, on the coast south of Aix, are red, white

218

and *rosé* wines. Bandol produces far better wine, but Cassis is picturesque and its wine is better known. With the possible exception of CHÂTEAU SIMONE at Aix, the red wines of Bandol are indisputably the finest of the whole southern strip.

The rest of the south produces mainly current-consumption wines; on the east side of the Rhône there are mostly *rosés* for the holiday resorts (the best coming from the hills, especially CUERS and PIERREFEU, rather than the fancy estates by the sea); to the west there are red wines (the best from the COSTIÈRES DU GARD, just a few miles from Arles).

This side of the Rhône, to the Spanish frontier, is the Languedoc where most of the ordinary wines for everyday consumption in French households are produced. It has been said that wine flows from the Herault plain, but it should not be forgotten that other wines of Languedoc, without aspiring to greatness, are of more than ordinary quality. Grenache and Carignan grapes, the bases here for red wines, approach each other from opposite directions. Close to the Rhône, Carignan is spoken of with disrespect, and only a small proportion is used among overwhelming quantities of Grenache. This is so on the Costières du Gard, for example, and also at ST. GEORGES D'ORCQ and ST. SATURNIN, north of Montpellier. Nearer to Spain the attitude changes and vineyards are 80 per cent Carignan or more. In the Corbières hills, which fit into a rough oblong bounded by Narbonne, Carcassone, Ouillan and Perpignan, wines of varied quality are produced depending on the slope of the grotesquely twisted landscape. The best red wines of this area are found around Tuchan delimited as FITOU within the Corbières: on the Minervois plateau, north of the Narbonne-Carcassone road; at PEPIEUX; and along the valley of the Agly, in particular at MAURY.

In addition there are the sweet dessert wines of FRONTIGNAN, LUNEL, BANYULS and RIVESALTES. Frontignan and Lunel are made primarily from the intensely aromatic small-grained muscat. The wines described as *vin doux naturels* are usually finer than the *vins de liqueur*. MUSCAT DE FRONTIGNAN itself, and MUSCAT DE BEAUMES DE VENISE, from a hill near Mont Ventoux, are the two best.

That part of the Rhône valley which forms a separate unit, particularly from the point of view of vine types, lies between Lyon and Montélimar. The Syrah and the Marsanne are vine stocks quite unrelated to the broader families of the larger zones. Even more exclusive is the Viognier, the capriciously delicate yet strangely long-lived vine of Condrieu and Château Grillet. In a tributary of the Rhône, but well to the east and halfway to the high mountains of Savoy, is the town of Die, producing a sparkling wine by the Champagne method from a mixture of Clairette and Muscat grapes.

Other still wines of Savoy are made from the Roussette and Blanc de Savoie for white wines and Gamay for red. Often they are sold simply as ROUSSETTE or GAMAY DE SAVOIE, but names of the communes that lie along the valleys are sometimes seen on labels—notably APREMONT and LES ABYMES. SEYSSEL, still and sparkling, is a clean, dry white wine with full *appellation* (whereas most other Savoy wines are *Vins Délimités de Qualité Supérieure*). CRÉPY, a crisp white wine, is from the shore of Lake Geneva. All Savoy wines, red and white, should be drunk young: there is no advantage in ageing them.

GERMANY

There is no doubt that the knowledge required for the production of wine reached Germany through the Graeco-Roman sources from Gaul. Gallic viticulture had been founded by Phocaean Greeks in pre-Roman times (approximately 600 B.C. in the region of what is now Marseilles), who extended it to cover the Garonne district and up the river Rhône. Apparently very soon after, viticulture spread towards the north and west, after Gallia Narbonnensis had become a Roman province (121 B.C.), and particularly under the influence of Caesar's

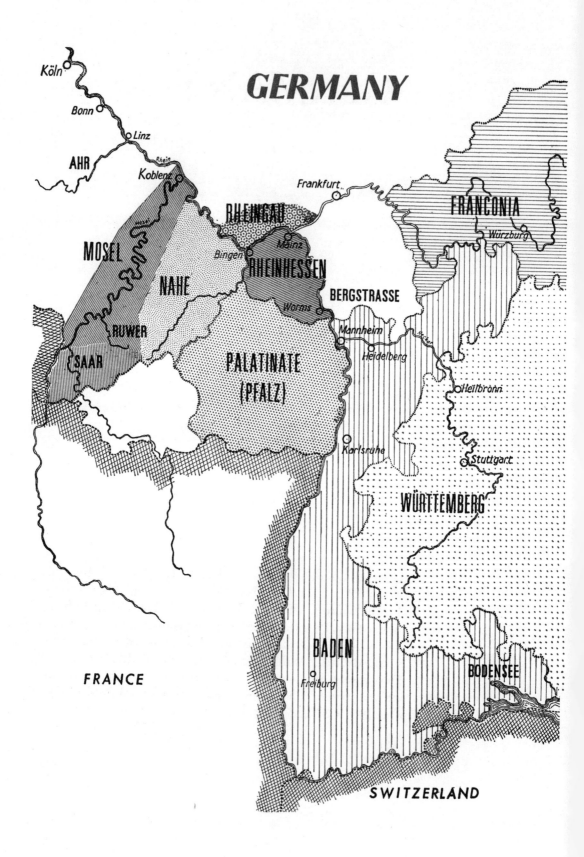

GERMANY

Köln
Bonn
Linz
AHR
Rhein
Koblenz
Frankfurt
RHEINGAU
MOSEL
Mosel
Bingen
Mainz
RHEINHESSEN
NAHE
Worms
BERGSTRASSE
RUWER
Mannheim
SAAR
Heidelberg
PALATINATE
(PFALZ)
Heilbronn
Karlsruhe
Stuttgart
WÜRTTEMBERG
FRANCONIA
Würzburg
BADEN
Freiburg
BODENSEE
FRANCE
SWITZERLAND

conquest of the whole of Gaul (58–51 B.C.). The Roman wine-merchant preceded the conquering soldier. These were followed by the colonist and the settler who never failed to plant vines, even if only for their own use. In this way, viticulture made its way to the North—probably near the Rhine–Rhône Canal—and into the valleys of the Rhine and the Mosel. All kinds of vines were introduced in this way, but it is quite possible that the cultivation of the native wild vines was also started about that time. Certain laws restricted the extension of viticulture in the Roman province, but apparently they were never properly enforced (for example the *lex Domitiana*, A.D. 91), and under the Emperor Probus (276–282) they were abrogated. And not only that, Probus rendered further service to the cause of viticulture by employing his legions to lay out extensive new vineyards.

In the Palatinate, seventy villages are known to have vines planted from Carolingian times.

The vineyards of the Rheingau were not planted until the reign of Charlemagne. The story goes that, one day, while standing in his Château in Ingelheim, he saw how on the other side of the Rhine the snow melted first on the hills of Johannisberg, and, on account of that, he gave the order to plant vineyards there. These were very soon extended to other sites in the Rheingau—in particular the Steinberg, which was planted in the eleventh and twelfth centuries by monks.

During the subsequent centuries German viticulture was widely extended, even to Northern Germany and the Baltic provinces, mainly through the monasteries, which were obliged to produce their own wines for celebrating Mass and Communion. It was, of course, easier for the monks to produce their wine for Mass at the place where they lived, where it was growing well. It was safer and cheaper than the imported wine from the South. In the same way, but in much more favourable conditions, monks of a thousand years later planted vineyards as far east as Silesia and East Prussia, and they planted red vines as produced round the Mediterranean. We understand that the production of red wine was much larger than that of white wine, even on the Moselle, where today there is no red wine at all to be found.

Later, the volume of the monks' production went beyond their own needs, and they began to trade in wine. In this connection it may be mentioned that many of the monks were sons of peasants who could read Greek and Latin essays and books on agriculture and viticulture, and, working in the vineyards, made good use of their studies.

Others beside monks began to perceive the value of possessing and enlarging vineyard properties. Such people included not only abbots and ecclesiastical princes, but also hard-drinking knights and secular authorities. And thus, in the early Middle Ages, the area devoted to the culture of wine increased considerably, reaching in the early fifteenth century a maximum which has never since been equalled. Giant casks and drinking vessels bear testimony to the immense consumption of wine at the drinking-bouts and various festivals customary at the time.

A second peak of prosperity of viticulture occurred in the eighteenth century. Better transport created better sales for the products of good wine districts, but the competition proved too formidable for the less favourably situated villages. Simultaneously, the increase in population led to a rise in the importance of agriculture, which, in many districts in the plains, began to displace viticulture. Gradually the restriction in the extent of the cultivation areas led to an improvement in the quality of the products, enforced by the planting of superior vine species.

When visiting Germany, you may come across some giant casks, and the best known of all is the giant cask of Heidelberg. Many authors mention these giant casks as a sign of how much wine was drunk in the Middle Ages, but they forget to mention where they were found—mostly in fortresses, where they served to store as much wine as possible, in as small a space as possible, as provisions in case of war.

Sculptured cask heads at the Julius Hospital, Würzburg.

Picking the grapes in a vineyard on the Rhine.

Over a hundred years old, the oldest vine in the Palatinate.

following p. 224

Grape cakes as they come from the wine press.

*Old style bottling
in the Nahe district.*

following p. 224

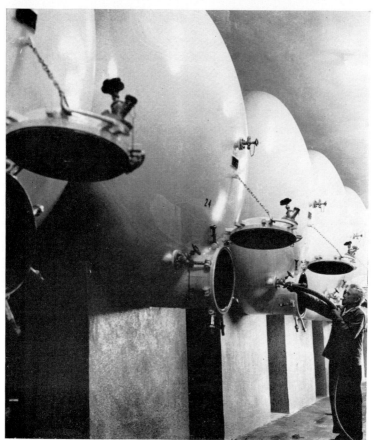

220,000 gallons of wine can be stored in this up-to-date winery at Eberstadt in Southern Germany. Weighing, sorting, de-stalking, pressing and storing is carried out in one work-operation in this modern cellar.

Old wine press in the museum at Würzburg.

following p. 224

Picking the grapes at vintage time in the district around Casale Monferrato, Piedmont. Some of the best Italian wines come from this area.

Vintage time in Piedmont showing the characteristic cone-shaped baskets and cart.

Modern mechanical presses are in use in most vineyards today but treading the grapes is still seen. These boots are worn by men in a Sherry vineyard. They are studded with nails to prevent the wearer from slipping.

The final pressing, in straw mats, of grape pulp for Sherry making. This is done under hydraulic pressure and leaves the pulp bone dry, ready to be sold as fertiliser.

following p. 224

Must, in the early stages of Sherry making, rising in the butts and flowing out of the top.

With an assistant standing by with dipper and glass, Maurice Gonzalez, member of the Gonzalez Sherry family, using a special Sherry glass gets the "nose" or bouquet of the Sherry.

following p. 224

A Sherry butt is weighed before despatch.

A wine store in Madrid showing the huge stone jars from which the customer fills his bottle.

In the seventeenth century great damage was done to German viticulture through wars; in particular the Thirty Years War (1618–1648), which left the country devastated to a large extent. Viticulture was nearly destroyed. Where vineyards once stood there were heather, weeds and bushes, and only slowly were the vineyards replanted. There were, however, difficulties in other centuries on account of over-production, crises on account of bad grapes, small grapes or no grapes at all.

Since 1900 the wine area in Germany has been reduced by about 40 per cent but the wine-production in Western Germany is nevertheless a most important branch of the German economy.

THE GRAPE
HARVEST

The most picturesque process in the production of wine is the gathering of the grapes. Many a traveller has been attracted to a particular locality in the hope of watching activities during the harvest season in the vineyards. Few, however, suspect how much the quantity and the quality of any vintage depend on the proper selection of the date on which the fruit may be gathered. And yet it is vitally important, a fact that has been recognised by wine-growers from time immemorial. In feudal times it was the *seigneurs* who set the date and kept a strict eye on the peasant to see that none entered the vineyard without special permission, particularly when the grapes were nearly ripe. This was not only to guard against pilfering, but in order to ensure delivery of a flawless harvest of fruit and grape-juice (Must), for no berry was allowed to come off the vine before it was fully ripe. Incidentally, even when the grape-harvest was in full swing, the vineyard might only be entered at specified times, the object being to hinder any grower from trespassing on his neighbour's ground and taking his fruit.

The same ancient rules are still in force, though for different reasons. Harvesting dates are set by the Commissions which exist in every grape-growing community and are composed of the leading growers. Their main object is to secure the best possible vintage in every respect by choosing the most favourable date. The riper the grapes, the more juicy they are and the

I

richer the wine, not only in sugar and acid content, but also in the etheric substances on which its bouquet and flavour depend. Even when the grape-gathering has officially started, the growers are not allowed to harvest their fruit when they please. Wine must never be watery, so the Commission, concerned to prevent the gathering of grapes which may be wet with dew or raindrops, takes careful meteorological observations and, in accordance with these and other conditions, orders the daily ringing of local church bells to denote the beginning and ending of picking-time. At the sound of the early bell, whole families—men, women and children—stream forth to the vineyards, their vine-cutters in their hands. There is work for all and to spare.

In order still further to enhance the quality of the wine, other special procedures are habitually taken during the harvesting. There is, for instance, the *Spätlese* (late gathering): one speaks of a *Spätlese* when the gathering of the grapes takes place a good time after the normal period of harvesting, so that all grapes of the vineyard are fully ripe. When *Auslese* of grapes is made only the choicest fully ripe bunches are used for the wine-making, to the exclusion of any specimens that may be diseased, damaged, or less than fully ripe. *Beerenauslesen* are *Auslesen* of berries, over-ripe and "sleepy" from good *Lagen* for separate pressing.

Trockenbeerenauslesen are *Beerenauslesen* as described above, but the collection of these "sleepy" berries takes place only after these have been semi-dried by the sun while still on the vines and have attained an almost raisin-like consistency.

"Sleepiness" in grapes is caused by the fungus known as *Botrytis cinerea*, which is apt to attack the fruit in a mild and sunny autumn. Its action is beneficial and greatly improves the quality of the grape. Needing for its existence large quantities of acid, it destroys the grape skin by means of its mycelial filaments, causing the water in the berry to evaporate in the dry, sunny autumn air; the fruit pulp thus becomes more concentrated with a relatively higher sugar content until the berry is finally sun-dried into a natural raisin. The dehydration process may

226

result in the evaporation of as much as three-quarters of the water content, bringing the harvest down to one-quarter of its normal amount.

When gathering the grapes, the harvesters collect these rarer dried-up raisin-berries in special sickle-shaped containers hung in the punnets into which they throw the rest of the fruit. A foreman in charge of every eight to ten (female) workers keeps careful watch to see that no ordinary grapes are mistaken for the genuine sleepy berries and are wrongly placed in the special containers. In this process, it takes anything up to 100 workers (varying with the size of the vineyard) a full two weeks to gather enough fruit from a vineyard of three hectares (nearly seven and a half acres) to make 300 litres of Must.

The highly concentrated Must from the over-ripe berries dried on the vine is so rich in sugar that it may fairly be described as syrupy, and this makes its fermentation and after-fermentation a difficult task which can only be entrusted to an expert with long experience and specialised knowledge. Once it has been accomplished, however, the result is a dream of perfection. The fineness, the delicate aroma, the rare bouquet, and the noble quality are indescribable. Honeysweet richness tempered by the clean, pure, finely-acidulated flavour of the grape make this wine the connoisseur's joy. Not easily obtainable, it is of course correspondingly high priced.

The partial dehydration of over-ripe grapes which turns them into raisins is an ancient process. It is mentioned in the Old Testament, and Homer has a description of it. He speaks both of allowing the grapes to hang on the vines till they are over-ripe and partially dried, and of the process by which they are dried (after picking) by being exposed to the sun on hurdles or beds of straw.

The ancient Romans were familiar with the respective processes of sorting out over-ripe and partially sun-dried fruit as already described, but in the course of time the knowledge was lost and was not recovered till the beginning of last century. The revival, so the story runs, was due to chance. The Bishop of Fulda, owner of vineyards in the Rheingau, is said to have delayed sending his permission to begin grape-harvesting until "too late": in other words, until the fruit had become over-ripe. To everybody's amazement, the resulting vintage was superb.

To the 1920 STEINBERGER belongs the distinction of having attained the record weight of Must of any selected dry-berry vine—its specific gravity was found to be 268 degrees Oechsle standard.

When the grapes have been gathered, they are tipped into large barrels and driven to the winepress. Here they are first crushed in grape-mills after which the juice has to be separated from the mash. In Germany, mechanical presses—worked hydraulically or by electricity—are generally used for this purpose.

By 1957 a new kind of press had made its appearance. It works on the principle of an accordion. The press rotates horizontally, the ends slowly moving inwards. The ends of the press are interconnected by several chains, which become interwoven with grape cake on pressing. Whereas with older types the grape cake had to be taken out and cut into smaller pieces for the second and third pressings, the cake is now fractured by the chains, as the press ends are restored to their normal position. This new process decreases the working time needed by no less than 80 per cent. Experiments and analyses have shown that the tannin content of the Must coming from the press is not greater than from any other type and there is no danger of oxidisation of the Must, as it is exposed to the air for such a short time.

This press has been greatly improved. The result is a press which crushes the grapes as smoothly as human feet used to do before the invention of the first presses.

The same press contains a rubber tube inside, along its whole length. When the press is filled with grape mash and closed, the rubber tube is pumped full of air with an electrical air pump and presses the grape mash against the inside walls of the press; the resulting Must flows through the slits of the press into receiving vessels. There is no danger of the pips being crushed and bringing more tannin into the Must.

The amount of Must obtained by pressing 100 kilograms of grapes varies from sixty-five to eighty litres, depending on the kind of grapes, the year and the degree of ripeness of the fruit.

NOMENCLATURE:
THE LABEL

Very strict regulations control the naming and marking of wines intended for sale. In fact, owing to the wide possibilities and the large number of rules that have been gradually evolved to prevent unfair practices, the subject has become very intricate. As an aid to understanding, it is well to remember certain basic principles on which the rules are founded and to regard all other regulations in the light of modifications of these principles, tending to greater or less severity, as the case may be.

The first principle is embodied in an enactment forbidding misleading nomenclature and all deceptive marketing devices. A second enactment is founded on the basic rule that topographical designations of wines may be used solely for indicating their origins. Blends are dealt with separately.

Thus, if extraneous sugar has been added to a wine, it would be illegal to call it by a name that might induce a purchaser to assume its purity or to believe that special care had been used in its production. Again, to put up a Rhine wine in a *Bocksbeutel* (a flask of distinctive and peculiar shape), which by long custom is used only for Stein wines, constitutes a clear case of fraudulent marketing. Similarly, when wines are designated by invented names, it is illegal to print a landscape on the label, as this might create the impression that the fancy *appellation* was a designation of origin.

A natural wine may have attached to it any description referring to its purity, vintage, etc., which is customarily used in marketing, providing it is in no way misleading.

The main examples of such descriptions (implying the purity of a wine or that especial care has been used in selecting the grapes), and which, as has been mentioned, may not be used in connection with sweetened wines, are the following:

Naturwein (natural wine)
Ungezuckerter Wein (non-sweetened wine)
Rein (pure)
Naturrein (purely natural)
Echt (genuine)
Durchgegoren (fully fermented)
Wachstum, Kreszenz (mY) own vineyard
Gewächs Eigengewächs (growth)
Originalwein (original wine)
Originalabfüllung—abzug (original bottling) or any other combinations with the word "original"
Kellerabfüllung—abzug (bottled in the cellar of the proprietor)
Schlossabzug (castle-bottled)
Fass Nr., Fuder Nr. (cask No.)
Spätlese
Auslese
Beerenauslese
Trockenbeerenauslese
Hochgewächs, Spitzengewächs, Edelgewächs (superb, supreme, noble growth)
Edelwein, Edelauslese (noble wine, noble select)
Cabinetwein or *Kabinettwein* (cabinet wine)

APPLICATION OF TERMS

The terms *Originalabfüllung* and *Originalabzug* may be applied only to unsweetened wine matured and bottled in the grower's cellars.

The term *Spätlese* is reserved exclusively for unsweetened wine from fully ripened grapes gathered later than the normal harvesting period.

The designation *Auslese* is strictly limited to unsweetened wines produced entirely from carefully selected bunches, to the exclusion of any that are not fully ripe or are in any way damaged or diseased.

Beerenauslese denotes a wine made from specially selected single berries which have been allowed to become "over-ripe" or "sleepy" in good vintages. *Trockenbeerenauslese* refers to wines made exclusively from the shrivelled raisin-like berries obtained by allowing over-ripe grapes to become partially dried on the vine. Only *Beeren-* and *Trockenbeerenauslese* may be designated *Spitzen-* or *Hochgewächs*.

One sometimes finds the terms *Goldbeerenauslese* and *Edelbeerenauslese*. Neither of these names is mentioned in the wine law.

A *Goldbeerenauslese* is an *Auslese* (not a *Beerenauslese*) of fully-ripe golden grapes (as a *Beerenauslese* is made of sleepy grapes, i.e. grapes attacked by the fungus *Botrytis cinerea*, which have passed the golden stage).

Edelbeerenauslese is synonymous with *Beerenauslese*. The term *Edelbeerenauslese* is used when the noble, honey-like bouquet produced by the noble rottenness is very "visible".

No wine may be marketed as "natural" if the unsweetened, that is natural, product has been adulterated by the addition of an "improved" wine, however small a quantity of the latter may have been added.

PLACE AND SITE NAMES

German wines are named after the villages, or other locality at or near which they are grown. Often the suffix "-er" is added to the name of the locality to designate the wine. Thus a wine may be called "Rüdesheim"—the actual place-name—or, more usually, "Rüdesheimer", meaning "the wine of Rüdesheim". (It has sometimes been mistakenly thought that the "-er" denotes the comparative form, indicating a better quality. This is not the case.)

The vineyards of a village are divided into several *Lagen* (sites) with special names distinguishing them from each other— for example Rüdesheim: Schlossberg, Roseneck, Berg, Burgweg, Häuserweg, etc.; Bernkastel: Lay, Altenwald, Doctor, etc. Any wine grown in the borough of Rüdesheim may be called "Rüdesheimer", but it may only be called "Rüdesheimer Roseneck" if it has been grown in that district of the borough of Rüdesheim which is known as Roseneck.

I have frequently been asked what significance should be attached to the site-names. What, I have been asked to explain, does *Lage* really mean? The term denotes a piece of land. Where one "site" or piece of land ends the next begins, and the sites keep their distinctive names even where they overlap the local community boundaries. In other words, the names of *Lagen* with the wine district are like the names of municipal districts within a town or city. Like all names, they are used to distinguish their owners and make them easier to recognise.

Despite the similarity of the geological structure and of the vineyard sites, the quality varies greatly. The slightest difference in soil, in the *Lage*, or its situation in respect to the sun, produces differentiations in the wine. Even Goethe bore witness to this when he wrote in 1814: "The quality of a wine depends on its *Lage*."

An investigation into the meanings and origins (with appropriate classification) yields an astonishing fund of discoveries and unsuspected connections.

1. There are names embodying historical memories:

> Cossack Hill (Geisenheim/Rheingau)
> Hindenburg Hill (Serrig, Saar)
> King John's Hill (Castel, Saar)

2. Names with ecclesiastical flavour that carry allusions to churches, church dignitaries, ecclesiastical institutions, monasteries:

Altar (Ürzig)
Deacon (Graach)
Deacon's Hill (Longuich)
Church Lane (Zeltingen)
Parson's Hill (Bernkastel)
Prelate (Erden)
Nun's Hill (Martinsthal) (Filzen) (Wehlen)

3. Names that recall theological conceptions, picturing for example various aspects of phenomena of heaven and hell:

Heaven (Graach, Zeltingen)
Paradise (Kröv)
Hell (Johannisberg)
God's Foot (Wiltingen-Saar)
Angel's Hill (Zeltingen)

4. At times a name has been inspired by the particular colour of some vine-bearing rock or mountainside:

Red Hill (Rauenthal)
Red Hill (Zeltingen)

5. And, naturally enough, vineyards specially favoured by the sun's rays are frequently the bearers of names indicating either the sun itself or the effects of its light and warmth:

Sunshine (Schweich)
Sunnyside (Wintrich)
Sunny Hill (Eltville, Canzem)
Sun Dial (Wehlen, Zeltingen)

6. Other sites have been given the names of birds or animals:

Bird's Hill (Longuich)
Cuckoo's Hill (Hatzenport)
Pigeon Garden (Piesport)
Cock Hill (Waldrach)
Swan (Bernkastel)
Bees' Garden (Winkel) (Senheim)
Hare's Jump (Winkel)
Wolf's Hill (Canzem)

Cock Hill (Forst)
Hare's Run (Brauneberg)

7. Then again we find **vineyards** with poetical, humorous or grotesque appellations:

Cupid's Lane (Bernkastel)
Gold Drop (Piesport)
Birds' Song (Nahe)
Spice Garden (Ürzig)
Bathroom (Bernkastel)
Little Heart (Briedel)
Bare Bottom (Kröv)
Rascal (Escherndorf)

8. The famous vintage FORSTER UNGEHEUER is derived from the name of former owners of the vineyard, a "patrician family" called Ungeheuer. Although the word *ungeheuer* (literally "monstrous") is commonly used to denote something overwhelming, it has in this case nothing to do with the fact that the wines from the Ungeheuer Estate are in truth "overwhelmingly" full and rich. So may many other sites have been named after their **proprietor.**

9. Names of *Lagen* were often taken from such obvious points of contact as the shape of a hill, the rock formation or other natural features *on* or *near* which they were situated. Hence the numerous combinations with: *berg* (hill, slope); *weinberg* or *wingert* (vineyard); *-feld* (field); *-acker* (field, etym. acre); *-bach* (brook, rivulet); *-lay* (form of *Lage*, site; etym. "lair"); *-stein* (stone); *-kopf* (head, summit); *-mauer* (wall); *-strasse* (road, highway); *-weg* (way); *-pfad* (path), etc.

There are many examples of original site names: *Am Hinkelstein, auf dem Domtal, am Geisenberg, Hinter der Warte, Ober dem Fockenberg, in der Rehbachersteig, im unteren Hipping, bei dem Kiliansberg, im unteren oder oberen Auflangen*, etc. In time these names were shortened to *Hinkelstein, Domtal*, etc.

234

10. Many mementoes of cultural history are preserved in the names of vineyard sites. Both the names themselves and the language from which they are taken point to the history of the Rhineland which in the course of centuries was in the hands successively of the Romans, the French and various Germanic races.

Latin names still survive as remnants either of the Roman viticulture period or of the monks' Latin of the Middle Ages. Here are some examples:

> Kranklay, from the *grande lay*, meaning "great site" (Ürzig, Bremm)
>
> Laudamusberg, from the first word (*laudamus*, let us praise) of a hymn (Neumagen)
>
> Pichter, from *petitura*, meaning "common land allotted to a vineyard" (Longuich, M, Forst P).

There are still a number of old Germanic or German names to be found either alone, or in combination with other terms.

> In Wüston (Ürzig); Neuberg (Forst P); *Olk Celtic*: originally meant fruit garden, later vineyard (Trittenheim, Bernkastel); *Brühl*, meaning meadow (Trier M, Erbach R); *Bungert*, meaning orchard (Baumgarten) (Poelich); *Steig* (Steeg), meaning footbridge.

11. In almost all Mosel districts, we find the name *Lay* or *Ley* sometimes alone, sometimes in combination—as in Urlay, Busslay, Rotlay, Münzlay, Baerlay, Stablay, Kirchlay, Hüttlay, Geirerslay, Günterslay, etc. The word *Lay* denotes the slate rock of the Devonian formation. It occurs particularly frequently on the Middle Mosel, on the Saar and the Ruwer, and on the Middle Rhine. The Devonian slate has its origin in the deposits of the Devonian Sea and can therefore be described as fossilised sea-foam. The slaty structure of the Mosel hills arose through the pressure of folds in the earth crust, and through the remnants of other (higher) strata which have since for the most part been removed. Indications of this origin are still to be found in the

slate in the form of fossilised flora and fauna: sea-lilies, sea-roses, sea-weeds, bracken, crabs, sea-spiders, etc. Their age is estimated at about twenty million years.

In the *Lagen* rejoicing in the name of *Lay* the vines stand on slate. Slate is both warm and moist, contains potassium, and promotes growth and maturity. To this, and to the species of grape from which it is grown, the Mosel wine owes the distinctive flavour that marks it off unmistakably from the other wines of any other district. *Lay*, then, means that the soil of the *Lage* thus designated has a pronounced slaty character. Wines from these sites are characterised especially by much bouquet and the typical delicate flavour of "slatiness". The name *lay* is usually applied to small sites situated round rocks, in places that are well protected and have a favourable aspect.

These site-names, some of which have great originality and charm, may be so strung together as to constitute an invitation to what might be termed the Rhineland equivalent of a merry pub-crawl. In Franconia, for instance, where the very names induce dreams of luscious wines, you can start by seating yourself on a *Kitzinger Sonnenstuhl* (sun-chair), magically placed in an *Iphofen Kammer* (parlour); here you converse gaily with draughts of Franconian nectar, and if the conversation has been a little too much for you, you take the Thüngersheim cure known as *Thüngersheimer Scharlach* (scarlet). Then soothed by the pleasant strains of a *Würzburger Harfe* (harp), you tread lightly across the *Randersacker Spielberg* (play hill), passing the *Eschendorfer Hengstberg* and, having descended into the valley, dawdle your way through the vinelands on the Main. Do not fail to look in on the *Rodelseer Küchenmeister* (kitchen-master), who will provide you with sustenance for your *Würzburger Innere Leiste* (Inner man). Possibly while you are thus taking your ease, someone will pluck a dunce's cap from the hill of the *Schalksberg* (imp of mischief) and cram it down over your ears; but most certainly that will not make such a fool of you that you will omit your visit to the *Würzburg Stein* (stone) where, with the help of the philosopher's stone, you will regain any wisdom you may have lost. And what fun you will have watching a *Sommeracher Katz-*

enkopf (cat's head) seeking its prey in the *Sulzfelder Maustal* (mouse valley). You are no snob and will therefore not object to sharing your table with the *Escherndorfer Lump* (ragamuffin), nor are you a coward to be frightened away by the flames ascending from the *Randersacker Teufelskeller* (devil's cellar). But should your participation in the sinful pleasures of the cellar at any time lead you too far astray, do not forget to seek forgiveness on the *Hörstein Abtsberg* (Abbot's Hill), after which you may pass blissfully into the Randersacker *Ewiges Leben* (Eternal Life).

It has already been mentioned that topographical descriptions of wines may only be used to designate their origin, that is, the country, the place or district, and also the name of the *lage* (site). To avoid confusion which might arise owing to the duplication of names (or pronunciation of names) in different winegrowing districts, it has been laid down that where this possibility exists, descriptions must include supplementary qualifications to show the actual geographical origin of the wine. Thus: Rüdesheimer is an insufficient *appellation* in itself—it is either Rüdesheimer-Nahe or Rüdesheimer-Rheingau; Zeller is either Zeller-Pfalz (Palatinate), Zeller-Mosel (Mosel), Zeller-Baden, or Zeller-Franken (Franconia). Wachenheim is either Wachenheim-Pfalz (Palatinate), or Wachenheim-Rhinehessia.

| WINE-GROWING CENTRES | The very large number of wine-growing localities and sites makes it impossible for all their names to be familiar to the public. In view of this, the law permits certain deviations from the basic regulations in order to assist the wine trade and facilitate marketing. It has, therefore, been enacted that certain wine-growing localities whose products are distinguished by their volume and quality should be looked upon as so-called "centres". This means that the names of these places designate particular brands of wines and have in fact become the generic names for the wines produced in whole districts. Such centres are: |

> (a) *All* wine-growing localities in the Rheingau, for example Rüdesheim, Johannisberg, Winkel, Geisenheim, Östrich, Hallgarten.

(b) In *Rhinehessia*: Alsheim, Bechtheim, Laubenheim, Bingen, Dienheim, Nierstein, Oppenheim, and others.

(c) On the *Mosel*: Zeltingen, Graach, Piesport, Traben, Wehlen, Bernkastel, and others.

(d) in the *Palatinate*: Dürkheim, Forst, Deidesheim, and others.

A wine grown in a locality "adjacent or near" to one of these centres may be labelled with the name of such centre, provided that the character and quality of the wine may fairly be described as identical with the products of the centre itself. A site is, as a rule, considered to be "adjacent" when it is actually contiguous to the locality in question. The term "near to" has not been strictly defined in this context—no fixed distance (as the crow flies) has been laid down as a maximum. Given, however, a reasonable similarity in growing conditions, it may be assumed that a minor locality in a radius of approximately nine miles of a centre would be entitled to use its name.

VINEYARD "CLASS-NAMES"

The regulations pertaining to nomenclature according to centres did not satisfy the wine trade, because they did not allow for distinctions (in the description) between the products of the various sites (*Lagen*). The trade's wishes were therefore met by further legislation to the effect that wines could be classed and named, not only according to topographical centres, but also according to the vineyard sites. Names thus given are not necessarily strictly individual designations of origin, but may be used for all wines coming from a group of adjacent or neighbouring localities in which vineyard products are similar in character and quality.

As has been noted, vineyard sites may belong to more than one village, and, in such cases, the vineyard "class-name" may be derived from either side of the local boundary. The Krötenbrunnen vineyard, for example, overlaps the boundary between Oppenheim and Dienheim, and the wines produced therefrom be called either "Oppenheimer Krötenbrunnen" or "Dienheimer Krötenbrunnen".

238

Some communities have started to simplify their vineyard names. One special line of simplification is the creation of one special name which may be used for *all* wines originating from one community. For instance, Alsheim (Rhinehessia) was formerly divided into thirty sites; these were reduced to ten site-names (Goldberg, Sonnenberg, Frühmess, Rheinblick, Fischerpfad, Römerberg, Friedrichsberg, Rosenberg, Öligstueck and Sonnenhaeuschen) with the further stipulation that wines from the first five named sites can all be named "Rheinblick".

The generic name for all NIERSTEIN wines is "Gutes Domtal"; for all wines from JOHANNISBERG "Klosterpförtchen"; from TRABEN "Liebeskummer". Other communities have reduced the number of site names without creating a generic name for all their vineyards.

BERNKASTEL (Mosel) intends to reduce its sites from fifty to fifteen with the generic name "Bernkasteler Kurfürst" for all Bernkasteler wines.

RESTRICTIONS ON NOMENCLATURE

The enactments outlined above allow a certain latitude in the giving of class-names to wines. But once a name has been given, the right to change it is lost. The classification of a wine under a particular designation is determined by origin, quality and characteristics, and it would constitute a breach of the law if, for example, a whole string of names were to be applied to products from one and the same vat. In exceptional circumstances, and *only* in exceptional circumstances, a second name may be chosen for a wine. Such an exceptional circumstance would be a change in the quality of the wine during treatment. The wine merchant who has occasion to lower the price of a wine may by law rename it according to its changed quality.

Where a wine is labelled *Originalabfüllung* (Estate-bottled), the regulations are extremely strict. No latitude is allowed in the use of the names of districts or sites; "class-names" are excluded, and the *appellation* must be an accurate indication of the wine's true origin. A GEISENHEIMER STEINACKER ORIGINALABFÜLLUNG, therefore, must have been grown at Geisenheim in the Steinacker vineyard, and bottled in the proprietor's cellars.

When a class-name is used for a wine grown elsewhere than in the named district, it would be misleading within the meaning of the law to print on the label a landscape of that district.

As can be seen, vineyard names are so numerous, and the possibilities of offending against the Wine Law as described previously so great, that many wines are sold under invented or fancy names: not that the Wine Law had nothing to say about this. Thousands of invented names have been registered and are being registered weekly. A shipper may just offer his X's "Weinzauber" without any indication of the geographical origin of the wine, perhaps just as "German White Wine" (*Deutscher Weisswein*).

INVENTED NAMES   Invented names must not be used in conjunction with a geographical designation, as this might be taken to indicate a district of origin. Chosen invented names may not be so formed as to mislead the purchaser, that is, the quality of the wine must not be inferior to that which he is entitled to expect from the label. If a wine should be sold as Mother Mosel, it must be a Mosel, if under the name Rheinliebchen, a Rhine wine. For German wines two invented names in general use come to mind:

LIEBFRAUMILCH. Liebfraumilch is always in great demand. Contrary to popular belief, Liebfraumilch is not a district at all, but an invented name which may be applied to any pleasant Rhine wine of good quality. The name is derived from the Liebfrauenkirche (Church of Our Lady) at Worms, which is surrounded by vineyards.

Liebfraumilch was originally "Liebfrauminch". *Minch* is an old word for *Mönch*, German for Monk. "Liebfrauminch" wines were the wines which belonged to the monks of the Liebfrauenkirche. Incidentally, the whole district round the church was known as the *minch*. The natural development of the language has changed the consonant "n" to "l", and Liebfrauminch into Liebfraumilch.

The vineyards round the Worms church, known as Liebfrauenstift, produce an average of 20,000 bottles a year, a quantity which is obviously insufficient to cover the demand for Liebfraumilch. And incidentally the wines produced in Worms in an average year are not even of specially good quality.

A wine sold as Liebfraumilch may be a Rhine wine from any Rhine district. It may come from the Rheingau, from Rhinehessia, from the Rheinpfalz (Palatinate), from the Nahe and the Middle Rhine (as far as Koblenz).

As Liebfraumilch is an invented name, nothing may be added to it that might be interpreted as an indication of origin. On the other hand, additions like *Spätlese* and *Auslese* are, of course, permissible where the implications coincide with the facts.

The fancy name Liebfraumilch is open to all and is not the monopoly, as most fancy names are, of a registered proprietor. So, to distinguish their choice of Liebfraumilch, shippers create their own "Brand". This may be either just an additional fancy name, or perhaps a distinguishing label.

MOSELBLÜMCHEN. A well-known fancy name for Mosel wines is Moselblümchen. No conditions regarding the quality of a wine under this label have been laid down by law or jurisdiction. Under this name one can expect a wine in the lowest price range from the Upper or Lower Mosel, and no more.

GENERAL CONCLUSIONS

Perhaps surprisingly, the main significance of all the above information of the law-nomenclature only deflects the literal truth in the case of estate bottlings. Quality is the only criterion to be considered. To judge the quality of a wine, the prospective buyer tastes it carefully and then takes into consideration the development of the product in the past and any well-founded expectations he may have had of its prospects for the future. For the rest, the wine-merchant's advice to a private buyer is—buy and store the wine you like whatever its name or vintage. You make your own work easier if you buy your wine from a trustworthy source and if the wine originates from a good exporter and shipper.

KINDS OF VINE

Even the most poetic titles are not worth very much. A vineyard name, though it may truly reflect and symbolise an ideal, carries no guarantee that the quality of the wine from that site will always remain the same. Vintages in Germany vary far too much from year to year for any such expectation.

A good pointer to the quality of a wine is to be found on its label in the designation of the *species of grape* from which it is produced in conjunction with that of the place of origin.

German wine-growers are aware that they can only justify the immense costs of their vocation and indeed their own right to exist if they produce high-grade wines. The authorities supervise the establishment of any new vineyard and have enacted general rules limiting the kind of grapes that may be planted. Some species of grapes may be planted anywhere, others only in certain districts, while others again may only be planted under a special licence from the authorities.

THE SYLVANER or SILVANER. The Sylvaner is said to originate in Austria, and in some districts is known as "Österreicher", meaning Austrian, but actually its origin cannot be reliably ascertained. It is the main strain used in many German viticultural districts, such as Rhinehessia, the Rheinpflatz (Palatinate) and Franconia. It is also cultivated in Baden, Württemberg, the Rheingau and on the Middle Rhine. It may safely be assumed that in Germany it is more widely planted than any other species of vine.

It is also one of the most valuable kinds, as it is very fertile and ripens comparatively easily. It is known to mature on sites and in

242

regions in which the Riesling never attains full maturity; in such places it yields fuller and mellower wines.

Its wine is mild and agreeable, often full-bodied. Its light table wines are fine-flavoured, and in good years and on good sites wines of rich sweetness with exquisite bouquet are produced from it, including the great Ausleseweine of the Palatinate and Franconia. The 1959 WÜRZBURGER STEIN SYLVANER TROCKEN-BEERENAUSLESE (Estate Bottling State Domain) is a giant.

THE RIESLING. The best-known of German white wine grapes is the white Riesling. The grape that has made the Rhine and Mosel wines world famous. It produces distinguished wines with a rich bouquet and its *Trockenbeerenauslesen* are the greatest of all German wines.

The Riesling vine is the noblest that anyone in Germany has hitherto succeeded in cultivating for the production of white wines.

It is distributed over all German wine regions; on the Middle Mosel, the Saar and the Ruwer, it is the only kind of vine that is cultivated at all.

It produces the small healthy berries that ripen to a brilliant brown-yellow colour; it grows more slowly and ripens later than other kinds of grapes.

Once the grape has attained its full, sweet maturity, it develops to highest perfection the delicate elements of its exquisite bouquet—the incomparable aroma, the entrancing taste which are somehow reminiscent of all the best in other kinds of fruit. Peach, walnut, pineapple, blackberries, blackcurrants—the Riesling fragrance seems compounded of them all. Pleasantly sweet, not too strong in alcoholic content, stimulating and refreshing through their acidity, the Riesling wines at their best have earned a world-wide reputation.

THE MÜLLER-THURGAU (Riesling × Sylvaner). This is a seedling vine raised by crossing the Riesling with the Sylvaner and called after its inventor, Müller-Thurgau. It has become popular in many parts of Germany, particularly in Rhinehessia, Franconia, Baden and Württemberg. Attempts to cultivate it are being made in all German wine-growing districts.

The wine produced from the Müller-Thurgau grape can be described as mild, aromatic and pleasant with a slight Muscatel flavour; grown on suitable sites its quality, particularly in a generally poor season, exceeds that of Sylvaner and even of Riesling wines. At auctions in Rhinehessia and on the open market it attains good prices and can be recommended if intended for consumption not more than two years after pressing. It is certainly not a wine that improves in the bottle. But that is not to say that, even in this particular, some Müller-Thurgau wines cannot compete with Riesling and Sylvaner products. Possibly their quality will one day surprise the connoisseurs when the vine-sites are older and can infuse a greater strength into the ripening grapes.

THE TRAMINER. Nowadays the main cultivation areas for the *Traminer vine proper* is in Baden where, particularly in the neighbourhood of Durbach, it is extensively grown, producing good, rich wines. It is seldom found in any of the other German wine regions.

THE GEWÜRZTRAMINER (spiced or aromatic Traminer), said to have been developed from the Traminer proper, and superficially very like it, used to be widely cultivated in Rhinehessia and the Palatinate, contributing greatly to the fame of many districts and many sites. Excellent Gewürztraminer wines were, for example, formerly produced in Deidesheim, Wachenheim, Ruppertsberg, and in Rhineshessia in Gau-Algesheim (near Nierstein and Worms). The famous Zeller Schwarzer Herrgott owes its great reputation to the Gewürztraminer vine. Except for fragmentary remains, all these cultivation centres have disappeared, but attempts are now being made to cultivate it in other districts. I have come across it in Guntersblum, in Bingen-Büdesheim (Hessian Domain, Binger Scharlachberg) and even in Hallgarten in the Rheingau. In these districts, the wine is not marketed as a pure Traminer, but blended with Riesling.

The ordinary Traminer is rich in alcohol, soft and velvety with a fine aroma. The Gewürztraminer has a truly magnificent bouquet, which may even become rather too overwhelming but which makes it eminently suitable for mixing with other wines with less natural bouquet. The result, even with small quantities of the stronger wine, is a delicate aroma; such blends are very popular in Germany. The Gewürztraminer is all the more sought after because it is so sparsely cultivated and therefore comparatively rare.

THE RULÄNDER. This strain comes from France and was formerly more widely cultivated in Germany than is the case today. The Ruländer is a genuine Burgundy, sometimes called Grey Burgundy, and is to be found mainly in Baden and Franconia. The grape has a recognisable Burgundy taste: delicate, noble, aromatic. The wine is mellow, with a delicate bouquet; its appeal is to a refined palate and its acid content is usually low.

THE MUSCATEL. This is nowadays seldom found in Germany.

THE GUTEDEL. This grape, like its counterparts (Chasselas) in France and Switzerland, produces agreeable, sweet table wines with low acidity and a delicate aroma.

THE ELBLING. This vine, which can be grown on the Upper Mosel in Württemberg, and in Baden, produces lower-grade wines which, in most cases, have to be "improved" before being sold for consumption.

NEW VARIETIES

German viticulturists have tried for the last fifty years to find new strains of grapes with characteristics necessary to produce quality wines in this northern climate; Germany needs vines suitable for the soil of each district and which are neither endangered by phylloxera or other pests, nor susceptible to damage through cold winters.

As a matter of fact the principal experiments are based on Riesling and Sylvaner. The best-known after the Müller-Thurgau are the SAMLING 88 (s88) or SCHEUREBE, called so after Mr. Scheu.

A further cross between Sylvaner and Pinot Blanc is the MORIO-MUSCAT (after Mr. Morio); the SIEGERREBE (also grown by Scheu) produces mild wine with a fine Traminer flavour.

THE WÜRZBURGER PERLE (Gewürztraminer × Müller-Thurgau). Franconia suffers annually from the continental climate, and frost and winter cold cause enormous damage, especially to vineyards lying in the hollows. Frost protection, which is only partially effective, costs £60 to £80 per hectare. The Perle can stand −35°C in winter and −6°C in spring, whereas the Sylvaner and Riesling freeze at −2°C. The wines are soft, fruity, and develop rapidly.

WINE JOURNEY Now we can start our journey through the various wine districts of Germany in order to learn more about the manifold characteristics of their wines. Let us remember once more that wine is a product of climate, soil, grapes, and the technique used in its making, and hence the great differences in quality.

We shall start in the well-known districts first and then visit the lesser-known wine districts of South Germany.

RHEIN PFALZ
(PALATINATE)

Coming from the Rhine into the Palatinate, the traveller sees a fertile plain spread out before him. This is, so to speak, the advance guard of the Palatinate—known as the "forward" (*Vorder-*) Palatinate. Towards the west this plain is separated from the Western Palatinate by a long chain of hills which (at its southern end) is a continuation of the Vosges mountains, while to the north it is known as the "Haardt" range, or simply the "Haardt".

The English designation Palatinate for the German *Pfalz* is linguistically and historically well founded, for *Pfalz* is derived from the Latin *Palatinus*, the name of the first seven Roman hills to be inhabited and the one on which the Imperial Palace was built under Augustus. Since 1838 it has been known (geographically speaking) as the Pfalz.

The Palatinate alone has more vineyards than the whole of the Rhine, Mosel–Saar–Ruwer and Nahe territories taken together. It also has more vine plantations than Hessia, Baden and Württemberg. The vineyards cover an area seven times as great as that of the Rheingau.

PFALZ
PALATINATE

Albisheim
Zell
Harxheim

Bockenheim
Worms

Dirmstein

GRÜNSTADT

SAUSENHEIM
Kirchheim

UNTERHAARDT
Dackenheim

HERXHEIM
Weisenheim

FREINSHEIM

KALLSTADT

UNGSTEIN

BAD-DURKHEIM

Fridelsheim

WACHENHEIM

MITTELHAARDT
FORST

DEIDESHEIM
Niederkirchen

KÖNIGSBACH

GIMMELDINGEN
RUPPERTSBERG

HAARDT
MUSSBACH

NEUSTADT

Hambach

St.MARTIN

MAIKAMMER

EDENKOBEN

Weyher
OBERHAARDT

Burrweiler

GLASSWEILER

Speyer

Rhein

MOSEL
RHEINGAU
RHEINHESSEN
NAHE
PFALZ

The wine region of the Palatinate lies about 210 metres above the chilly mist-wrapped Rhine valley. The eastern slopes of the Haardt afford a natural protection against the cold winds from west and north.

The vineyards of the Palatinate are nowadays almost entirely confined to sites which are particularly suitable for grape cultivation and, as a rule, guarantee a good mature crop.

A good many of the vine plantations are to be found in the plain. In consequence, the inhabitants of the Palatinate seldom speak of their Weinberge (lit. Vine hills—the usual German word for vineyards), but mostly of Wingerten—that is, Weingarten, meaning wine gardens. The geological and climatic conditions in the Palatinate account for this difference. The Rhine valley from Mühlhausen to Bingen is like an immense sunken trench. The Vosges and the Haardt on the one side, the Black Forest and the Odenwald on the other, form the sides of this mighty "ditch" through which the River Rhine flows. In the whole region of the Rhine plains the climate is outstandingly warm and dry, but particularly so in the Palatinate. In the summer there is almost tropical heat, and the winters are mostly mild and free from snow, so that the traveller may well think he has struck a patch of the "warm south".

Such a favourable climate obviously promotes the growth of vines, which here put out their shoots and blossom earlier, and bring their grapes to an earlier maturity than in any other German district.

Particularly in years when the sun has been sparing of its rays do the wines of the Palatinate usually outshine their rivals in other German wine regions. As a rule, they are milder, have less acidity, are somewhat mellower but also richer than comparable products of different regions. Anyone therefore whose digestion is inclined to be intolerant of acids will find that these wines suit him better than others. The present tendency to prefer sweeter, richer wines has enlarged the market for Palatinate products.

The nature of the soil in the whole of this Palatinate wine region varies considerably, sometimes changing more than once within a very short distance.

The main species of grapes to be found here are Sylvaner (in this district known as Österreicher or Franken—Austrian or Franconian); then the Riesling, which is grown in large quantities, mainly in the finest production region of the Middle Haardt; the Traminer (and the Gewürztraminer) which used to be the main product of the Palatinate, but is now only sparsely grown as a pure strain; and the blue Portuguese, from which a light red wine is made. The Palatinate (Rheinpfalz) is divided into three unequal parts: the Oberhaardt (Upper Haardt), the Mittelhaardt (Middle Haardt) and the Unterhaardt (Lower Haardt). The largest is the Oberhaardt. It reaches from the French frontier in the south to Neustadt in the north. The Mittelhaardt stretches from Neustadt to Herxheim along the Weinstrasse (Wine Road). The Unterhaardt is the smallest of the three, stretching from Herxheim to Zell in Hessia.

OBERHAARDT (UPPER HAARDT)

The Upper Haardt is the wine-cellar of the Palatinate, or rather of the whole of Germany, for nowhere are such record harvests gathered as here. Medium wines are produced which are marketed as "small" to "medium", mostly in casks, but sometimes in bottles. A goodly proportion is devoted to the preparation of sparkling wines.

A few sites in the upper country may be said to produce medium —more rarely good—table and bottle wines (Hambach, St. Martin, a few sites in Weyher and Burrweiler, in Edenkoben and Maikammer have a good reputation); but for the German exporter and the foreign importer the wines are uninteresting and classed as "mass-produced". During the last few years, many of these wines have been shipped as cheap Liebfraumilch to the

U.S.A. Should any drinker of the cheap Liebfraumilch read this paragraph, I would advise him to buy next time a wine with a geographical denomination exported by a reputable house, so that his impression of German wine is rectified.

MITTELHAARDT (MIDDLE HAARDT)

North of the Upper Haardt and adjoining it, we find the Middle Haardt which is about 18 miles in length. It is the region where the quality wines of the Palatinate are produced.

Less rain falls in the country between Neustadt and Bad Dürkheim than anywhere else in Germany and it has more sunshine than any other part. Moreover, this soil is unsuitable for anything but the growing of vines, so that the whole region has been turned into what seems to be one vast vineyard. The main species grown is the Riesling, cultivated as a pure strain and selectively gathered, and producing Auslese wines, Beeren- and Trockenbeeren-auslesen of superb quality. Gewürztraminer and white muscatels are also cultivated here. In the lower, moister sites there are Sylvaner plantations.

NEUSTADT Neustadt is the hub of the Palatinate wine trade, and a tourist centre. The sites are Vogelsang, Grain and Kies. The communities between Neustadt and Bad Dürkheim and their sites are all worth knowing. The most important in quality are: Ruppertsberg, Deidesheim, Forst and Wachenheim, in the very centre. The next best wines are from Königsbach south of Ruppertsberg, and Bad Dürkheim, Ungstein and Kallstadt which are north of Wachenheim. Other villages are Haardt with sites Herzog and Mandelring; Gimmelding with sites Meerspinne, Schild, Kieselberg, Hofstück, Schlössel, Neuberg; and Mussbach with sites Pabst and Spiegel.

Königsbach	Produces wines next in quality to the greatest; the sites are: Idig, Satz, Bender and Weismauer.

RUPPERTSBERG   Fine quality wines are produced on the sites:

Reiterpfad	Goldschmidt
Hoheburg	Linsenbusch
Spiess	Hofstück

DEIDESHEIM   This is the site of the Bassermann-Jordan wine estate, to whose late owner (Dr. Friedrich von Bassermann-Jordan) we are indebted for an historical survey of German viticulture.

The soil in Deidesheim is suitable for fine quality wines, consisting as it does of volcanic primary rock, shingle, sand and lime. Deidesheim is the centre of the highest grade wine production in the Rhine Palatinate. The best "peak" wines in the world prosper here on the sites:

Grain	Kieselberg
Hohenmorgen	Kraenzler
Kalkofen	Langenmorgen
Leinhöhle	Rennpfad

In the Middle Haardt, near Forst, there is an impressive natural formation which is of inestimable importance for the local wine production. This is the so-called "Pitchstone Head" (Pechtsteinkopf), a basalt cone created by eruptive rock. The dark-coloured basalt rubble from basalt quarries is frequently used (as mentioned earlier) for treating the soil of vineyards. It has the effect of generating warmth in the shingle soil, and this is extremely favourable to wine production; the vintages from soil thus treated are particularly good, sweet, full and fiery.

FORST   The Forster wines are the only ones that can compete with the Deidesheimer. World-famous are the sites:

Kirchenstück	Elster
Freundstück	Ziegler
Jesuitengarten	Langenmorgen
Ungeheuer	Pechstein
Fleckinger	Musenhang

The Reichs Valuation Law of August 10th, 1925, which fixed values per hectare of wine producing lands, assessed the site FORSTER KIRCHENSTÜCK at 16,000 marks per hectare; a higher value than that given for any other site. It is here that the grapes reach their highest degree of maturity. The Forster Auslesen and Trockenbeerenauslesen are world-famous.

If you visit cellars, the cellarmaster may point with pride to a blackish substance covering the wall and will explain that the excellence of his wines is in part due to this. The substance is cellar-mould. This fungus is only to be found in good cellars. It cannot develop if the cellar is either too dry or too moist. It cleanses the air of the cellar, lives literally on air, mainly on alcohol in gaseous form. Thus the fungus absorbs the volatile components of wine which are given off in the process of fermentation, tapping, etc.

WACHENHEIM

This is one of the four villages which produce great wines on the sites:

Goldbächel	Altenburg
Bächel	Böhlig
Gerümpel	Wolfsdarm

Bad Dürkheim

The wines produced here on the sites:

Spielberg	Hochmess
Michelsberg	Geiersboehl
Fronhof	Schenkenboehl
Feuerberg	Proppelstein

are second only in quality to those produced at Wachenheim.

| **Ungstein** | The wines produced in this ancient village are of a similar character to those of Bad Dürkheim. The sites are: |

Spielberg	Kreuz
Herrenberg	Kobnert
Nussriegel	

The vineyards on the last-named site extend to the neighbouring village of Kallstadt.

| **Kallstadt** | Excellent wines are produced on the sites: |

Horn	Steinacker
Nill	Trift
Saumagen	Kronenberg

UNTERHAARDT
(LOWER HAARDT)

Merging into the fertile Rhinehessian plain, the German Wine Highway comes to an end with the following well-known viticultural communities in the Unterhaardt region:

DACKENHEIM	SAUSENHEIM
WEISENHEIM	DIRMSTEIN
KIRCHHEIM	BÖCKENHEIM
	GRÜNSTADT

The soil on which the Unterhaardt vines grow is heavy and rich in lime (clay, loess and sand). This tends to produce milder wines, less elegant and patrician and with less body than those from the Mittelhaardt, but nevertheless fruity and racy and extremely pleasing to some palates.

| **Grünstadt** | Grünstadt is distinguished by a "Wine-Market Association". The wines produced by members of this organisation are judged |

annually during the Grünstadt Wine Festival by a special panel of experts, and are drunk in enormous quantities by tens of thousands of visitors to the Festival.

Grünstadt is the end-point of the Wine Highway, but not of the viticultural area of the Palatinate. Adjacent to it lie the wine-lands of the Northern Palatinate. There in the Zell valley, on lime-soil mixed with clay, grows a wine very different from all other Palatinate wines, a wine both robust and steely. The Zell product known as SCHWARZER HERRGOTT has an excellent reputation in Germany itself, but is so far unknown in other countries. (Place of production: Harxheim-Zell.)

In conclusion it may be said that of all Palatinate wines, those from the following communities are in the *top class*:

FORST	RUPPERTSBERG
DEIDESHEIM	WACHENHEIM
KÖNIGSBACH	

The second class is composed of those from:

DÜRKHEIM	MUSSBACH
UNGSTEIN	NEUSTADT
GIMMELDINGEN	WINZINGEN
HAARDT	NIEDERKIRCHEN
KALLSTADT	

while all others are third class.

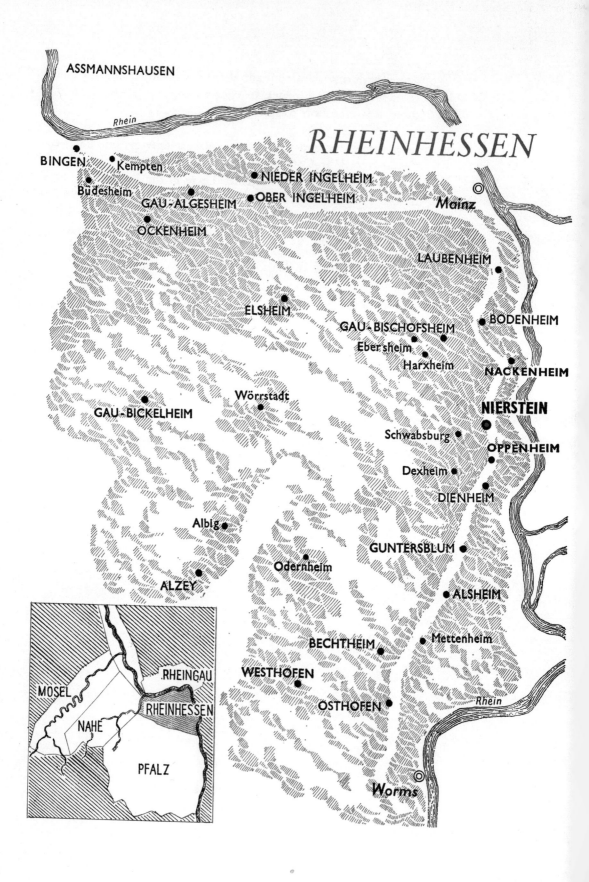

ASSMANNSHAUSEN

Rhein

RHEINHESSEN

BINGEN
Kempten
Büdesheim
GAU-ALGESHEIM
OCKENHEIM

NIEDER INGELHEIM
OBER INGELHEIM
Mainz

LAUBENHEIM

ELSHEIM

GAU-BISCHOFSHEIM
Ebersheim
Harxheim

BODENHEIM

NACKENHEIM

Wörrstadt

GAU-BICKELHEIM

NIERSTEIN

Schwabsburg

OPPENHEIM

Dexheim

DIENHEIM

Albig

Odernheim

GUNTERSBLUM

ALZEY

ALSHEIM

Mettenheim

BECHTHEIM

WESTHOFEN

OSTHOFEN

Rhein

Worms

RHEINGAU

MOSEL

RHEINHESSEN

NAHE

PFALZ

In the Hallgarten cellars, in the Rheingau.

facing p. 256

Typical bottles used for Schloss Vollrads wine. The German antique Hock glasses from the collection of the schloss date from the seventeenth to the nineteenth century.

RHEINHESSEN
(RHINEHESSIA)

Emerging from the Palatinate, we immediately find ourselves near Worms in the wine district of Rhinehessia.

The designation Rhinehessia is used to denote the origin of all wines grown in the province of Rhinehessia with the exception of a small area along the River Nahe.

It is often forgotten that Rhinehessia formed part of the French Republic (1797–1816). Rhinehessia is today part of the Federal Republic "Rheinland-Pfalz", the greatest wine-growing state of Western Germany.

Round the east and north of Rhinehessia flows the River Rhine in a wide semi-circle (Worms–Mainz–Bingen), while the Nahe flows to the west of the province. The region comprises 30,000 acres of cultivated wine-lands, and here we find the greatest possible variety of wines ranging from "small" table wines to the most exquisite "peak" wines (Spitzenweine) produced not only in Germany but all over the world.

Rhinehessia has been called "God's Garden". Its fertility and wealth have been known from time immemorial.

In considering the wines of Rhinehessia with its 165 wine-growing communities, from the point of view of soil, it is necessary to distinguish between the wines of the "Rhine Front" from Worms to Oppenheim and Nierstein-Nackenheim, the wines that originate near Bingen on the Rhine, and those from the high plateau lying farther back, and of Alzey and Gau-Bickelheim.

On arriving at Worms, we find, near the Rhine bridge, the Church of Our Lady (Liebfrauenkirche) which is surrounded by a few vineyards. It has already been mentioned that the wine marketed under the designation Liebfraumilch does not come from these vineyards. Incidentally, the entire annual output amounts to only about 110,000 litres. The wine is of medium quality and has a decidedly earthy taste to which most wine drinkers object.

In the extensive vine-covered hill-country to be found on the left bank of the Rhine from OSTHOFEN to OPPENHEIM, vines are planted almost exclusively on loess. This applies to BECHT-HEIM, ALSHEIM, NETTENHEIM, GUNTERSBLUM, DIENHEIM and OPPENHEIM. Here the tertiary marl and lime assist the growth of first-quality vines, particularly in dry years, as this kind of soil is capable of storing considerable amounts of finely distributed moisture. Red sandstone striated with sandy clays is also found. It is easily warmed by the sun's rays, and in wet seasons is capable of storing superfluous moisture in such a way that the vines are not harmed.

OPPENHEIM Oppenheim is the seat of a viticultural college and with Bodenheim, Dienheim and Nackenheim produces some fine quality wines on the sites:

Sackträger	Reisekahr
Kreuz	Goldberg
Krötenbrunnen	Schlossberg

258

DIENHEIM   This is one of the five localities of Rhinehessia which produces some quality wine on the sites:

> Krötenbrunnen   Goldberg
> Saar

NIERSTEIN

Nierstein boasts a population whose ancestors have been settled there for many generations and all its families are dependent either directly or indirectly on the cultivation of vines. There are about 500 individual owners of vineyards—both large and small plantations. Almost every Nierstein family owns at least part of a vineyard, but only about twenty of the wine estates play a significant part as producers of world-famous "peak" wines. It is almost entirely owing to them that the name Nierstein has such a good reputation as designating the place of origin of superb vintages. Foremost are the estates Franz Karl Schmitt (whose owner is the president of the Rhinehessian wine growers), Anton Balbach Erben and the State Domain.

Vineyard sites of NIERSTEIN on the Rhine are:

> Rehbach   Auflangen
> Spiegelberg   Ölberg
> Fockenberg   Heiligenbaum
> Hipping   Bildstock
> St. Kiliansberg Patersberg

Generic site names:

> Domtal   Monzenberg

NACKENHEIM   Where, leaving Nierstein behind them, the Rhinehessian hills draw quite close to the Rhine, we come upon NACKENHEIM, clustered around its vineyards in the form of a horseshoe: at one point the well-known Rothenberg: at another the Engelsberg with an old mountain chapel, and, pushing right down into the village, the Kirchberg with its baroque church. The houses are built down to the very bank of the river, crowded close together, among them imposing homesteads with tall stone-arched gateways.

It was not until the end of the eighteenth century when the growers were freed from serfdom that the whole of the land to the last patch became dedicated to the cultivation of the vine.

Today there is no room for the cultivation of any but the highest quality products. Climate, situation, nature of the soil, these are three determinants for the character and quality of a wine, all so favourable in Nackenheim that nothing but the best need be or is produced. Sun-kissed slopes and hills of red sandstone and clay slate (so-called "Red-lier") are here the homes of the Riesling and Sylvaner grape which are also favoured by the vaporisation, light reflexes, and warmth-conveying influence of the broad stream of the Rhine. Small wonder that they bring forth a wine which combines depth, fire, spiciness and delicacy in delicious and noble harmony. Hard work is needed to attain these results. In an average year the quantitative yield in this region is less than in any other part of Rhinehessia.

For a long time, far too long, Nackenheim wines were used for blending with others. In giving of their maturity and sweetness to wines from other regions which were deficient in these qualities, they descended into anonymity: the name of Nackenheimer was lost. It is only in recent years that people have begun to recognise the peculiarity, the special qualities and the exquisite taste of the wines fathered on the Nackenheim slopes. (The estates of Gunderloch-Lange, Dr. Gunderloch-Usinger, produce wines which, showing all the finesse of the best Rhinehessian wines, have some of the characteristics of good Rheingau wines.)

BODENHEIM   Next we come to Bodenheim which produces mild wines with a fine bouquet. They are good, wholesome wines, though they never attain the excellence of a top quality Niersteiner. Sites of Bodenheim:

Westrum	Hoch
Burgweg	Kahlenberg
Hasenmaul	Ebersberg
Leistenberg	Bock
Neuberg	

The same applies to the wines of LAUBENHEIM with its sites:

Hitz	Edelmann
Dammsberg	Seckergrund
Kirchenstück	Kalkofen
Steig	Johannisberg
Burg	Hausschen

Journeying along the Rhine we come first to Mainz, a centre of the Rhinehessian wine trade. Not very much can be said about the wines of Rhinehessia between Mainz and Bingen and the plateau lying to the south of this strip, with not less than ninety-eight wine-growing communities. Names connected with this region are:

Elsheim	Gau-Bischofsheim
Ingelheim (the red wine centre of Rhinehessia)	Gaubickelheim
	Wörrstadt
Gau-Algesheim	Alzey
Ockenheim	

The vineyards of ALZEY are to be found widely scattered over the sites of the Selz valley and the plains of the Alzey plateau. The wines produced there are: Sylvaner and Müller-Thurgau (white), and St. Laurent (red). Their quality varies. The district is cold and windy and therefore unfavourable for the production of quality wines. It is the "little" wines that are cultivated here, those sold *en carafe*; they are seldom bottled (except when blended with other wines).

BINGEN   The municipality of Bingen-Rhine lies actually on the Rhine and Nahe and comprises the vineyard sites:

BINGEN-STADT:	Schlossberg	Rosengarten
	Eisel	Mainzerweg
	Schwätzerchen	Rheinberg
	Morsfeld	Ohligberg
	Rochusberg	Mittelpfad
	Rochusweg	Kalbskopf
	Hungerborn	
BINGEN-KEMPTEN:	Kempten Berg	Hofwingert
	Gänsberg	Mauer
	Schnack	Treffelsheim
	Wolfskraut	Mördershölle
	Pfarrgarten	Hagelkreuz (red wine)
	Kapellenberg	Grosse Lies

Although the Bingen vineyards are separated from the Rheingau only by the width of the river, they produce quite different wines. The vines along the railway line and on the slopes around Bingen are distinguished by a certain "smokiness", derived from the smoke of the engines. I myself do not care for the taste, but the wine has found many lovers; it is well suited to the preparation of a good, racy, sparkling wine.

Bingen is a city with a long wine tradition going back to the fourteenth century.

On the *Rochusberg* near Bingen we find clay-slate, lightly mixed with Devonian quartz. The slate disintegrates easily, producing a clayey soil which though poor in lime is rich in vegetable mould and has a medium potassium and high nitrogen content. The large dark slabs of slate and the quartz keep the soil loose, which is a good quality because it permits the passage of air, the easy circulation of water, and the rapid assimilation of warmth—all of which have an excellent and characteristic effect on the surface soil of these vineyards.

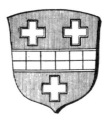

NAHE

Leafing through an old book of student drinking-songs, I found one commending the wines of the Nahe. This is how it begins:

> Here's to Monzinger—smooth and fine,
> Like satin (only wetter),
> First cousin to a Rhenish wine—
> I don't know which tastes better.

It might have added that the Nahe wines are also first cousins to the Mosel products. This would have made the description accurate, as Nahe wines are reminiscent of both Rhine and Mosel wines, which is not surprising when it is remembered that their geographical origin lies between the two.

Looking down from the Rüdesheimer Berg vineyards on to the Rhine, you will see—just opposite and coming from the south—a little stream slipping past the two watchful hills known as the *Scharlachkopf* and the *Elisenhöhe* and winding its peaceful way towards the Rhine. That is the Nahe. Its source is near Birkenfeld on the Hunsrückhöhe and its path to the Rhine takes it through one of the most beautiful valleys in the region.

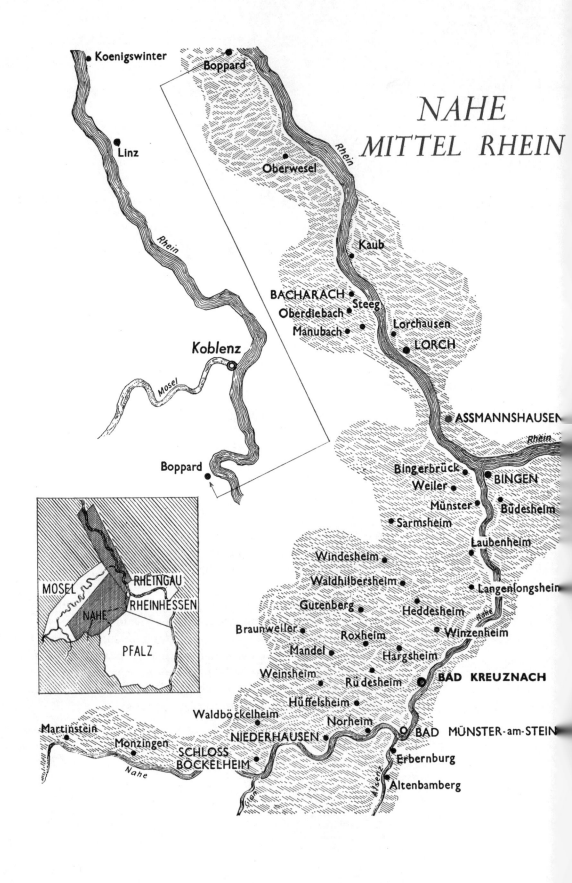

NAHE
MITTEL RHEIN

The products of this valley, however, are not the only ones sold under the name of "Nahe wines". The name includes those from the districts of Kreuznach, Baumholder, and the Alzenthal.

Nowadays quality is more important than quantity, and in this the Nahe can certainly hold its own in competition with other German wine regions. Both the Domains and the carefully cultivated ancient private estates produce wines which have a distinct character, which are racy, fiery, and patrician. But more on this subject later.

What does the Nahe region look like?

Dominating the landscape is the height known as the *Burgklopp* rising up from the town of Bingen and standing out behind the vine-covered *Scharlachkopf*. The *Scharlachberg* belongs to the community of BÜDESHEIM and the inhabitants claim its robust products as their own. They are probably right.

The ancient Roman Drusus Bridge that once spanned the Nahe was destroyed by the Nazis during their retreat in 1945; but it has been rebuilt in its old style. Crossing this from Bingen, we reach the western bank with its numerous picturesque villages: MÜNSTER near BINGERBRÜCK, SARNSHEIM, LAUBENHEIM (not to be confused with the other wine-growing locality mentioned above, namely Laubenheim near Nierstein), and LANGENLONSHEIM with its rich, sun-drenched slopes.

At Langenlonsheim the Guldenbach valley rises to Stromberg and on to the Hunsrück. In this valley we find the villages of HEDDESHEIM, WALDHILBERSHEIM and WINDESHEIM.

In all these, there is extensive vine cultivation. WINZENHEIM is the next wine village with its famous sites: Rosenheck, Honigberg and Metzler.

Vines are also widely cultivated in the lateral valleys branching out from the Kreuznach district. Here, for example, is the territory of the Amtsbezirk Rüdesheim/Nahe. It lies in the heart of the Nahe vineyard country, about ten miles as the crow flies from Rüdesheim/Rhine. Its wines are of good quality.

NIEDERHAUSEN ON NAHE

This is the most important of the twelve communities belonging to this *Amtsbezirk* (local government centre). Its best and most widely known sites are:

Hermannshöhe	Rosenheck
Klamm	Rosenberg
Kerz	Steinberg
Hermannsberg	

As a viticultural Domain (State Property) it is world-famous and worth a visit. The administrative buildings of the Domain are picturesquely situated on the western spur of the hill and afford a delightful view of the River Nahe framed in vine-covered banks.

Straight ahead lie vineyards rising in a series of terraces to the highest point of the Kupferberg (Copper Mountain). The terraces are separated from each other and buttressed by strong fortress-like walls; they run from north to south so as to catch every ray of sunlight, thus giving the grapes the best possible chance of ripening.

Its copper content has given the soil of the "Kupfergrube" a curious earthy colour. (The name *kupfergrube* means "coppermine"—and, at one time, it was actually mined, but uneconomically.) The wine has a taste which is reminiscent of blackcurrants. For this reason, when I first tried it, I thought it was impure, but later I gladly and wholeheartedly changed my opinion. The earthy element gives the beverage a certain delicate piquancy. To be understood and enjoyed, this particular wine must be sipped rather than drunk in the normal way.

The vineyards on these slopes are now at the height of their productive capacity.

266

SCHLOSS BÖCKELHEIM

This village near Niederhausen produces wines which are among the best to be found along the whole of the Nahe. The sites are:

Kupfergrube   Mühlberg
Felsenberg   Königsfels

The Schloss Böckelheimer Kupfergrube Trockenbeerenauslese 1945 sold at the 1948 auction for £5 10s. a bottle.

Norheim

This village ranges close behind with its sites:

Dellchen   Götzenfels
Kirschheck   Hinterfels

Traisen am Rotenfels

Here are some glorious vines which grow from among porphyry rocks.

The other villages in the Amtsbezirk produce wines of the same or very similar quality. They are: HÜFFELSHEIM which once changed hands as the result of a wager when one Ritter Boos von Waldeck drank a whole bootful of Must in one draught.

WEINSHEIM, the wine village *par excellence* as its name indicates, with sites named after the hills, here rather grandiosely called "mountains" (*Berge*):

Kellerberg   Nauenberg
Mühlberg   Holzberg
Hinterberg

RÜDESHEIM, which produces simple luncheon wines with Rosengarten, Wiesberg and Haardt heading its list of sites.

MANDEL likewise has a Rosengarten and also Schlossberg and Dellchen.

HARGESHEIM is another village in the area.

ROXHEIM comes next with the site name: Kronenberg.

SANKT KATHARINA was formerly a convent.

BRAUNWEILER calls its best vineyard site simply Weingarten (wine garden).

GUTENBERG has the sites:

> Schlossberg (on which an old castle stands)
> Rosengarten
> Margarethenberg
> Bangenberg
> Bingergrube

BAD MÜNSTER AM STEIN is reached through the beautiful Salinen valley; its wine sites are:

> Rotenfels   Felseneck

EBERNBURG. The ruins of Ebernburg, the mighty fortress that belonged to Franz von Sickingen, are on the heights of the opposite bank. There on the sites

> Weidenberg   Schlossberg
> Erzengrube   Pfarrwingert

grow the vines that produce Sylvaner, Riesling, Traminer and Portuguese grapes.

On the warm slopes of the porphyry rocks we find sites that bear signs of high-grade cultivation. The wines produced are peculiarly racy, have an individual bouquet, are steely, fruity, and, in the case of Rieslings, of a fine piquancy.

Farther south, in the valley of the lively Alsenz, there are many more wine-cultivating areas.

ALTENBAMBERG is one that deserves mention.

WALDBÖCKELHEIM, slightly off the route along the river, is known for its good sites, exemplified by:

Königsberg
Mühlberg
Welschberg

At Monzingen we enter a new viticultural region of good repute; this fairly extensive district, which includes WEILER, and MARTINSTEIN with its site, Burgwingert, is practically the end of the Nahe wine-lands.

In the valleys on both sides of the Nahe there are many more places with a thriving wine culture—for example, on the Glan near Offenbach, and Odernheim. Although the vine centres on the Alsenz and some of those on the Glan are, politically speaking, in the Palatinate, their wines belong in the Nahe category.

In 1959, Nahe wines were real beauties. They had the charm of a good Mosel, the aroma of a Rheingau and the fruit of Rhinehessian wines.

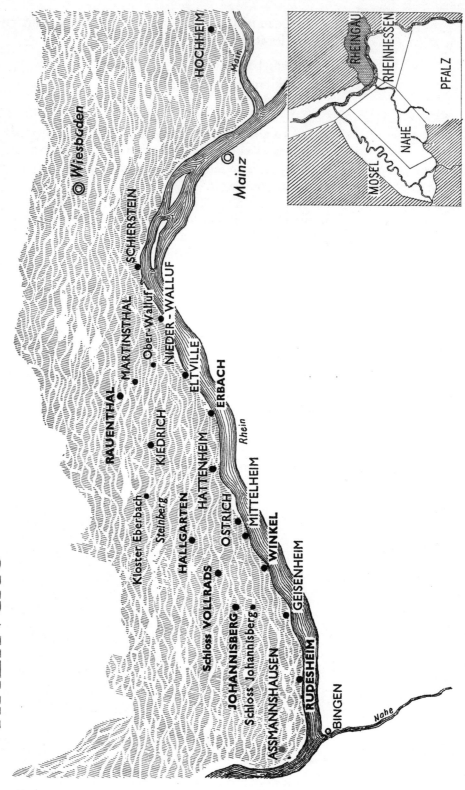

RHEINGAU

The natural conditions for wine-growing are very favourable in this district. The cluster of vineyards on the right bank of the Rhine (which at this point flows from east to west) has a southerly aspect and is protected against the biting east and north winds by the semi-circular wall formed by the thickly wooded Taunus mountains. The effect of the sun's rays on the more or less steeply inclined vineyard slopes is heightened by their reflection from the surface of the Rhine. Moreover, the high proportion of moisture in the air, caused by the broad surface of the river, has an extremely stimulating influence on the whole development of the plantations, being particularly helpful when the grapes are ripening in the autumn. And, finally, the advantages of the site are still further increased by the composition of the soil; this is for the most part very fruitful and particularly well adapted to viticulture.

The designation "Rheingau" is used for wines originating in the wine-growing communities of the district of Rüdesheim (Rheingau-Kreis), and extended to include those from the municipal district of Wiesbaden, the localities Frauenstein and Schierstein, and even the wine-growing centre of Hochheim together with its immediate surroundings; these are situated on the right bank of the River Main and, strictly speaking, therefore, belong to the Main rather than the Rhine.

The Rheingau is still the home of descendants of old patrician families who devoted their lives to furthering viticulture. In ELTVILLE we have Freiherr Langwerth von Simmern; Graf zu Eltz; in HATTENHEIM, Graf Schoenborn; in HALLGARTEN, Fürst Löwenstein; in JOHANNISBERG, Fürst Metternich; in WINKEL, Freiherr von Brentano and Graf von Matuschka-Greiffenclau—and many others.

Then there are many small, medium and large Growers' Associations whose work is entirely devoted to the cultivation of wines. They look upon it as their duty to produce high-grade wines.

Hochheim

The most easterly town of the Rheingau is, as has been mentioned, Hochheim, and it is odd that this place on the River Main should have given the name "Hock" in English-speaking countries to Rhine wines as a whole. But it is a fact and perhaps not so strange as it seems, for Hochheim wines have all the typical features of the Rheingau products.

Several dozen sites in Hochheim produce wines which, together with a slightly earthy taste, are found to be mellow, delicate and well balanced. Here are the names of some of these sites:

Hölle	Neuberg
Stein	Wiener
Kirchenstück	Daubhaus
Domdechaney	Stiehlweg
Rauchloch	Weiler
Bettelmann	

Up to 1273 Hochheim and its vineyards belonged to the Chapter of Cologne Cathedral; from then until 1803 to the Chapter of

Mainz Cathedral. Since 1803 a large part of the Hochheim vine estates has belonged to the city of Frankfurt. Many of the ecclesiastical names still survive—for example, Domdechaney (cathedral deanery) and Kirchenstück (church piece). To this very day Hochheimer Hölle (Hochheim Hell) is drunk in the Frankfurt "Ratskeller" as the city's own home-grown wine.

Just a word about the estate known as the "Queen Victoria Vineyard" (Königin-Viktoria-Berg). Not that I think particularly highly of this wine; on the contrary, I have always found its earthy taste so prevailing and penetrating that its other qualities are submerged. But this vineyard was christened after Queen Victoria. In 1850 she visited the vineyard which produced her favourite wine. This visit was the cause for asking the permission of the Royal Court to give the "Lage" the new name. It displays a monument to her within its own precincts. That is its main claim to interest. On December 5th, 1950, the town of Hochheim celebrated the centenary of the *Lage* "Königin-Viktoria-Berg".

Passing over Schierstein (which incidentally possesses one of the oldest and formerly most important Rhine harbours) and the little village of Nieder-Walluf, which is better known for its horticulture than for its wines, we come to the Rheingau proper.

Eltville

The town derives its name from the Latin *alta villa*. Its vineyard area comprises 740 hectares and is the biggest in the whole Rheingau. Sites belonging to it are:

Kalbspflicht	Sonnenberg
Taubenberg	Bunken
Messwingert	Grimmen
Langenstueck	Sandgrub
Mönchhanach	Steinmacher
Neuweg	Auf'm Ehr
Klimchen	Pellet
Freienborn	Grauer Stein

Three well-known wine centres, KIEDRICH, MARTINSTHAL and RAUENTHAL, are situated on the heights at the foot of the Taunus mountains.

Kiedrich

Kiedrich sites include:

Wasserros	Turnberg
Gräfenberg	Gangolfsberg
Sandgrube	Klosterberg
Heiligenstock	Scharfenstein
Berg	

Wines from these sites are compact and have a fine aroma of spicy herbs. When they have been bottled for some time they are found to have gained in refinement and elegance. At the wine auction in Eberbach in 1906 a Gräfenberg vintage broke the world price record for any wine sold up to that date.

RAUENTHAL

Wines from these vineyards always cost 10 to 15 per cent more than any other Rheingau products—and rightly so. Here, on the steep mountain slopes, are produced wines of supreme elegance—mild and aromatic, rose-scented, with a taste suggesting fruits and spices, and often honey-sweet. Rauenthal sites are:

Rothenberg	Langenstueck
Burggraben	Siebenmorgen
Pfaffenberg	Wülfen
Nonnenberg	Baiken

The 1953 and 1949 wine of Rauenthal, produced from old European vines, have kept all their early promise.

Martinsthal

Martinsthal is situated in a valley between Rauenthal and Eltville. The community was known till 1935 as Neudorf. The inhabitants of Neudorf considered that the name Neudorf (new village) was too common: it allowed the distinctive quality of their own wines too little chance of becoming known and appreciated. A 1933 Martinsthal which had won a special prize for its superb quality was a wonderful wine—mature, sweet, fruity, with a delicate bouquet.

ERBACH

Lower down the Rhine about half a mile from Eltville is Erbach. Sites are:

Marcobrunn	Michelmark
Honigberg	Seelgass
Brühl	Langenwingert
Siegelsberg	Rheinhölle
Herrnberg	Steinmorgen
Hohenrain	Pellet

In my opinion, the Marcobrunn wines are neither as elegant nor as mature as the Rauenthaler, they are particularly robust and spicy and overrated. They are no better in quality than many other Rheingau wines, but much higher in price.

Hattenheim

This is a picturesque village close to Erbach. It is the only community in the Rheingau which owns vineyards. The sites belonging to Hattenheim are:

Bergweg	Schloss Reinhartshausen
Hassel	Rheingarten
Heiligenberg	Schützenhauschen
Kilb	Stabel
Mannberg	Willhorn
Nussbrunnen	Wisselbrunnen

KLOSTER EBERBACH (Monastery of the wild boar stream) is equidistant from Hattenheim and Erbach, but farther from the river, idyllically situated in a wooded valley. It was founded by

Augustinian monks in 1116 and "modelled" on a wild boar shown with its tusks.

In the year 1200, the monks built a wall encircling their whole premises, including the courtyards and gardens. Most of this wall is still standing. Their most famous vineyard was the Steinberg (twenty-seven hectares) which is still surrounded by a wall two to two and a half metres high and nearly two kilometres long.

The Steinberg vineyard now belongs to the Hessian State Domains. It has up-to-date equipment and keeps pace with all modern scientific and technical improvements. The cellar alone is worth a visit. It contains nearly 800 Half-Stück (48,000 litres) of wine, but unfortunately special written permission by the Minister of Agriculture is needed and can only be obtained if applied for a good time before the intended visit.

The favourite Rheingau wine in Germany today is the STEIN-BERGER. And certainly its Trockenbeerenauslesen represent the noblest and finest of any produced in the whole country.

A 1921 Steinberger fetched 15.10 RM; Auslese: 24 RM; hochfeine Auslese: 28 RM; Edelbeerenauslese: 89 RM; and the best Trockenbeerenauslese 172 RM per bottle (£1 = 20 RM). The price difference shows how little importance can be attached to a name of a wine, even in combination with a particular vintage year. The content of the bottle is the only thing that matters.

The 1949 Auslese and Beerenauslese were admired and enjoyed by my friends and their friends. The 1953 was a worthy successor. In 1959 a great quantity of Beerenauslesen and Trockenbeerenauslesen was produced, proportionately too much, so that most Spätlesen and Auslesen of this vintage are below the expected quality.

HALLGARTEN   The village of Hallgarten shelters beneath the Hallgarter Zange ("Pincers"), sunbathed, glorying in the fertility of its vineyards.

The growers who live there are born and brought up in the wine tradition and produce the racy and distinguished wines that prove an attraction on any wine list. In the year 1921, that famous year which brought forth fine wines everywhere, the Hallgarten products were superior in body, bouquet and elegance to any others from the Rheingau. The Hallgarten sites are:

Jungfer	Würzgarten
Schönhell	Hendelberg
Deutelsberg	Rosengarten
Mehrhölzchen	Kirchenacker
(adjoining the	
Steinberg vineyard)	

In Hallgarten most of the growers belong to one of the four local Associations, called respectively the "English", the "Boers", the "Germans", and the "Boxers". The *appellations* are now used officially, but have a popular origin, dating from their foundation during the Boer War. The poorer growers, having dubbed the large owners "Englishmen", themselves automatically became the "Boers".

In the parish church at Hallgarten stands the famous "Wine Madonna", a piece of fifteenth-century sculpture and one of the most delightful monuments to Rhenish wine culture.

Nestling close together in the valley are the villages Östrich, Mittelheim and Winkel.

Östrich

This village is blessed with very good vineyards which slope gently down to the Rhine from the Hallgarten vineyards. It shares a railway station with Mittelheim. The sites are:

Doosberg	Lenchen
Pfaffenberg	Klosterberg
Räuscherberg	Klostergarten
Eiserberg	Magdalenengarten

| **Mittelheim** | The wines produced here are of fair to fine quality. The sites are called: |

| | Edelmann   Honigberg |
| | Gottesthal |

| **WINKEL** | The village of Winkel adjoins Mittelheim, the boundary being practically non-existent. The following are some of the sites: |

	Gutenberg Dachsberg
	Jesuitengarten Honigberg
	Steinchen Eckberg
	Hasensprung Oberberg
	Ansbach Ensing

The vineyard estate of SCHLOSS VOLLRADS, above the village of Winkel, is tucked away in a little vale half-way up the slope of the wooded Taunus hill. Its wines rank high among the best Rheingau products. Established at the end of the seventeenth century, Schloss Vollrads is justly proud of its press-house. This contains, in addition to some modern presses, one very old press made from the trunks of old oaks on which a coat of arms has been elaborately carved. The castle is owned by Graf Matuschka-Greiffenclau, the leading figure in German viticulture. His family formerly inhabited the oldest existing German residence —the "Grey House" in Winkel.

Schloss Vollrads' 1933, 1934, 1935, 1949 and 1953 vintages are wines of pleasant memories, and its 1959 products are "grand". They have an exquisite aroma.

May I just say here that, in good vintages, Schloss Vollrads is unbeatable for wines of character, breeding and staying-power.

| **JOHANNISBERG** | The famous SCHLOSS JOHANNISBERG is spectacularly situated above its steeply sloping vineyards. It is blessed with fruitful |

vines, and has had a colourful history. The first Benedictine monastery in the Rheingau was erected at Johannisberg on the initiative of Archbishop Ruthard of Mainz (1088–1109). They planted the first vineyard on the hill, which was then named the Bischofsberg. Beyond the castle lies the village (*dorf*) of Johannisberg with its vineyards:

Nonnenhöll	Erntebringer
Hölle	Klaus

Its wines fully deserve their universal popularity.

Johannisberg wine graced the historic occasion when, at the 1858 Berlin Congress, the Russo-Turkish war was brought to its formal conclusion. At the close of the proceedings Bismarck invited the members of the Congress to his house and, raising his glass of 1811 Johannisberger smilingly to Disraeli, gave the toast to "perpetual world peace and increasing understanding among the European peoples". He compared the gold of the wine to the honest work accomplished by the Congress.

Geisenheim   Close to the river lies the old town of Geisenheim with its two (dissimilar) open-work Gothic towers. It is widely known as the home of the largest German Training Centre for Viticulture, Fruit-growing and Horticulture. The vineyards of Geisenheim extend for almost two miles from Johannisberg in the east to those of Rudesheim to the north and west. They produce a great deal of wine—some on occasion very fine. Geisenheim sites are:

Rotenberg	Schroederberg
Kapellengarten	Spitzenlehn
Mauerchen	Steinacker

RÜDESHEIM   This famous town extends a considerable length along the Rhine. Its very numerous and far-famed sites are:

Bischofsberg	Kreuzgarten
Bronnen	Kroonest
Burgweg	Lay
Dickerstein	Mühlstein
Engerweg	Pares
Hellpfad	Platz
Hinterhaus	Rammstein
Klosterkiesel	Rechacker
Stoll	Roseneck
Wüst	Rottland
Kiesel	Stumpfenort

Here in this district you find the typical Rhenish wine taverns, where all the Rheingau wines may be tasted. The Rheingau is far too proud of its products to serve wines from any other region.

The wines grown on the Rüdesheimer Berg, particularly on the sites Schlossberg, Burweg, and Bischofsberg Roseneck, are famed for their incomparable bouquet and their fruity taste.

The Rüdesheim wines have one characteristic which sets them apart from most others: in so-called "good years" they are seldom at their best, and vice versa. There is a very simple explanation for this. The Rüdesheim sites, like many on the Mosel, are on steep slopes; consequently, the moisture in their soil is apt to leave the higher regions comparatively quickly. The vineyards have little natural moisture, so, in hot summers, the warmth is not offset by sufficient water to feed the ripening grapes: this, in turn, retards the development of their sugar content. The 1921 and 1949 Rüdesheim wines from the best sites were too dry.

Red Hocks   These observations would not be complete without a reference to red hocks. In 1962, 83 per cent or 55,466 hectares of the wine-producing area were producing white wine; 17 per cent or 11,671 hectares red wine.

In good vintages the wines show a soft and delicate flavour, and though the red grapes ripen earlier than the white ones under no circumstances can they be compared with the French growths. It is, therefore, easily understandable that there is no export of these wines; they are consumed within Germany, whereas foreign countries will, in any case, look for the fine red wines of Bordeaux or Burgundy, and not for Assmannshausen or any other German red wine, as they would have to pay the same duty.

The red-wine grape most favoured in Germany is the Blue Burgundy (*Spätburgunder*). Its wine is dark, strong and finely spiced. It flourishes on the Rhine, on the Ahr, and above all in Baden. Next in favour comes the Müller-vine (Schwarz-Riesling) in Württemberg.

Lesser red wines are produced from the Blue Portuguese grape in the Palatinate (the Palatinate is the biggest red wine region in Germany), in Rhinehessia and in Württemberg; and from the Limberger vine and the Trollinger (originating in the Tyrol) in Württemberg. The last-named produces a somewhat sour table wine. Then there is the Affenthaler, which is produced near Bühl in Baden.

On account of a monastery which was situated in the valley, this village was called *Ave Thal*, that is, *Ave-Marie-Thal* (Thal means valley). In this part of the country "V" is pronounced "F" so that people called the village *Affenthal*; *Affe* in German means a monkey. As a result of all this manipulation of the language, and in order to distinguish their wine from other districts, the growers used, and still use, a bottle on which a monkey is embossed.

Red wines in Germany—like the French red wines from Bordeaux and Burgundy—are obtained by fermentation of the grape "mash". Under the German Wine Law it is permissible to add to a German red wine a quantity of foreign red wine not exceeding 25 per cent of the total volume. This licence constitutes a great commercial advantage to growers and wine-merchants in Germany, as, with the exception of Württemberg and Baden, practically no region producing German red wines would otherwise be able to condition its products for a ready sale.

The German red wine region *par excellence* is the Ahr valley, which is also the most northerly wine region in the world. The wine produced there is called Ahr Burgundy. Owing to the lack of foreign wines in Germany, the Ahr products have an almost clear field and the chance to reign supreme. It seems doubtful, however, whether they will be able to maintain this position, even inside the country. The foreign consumer is certain to prefer a genuine Burgundy to the Walperzheimer.

Moreover, the cultivation of red wine on the Ahr is on the wane. The growers are of the opinion that the vineyards on the Ahr are "Burgundy-weary", an opinion based on the discovery that, in many places, new cuttings lacked vigour in their development, while other species, when planted in vineyards earlier devoted to Burgundy vines, bore good fruit. Just as a farmer rotates his crops, so the vine-grower must, from time to time, change the species of vines in his vineyards. As a result of these considerations, the growers on the Ahr have begun to plant grapes which produce the white wines. At the present day, red and white wines are being grown in about equal proportions. There is no need to go into detail about these white wines whose origins are nearer to the North Pole than any others.

Assmannshausen

This village still belongs to the Rheingau officially but produces wines more like the style and quality of the Mittel Rhein wines. It is the city of Rhenish red wines. The sites are:

Höllenberg	Frankenthal
Hinterkirch	Bohren
Eckerstein	Bomberg
Steil	

Assmannshausen red wines are all derived from the "Late Burgundy" vine. As the best red wine produced in Germany, the Assmannshauser has been praised in many writings. It is no

Burgundy—despite the fact that it comes from a "Burgundy" grape—but a Rhine wine with some of the qualities of a Burgundy. The difference is no doubt due to the difference in soil. The slate hills of the Rhine produce something less fine than the French Burgundy but possibly for the same reason rather stronger.

Unfortunately, what Assmannshausen has to say of its soil, the Burgundy growers can say rightly of their soil and climate. So the Assmannshauser is a red wine, but no Burgundy.

The Assmannshausen sold pre-war in London at 660s. per dozen bottles (which then included only 12s. duty) was the most interesting wine I ever tasted. It was the 1934 ASSMANNSHAUSER HÖLLENBERG SPÄTBURGUNDER ROT-WEISS, FEINSTE TROCKEN-BEERENAUSLESE, Estate Bottling Prussian Domain. This is a wine resulting from a very special kind of Beerenauslese of the late Burgundy grape.

This red-white wine must not be confused with the *Schiller Wine*. Schiller wine is the name given to a wine pressed from a mixture of red and white grapes. The name has nothing to do with the poet Schiller, but derived from the red-white (merging into pink) radiance or "shimmer" of the wine. (The German verb for "shimmer" is *schillern*.)

This species of wine was developed mainly during the worst crisis ever suffered by German viticulture—after the Thirty Years War. During that period, the many devastated vineyards were hastily replanted with any kind of vine likely to afford a good crop, whether it was a red wine or a white wine grape. Even nowadays the Swabians are very fond of their "Schiller", but its production has been drastically reduced. In Württemberg as elsewhere there is a very strong tendency—wholly admirable from the viticulture point of view—to keep grape strains and wines pure by selective planting, selective harvesting and selective wine production. This tendency will no doubt lead to a still greater improvement in the quality of German wines.

In bad vintages, as in 1954, when grapes cannot ripen and therefore do not produce colour substances, white wine is produced
from the red grape which is either used locally or for the production of sparkling wine.

Best Known German Red Wines

AHR	Walporzheimer Honigberg
	Ahrweiler Daubhaus
RHINEHESSIA	Ingelheimer Hundsweg
	Ingelheimer Langenberg
	Ingelheimer Hirschtal
	Ingelheimer Bein
	Ingelheimer Höllenweg
	Ingelheimer Steinacker
	Ingelheimer Sonnenberg
PALATINATE	Dürkheimer Feuerberg
	Forster Neuberg
	Kallstadt
	Herxheim
RHEINGAU	Assmannshauser Höllenberg
WÜRTTEMBERG	Brackenheim
	Schwaigern
BADEN	Oberrotweiler Kirchberg
	Affenthaler Klosterreberg
FRANCONIA	Klingenberg am Main

MITTELRHEIN
(MIDDLE RHINE)

After this short digression we return to the Middle Rhine, the district extending along the left bank of the Rhine from Bingerbrück to Rolandseck, and on the right bank from Kaub to Königswinter.

LORCH AND LORCHHAUSEN

These places immediately follow Assmannshausen and really belong to the Rheingau, but as the character of their wines has nothing in common with the products of the Rheingau, we need have no hesitation in including them in our survey of the Middle Rhine.

Lorch, with sites:

Bodental	Flur
Pfaffenwiese	Kapelle
Krone	Schlossberg

is actually the largest vine-growing community of the Rheingau.

There cannot be many river valleys in existence whose natural beauty rivals that of this stretch of the Rhine. This is where the beautiful Rhine really begins and anyone singing the praises of the Rhine is almost sure to be thinking of the Rhine valley from Bingen to Bonn. But unfortunately the same cannot be said of the wines of the Middle Rhine. The surface structure and the geological composition of the soil differ from that of the Rheingau. The vines grow on quartzite and Devonian slate and at best produce wines of medium quality. These are either drunk locally, or else they find their way into the sparkling wine factories, where they are welcome for their steely taste.

BACHARACH

On the left bank is Bacharach which, for our purpose is the main locality on the Middle Rhine. At one time there was a popular saying:

> "At Würzburg on Stein, and at Bach'rach on Rhine,
> You will find the best wine".

That alone would show that in earlier days the Bacharach wine was famous. But the town of Bacharach owes this reputation less to its good vineyards than to the circumstance that it was a reloading station for the big ships. Only little ships could pass through the so-called Binger Loch ("Bingen Hole"). And so it came about that the Bacharach stocks were the general repository for the Rhine wines from Rhinehessia, the Rheingau, and the Rhenish Palatinate—and these wines were then sent into the world as Bacharacher. CITY OR BACHARACH, sites are: Posten and Untere Wolfshöhl.

STEEG

Closely connected with Bacharach are Steeg and Oberdiebach. Their wines are among the best produced on the Middle Rhine. STEEG sites are St. Jost and Flur.

OBERDIEBACH

OBERDIEBACH sites are: Fürstenberg and Mittelberg.

KAUB

KAUB, on the right bank of the Rhine, comes next. The best sites are Blüchertal, Bachofen and Pfalzgrafstein.

BOPPARD

As a formidable stream, the Rhine races past Boppard, the city with a Royal Court of its own.

The waves are then broken on the Altenberg, where the river turns sharply to the east, forming (in the Boppard Hamm) its biggest bend north of Bingen.

Looking down from the Schützen we can survey "wine-soaked" Hamm, which, more than five kilometres long and sited due south all the way, is (next to the Rheingau) the best situated tract of wine country on the Middle Rhine.

Strong Riesling wines with a fine bouquet flourish here on the upper Koblenz levels.

KLOSTER EBERBACH in the Rheingau, whose wines are world-famous, used to possess more than 64,000 vines in the Boppard Hamm. The "Eberbacherhof"—the memory of which is kept alive by the picturesque "Ebertor" on the Rhine—attended to the cultivation of the vines, and pressed and matured the wines in its own cellars (which incidentally are still extant).

Before we pass on to the Mosel which we are now about to reach at Koblenz, it should be noted that the Middle Rhine wine-lands extend farther to the north: here they comprise, in particular, LINZ, with its sites: Auf der Rheinhölle and Im Langhaelschen; and KÖNIGSWINTER, with its sites: Bocksacker and Vitzenberg.

Just before the vintage at Urzig on the Mosel.

facing p. 288

Against the background of a carved cask, the tall Reisling bottle of the Palatinate with antique glasses, and in the foreground bunches of grapes showing the "Edelfäule" or "Noble Rot".

MOSEL

The collective designation "Mosel" includes, besides the wines of the Mosel proper, those of the Mosel tributaries, the Saar and the Ruwer.

The Rhine provides us with wines which may be described as mighty, massive, weighty, and full. His daughter, Mosella, supplements his gifts with wines which vary in character according to their place of origin. These wines have had a changing fate on foreign markets.

Unfortunately, particularly after the war, many natural wines (especially of the 1946 vintage) were shipped which ought to have remained in their country of origin, for a scarcity of sugar had prevented the growers from supplementing the lack of sugar of the grapes, and many lovers of Mosel got very suspicious of them. The vintages 1947, 1948 and especially 1949 made up for it, and these wines have now come back to fashion.

The Mosel valley from Trier to Koblenz is a very long and narrow strip of land—100 kilometres in length—but, when measured across from the vine-covered slopes on one side of the

L

valley to those on the other, the average width works out at no more than seven and a half kilometres. The whole area therefore comprises about 750 square kilometres.

But the Mosel, once it has joined up with the Saar, near Trier, winds in and out so much that the distance from Trier to Koblenz—100 kilometres as the crow flies—is just about doubled, giving that much more space for vine cultivation. To this must be added the vineyards of the Saar and the Ruwer. On the strip of land just described there are at least two hundred inhabited places—towns, hamlets, villages, parishes, castles, monasteries; 176 communities grow wine. The general direction of the river's flow is toward the north-east, but some of its windings are at such an acute angle that, in some places, the flow is actually in the opposite direction. Most of these windings are very short: in nearly all cases the river very soon turns back to continue its original course. The windings result in the formation of a number of peninsulas, which jut out from the mainland into the river: most of these tongues of land are broad-tipped, sometimes being very long.

If the Mosel from Trier to Koblenz had kept to a straight line in a north-easterly direction instead of indulging in all these fluctuations, it would have had a left bank facing south-east and thus continuously turned to the sun, while its right bank would have faced north-west and been just as consistently deprived of much sunshine. But owing to the multitude of curves, the banks of the river on both sides show the greatest possible variety in their relation to the sun, so that climatic conditions on the riverside and in the valley vary from point to point, often at very short intervals. Here you may have a little hillock whose slopes face due south, where the sun's rays, caught in rock crevices, are thrown back, their intensive warmth being of the greatest possible benefit to the vines. On such slopes vines are planted on all available space, and not a corner is left free. At one time these favoured hillocks may be on the right bank, while the next is found on the left. The best wines are derived from slopes such as these which face due south. There are other rocky promontories with slopes facing south-east and east, or south-west and west, which, in the course of a year's changes, are exposed to the sun's rays in all sorts of crannies and crevices. It is here that the medium grades of wines are obtained. And finally there are the slopes which, turned away from the south, get no sun at all. They are cold, and useless for vine-growing purposes.

Because of this curious structure, the inhabitants of the region usually have their villages and dwellings on one side of the river and their vineyards on the other. This has given rise to a complicated system of property ownership on both banks and also explains the very large number of bridges over the Mosel.

The slopes bordering the Mosel are much higher than those on the Rhine or, for that matter, on any other German river. Up and up go the steps, innumerable are the terraces, one above the other, and even the topmost levels are covered with vines. This means hard work for the wine-grower.

For one thing, the Mosel wine-grower has a task peculiar to this region. Throughout the whole winter he has to prise slabs of slate out of the rocks, chop them up small and distribute the pieces in the vineyards—right up to the top level. These slates not only give the Mosel wines their basic taste, but the slabs hewn from the rock have a certain vital energy which they communicate to the vines. They help to keep the soil moist and act as fertilising agents when they disintegrate. But of course their disintegration means that they have to be constantly replaced. Their usefulness does not end there. In the summer time—on hot days—the slate stores up the heat of the sun during the day, and when evening comes the warmth is radiated back on to the grapes, so that even by night the vines—through the action of the slate—indirectly get the benefit of the "sunshine" they need to complete the maturing process.

Another hard task for the Mosel wine-growers is the transportation of loads of fertiliser from the riverside to all the vineyards, including those at the top of the long slopes.

It seems likely that, within a reasonable time, these tasks will be alleviated. Plans have been mooted to build funicular railways modelled on the Swiss ski-lifts—some indeed have already been constructed, notably at Enkirch—which by connecting the valley with the mountain paths will make both the slate distribution and the transportation of fertiliser a much less strenuous task.

On the Mosel, they cultivate nothing but vines and market nothing but the wines they produce. They have hardly any cornfields. In so far as they have meadows or keep cattle, it is only in the interest of their viticulture.

Except on the Upper Mosel, the only kind of grape grown is the Riesling, even though this species has only been cultivated there since the sixteenth century. Its triumphant progress on the Mosel, to the final exclusion of all other species, is due on the one hand to the much appreciated taste which it imparts to its wines and its allegedly health-giving properties—it is jokingly known as "Riesling tea"—and on the other to the reliability of its yield.

On the whole the climate is favourable to grape-growing, with a good average temperature and good atmospheric conditions. Apart from evaporation from the river, the vines obtain moisture from a varying number of rainfalls, and warmth from the heat-absorbing action of the slate-stone.

In addition, in those vineyards where quality wines are produced, the vines are mostly kept close to the ground, in order that the grapes may ripen earlier and more evenly.

To ensure that the Riesling grapes reach full maturity, even in poor seasons, the grape harvest is delayed as long as possible—until October or even November. The grapes are not left on the vines—as in the Rheingau—until they reach *Edelfäule*, but only until they have reached full maturity and are then pressed immediately in order to preserve the effervescent and racy qualities of the wine and its golden-green colour.

292

The vine country falls naturally into three parts, based on the differences in soil and the resulting differences and peculiarities of the vines cultivated thereon:

The Lower Mosel
The Middle Mosel
The Upper Mosel

The region of the Middle Mosel produces a wine which has the lowest alcohol content of any German, or indeed any European wine: but, at the same time, it boasts the greatest wealth in "bouquet" substances and a pleasant refreshing acidity.

Mosel wines have always been considered an asset at any dinner-table, and today they are to be found on any and every wine-list.

LOWER MOSEL

On the Lower Mosel from Bullay to Koblenz we find that ferrous combinations in the crumbling yellow efflorescent soil (which in some parts forms a layer of rubble one and a half to two yards deep) have given it a reddish or a yellowish-brown tone. The soil dries out quickly and the layer of yellow, grey or bluish dark-grey rubble which covers it is very thin. Moreover, it has to be supported by numerous buttresses, being very liable to slip on the steep slopes. The wines produced in this district are of a poorer quality than those from the Middle Mosel.

The Silurian stratum is of hard slate with large fragments of rock. Its disintegration is slow, on account of its high content of silicic acid. The slopes are poorly nourished along here. Worthy of mention are only the following places:

WINNINGEN, with its sites: Hamm and Uhlen (of which Uhlen belongs partly to Kobern); POMMERN which is farther up the Mosel with the sites Kern and Kapellenberg; COND, COCHEM, and VALWIG with the sites Hahnenberg and Hüttenberg; and BREMM. Notable among the sites of the locality of Bremm is Calmont (part of which belongs to Eller). Calmont is the steepest vineyard site I have ever seen, and most laborious to cultivate. It is probably the steepest in the world.

MIDDLE MOSEL

Here we find wines that are aristocratic and spicy and have an exquisite bouquet.

Best known among Mosel wines is the Bernkasteler Doktor which became world-famous after it had been warmly recommended by King Edward VII's personal physician. The vineyard site is not very large and is moreover cut up into three estates (owned respectively by Dr. Thanisch and Messrs. Deinhard and Lauerburg). In a good year the site will produce no more than from 1,500 to 2,000 dozen bottles, so that it is easy to understand why very high fancy prices—one might almost call them monopoly prices—are paid for them. Sold on the value of the wine alone—despite the fact that the Bernkasteler Doktor has by far the greatest "name"—the wines from the Wehlener Sonnenuhr have often attained prices higher than those achieved by the famous Doktor. Inside Germany the Wehlener Sonnenuhr is accounted easily the best of all Mosel wines. Fifty to seventy years ago it was the Brauneberger Brauneberg. So even vineyards have their changes of fortune! Incidentally, Lauerburg's Bernkasteler Doktor vineyards are still planted with old European stock and well cared for by its enthusiastic owner. As a matter of interest, another Doktor vineyard exists, at Dexheim, near Nierstein (Rhinehessia).

All the wine communities of this region are worthy of mention, but we must content ourselves here with naming the best among so many that are good, namely:

On the right bank of the river

ZELL	BERNKASTEL
ENKIRCH	MÜLHEIM
TRARBACH	BRAUNEBERG
ERDEN	NEUMAGEN
ZELTINGEN	DHRON (Inland, belongs to Neumagen)
GRAACH	LEIWEN

On the left bank of the river

TRABEN	KUES
KRÖV	LIESER
ÜRZIG	PIESPORT
WEHLEN	TRITTENHEIM

The large-scale wine-growers on the Middle Mosel have combined to form two Associations—the Large Ring and the Small Ring—the Bernkasteler Ring. The largest owners are the State and the Church—a remnant of the days of feudal and ecclesiastical power. They are the State Domain and the Bischoefliches Seminar (Episcopal Seminary), the Hohe Domkirche (Cathedral), the Priester Seminar (Priests' Seminary), Vereinigte Hospitien—all situated in Trier, but owning land in many communities. Then there are a large number of lay enterprises, among which may be mentioned the wine estates of Lauerburg and Dr. Thanisch in Bernkastel; of Zacharias Bergweiler-Prüm, successors to Johann Josef Prüm, Peter Prüm, and S.A. Prüm in Wehlen.

The Hunsrück mountains crowd so far into the valleys along the curving stretches of the River Mosel that little space is left for habitation and cultivation. Whenever a community grew up there, it could only manage to straggle along two or three parallel roads.

This applies, for instance, to the little town of Zell in Hamm (as that curve of the Mosel has been called from time immemorial).

Zell Zell was a Roman settlement. This has been proved by various objects dug from its soil and now housed in museums at Bonn and Wiesbaden, and is also attested by a Roman sarcophagus erected in the upper part of Zell itself—the part known as Brandenburg. The sites are:

Zeller Schwarze Katz	Domherrnberg
Burglay	Klapertchen
Nussberg	

Although Zell wines have never been in the top class, *Zeller Schwarze Katz* is to be found on all German wine lists. Everyone knows the label showing a black cat on a barrel. There is not so much produced in the whole of Zell as is sold under the "Black Cat" label. The name (Schwarze Katz—Black Cat) is nowadays nothing more than a generic title, and, in my opinion, a name under which often a better species of wine is sold than that which originally gave it its designation. It would be unfair if I did not mention that high awards have been presented to two growers of Zeller Schwarze Katz and that the Zell Council has taken steps to stop the misuse of this much-loved site name.

The next village is REIL, with its sites:

Stein	Weingrube
Falklay	Sorrentberg

It produces steely, robust wines.

Enkirch The name is derived from the Latin *ancora* (possibly connected with the Greek *agkura* and means "anchor"). People began to settle here—below the fastest rapids—as it was the landing-place for Mosel boatmen who were being towed up the river; it was here that they would make their preparations for overcoming the rapids. Enkirch has the largest cultivated vineyard acreage (165 hectares) of any single locality, and in good years produces 1,200 to 1,500 *Fuder*. The only estates which exceed this quantity are those belonging to more than one community with such double names as: Bernkastel-Kues, Traben-Trarbach, or Zeltingen-Rachtig.

The most famous of its sites is the Enkircher Steffensberg, with its subsidiary sites: then comes the

Herrenberg (with its subsidiaries)
Edelberg

Kröv This ancient wine village, situated at the foot of a wide range of vineyard-covered slopes, close to the motor highway through the Middle Mosel, has a colourful past. Here we find ancient timbered buildings, picturesque courtyards and quaint corners, besides a really beautiful baroque church. The sites are named:

Steffensberg   Bockskopf
Paradies   Nacktarsch

The last name has indelicate implications, but—as must be regretfully recorded—that fact has apparently added to its popularity. It is to be found on every wine list in Germany.

ÜRZIG This village lies on a bend of the Mosel river. It is open to the south and, on its other three sides, is cut off and completely sheltered by mountain ridges. On this spot, clay and coloured sandstone from the Eifel breaking through the slate strata, give the rocks a peculiar red colour and the local wine a characteristic flavour.

Ürzig is one of the earliest documented wine-producing communities on the Mosel. In the year 690 the daughter of King Dagobert of the Franks owned a wine estate there. The name—*Ursiacum*—is of Celtic-Latin origin. Its best sites are:

Kranklay   Würzgarten
Urlay   Urglück
Michelslay   Goldwingert

They are situated around a picturesque group of rocks, crowned by a mountain-top, which is one of the most beautiful spots on the Mosel. This is attested by one Von Stramberg who, in 1837, wrote a description of the Mosel. He called Ürzig "one of the classic places of Germany" on account of its particularly charming situation and the good quality and unique character of its wines. These wines have a bouquet and spiciness which I find astonishing in view of the fact that they are lighter than those of neighbouring communities.

ERDEN Next to and below the Ürzig vineyards we find the famous Erden plantations; most of these, however, are owned by inhabitants of Ürzig. The sites here are:

Treppchen	Busslay
Herrenberg	Hötlay

The Erden sites are very sunny, the wines full and spicy, with a pleasant, slightly earthy taste.

And this brings us to the Mosel bend *par excellence*, on which are situated the best known of all Mosel wine-growing localities.

ZELTINGEN First and foremost is Zeltingen, with its modern bridge joining the Eifel and the Hunsrück. Here, beginning far below the place itself, is a veritable parade of vines, stretching farther than the eye can see, beyond Zeltingen up the river, merging with those of neighbouring communities until they reach Bernkastel, and forming the largest unbroken vineyard area in all Germany. To Zeltingen itself belongs the biggest stretch; in a good year its produce amounts to over 2,000 *Fuder* of wine. The long viticultural tradition of the place and its good slaty soil have given Zeltingen wines their reputation, and maintained it. Usually they are the cheapest on the wine list, placed among the smaller, lighter wines of the Middle Mosel, and, consequently, many drinkers of Mosel look on Zeltingen products as nothing more than cheap table wines. They are quite wrong, however, because Zeltingen wines are produced in a wide range

298

of qualities, from the simplest to the very best; from the light and volatile to the full and heavy with plenty of body and vigour—wines in fact for everyday use, but also wines to be brought forth as special delicacies on festive occasions.

One of the most intriguing factors in the nomenclature of German wines is the naming of German vineyards, of which there are no less than ten thousand!

In view of this enormous number of vineyards it is a good policy that various authorities are trying to simplify matters. The latest decision was made by the Council of Zeltingen (Mosel) and its sister town Rachtig. This latter is a Riesling wine-producing village of just over 200 hectares, yet the growers market their wines under no less than nineteen different vineyard names. By the decision of the Council, the Zeltingen and Rachtig vineyard names are reduced to four, namely:

KIRCHPFAD. Simple, wholesome wines, not exciting, but thoroughly dependable. Good foundation, harmonious.

HIMMELREICH. This lies above the village in the best position. The soil is ideal—pure slate—exactly what the vines need. It produces finest wines of great elegance and with a rich spicy bouquet.

SCHLOSSBERG. High-class wines, heavy and yet aristocratic.

DEUTSCHERRENBERG. We have now reached the élite among Mosel wines.

WEHLEN

Wehlen is situated on the left bank of the Mosel in a grove of fruit-trees. It is over a thousand years since the inhabitants of this little community first started to plant vines. The Wehlen wine rejoices in a splendid maturity and a spicy bouquet, due in part to intensive cultivation for quality, but particularly to the nutritive durable soil and the favourable sunny aspect of the sites. The sites are:

299

Sonnenuhr   Rosenberg
Nonnenberg   Klosterberg
Lay   Klosterlay

The best of these sites (and, in my opinion, the best site on the Mosel) is the Wehlener Sonnenuhr, but the other sites also produce spicy "quality" wines of great value. The Sonnenuhr is a large vineyard and owned by many proprietors. There are great differences in the quality on account of the different situation of the part vineyard (vineyards lying in the centre of the hill produce the best wines.)

Traben-Trarbach

These are little twin towns on the right and left banks of the Mosel. At the foot of the Grafenburg on the sites Schlossberg, Halsberg and Hühnerberg, good wines are produced. These Trarbach wines are firm, steely, and have an agreeable bouquet. The Traben wines produced on the sites, Steinbacher, Bergpächter, Rickelberg, Backhaus, Würzgarten, Geiersberg, mature too early and do not keep well.

GRAACH

This produces weighty, full, heavy wines that keep well but are coarser than those of the surrounding communities. Sites are: Münzlay, Lilienpfad, Stablay, Goldwingert, Kirchlay, Abtsberg, Bistum, and, above all, Domprobst and Himmelreich.

The estate known as Josephshof lies between Graach and Wehlen in the heart of the Middle Mosel. It belongs to the Reichsgraf von Kesselstatt.

BERNKASTEL-KUES

The viticultural area of the town includes that part of it known as Kues, on the left bank of the river. It is among the most valuable vineyard districts on the Mosel and produces wines of superb quality. Sites (on the Bernkastel side) are:

Doktor   Amorpfad

Olk	Johannisbrünnchen
Lay	Schlossberg
Rosenberg	Held
Schwanen	Teurenkauf
Pfalzgraben	Matheisbildchen
Badstube	

The name of the site "Bernkasteler Doktor" is attributed to a legend. Archbishop Bömund II, Elector of Trier 1351–62 (so runs the tale), lord of large tracts of vinelands on the Mosel and the Rhine, and owner of a castle situated on the windy heights above Bernkastel, was addicted to spending much of his time in this favoured spot. One day he fell ill there. He was grievously sick and his doctors plied him with medicines in vain. As he lay on what was thought to be his deathbed, a flask of wine was brought to him from one of the best sites in the neighbourhood. He drank, and a miracle was wrought. The dying prelate recovered and in gratitude bestowed on the wine—and the site— the appellation "Bernkasteler Doktor".

> Ye who are sick and sorrowful
> Arouse yourselves and take a pull
> of Wine—the finest "Doctor".
> It's better than the best of pills,
> For "Doctor" Wine can cure all ills—
> A great and kindly doctor!
> For cheering draughts so justly famed,
> its native hill is proudly named
> (just like the wine) "The Doctor".

There is so little Bernkasteler Doktor produced and the demand is so big that two of the three growers to whom the Doktor vineyard belongs gather the grapes with adjoining vineyards and market it as BERNKASTELER DOKTOR UND GRABEN and BERN- KASTELER DOKTOR UND BRATENHÖFCHEN, and the third grower has the same procedure for a part of his crop. The result is BERNKASTELER DOKTOR UND BADSTUBE.

None of the wines of German vineyards is so overrated as the

Doktor. In blindfold tastings, wines of adjoining vineyards costing only half the price are of equal quality.

Bernkastel wines often show the same peculiarity as those from Bingen, that is, a smoky flavour.

On the KUES side the sites are: Weissenstein, Herrenberg, Rosenberg and Königstuhl.

Lieser This very small village with a population of 1,500 lies on the River Mosel at the mouth of the little stream known as Lieserbach. Sites are:

Lieserer Niederberg, with its subdivisions:

Held	Die Pichtern
Hutlay	Bärlay
Süssenberg	Mariengrube

Lieserer Schlossberg with its subdivisions:

Rosenberg   Lay
Lieserer Paulsberg and Kirchberg

Lieser wines are justly famed for their wholesome qualities, their excellent flavour and the stimulating "prickle".

BRAUNEBERG Brauneberg owes its fame to the very high quality of its wines on the sites:

Hasenläufer	Juffer
Falkenberg	Bürgerslay

Until 1925 the place was called Dusemond, the name being a popular distortion of the Latin *dulcis mons* (sweet mountain). The Romans who planted vines on the Mosel bestowed this name on the place because of the excellence of the Brauneberg wines. In the year 1806, when Mosel vineyard sites were divided into classes according to the quality of their products, Brauneberg was the only name in the first class. The list can still be seen in the Landrat's office at Bernkastel.

Brauneberg wines frequently have a strong but pleasing earthy taste which gives them a fullness commended by many consumers, particularly by those partial to the combination of the specific Mosel bouquet with a heavy wine.

PIESPORT   This village nestles among steep vineyard slopes, in a graceful bend of the Mosel. Its sites are:

Grafenberg	Treppchen
Falkenberg	Pichter
Hubertuslay	Taubengarten
Lay'chen	Hohlweid
Weer	Günterslay
Goldtröpfchen	

Of these sites, the following belong in part to another community and are therefore used as collective site designations: Piesporter Grafenberg, Taubengarten, Günterslay. Piesport wines are liable to have a slight tarry flavour which gives them an agreeable fullness.

Neumagen   This is the oldest wine-growing locality in Germany, the place in which the oldest evidence of German viticulture was discovered, including "The Wine Ship", which is more famous than any other. The Roman poet Ausonius sang the praises of this spot—under the name *Nociomagus*—in a long poem entitled "Mosella". Its best-known and best sites are:

Engelgrube	Laudamusberg
Rosengärtchen	

303

All other sites are combined under the heading of Katerloch.

The peculiarities of the Neumagen wines are a flavour of bitter almonds and often a suggestion of the taste of blackcurrant.

Dhron

Dhron lies on the Mosel at the mouth of the pretty little stream called Dhronbach. The Roman poet Venantius Fortunatus extolled the place in verse. Sites are:

> Dhroner Hofberg (Dhronhofberger). This takes its name from the court (at the foot of the hill) which was formerly part of the property of the Tholey Monastery (Saar). Its wines are aristocratic, have a noble bouquet and unusual spiciness.
> Dhroner Rosenburg
> Dhroner Sängerei
> Dhroner Roterd—which derives its name (meaning "red earth") from a vein of reddish sand which here traverses the slaty soil.

Stramberg says of Dhron wines that they have "the most agreeable bouquet". Generic name: Dhroner Eselsmilch (Ass's milk).

Niederemmel

Roman remains have also been found at Niederemmel, the starting-point of the famous Roman road to Bingen. Its vineyards are all on the left bank of the Mosel and all its sites are Piesporter. Within the Niederemmel precincts lie the famous Piesport sites of:

Taubengarten	Güntherslay
Hohlweid	Lay

Hohlweid includes the district of Aurenkomp, a name derived from the Latin and meaning "gold beaker" or "gold mine".

Trittenheim

Next comes Trittenheim with its rather light but firm wines. Sites:

Laurentiusberg   Falkenberg
Neuberg   Altärchen

LEIWEN with sites:

Steinmaurchen   Klostergarten

has wines more rounded than those of Trittenheim; and
LONGUICH (the long village) with its sites:

Probstberg   Herrenberg
Hirschberg

produces amiable, delicate wines of medium quality.

Here the State Domain AVELSBACH deserves mention. It is
situated in a little valley where dry Riesling wines are produced,
wines with some special earthy flavour but wines which with
some bottle age are very enjoyable partners to hors d'oeuvre.

And herewith we take our leave of the Middle Mosel to which
we shall return later for the purpose of visiting its two tributary
valleys, those of the Saar and the Ruwer.

UPPER MOSEL

The vines of the Upper Mosel, like those of Champagne, are
rooted in shell-limestone. The wines they produce are "small"
wines, mostly sour and, on account of their meagre alcohol
content, not suited for consumption in their pure form. As a
rule they find their way into cheap blends or manufacture of
Sparkling Mosel.

The frontier delimitation of the autonomous Saar district has
cut off the communities of Weis-Nenning, Besch, and Perl from
the Upper Mosel wine-growing region. The territory of the

"Saar" does not include a single vineyard devoted to the cultivation of Saar wines, so that the three communities of the Upper Mosel represent the modest viticultural efforts of the whole of the Saar territory ("Mosel Viticulture in the Saar").

In the "Three-Country-Corner" (Germany, Luxembourg, France) the vineyards sustained heavy losses during the war. But the general economic situation, in particular the wine market in the Saar, has encouraged the growers to devote themselves with greater intensity to cultivating their plantations. The destroyed vineyards have been restored, while those that escaped damage are being tended devoutly. In its climate, the region of the Upper Mosel is extremely favourable, so it is reasonable to expect that the efforts of the growers will meet with success. They plant the Sylvaner, Ruländer and Auxerrois grapes, and all these wines enjoy popularity on the Upper Mosel for though they do not yield such large quantities as the Elbling, they are qualitatively far better. In the Saar itself the newly acquired territory on the Upper Mosel is known as the Riviera of the Saar, because many foreign tourists make for this part of the country, and the demand for Mosel wines plays a part in their choice.

SAAR

The younger Saar wines in comparison with others may be designated as the tomboy of this wine family, being steely, elegant, and volatile with a delicate bouquet; while the youngest scion of the Mosel—the product of the Ruwer—is racy, steely and fragrant.

The vine-plantation area comprises 1,000 hectares and stretches from Saarburg to Konz. In the lower reaches of the Saar the soil is slaty, while above Saarburg it consists of shell-limestone. The grape species commonly planted here is the Riesling. Owing to the comparatively high situation of the vineyards (over 600 feet) and the harsh winds coming from Lorraine and Hunsrück, the average wine produced in this region is of no more than medium quality, but in a good year Saar wines are nevertheless in fairly great demand on account of their distinctive bouquet and flavour, their superior breed and elegance. The 1949 vintage attained an unprecedented maturity, and wines were the best ever made there. But May frosts destroyed two-thirds of the crop, so that only a small quantity of this desirable wine was produced.

The best Saar wines ever made are the 1959s—such harmony,

finesse and elegance has never before been witnessed—and many of the 1964 Saar wines reached the same quality; their bouquet may prove better than that of the 1959s.

SERRIG AND OCKFEN These villages own good sites and produce wines that are much sought after, such as the OCKFENER BOCKSTEIN.

AYL This is a small village on the left bank of the Saar with a stretch of vineyards still mostly ecclesiastical property with sites:

Kupp   Neuberg

WILTINGEN This is the largest wine-growing locality in the Saar, with its sites:

Scharzhofberg   Rosenberg
Scharzberg   Kupp

Wawern A small village below Kanzem on the left bank of the Saar, with its site:
Wawerner Ritterpfad

KANZEM An important village on the left bank but its vineyards are on the slope of a hill facing south on the other side of the river. Its sites are:

Altenberg   Kelter and Wolfsberg
Hörecker   Sonnenberg

Oberemmel In a side-valley of the Saar near Wiltingen lies Oberemmel which produces good wines. Its sites are:

Agritiusberg   Huette
Rauler   Junkerberg

RUWER

On the narrow slopes of the slate-strewn valley of the Ruwer the Riesling grape seldom reaches full ripeness. The accusation usually levied against Ruwer products is perfectly justified and they are in consequence less popular than Mosel wines. But in good years like 1921, 1934, 1949, 1953 and 1959 they rank with the finest. These vintages have a volatile elegant bouquet reminiscent of blackcurrants combined with a touch of "earthiness".

The ordinary 1959 Ruwer wines are the perfection of a fine table wine, light, elegant, dry, whereas the Spätlese and Auslese wines were, on account of their unbalanced richness, most disappointing. The Ruwer produced in 1964 the best of all German wines.

KASEL   This is the largest of the wine-producing villages of the Ruwer and its vineyards produce some very fine wines. Its sites are:

Nieschen   Hitzlay
Taubenberg

EITELSBACH

On the right bank of the Ruwer is Eitelsbach which produces the world-famous Karthäuserhofberg (Carthusian Castle Hill). The Karthaus Hof was originally a Dominican property, but was owned by the Carthusians from the fourteenth century until 1802 when Napoleon gave it to the Rautenstrauch family who have owned it ever since.

Other wine localities in the Ruwer are: MERTESDORF, WALDRACH, MORSCHEID, and MAXIMIN-GRÜNHAUSER HERRENBERG.

VITICULTURE IN SOUTH GERMANY

When discussing with Director Goedecke (in the Domain of Niederhausen) some questions of viticulture on the Nahe, I expressed my amazement at its extraordinary development in the course of the past twenty years. He replied that I should be still more amazed if I were to study viticultural developments in Southern Germany, particularly in Württemberg.

A glance at the viticultural map will show that South German vineyards cover a considerable area. But, it must be noted that the local consumption is high and that there is an immense tourist traffic from other parts of Germany and from abroad. These visitors consume most of the local wines served in the hotels and restaurants of the southern wine area.

The region, like Alsace, produces a great many different kinds of wine, some of which bear names other than those used for similar Alsatian products. In South Germany we find the Elb-ling white wines (sometimes known as Rauschling): Gutedel; Ruländer; Sylvaner; Müller-Thurgau; Traminer (sometimes called Clevner); Muscatel; White Burgundy, and Riesling. Also the red wines: Trollinger, Schwarzriesling (Müller-Rebe), Limburger and Spät (late) Burgundy. All these wines have qualities characteristic of the district.

A few words about the region itself and its individual products: Politically speaking, the region comprises Bavaria, Baden, Württemberg and Hessia. But the law groups the wines from these parts rather differently, as follows:

310

The designation WÜRTTEMBERG is used to denote wines originating in Württemberg wine-growing communities with the exception of those produced near Lake Constance.

The designation LAKE CONSTANCE (*Bodensee*) for wines from those parts of Baden, Württemberg, and Bavaria that are adjacent to the Lake.

The designation BERGSTRASSE: (*a*) for wines from those parts of Baden situated on or near the Bergstrasse from Wiesloch to Weinheim; and (*b*) for wines from the wine-growing communities of the Hessian Province of Starkenburg.

BADEN is used to denote wines from Baden's wine-growing communities except those around Lake Constance and those in the neighbourhood of the Bergstrasse.

There are only a very few large wine estates in Württemberg—most plantations are on a small scale and have been owned by the same families for generations. The centre of Württemberg's viticulture is Stuttgart, which is also the seat of the Winegrowers' Central Organisation. Small wonder! The City of Stuttgart is a child of the Neckar, and it is in the valley and side-valleys of this river—and beyond them in the valleys of the Rems, Enz, Kocher and Jagst—that most of the Württemberg wine is grown.

In the *Rems* valley the most important villages are:

Beutelsbach	Schnait
Endersbach	Stetten
Grossheppach	Strümpfelbach

In the *Enz* valley:

Horrheim	Rosswag

In the *Kocher* valley:

Künzelsau	Niederhall
Belsenberg	Weissbach
Bad Ingelfingen	Forchtenberg
Criesbach	Ernsbach

In the *Jagst* valley:

Ailringen	Klepsau
Eberstal	Krautheim
Dörzbach	Bieringen

The following are important wine centres:

UNTERTÜRKHEIM	NECKARULM
FELLBACH	REUTLINGEN
HEILBRONN	EBERSTADT
WEINSBERG	GRIMSBACH
WALHEIM	

Last, but not least, Stuttgart's own vineyards must be mentioned, the "Zuckerte" in Stuttgart-Cannstatt, and Lemberg and Hohe Warte in Stuttgart-Feuerbach.

In the years from 1865 to 1870 Baden, with its 22,000 hectares of vineyards, was the largest vine-growing district of Germany. The present total for Baden (Old Baden) may be assessed at 8,000 hectares.

The best-known wine-producing district is LAKE CONSTANCE (*Bodensee*) with its sites Meersburg and Hagnau. The best-known wines from Lake Constance are the so-called Weissherbste which are white wines slightly tinged with red.

An extensive unbroken viticultural area reaches from the south side of Basle to Freiburg. It is called the MARKGRAFSCHAFT. The most important communities and sites are:

HALTINGER Stiege
OTLINGER Pflanzer, Weingarten and Fischeninger

EFRINGE-Kirchener Weingarten
SCHLIENGENER Sonnenstück
AUGGENER Letten
LAUFENER Altenberg
SCHALLSTADTER Batzenberg
KIRCHHOFENER Kirchberg
EHRENSTETTENER Ölberg
EBRINGENER Sommerberg

On the massif of the Kaiserstuhl, a kind of island of volcanic origin to the west of Freiburg Bay, we find the Baden speciality known as the Ruländer (grey Burgundy) grape. Its wines are heavy, rich in alcohol, and of medium acidity. The most important communities are:

ACHKARREN	IHRINGEN
BAHLINGEN	KÖNIGSCHAFFHAUSEN
BICKENSOHL	OBERBERGEN
BISCHOFFINGEN	OBERROTWEIL
BÜRKHEIM	WASENWEILER
EICHSTETTEN	

In the Middle Baden viticultural area—that is the region around OFFENBERG known as ORTENAU—mainly high-grade wines are produced. Riesling is cultivated here, but known under the name of *Klingelberger*, so are Traminer (Clevner) and Ruländer. The most important communities here are:

DURBACH	WALDULM
FESSENBACH	ZELL-WEIERBACH
ORTENBERG	

In the neighbourhood of BÜHL—well known for its rich stone-fruit harvest—we find extensive Riesling plantations. It is here that the wines called Mauerweine are bottled in "Bocksbeutel" (for "Bocksbeutel" *cf. sub* Franconian wines, p.317). Most important communities and sites:

KAPPELRODECKER Dasenstein
WALDULMER Russhalte

BÜHLERTALER
NEUWEIERER Altenberg
VARNHALTER Klosterberg
VARNHALTER Klingelberg

not to forget AFFENTHAL, with its special "Affenflasche" (mon-
key-bottle).

In the midst of this South German wine-country stands HEIDEL-
BERG with its castle. Inside the castle, in the Königssaal (King's
Hall), is the famous "Great Cask" capable of holding 220,000
litres (300,000 bottles). It was only filled three times and has
long ago become leaky.

From Heidelberg we turn to the Bergstrasse, which is partly
Rhinehessian and partly Baden territory.

The wines of:
| ZWINGENBERG | BENSHEIM |
| AUERBACH | HEPPENHEIM |

are comparable to the lesser Rhinehessian wines. The best comes
from Heppenheimer Steinkopf generally known as *Steinkopfer*.

FRANKEN
(FRANCONIA)

The study of Franconian wines takes us eastward along the Main towards Aschaffenburg. I have found that the proper occasions for drinking these so-called Stein wines are those where the textbooks suggest Chablis. Stein wines are finer and stronger, firm and nutty. It is always said that a Chablis can only be properly understood and enjoyed when drunk on its ground, but that does not apply to Stein wines. The latter travel well and deserve to be more widely known.

The Sylvaner vine, which is more intensively cultivated in Franconia than any other, produces wines with qualities varying according to the site. They may have an exquisite bouquet, or a juicy freshness, or again they may be racy and invigorating, or pleasantly full-bodied.

Many wine historians have pointed out that Franconia produces a large number of rare wines. There are very considerable differences between, for instance, the great first-grade products of WÜRZBURG, STEIN and LEISTEN.

And as to the other Franconian wines, there are:

the fine, racy STEIGERWÄLDER;
the rich, succulent ESCHENDORFER;
the elegant wines from the neighbourhood of KITZINGEN;
the delicate SAALE products;
the aromatic KALLMUTH;
the pungent wine from the TAUBER and LOWER MAIN;
the spirituous HÖRSTEINER;

and many others with varying characteristics. And, of course, each year the vintages differ, even from the same localities.

Franconian wines are traditionally bottled in a peculiarly shaped flat-sided flask, known as a *Bocksbeutel*, the origin of which is obscure. Possibly a glass-blower may once have turned out a strange shape, either accidentally or intentionally, or maybe the Low German "Bockesbeutel" (a bag in which prayer books or other volumes were transported) had something to do with the original invention, and its name. It must be remembered too that there is a grape called "Bocksbeutel", possibly a reference to its shape.

The Bocksbeutel is almost exclusively reserved for Franconian wines, but is also used for certain high-grade Baden wines—the so-called "Mauer wines". It is an old custom that these too should be sold in Bocksbeutel. By special agreement between the Bavarian Wine Trade Association of Franconia and the four Wine Growers' Co-operatives of NEUWEIER, STEINBACH, UMWEG and VARNHALT these communities are allowed to bottle and sell 30 per cent of their crop in average years and 50 per cent in excellent years in Bocksbeutel. They have combined to fight any other "users" of Bocksbeutels in Germany.

WÜRZBURG This is the home *par excellence* of Franconian wines, and Würzburg's site STEIN has given to Franconian wines the name by which they are known in other countries—Stein wines. Under the German Wine Law, the name "Stein Wine" is reserved for wines from the Würzburg sites "Stein and Steinacker" and may not be used for Franconian wines as a whole. Any wine bottled

317

in a Bocksbeutel with nothing on the label but the word "Stein" (or "Stein Wine") is assumed to be a Würzburg Stein and must conform to this expectation.

Except for Rüdesheim on the Rhine, no German vineyards suffered quite so much from bomb damage as those in Würzburg.

The State wine estate in Lower Franconia originated in the vineyards owned by the former Prince-Bishop in Würzburg. Apart from the vines grown on their own estate, these princes had enormous quantities of wine in their cellars which had been collected as tithes from the wine-growing population. When the rule of the Prince-Bishops came to an end, their large wine estate was made over to the Duchy of Würzburg, and in 1816 it was transferred to the Bavarian Crown as State property. With it went the one-time princely, later State Court cellars (Hofkellerei) in Würzburg, which from time immemorial had been linked to the estate. At present the State vineyards cover about eighty hectares, divided between the estates of Stein, Leisten, Randersacker and Hörstein. A great variety of vines are grown on the State winelands: the Riesling, the Sylvaner, Müller-Thurgau, Scheurebe, Rieslaner (Mainriesling), Spätburgunder.

CLASSIFICATION AND VINTAGES
OF
GERMAN WINES

CLASSIFICATION

Now that we have come to the end of our journey through the wine country of Western Germany—the Rhineland—let me say a few words about the classification and the vintages of wines.

In France, the *Chambre Syndicale des Courtiers* in Bordeaux have classified the wines of Bordeaux in order of merit—the red wines in five growths, the white wines in two. Nothing of the kind is possible respecting German wines. Bordeaux Château-bottled wines are all a product of one *cuvée*, but there is some analogy with Burgundy where many vineyards are divided between a number of proprietors, each of whom makes a different wine.

In a book called *A History and Description of Modern Wines* (London, 1851) I have found a classification which is worth reading. No such classification and no similar one can, however, be of any real use.

In Germany the situation is quite different. German growers, large and small, stock their wines in individual casks as they come from the press. On the Mosel they usually use *Fuders* (960 litres) and half-*fuders*; *Stücks* (1,200 litres), half-*stücks* and quarter-*stücks* are customary in Rhinehessia and the Rheingau; while in the Palatinate they use *fuders* of 1,000 litres capacity. The wines mature in the casks and keep their individuality at least as long as they remain in the wine-growers' cellars. For this reason, wines from the same growers differ greatly in quality. The differences are due to various circumstances—the grapes may have been gathered in the early or the late harvest period; they may have been gathered with particular care, for instance by the selection of special bunches of the fruit, or even of specially ripe or over-ripe single berries, etc.

MOSEL-SAAR-RUWER
1966ᵉʳ
Josephshöfer Auslese
Riesling
Fuder Nr. 6811 — Original Abfüllung
Produce of Germany
WACHSTUM: REICHSGRAF VON KESSELSTATT, TRIER

The *Lagen* are divided into a great many smallholdings of various sizes. Only a few *Lagen* are in the hands of one owner, the best examples of these being: Schloss Johannisberg (Fürst von Metternich), Schloss Vollrads (Graf Matuschka-Greiffen-clau), Josefshof (Reichsgraf v. Kesselstadt), Steinberg (State Domain). These subdivisions afford another reason for the differences in wines from the same *Lage*. One owner may tend his vineyard more carefully than the other, may manure it at shorter intervals, and this makes for great differences in taste—quite apart from the different dates and selective methods of gathering the fruit already mentioned.

Some growers have for these reasons adopted a method of classifying their own wines by furnishing them with different labels, caps or seals, and some use the word "Cabinet" (or Kabinett) to designate wines which fetch a certain price (laid down by the individual growers).

As a matter of fact the recent change-over to fermentation and storage in large vessels may bring about a change in this classification. Schloss Johannisberg has in any case made a start with this method by using tanks of 5,000 litres each for the 1950 vintage. The State Domain in the Rheingau has, at present, nine tanks of 8,500 litres each and one tank of 21,000 litres; the balance of the crop is still kept in casks of 600 litres.

The growers themselves are well aware how misleading it is for the consumer when two wines of the same name vary so greatly in all their characteristics, as I have shown above. The consumer should always protect himself when re-ordering by insisting on a supply from the same cask.

It has been suggested in some quarters that German growers should accept the French method. It would certainly deprive us of the Auslese, the Beeren- and Trockenbeerenauslese wines, but it would increase the average overall quality to a high degree. Those who are of this opinion hint specially at the Steinberger wines. If you taste the whole range, you will find that the "Steinberger" is no more than a *vin ordinaire*—not worth drinking—because all that is best in the vineyard has gone into the Auslese, the Beerenauselese, and the Trockenbeerenauslese, and the latter is considered the best wine of the Rheingau. They argue what a grand wine the "Steinberger" would be if all the vineyard products were to be used for one *cuvée*, and it would help to bring an exquisite wine within range of thousands instead of the few who can afford to buy the extract, the Trockenbeerenauslese. And what is true of the Steinberger applies of course to all vineyards.

It is true that the price differences are sometimes colossal. At the auctions in January 1951, for example, the best cask of 1949 Steinberger (the ordinary Steinberger) cost 50 per cent more than the cheapest. When bottled they look exactly alike, therefore, the argument goes on, the unfortunate consumer, having had and enjoyed one consignment of bottles from the best cask, may get his next consignment from the cheapest, and is due for a sad disappointment. Is it false pride on the part of the German grower when he boasts of the high price his best cask has attained if, at the same time, his other wines are the poorer for it? Whoever has tasted the Auslese, Beerenauslese and Trockenbeerenauslese wines cannot and will not agree with these arguments. These wines are the nectar of the gods, wines to be sipped on a festive occasion, and represent the finest nature can produce.

It is of course true that this method reduces the average quality, as was only too clear when too many Beerenauslesen were made in 1959 in the Steinberg vineyard, reducing the quality of even the 1959 Spätlese and Auslese wines of this vineyard to below standard.

It would be a loss should we ever be deprived of these enjoyments, and it is not likely that the growers will listen to such arguments. They may reduce the ordinary wines to one or two *cuvées*, but will never give up their endeavour to produce the best. The competitions arranged by government bodies and Viticultural Associations will contribute to increase the growers' ambition still more.

Some growers have made a start with equalisation of their wines, but have not gone the whole way, namely, Schloss Johannisberg produces three different *cuvées* blending—in *cuvée* one the ordinary Schloss Johannisberg, in *cuvée* two the Spätlese, and *cuvée* three the Auslese wines. The better wines—the Beerenauslese and Trockenbeerenauslese—are individually treated and sold.

As a matter of fact, part of these *cuvées* are sold with the designation "Cabinet" and the same quality may appear with different make-up—it depends how the wines are marketed. The Estate Bottling are generally sold through all wholesale houses, and the Cabinet wines through appointed agents—there is even an agent for Germany! A classification table reads as follows:

SCHLOSS JOHANNISBERGER

Estate Bottling

Red Seal
Green Seal (Spätlese)
Pink Seal (Auslese)
Pink Seal (Beerenauslese)
Pink Seal (Trocken-
    beerenauslese)

Cabinet Bottling

Orange Seal
White Seal (Spätlese)
Blue Seal (Auslese)
Gold Seal (Beerenauslese)
Gold Seal (Trocken-
    beerenauslese)

SCHLOSS VOLLRADS

Schloss Vollrads: green, green-silver
Schlossabzug: red, red-silver, red-gold
Kabinett: dark blue, blue, blue-silver, blue-gold
Auslese: pink, pink-gold, pink-white
Beerenauslese: white
Trockenbeerenauslese: white-gold

HESSIAN STATE DOMAIN ELTVILLE

Black
Black-Silver
Black-Gold

FREIHERR VON SIMMERN

Yellow with black stripes—sweetened wines
Red with black-yellow-black stripes
White with red-yellow-red stripes
Blue with red-yellow-red stripes
Orange with blue stripes

One must strongly warn against the conception that, because a wine is produced by Mr. X or comes from this or that site (*Lage*) or village, it *must* be good. It would be still less justified to speak of a grower as *the* leading grower and therefore expect the best only. These ideas must lead to great disappointment.

The Steinberg vineyard is considered the best site of the Rheingau, a most impressive site, but the qualities of its wines coming from one grower—the State Domain—differ as much as in Burgundy, the Clos de Vougeot wines belonging to more than a dozen growers. The 1961 Steinberger should never have been bottled; its Kabinett was just good enough as an aperitif. The 1959s were all good—reaching from the ordinary table wine to the Feinste Trockenbeerenauslese.

A grower of the Mosel was especially successful with his 1949, 1950 and 1953 wines and soon he was called "the leading grower". 1954/1962 were not at all successful, including the 1959, with the exception of a few casks, but he received much higher prices for all his wines because somebody had stamped him the leading grower.

It is a great pleasure to find in bad vintages *the* really good and excellent wines; it is an even greater pleasure to find in the cellars of the medium-sized growers qualities which beat those of their aristocratic neighbours. The individual care and skill often produce qualities in the wines without pedigree which are far above those of the Doctors, Sonnenuhr or Steinbergers.

To sum up:

Only his own palate and purse can decide for any individual consumer which wine is best for him. As long as he is inexperienced, he cannot do better than follow the advice of his wine merchant who has tasted and selected the wines on his list with a view to satisfying his clients' needs. One cannot classify village against village, and site name against site-name. If one would compare, one could only do so with ordinary against ordinary wines, Spätlese against Spätlese, Auslese against Auslese. The classifications in the olden days were mostly made according to the best cask which was produced. If one vineyard produced the best cask, it was considered the best vineyard.

As already indicated, the only classification is by the taste and value of each single cask. There are of course specially favoured *Lagen* which enjoy suitable soil and much sunshine and therefore produce genuinely good wines, provided nature in the respective vintage has ripened the grapes. Knowledge of these factors will assist the consumer and help to avoid disappointment. The following are some of these favoured sites:

Palatinate

FORST Kirchenstück
    Freundstück
    Jesuitengarten
    Ungeheuer
DEIDESHEIM Herrgottsacker
    Leinhöhle
WACHENHEIM Gerümpel

Mosel

BERNKASTEL Doktor
PIESPORT Goldtröpfchen
GRAACH Himmelreich
ERDENER Treppchen
WEHLEN Sonnenuhr
BRAUNEBERG Juffer
ZELTINGEN Himmelreich

Rhinehessia

NIERSTEIN Auflangen
    Rehbach (Pettenthal)
    Ölberg
OPPENHEIM Sacktraeger
    Reisekahr
    Krötenbrunnen
NACKENHEIM Rothenberg
    Engelsberg

Saar

SCHARZHOFBERGER
WILTINGER Kupp
OCKFEN Bockstein
AYLER Kupp
    Herrenberg

Ruwer

EITELSBACH Karthäuserhofberg
MAXIMIN Grüenhäuser
    Herrenberg
KASELER Nies'gen

Rheingau

RAUENTHAL Baiken
HALLGARTEN Jungfer
ERBACH Marcobrunn
JOHANNISBERGER
WINKELER Hasensprung
SCHLOSS VOLLRADS
RÜDESHEIM

Franconia

WÜRZBURGER Stein
    Leisten
RANDERSACKERER Spielberg
HÖRSTEINER Abtsberg

324

Nahe

SCHLOSS BÖCKELHEIM Kupfergrub
BAD KREUZNACH Kauzenberg
NIEDERHAUSEN Hermannshöhle

Furthermore, a Spätlese or Auslese wine is always apt to give full satisfaction on account of its special ripeness and fruitiness.

Some enthusiastic wine-drinkers—and not by any means the least knowledgeable—prefer the old well-seasoned wines to any others. Nowadays such wines are difficult to find. Pre-war wines are unavailable.

One of my friends still has a good stock of 1933, 1934, 1935 and 1937 wines, which we tasted in Spring 1963. In our tasting result, we placed 1934 the highest and came to the conclusion that the 1934 proved to be a finer vintage than the much-praised 1921. The staying-power of the 1934 is astonishing. A Hallgartener Jungfer Riesling Spätlese 1934 showed such light fresh colour and taste that it may have another 20/30 years and still be enjoyed.

Even the most fastidious taste should be satisfied with the 1945, 1947, 1948—and with the 1949, 1952, 1953 and 1959 vintages. The last decades have given us a good range of vintages.

Personally I am of the opinion that the connoisseur has given up the idea of valuing the wine according to its age; it is certainly interesting to observe a wine ageing and its development, but a young wine can give so much pleasure; it has finesse and elegance so that it outclasses older wines of the same vineyards —it is just as if you compare a young lady, just coming of age, in all her freshness, beauty, etc., with a more matured person. In exactly the same way as we become wrinkled when we are getting old, so do wines after having reached their best. The 1921, 1934 and 1937 wines have, of course, great names, but I personally prefer the 1945s, 1949s, 1952s, 1953s and 1959s to their older brothers.

It has generally been considered that Mosel wines keep in flourishing condition for seven years, but I have drunk much older Mosels which had lost nothing of their vigour. On the whole, however, I prefer younger wines with their freshness and delicate flavour—a two- to three-year-old Mosel or a four- to ten-year-old Rhine wine should be able to fully satisfy even the most captious consumer.

Wines are living organisms and must be treated as such—that is, account must be taken of their individual peculiarities. Rheingau, Rhinehessian and Palatinate wines often reach a ripe old age without deteriorating. But their development is partially dependent on the cellar temperature. It is a universal rule that chemical and biological development is hastened by a high, and slowed down by a low, temperature. If, therefore, a wine is housed in a warm cellar, it will mature more quickly, age more quickly and suffer deterioration earlier than if the cellar is cold. It is advisable to keep bottled wines in a cellar in which fluctuations of temperature are reduced to a minimum. For white wines the optimum temperature is about 50°–54°F, for red wines at least 64°F.

Bottled wines do not stay static in quality; they continue their development till it reaches its peak. Having reached this stage, the wines remain at their best for years, or even for decades, and then gradually deteriorate.

VINTAGES   The fact that wines are designated by their *Lagen* and by the year of origin is sufficient indication that in all stages of their development in cask and in bottle they are dependent on Nature. Anyone, therefore, who expects the wine-grower to deliver him identical products year after year, as if they were machine-made, is depriving himself of the exquisite enjoyment that can only be provided through the great variety of the offerings from different sites under the changing conditions of different seasons. No year is the same as the next; the degree of sunshine varies, and with it the characteristics of that season's wines. The real wine connoisseur makes it his aim and his pride to pick out the finest product among the manifold kinds set before him and—renewing this delightful occupation every season—to enjoy these "peak" wines to the full. His cultivated wine palate may be compared with the finely attuned sound sense of the musician or the colour-conscious eye of an artist, and affords him similar possibilities of artistic appreciation.

The general quality of German wines in recent years—to which we now turn our attention—has been very good. Nature has been very kind to German viticulture. The 1945 and 1946 vintages were fully satisfactory in quality, particularly in view of the fact that the war took heavy toll of German vineyards. During the war there was very little labour to be had, there was a great shortage of everything needed for protecting the plants, etc., and this makes the reasonably good quality of the wines little short of astonishing. In 1945 there were late frosts during the first days of May and the late summer was fine and sunny; but it was July that brought the storms and sudden showers to which we owe the exceptional qualities of that year's vintage. The velvety taste, fruity richness and bouquet of these wines will distinguish them above all others for many years to come. The weather in 1946 was very similar in many respects; that year's wines owe their characteristic traits to the autumn. Full of body but fruity, they contain more acidity than usual, but are well balanced and elegant and, in general, fully representative of the typical Rhine wine flavour. Next came the great year 1947, noted for what was almost excessive sunshine. All wine-growers had fine harvests and produced heavy wines of a very pronounced character whose delicious bouquet will be the delight of every wine connoisseur now and in the future, even though many wines of this vintage show a lack of acidity. It was an outstanding year, in which the specific gravity of the Must was particularly high. It should, however, be noted in passing that this quality alone is not sufficient indication of the greatness of a wine. In the harmonious blending of sweetness with sufficient acidity the 1947 is a worthy successor to the famous 1921, and altogether a wine that will long be remembered by producers and consumers.

The 1948 harvest produced a wine which in some places outshone the 1947 in its harmony and raciness. Its quality may be described as great, and quantitatively the crops were outstanding. Both quality and quantity were due to the beautiful weather which prevailed while the vines were in flower. The summer was followed by a mild and sunny autumn. The delightful flavour of the 1948 wines coupled with their general harmony and delicate bouquet have been greatly appreciated by the connoisseurs. When allowed a suitable period for maturing, their quality will improve still more.

It is well known, even in lay circles, that a rich, and still more an excessively rich, crop is in general obtained at the expense of quality. Despite this undoubted fact, the 1948 can compete on equal terms with its predecessors, even in some cases being preferred to them. Thus, 1945 to 1948 constitute four successive good years, and the 1949 products bid fair to equal them. Wherever the grapes were able to ripen undisturbed by natural phenomena, and wherever their subterranean store or supply of moisture was sufficient to offset the lack of rain in that year, the wine produced had an elegant fullness and harmony that may make it the wine of the century. On the other hand, dry sites produced wines of only medium quality which can at best be compared with the 1928 vintages. A notable feature of the year 1949 was the frequent appearance of the *Edelfäule—Botrytis cinerea*—on the berries, some of which had shrivelled to raisin-like consistency. Whenever this happened and the berries that had been so attacked were gathered or pressed separately and the wine was appropriately treated, a really superb product was achieved.

The 1950 products have been high in quantity, but qualitatively they fall far below those of previous years. When sunshine was needed there were rainfalls, and many berries began to rot before they had reached the required maturity so the wine could only be made durable and drinkable by the addition of sugar.

The 1951 vintage was the worst since 1941 and was similar in quality to the 1931; it has been surpassed still by the 1954—a vintage which the grower will remember for a long time, be-because everything went wrong with the weather—spring frosts, much rain and no sunshine, a vintage which the wine-lover will not look for. If wine is captured sunshine, there can be no "wine" in 1954.

The more we can rejoice at two vintages which we can enjoy, the 1952 and 1953. 1952 was a satisfactory vintage and some really good wines were made. After a fine July and August, many people expected a fine year and one even dreamt of better wines than 1949 and 1921. Unfortunately the weather in September and October was disappointing; but an Indian summer brought us, if not great, still good Spätlese and Auslese wines, similar in quality to 1948—ideal luncheon wines.

1953 is a fine successor to the 1949 and everything I said about 1949 applies to 1953. Ripe wines with fruit, finesse and elegance. A good vintage needs thirteen months' good weather, and good weather means rain and sun always at the right time and in the right quantity. The vintages 1955 to 1958 are not worth mentioning; they are in any case overshadowed by the vintage of the century, the 1959.

The Statistical Office, which receives detailed reports about the quality of the grapes during the harvest, has issued very interesting figures about the quality of the 1953 and 1954 vintages in comparison. Let figures speak for themselves. The following points were awarded:

	Very Good	Good	Medium	Inferior	Very Inferior
1954	1%	17%	48%	28%	6%
1953	39%	44%	14%	3%	—

1960 An enormous harvest of average quality.

1961 Half the quantity of 1960, but fuller wines. "Ice wine" year of excellent quality.

1962 Another Ice Wine year, larger quantities of Ice Wine made with still more concentration than 1961. Otherwise quality like 1961.

1963 A quantity harvest with quantities above the 1960 quality. Quite useful fruity wines!

1964 The best since 1959, actually the best since 1953, with the exception of 1959, some reaching 1953 quality.

1965 Worst of the century, a few Ice Wines only on best sites.

1966 Very good vintage which proved very balanced and harmonious. The first place is taken by Mosel, Saar and Ruwer and the second by the Rheingau.

Sekt (Sparkling Hock & Mosel)

The inventor of Champagne is said to have been a monk by the name of Perignon who was cellarmaster in the Benedictine Abbey of Hautvillers, Champagne (France), from 1670 to 1715. It may be remembered, however, that long before this—in Roman times—many poems and songs were written in praise of "sparkling" wines.

Dom Perignon bottled young wine and mastered the secret of clearing the sediment formed in the bottle without allowing the carbon dioxide to escape. And that is the vital basis of all sparkling wine production.

Because this effervescent wine was first produced in the Champagne country, it became known as *Champagne* and has retained the name to the present day. In Germany, however, the word *Sekt* began some time ago to replace the more general *appellation*. The change-over from *Champagne* to *Sekt* in Germany has a somewhat peculiar history. It came about thus:

When in 1815 the actor Ludwig Devrient came to the Berlin Court Theatre he would often play Falstaff in *Henry IV*. In the scene at the "Wild Boar's Head", when he ordered the servitor to bring a "cup of sack", he used the German word *Sekt* to denote "Sack". Obviously this was not meant for Champagne, a beverage unknown in the days of Henry IV, but for Sherry. The Shakespeare translators had, however, rendered "sack" with "sekt". From the stage Devrient carried this nomenclature into his Berlin "pub", or rather into the wine-restaurant of Lutter and Wegner, where he used to sit imbibing Champagne with his friend and crony, the world-famous E. T. A. Hoffmann.

The waiter became accustomed to bring Devrient his Champagne whenever he called out "Hey, villain, bring me a glass of *Sekt*." Since then the word has established itself in Germany as the correct designation for sparkling wine.

Theoretically, Germany should be able to produce the finest of sparkling wines. No law hampers the activities of their manufacturers, who are at liberty to use any wine in the world for their blends in attempts to find the right *cuvée*. They may even use pure still champagnes, and certainly in former times many a brand contained a percentage of real champagne. Nowadays the sparkling wines of the Saar, the Lower Mosel, and the Middle Rhine are used for these brands, blended with the cheaper wines of the producer's home region. Manufacturers of sparkling wines are to be found in all parts of Germany. Some of their products are world-famous and named on the wine lists of good hotels in all countries under the heading "Sparkling Hock" or "Sparkling Mosel". In addition to these, there are the "Special Cuvées", such as Sparkling Bernkasteler, Sparkling Johannisberger, etc. These brands of sparkling wines are produced from blends which, were they to be marketed as still wines—would have a right to these names.

It may happen that a *cuvée* is prepared exclusively from wines originating on different sites: if then two-thirds of the blend comes from one site only, the sparkling wine may be (and is) marketed under the name of that site—for example, Sparkling Steinberger.

But unique among the sparkling hocks are those made solely from wines of a famous site or from wines of one estate and therefore on an equal footing with the German "Estate Bottled" wines.

Under the name of Perlwein (bubbly) a wine containing carbon dioxide is at present being marketed in Germany. Instructions for its manufacture were given by Kielhöfer thirty-five years ago in his *Cellarage Reports*. They are as follows:

Must or sugared still wine is allowed to ferment in tanks until the sugar content has been reduced to 15 to 20 grammes per litre. The liquid is then cooled down to 3°–5°C, so that the "shocked" yeast works with reduced energy. At the same time, the pressure is set at 1·5 atm. Most of the yeast is deposited, and the wine, saturated with carbon dioxide, is drained off under counter-pressure into an empty tank. At the same time, the necessary finings are carried out. Clearing by filtering is conducted isobarically in order that none of the carbon dioxide may escape, and the final bottling (long-necked bottles) is similarly accomplished with the help of the sterilising filter. The bottled wine is under approximately 1 atm. carbon dioxide pressure and is served like sparkling wine at a temperature of 41°F. The bottle needs no wire netting to keep the cork in place.

Perlwein is quite a formidable rival to the lesser brands of sparkling wine because it has hitherto remained tax-free in Germany. A bottle of *Perlender Saarriesling* (Bubbly Saar Riesling) as supplied by the producer costs about one-third to one-half the price charged for the cheapest brand of *Sekt*. *Perl* wines are greatly in demand in Germany today, and they are certainly very pleasant to drink on a warm summer's day. A bye-law of July 25th, 1963, decrees that Perlwein must not be too sweet, as it must not have more than 40 grammes unfermented sugar per litre.

Since this chapter was written there have been several changes in the German Wine Law. See appendix following page 699

LUXEMBOURG

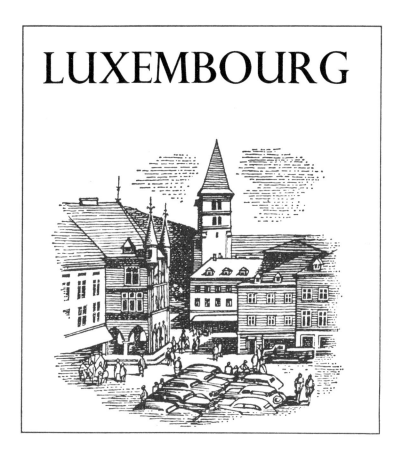

The origin of the Luxembourg vineyards goes back to Roman times. The Roman soldiers were used to drinking wine, and therefore they planted vines in the districts which they occupied. In the course of the centuries, Luxembourg viticulture experienced the depths and heights, it knew good and bad times. Also today, even at this moment, the European economy is in a transition stage, where one cannot see what will follow.

CLIMATE   The Luxembourg vineyard district is in an area where a sea
              climate with west winds prevails. The mid-year temperature in
              the town of Luxembourg is 8·6°C, although the average in the
              Moselle valley is 9·5°, and in especially sheltered positions as
              much as 10°. The canalised Moselle had a favourable influx on
              the microbial climate of the valley. Deep troughs of low pres-
              sure reach, on the average, 650 mm. As the Luxembourg vine-
              yards are on the northern wine-growing frontiers, they are
              especially vulnerable to frost, and on an average the plants suffer
              from this two or three times in a decade.

GEOGRAPHY   The vineyards are situated along the Moselle with a length of
AND GEOLOGY   40 km and an average width of 3,000 m, from Lorraine to the
              German frontiers. The best plants are on the southern slopes,
              where the vineyards are often terraced. These vineyards have an
              average height of 150 to 250 m above sea level. The soil belongs
              to the Triasformation group.

THE LUXEMBOURG WINE ROAD

WINE GROWING COMMUNITIES WITH THE BEST SITES AND AREA OF PRODUCTION

Name of Village	Area of Production	Best Sites
SCHENGEN	75 hectares	
REMERSCHEN	86 ,,	Kreitzberg
		Jongeberg
WINTRANGE	42 ,,	Felsberg
		Hommelsberg
SCHWEBSINGEN	65 ,,	Kolteschberg
		Letscheberg
BECH–KLEINMACHER	108 ,,	Roetschelt
		Fousslach
WELLENSTEIN	70 ,,	Kourschels
		Fulschette
REMICH	39 ,,	Primerberg
		Hôpertsbour

334

STADTBREDIMUS	65	,,	Primerberg
			Dieffert
GREIVELDANGE	48	,,	Huette
			Herrenberg
EHNEN	56	,,	Kelterberg
			Broomelt
			Wousselt
WORMELDANGE	159	,,	Koeppchen (Koepp)
			Nussbaum
			Elterberg
AHN	78	,,	Palmberg
			Vogelsang
MACHTUM	67	,,	Ongkaf
			Gollebour
GREVENMACHER	47	,,	Fels
			Groerd
			Rosenberg
NERTERT	25	,,	Syrberg
			Herrenberg
WASSERBILLIG	13	,,	Bocksberg

Administratively, as well as geologically, the Luxembourg vineyards are divided into two parts:

1. The soil in Canton Remich consists mainly of "keuper" with *tonmergel,* from which the best quality grapes can be grown. The wines from this district are as full and harmonious as the landscape of rounded and soft formed hills. The varieties of grapes planted here are Riesling × Sylvaner (Rivaner, Müller-Thurgau), Auxerrois, Ruländer, Weissburgunder (Pinot Blanc), Traminer, and also cultivated Riesling and Elbling.

2. The landscape in Canton Grevenmacher is quite different. Mussel-lime dominates in this region. Dolomite-type rocks climb steeply upwards, the valley is narrow, the soil is often poor, and protective lime walls have to be built to prevent flooding. The wines are very dry and racy, but sometimes also elegant. Normally their quality grows with maturity and they often show a special soil tone. The wine grower

plants especially Elbling, Riesling × Sylvaner (Rivaner), Auxerrois, Pinot Blanc, Riesling, but also Traminer or even Ruländer (Pinot Gris).

THE VITICULTURAL
INDUSTRY

At the census dated December 1st, 1964, 1,675 viticulturists (wine-growers) were counted as compared with 2,050 in 1956. The actual vineyard area has not gone down during these eight years, although the number of growers has decreased by twenty per cent. The average sized enterprise owns 0·72 hectare of vineland belonging exclusively to families, which for the most part are occupied with other kinds of agriculture.

As in other wine growing countries, there is a strong co-operative movement among the wine-growers. They are well aware that, to give the wine the best treatment, modern machinery is absolutely necessary and the single grower cannot afford to buy these—the co-operatives in their large cellars employ technically skilled viti- and viniculturists. Co-operatives of some size (1,400 co-operators) can be found in Remerschen, Wellenstein, Greiveldange, Wormeldange, Stadtbredimus and Grevenmacher. They arrange wine festivals combined with wine markets and wine tastings to make their products better known.

PRODUCTION

Thanks to technical advancements, production rises annually. Some post-war harvests are detailed below:

1945	32,000 hectolitres of wine		30·4 hectolitres/hectare		
1951	115,000	,,	,,	104·5	,,	,,
1960	133,000	,,	,,	116·6	,,	,,
1964	165,000	,,	,,	142	,,	,,

The average for the last twenty years is 114,500 hectolitres, which is a yield per acre of 104 hectolitres/hectare. The value for an average harvest is about £1½ million. Included in this figure are all kinds of grape, including Elbling and Riesling × Sylvaner, which are known to have the greatest production.

336

GRAPES   Set out below are characteristics and statistics of various grapes grown; all are white wines and all are light and dry with very low alcohol content:

Kind of Grape	Total Production 1964 Fuder	Highest alcoholic contents grams/litre per cent vol.
Rivaner (Riesling × Sylvaner) (Müller-Thurgau)	7,300	82 g/l = 10·3
Elbling	6,000	80 „ = 10
Riesling	1,400	86 „ = 10·8
Auxerrois		84 „ = 10·5
Pinot Blanc	1,800	84 „ = 10·5
Pinot Gris (Ruländer)		88 „ = 11
Traminer		92 „ = 11·5

Wine is usually drunk in the first year, yet the quality of the wine increases with maturity. Often, after three years, wine reaches its peak; very good wine remains there for years. All the wines are principally dry and should be served at a temperature of from 8° to 10°C.

Since the First World War, the Luxembourg wine production has greatly changed. Until then, ninety-five per cent of the vineyards were planted with Elbling, which for the most part was exported to Germany, with whom Luxembourg had a customs union. About the same time that the Belgian–Luxembourg Economic Union came into force, phylloxera was found in the vineyards. These two factors resulted in the wine grower having to transplant his vineyards and find a different market for his wine. Because these things occurred together, it was possible to solve the problem. The State helped and the companies were also built up.

SPARKLING WINES   As the Luxembourg wine is especially good for the production of sparkling wine, production has increased accordingly. After

337

the last war, production decreased to less than 100,000 bottles annually. However, in 1964 more than 600,000 bottles were produced, which constitutes more than two bottles per head of population. The leading House is Cave St. Martin in Remich. Another wine with just some effervescence—Perlwein—is bottled in ordinary Moselle bottles with "crown corks" and makes a refreshing drink. It carries in Great Britain, as a rule, ordinary table wine duty.

Wine consumption per head of population averages thirty-five litres. In spite of this, the majority is exported, as can be seen below:

Year	Belgium	Holland	Germany	Other Countries	Total Hectolitre
1933	21,287	568	1,593	2,806	25,534
1950	18,340	1,020	63	147	19,570
1960	30,480	5,810	23,650	120	60,060
1964	50,940	9,700	6,230	110	66,980

VITICULTURAL INSTITUTIONS

In 1907, when the first grape louse was discovered in the Luxembourg vineyards, the viticulture schools in REMICH and GREVENMACHER were founded. Through a law in 1926, a viticultural institution in Remich was opened. It moved to a new building in 1962, and in 1963 a law came into force which gave this reorganisation a special interest. The reason for the institution became clearer.

The inland wine comes under the control of the viticultural institutes from the time of production to the time when it reaches the retailer. They also control imported wine and a special quality control has been introduced.

A special decree regulates the denomination of Luxembourg quality wines. In this decree it is laid down that wines made of noble grapes, namely the Riesling, the Traminer, the Ruländer

338

(Pinot Gris) and the Auxerrois grape are the only grapes which can serve for the making of quality wines. Quality wines are sold under the denomination *Cru Classé, Premier Cru, Grand Cru, Réserve, Grande Réserve*. Apart from these no other statement must be made. In order to be permitted to use these denominations, growers or co-operatives or wine merchants have to supply samples with an application for permission to use this denomination. In the application they have to give details of the original sugar content, the specific grade of the Must and the quantity harvested in the special vineyard. If permission is granted, the control number and the number of the cask have to be printed on the label and the following is important. The best quality, namely Réserve and Grande Réserve, cannot be applied for before the wine is at least more than a year old, that is, it cannot be applied for before the last day of the year following the vintage. The other denominations can be applied for as early as 15th March following the vintage.

In addition to the statements just given, the *Marque Nationale* has to be affixed to the bottle. Since its creation and particularly in the immediate post-war years, the *Marque Nationale* has constantly gained in popularity in Luxembourg and in Belgium to such a degree that the connoisseur would not have the quality bottles of his choice without the official label. Incidentally, the Luxembourg *Marque Nationale* is an institution created by the State in 1935 in order to protect the authenticity and quality of wines. It is only conferred after a conscientious tasting by a Commission of expert tasters who are not informed beforehand of the origin of the products. The label *Marque Nationale* is the official emblem for the selected wines, the naming of whose origin is guaranteed as a result of serious tests, and is reserved exclusively for the bottles. The label can be applied for by the following bodies: private producers; Caves co-operatives; wine merchants and innkeepers and hoteliers. The bottling is supervised by a Government control officer. Each type of wine bears its individual control number. The labels should be affixed in the cellar of the bottler in the district of origin, and each bottle should be furnished with the cork-mark of the producer or of the Luxembourg seller or of the foreign seller. It is nevertheless permitted to replace the address of the seller marked on the cork by details of the variety and year of the grape, as approved by the Commission.

When wine is exported, a certificate is given to prove that it has undergone an organic and chemical analysis. Statements regarding its origin are also examined.

In the last few years, viticultural instruction has greatly increased and the young wine grower attends the school in Remich during two winters or for a period of five months.

Gastronomical specialities of Luxembourg include: Black pudding and sausages, mashed potatoes and horse-radish; smoked pork and broad beans; Ardennes ham, cooked and uncooked; jellied sucking pig; calf's liver *quenelles*, sauerkraut, boiled potatoes; from April 1st to September 30th: trout and crawfish, Luxembourg fashion. During the shooting season: civet of hare and thrushes, Luxembourg fashion.

Vintage Chart

Excellent	1921	1947	1953	1959	1964
Very good	1933	1934	1937	1943	1948
	1949	1952	1958	1962	
Good	1920	1928	1929	1935	1938
	1942	1945	1951	1955	1961
Average	1925	1926	1927	1931	1932
	1940	1941	1946	1960	1963
Inferior	1922	1923	1924	1930	1936
	1939	1944	1950	1954	1956
	1957				

ITALY

Italian wine production has been the largest in the world for the last few years, averaging 1,550 million gallons per annum. 1967 was a record year, with an excellent vintage of good quality and quantity reaching 1,650 million gallons.

In order of production, the most important of the eighteen regions are: Puglia, Sicily, Veneto, Emilia-Romagna and Piedmont.

But Italy is not only a great wine-producing country; it is also a

country producing great wines such as those celebrated ones of Piedmont and Tuscany which enjoy a world-wide reputation.

CLASSIFICATION

In 1963 an Act of Parliament came into force, basically instituting three different classifications for Italian wines:

a. plain denomination of origin;
b. controlled denomination of origin;
c. controlled and guaranteed denomination of origin.

The plain denomination of origin or *Denominazione di Origine Semplice*, applies to wines obtained from grapes produced by typical vines growing in specific areas from which these wines can take their name: i.e. the region of Toscana (Tuscany); Rosso Toscano, etc.

The controlled denomination of origin or *Denominazione di Origine Controllata*, known as D.O.C., is applicable to those wines that comply with the conditions and qualifications stated for each of them by the various Presidential Decrees, and is reserved to those wines of particular reputation and value. D.O.C. means that the wine is produced within a specified area, with traditional methods and using the percentages of different grapes admitted by the law; the yield of wine per ton of grapes is within the permitted limits; the wine has been aged for a set minimum period of time before being allowed to be sold; the inspectors have sampled the wine during the various stages of preparation; the wine meets the requirements of the National Committee and has reached the minimum natural alcoholic content.

D.O.C. wines will also be known within the E.E.C. as V.Q.P.R.D. or *vins de qualité produits dans des régions déterminées* and they are accompanied by a certificate of analysis.

Because of the considerable work involved, it took about four years from the 1963 Presidential Decree to have the first D.O.C. wines; to date, about 80 wines have been awarded the right to the D.O.C., some 15 have been approved by the Committee and over 20 have been rejected.

The controlled and guaranteed denomination of origin or *Denominazione di Origine Controllata e Garantita*, will apply only to very special wines, selected among those that have gained the D.O.C.; these wines will bear a Governmental seal. It will not be possible to sell such wines in containers exceeding 5 litres or 1·1 gallon.

Plain misuse of denominations of origin or forging of labels carry fines of up to £6 sterling per gallon and imprisonment.

PIEDMONT

Asti Spumante	Sw. Sp. W. Moscato		D.O.C.
Barbaresco	R. Nebbiolo		D.O.C.
Barbera d'Alba	R. Barbera		D.O.C.
Barbera del Monferrato	R. Barbera		D.O.C.
Barbera d'Asti	R. Barbera		D.O.C.
Barolo	R. Nebbiolo		D.O.C.
Brachetto amabile	S. Sw. R. Brachetto		D.O.C.
Carema	R. Nebbiolo		D.O.C.
Cortese di Gavi	W. Cortese		D.O.C.
Dolcetto	R. Dolcetto		
Erbaluce di Caluso	W. Erbaluce		D.O.C.
Freisa	R. Freisa		
Gattinara	R. Nebbiolo		D.O.C.
Ghemme	R. Nebbiolo-Bonarda		D.O.C.
Grignolino	R. Grignolino		
Lessona	R. Nebbiolo		
Moscato d'Asti	Sw. Sp. W. Moscato		D.O.C.
Nebbiolo d'Alba	R. Nebbiolo		D.O.C.

Sw. = sweet; Sp. = sparkling; W. = white; R. = red;
S.Sw. = semi-sweet.

Piedmont is a region of north-western Italy, that borders France on the west and Switzerland on the north. Some of the best Italian wines are produced in this region where vines thrive particularly on the hills of Monferrato and the Langhe.

344

ASTI SPUMANTE. This is a sweet, sparkling white wine, made from selected grapes of the muscat variety. Rich in sugar and of low alcoholic content, Asti Spumante is one of the finest sparkling wines of the world. Its natural amber colour is made lighter for better appeal. It is a delicate wine to be drunk fresh and not for keeping. Alcoholic content 6 per cent by volume; total acidity 0·6 per cent.

BARBARESCO. One of the best wines of Piedmont. A red, ruby-coloured wine of dry taste with a delicate aroma of violets; not as austere as Barolo, the great aristocrat of this region. Like Barolo, though, and indeed other red wines of Piedmont, Barbaresco is made from the Nebbiolo grape.

Barbaresco can be described as a fine burgundy-type wine, generous in nature and of a delightful nose. It is shorter lived than Barolo and ages more quickly. Alcoholic content 12/14 per cent by volume; total acidity 0·7 to 0·9 per cent.

BARBERA. A good, generous wine, quite popular in Italy, particularly in the north. It is produced on a vast area and there are basically three types, named after their districts. The alcoholic content is between 13 per cent and 14 per cent by volume; the total acidity 0·1/1·0 per cent.

A rich wine, with a deep red colour and a bouquet of violets and Morello cherries, especially the type produced near Asti. This wine can be found in Italy in a *frizzante* condition. It is made from Barbera grapes. If of a good year it can age moderately, in which case its ruby red colour turns into garnet.

BAROLO. In Italy Barolo is considered the king of wines. It is in fact one of Italy's best wines; an excellent companion for roasts of red meat and for game.

Barolo is made from Nebbiolo grapes grown in the district near Alba. It is a wine suitable for ageing as it matures after some years, when its colour is bright ruby red, and in six or eight years becomes perfect, with the colour acquiring orange undertones, and the bouquet of violets and faded roses is even more accentuated.

345

By law, Barolo has to age for at least three years from January 1st following vinification, with at least two years in cask. When bottled, the bottles are left to lie in deep cellars where they remain for some time. The alcoholic content of Barolo is 13/14 per cent by volume; the total acidity 0·7/0·8 per cent.

BRACHETTO A typical red dessert wine of limited production, this is immediately ready for consumption. Made from Brachetto grapes, it has a clear bouquet of roses and an excellent velvety taste. It is mellow and generous and has a delightful gentle frothing. Alcohol 11/13 per cent by volume; total acidity 0·6/0·8 per cent.

CORTESE DI GAVI. This is a white wine made from the Cortese grapes grown in the province of Alessandria. Delicate and light, dry and almost sharp, it is suitable for moderate ageing. Alcohol 10/11 per cent volume; total acidity 0·7/0·9 per cent.

GATTINARA. Another great red wine produced in the province of Vercelli, also from Nebbiolo grapes, known locally as Spanna. It matures after four years and improves with age. It has an aroma of raspberry that fades into roses and violets.

The use of the *denominazione Gattinara* is allowed only for those wines produced within the commune of Gattinara, from grapes grown on the sunny hillsides and excluding those growing on level ground. The alcoholic content of this wine is 13/14 per cent by volume; the total acidity 0·6/0·8 per cent.

GHEMME. This is a good red wine made from the following grapes grown in the territory of the commune of Ghemme and part of the commune of Romagnano Sesia: Nebbiolo (Spagna) 60/85 per cent, Vespolina 10/30 per cent and Bonarda, maximum 15 per cent.

It ages well and has a deep garnet colour with amber undertones and a bouquet of violets. By law it cannot be sold before four years, starting from January 1st following vinification; during this time the wine has to be aged in wood (oak or chestnut) for a minimum period of three years.

Alcohol 12/13 per cent by volume; total acidity 0·6/0·8 per cent. Adjectives such as "superiore", "extra", "fine", "scelto", "selezionato", are not allowed on the label.

LOMBARDY

Colli dell'Oltrepo Pavese	R. Barbera, Croatina, Ughetta	D.O.C.
Franciacorta Rosso	R. Carbernet, Barbera, Nebbiolo	D.O.C.
Grumello	R. Chiavennasca (Nebbiolo) Sassella	D.O.C.
Inferno	R. Chiavennasca, Sassella	D.O.C.
Lugana	W. Trebbiano di Lugana	D.O.C.
Sassella	R. Chiavennasca, Sassella	D.O.C.
Tocai di S. Martino	W. Tocai	D.O.C.
Valgella	R. Chiavennasca, pignola	D.O.C.
Valtellina	R. Chiavennasca	D.O.C.

Lombardy is a region east of Piedmont. It borders Switzerland to the north, Veneto to the east and Emilia to the south. The northern part is mountainous, the central part hilly, the southern part very flat and fertile. Vines are grown in the north, particularly in Valtellina, the valley that, from Lake Como, runs almost due east, and also in the south, in the province of Pavia, across the River Po.

GRUMELLO, SASSELLA, INFERNO AND VALGELLA These are four outstanding wines made from the Chiavennasca grape, which is the name given in Valtellina to Nebbiolo. They are all red wines. Grumello and Inferno are superior table wines that mature after a couple of years. Sassella is a great wine that matures after three years and improves with age; alcoholic content 12/13 per cent by volume; total acidity 0·7/1·0 per cent.

COLLI DELL'OLTREPO PAVESE. The *denominazione Oltrepo Pavese* with no other specification, applies to a red wine made from Barbera, Croatina and Ughetta grapes. If 90/100 per cent of a particular grape is used for vinification; additional specification

will appear on the label, to define the wine. This can be: Bonarda, Barbera, Riesling, Cortese, Moscato and Pinot. These wines are produced south of the River Po, in the province of Pavia.

LUGANA. This is a white wine made south-west of Lake Garda, in the province of Brescia. It is pleasantly dry. Alcohol 11·5/12 per cent by volume; acidity 0·5/0·7 per cent.

TRENTINO-ALTO ADIGE

Lago di Caldaro	R. Schiava, Grossa	D.O.C.
Marzemino	R./Ro. Marzemino	
Santa Maddalena	R. Schiava, Lagrein	D.O.C.
Silvaner	W. Silvaner	
Terlano	W. Terlaner, Riesling, Pinot	
Teroldego	R. Teroldego	

It is the northernmost region of Italy, very rugged and mountainous. Some excellent wines are produced.

LAGO DI CALDARO. This is a ruby red wine, fruity and pleasant, with a light bouquet of almonds. It can be called *classico*, if made from grapes grown and vinified in the communes of Caldaro, Appiano, Termeno, Cortaccia, Vadena, Egna, Montagna, Ora and Bronzolo, south of Bolzano. A full-bodied wine of low acidity (0·4 per cent).

VENETO

Bardolino	R. Corvina, Rossara, Negrara	
		D.O.C.
Breganze Bianco	W. Garganega	D.O.C.
Breganze Rosso	R. Marzemino, Negrara	D.O.C.
Colli Euganei Bianco	W. Garganega, Riesling	D.O.C.
Colli Euganei Rosso	R. Merlot, Cabernet	D.O.C.
Gambellara	W. Garganega, Trebbiano	D.O.C.

Pinot del Collio	R./W. Pinot Nero, Pinot Bianco	D.O.C.
Prosecco Spumante di Conegliano	Sp. W. Prosecco	D.O.C.
Recioto Amarone	R. Corvina, Rondinella	D.O.C.
Recioto di Soave	W. Garganega, Trebbiano	D.O.C.
Recioto della Valpolicella	R. Corvina, Rondinella	D.O.C.
Riesling Italico Collio	W. Riesling Italico	D.O.C.
Sauvignon Collio	W. Sauvignon	D.O.C.
Soave	W. Garganega, Trebbiano di Soave	D.O.C.
Tocai del Collio	W. Tocai	D.O.C.
Traminer del Collio	W. Traminer	D.O.C.
Valpantena	R. Corvina, Rossara, Negrara	D.O.C.
Valpolicella	R. Corvina, Rossara, Negrara	D.O.C.

Veneto borders with Austria to the north, Yugoslavia and the Adriatic sea to the east, Emilia to the south, Trentino-Alto Adige and Lombardy to the west. A large number of wines is produced in this region: a variety of red, white, *rosé* and sparkling wines of good quality.

BARDOLINO. It is named after a village on the eastern shore of Lake Garda, and produced from grapes grown nearby on the hills and gentle slopes where the soil gives, to the very same grape varieties used to make Valpolicella, a personality of their own which is transmitted to this delightful red wine. This is a wine with 10/11 per cent of alcohol, average acidity and a good bouquet, to be drunk in two, three years.

RECIOTO. This wine is made from selected grapes left to dry for a brief period. Only the upper part of the bunch of grapes is used; this is called *recia* in the local dialect, and means "ear", hence the name of the wine. Deep in colour and full bodied, this red wine is produced with the same grape varieties as Bardolino and Valpolicella. There is also a Recioto Amarone and a white Recioto di Soave.

SOAVE. This very pleasant white wine is named after the village of Soave; it has a clear bouquet of almonds and is an excellent wine with *hors d'œuvre* or fish. Its colour is greenish-yellow; the taste is dry almost bitterish. Alcohol 10·5 per cent by volume, acidity 0·5 per cent minimum.

VALPOLICELLA. This is a red wine, made from Corvina, Rossara, Molinara, Negrara and Rondinella grapes. It is fruity and can age moderately. A superior table wine extremely pleasant.

PROSECCO. Further north, in the province of Treviso, in the commune of Conegliano Veneto, with the snow-covered Alps in the distance, the Prosecco grape grows. From it a delightful sparkling white wine is produced: Prosecco Spumante di Conegliano, an excellent dessert wine.

EMILIA-ROMAGNA

Albana	W. Albana	D.O.C.
Gutturnio	R. Barbera, Bonarda	D.O.C.
Lambrusco	R. Lambrusco	D.O.C.
Sangiovese	R. Sangiovese	D.O.C.

Emilia-Romagna is a region that stretches from Piedmont across to the Adriatic Sea.

ALBANA This white wine has a golden yellow colour and can be dry or *amabile*, semi-sweet.

LAMBRUSCO. Lambrusco Grasparossa di Castelvetro, Lambrusco Salamino di Santa Croce, Lambrusco di Sorbara, these are the three Lambruschi recognised by the law and named after the localities where they are produced and the varieties of grape. Lambrusco is a red wine with a thick natural froth; whether dry or semi-sweet this is "the wine" of this region.

SANGIOVESE. A ruby red wine, with a vague bouquet of violets

and a slightly bitter after taste. If aged for two years it can be
called *riserva*. It is produced in the provinces of Forlì, Ravenna
and Bologna.

LIGURIA

Cinqueterre	W. Bianchetta, Vermentino
Dolceacqua	R. Rossese, Dolcetto, Vermentino
Polcevera	W. Bianchetta, Vermentino
Vermentino	W. Vermentino

Liguria is a small region, shaped like the waxing moon, with the
Mar Ligure to the south and the Alps and the Apennine mountains to the north. Viticulture here is a vocation as the vines are
often grown on terraces almost hanging over the sea. The wines
are mainly white and produced in small quantities.

CINQUETERRE. This means "five lands" and is the best known of
the wines of Liguria. It is white with a golden colour and can be
dry and sweet, in which case it is known as Sciacchetrà, a *dolce
passito* wine for dessert.

TUSCANY

Aleatico di Portoferraio	R. Aleatico	
Brunello di Montalcino	R. Brunello	D.O.C.
Chianti Classico, Chianti dei Colli Aretini, Fiorentini,		
Pisani Senesi, Rufina, Montalbano		
	R. Sangiovese, Canaiolo,	
	Trebbiano, Malvasia	D.O.C.
Nobile di Montepulciano	R. Sangiovese, Canaiolo,	
	Malvasia	D.O.C.
Vernaccia di S. Gimignano	W. Vernaccia	D.O.C.

This region of central Italy was part of Etruria, once inhabited
by the Etruscans.

BRUNELLO DI MONTALCINO. This is a full-bodied red wine of great character that improves considerably with age. It is produced in the province of Siena in the commune of Montalcino and is one of the great wines of Italy, capable of living up to half a century. High in alcohol, Brunello matures in casks and is then bottled after five or six years.

CHIANTI. A wine usually associated with the Tuscan flask. It is made from Sangiovese 50/80 per cent, black Canaiolo 10/30 per cent, Trebbiano and Malvasia 10/30 per cent and undergoes the *governo* which is a secondary fermentation to give freshness to the wine with the addition of fermenting juice from the Colorino variety.

The grapes must come from vines growing on hilly terrain not higher than 1,800 feet, but not from the plain. If produced in the area around the communes of Radda, Gaiole and Castellina, first defined in a Ministerial Decree issued on July 31st, 1932, it can be called *classico*.

Both Chianti and Chianti Classico can be called *vecchio* if aged for more than two years, and *riserva* if aged for three years or more. The *denominazione Chianti* is applicable only to red wine.

Minimum alcohol 11 per cent for Chianti, 11·5 per cent for Chianti Classico; for Chianti Vecchio and Riserva 12 per cent, for Chianti Classico Vecchio and Riserva 12·5 per cent.

VIN NOBILE DI MONTEPULCIANO. This red wine is from the same grape varieties as Chianti but made without the *governo* system. Similar in character to Brunello di Montalcino but not as great.

VERNACCIA DI SAN GIMIGNANO. This wine was produced already ten centuries ago in the territory of San Gimignano. A white wine of pale golden yellow colour, fresh and slightly bitter. If aged for one year it can be called *riserva*. Alcohol 12/13 per cent; total acidity 0·5 per cent minimum.

Alfresco lunch with Chianti.

facing p. 352

Top, from left to right shows Brown, Dark Golden and Golden sherries
Bottom, from left to right shows Pale, Very Pale and Very Very Pale. (See pp. 368-371)

UMBRIA

Orvieto	W. Trebbiano, Verdello, Malvasia	D.O.C.
Torgiano Bianco	W. Trebbiano, Grechetto, Malvasia	D.O.C.
Torgiano Rosso	R. Sangiovese, Canaiolo,	
	Trebbiano	D.O.C.

ORVIETO. *Urbs vetus*, old city, is also a white wine either dry or *abboccato*, semi-sweet, usually sold in *pulcianelle*, squat straw-covered flasks. It is a delicate wine, traditionally drunk by the Popes, very pleasant and, if dry, a slightly bitter after-taste.

MARCHE

Bianchello del Metauro	W. Bianchello	D.O.C.
Rosso Conero	R. Montepulciano, Sangiovese	D.O.C.
Rosso Piceno	R. Sangiovese, Montepulciano	D.O.C.
Verdicchio	W. Verdicchio, Trebbiano, Malvasia	D.O.C.

The western boundary with Umbria is the watershed of the Umbro-Marchigiani Apennines. To the east is the Adriatic Sea.

BIANCHELLO DEL METAURO. This wine is produced in the area between Fano and Urbino and named after the grape variety from which it is made and the Metauro river. It is a white wine of straw colour, with a delicate bouquet and a dry fresh taste. Minimum alcohol 11·5 per cent; total acidity 0·5/0·8 per cent.

VERDICCHIO DEI CASTELLI DI JESI. Is a great white wine with a long history behind. An "ally" of the Romans, as the half-drunken army of Hannibal pushed south through Marche!

Verdicchio is an excellent wine for fish dishes; clear and dry, it ages moderately. It takes its name from the grape variety from which it is made and also the name of the place, Jesi.

353

LAZIO

Colli Albani	W. Malvasia, Trebbiano	D.O.C.
Est! Est! Est!	W. Trebbiano Toscano, Malvasia	D.O.C.
Frascati	W. Malvasia, Greco, Trebbiano	D.O.C.
Marino Bianco	W. Malvasia, Trebbiano	D.O.C.
Sangiovese d'Aprilia	R. Sangiovese	D.O.C.
Trebbiano d'Aprilia	W. Trebbiano Giallo, Trebbiano Toscano	D.O.C.
Velletri Bianco	W. Malvasia, Trebbiano	

In Lazio, a region of west central Italy, corn, wheat and fruit are grown, but it is on the hills that the vines thrive, together with olive trees. Vineyards cover the slopes of the Alban hills and especially those in the area around Montefiascone.

EST! EST! EST!. This is a white wine of which there are two types: a dry with a pale straw colour and a semi-sweet, more yellow and with a strong vinous aroma. These wines are made in the territories of Montefiascone and Bolsena; the dry is very suitable with the eels of the Bolsena Lake, the other is more of a dessert wine. Alcohol 11 per cent; total acidity 0·6 per cent.

FRASCATI. This is a town a few miles from Rome and Frascati is the wine produced from the vines growing around it, on the gentle slopes of Grottaferrata and in the commune of Monte Porzio Catone. This area was defined by a decree in 1966.

Frascati is a white wine of clear yellow colour; a full-bodied table wine, dry or sweet. The two principal qualities produced are Frascati and Frascati Superiore, the latter having a higher degree of alcohol. The sweet is known as Canellino and is considered the best wine produced in the district. Minimum alcohol 11·5 per cent.

VELLETRI. This is a white wine named after the town of Velletri, near Rome, and produced with the grapes grown in the communes of Velletri, Lariano and Cisterna di Latina. There is also a semi-sweet type.

354

Velletri is made from 70 per cent Malvasia and 30 per cent Trebbiano, maximum 10 per cent of Bellone and Bonvino varieties is allowed.

ABRUZZI e MOLISE

Cerasuolo	R. Montepulciano	
Montepulciano	R. Montepulciano	D.O.C.
Trebbiano d'Abruzzo	W. Trebbiano	

This is a very mountainous region, situated in south central Italy. The Apennines cover most of the territory that slopes east towards the Adriatic Sea, where the towns of Chieti and Pescara are situated. Here are also the vineyards.

MONTEPULCIANO. This is a good red table wine, dry and pleasant, with a very slightly sweet after taste, not as accentuated as in Cerasuolo, the other red wine from this area. It can age for a short time and preserve a certain *petillance*. If aged for at least two years it can be called *vecchio*. Alcohol 12 per cent.

CAMPANIA

Capri bianco	W. Greco, Fiano	
Gragnano	R. Aglianico, Strepparossa, Nufriello	D.O.C.
Greco di Tufo	W. Greco del Vesuvio	D.O.C.
Ischia bianco	W. Forastera, Biancolella	D.O.C.
Ischia rosso	R. Guarnaccia, Piedirosso, Barbera	D.O.C.
Lacrima Christi	W./R./Ro. Aglianico, Strepparossa	
Taurasi	R. Aglianico, Piedirosso, Barbera	D.O.C.

Campania is south of Lazio and Abruzzi e Molise.

GRECO DI TUFO. This white wine of yellow golden colour, is dry and smooth, suitable with fish dishes. It is made from the Greco di Tufo grape, with a possible addition of up to 20 per cent of Coda di Volpe, growing in the communes of Tufo,

Altavilla Irpina, Torrioni and others specified in a Presidential Decree. Minimum alcohol 11·5 per cent; minimum total acidity 0·5 per cent.

The D.O.C. Greco di Tufo can apply to sparkling wines produced according to the Presidential Decree, within the territory of the province of Avellino.

A white and a red wine are produced on the island of Ischia. These two wines were among the first to receive the approval of the Special Commission and a presidential decree to define them was passed on March 3rd, 1966. The ISCHIA BIANCO has a brilliant straw colour and a delicate vinous aroma; it is dry and has a minimum alcoholic content of 11 per cent.

There is also an ISCHIA BIANCO SUPERIORE, made from grapes produced in specific localities within the defined communes; this has a more aromatic bouquet and 12 per cent of alcohol is the minimum allowed.

The ISCHIA ROSSO is a brilliant ruby-coloured wine, dry and well balanced; it ages moderately and becomes a good table wine for roasts. Minimum alcoholic content 11·5 per cent.

LACRIMA CHRISTI. The white is dry and has an amber straw colour; a good wine for fish dishes and white meat, particularly if moderately aged. The red is an excellent wine for white meat roasts and has a deep ruby colour. There is also a *rosé* Lacrima Christi. Unfortunately many spurious Lacrima Christi are to be found lately, made in other areas.

PUGLIA

Castel del Monte
        Ro./R./W. Uva di Troia, Bombino,
           Montepulciano, Sangiovese   D.O.C.
Locorotondo   W. Verdea, Alessano   D.O.C.

Martina Franca	W. Verdea, Alessano	D.O.C.
Rosato del Salento	Ro. Negramaro, Malvasia	
Sansevero	Ro./R./W. Bombino, Trebbiano, Montepulciano	D.O.C.
Squinzano	R. Negramaro, Malvasia	

Puglia is the first wine-producing region of Italy and some of its wines are often used for blending as their natural alcoholic content is quite high. This region is situated in the "deep south" and enjoys a very mild climate in winter and quite hot spells in summer; these account for full maturation of the grapes from which wines of high alcoholic content are obtained.

CASTEL DEL MONTE. The red Castel del Monte has a deep ruby colour, vinous bouquet and dry taste; minimum alcohol 12 per cent. If aged for three years of which one in cask, this wine can be called *riserva*. The *rosé* is a fruity wine, with a delicate bouquet and a pale ruby colour. The white Castel del Monte is a dry wine of marked straw colour with a delicate vinous aroma. It is made from the Pampanuto grape variety, with addition of Trebbiano, Bombino and Palumbo grapes to a maximum of 35 per cent. These wines are produced north of Bari in the communes of Trani, Ruvo and others.

LOCOROTONDO. This is a white wine with a pale green colour often fading into light straw colour. With a dry delicate taste and an agreeable bouquet, this wine is suitable for grilled fish dishes and soups. It has a minimum alcoholic content of 11 per cent and is produced in the communes of Locorotondo and Cisternino, between the towns of Brindisi and Bari, from 50/65 per cent Verdea grapes and 50/35 per cent Bianco d'Alessano.

MARTINA FRANCA. This is very similar in character to Locorotondo; this wine is produced from the same grape varieties in the communes of Martina Franca and Alberobello.

The *denominazione Martina Franca* can be applied also to a white sparkling wine produced in the provinces of Bari, Brindisi and Taranto.

357

CALABRIA

Cirò	W./Ro./R. Greco Bianco; Gaglioppo	D.O.C.
Greco di Gerace	D.W. Greco di Gerace	
Savuto	R. Magliocco, Greco, Malvasia	

Calabria is the southernmost region of Italy, "Italy's toe".

CIRÒ. A Presidential Decree issued on April 2nd, 1969, sets forward the regulations controlling the production of this wine of which there are three types: a red, a white and a *rosé*. The red and *rosé* are made from the Gaglioppo grape variety and cannot be sold before June 1st following vinification. The red can be called *classico* if it is produced in the communes of Cirò and Cirò Marina; *riserva* if it is aged for a minimum period of three years and has at least 13·5 per cent by volume of alcohol.

GRECO DI GERACE. This is a white wine produced in the province of Reggio Calabria, north of Aspromonte in the district of Gerace. It is a dessert wine of high alcoholic content, between 16 and 17 per cent; it has a golden colour and a fragrant bouquet.

SAVUTO. This is an excellent red wine, with garnet and orange reflections, and a warm and velvety dry taste. It is produced between Nicastro and Cosenza, on the hills north of the river Savuto. A superior table wine that improves with age.

SICILY

Alcamo	W. Catarrato, Inzolia, Grillo	
Etna Bianco	W. Carricante, Catarrato	D.O.C.
Etna Rosso e Rosato		
	R./Ro. Nerello Mascalese, Nerello Mantellata	D.O.C.
Faro	R./Ro. Nerello, Nocera, Citana	
Mamertino	W. Catarrato, Grillo	
Marsala	D. Catarrato, Grillo	D.O.C.

In 1773, the Woodhouse Brothers, from Liverpool, started Sicily's international Marsala trade, having discovered this wine they considered similar to Sherry and Madeira.

Other excellent wines are produced in Sicily; they are mainly table wines, both red and white.

ETNA BIANCO. This is a white wine, dry with a delicate bouquet, produced in the province of Catania, around Mount Etna. It is made from 60 per cent Carricante and 40 per cent Catarrato; the BIANCO SUPERIORE is made with 80 per cent Carricante and has a minimum alcoholic content of 12 per cent.

ETNA ROSSO AND ROSATO. These are made from 80 per cent of Nerello Mascalese and 20 per cent of Nerello Mantellata. The red is a very good table wine suitable for moderate ageing; alcohol 12·5 per cent by volume. The Rosato is a more delicate wine also produced around the Etna volcano.

Marsala is a town situated at the westernmost point of the island; its name, which was later given to Sicily's most famous wine, derives from the Arabic *Marsh el Allah*, port of God. The wines produced here are of the Madeira and Sherry types; the grapes are dried and used to produce dry and sweet dessert wines with a very attractive character. The dry wine is fortified with high proof grape brandy and then to the desired degree of sweetness by the addition of an extremely sweet, concentrated grape juice. The grapes used are Catarrato and Grillo, separately or together.

There are various types specified by the law: MARSALA FINE (Italia, I.P.), with a minimum alcoholic content of 17°; MARSALA SUPERIORE (Garibaldi dolce, S.O.M., L.P.), minimum alcohol 18°, minimum age two years; MARSALA VERGINE (Solera), with a minimum alcoholic content of 18°, aged at least for five years; MARSALA SPECIALI are those with various flavours such as almond, strawberry, banana. They, too, have to have a minimum of 18° of alcohol.

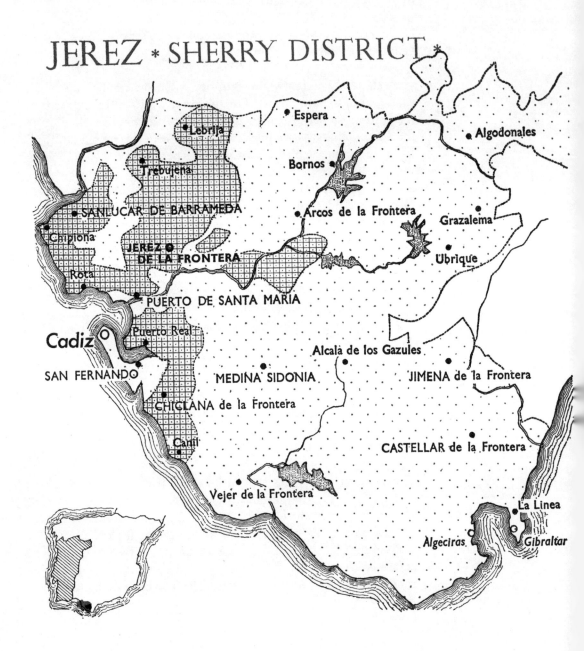

JEREZ * SHERRY DISTRICT *

Espera

Lebrija

Algodonales

Trebujena

Bornos

Sanlúcar de Barrameda

Arcos de la Frontera

Grazalema

Chipiona

JEREZ DE LA FRONTERA

Ubrique

Rota

PUERTO DE SANTA MARÍA

Cadiz

Puerto Real

Alcalá de los Gazules

San Fernando

MEDINA SIDONIA

JIMENA de la Frontera

Chiclana de la Frontera

Conil

CASTELLAR de la Frontera

Vejer de la Frontera

La Línea

Algeciras

Gibraltar

SPAIN

SHERRY

Sherryland's soil, the special vines which grow on it and the glowing Andalusian sun which ripens the grapes are the three inseparable allies which produce this unique wine—Sherry.

The oldest reference to the town of the Jerez of today is in the fourth century B.C. by the Greek Theopompos which runs: "Xera, city situated in the proximity of the Columns of Hercules". Evidence suggests that the Phoenicians brought the vine to the Iberian Peninsula from the East several centuries before the Christian era, and in 133 B.C. the Romans converted Spain into a Roman colony, their domination lasting till A.D. 409. Then the Goths settled down in the south of Spain, which they named Wandalusia, and peopled the peninsula till A.D. 711, when the tribes of North Africa crossed the strait of Gibraltar and conquered the Goths. The Moslems remained in occupation until Xera was recaptured by Alfonso X (The Wise) in 1264. The original Greek name *Xera* was changed by the Romans to *Ceret*, which the Arabs later converted to *Sherrish*. The modern name, Jerez de la Frontera, derives from the fact that it was the frontier between the Christians, that is, the domains of the kings of Castile, and the Moslems.

VINEYARDS   Under the Romans, the wines from the Betica or Southern Spain were exported to Italy, where they were much appreciated. Though the Arabs, according to the Laws of the Koran, should not drink wine, there is evidence that they did keep the vineyards under cultivation, probably for eating as grapes or raisins.

The Sherry area is the land lying within the triangle where Sherry is matured and exported, the apexes of which are the towns of JEREZ DE LA FRONTERA and PUERTO DE SANTA MARIA, both on the right bank of the Guadalete river, and SANLUCAR DE BARRAMEDA on the left bank of the Guadalquivir river.

TYPES OF SOIL   The soil of this area is partially white clay with a large, though varying, proportion of lime (calcium carbonate). This soil is called *Albariza*, though there are other soils called *Barros* (dark clay) and *Arenas* (sandy), but these last two are not nowadays generally used for planting the vine, as the first-named produces the best wine.

VINE VARIETIES   There were many varieties of vine in the Xerez area in ancient times, but today these have been practically reduced for wine-making to the Palomino variety (Listan) and the Pedro Ximenez. The first produces most of the dry Sherries and the second the sweet blending wines.

As elsewhere in Europe, at the end of the last century, the phylloxera devastated the vineyards, so phylloxera-resistant American vine roots were planted and grafted with the Palomino or Pedro Ximenez varieties.

The Sherry vine is only about 15 in. high, and one of the most important tasks to be carried out is the pruning of each plant, which is done by experts, who leave only one long branch to carry the crop and a short knob which, in the following year, will be left to grow and carry the grape, then cutting the long branch which carried it the year before. It takes about four years for a vine after planting to bear a reasonable amount of grapes, so the investment of capital in a vineyard (apart from the value of the land which nowadays is very high) is really exorbitant. It can be said, however, that the yield is high, compared to the production in other wine districts and should be well worth the investment.

THE VINTAGE   The vintage, or picking of the grapes, takes place a little earlier than in the rest of the wine countries of Europe and is naturally done by hand. As regards the pressing of the grape, up to quite recently it was executed by men wearing hob-nailed shoes in *lagares* or troughs in the vineyard buildings, but now this has been mechanised and many firms bring the grape to Jerez, Puerto or Sanlucar where modern mechanical presses are used.

If the grape is pressed in the vineyards the butts of Must are transported to the different *bodegas* where the violent fermentation in all likelihood has already set in, and this violent fermentation lasts for about a week or ten days when the sugar content of the Must is converted into alcohol, leaving the wine completely dry. This fermentation generally takes place in casks, although some wine-growers use vats or tanks for this purpose, but it has always been considered that fermenting the wine in butts also has an advantage, if new butts are used, because the fermentation of the Must or new wine seasons the cask, giving no woody taint to the Must. The tannin in the wood of the cask is also a favourable factor for fermentation.

After the violent fermentation has ended a second slow fermentation sets in, which is really most important as it is then that the different esters and aldehydes are developed in the wine. During the pressing of the grape a small amount of pure gypsum (calcium sulphate) has always traditionally been added to the grapes in the press; the amount generally is under 1 kilo per butt of Must produced. The sugar content of the Must obtained from the Palomino grape is between 12° and 13° Baumé, which is converted into about the same percentage of alcohol by volume. With the Pedro Ximenez variety the strength sometimes exceeds 15 per cent, but when sweet Pedro Ximenez wine is required, the grapes are left in the sun for about a fortnight and the degree of sweetness obtained is generally between 22° and 25° Baumé, but, of course, the yield of the grapes, which have lost a great part of their juice, is reduced to about one-fourth of what they would have produced had they been pressed soon after they were picked.

BODEGAS   There are no underground cellars in Jerez and the most appropriate buildings for storing Sherry are above ground level, well ventilated, high-ceilinged structures, supported by pillars or columns, generally with four to six aisles, the butts being placed on either side of these aisles, generally three to four tiers high. After the Musts have fallen bright and the lees have deposited at the bottom of the casks, the wines are racked and fortified by adding some spirit which is generally blended with the same wine before adding it to the wine to be strengthened. Before this is done, the new wine has to be classified, and this is always carried out by experts who mark the different casks, consigning them into one of three categories according to quality. Later the casks will again be classified according to the class of wine into which each cask is developing. This is done with the *venencia* which is used in Jerez for drawing Sherry from the oak casks and pouring it into a glass. As the wine is poured from a certain height, depending on the skill of the *venenciador*, it mingles with the air and the bouquet of the wine is thus enhanced. Much practice is needed and the expert use of the *venencia*—without spilling a drop of wine—can be considered an art. The stem of the *venencia* is usually made of whalebone and the cup is silver or stainless steel.

THE SOLERA SYSTEM

Sherry alters with age from one year to another, varying in quality gradually as it matures, usually acquiring higher alcoholic strength, body and colour. The object of the *Solera* system is to compensate the changes produced in the wine due to age by refreshing or rejuvenating the older wine by blending it with a younger one. To maintain the quality uniform it is, therefore, necessary that periodical drawings should be made; these drawings are generally carried out several times a year. There is an old Spanish saying: *"El trigo en la pala y el vino en la jarra"* (A scoop for the wheat and a jug for the wine). This refers to the advisability of drawing from a *Solera* several times a year in small quantities instead of at once, all that is required for the whole year, and, in actual practice, this has proved to be good counsel. Apart from this, the aeration resulting from the racking of the wine from one cask to another also has a favourable effect on the wine and has contributed, in no small way, to the success of the *Solera* system. People are sometimes confused with the name *Solera* and it should be noted that this word *Solera* does not mean a matured wine of dark colour, as many erroneously believe, but just a system of development which can be used for all kinds of wines and is certainly indispensable for the production of Finos so as to allow a perfect growth of *flor* and to attain uniformity in the quality of the brands sold on the market.

In some wine districts of Spain, outside the Sherry area, the word *Solera* is at times used to describe an old wine and also to convey the idea of continued quality in matters other than wine:

that is, a writer of established prestige, whose father was also a writer, would be called *un escritor de solera*.

The system consists of tiers of casks or scales of different ages, and to give an idea of how the system works, it is worth while describing an example of a *Solera* with, say, six scales, each one containing, say, forty or fifty butts, an equal number to those in the first scale which is the *Solera* proper. The wine from this first scale is the one ready to be sold—naturally after fining and filtering—whilst the scale above has an equal number of butts of wine which is about a year younger, and so on consecutively until the sixth and the last scale where the wine will be about five years younger than that of the bottom tier or first scale of the *Solera*. The wines in the different scales should always be of the same class or kind, although different in age and wherever possible, from the same vineyard. As mentioned before, the first scale is generally called the *Solera* (derived from the Spanish word *suelo* or solar—floor or ground, due to it generally being on ground level), and the second, third, etc., are sometimes called *criaderas* (nurseries) and in some *bodegas* they are called second, third, etc., scales of the particular *Solera*). The number of scales or *criaderas* for Fino wines is naturally larger than those in the fuller bodied Oloroso wines because these latter wines vary much less from one year to another than do the Finos.

The more one thinks about the gradual changes which occur in Sherry during the maturing of the wine and later, its ageing, the more one realises that it is very like a living being. From the time that the wine is born, that is, when the sweet juice of the grape is converted into wine, it commences a continuous change from year to year, during which a certain guidance is required so that it takes the best possible course. The process followed in Jerez is:

First the wine goes into the *criaderas* or nurseries of one of the two basic classes of Sherry—Fino or Oloroso: after its initial breeding it runs through the different scales of the *soleras*, which can be compared to the different forms in a school, until it gets

366

to the first scale or ground tier of the *solera*, which can be compared to the university, and it is there that the scholar gets his degree and becomes a graduate. The year when the *solera* was founded, which is often shown on the labels of bottled wines by some wine shippers, should not be confused with the age of the actual wine. The wine of the first scale will undoubtedly have some proportion, although extremely small, of the original wine when the *solera* was founded, but with this system one can never assert that the wine is of any particular vintage or year and the main objective of this process of maturation, which is a perpetual cycle, is to obtain from one year to another a wine that does not vary in quality or age.

This is why the term "vintage wine" is never used for Sherry on the market—as once the wine enters a *solera* it loses the identity of the year in which it was produced.

The new wine which is classified for the Fino *criaderas* generally goes into these the year after it was pressed, but those wines which are prone to the Oloroso group are sometimes left as *anadas* by certain shippers. They are really on the waiting list to be applied later to the fuller bodied Oloroso *soleras* as and when required by the different scales of the Oloroso *soleras*.

THE FLOR IN JEREZ WINES

Fino wines when in cask develop a film on the surface of the wine which is called *flor* in Sherryland and which is formed by yeast cells which periodically rise to the surface. The growth becomes more active twice a year and in between these periods the cells sink to the bottom of the cask. The most active periods of this *flor* development are April to May and again in the autumn. This *flor* continues to increase each year and the film gradually gets thicker, but Fino wines generally have a film of yeast cells floating on the surface all the year round. The Amontillados also develop *flor* and the Olorosos slightly at the beginning of their life, but in all fuller-bodied wines the *flor* is generally darker.

Sherry can be divided into two main groups, the Finos and the Olorosos, but there are also some intermediate categories. The Fino Sherries are generally lighter, both in alcoholic content and shade, than the Olorosos which are fuller bodied and darker in shade. These two main categories may be further sub-divided:

F.   Finos   — Manzanillas and Amontillados.
O.   Olorosos — Palo Cortados and Rayas.

Apart from these, there are the medium sweet wines or *abocados* which are among the aforementioned and the very sweet wines made from the Pedro Ximenez and Moscatel grapes. It will be realised that it is far easier to sample the wines in question than to attempt to describe them. However, the following explanation is as succinct as is possible and may help to understand the different classes of wine mentioned.

FINOS: These are of a pale straw colour and very dry, though low in acidity. Like topaz, their colours differ in shade whilst the alcoholic content of the wine ranges between 15·5° to 17° Gay Lussac. The bouquet is delicate yet pungent because of the *flor* or veil of yeast cells which develops on the surface of the wine. Fino Sherries are notably distinguished for their clean nose, elegance and delicate aroma. This wine has only become popular since the last quarter of the nineteenth century and then mainly in Spain and other warm climate countries. Now, however, they are also extremely popular abroad, even in those countries where the climate is decidedly not warm.

The shade of the above-mentioned wines is generally V.P. (very pale). See Colour Plate facing p.353.

MANZANILLA: This is the name given to a Sherry which is produced within the rural limits of SANLUCAR DE BARRAMEDA, a small coastal town about 20 kilometres from Jerez Although the vine-growing lands of Jerez and Sanlucar are separated by a strip of farmland, the actual rural borders of these towns are

368

themselves adjacent and many Sanlucar owners have vineyards in Jerez and vice versa. The sea air of Sanlucar has a decided effect upon the wine, making it lighter in body than the Finos and imparting a delicate and markedly characteristic aroma. The wine is completely dry, leaving a clean but slightly bitter aftertaste on the palate, without being so rounded and full as the Fino. In fact, if the Jerez wines were taken to Sanlucar, as they sometimes are, they usually develop into Manzanillas, whilst the Sanlucar wines brought to Jerez sometimes take on certain characteristics peculiar to Jerez wines. Manzanilla is a very pale straw colour, although, as it matures, it acquires an amber shade similar to that of the Amontillados. Its degree of alcohol varies between 15·5° and 16·5° Gay Lussac and some very old Manzanillas called *Pasadas* sometimes reach 20° Gay Lussac. The shade of Manzanilla is V.V.P. (very very pale). See Colour Plate facing p.353.

AMONTILLADO: This is a wine which also belongs to the Fino class, but which generally acquires Amontillado characteristics with age. Amontillados, like the Finos from which they are derived, are dry to the palate in *Solera*, but in general less pale in colour, having an amber tone which, as they mature, gains a deeper hue. They also have the same pungent bouquet as the Finos, but are nuttier owing to their higher alcoholic content —17° to 18° Gay Lussac. In rare cases, with age, the strength naturally increases to 20° or even 24° Gay Lussac, although this limit is rarely reached. These wines are extremely crisp, clean on the nose and the palate, and, although naturally dry, are usually blended with a little sweet wine prior to shipment, so that Amontillado has now come to mean, in the British màrket, a medium dry Sherry. A Fino usually becomes, with age, an Amontillado, that is if the Fino is allowed to lose its characteristic features by not being periodically drawn from the *Solera*. The earliest known reference to Amontillado in the Sherry trade is said to be in the year 1796.

OLOROSO: This, as the name implies, is given to wines that have a strong bouquet, but only those wines which are clean on the nose should be called by this name. Its bouquet is not as pungent as the Finos and Amontillados and is distinguished by being a fuller wine both on the nose and palate and having more vinosity—full-bodied. Although the wines are dry, a trace of sweetness often appears on tasting them, thus differing from the Amontillados which leave a completely dry aftertaste. Olorosos usually have an alcoholic strength of 18° to 20° Gay Lussac and this increases with age, sometimes reaching 24° to 25° Gay Lussac. The colour is usually more golden than the Amontillado, looking rather like burnished gold and deepening in shade with age. The normal colours range between G (golden) and D.G. (dark golden). See Colour Plate facing p.353.

The flavours of the Fino, Amontillado and Oloroso wines have been compared by the author to the taste of certain nuts. Thus the Fino is likened to the almond, the Amontillado to a hazelnut, and the Oloroso to a walnut. These are obviously only approximate comparisons, since it is impossible to obtain an exact parallel, so that, regardless of what is written, the most satisfactory method of differentiating each subtlety of taste and colour really is only obtained through continued practice.

PALO CORTADO: This name is applied to certain wines of the Oloroso group which, in general, are rare and not obtained at every vintage. These wines have a very clean bouquet and, in this respect, are like the Amontillados, whilst on the palate they are full-bodied and have the beefiness of an Oloroso. The Palo Cortados class comes between the Oloroso and the Amontillado and is usually graded according to its vinosity by marking the casks: one Palo Cortado (⊥), two, three, up to a maximum of four (≢). The Palo Cortados are generally in the G shade (golden) unless they are very old and they then get darker. See Colour Plate facing p.353.

RAYA: These are wines belonging to the Oloroso group but lacking the fragrant bouquet and crispness on the palate, being slightly less delicate. If on the nose they are cleaner, yet not enough so to be an Oloroso, the wine in question is classified

370

as a Raya Olorosa. Both Raya and Raya Olorosa are usually full-bodied with a deep golden colour and a maximum of 18° Gay Lussac. On the palate they are usually full, sometimes retaining a trace of sugar, perhaps through not having completed their fermentation. The colour is generally D.G. (dark golden). See Colour Plate facing p.353.

Although the wines of the different classes mentioned show variation in their components, chemical analysis alone does not suffice to classify them, especially when they are young. Apart from the wines given in the preceding paragraphs, there are also several other blended Sherries which are important. The following are some examples, CREAM which is a full sweet Oloroso, AMOROSO a medium-sweet and velvety Oloroso D.G. (dark golden in colour), and OLD EAST INDIA which the British generally call a somewhat sweet old Oloroso and is brown in colour. This name is derived from the old practice of shippers sending Sherry in casks on long voyages so that, by the time the wine had been on the outward and return journey in the ship, it was believed to have been improved in quality through having doubly crossed the Equator. The real cause of the improvement was, probably, the oxidation which the wine underwent buffeted about by the ship's roll whilst in casks with some ullage. This old custom might perhaps be the origin of the well-known saying *Mareado el buen vino de Xerez, si valia cinco, vale diez* ("A sea-tossed Sherry, if it was worth five, is worth ten"). Although the practice has fallen into disuse, there are still a few instances when it is done at the client's request. It seems the custom was also known in Pliny's time, since he mentions it in Book XIV, chapter 18: "It also happens to wines that travel by sea which are felt to double in vigour from the movement of the ship." It seems quite likely as well that Cervantes was referring to these wines in his book *Persiles y Segismunda* (Book 1, chapter 15) when he writes: "They went with the girl to the inn for refreshments, where the feasting tables were laden with food and where their souls were brimming with merriment as much as their goblets were charged with noble wines which are improved in such a miraculous way by being sailed across the sea from one

point to another in such a way that there is no nectar to equal them."

Mention must also be made of the sweet and colour wines that are essential accessories in the Jerez blending. The best sweet wines are obtained from the Pedro Ximenez grapes which are gathered when they are very ripe and then left to bask in the sunshine for about ten to twenty days before being pressed. This increases the sugar content and as a result the fermentation is only partial, producing a sweet wine of low alcoholic strength. Throughout the time the grapes are exposed to the sun, it is normal to cover them at night with round *esparto* grass mats to protect them from the dew. The sugar content of a good Pedro Ximenez is usually 22° to 24° Baumé, which comes to approximately 400 grammes of sugar to a litre. As may be imagined, these wines are extremely expensive to produce, owing to the scant quantity of juice obtained from the grapes after they have been dried in the sun. The wines are, of course, very sweet, dense, of a dark colour and having a pronounced flavour of raisins. It is offered as a dessert wine which is much appreciated as a substitute for a liqueur.

A similar wine is obtained from the Moscatel grape, although this variety of grape is not exposed to the sun as long as the Pedro Ximenez generally is. The main feature which distinguishes a Moscatel wine from a Pedro Ximenez is the characteristic fruity bouquet of the former which is due to certain essential oils which are present close to the pip of the grape, and it is not generally as sweet as the Pedro Ximenez. The Moscatel wine is also very popular as a dessert wine. (The colours of the two above-mentioned wines are brown.)

SHERRY EXPORTS

For the last two centuries the British Isles has undoubtedly been Jerez's best customer, but it is difficult to trace figures of what was shipped from Jerez prior to this period, although undoubtedly Sherry must have been well known in Britain, judging by what Shakespeare wrote about Sherris Sack. It has always struck me as strange that Shakespeare, being an Englishman, should have mentioned Sherry so often in his writings, and Cervantes, a Spaniard, who was contemporaneous with Shakespeare (although different ages—both eminent writers died on the same date in April 1616), never mentioned anything about our wine. There are certain notes in Cervantes' works which may refer to Sherry, but, generally, when he speaks about wine he refers to the *vin ordinaire* of the Mancha district in the centre of Spain, which was the scene of Don Quixote's exploits. In those times Sherry was exported abroad from Xerez, but was surely not sent from there to any other province of Spain, as roads and means of transport must have been scarce in those days.

We are indebted to that genius William Shakespeare who made Sherry so popular in England then, and gave sound advice in quoting Falstaff: "A good sherris-sack hath a twofold operation in it. It ascends me into the brain; dries me there all the foolish and dull and crudy vapours which environ it; makes it apprehensive, quick, forgetive, full of nimble, fiery and delectable shapes; which delivered o'er to the voice, the tongue, which is the birth, becomes excellent wit. The second property of your excellent sherris is the warming of the blood; which, before cold and settled, left the liver white and pale, which is the badge of pusillanimity and cowardice; but the sherris warms it, and makes it course from the inwards to the parts extreme. It illumineth the face, which, as a beacon, gives warning to all the rest of this little kingdom, man, to arm; and then the vital commoners and inland petty spirits muster me all to their captain, the heart, who great and puff'd up with this retinue, doth any deed of courage—and this valour comes of sherris. So that skill in the weapon is nothing without sack, for that sets it a-work; and learning, a mere hoard of gold kept by a devil till sack commences it and sets it in act and use. Hereof comes it that Prince Harry is valiant; for the cold blood he did naturally inherit of his father, he hath, like lean, sterile and bare land, manured, husbanded, and till'd, with excellent endeavour of drinking good and good store of fertile sherris, that he is become very hot and valiant. If I had a thousand sons, the first humane principle I would teach them should be to forswear thin potations and to addict themselves to sack. . . ."

A lot has been said about the etymology of the word "Sack" which, because Sherry is dry, has generally been attributed to the French word *sec*, but I have always wondered if this is so, because Shakespeare also referred to Malligo Sack and also to Canary Sack, and, undoubtedly, Malaga was never a dry wine. Going through the wine history of Xerez with the eminent English writer on wines, Mr. Warner Allen, we noticed that Sherry to be exported from here was always referred to as *Vinos de Saca*, which translated into English really means Export Wines, because the word *sacar* in Spanish means "to draw from" or "extract". In the municipal archives of Xerez, the Regulations regarding the granting of permits for Sherry to be shipped always referred to these wines as *Vino de Saca*, and it is much more likely that the word "Sack" has its derivation from the Spanish word *saca* than from the French word *sec*, and this would explain why the wines exported from Malaga were called Malaga Sack.

In the last decade of the nineteenth century, Sherry exports to England fell, perhaps due to the invasion of the phylloxera in Europe, which later reached the Sherry district in 1894, but shortly after, at the beginning of the present century and coinciding with the wedding of King Alfonso XIII to Princess Ena of Battenberg, the shipments to England started rising again. We must place on record that this was greatly due to King Alfonso's personal efforts to popularise this wine again in England, and it is only fair to acknowledge that the Sherry trade owes a debt of gratitude to this Spanish monarch who, unfortunately, died in exile, in spite of the good work he did for Spain during his lifetime. In an article "Fashion in Wine— King Alfonso re-introduces Sherry in England" which was published in London in the periodical *The Tribune* of August 16th, 1906, the following reference appeared:

"The visit of the King and Queen of Spain to this country has already had some influence upon society in one respect at all events: it has done much to revive the declining taste for Sherry in England. At all the dinners and parties given by King Alfonso at Cowes, Sherry occupied a prominent place in the menus.

374

Out of a selection of eight or nine wines, four were usually Sherries, and, as the wine was of unusually fine quality, it attracted a good deal of attention. King Edward complimented His Majesty upon possessing the wine, saying that he had not tasted such excellent Sherry for many years."

For the last quarter of a century, shipments to foreign countries from Jerez have been on the increase and in 1969 they exceeded a total of 130,000 butts.

SHERRY CASKS

The casks mostly used in Jerez are butts. A shipping butt has a capacity of about 110 gallons, that is, 500 litres. Hogsheads, which hold half this amount, are also used, as well as quarter casks and octaves. The butts used for maturing the wine in the bodegas are of larger capacity, about 20 per cent more, but, as the development of the *flor*, which is essential to the maturing of Sherry, requires a certain amount of ullage for aeration, the usual amount of wine which the *bodega* butt contains is also about 110 gallons.

The wood which is preferred in Jerez and, as a matter of fact, in most wine countries of Europe for the maturing of wine is the American white oak. Before America was discovered different woods were used in the Sherry trade and some ancient casks still exist which were made of cherry wood. It is said that the first oak wood that came from America was really sent as ballast for the ships which returned from the new colonies, and it is said that on the *Mayflower*, when the pilgrims went over, one of them was a cooper, so we might presume that he was the first Englishman to build a cask with American wood.

Sherry casks are greatly appreciated for maturing whisky, and, as the Sherry area's coopers are very efficient in their craftsmanship, these casks at times fetch a fairly high price abroad and are even shipped empty to Scotland, and other places.

BOTTLED SHERRY

Most of the Sherry exported to the United Kingdom is shipped in bulk and very few firms send bottled wines over, but Sherry is shipped in bottle from Jerez, Puerto and Sanlucar to other European and American markets.

There is always, however, a possibility of bottled Sherry throwing a deposit in the form of potassium bitartrate which the wine naturally contains. Nowadays, this can be avoided with certain wines by subjecting the Sherry to low temperatures for a short period and filtering it afterwards so that the wine keeps bright.

As regards the Sherry which is drunk in Spain, the principal shippers sell all their brands in bottle, but it should be said that Sherry does not keep as well in bottle in hot countries like Spain, where temperatures fluctuate more, as it does farther north, and pale dry Sherries are more apt to get bottle flavour in warm countries due to the oxidation of the wine, which is also affected by light, if they are not bottled in very dark bottles or kept in cool and dark cellars.

THE NAME OF SHERRY

Sherry, mainly due to its versatility and the many markets where it is justly appreciated, has had many imitations and for many years back, in many wine districts of the world, "sherry type" or "sherry style" wines have been put on the different markets where Sherry had customers. It must be said that, although imitation is the sincerest form of flattery, we are sure that many people will agree with an eminent writer on wine questions, Mr. André Simon. In his book *The Blood of the Grape*, on page 119, he writes: "Pedigree wines should always be sold under their legal denomination of origin." Mr. Simon, in this paragraph and others, explains that the denomination of origin not only applies to the place where the wine comes from, but also to the maturing and developing processes or practices employed. "Bordeaux and Cognac, Champagne and Burgundy, Port and Sherry are geographical names of origin which should never be used in a generic sense as simply representing certain classes of wine; the significance of these names is firstly geographical and should be applied exclusively to the wines of well-known

376

European vineyards, the boundaries of which are fixed by long-standing international commercial practice and by national legislation in force."

It is also interesting to note what was written by Mr. Cuthbert Burgoyne in April 1905 in the *Australian Vigneron and Fruit Growers Journal*. Mr. Burgoyne, who belongs to a well-known Australian wine shipping firm, when referring to the imitation and misuse of European wine names by the Australians, said: "These wines (the European ones) have made their brands known with their original names, which other countries have tried to imitate afterwards; and it is a well-known thing that he who imitates will never be a leader, and it is evident that the Australian growers should adopt their special denomination for the wines which are better produced on their soil, instead of usurping the names of wines from other countries."

COURT DECISION

Since the preparation of this chapter, a famous lawsuit about Sherry has been heard in London. The case was brought by Vine Products Ltd., an important British wine producer, and two associated companies against four Sherry companies Mackenzies, Gonzalez Byass, Williams & Humbert and Domecq. The plaintiffs asked for declarations that the expressions "British Sherry", "Australian Sherry", "South African Sherry" and "Cyprus Sherry" might be permitted to continue, and they put forward a definition of Sherry which totally ignored, and indeed denied, the historical and geographical rights of Jerez.

The Jerezanos naturally counter-attacked, and after years of preparation for the case and a hearing which lasted more than six weeks, the judge resolved the long argument (which had been simmering in the wine trade for most of this century) by giving something to each side. To Jerez he gave the exclusive right to use the word Sherry by itself. Sherry is not, he found, a word for a type of wine, made anywhere in any way. It is a geographical name, meaning wine from the Jerez district of Spain. Wines of sherry-type made elsewhere than Jerez are not Sherry; but because such wines, made in Britain, South Africa,

Australia and Cyprus have for so long been known as "British Sherry", "South African Sherry", "Australian Sherry" and "Cyprus Sherry" without objection, it would now be unfair to prevent such use, and the judge therefore permitted them to continue.

The transcript of the case will for long provide a rich mine of information for the student of Sherry and its imitators. Every conceivable point was contested and argued. Jerez even had to prove the connection between its name and the English word "sherry". A professor from Madrid gave evidence that the Moorish name was "Scherish"; and a rare and early book in the library of Emmanuel College, Cambridge, showed that at that time the town was called "Sherrys". In Castilian Spanish, "Sherrish" became "Sherrys" or "Sherris", then "Sherry". (Did the English think it was a plural and invent the singular?) Thus modern English is closer in form to the old name than the modern Spanish.

Judgement was given in 1967; and already (1971) the effect has been marked. Our imitators may still sell their wines of sherry-type as "British Sherry", "Australian Sherry", "South African Sherry" and "Cyprus Sherry". But no longer can they advertise, or in any way refer to, these wines as Sherry. "Real Sherry comes only from Spain" was something which to Spaniards was self-evident. To others it had previously seemed a somewhat contentious assertion. Now it is a judicial finding of fact. To say in course of trade that "British Sherry" is good Sherry is no longer permitted; and if anyone objects, said the judge, that this seems rather hard, he may be reminded that there is no obligation to call the product "British Sherry", "and so saddle it with a suggestion of inferiority which it may not deserve. He can—and indeed he sometimes does—sell it under a brand name without using the word 'sherry' at all."

We had waited fifty years too long to get all we wanted, the central prize was still ours; Sherry means in England the wine of Jerez and nothing else.

SPANISH
TABLE WINES

"One sleeps where Southern vines are drest
Above the noble slain;
He wrapt his colours round his breast
On a blood-red field of Spain."

(Felicia Hemans, 1793–1835)

GEOGRAPHY When the Duke of Wellington complained, "With small armies you do no good here and with a large one you starve to death", he had acquired a knowledge of the climate and terrain of Spain which is an essential prerequisite to an understanding of the reasons her countless vineyards produce such a great variety of wines.

Next to Switzerland, Spain has the highest average altitude in Europe and it is to the coastal areas surrounding the *meseta*, the high arid tableland of Central Spain, that we look for the greater production. But such is its sturdy nature that even in New Castile, all of which is over 2,000 feet above sea level, the vine flourishes in temperatures which, in July, can vary up to 30°F. between day and night. The air is hazy with dust, the *calina*, in this semi-desert which has to its west and north the ranges of the Montes de Toledo, Sierra de Gredos and the Sierra de Guadarrama, while to the east it is separated from Aragon by the hills of the Serrañia de Cuenca. Truly a hot spot!

379

But if the one great wine of Spain is Sherry, blessed by the quality of the light in Andalusia, the 500 million gallons of table wine produced every year (because the uniformity of the climate ensures every year is a good year for wine in Spain) can sometimes be very interesting and always good.

Also, because the country, with an area twice the size of Great Britain, supporting a population of only about 30 millions, has a production of wine, *per capita*, double that of France, and a consumption less than France or Italy, it is well placed to export the genuine surplus.

Of the 28 million gallons of wine Great Britain imported during 1964, 8 million gallons came from Spain, with the finer ones being "about the best wines for the money in the world".

Not all of Spain enjoys the commercial cultivation of the vine, and in the north-west province of Galicia, where the mountains of its neighbouring province of Léon and of Northern Portugal act as a barrier to the Atlantic winds, we find farmers, with Irish-like faces, reminding us that the Celts settled in this northern strip of Spain tending their haystacks and granaries in the cool and wet climate. In the province of Asturias, which looks north to the Bay of Biscay, the mountains of the Cordillera Cantabrica precipitate so much moisture that, before industries came to raise the standard of living and provide money for drainage, the common footwear was the *almadreñas*, or wooden shoes of the rainy north, with three legs like a milking stool to prevent sinking ankle-deep.

If the Cordillera Cantabrica mountains restrict wine-making to the north, immediately south, ample compensation is received in the valley of the River Ebro, especially in the district of Rioja, which centres on the towns of Haro and Logrono.

RIOJA

Before 1875 the Rioja district produced good wine but perhaps only a little better than *vino corriente*—ordinary wine. Then, when the phylloxera blight was laying low the vineyards of France, and failed to cross the Pyrenees to Spain, French viticultural experts—with capital, good equipment and sound scientific knowledge (Pasteur had just finished his experiments)—descended on the area and greatly improved the wines.

The Golden Age for Rioja wines followed for thirty years until the phylloxera bug eventually arrived. Gradually the vines have been grafted and planted on American stocks and now, once again, the sturdy and heavily productive vineyards are producing the quality wines for which Rioja is justly famous. The trade is largely in the hands of families with sufficient capital to allow them to fully mature their wines, and seldom is a Rioja bottled before spending at least three years maturing in cask—a useful pointer to quality but a sure indication that the wines cannot possibly be as inexpensive as those in some other parts of Spain.

Of the families producing great wines, perhaps the most famous vineyard owners are the Marques de Riscal, and Lopez Heredia near HARO, and the Bodegas Francos Espanolas at LOGRONO.

Certainly the notes of my first tasting in the district are liberally spattered with suggestions of flavours comparing with great names of France. This is perhaps not surprising when one considers the admirable vine producing qualities of the district and

SPAIN

ALELLA
CATALONIA   Alella
Barcelona

Panades
PrIorato   Reus
TARRAGONA   Tarragona

VALENCIA
Valencia

CARINENA
Zaragoza

Utiel
Requena
Cheste

ARAGON

VALENCIA

Monovar
Jumilla
Yecla
ALICANTE
Alicante

MURCIA

RIOJA
Haro   LOGRONO

Guadalajara

MADRID
Aranjuez

Segovia

Manzanares

VALDEPENAS

Valladolid

Toledo

Ciudad Real

CASTILA

ANDALUSIA

Cordoba   Moriles
Montilla   Montilla

Lagrima
MALAGA
Malaga

LEON   Salamanca

ESTREMADURA

Manzanilla

Sevilla

Jerez de la Frontera
JEREZ
Cadiz

Badajoz

LOGRONO
Calahorra
Alfaro
Arnedo

Haro

RIOJA

Santo Domingo de la Calzada
Najera
Torrecilla en Cameros

Requena   *Red wine*
ALELLA   *White wine*

the great care taken by the French when they introduced the root-stocks, which still carry the names Cepa Chablis, Cepa Médoc, Cepa Borgona, that they grew from disease-free vines of their native land.

The red wines, which are often better than the whites, live to a good age and although vintage years are not of great consequence in Spain, the words *consecha de*, followed by the year, on a bottle of Rioja is a sure guide to a good bottle, this being a district like Jerez, Tarragona and Malaga having an "Official Board Controlling the name of Origin", which controls the making and quality of the wine and will only give its seal to approved wines.

Extra special bottles are sometimes decorated with *Alambrado*, that fine wire mesh sealed with a tiny lead seal, and may carry the word *Vina* (vineyard) followed by the name of the vineyard. But whether you select a "great" bottle, a simple "clarete" or a fuller burgundy type, with the red wines of Rioja you will not be disappointed; while, with the whites, you will find as great a variety as can be found along the length of the Loire in France, and all of them drinkable!

CASTILE AND LEON

To the south and to the west of Rioja the province of Old Castile produces more than 20 million gallons of wine each year, while its neighbouring province of Léon has a production of half that quantity. These are the carafe wines the visitor may drink in Valladolid and Salamanca, or while waiting for that baby lamb to be roasted in the restaurant which faces the Roman aqueduct at Segovia. Light wines, clean on the palate but without the character necessary to bring acclaim far from their native home.

ARAGON

In Aragon, which is to the east of Rioja, the more than 10 million gallons produced annually along the valley of the Ebro have some wines of quality, especially the CARIÑEÑA. This extremely sweet white wine is greatly enjoyed in Saragossa, the capital of the province, and the surrounding district. Little is exported, however.

CATALONIA

Between Aragon and the Mediterranean lies Catalonia, with the Pyrenees and Andora to the north and the broad Ebro valley to the south. This is one of the main wine-producing areas in Spain with an output approaching 100 million gallons each year. Records show that it was in about 600 B.C. that the Greeks came, bringing the grapevine and olive root, and it was already a flourishing district when Caesar Augustus ruled the Roman Empire and ordered the 10,000 miles of Imperial Road in Spain, which today still marks the main highways.

TARRAGONA

Tarragona gives its name to the most famous wine of the area, and, as a port, remains the centre of a very extensive wine trade. From here are shipped large quantities of sound, inexpensive wines as well as the very full-bodied dark red PRIORATO produced mainly around REUS about eight miles inland at the foot of the hills. The vineyards of VILLAFRANCA DE PANADES and VALLS add their quota to the quantity exported to the world, but when 200 to 300 happy Catalans join hands on the Plaza

The decanter in the photograph is old Irish glass dated around 1770 and the coaster in English silver is of the same period. The bottle shows the customer's initialled plaque and the glass (still preserved at the Cambridge branch of Barclays Bank) is the one from which William Pitt drank his port when he visited the directors of the bank.

facing p. 384

Loading the newly pressed wine on to the Douro boat for shipment to Oporto.

Douro vineyard workers in single file with baskets slung high, carry down the grapes from the steeply terraced vineyards.

or in a leafy *Rambla* to dance the light rhythmic *Sardana*, there
will always be a flask remaining to quench the dancers' thirst,
and even one for the British holiday-making along the most
famous part of the Catalonian coast—the Costa Brava!

BARCELONA

Barcelona, too, has its share of the wine trade and just north of
here at ALELLA a very pleasant, strong earthy white wine is produced, as well as a fine red wine which, although taking some
time to mature, is well worth the waiting. And in the hills
around SAN SADURNI the fresh white wine, with a natural
tendency to sparkle, is handled by traditional methods to produce the sparkling wine of Spain which, although not so "fine"
as its competitors from northern countries, is nevertheless sound,
a refreshing aperitif in the cool of the evening and a happy base
for many iced fruit drinks.

VALENCIA

There are no difficulties in producing wines along the Mediterranean coast, and in the south-east the districts of VALENCIA and
MURCIA combine to provide the forty-five million gallons of
LEVANTE wine annually. Valencia, the third largest city in Spain,
is sited on an extremely fertile plain, and the sweet red wines
from here were once very popular in England. The whites, however, lack acidity and few are exported. The wines of the district marry well with *paella*, the chicken, rice and seafood dish of
Valencia, and are ideal to drink a toast to El Cid, the knight who
in the eleventh century fought the Moors and became the idol
of Spanish chivalry.

ALICANTE

At Alicante the castle, first built by the Carthaginians in 400 B.C., looks down on a busy port from the rock 700 feet high and right in the town. The wines from here, too, were once very popular in England but have lost place to those from farther north. But inland from YECLA comes a powerful *rosé* wine which is much admired in France, and whose fame will probably spread.

MALAGA

On the Costa del Sol, Malaga, another town rich in history, with many Roman remains, produces rich, sweet, sometimes walnut brown wines in its remarkably mild climate. This is the wine which was popular long before the Sherry of Jerez, but is now not so fashionable as its Andalusian cousin.

LAGRIMA, the finest type, made from sun-dried grapes, is a nectar, while MOUNTAIN, a variety made from the grapes grown on the mountains, is much lighter and drier in character, and was very popular in England in the eighteenth century. The driest wine is VIRGIN, which can be very pleasant, but Malaga is above all renowned for the finest sweet wine of Spain; it ages in wood and improves with age.

MONTILLA

To the north and towards Cordoba we discover MONTILLA—"only great wine of Europe hardly seen in England". The area of production is large and the wine is produced on the same solera system as Sherry except that it is less fortified or not at all. A feature of the *Bodegas* are the enormous earthenware jars of amphoral shape made of glazed pottery or smooth cement, called *tinajas*. Standing seven to ten feet high and holding anything from 600 gallons to 1,200 gallons, they are built *in situ* and left open at the top. *Flor* grows on the wine and produces very delicate flavours. This is the same special kind of yeast which is also responsible for the distinctive taste of Fino Sherries. To be sold as MONTILLA, regulations require that the wine has had at least one year's maturation and has a minimum of 15° of alcohol —or if in bottle, 16°. These strengths attract the higher rate of duty in England, which makes Montilla wines costly when compared with their more robust counterparts from Jerez. But the wines from the town which gave AMONTILLADO its name are attractive and worthy of a place in a wine-lover's library.

NEW CASTILE

Great quantities of wine are also produced in the central area of Spain, as instance the approaching 100 million gallons of NEW CASTILE and LA MANCHA. This is an area heavy with history: Toledo, the beloved city of El Greco on the River Tagus, where, taught by the Moors, swords have been hand forged for military men since the first century B.C.; the home of Don Quixote; the palace at Aranjuez, summer residence of the Bourbon kings; and one of the most photographed old castles of Spain at Manzanares. Much of the wine of the area goes to the capital, Madrid, red and white wine, produced in great quantity, which is inexpensive and does not improve with age. But there is an exception at VALDEPENAS (Valley of Stones) where the big, full-bodied wine VINO DE LA TIERRA enjoys a reputation known the world over.

To complete the tour of Spain, today, even in Estremadura, the "dust bowl", the western province which borders on Portugal, vines flourish, and with the irrigation scheme at Badajoz nearing completion, we may soon see an extension of intensive farming where fields of irrigated rice give way to drier roots of long staple cotton, next groves of glossy orange trees, then vineyards clinging to the steeper slopes, while above, in nearly perpendicular hills, shepherds graze their flocks.

PORTUGAL

I can never understand why it is necessary to describe a wine as a "type" of wine. Every wine-producing country produces its own style of wine, be it red or white, sparkling or still, sweet or dry, fortified or unfortified. Thus each country should be proud of its individual wine and describe these wines by their individual district. This the Portuguese have very sensibly done, as they are, and rightly so, proud of their wines.

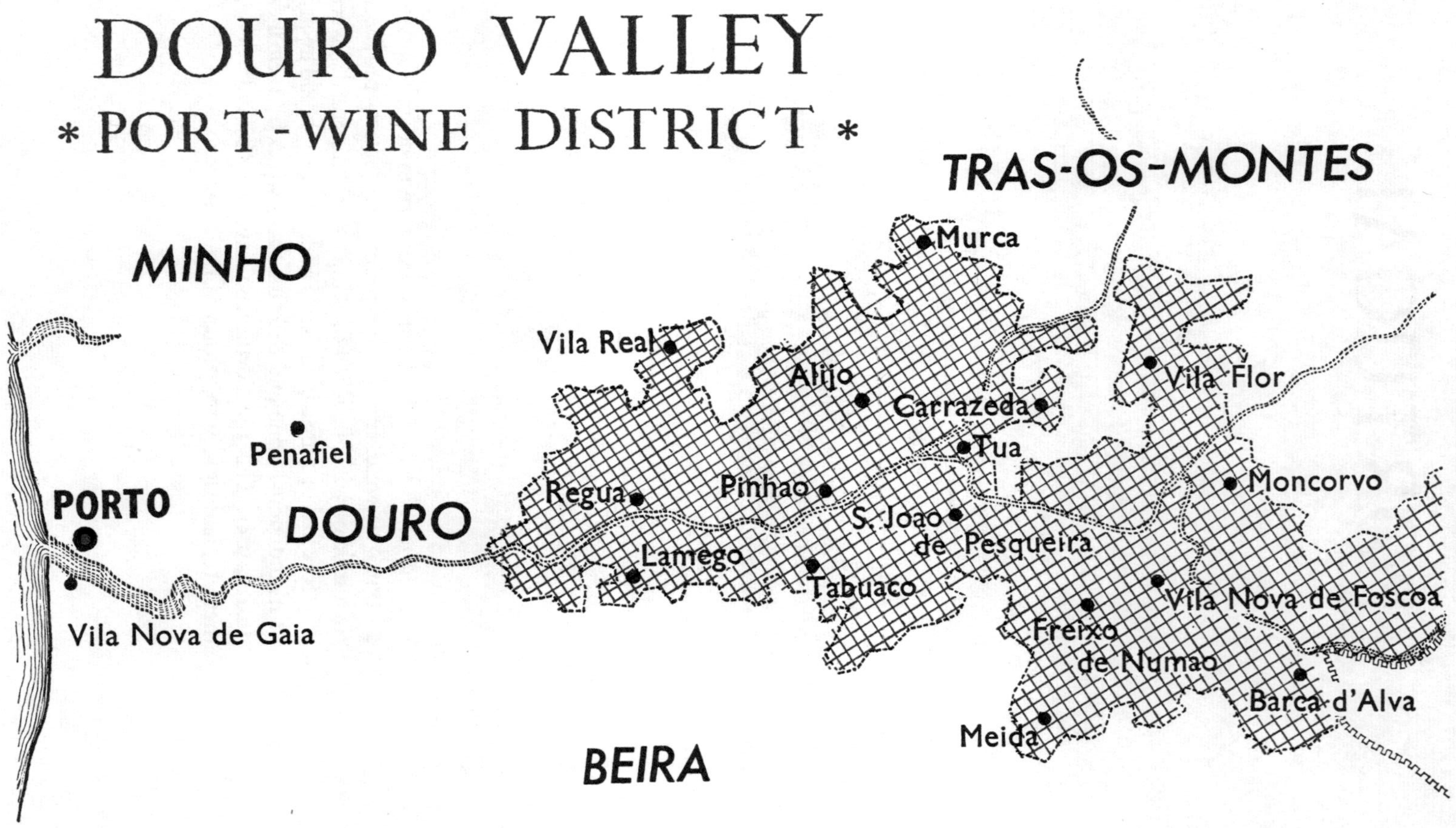

DOURO VALLEY
* PORT-WINE DISTRICT *

MINHO

TRAS-OS-MONTES

DOURO

BEIRA

PORTO

Penafiel

Vila Nova de Gaia

Vila Real

Regua

Lamego

Pinhao

Tabuaco

S. Joao de Pesqueira

Alijo

Murca

Carrazeda

Tua

Vila Flor

Moncorvo

Vila Nova de Foscoa

Barca d'Alva

Freixo de Numao

Meida

PORT WINE

The Supreme Dessert Wine! The King of Wines! The English-man's Wine! or should I say the Britisher's Wine! These are only a few rightful descriptions of the nectar produced in the region of the Upper Douro in the north of Portugal.

History was never one of my best subjects at school, but I feel it is right to give you some background on the discovery of Port as such, and try to describe to you why Port should be called the Britisher's Wine.

We all know that Portugal and Great Britain are the oldest allies in existence, and it is probably due to this factor that Port came to this country in the seventeenth century. In 1679 the importation of French wines was prohibited, and the ban, which lasted for seven years, gave the Portuguese their chance and in four years the quantity imported considerably exceeded that of the French wines imported during the previous years. This wine was all unfortified and of the Claret style. Unfortunately, due to the sudden tremendous export from Portugal of these table wines, the quality was not maintained, and, although they may have been palatable to the Portuguese peasant, they certainly did not suit the British palate which was used to the French Clarets. In 1686, the ban on French wines was lifted, and France recaptured the market from the Portuguese, but this was short-lived when France and Britain began their long hostilities which lasted until 1815.

On December 27th, 1703, the Methuen Treaty was signed between Britain and Portugal which stated that "Her Sacred Royal Majesty of Great Britain shall in her own name and that of her Successors, be obliged for ever hereafter to admit the wines of the growth of Portugal" on payment of a duty one-third less than that levied on French wines.

It is interesting to note that the three oldest shippers are as follows: KOPKE 1638, WARRE 1648 and CROFT 1678. This could have meant that the owners of Croft had some inside information, as they became established one year before the ban on French wines into Britain!

It is also interesting to note that in those days wine was shipped from Viana, a flourishing port about sixty miles north of Oporto.

The grapes in the Douro were found to be rich in sugar and colour, and due to the great heat, fermentation was quick, transferring them into strong, robust but harsh wines. This brings us to the most important date of all—when was brandy first added to the wine to stop this fermentation and thus obtain a sweet wine? A handbook published in 1720 recommends the addition of a very small dose of brandy to fermenting Must, three gallons to the pipe, and about 1727, when the Oporto Shippers' Association was formed, it was discovered that sugar could be retained in the wine to correct its unpalatable harshness if enough spirit were added during the fermentation to arrest the process.

So it can be taken that between 1720 and 1727 the birth of Port Wine, as we know it today, took place.

Another interesting date is 1775 when probably the first Vintage Port was shipped and bottled, and at the very end of the century British drinkers of wine began to ask for Vintage Port as well as Vintage Claret.

Port, therefore, as we know it today, is a medium sweet wine, in which the natural sugar content of the grapes has been retained, the sweetness thereof entirely controlled by the timing of the addition of brandy to arrest the fermentation.

GEOGRAPHY

Sixty miles by road due east from Oporto on the coast there lies the town of Regua. This is the administrative town and heart of the Douro or Port Wine district of Portugal. The district is hard in every meaning of the word—mountainous, lacking in water other than the river and a few springs, freezing in winter and a furnace in summer. No other wine-growing district is quite like the Douro with its schistous soil which needs to be blasted to be broken up. No other district needs the terracing and walls built to preserve the rainfall and prevent the soil being washed down the mountain-sides, together with the precious vines.

The mountain ranges normally run north and south, thus the great difference between the wines produced in the vineyards of the "Rising Sun" and those of the "Setting Sun". The former should be "greener" and the latter "more mature". Thus the blend of the two creates a perfection in a good year of perfect weather.

Very roughly, the district is divided into two parts—the Cima or Upper Corgo and the Baixo or Lower Corgo. Regua lies on the River Douro, at the mouth of the River Corgo, and it is said that wine from the east of the Corgo or the Upper Corgo is better in quality but lower in production than the wine from the west or the Lower Corgo. This is a very rough generalisation but it will serve to illustrate the regions within the district as a whole. Roughly, 1,000 vines produce one pipe (550 litres) of Port in the Cima Corgo, whilst the same quantity of vines in the Lower Corgo could produce up to two pipes. The price of the Must is obviously higher in the Upper Corgo. Again, the reason for the lower production in the better district is also due to the soil. The permitted quantity of Must to be made into Port is dependent upon the category of the soil and the position of the vineyard. The first-class type of soil is one hundred per

393

cent schistous, à hard, rock-like slate, ochre in colour. The walls of the terraces are also made with this soil. In the higher quantity areas there is a large proportion of earth mixed with the soil, which, although producing more wine per 1,000 vines, lowers the quality.

It is strange that in this Port district, comprising an area of some 900 square miles, there can be such a varied range of temperatures. In winter it has been known to snow and a heavy mist usually hangs above the river for the months of November and December. We all pray that the rains will fall during the first three months of the year to permeate the soil, ready for the long drought in the summer. The spring in the Douro is usually ideal, warm and sunny with a few showers. The summer should be hot to mature the grapes, and a few showers to swell the grapes and "lay the dust" at the end of August or beginning of September should give us perfect vintage weather around the middle of September. Cool nights and hot days during the vintage would then be the end of a perfect climatic year! I can remember in 1948 the temperature in the shade reached 112°F, and this dropped to 102° at 3 a.m. The sun temperatures soared to between 165° and 170°F at midday, and still the women continued to sing whilst they picked the grapes in the vineyards and the men cheerfully shouted at each other with their 130 lb. grape-laden baskets on their backs.

VITICULTURE   This is a subject about which many pages could be written. But the Portuguese farmer is a simple man, the climate in the Douro is hard as is the soil, so common sense and brawn are used generally in lieu of academic terminology. The vines are treated expertly by men of experience, the rotation of seasonal work is annually accomplished, and in the end—the product is perfect.

In November a *roga* or band of pruners cut back the vines which are 1 metre high, planted 1 metre down and 1 metre apart. In the spring there is the grafting of the Portuguese vine on to the

394

American vine root when the latter is one year old. This is necessary because in 1868 the phylloxera destroyed the vineyards in the Douro, but the beetle will not attack the American vine. Strangely enough, this beetle originated from America. Between the pruning and the grafting, the soil is hoed around the roots of the vines and small "wells" are made ready to retain the rain which one hopes will come in January to March. In April, when the leaves appear, a mixture of copper sulphate and sulphur is sprayed on the vines to prevent mildew, and this is normally carried out in rotation until the end of May, again depending upon the weather and the unpredicted rainfall in May. Artificial manure is used in rotation in the vineyard when natural compost is not used, but the former is an extremely costly affair when only one pipe is produced from 1,000 vines.

Should the year be a cold one and there is a lack of sun, a certain percentage of the leaves are stripped to allow the bunches of grapes to mature. This seldom happens, fortunately. A light shower every now and then before the end of August is good to swell the grapes and mature them, also to settle the dust which is everywhere.

This is a normal year's work and everyone by the beginning of September is wondering when the actual date of the vintage will be. A rough average is between the 15th and the last week in September, but in very hot years it has started during the first week of this month.

THE VINTAGE   We have now arrived at the culmination of a year's work, weather and, principally, hope! The weather is still hot, the grapes have been examined and the decision to start picking has been made and the personnel for the festival have arrived.

These peasants are an amiable and happy crowd. They are not local and usually come from many miles away, either on foot or by train. They laugh and sing as the vintage to them, apart from hard work, is, in a way, a holiday. They are humble folk but respectful and work from dawn to dusk. The women-folk carry the luggage, usually in baskets on their heads, as it is not done for the men to carry any parcels when there are women present.

The actual start of the vintage depends very much on the geographical situation of the vineyard or *quinta*. These lie usually north and south, thus there are the *quintas* of the "rising sun" and those of the "setting sun". This makes a great difference in the maturing of the grapes as the first will take longer than the second, due to the heat of the sun being at its greatest in the afternoon, or rather from noon onwards. There are some like Croft's Quinta da Roeda which is relatively flatter than many others and the rays of the scorching sun shine on it all the day long—thus it is usually the first one to start, that is, normally a week before the general beginning of the vintage.

Pre-vintage work is arduous for the tasters and technicians in the Port Trade, as they have to visit every *quinta* they are buying wine from and examine the grapes, giving orders when to start their vintage, taking the sweetness of the grapes, examining all the vats and casks which will be used for the wine when it is made. This is really rather interesting, as you can determine whether a vat is clean or not by sticking your head inside it through the narrow entrance at the base of the head, which in Portuguese is called the *portinhola*, and with your right arm banging the outside of the vat to rouse all the vapours within. I may warn you before doing this that, if the vat has been perfectly sealed from air during the whole year from the last vintage, and you take a very sharp intake of breath, you will come out spluttering and coughing, as the smell is very concentrated. This is just a tip when you have the pleasure of visiting the vineyards of Portugal before the vintage.

All vats which have been passed for use must be initialled by the expert, and no utensil may be used which is not scrupulously cleaned and disinfected.

There are many types of grapes used in the Douro valley. The main thing about these grapes is that a blend of certain qualities

396

which are grown in the individual *quintas* produces the necessary style of wine required. For instance, there are grapes which produce a lot of colour and much juice, but these are not as sweet as others which have a small production. There are the Tinta Francisca, Mourisco de Semente, Malvasia Preta, Malvasia Branca, Rufete, Tinta Francesa, and many others. Each one has its own character, sweetness, colour and many other qualities which add up to the perfect wine in the opinion of the individual farmer. Also, curiously enough, some of the types of grapes do not grow as well in the Cima Corgo as the Baixo Corgo and vice versa.

The final decision to start the vintage is really governed by the *lagrima* of the grape. Selected bunches of grapes of different qualities in the *quinta* are picked, and squeezed into a glass tube. A saccharometer takes the actual sugar content of the juice or "tear" (*lagrima*) of the grape. When this has reached its peak, a decision can be reached fairly accurately to start the general picking.

The women pick the grapes, every bunch selected by hand; they place these in small baskets which are transferred to large baskets which the men carry on their backs suspended by a small cloth strap round the forehead. When quite full they can weigh approximately 60 to 65 kilos (130 lb.)

There are two methods of crushing the grapes today and the first one which I shall describe is rapidly overtaking the old method of treading by foot. Due to personnel difficulties and many other reasons, crushing by machine is one of the modern methods now in use.

At Croft's Quinta da Roeda there is now installed one of the most modern installations in the Port Wine production world. When the grapes are picked and brought to the lodges, they are emptied into tanks which feed the pressing machines. This is a very simple and easily worked machine, electrically driven, which receives the grapes from the tank, crushes them in an enclosed revolving cylinder which has three plates centrifugally operated. This smashes the grapes against the sides of the cylinder, but does not crush the pips. Then it automatically shoots the already completely mashed Must, via plastic pipes, into either the awaiting fermenting vats, which are specially lined cement vats holding up to twenty-five pipes, where fermenting takes place, or into *lagars*. These latter are the stone treading tanks, usually square, which can hold up to twenty-five pipes of Must. They are shallow tanks which are approximately the depth of a human leg, and when they are filled the Must would be just above the knee.

This mashed grape pulp is then kept aired by only a few men who, standing on the edge of the tanks with the *macacos* (wooden paddles), continually keep the Must stirring. The colour which comes from the skins is already appearing and soon the fermentation begins pushing up all these crushed skins, pips, and stalks to the top and forming a *manta* or "blanket". The natural sugar of the grapes (*lagrima*) is continually reducing and automatically turning into alcohol. Sugar tests are taken the whole time and when the required sweetness has been attained the tap is opened in the base of the *lagar* and the fermenting juice or Must is drawn off through a filter and flows directly into the waiting vat. As this flows in, brandy is immediately added to arrest the fermentation. This brandy or *eau de vie* is a distilled local wine or port having a strength of 77° alcohol and of an age of two years. It is colourless and very pungent. When I say a Douro pipe holds 550 litres, 100 litres of this brandy is added to 450 litres of Must, thus making up the Douro Pipe. Therefore, one can say that approximately 20 per cent of Port Wine is fortified by this brandy.

It depends entirely upon outside temperatures when the fermentation reaches the exact point of drawing off. Obviously, if the temperatures are extremely high outside, the fermentation will be much quicker than when these temperatures are low. If the fermentation is too rapid, it must be checked by adding a certain amount of tartaric acid into the *lagars*, as the shipper wants the maximum amount of colour from the grapes and a too rapid fermentation would mean too little work with the Must.

The old-fashioned method of treading by the human foot is gradually dying out as I mentioned earlier, due to the lack of personnel and other reasons. It is sad to see this happening as this method has been used by all wine-growers for very many centuries, but modern methods must take precedence these days. It must still, nevertheless, continue for some years to come, as, due to the geographical position of the Douro Port Wine district, electricity and water in very many *quintas* are still non-existent.

Whether the machine or the human foot is used, the results are the same and the blend of Must and brandy lies in the vats up the Douro until November. The wines are then racked or turned over, the strength taken plus all the usual tests of acetic acid, etc., and not forgetting the actual tasting.

I must stress that nothing is added to Port other than grape brandy, no colouring matter, and the amount of natural sweetness is controlled entirely by the fermentation. The longer the fermentation the drier the wine, and the shorter, the sweeter. In fact, Port is grape and grape only! Even the yeasts which produce the fermentation are the natural yeasts which exist on the outside of the original grape.

When I mentioned before that other *quintas'* produce was purchased, you must not think for one moment that any single shipper of Port can produce all his requirements from his own *quinta*. Depending entirely upon his shipments and sales to the world, he purchases from different regions of the Port Wine district in the Douro every year, and universally he always purchases his grapes from the same regions and *quintas*, as he wishes to maintain the style of his House. These farmers are always very willing to sell annually to him, as, apart from having a guaranteed sale, they like to "belong" to a well-known shipper. They are controlled by the Port Farmers' Association (*Casa do Douro*) in Regua, which is the capital of the Douro district. This I will come on to later.

Once the wines are safely stored in their vats, the grapes picked and the vintage over, the personnel then prepare themselves to bid the owners farewell until the next year and vintage. They line up in two files and dance and sing towards the lady of the house, and the fortunate girl to be chosen amongst her companions then presents her with a *rama*, which is a decorated bamboo stick with flowers (paper) and streamers and the traditional bunch of grapes. This is blessed and kept in the house or bungalow of the owners until the following year. Accompanied by the traditional rockets, drums and music, they then all disperse and dance away to their respective homes for yet another year.

The wine lies in the vats, settling down and "getting together", until the cold comes in November. They are then tested again for strength and more brandy added to bring them up to reasonable strength before sending them down the river to Vila Nova de Gaia to the Shippers' Lodges. They are drawn off their lees, refreshed and then allowed to settle once more before their departure to Gaia in February of the following year. This procedure is called the *lota*. After the vintage, the Douro district settles down once more to its cycle of pruning, grafting, planting, etc., for one more year.

TRANSPORTATION TO VILA NOVA DE GAIA

The new wines come down to Vila Nova de Gaia, which lies on the south side of the River Douro opposite the city of Oporto, from early February until early May. Normally they travel in cask by train, but there are still a few flat-bottomed boats (*bardo Rabelo*) in existence which also transport the casks down by river. The journey takes three days and the boats are rowed down by the men, who spend the nights on board. The bigger boats can carry up to thirty-four full casks. In the early part of the year the currents are fairly strong and the boats are swept down at speed, especially over the many rapids. This method is still romantic and picturesque, but merely kept on for the sake of the owners of the boats. Very soon now the wine will be transported down in steel tanks by rail or lorry and even in tankers. The constant duel between the ancient and modern.

We now come to one of the most interesting parts of the Port trade, and that is the blending and tasting. I will set out as simply as possible what happens to the wine from the time it arrives at the lodges in Gaia from the Douro in the early spring of the year following the vintage. You will remember that the shipper has purchased port from different *quintas* in the Douro district in order to maintain the style of his House. These then come down in casks and every one is tasted and examined in the tasting room.

They are then selected for their different qualities and charcteristics and separated into what we call "Lots". Each Lot is given a number and a name or a series of letters. For instance, a Lot made up from the Quinta da Roeda in 1963 would be labelled or marked as follows:

V T

R D A

1963

This means: VT—*Vinho Tinto* or Red Port (VB—*Vinho Branco* or White Port); then RDA—Roeda; and after that the year. The Lot would be given a running number and called, for example, Lot No. 2468. This title and number would remain with this Lot for ever. The wine from the casks, having been examined and tasted, would then be blended into a vat, the strength brought up to shipping strength (normally 20° alcohol) by adding a very small percentage of grape brandy at 77° alcohol, then transferred back into Lot casks each holding on an average 630 litres. These casks are then all marked with the above-mentioned mark and Lot number, stacked in three tiers and left in the lodge for maturing. It is continually supervised, tasted and examined and when it is young it is racked every nine to twelve months. This racking involves drawing the wine off the lees in the cask, airing and replacing in fresh casks, which are old, very well-seasoned oak casks. Gradually, after years of racking and maturing, the wine losses colour and becomes a Tawny wine. The original colour of the new wine is a rich purple colour with a very strong fresh bouquet of grape and brandy, and the brandy takes some time to "marry" in with the new wine.

Having settled this particular wine down for maturing, we must not forget that many thousands of casks of different wines are all maturing in the same Lodge, all with their respective titles or marks and Lot numbers. Some are brand-new wines, some are old and mature tawnies. Others are White Ports, both old and new. Before I come on to blending for shipping, I must remind you that, if you left a wine in cask for, say, thirty years, without racking or refreshing, this wine would lose a tremendous amount of colour, become rather flat, the cask would be on ullage as there is a natural evaporation annually of between 1·5 per cent to 2·5 per cent (depending upon the coolness of the Lodges), and the strength would naturally become lower every year. So they are racked to maintain their freshness, the casks, are always kept full, every year or two an extremely small percentage of brandy is added to replace the evaporated strength, and when the wine becomes extremely old and yellow, it is "fed" with a slightly younger wine to maintain its maturation. It must be a slightly younger wine, because if you "fed" a thirty-year-old wine, matured in cask, with a two-year-old wine, it would swamp it completely and ruin and lose all the wonderful character which it had been slowly acquiring during these many years.

BLENDING

So, remembering we have many hundreds of Lots maturing in the Lodge with which to make up our shipping Lots, we can now come down to the art of blending for shipments. Many Houses have different ways of doing this, but generally speaking the following system is normally used:

When the shipper receives an order from the wholesaler, this is registered in his shipping book. As an example, let us say the order was for ten pipes of a certain mark of Ruby Port with average age of say five years. We shall also state that this was not a new order which would have to be matched against samples sent by the wholesaler. It is merely a repeat order of a wine the wholesaler has had for many years.

When the wine was originally shipped, the colour was registered in a tintometer, the sweetness and strength registered, and a reference sample taken and kept on shipment. Therefore the shipper, on receiving the order, looks up in his blending book to see how the last shipment was made up, and proceeds to make up a new blend. Should this be only an annual order, we must not forget that the wines are one year older and thus lighter in colour. We know the average age, the colour, the sweetness, strength and style and price. So we use the same Lot as shipped previously, but blending in at the same time some younger wines so that the colour on shipment will be identical to the colour on shipment the previous year. This is not complicated in any way, the only thing that is really necessary is that the taster knows his own wines and the styles of these different wines in order to make up the order or shipment so that it will be identical to the previous shipment, which is essential for the wholesaler to maintain the continuity of the style of wine he bottles and sells.

Although the mechanical elements of the blend are registered and essential, the final resolution before shipping must be on the nose and the palate. It must be remembered that, in this particular order, which is an annual one, the reference sample is one year old, the colour in this sample has lost one year's depth, so all this must be taken into consideration when tasting the new shipment against this reference sample.

Through experience, one can judge the loss of colour, but the style, taste, and "nose" must be identical, as the final judge is the customer who buys the bottle. If the order were a new one to be shipped against a sample sent by the wholesaler to match, a new blend would have to be made up of perhaps four or five wines to obtain an average age of the wine in the matching sample, and to produce the colour.

Normally speaking, the shipper knows approximately what he will be shipping during the year and will always have many Lots made up of various shipping marks made up to "follow on", which means the wines are "married" before actually shipping, and this helps considerably when the wine is eventually shipped and bottled as it remains brighter for a much longer period.

When the shipping order has been made up, it is then fined, normally with gelatine, drawn off the vat into shipping pipes (534·24 litres), and then samples of this wine are sent to the *Instituto do Vinho do Porto* (The Portuguese Government Port Wine Institute) for final tasting and approval before the Certicate of Origin is signed by them. No Port can be shipped without this document, which is a complete guarantee that the wine is in perfect condition in every way for shipment. These rules are extremely strict, which is an excellent proof of the highest possible standards of Port.

There is only one wine which is not matured longer than two years in cask in the Lodges and that is Vintage Port, which is bottled after two years and remains all its life in bottle. But I shall come on to that later when I define the various types of Port.

TASTING

Many people ask, how do you taste wine? The sensation of tasting is a very personal and elusive thing. To try to convey to someone else exactly what it is you taste, in a wine for instance, is quite a difficult feat. "This wine is sweet" you may say, and that is simple. "It is round", you add (but roundness is a shape, not a taste). "It is flowery", you try to explain (but floweriness is surely mostly a matter of smell rather than taste). The actual sensations of taste are said to be four: sweetness, bitterness, sourness and saltiness (some experts add tentatively two more: alkaline and metallic tastes). All tastes are some sort of combination of these basic half-dozen. Indeed, an experienced taster hardly tastes at all in the strict sense of the word. Practically all his work is done "on the nose" and the palate only gives confirmation to what his nose has already conveyed.

As to the actual procedure of tasting, there is nothing that can equal the experience you gain by you yourself trying to taste. What I can do is to suggest how to make the best use of such opportunities of tasting wines as come your way. One should always taste against a standard set in one's own mind. "I like this", you may say of a wine; "it reminds me of a '34 I tasted last month, but it seems sweeter" (or less "round" or not quite as rich, etc.). You have begun to assemble your "wine memory", to which you add with one more experience every time you critically taste any wine.

Let us now see how we can best begin tasting Port, for instance. First you must obtain the right glass, and this is a tulip-shaped one with a short stem. See that it is sparkling clean with no extraneous odour from drying with a dirty cloth. Wipe the lip of the bottle and pour out about a third so that you can swill the wine around the glass so that it mixes with the air. Look at the colour. Is it bright and clear, as every wine should be? Is there a hint of the brownness of age along the edge of the wine? In some rare old Ports there will even be a sort of "greenness" of extreme age. The swirling of the wine will now have released the ethers, so gradually bring the glass up until you eventually put your nose right in the top of the glass. Then sniff, trying to close down your senses to the pinpointed moment of assessing what you find in the wine. Be blind and deaf to all outside impressions for a moment and try to place exactly the sensations which the wine conveys. Is it "clean" with no unpleasant undertones; does it suggest sweetness or acidity, floweriness of bouquet (which reminds you of the gum-cistus flowers in the Douro valley)? Try to identify all the delicate impressions and try too to impress them on your mind for future comparison.

Having obtained all you can from the nose, now take a sip. Hold it in your mouth, rolling it around and swilling it against the top of the palate over the tongue. At the same time, through drawn lips, suck in a little air so that it slightly hisses as it meets and mixes with the wine. This air is necessary in order to allow the wine to give up its flavours and ethers to your taste cells. You then get the sensations which the wine is able to give—its sweetness, roundness and completeness. Only then should the wine be spat out, that is, if you are tasting and not drinking.

You must remember one maxim only: be completely honest with yourself. Whatever the reason, if you taste with an open mind and reach an honest opinion of what you personally find, that is what you must hold fast to. Be humble, because tasters, tasting every day for years as part of their profession, confess themselves liable to error. But above all, be honest.

DEFINITIONS   Now to give you a short explanation of the different types of Port. Unfortunately, many people think that Port is rich, red and sweet and gives you a headache, and even more people think that Sherry is a more attractive wine because there are so many different types. This is completely wrong, because the following are some of the many types you may find in Great Britain.

RUBY: This is a blend of young wines, made from red grapes, blended and matured in cask for four or five years, fined and bottled. There are various types of Ruby as some are far heavier than others; some sweeter than others.

TAWNY: This is a blended wine which has been allowed to mature in cask in the lodges of the shipper until such a time that the wine has attained a Tawny colour. Therefore, normally it is older than the Ruby, as all red Ports start as a ruby wine, being full when they are young. But a Tawny being old is more expensive, so there is another type of Tawny Port which is cheaper and can be the same price as a Ruby. This latter Tawny is a blend of white and red Ports, younger on the palate and nose, but it can be blended to resemble an old Tawny quite easily. If the customer wishes a Tawny but cannot afford the price of an old Tawny, he can obtain the same style with this younger blend. There is nothing to hide as both wines are Port made in exactly the same way, the only difference being that part is white Port and the other red Port.

WHITE: This is a blended wine made entirely from white grapes. It is made in exactly the same way as Red Port, the only difference being that the wine, or rather the Must, is not "worked" as hard as the Red Port at the time of the vintage as it is not necessary to obtain the colour which comes from the skins. This can be dry or sweet, depending entirely upon the control of the fermentation originally at the vintage time. There is no such

406

thing as a vintage White as it does not improve in bottle. A dry White Port, chilled, is an extremely good aperitif wine because, although this wine is much drier than normal, the type of grapes which make White Port always produces a certain "fullness" in the mouth when you drink it.

VINTAGE CHARACTER: This is a full-bodied wine made and blended from first-class years and first-class Cima Corgo wines which take longer to lose their colour in cask. Therefore, when they are bottled, they are ready for drinking, but have that fullness and breeding which you will notice when you taste them against a young Ruby Port of a quality.

CRUSTING PORT: This is a first-class blend of two or three years which is kept for a few years in cask, say up to five or six years, then bottled. As they are big wines, after a time in bottle they will throw a crust and they will have to be carefully decanted. If kept long enough in bottle they will gradually obtain a definite vintage nose, but of course will not achieve the perfection of the real Vintage Port.

LATE BOTTLED VINTAGE: This is a wine of one year selected by the shipper, and matured in cask for over three years but not more than six years. It will be ready for drinking when bottled and sold and will normally have the date of the vintage and date of bottling. It is a much lighter wine than the real vintage, and of course less expensive.

VINTAGE PORT: This is the nectar of all Ports as it is a blend of wines of one year only, kept in cask for two or a maximum of three years, then bottled, and spends the rest of its life in bottle. Only in a very special year will the shipper decide to declare the wine, or a certain quantity, as a Vintage Port, because the name of his House will depend upon this wine amongst the connoisseurs in the trade and most especially outside. Before the shipper declares the wine as a Vintage, he must think of at least fifteen years ahead when it should be coming ready to drink. Mind you, it is not for us to judge, as some wines may last thirty or more years and still improve, whilst others reach their fifteen years of age and will be ready to drink. Also the customer may like to drink a younger vintage, and who are the shippers to tell a customer his taste? Whilst the 1947s and 1950s are ready for drinking now, the 1945s will improve for very many years to come. There can be no rules and regulations regarding the drinking of Vintage Ports—that is, the order in which to drink them—because it is the wine which eventually governs this order.

I maintain that a "wood Port" should be served straight from the cask, and that a bottle is used only for transporting the wine from the cask to the glass. But Vintage Port must be treated with respect, decanted correctly, and at the right time. The latter remark is important because a very old Vintage Port can lose all its bouquet if opened too early before the meal, and a younger one will improve as it will "breathe". I am frequently asked how long a Vintage Port will last when it is decanted. This depends entirely upon the year, as it is only natural a very old wine will die quickly, whilst a big and fruity one will last longer decanted. When I say "old", I mean a thirty- to fifty-year-old Vintage, and, anyway, I do not think there would be any trouble regarding the keeping open of this wine, because it will surely be finished and drunk before it would be allowed to ever lose its glorious characteristics!

WOOD

This could be a very long chapter as the making of a cask, and the selection of the wood for casks and vats is a story in itself. But I shall not delve too deeply in this matter and shall tell you that all Port casks are made from oak or chestnut, and the vats from *macacauba* or Brazilian mahogany and oak and chestnut. Before the 1939–45 war the great majority of the oak was grown in Lennin and Stettin, but nowadays this is produced locally in Portugal, as well as the chestnut. The latter casks are used for transport only as they are not as strong as oak casks and not as good in quality. A shipping pipe has approximately thirty-seven staves which are kept together with iron hoops, no nails being used at all. This is a wonderful art and it is passed on from generation to generation of coopers. When the new cask is made, it is

408

measured by filling with water in a measuring tank, then emptied, thoroughly cleaned and filled with a very young and full wine for seasoning for a period of at least six months, as the wood must never give a "woody" flavour to the wine which will eventually be shipped in it. When pipes are shipped back to Portugal for re-exportation, they are thoroughly examined, broken down, and then re-assembled.

Before the casks are made up originally, the wood is cut into staves and seasoned for at least two years in the open air. The following measurements in litres will give an idea of the type of casks in which Port is shipped and stored in Lodges.

Lodge LOT Cask	=	Normally about 630 litres
Douro Cask	=	550 litres
Shipping Pipe	=	534·24 litres
Hogshead	=	267 litres
Quarter Cask	=	134 litres

Sometimes Octaves and Sixteenths are also shipped, but this is not normal as, if kept for a long time in these small casks, Port will quickly acquire a "woody" nose due to the high proportion of wood to wine.

Vats in the lodges which are kept for blending Lots can hold anything up to 200 pipes of Port. When they are situated in the Douro district and kept empty from one year to another after the new wines have been shipped down to Gaia, the *portinholas* are tightly shut to make the vat air-tight and some wine left in at the bottom of the vat to keep it fresh. Also, sticks of sulphur are left to keep it completely clear of any acidity-producing insects. It is always a great tragedy that some farmers can, due to negligence, lose a whole vat of wine, thus the shippers' stress on complete cleanliness at the time of the vintage.

GOVERNMENT
DEPARTMENTS
AND LOCAL
ASSOCIATIONS

In Great Britain the Port Wine Trade Association comes under the auspices of the Wine and Spirit Trade Association of Great Britain. In Portugal the *Casa do Douro* or Farmers Association and the *Gremio dos Exportadores do Vinho do Porto* or Shippers'

Association come under the auspices of the government body, the *Instituto do Vinho do Porto* or the Port Wine Institute.

CASA DO DOURO   The Casa do Douro deals entirely with the farmers and owners of the many *quintas* in the Douro district, inspects and regulates the quantity which each farmer can produce of Port Wine, issues the brandy for the vintage, and acts as bankers for the farmers. This latter remark means that by law the shipper or the buyer must deposit one-third of the total cost of the wine purchased in June when the contract is signed, one-third when the wine is made immediately after the vintage, and one-third on delivery in the spring when the wine is measured. This deposit must be made in the *Casa do Douro* to ensure the farmer will be paid. It also deals with the viticulture and viniculture of the district, inspection of the different grades of soil and types of grapes. Only a certain amount of planting and re-planting is allowed in the various vineyards, and this is all governed by this Association.

GREMIO   The *Gremio* or Shippers' Association deals with everything pertaining to the shipping side of the Port Wine trade and represents them at foreign associations whenever the subject of Port is discussed where policy is concerned. Prices, stock and all other matters are ruled from this Association.

INSTITUTO   The *Instituto* is the government body which has the final say in all policies pertaining to the Port Wine trade as well as embodying the official government tasters who decide whether a wine is fit for shipment or not. The Certificate of Origin which guarantees the quality for all shipments to the whole world is signed here. It also has a completely modern and up-to-date laboratory where every sample of every shipment, be it in cask or bottle, is thoroughly examined, the strengths and sweetness taken again, which adds once more to the guarantee of the quality of Port Wine.

The Port Wine Association of Great Britain is always in close co-operation with the *Gremio* and the *Instituto* in Portugal.

410

VINTAGES   The following is a list of vintages from 1900 to the present day, but it must be noted that many of these dates were not universally declared as Vintages by all shippers. It is always possible that a certain year can favour one shipper or producer more than another, due to the many reasons of the position of their respective *quintas*.

1900, 1904, 1908, 1911, 1912, 1917, 1920, 1921, 1922, 1924, 1927, 1931, 1934, 1935, 1942, 1943, 1945, 1947, 1948, 1950, 1954, 1955, 1958, 1960.

At the time of writing, the 1963s are looking extremely good and are developing well.

A question I am being continually asked is: "Between you and me, honestly, which shipper produces the best Port?" and my reply to this is completely honest: "Every shipper has his best Port— it depends upon *your* taste." Every shipper has his best, he also has his own style of Port, and therefore competition is great, which, in all walks of life, produces quality, care and excellence. God has given us the material with which to work, let us now all appreciate it.

PORT

PORTUGUESE TABLE WINES

VINHOS VERDES

The literal translation, Green Wines, is slightly misleading as there are White Green wines as well as Red. Therefore the description "green" is not really kind, as, although they are normally drunk young and fresh, they are mature and made from mature grapes and certainly not immature and green!

They can boast of a long history which goes back to the days when the Romans came to Portugal and they are recognised officially as a definite class of wine which is supervised and protected by strict legislation.

The district stretches from the Spanish–Portuguese border in the north divided by the River Minho, to slightly south of the River Douro. It follows the coast from Caminha down to Oporto, and stretches inland about forty miles.

The unique peculiarity of the viticulture of this wine is that the vines are grown up trees and along the branches. They are also allowed to grow very high on posts and then trained along wires so that the grapes are all hanging from a height and not from the normal three-feet-high vines.

These are light wines in body with an average alcoholic content of between 8° and 11·5°, rich in fixed organic acids, the red being bright red in colour and the white almost lemonish, but both have a characteristic taste of the grape with a natural and pleasant sparkle in it.

These wines are subject to strict supervision by the *Comissão de Viticultura de Região dos Vinhos Verdes* and are only allowed to be produced in the aforementioned delimited area of the north of Portugal.

They are extremely pleasant wines, light and sparkling and especially appreciated in the summer months, and due to this sparkle they are always shipped in bottle.

DÃO

It is very difficult to trace back the history of the Dão wines (pronounced "Dong", the 'o' being the same as used in the word "don't"), since they were well known even in the days of the Roman province of Lusitania. Nevertheless, both King John I and John III are known to have protected the Dão wines, forbidding any other wine to enter Viseu (the capital of the district) whilst the inhabitants had supplies of their own. The present outline of the region dates from 1912 and lies approximately thirty to forty miles south of the River Douro between the Estrela and Caramulo mountain ranges. It is sheltered from the maritime influence and from the continental climate further inland by these mountain ranges, allowing it to retain a climate of its own. The soil is granitic, with small schistous outbursts, and the vines grow mainly on the rocky slopes, making it more difficult to work them.

The excellent red wines, with an alcoholic content of about 12°, are full bodied with a splendid ruby colouring, a delicate bouquet and velvety taste. They are mainly produced from the Tourigo-do-Dão, Tinta Pinheira, Tinta Carvalha, Alvarelhão and Bastardo grapes.

The delightful white wines are fresh and of a light colour and have a very pleasant bouquet.

These wines are again guaranteed as genuine Dão wines by the Federation of Dão Viniculturists who issue Certificates of Origin to all those wines which are entitled to them. Their head office is in Viseu.

BUCELAS

Coming south again, we reach the districts of Alcobaca, Ribatejo, Torres and Bucelas which lie north of the River Tagus and Lisbon. It is said that Bucelas produces one of the best table wines in Portugal, but everyone has his own taste! The most characteristic type is the white wine that has a delicate bouquet of a very light, fresh and acid type, which acquires a special aroma with age as it becomes slightly sparkling. The average alcoholic content is 11·5°. As this wine is light it should be served with shellfish, hors d'oeuvres and grilled fish.

Strangely enough, the climate in this wine-growing region is quite different from the surrounding area, being cold in winter and temperate in summer. Furthermore, since this region is hemmed in by mountains, it is sheltered from the winds and therefore benefits from a mild climate which gives the wine certain unique characteristics.

The excellent quality of the Bucelas wines stems from the *arinto* grapes that are specially treated for the purpose, and, although the region produces a first-class red wine, it is not so well known as the white. Strangely enough, with age, this red wine, when its colour gradually lessens, takes on a topaz colour.

The Bucelas district is again subject to strict control and this time the Regional Wine Union of Bucelas checks all wines and co-ordinates the activities of the producers in order to certify that the wine is genuine and typical of that region.

COLARES

Going west from the Bucelas district, we come to the sandy area of Colares, just north of Lisbon. It forms part of one of the most lovely tourist regions of the country, bordering on the splendid Sintra range of hills on the one side, and the Atlantic Ocean on the other.

Wine has been produced in this district before the Age of the Discoveries, and there are documents to prove that Colares wine was one of the favourites on ships sailing to India.

The sandy area where the vines grow in Colares is almost exclusively composed of dunes, interspersed with some layers of Pliocenic sand. Since the sand is not rich in organic matter and quite incapable of retaining any rain water, the vines usually take root in the layer of clay. On account of the winds blowing in off the sea, the vines are stumpy and have to be shielded with special shelters made of cane.

Not only is the wine very smooth, but it has a vivacity and bouquet all of its own, giving it a strength and energy such as a strong nectar, whilst it simultaneously appears fresh, delicate and attractive like a precious wine. The average alcoholic strength is 11°. The region actually produces two types of wine —*chão de areia* (sandy bed) and *chão rijo* (solid bed). It is curious to note that the latter is produced from the former, but can only be sold in demijohns, whilst the *chão de areia* can only be sold in bottles. Due to the sandy soil, phylloxera does not exist.

The terraced vineyards of the Douro Valley, home of Port Wine.

Vintage time in Portugal. Workers with full baskets leaving the vineyard.

The cooperage at Croft & Co.'s lodges at Vila Nova de Gaia, Oporto. Croft, established in 1678 is one of the very oldest Port Wine shippers. Its vineyards at Quinta da Roeda are among the showplaces of the Douro Valley.

following p. 416

The highest vineyards of Europe at Visperterminen in the Valais, Switzerland (3,936 feet above sea level).

Emptying grapes into a barrel from one of the characteristic hods in a Swiss vineyard.

following p. 416

The cellar master takes a
sample of wine in a Tokay
cellar in Hungary. The black
fungoid growth on the walls
is essential to produce the correct
conditions in the wine cellar.

Tokay wines in the Budafok State Wine Cellars, Budapest, are labelled by hand.

following p.

Vintage time in the Tikves vineyard, Yugoslavia.

A view of the Tikves vineyard, Yugoslavia.

following p. 416

Grape picking at the Biruintsa collective farm vineyards in Moldavia, U.S.S.R.

Holidaymakers sampling the wine at a wine-tasting hall in Yalta, U.S.S.R.

following p. 416

Vintage time near the village of Omodhos on the slopes of a hill in the Troodos range in Cyprus.

A large vineyard on the outskirts of the town of Renmark, S. Australia.

following p. 416

Grape picking in a South African vineyard in Constantia.

CARCAVELOS

Literally a few miles south and still north of Lisbon, we come across another famous wine district. This produces a strong and fortified wine of 19° alcoholic strength. The full-bodied Carcavelos wine has been famous since the thirteenth century and its subsequent expansion is mainly due to the Marquis de Pombal (who created the Port Wine district of the Douro) and, about fifty years later, to the British who fought in the Peninsular War. The officers who came out to Portugal with the Duke of Wellington took such a liking to the pleasant taste of this wine that, after the war, they imported large quantities for their own tables at home.

The official Carcavelos wine district was established by law in 1908 to include the parishes of s. DOMINGOS DE RANA, CARCAVE-LOS and part of OEIRAS and ESTORIL. The proximity of the River Tagus and the sea make the climate temperate, and the north winds which are especially prevalent during the summer months help to prevent the grapes becoming damp, with the resultant precipitated ripening. These factors allied to the position of the vineyards, which all face south and are planted in limestone soil, provide a warm climate which allows the grapes to ripen in such a way that the wine is of excellent quality. Amongst the various soils in this region, special mention should be made of those known as the *lombos de Carcavelos* which are small hills along the coast which are well drained, but sufficiently damp, and face south-east.

The most important of the grapes grown and which form the basis of the regional Must is the Galego dourado grape. As the first-class Carcavelos wine has an average strength of 19°, it is most suitable for serving as an aperitif or dessert wine, depending on the degree of sweetness. It has a pleasant bouquet and is very smooth to the taste. It also ages well, during which it acquires a stronger "nose" or aroma.

The official region and quality of CARCAVELOS wine has been established by legal regulations, and in 1930 the competent

P

authorities set up the Union of Wine Producers and Exporters for this region which safeguards the interests of the producers and traders. The Union is further responsible for supervising the quality of the wine and issuing seals of guarantee and Certificates of Origin.

SETUBAL

This district, which lies a few miles south of the River Tagus and Lisbon, can be divided into two parts—the one covering the northern slope of the Arrabida hills with their clayish-limestone soil and open to the north wind; the other being a sandy soil fanned by the warm breezes of the south.

The golden SETUBAL MUSCATEL with its delicate bouquet and delicious taste is considered by many people to be the best muscatel wine in the world. This is produced from the Muscatel grape and grown in the steepest part of the region. Like the Carcavelos wine it is fortified with local brandy and the average alcoholic content is normally 18°. The same species of grape is used in the flat part of the region and is more full-bodied and very sweet. There is also a red Muscatel quality made from the red grape, but this is less known than the white. As a fortified wine it is especially suitable to be served with dessert as it has a very pleasant aroma of fruit when young and acquires a special taste and "nose" with age.

Apart from this Muscatel, the district is famous for its good quality table wines, the majority being red and made from the excellent and well-known Periquita grape.

Again the control of the wines produced in this district is as thorough as all the other regions already mentioned, and the head office of the Producers Union of Setubal Muscatel is situated in Azeitão.

418

GENERAL   These are the principal districts of table wines and fortified southern wines of Portugal, and the main interesting point is that they are completely controlled by their individual Unions so that the customer eventually is guaranteed the quality of the wine produced in each area. This means that there can be no blending of wines from the various districts, and that a wine with the district marked on the label is a guaranteed wine from that district, which, in itself, is a great comfort to any wine-lover.

The day will come when the British wine-drinker will order green wines, DÃO, COLARES and so on, with the same confidence as he has ordered for years Médoc, St. Émilion or Pommard. This classification at present includes:

Dessert and Aperitif Wines with a legal geographical status:

PORT, MADEIRA, CARCAVELOS, MUSCATEL DE SETUBAL.

Table wines with a legal geographical status:

VINHOS VERDES from the north-west of Portugal; MONCÃO, BRAGA, BASTO, LIMA AMARANTE and PENAFIEL.

Natural wines from the Douro region, DÃO, COLARES, BUCELAS.

Other wine regions with distinctive characters in the process of being officially classified:

PINHEL (*vin rosé*), AGUEDA (still table wine) BAIRRADA (good beverage wines and sparkling wines), ALCOBAÇA (good beverage wines—OBIDOS noted for white wines), RIBATEJO, TORRES VEDRAS, SETUBAL WITH PERIQUITA (excellent red wine and other table wines), LAGÕA in the Algarve, where a wine long ago popular in Flanders is being revived.

I have not mentioned the sparkling wines which are produced in Portugal at LAMEGO and BAIRRADA, which are prepared by the classic process of fermentation in the bottle. These are again excellent and are produced in varying degrees of sweetness,

419

Brut, Dry, Medium-Dry, Medium Sweet and Sweet. The production of this type of wine began in the last quarter of the past century and has reached the highest degree of perfection.

With this last wine, I can sum up, pointing out to readers the many varied types of wines produced in this lovely country of Portugal, a small country but blessed with the proper climatic conditions, soil and geographical districts. There are wines to accompany every meal from the aperitif stage to the final dessert wine; there are wines to be drunk at all times of the year, for festive reasons or normal daily drinking. Sparkling wines, aperitif wines, green wines, gay and light, red and white table still wines, *rosé* wines, fortified wines from the Estremadura, and, finally, the nectar of all wines—Port.

Before I finish, may I add a small but to me very important postscript: Never drink table wines, be they red or white, without accompanying them with a small scrap of food; you will always find the native of a wine-growing country will always eat something when he drinks wine—even if it is only an olive.

SWITZERLAND

Only a relatively small quantity of Swiss wines are imported into England and they have never received the accolade of greatness in comparison to the white wines of Germany or the red wines of Bordeaux and Burgundy. This is due to the geographical difficulties (many of the vineyards are on steep terraced slopes over four thousand feet high) and the erratic climate. The vineyards cover an area of about fifty square miles and the average production is fifteen million gallons per annum. The Swiss themselves drink wine mainly as an aperitif and this is indicative of the quality of the wine.

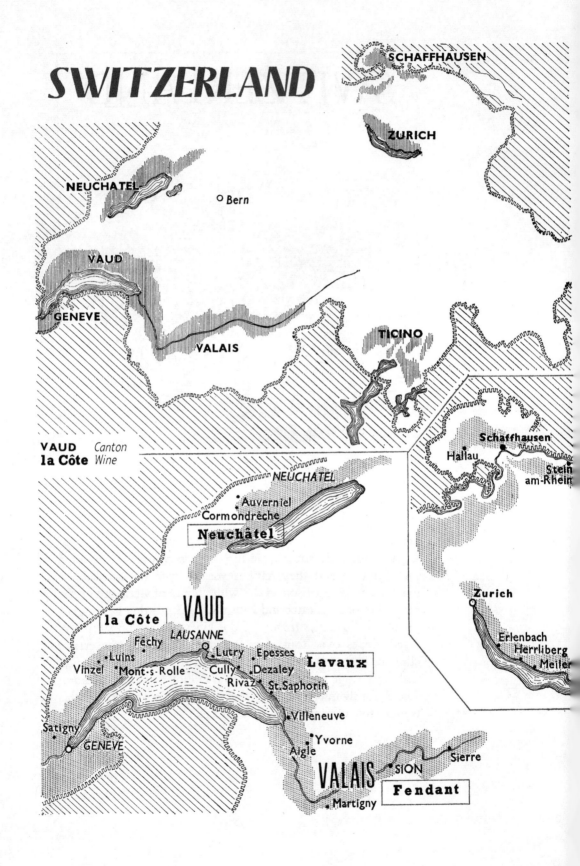

SWITZERLAND

SCHAFFHAUSEN

ZURICH

NEUCHATEL

Bern

VAUD

GENEVE

VALAIS

TICINO

VAUD *Canton*
la Côte *Wine*

NEUCHATEL

Auverniel
Cormondrèche
Neuchâtel

Hallau
Schaffhausen
Stein
am-Rhein

Zurich
Erlenbach
Herrliberg
Meilen

VAUD

la Côte
LAUSANNE
Féchy
Luins
Vinzel
Mont-s-Rolle
Lutry
Cully
Rivaz
Epesses
Dezaley
St.Saphorin
Lavaux

Villeneuve

Satigny
GENEVE
Aigle
Yvorne

VALAIS
SION
Sierre
Fendant
Martigny

There are fourteen main *cantons* where wine is produced in Switzerland. Three of them, the cantons of VAUD, NEUCHÂTEL and VALAIS, produce wines which are relatively popular in Great Britain. The wines of Geneve, Ticino and Eastern Switzerland are mostly consumed locally.

VAUD

This is the major wine producing area of Switzerland. The terraced vineyards extend along the slopes on the sunny northern shores of Lake Geneva from Vevey to Lausanne. On the steeply terraced hillsides east of Lausanne are the very picturesque Lavaux vineyards. Most of the wine produced is white from the Chasselas grape. In the Lavaux are many different wines. The CHABLAIS VAUDOIS white wines are produced in the region of Aigle, while at LUTRY, CULLY, GRANDVAUX, LE DÉZALEY and ST. SAPHORIN are wines which take their names from these villages in the Lavaux proper.

La Côte vineyards, which begin at Morges west of Lausanne, are on gentle slopes which makes cultivation less arduous. FECHY, MONT-SUR-MOLLE, VINZEL and LUINS are only some of the pretty villages which give their names to the wines.

The northern part of Vaud around the southern end of Lake Neuchâtel produces both red and white wines at ORBE, GRANDSON, BONVILLARS and VULLY.

NEUCHÂTEL

This district produces both red and white wines and most of the vineyards are cut ledge-wise along the very steep foothills of the Juras. The white wines show sparkle and are better iced. The pale red wines of CORTAILLOD are also popular and, in particular,

OEIL DE PERDRIX (Eye of the Partridge), a *rosé* of repute which is unfortunately rather expensive in England. Other vineyards are AUVERNIER, SAINT BLAISE and CRESSIER. All the Neuchâtel wines being fresh and aromatic are excellent as an accompaniment to fish and all cheese dishes.

VALAIS

The canton of Valais, especially the part lying along the right bank of the Rhône, is ideal for wine production. It has a dry climate with hot summers and mild autumns. The vineyards are in many places irrigated with small aqueducts which they call *bisses*.

The red DÔLE, made from the Pinot Noir and Gamay grape, is indisputably the finest red wine of Switzerland. It is a very pleasant table wine, deep coloured and fairly high in alcohol. Dôle has a rather scented flavour and is generally compared to a good bottle from the Côte du Rhone.

FENDANT: The Swiss name for the Chasselas grape from which the wine is made. It is a light, dry, white wine, pleasant and reasonably inexpensive.

JOHANNISBERG: A white wine made from the Sylvaner grape from vineyards on the Lavaux ridge at the eastern end of Lake Geneva.

MALVOISIE: A rich sweet dessert wine made from the Pinot Gris grape and similar to the Malvasia grape which produces the sweet fortified wines of Madeira, Cyprus, Italy and Greece. The grapes are picked late which produces a high sugar content in the wine. Malvoisie is also very popular as an aperitif.

Although not sold in England, it would be churlish not to mention the well-known Glacier wines produced near SIERRE, also in the canton of Valais. They have an unusual and somewhat bitter taste. These are white wines kept from ten to fifteen years in thirty-seven litre casks made of larchwood staves, and, after the *vendange* is over in October, carried high up to the mountain villages. Glacier wines are much thought of and worth looking for on a holiday in this district.

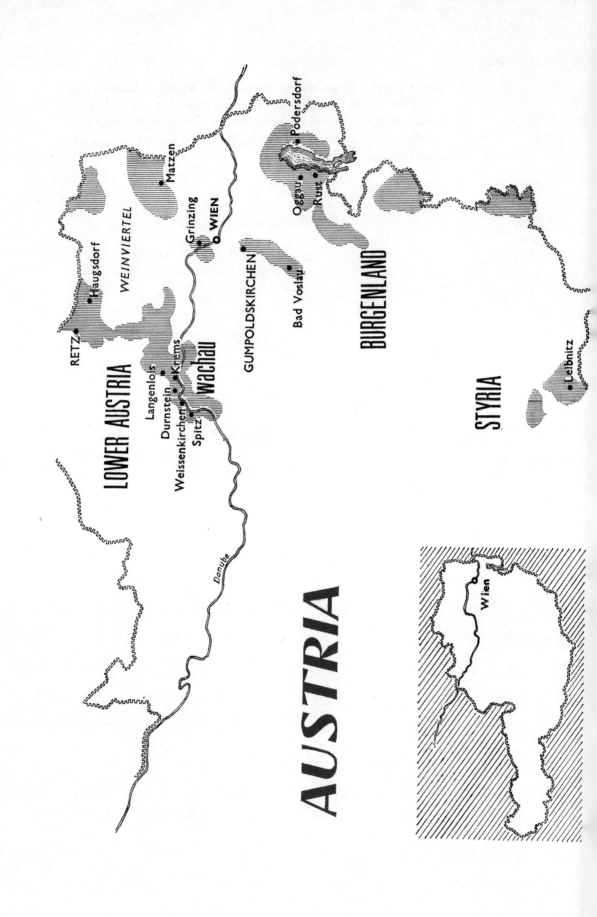

AUSTRIA

The annual production is twenty-five to thirty million gallons of table wines—White 85 per cent; Red 15 per cent. With the Alps occupying the west and southern parts, the vineyards of Austria are all on the eastern side. There are four districts: Lower Austria, Burgenland, Styria and Vienna.

LOWER AUSTRIA

This is the main district contributing sixty per cent of the total production. It includes the famous Wachau vineyards.

WACHAU Of recent years the Wachau vineyards, running upstream along the steep sides of the Danube from Krems, have become the best known outside Austria. This is not only due to the quality of the wines but to the energy of one of the principal growers, Lenz Moser, and, in Britain, to that of the shippers, Lawlers of London, who have introduced his wines to the public. WACHAUER SCHLUCK, a fresh dry white wine with a slight sparkle, made from the Sylvaner grape, is now sold by most wine merchants. Though the name "Schluck" merely means "a drop of wine", consumption is now far from being a drop in the ocean. A Traminer wine, TRIFALTER, and the sweet estate-bottled EDEL-FRAULEIN from the Muscat Ottonel grape, are among other Moser wines shipped.

Mosers have been wine people since 1124. As a boy working on his father's estate, Lenz decided that cultivating between rows of vines placed only three feet apart was singularly uncomfortable and grossly inefficient. There was barely room for an ox or horse to pass. In due course, when the business became his, he planted *his* rows three yards apart, allowing the vines to grow up on trellises.

For twenty years controversy raged. The wine would not be good; there would be more trouble from pests; frost would be more devastating. But the critics were wrong: and nowadays, with tractors, the "high, wide and handsome" system allows one man to work ten acres in place of ten men before. Moreover, fewer plants are needed to produce the same amount.

Another firm of Austrian shippers, Alois Morandell, offers a wide range of estate-bottled white wines, some sparkling wines and some reds, through their London agents. One of these, a dry Riesling wine, is named STEINER HUND. Possibly the Boston bull terrier on the label has a sporting chance of taking the place in British hearts left vacant by the departure of the Hennessy St. Bernard!

GUMPOLDS-KIRCHEN Until Wachauer wines challenged its position, Gumpolds-kirchen was the best known of Austrian wine towns. The vine-yards making its full golden wines are on the slopes which fall to the Vienna basin of the Danube only fifteen miles from the capital. Auslese, Spätlese and Beerenauslese varieties are made, but these expressions do not bring forth quite the standards associated with Germany. A restaurant specialising in Austrian food would certainly not omit GUMPOLDSKIRCHNER, but price for price others will not easily be dissuaded from Hocks and Moselles.

BURGENLAND

This is a warm flat area round Lake Neusiedl on the Hungarian border south-east of Vienna which makes thirty-three per cent of the wine, WELSCHRIESLING, MUSCAT OTTONEL and TRAMINER being among the best types.

STYRIA

Contributing a mere six per cent of ordinary wines, Styria in the south is not important, yet it is only fifty miles from the Yugoslav town of Lutomer and the River Mur flows through both districts. By replanting with the Riesling vine, a comparable success might possibly be achieved.

VIENNA

More famed for wine drinking than making, Vienna produces the final one per cent of the total. In the taverns, vast quantities of GRUNER VELTLINER wine are consumed. White, dry and fresh, some examples are now shipped to Britain notably a Schloss Grafenegg (Estate-bottled), and Mayerling rather lower in price.

HUNGARY

Many centuries ago, the Romans invaded that part of the Continent now known as Hungary, and it was probably the Emperor Probus (A.D. 276–82) who ordered his legionnaires to build roads and bridges and extended the viniculture by planting thousands of acres of vines, imported from their own stock. Roman pruning knives and drinking vessels have been found in the Balaton area, and in the south of Hungary a Roman altar has been preserved, with an inscription in Latin to Bacchus, the god of wine.

After the Romans came the Huns, under Attila, who was reputed to be fond of wine. In the seventh and eighth centuries came the Magyars. They swept into eastern Europe from the south-west of Asia, with a tribe called Kaliz from the lower Volga, and soon gained a reputation for excellent wine-making.

About the year A.D. 1000 Hungary was ruled by Stephen I, their greatest king, and under his rule the whole country accepted the Christian religion. He had monasteries built and the monks employed themselves diligently in viticulture and viniculture. The land was peaceful and prospering until the invasion of the Turks at the beginning of the sixteenth century, and for 150 years Hungary laboured under their yoke. This was one of the many sad periods of their history, as wine drinking was forbidden on religious grounds by the Mohammedans. It was not until they were driven out by the Hapsburgs in the seventeenth century that the wine-growers were able to start cultivation again.

The climate of Hungary is ideal for wine-growing as it has long hours of sunshine, but without the fierce heat of the Mediterranean countries, and its grapes can ripen slowly to maturity. The wines are usually classified into two categories—mountain and sand wines. The mountain wines include those from the vineyards of LAKE BALATON, EGER, TOKAY, MOR and many other districts, where the soil is volcanic, and this gives Hungarian wines their characteristic flavour. The "sand" wines grow in the vineyards of the Trans-Danubian plain. Once a sandy waste, but irrigated and planted with vines in the eighteenth century, it is now the most fertile area of Hungary.

TOKAJ-HEGYALJA   TOKAY ASZU, famous internationally for centuries, is the best known of all Hungarian wines. It was called by Louis XIV "The King of wines, the wine for Kings!" This rich, golden dessert wine, from the hilly vineyards of Tokaj-Hegyalja, is produced by a unique method originated over 300 years ago. Three different grapes are used, mainly Furmint—of French stock—with some Hárslevelü (Linden-leaf) and about 10 per cent Muscat.

Traditionally the vintage does not begin until the Feast of SS. Simon and Jude on October 28th, and it should be finished by the end of November. The late picking increases the sugar content of the Aszu grapes, as they shrivel slowly in the autumn sun. After careful selection, the grapes are hand-picked into hods or *puttonyos*. Tokay Aszu is made by pouring grape Must into a *Gonc*—a cask of about 140 litres—into which have been measured three, four or five *puttonyos* of a sort of paste, made by crushing the over-ripe grapes. This is a very important process and it is still done by hand, so that the pips remain whole. Today they mostly produce three or four *putts.*, but a certain quantity of five *putts.* is also made.

The Must is then stored in these small casks in very low "stone holes" often less than 6 feet high, hewn out of the volcanic rock of the mountains, This was done purposely to hide these fine wines from the constantly invading enemy troops. The temperature is not more than 45° and the Must ferments very slowly, taking four to eight years, and the bungs are left out of the casks. The high sugar content of the wine and the slow fermentation results in unparalleled keeping powers.

TOKAY SZAMORODNI, Sweet and Dry, comes from the same vineyards, but the grape clusters are pressed in their entirety and not specially selected. Szamorodni means "born of itself" and the name is of Polish origin. The Must is fermented in larger vats and then racked into a small *Gonc* for further fermentation and maturing. The dry Tokay is made from grapes picked before they are over-ripe. It is a wonderful wine, very dry with a beautiful aroma, and it is mostly drunk as an aperitif or with shellfish. SZAMORODNI SWEET is a very pleasant dessert wine. Tokay wines must all be served at room temperature, and never iced, as this would destroy their perfect character.

TOKAY ESSENCE, about which many people still enquire, was well known as a restorative, particularly in Victorian times. Alas, it is no longer produced for consumption, but only to improve the Aszu wines. Here, only shrivelled berries are used and put into a special hod with a sieve at the bottom, and the juice is extracted by the pressure of its own weight. The yield from 30 lb. of over-ripe berries is just about three to four pints, and under present-day conditions this is not an economic proposition.

TOKAY FURMINT, although from the same district, should not be included in the "Tokay" group, as only the Furmint grape is used in its production. It is a very rich table wine with a distinctive flavour of raisins, and is shipped in a hock-type bottle, whereas the other Tokay wines are in 50 cl. bottles of a traditional shape, similar to a dumb-bell.

LAKE BALATON

In the west of Hungary lies Lake Balaton, the largest lake in Europe, and its terraced vineyards are situated on the northern slopes, coming right down to the edge of the water. The climatic conditions are very favourable with the night and early morning dews, and the sunlight, reflected in the surface of the lake, is thrown back on to the grapes. Many excellent wines are produced here and, after Tokay, it is the most famous wine-growing region of Hungary.

The most outstanding wines come from BADACSON, especially the famous BADACSONYI SZURKEBARAT, which means "Grey Friar", produced from the original French grape, Pinot Gris. It is a full-bodied white wine, rich in glucose. Two other well-known white wines from these vineyards are the medium sweet BALATONI RIESLING and medium dry BALATONI FURMINT, with its delightful fresh bouquet.

MOR

MORI EZERJO comes from the vineyards of Mor and, like most Hungarian wines, it is named after the district, followed by the name of the grape. Ezerjó, which means "a thousand boons", is a traditional Hungarian grape. It produces this very dry, delicate white wine with a most interesting bouquet, perfect with all fish dishes and appreciated by connoisseurs everywhere. It should be well iced before serving.

434

DEBRÖ DEBROI HÁRSLEVELÜ—"Linden-leaf"—from the vineyards of Debrö, is another outstanding white wine. It is a medium dry table wine, worthy of a banquet.

PÉCS-VILLÁNY The vineyards of Pécs-Villány, in the angle of the Danube and the Drava near the southern frontier, produce some notable wines, and the two available here are PÉCS RIESLING, a sweet white wine, and MAGYAR ROSÉ, a pleasant *rosé* wine.

EGER In the northern hills of Hungary is the ancient baroque walled town of Eger, surrounded by vineyards which produce that splendid dry red wine, BULL'S BLOOD OF EGER (*egri Bikavér*), with its own robust character. It is a blend of grapes, mainly Kadarka with some Pinot Noir and Médoc Noir, and is perfect with goulash or grilled steak and very popular at wine and cheese parties. According to legend, Eger was besieged in the sixteenth century by a horde of about 150,000 marauding Turks, but the people of this little town, led by the heroic Istvan Dobo, successfully held the fortress, and repelled the invaders by pouring burning pitch down on them. Their superhuman strength was said to be gained from large draughts of the local red wine, later named EGRI BIKAVÉR!

Hungary produces a very interesting and unusual *rosé* wine called NEMES KADAR, made from the Kadarka grape. It is garnet in colour, with more sweetness and body than one expects from a wine of this type, and it has become very popular.

Finally, a wine for parties—Sparkling HUNGARIA, *demi-sec*—for occasions when the price of Champagne might be prohibitive.

Hungary of course produces many more excellent wines, but for obvious reasons I have concentrated on the wines available here.

On my annual visits to that beautiful country, quite apart from their wonderful food, romantic gypsy bands and attractive peasant costumes, I have been most impressed by their viniculture

435

and their dedication to producing wines of such outstanding quality, and this is one of their major exports. To summarise, below is a list of the wines exported to Gt. Britain and serving instructions. R.T.=Room temperature. C.=Chilled.

White

Estate Bottled	Vintage	Serve
TOKAY ASZU 3 putts.	1959	R.T.
„ „ 4 putts.	„	„
„ „ 5 putts.	„	„
TOKAY SZAMORODNI—Dry	„	„
„ „ Sweet	„	„
TOKAY FURMINT	1959	„
BADACSONYI SZURKEBARAT	„	C.
DEBROI HÁRSLEVELÜ	„	C.

Red and Rosé

EGRI BIKAVÉR	1961	R.T.
NEMES KADAR	1959	Cool

Sparkling Wine

HUNGARIA, Demi-sec	N.V.	C.

White

London-bottled		
BALATONI RIESLING	1959/61	C.
BALATONI FURMINT	„	C.
MORI EZERJÓ—Very dry	„	C.

Red

BULL'S BLOOD OF EGER (Egri Bikavér)	1959	R.T.

White

PÉCS RIESLING	N.V.	C.

Rosé

MAGYAR ROSÉ	N.V.	C.

YUGOSLAVIA

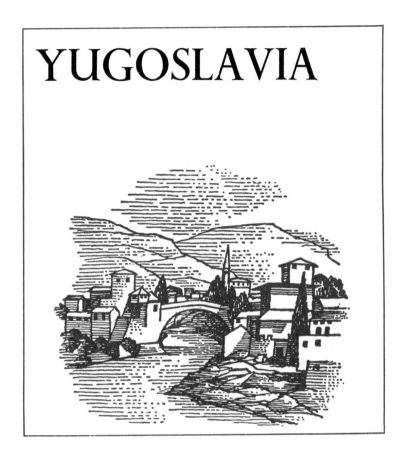

The wines of Yugoslavia are of particular interest at this time because the demand in England is for good wines at modest prices.

Most of the wines imported here are white and come from Slovenia, which was formerly part of Austria and is only separated from that country by the Julian Alps. Because of the nearby mountains and the warmth which comes from the Adriatic to the south, Slovenia enjoys great advantages for the production of white wines.

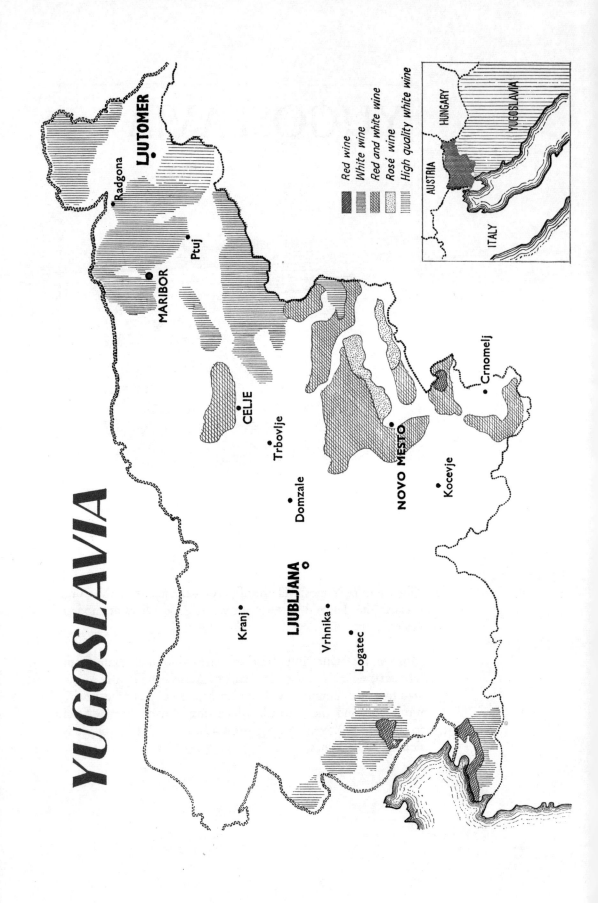

RADGONA It is only since the war that Yugoslavian wines have been imported here in quantity. Because of their quality and very reasonable prices sales of these wines have become very considerable and most wine merchants sell increasing quantities each year. The main sales are for the Riesling wines, although there is some demand for the Sylvaner, Muscat, and more recently for the sweeter wine from Radgona near Maribor and called RANINA, perhaps better known as TIGERMILK. Were this wine tasted without it being known that it came from Yugoslavia it could be mistaken for a Rhine wine of a good year and of some quality. The price for this is more than for the Rieslings, but is still very reasonable.

The historic town of Ptuj with its famous castle is not far from the important city of Maribor, which was formerly known as Marburg. Ptuj is also the important wine centre, being adjacent to the famous vineyards of LUTOMER, ORMOZ and RADGONA. In the fine cellars at Ptuj are large stocks of these wines ready for despatch and shipment to all parts of Europe. The wines for England, which come mostly in cask, are shipped in Yugoslavian steamers from Rijeka, the well-known port on the Dalmatian coast. The fine oak casks which are used for this trade are returned by the same route.

LUTOMER There was already a flourishing trade in wine at Ptuj in the Middle Ages and the wines of Luttenberg, now called Lutomer, and adjacent vineyards were famous during the period of the Austro-Hungarian Empire. They are even better known today.

One of the fine wines grown at Lutomer is named JERUSALEM, the reason being that some of the would-be Crusaders when they arrived at this place decided to go no farther, being much pleased with the wines and the surroundings there, and in consequence the vineyards were thereafter called Jerusalem.

Although the vintages do vary in quality the aim of the exporters is to provide wines which maintain their quality year by year. In this endeavour they are much helped by the *pourriture*

439

noble, the "noble rot" which develops in the grapes which are picked last as a result of the warm days with great air humidity and provides quality wines with a great amount of fruitiness. Slovenia did not escape the phylloxera and when the old native vines were lost as a result, they were replaced by the Laski and Renski Riesling vines, also the Sylvaner, Sauvignon, Traminer, Ruländer, Pinot and Muscat—vines all of which produce wines of quality.

Although some red wines are produced in Slovenia, the best area of production of red wines is along the Adriatic coast where the exceptional sunshine and weather conditions greatly assist. Some of these wines have been shipped to England, but as yet they have not made nearly the progress in sales that the white wines of Slovenia have achieved.

RUMANIA

Rumania produces red and white table wines and dessert wines; the annual production was 130 million gallons (1959).

The chief drawbacks to making fine wines in Rumania are extremes of climate. Soil and position are good, but a shade temperature sometimes over 38°C in summer and a winter which can leave the Danube icebound for months are disadvantages. Nevertheless, *Fructexport*, the state-run organisation, is making enormous strides, expanding vineyards, planting new vines and installing modern machinery, with the result that wines are already exported to thirty-two countries and the annual production figures may have topped the 200 million mark by now.

Like Bulgaria, Rumania only threw off Moslem rule in 1878. In 1945 Russia took back Bessarabia and with it 40 per cent of Rumania's pre-war wine production, so achievements since the war are all the more remarkable.

The country is mountainous except in the great coastal plain of Wallachia and Moldavia. The Carpathians sweep in a sickle-shaped curve from the north-west, meeting the Transylvanian Alps in the centre.

VALEA CALUGARESCA

Although there are vineyards all over the country, the best are apt to be on the lower slopes of the hills facing the Black Sea where the mountains descend to the plain. A typical example is Valea Calugaresca ("Valley of the Monks") fifty miles north of Bucharest. In this hot summer climate the grapes develop a high sugar content so that sweet wines tend to result. MUSCAT OTTONEL, a highly flavoured dessert wine, is one of these and the sweet, soft red SEGACEA CABERNET another.

TIRNAVE

Quite different from these two are the wines of Tirnave, an inland district in the heart of the Carpathians. Tirnave is a river which flows west, eventually to join the Danube beyond the Hungarian border. White wine grapes—Traminer, Pinot Gris, Italian Riesling and Furmint—are the main plantings along its banks. TIRNAVE RIESLING and TIRNAVE PERLA are the two best white wines, their style being broadly similar to the Yugoslav and Hungarian Rieslings selling at about 50p a bottle, though they have their own distinctive flavour.

The four wines mentioned, all shipped by Norton and Langridge Ltd., of Wood Street, London, are stocked by many retail shops. Capital Wine Agencies, Knobs Hill Road, London, E.15, also ship some Rumanian wines, notably the red KADARKA and the white RULANDER. At prices under 75p it is to be hoped that these bottles succeed in pleasing the public.

Principal shippers of Rumania wines to Britain are Wines of Rumania Ltd., 4/9 Wood Street, London, E.C.2. Riesling, Perla, Muscat and Cabernet wines are among those obtainable. At low prices, it is to be hoped that these wines succeed, for the Rumanians declare that up their sleeves they have far better ones to come.

BULGARIA

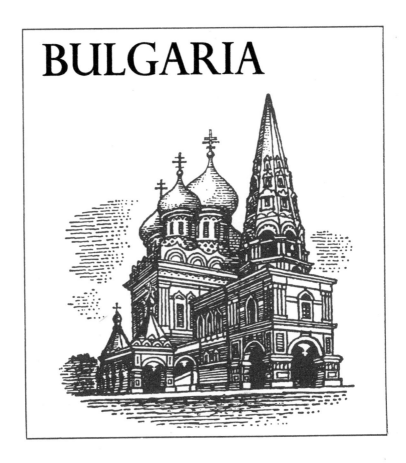

The annual production of Bulgaria is 46 million gallons of table wines, 60 per cent being red and 40 per cent being white and sparkling.

From 1396 to 1878, Bulgaria was under the Moslem rule of the Turkish Empire, so that from religious principles wine was altogether discouraged. Her independence coincided with the plague of the root-eating bug phylloxera, which at that time was sweeping Europe. Adding the Balkan wars of 1912 and 1913 and the two World Wars, it becomes clear that conditions have not been exactly ideal for building a wine trade. The rapid rise in production since 1945 to forty-six million gallons (much the same figure as Australia) is no mean achievement for which the State organisation Vinprom in Sofia can take credit.

A brief look at the map of Europe shows that Bulgaria is a small country, 300 miles long by 200 miles wide, bordering the Black Sea along whose shores some white wines are made. But the chief vineyards lie inland in the deep valleys. Bulgaria is in fact split into north and south by the high Balkan range running east and west across the middle. On the northern side, these valleys, carrying fast-flowing streams and rivers, descend to the Danube; on the southern side the valleys descend to the River Maritsa. The two "halves" are linked by the Skipka pass carrying the railway up the Yantra valley to a summit of 4,363 feet.

TRNOVO

On the northern side, in the province of Trnovo with its good communications, the main vineyards and wine co-operatives have been established. Four million bottles of sparkling wine are produced here annually, besides a variety of red, white and dessert wines. They are even contemplating installing the latest Russian device, which produces sparkling wine continuously!

MARITSA VALLEY

The Maritsa valley in the southern "half" is less important. Here, on the right bank around Plovdiv—the largest town after Sophia—they make chiefly a red wine called MAVRUD.

In Bulgaria the wines are sold by the name of the grape, most of these being traditional, for in the days before the Turkish occupation the vine had been cultivated widely. Of these,

446

GAMZA and KADARKA are the best of the reds, DIAMIAT and MISKET of the whites, but to Western European tastes they may not appeal greatly.

Plantings of the Cabernet Sauvignon (the great Claret grape) and of Riesling and Chardonnay (white Burgundy) are now being made with good results. There is no reason why they should not be successful; Bulgaria, whose latitude is much the same as southern France, has the right weather and soil for the vine.

Although 80 per cent of the total production is exported, chiefly to Communist countries, Bulgarian wines have only recently reached Britain.

The RILA range—a RIESLING, a CHARDONNAY, a KADARKA and a GAMZA—is being shipped by Duthie & Co. Ltd., of Croydon, who have chosen some gay, attractive labels for their quartet. KADARKA is sweet, GAMZA dry; but the two white wines seemed to me the more attractive. They certainly catch the eye in a shop window and could well become popular with the public.

448

GREECE

The annual production is eighty-five million gallons. This includes dessert wines and red and white table wines.

Interest in Greece as a wine country centres more on what the Greeks did in the past rather than what they are doing in the present. The writings of Homer and Hesiod, Xenophon and Plato testify to their prowess both as wine makers and drinkers during the 800 years before Christ. They invented the God of Wine, Dionysus, who held sway for some centuries until we find Bacchus taking his place.

But the Greeks' great achievement was as a seafaring people. They carried the cult of the vine east to the Crimea and the Caspian shore and west across the Mediterranean. It is to them that we owe the wines of Jerez, Malaga and Sicily. In their colony at Marseilles they perhaps found their keenest pupils, for we know that the vineyards up the Rhône valley were started well before the Romans.

The extent of Greek vineyards today is 527,000 acres of which 60 per cent are planted for making wine and the rest for sultanas, currants and table grapes. Annual production of eighty-five million gallons puts Greece about twelfth—between Yugoslavia and Hungary—in the "international producers' league table".

Table Wines

RETSINA: The most likely table wine to be stocked by wine merchants is RETSINA, which has its advocates outside Greece, although it is an acquired taste. Retsina is a white wine to which they add a special resin from the local pine tree, *Calitris quadrivalvis*. After about a year, the wine begins to taste musty, which disproves the popular theory that resin was originally added to remove the flavour of goatskins, in which wine was carried. Even so, resinating does not seem to have been adopted outside Greece and Turkey. Perhaps the resin from other types of pine was too unpalatable or perhaps they just preferred a bouquet of straightforward goat. Suffice to say, then, that though Retsina is an acquired taste, acquiring it will not cost very much.

Best known among the normal table wines widely distributed in Greece itself are DEMESTICA, SANTA HELENA and ANTIKA, all made in Patras. The dry white varieties are pleasant. The enthusiast should find these and other sound low-priced Greek wines in Soho as well as in Athens.

Dessert Wines

MAVRODAPHNE: This sweet, Malaga-like dessert wine is deservedly well known. Gustav Claus, a Bavarian refugee who set up in business in Patras in 1861, began to make it soon afterwards, choosing, so they say, the name of a lady with whom he was in love. His business, now the Achaia-Claus Wine Company, has always kept a distinguished visitors' book whose names now include characters as divergent as Lord Montgomery and Franz Liszt, the composer.

But Mavrodaphne is made in many parts of Greece and Greek scholars prefer to think the name originates from the disappearing Daphne, who, pursued by Apollo, prayed for aid just as he was overtaking her and was transformed into a laurel.

SAMOS MUSCATEL: The second Greek dessert wine which some wine-merchants find worth stocking sells at much the same price as Mavrodaphne, though the varieties we import seem to be less good. On the island itself, barely a mile from the Turkish coast of Asia Minor, the wine may be better. Certainly it impressed Byron, who made Don Juan demand it by the bowl. It must also have had something to do with the square of the hypotenuse, for Pythagoras, the creator of that geometrical theorem, was a distinguished son of Samos.

Spirits

Greek Brandy compares favourably with other "lesser country" brandies, CAMBUS being a well-known mark. But the national spirit is OUZO, distilled from grapes with aromatic herbs added. 70° proof, it can be described as a spirit aperitif, best drunk cold with water added.

CYPRUS

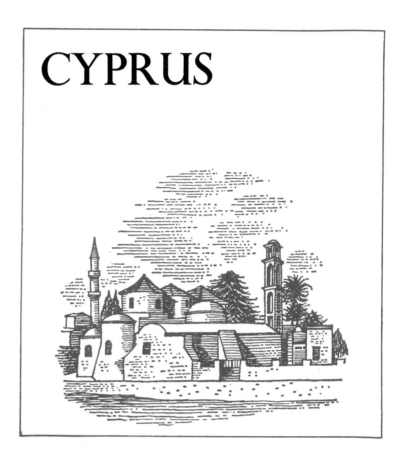

The wine industry of Cyprus is one of the most ancient in the world. Cyprus appears to have been fought over at various times by the Persians, Assyrians, Egyptians and others until its annexation by Rome in the first century B.C. Wherever Graeco-Roman influence has been strong, viticulture and wine-making have been developed and Cyprus, no less than France, Spain and the Rhineland, owes a debt in this respect to the Romans.

Richard Coeur de Lion, who conquered the island in 1191, sold the sovereignty to the Templar Knights. The Templars

453

retained control of certain areas known as Commanderies, and it is to the largest of these, the Grande Commanderie, that COMMANDARIA owes its name; probably the oldest of wine names still in current use. The first exports of Cyprus wines to England date from this time.

In the Middle Ages it is related that Count Thibaut IV of Champagne, on his way home from the Holy Land, stayed in Cyprus to visit his cousin the Queen. While there, he rescued a young nobleman who was in prison there and took him back to France. Later the young man fetched his fiancée and returned to Champagne with gifts for the Count, among them cuttings of the best vines of Cyprus which, according to a local tradition, were the foundation of the great vineyards of Champagne.

During Venetian rule in Cyprus the export trade in wine appears to have thrived, but after the conquest by Turkey viticulture was discouraged, though it never died out.

After the cession of Cyprus to Great Britain in 1878, the wine industry was still in existence and, in recent years, efforts have been made to improve and modernise it and vine cuttings have been imported from Europe and South Australia.

VINEYARDS   The vine-growing areas are mainly at the foot and on the slopes of the Troodos mountain range, and, to a lesser extent, on the slopes of Makheras. The vineyard area of the Troodos falls in the districts of LIMASSOL and PAPHOS and a small part in the district of NICOSIA (Marathassa and Pitsilia).

The mountainous areas are relatively densely populated, the people living mostly in large villages and going out to work their holdings in the surrounding land, where the growing and tending of the vines is carried out almost entirely by family labour. Vines, in fact, are the principal if not the only possible crop for such areas, which emphasises the great importance of viticulture to the people of Cyprus.

The vine is a hard taskmaster wherever it grows and in Cyprus it is no exception. There is, however, one consolation often lacking in other vineyards: there will always be enough sun to ripen their grapes. In fact neither the quantity nor the quality of the Cyprus vintages vary from year to year—to the extent they do in Europe, and if the vintage appears on the label of a bottle of table wine it is more an indication of its age than of any other characteristic.

It is interesting that the practice of plastering was general and it is still used in the making of some village wines. This consists of the addition of gypsum to the pie or mash left after the first pressing before the final pressing is done. For various reasons this is no longer permitted in France, but it is usual to add *yeso* in the course of the pressing of Sherry in Spain. The object is to remedy certain deficiencies in the Must and thus produce a better wine.

Table Wines

The wines people drink with their food are of great interest because such an immense variety is available to an ever-growing wine public, particularly in England, and although the table wines now coming from Cyprus form only a small part of her wine exports they are none the less worth describing both for their merits as they are now and because of their future possibilities.

It is important to remember that a large proportion are made to appeal to local taste which, in reds, is for very full deep-coloured wines with a high tannin content. These go well with the strongly flavoured spicy foods eaten in Cyprus, but they are rather strong for northern European palates. It must not be forgotten, however, that wines of such strength and so high in extractive value must be the envy of many producers in more northerly parts where thinness sometimes has to be passed off as finesse. Larger quantities, however, of types closer to the Southern Burgundy (Mâcon-Beaujolais) style are being produced as trade develops. The colour of these is lighter and the wine smoother on the palate, but the substantial nature of Cyprus wines remains and the alcoholic strength is seldom below 13° Gay Lussac.

Between these two extremes are many degrees of difference and finding the best is largely a matter of trial and error as with all wines.

Red wines are made principally from the local black grape which some experts consider to have common stock with the Malvoisie of Madeira, reputedly transported thither from the Eastern Mediterranean in the Middle Ages. Other species are, however, introduced to give acidity, colour, and a better balanced Must, notably an oval grape named Opthalma, and the Maratheftika, so named because it was grown originally in the Marathassa area mentioned above. The area includes the villages of YERADJES, PRODROMOS, KALOPANAYOTIS, PEDHOULLAS and about ten others on the north-western slopes of the Troodos.

The local black or Mavron vine is predominant, being grown practically throughout the vineyards of Cyprus. It is difficult to give specific areas in this case beyond saying that some of the finest of the variety are grown on the slopes of a hill named Afames near the village of PLATRES and some of the best red wines are made from grapes from this area.

A wine which is particularly successful is the local *rosé* known in the Island and in Greece as KOKKINELI. For a *rosé* it is deep in colour, fresh to the palate and usually entirely dry. When iced, it can be drunk with almost any food. Here again, there is none of the over-lightness so often found in *rosé* wines. The Mavron grape, already mentioned, is used in the production of this wine having the characteristic that the skins are only lightly pigmented. This makes it particularly suited to the production of

456

this type which, like many natural things, is much to be recommended.

First shipments of this *rosé* have arrived in England from an old-established winery in Limassol, and it is to be hoped that many wine merchants will offer it on their lists.

It is significant that when there were French troops stationed in Cyprus during the Suez crisis of 1956, it was this wine which was particularly popular with them.

The local white Xynisteri vine is cultivated in many areas. PITSILIA and the vineyards of the PAPHOS district on the west are noted for this variety and it is 90 per cent of the production of the FAMAGUSTA and LARNACA vineyards. The finished white wines are full bodied, with a flavour entirely their own. The majority are dry partly because they are preferred like that and partly because the local yeasts are capable of fermentation in the presence of even the high degree of alcohol usual in Cyprus if any free sugar is present.

To give themselves greater control over the end product, the principal wineries are importing some of the most elaborate apparatus from Europe, much of which is already installed. This will enable their technicians to produce a far greater range in the near future than has been possible up to the present and wine will be offered on the United Kingdom and other markets varying greatly in sugar content, colour, freshness, acidity and alcoholic strength. This is far-sighted and promises well for the future.

Sherry Types

The natural white wines, apart from their properties as table wines, have a tendency to "maderise" in the heat of Cyprus and are, therefore, particularly suitable raw material for the production of Sherry types. A large range of these is made for home consumption and export and varies greatly in style. Experiments are being conducted in the production of Fino and Amontillado types by the agency of the *flor* yeast which is responsible for them in Spain.

Cyprus Sherries available in this country fall into three categories:

1. Those imported at full Sherry strength as from Spain, and bottled here after normal clarification.
2. Those which are imported at two strengths and married by the importers.
3. Low strength wines, nearly always sweet.

The best of those in category 1 can compete with any Sherries from the Commonwealth. Their price makes them the least expensive in their class. They vary from Pale Dry to Medium.

In the second category they tend to vary in strength according to the requirements of the blender, but are seldom noticeably lighter in alcohol than those in the first group. The object here is to produce a wine at high strength, having only paid the high rate of duty on part of the total, and thus be able to offer to the public a bottle of Cyprus Sherry at proper strength at a low price. Generally speaking, the finished article is excellent.

The taste for dry Sherries is a comparatively recent one, so that the sweet wines in the third group are not so out of character as might at first appear. Although subject to the lower rate of duty they are able to be imported at a higher strength than foreign wines so that they are very reasonably priced for what they are. This class, together with other dessert wines at the same strength, forms, at present, the bulk of wine imports to the United Kingdom from Cyprus. For those who watch their budget carefully and who have a taste for sweet things, these wines are a good buy, being entirely natural; their high sugar content, up to 4°–5° Baumé, is the product of the abundant sunshine of Cyprus and nothing else.

458

Dessert Wines

COMMANDARIA: Conditions in Cyprus are particularly suited to the production of dessert wines, the most generally known of which is Commandaria. It has been made from time immemorial in certain of the mountain villages, the three best known being KALOKHORIO, ZOOPIYI and YERASSA; also AYIAS MAMAS, LANIA, SYLIKOU, DHOROS, MONAGRI, AYIOS GEORGHIOS and some eleven others are recognised producers. For sale in Cyprus and for export, village Commandarias are frequently blended with certain wines traditionally used for the purpose as the very high degree of concentration makes them unpalatable by the standards of the general public; in fact, the sugar content is often as high as 14° Baumé compared with about 3° Baumé in Port as shipped to the United Kingdom. However, the interesting flavour of this traditional wine of Cyprus remains. In many of the villages it is stored in large earthenware jars suggestive of Ali Baba's forty thieves and some of it is kept in this manner until it reaches a great age.

It can be seen how important is the role of the blender in the production of the finished wine, which varies according to what villages the shipper buys his Commandarias from, their various ages and styles, and the types of wine used in the breaking-down process by which the high degree of concentration is reduced.

Commandaria is made traditionally from a mixture of red and white grapes, the proportion varying from village to village. The amount of white grapes used in the best is generally about 10 per cent of the total.

ISRAEL

I am sure the present effort to introduce the wines of Israel to a wider public will be welcomed by wine-lovers everywhere. Israel may be considered the cradle of the wine industry. The Bible is strewn with references to vineyards, and I quote: "And Noah began to be a husbandman and he planted a vineyard." It was the first of many that were to become such a characteristic culture in the ancient husbandry of Israel.

HISTORY   Much of our knowledge of the far-distant beginnings of wine-making are fragmentary and uncertain, but in Scripture we get ample evidence of the respect accorded the vine, of methods of cultivation, and of the existence of vineyards in all parts of the Holy Land. A typical verse is that in Isaiah: "My well-beloved hath a vineyard in a very fruitful hill, and he fenced it, and gathered out the stones thereof, and planted it with the choicest vine, and built a tower in the midst of it, and also made a wine-press therein." And who does not know of Micah's dream of peace when "shall sit every man under his vine and under his fig tree, and none shall make them afraid"?

The importance of viticulture and the esteem which the vine enjoyed in ancient Israel can best be seen from the fact that wine-growing was recognised in war as (perhaps the only one) a "reserved occupation". A decree issued by Moses said that he who planted a vineyard should stay at home and not join an army, so that he should not die before the vineyard had borne its first fruit and another man gather the fruit.

Centuries passed and then came the tragic destruction of Jewry and the dispersal of the Jews. Most of the laboriously cultivated vineyards fell into disuse and the arrival of the Moslems with Mohammed's strict ban on the production and drinking of alcohol completed the ruin of the industry.

The turn of the tide came eighty years ago with the drifting back of the Jews to their ancient homeland. Thanks to the interest and benefaction of Baron Edmond de Rothschild, viticulture was made an important part of the agricultural resettlement. He encouraged the settlers to copy Noah and plant vineyards, and from his Paris headquarters he arranged for French experts to go out to Palestine and instruct the farmers in wine-making. So energetically did they put the lessons into practice that in a short time vineyards began to sparkle like jewels in the Plain of Judaea, the Valley of Sharon, and the hills of Samaria, and lushness and colour spread over formerly barren lands. Wine cellars were built in various places and a corresponding variety of types of wine produced.

Over the years these have been improved through experiments with many kinds of vines and the selection of those best suited to the soil and climate, as well as by improved viticultural methods.

TYPES OF WINE
Today Israel produces a fairly wide variety of wines, as can be seen from the now-discarded former names—Alicante, Haut Sauternes, Tokay, Sherry, Port, Malaga, Champagne. (There are other types also.) These names have been dropped following Israel's adherence to the Madrid Pact and the passing of a law forbidding the use of foreign place-names for wines and spirits. Each grower takes his own brand names, and these are generally local ones.

In Israel one sometimes comes across a name of a town or village, but this has not the significance as the birthplace of the wine, but the place of establishment of the wine merchant— in other words, the name of the village is used as a brand name.

At the end of 1962 Israel had 23,500 acres of vineyards of which 9,500 acres were under wine-grape vines plus 1,500 acres of young vines (the balance being table-grape vineyards). The wine districts are:

THE HILLS OF UPPER GALILEE (near the Lebanon frontier)
THE HILLS OF LOWER GALILEE (near Nazareth)
THE HILLS OF SAMARIA (Zichron Ya'aqov, Binyamina)
THE COASTAL PLAIN BETWEEN HAIFA and TEL-AVIV
THE PLAIN OF JUDAEA (Gezer, Ramla, Rehovot, Gedera)
THE HILLS OF JERUSALEM
THE NEGEV (Gilat, Rannen)

Actually, as mentioned above, no geographical names are used, but only brand names (CARMEL, ELIAS, KING SOLOMON). This enables the growers, and especially the large co-operatives with properties in all districts, to blend wines from various districts, and guarantee continuity of quality much better than if they had to rely on the vintage of a special district.

KINDS OF VINES   The principal vines grown for the making of wine are:

> BLACK: Carignan, Alicante Grenache, Alicante Bouschet, Malbec.
>
> WHITE: Sémillon, Clairette egreneuse, Muscat d'Alexandrie.

Other vines, including new crossings, have been planted, for instance Riesling, Sauvignon, Ugni Blanc, White Grenache.

As in all wine-producing countries, Israel produces its own brandy. The production in most enterprises is done by distillation in pot stills, followed by a second distillation.

The brands of wine available in Gt. Britain are: King Solomon, Palwin, Bozwin, Elias, Carmel and Camel.

U.S.S.R.

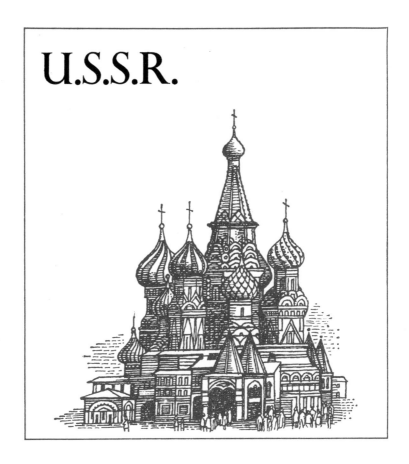

A rough estimate of the annual production of wine in the U.S.S.R. is 300–400 million gallons including table wines, red, white and sparkling.

The Russians certainly do things in a big way. A current news item describes a crisis caused by six million empty "Champagne" bottles cluttering up the republic of Uzbekistan. They are worth £400,000, but to remove them to a dumping ground would require 600 railway waggons, and so they remain.

In the last decade the U.S.S.R. has extended her vineyards until she may now be the largest producer of grapes in the world. The proportion used for wine puts her about fourth in the international table after France, Italy and Spain. Probably little attempt has yet been made towards quality, and such wines as are exported seem inferior to those of her satellites, Rumania and Bulgaria, price for price.

In this vast "Socialist Sixth" there is every variety of climate except tropical. Vineyards are widespread; experiments have even been made as far north as Moscow. But, as is only to be expected, the best wines come from the south not far from that world *route des vins* the 45° latitude parallel on which Bordeaux itself is situated.

A few British firms have shipped Russian wines in recent years. The selection of course varies, those proving insufficiently popular being discontinued and possibly replaced by others. The districts of the U.S.S.R. where they are made are as follows:

MOLDAVIA

Vines are grown almost everywhere in this strip along the Rumanian border between the Dnieper and the Danube. Wines are of ordinary quality, the possibility of advance not being improved by a heavy annual rainfall in summer which washes away the top soil.

NEGRI DI PURKAR is a red wine from Cabernet, Saparvi and Rara-Njagra grapes from the lower reaches of the Dnieper. KABERNE is a typical Cabernet red wine. FETIASKA is a dry white wine; likewise ALIGATE, less dry than Fetiaska.

CRIMEA

Only one Crimean wine seems to be shipped to Britain, MAS-SANDRA MUSCATEL, a rich sweet dessert wine. ANAPA RIESLING, medium dry white, is made at ANAPA, a wine centre across the Straits of Kerch on the mainland.

The south-eastern coast of the Crimea is the Russian riviera enjoying a Black Sea climate with high mountain protection. YALTA is not only a famous resort but makes the best wines and has very large maturing cellars.

GEORGIA

At those wartime banquets given in the Kremlin to Sir Winston Churchill and other Heads of States, Stalin was always reported as drinking a "light" Georgian wine. The son of a poor Georgian shoemaker, this was more than likely, but the description "light" was more politically expedient than vinously accurate, as Georgian wines do not lack strength.

The vineyards of this republic are mainly in the valley of the river Rion, which flows into the Black Sea. There is mountain protection on both sides, particularly important to the north where the great mountains of the Caucasus, rising to the 18,470 feet peak of Mount Elbruz, take the worst of the Siberian blast.

The wines tend to be full and the red ones dark. MUKUZANI and SAPERAVI are two dark strong red wines of 14° alcoholic strength from the eastern side of Georgia in the Tiflis region. GOORJUANI and TSINANDALI are two straw-coloured white wines from the Rion valley district.

As may be gathered from the six million empties already mentioned, the Russians' favourite wine is Champagne. The variety they make, which we very rightly cannot call Champagne since this name is now protected by law, is really very sweet sparkling wine. KRASNODAR, a brand which has appeared in this country, is described as *Champanski*.

Spirits

Mexicans, Indians, Africans . . . all have found some form of vegetable matter from which to distil spirits, which can in fact be made from almost anything containing starch, except a laundered shirt which *should* lack the quantity. The impoverished Russian peasant turned to grain and Vodka became the national drink.

CANADA

Although grapes are believed to have been grown in Nova Scotia in the days of the Vikings, the wine industry did not develop until many years later. There are records which confirm that wine was made in Canada in 1636 from the "fox" grape which grew wild at the time and it is known that Jesuit missionaries used the grapes to make wine for the sacrament.

It was not until the nineteenth century that the Labrusca vines of the Eastern United States were introduced into the Niagara

Peninsula where most of the Canadian wine is still made. The area is about 45 miles long stretching by the shores of Lake Ontario from beyond Hamilton in the west to Niagara and Crystal Beach in the east. The chief centres are Niagara Falls Welland, London, Grimsby and St. Catherines.

Ontario, one of the most important fruit growing areas of Canada, has grapes as the main fruit crop and most of these grapes are made into wine. The wines resemble those of New York State, being from the same varieties of grapes, the Labrusca, the Concord, the Delaware and the Niagara.

The next largest area of vineyards is in British Columbia which in 1970 had six wineries. There are also two in Alberta, one in Saskatchewan, one in New Brunswick and one in Nova Scotia.

The vineyards of Canada cover some 30,000 acres and the annual production of wine is in the neighbourhood of six million gallons. New varieties of grapes are constantly being researched and tested and experiments with French hybrids, since World War II, seem to promise a much better quality in the future. Although practically all the wines produced are consumed in Canada there has been some exported to Britain since 1965.

The soil and climatic conditions are second to none, this notwithstanding the winters which leave a lot to be desired. Many wine experts believe that because of the Canadian winters the culture of Vitis Vinefera is impossible. This no longer applies as the vine strains from Canada replaced many Europeans when they were destroyed some years ago. The variety of grapes and the technology surrounding their growth and care are the pride of the *vignerons*. The acreage of the vineyards is growing annually as is the tonnage of the grape yield but so great is the demand for grapes and wine in Canada that grapes have to be imported for domestic use and, with the exception of Ontario, by the wineries themselves.

The conditions and manner of the sale of wine in Canada is through the various Provisional Governments who control sales through their respective Liquor Control Boards. They in turn import all other brands of Liquor and Wines and in most provinces actually do the selling as well.

APPETIZER WINES

CANADIAN SHERRY: a very popular wine with a delicious nutty flavour; they range from light to dark amber in colour and may be dry, medium dry or sweet.

CANADIAN VERMOUTH: can be dry or sweet, ranging from white to golden amber in colour.

CANADIAN APERITIFS OR FLAVOURED WINES: specially prepared and varying considerably in colour and flavour.

WHITE TABLE WINES

These may be labelled as such, or as described below. They are light in body, delicate in flavour, pale to deep yellow in colour, sweet, medium dry or dry. Alcoholic content does not exceed 14%.

CANADIAN SAUTERNES: varying from sweet to medium dry.

CANADIAN RHINE (OR RIESLING): dry and delicately tart.

RED TABLE WINES

They may be labelled as such or described as below. They are light-bodied but robust in flavour and usually dry. Alcoholic content does not exceed 14%.

CANADIAN CLARET: dry with a balanced tartness.

CANADIAN BURGUNDY: dry and full-bodied.

CANADIAN ROSÉ: light, all-purpose dinner wine, dry to medium sweet.

DESSERT WINES

This is a North American classification of wines of higher alcoholic content than table wines. They vary from sweet to dry. Alcoholic content 16 to 20%. The principal wines in this group are:

471

CANADIAN SHERRY: the most popular dessert wine varying from richly sweet to dry.

CANADIAN PORT: rich ruby red or tawny in colour, sweet and full-bodied.

CANADIAN TOKAY: sweet and amber-coloured.

CANADIAN MUSCATEL: has the sun-dried, rich flavour of raisins.

CANADIAN KOSHER WINES: produced under rabbinical supervision, generally sweet.

CANADIAN FRUIT WINES: made from fruits other than grapes.

CANADIAN WINE COCKTAILS: wines to which herbs have been added. Sweet or dry.

CRACKLING WINES

Sometimes referred to as petillant, rosé or white, have a mild effervescence, more apparent to the tongue than the eye. Less than 14% alcoholic content.

SPARKLING WINES

These are fully effervescent, less than 14% alcoholic content.

CANADIAN CHAMPAGNE TYPE WINE: pale, straw-coloured or pink, dry to medium sweet, light and bubbly.

CANADIAN SPARKLING BURGUNDY: dry, red, fuller bodied than the champagne.

CHILE

The annual production of red and white table wines is ninety million gallons.

First priority to the English colonist was allegedly the construction of a cricket ground. To the Spaniards conquering Mexico and South America in the sixteenth century it was—so Edward Hyams declares*—"the establishment of the vineyard". Cortes was demanding vine cuttings from Spain in 1522 even though it

* *Dionysus, A Social History of the Wine Vine.*

473

took him another eight years to pacify Mexico. Wine was needed for religious purposes as well as for Spanish morale. Vineyards sprang up everywhere in the wake of the conquerors to such an extent that the vine became the hated symbol of the invader, to be destroyed whenever possible.

By the end of the sixteenth century there was so much South American wine that Spain, fearing for her own exports, clamped down on her settlers, imposing regulations impossible to enforce and therefore largely ignored. The vine continued to spread and still thrives in all the South American states except those in the north, which are too near the Equator. Argentina, Peru and Chile are the principal countries; the first named for quantity, the last for quality. But a century or more ago there was a setback. Edward Hyams cites a theory that long-continued propagation of a plant, without new graftings or raisings from seed, ends in its degeneration. Certainly something of the kind occurred in ancient Greece and other Mediterranean countries.

The Chileans, however, turned their misfortune to excellent account. They replanted with Cabernet, Merlot and Malbec from Bordeaux and with the great white wine grapes, Sémillon and Sauvignon. By 1900, Chilean wines had taken medals in Paris and Vienna; one "impertinent" grower even shipped his wine to Bordeaux, selling it there at an excellent price.

Today Chilean viticulture gives employment to 30,000 smallholders and their families, a typical holding being about three to five acres, although there are a few large estates. The astonishing thing is that Chile entirely escaped the phylloxera, so that all her vines are on their own root stocks. Neither, for some reason, are the growers troubled with mildew. These facts led Edward Hyams to suggest that if there is another "golden age" in wine it may come from Chile in the next four hundred years during which the *encépagement* should reach its peak of development.

The land of Chile, wedged between the Pacific and the Andes, is only 100–200 miles wide but 2,800 miles long. In parts of the north there is no rain and in parts of the south it never ceases;

but in the centre, over a 700-mile stretch from Coquimbo (30° latitude S) to Valdivia (40° latitude S), the vine does well. The best red wines are said to be from O'HIGGINS, south of Santiago, the capital. Other districts are at ACONCAGUA and MAIPO, where there are rivers to provide the irrigation necessary. With France and other European countries on our doorstep, it is hardly surprising that the merits of Chilean wines have never been recognised here. Freight charges are of course high and importing from hard currency countries difficult. Nevertheless there are available Chilean "Clarets", "Burgundies" and "Reislings". Southard & Co. of Moseley, for example, ship ones from the Santa Rita Company in Santiago.

TUNISIA

As in Algeria, the Tunisian vineyards owe their origin to French growers, although in this case Italians have also played an important part. The Tunisian wine industry started to develop on a large scale about sixty years ago and originally the classic French varieties of vine such as the Cabernet and Pinot were planted.

Experience showed, however, that these varieties were not suited to Tunisian conditions and when the vineyards were attacked by the phylloxera in the 1930s, a complete reorganisation of the Tunisian vineyards took place which resulted in the pattern which now prevails. The principal *cépages* are as follows:

For Red wine: Alicante Bouschet, also known as Petit Bouschet, Alicante Grenache, Carignan and Cinsault. The same varieties, with the exception of the Bouschet, are also used for the making of *rosé* wines.

For White wine: Clairette, Pedro Ximenez and Beldi.

The bulk of Tunisia's wine production, which approaches forty million gallons a year, is now in the hands of co-operatives, and the best of these use modern and efficient methods of vinification and are well run. Temperature control plays, of course, a vital part in wine making in such a hot country and methods of continuous cooling are part of the normal routine of vinification in the larger establishments.

The vineyards, which cover an area of 130,000 acres, are concentrated principally in the Cap Bon area and around Bizerta. Owing to the hilly nature of the country one does not normally see vast flat expanses of uniform vineyards which are such a feature of the Midi and even parts of the Côtes du Rhône. On the contrary, the landscape is pleasantly broken up with cypress and olive trees and the mountains form a background to most vineyards. The pleasantly undulating countryside is at times extremely fertile in appearance and very reminiscent of parts of Spain. It is common practice to grow rows of vines between olive trees in new plantations until the trees are sufficiently mature to begin bearing a crop, which usually takes some ten years. In general aspect the vines closely resemble those in the Côtes du Rhône and are pruned in the form of a bush without any staking or wiring. The vintage in Tunisia usually commences early in September and takes about a month to bring in.

There are considerable variations in the quality of Tunisian wines determined principally by the care and skill of the vinification. The best quality is undoubtedly achieved with the red wines which have the alcoholic strength (13° or more) and the vigour of the wines of the Côtes du Rhône, but are softer and more velvety in texture like a rather full-blown and plummy Côte d'Or wine. The *rosé* wines are quite pleasant although many tend to lack acidity. The best are quite firm although high in alcoholic strength. Most white wines are rather golden in colour and tend to be a little flat, although one or two excellent wines, light in colour and quite crisp on the palate, are to be found, but they are an exception rather than the rule.

Until very recently virtually the whole of Tunisia's wine production was exported to France. Local consumption is small as the country is predominantly Moslem, although the years of French influence have done something to erode strict observance amongst educated Tunisians. The recent increase in the tourist trade is also helping to increase local consumption. There is now an effort being made to reduce the complete dependence on France which has previously existed for a product which forms one-fifth of the value of all Tunisia's exports. As a result of this, their wines are now being successfully marketed in Germany, Switzerland, Poland, and the first important sales to England began in 1965 with the importation of a red wine which is sold under the brand name of CAP BON.

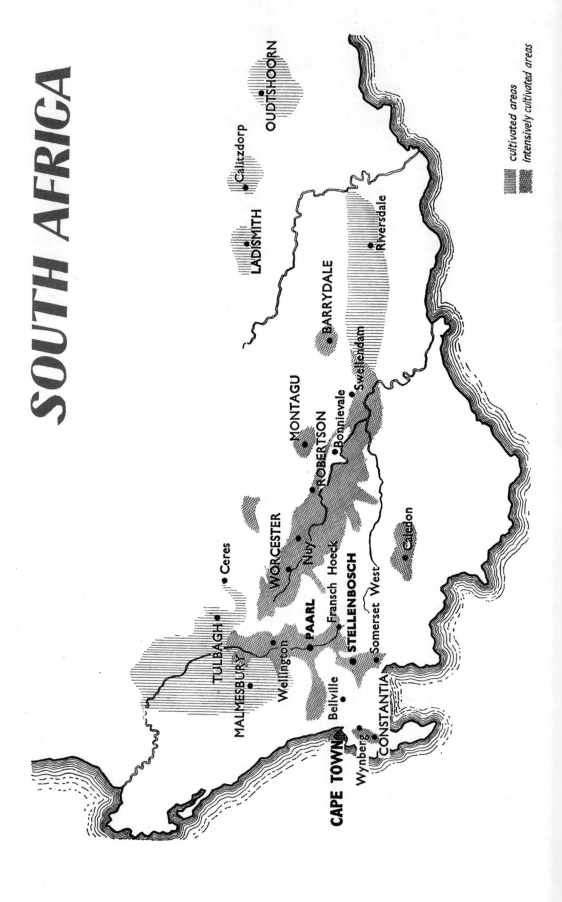

SOUTH AFRICA

OUDTSHOORN
Calitzdorp
LADISMITH
Riversdale
BARRYDALE
Swellendam
Bonnievale
MONTAGU
ROBERTSON
Ceres
WORCESTER
Nuy
Fransch Hoeck
Caledon
PAARL
TULBAGH
STELLENBOSCH
Wellington
Somerset West
MALMESBURY
Bellville
CONSTANTIA
CAPE TOWN
Wynberg

cultivated areas
intensively cultivated areas

SOUTH AFRICA

The wine industry in South Africa is practically as old as is European civilisation in this part of the South African continent, and is more than three centuries old.

In 1655 Jan van Riebeeck, Commander of the first Dutch settlement of the Cape of Good Hope, planted the first vines in Cape soil, and in the year 1659 wine was made for the first time from Cape grapes.

R

Later, in the seventeenth century, French Huguenots fleeing from Europe for religious reasons settled in the Cape, predominantly in the Fransch Hoek, Paarl, Drakenstein and Stellenbosch areas. These settlers extended the vineyards and improved the quality of the wine so much that by the first decade of the eighteenth century the "Wines of Constantia" were world famous.

At about this time brandy was also distilled for the first time in the Cape. This was a very raw and uncouth product, but it laid the foundation stone of a very important section of the liquor industry in South Africa.

By the nineteenth century exports to Britain were flourishing, the wine trade was prosperous, and wine merchants were investing substantial sums of money in the industry. Suddenly, however, they faced ruin. In the latter half of the nineteenth century the preferential tariffs on wines entering the United Kingdom were abolished by the Gladstone Government and the export trade collapsed.

The dreaded vine disease, phylloxera, also struck and destroyed a large portion of the Cape vineyards and the wine farmers were in dire straits. The threat of the phylloxera was overcome, as in other parts of the world, by planting vineyards on to disease-resistant American root stocks. Production slowly recovered but local consumption of wines was small and the loss of the export trade resulted in over-production and a slump in the price of wine. A leaguer of wine (127 gallons) was selling for as little as £2 10s.

This eventually led to the founding of the Co-operative Wine Growers' Association of South Africa Ltd., in 1918. This organisation is now better known as the K.W.V. (*Ko-operatieve Wijnbouwers Vereniging*) and is the controlling body of the South African wine industry.

By Act of Parliament, the K.W.V. is empowered to fix the minimum price for all wines, including wines for distillation into spirits and brandy. The K.W.V. fixes annually the percentage of the vintage which they estimate is not saleable on the local market, and it must take all wine produced which is not purchased by the wholesale merchants. The function, therefore, of the K.W.V. is to stabilise the wine prices on the local market and to obtain control of the surplus production. It is the duty of the K.W.V. to keep this surplus off the local market and to endeavour to obtain a sale for it on the export market.

All wines purchased by merchants from wine farmers or primary producers are bought on a contract basis and the K.W.V. controls these contracts. The merchant pays to the K.W.V. the full fixed minimum price for all wines purchased, but the grower only receives an amount which is the fixed price less the estimated surplus production. Should the surplus prove to be less than estimated, or if the K.W.V. manages to sell the surplus profitably on the export market, the grower will receive a further back-payment in respect of wines sold by him. Wine merchants are therefore controlled as to the minimum prices they pay for wine, spirit and brandy and, as the K.W.V. is not subject to this control, competition by the K.W.V. on the local market would be unfair. The K.W.V. is therefore prohibited by law from selling its products in any territory in Africa, south of the Equator.

Production of wine and the planting of vineyards is also controlled by the K.W.V. by means of a quota system. A production quota is allotted to each grower to prevent injudicious planting and consequent over-production.

Most of the surplus wine taken in by the K.W.V. is taken in as distilling wine and most of the K.W.V. export market is therefore built up on dessert wines (wines fortified with the addition of spirit) as well as brandies. The reputation of South African wines on the export market has therefore been built up mainly on these fortified types of wine, particularly the South African sherry types.

The quality of all wines exported from South Africa, including those of the K.W.V. and wine merchants, is subject to very strict governmental control. Samples of all wines intended for export are submitted to a government analyst and to a government panel for tasting purposes. The approval of this Export Control Board must be obtained before any wines can leave the country. This ensures that no wines of inferior quality can leave the country and jeopardise the reputation of South African wines abroad.

The wine industry is at present a very stable and buoyant one. Local consumption of wine is in excess of 24 million gallons per annum and more than four million gallons are exported. South Africa is experiencing an economic boom and local consumption of wine has increased phenomenally. The South African is traditionally a spirit drinker, but due to the improvement in the quality of the *vin ordinaire* type wines, the sales of these types of wines have more than doubled in the last few years.

South African wines, Sherry types in particular, have become increasingly popular on the export market, with the result that there is a wine shortage. Insufficient wines are being produced to satisfy the local and export markets and, although additional production quotas have been issued, it will be many years before the supply meets the demand if boom conditions continue.

GEOGRAPHY

The vineyards of the Cape are confined to the south-western districts, which enjoy a temperate Mediterranean climate. The winters are cold and wet enough to ensure full dormancy for the vines and the warm, dry summers ensure sound and healthy growth of the grapes.

The wine-growing areas can be divided into two distinct climatic areas. The first and best is the coastal region, confined by the awe-inspiring Drakenstein mountain range. This area has warm, sunny summers and the average rainfall is between twenty and thirty inches per annum. Vines are grown on the slopes of the mountains and hills, in soil of medium depth and fertility.

Outstanding dry white and red wines are produced in this area, as well as Port and Sherry types. The best-known districts of this coastal area are CONSTANTIA, STELLENBOSCH, PAARL and the beautiful TULBAGH VALLEY.

The second area is the one north of the Drakenstein range and is called the LITTLE KARROO. The climate here is more extreme; the summers far hotter and the average winter temperature lower. The average rainfall is usually not more than ten inches a year and all vineyards must therefore be irrigated. The alluvial soil is, however, very fertile and, with irrigation, high yields of up to ten tons per acre are obtained. Soils in this area are also high in lime content and excellent muscadel wines are produced, with a very high sugar content.

Wines eminently suitable for distillation into brandy are also produced here, as well as the basic wines for the well-known South African sherry types. The best-known districts in this area are WORCESTER, ROBERTSON, BARRYDALE, MONTAGU and the LADISMITH–OUDTSHOORN districts.

Dessert Wines

The reputation of Cape wines from the early eighteenth century has been founded on the heavier dessert types. The renowned CONSTANTIA wines come from the beautiful Constantia valley adjoining Table Mountain. This, the real birthplace of South African wines, has now become an élite residential area of South Africa, with beautiful homes and estates. The old farms have been cut up and subdivided into smallholdings and more emphasis has been placed on table grapes than on wine grapes.

The muscadel types, which produced such wonderful varieties in the past, are now mainly cultivated in the Little Karroo area. The warm sun and fertile soil of the Little Karroo produce grapes with a sugar content of up to 30 per cent. Rich, velvety wines with a full grape character are produced, as well as robust sherry types. The main grape varieties used for these wines are Muscadel and Hanepoot, as well as the Stein grape.

The grapes are normally picked with a high degree of sugar, usually about 26 per cent by weight but never below 22 per cent. After crushing, the stems are removed. Some producers prefer to ferment the fresh juice in contact with the husks for a very short period of time (usually sufficient to produce two to four degrees of proof spirit alcohol), but normally the free run juice, together with the juice produced from a light pressing of the husks, is immediately fortified by the addition of pure grape spirit to about thirty to thirty-two degrees proof spirit. This fortified juice, which in South Africa is called *Jeripego*, is then allowed to settle, subjected to clarification by the addition of fining, and racked into wooden vats for a maturation period of from one to three years. These *Jeripegos* are very sweet and are usually blended with a dry white wine before bottling. Prior to bottling, the wines are stabilised by refrigeration.

Port Types

The Port type wines are made mainly from Portuguese varieties introduced from the famous Douro valley and planted in the PAARL and STELLENBOSCH areas. Almost invariably the wines from these Portuguese varieties are blended with wine from Hermitage grapes. Hermitage vines are planted extensively throughout the wine-growing areas of the Cape and do very well.

Local consumption of Port type wines is very small and there is therefore little incentive for local merchants to improve the quality of this wine type or for growers to improve their varieties and extend their Port vineyards.

The best Port types are undoubtedly produced by the K.W.V., which has a fairly good export market and specialises in this type of wine.

Sherry Types

Excellent Sherry-type wines are made in South Africa, mainly from the Palomino grape, which is locally known as French grape. Wines from the Stein grape have also been used extensively and successfully.

486

The areas in which these grapes are grown are, for the lighter Fino types, PAARL, STELLENBOSCH and the TULBAGH VALLEY (in fact the same areas that produce the best table wines), whereas the more robust sherries are produced from vines grown in the Little Karroo area.

The South African Sherry-type wines resemble wines produced in Andalusia, Spain, as climatically these two areas are very similar. The same grape varieties are used and the *flor* type of yeast, which grows on top of the young maturing sherry and occurs naturally in Andalusia, is also indigenous to the Cape vineyards.

METHODS OF PRODUCTION

For the Fino type sherries, grapes are usually picked with a sugar content of from 18 to 22 per cent. Grapes are crushed and de-stemmed and usually the free run juice only is used. The juice, extracted from the husks by pressing, is converted into distilling wine for the manufacture of neutral spirits. The wines are always fermented with special *flor* yeasts, obtained from the government laboratories and, as in Spain, it is common practice to plaster the sherries with *Yeso* or *Gypsum*. This plastering causes a more rapid clarification of the young wine and, by increasing the free fixed acidity, promotes a typical sherry flavour.

After fermentation the wine is racked, fortified with neutral spirits to about twenty-six degrees proof spirit and then begins its long journey through the *Solera*. Some really superior Finos are produced, but as the South African climate is very warm, there is an unfortunate tendency to mature these Finos too long and they quickly oxidise and lose their delicate character. The South African sherry varieties, especially the heavier types, usually lack acidity and it is standard practice for the producers to rectify this by adding tartaric acid.

For the heavier brown sherries, grapes are picked with a higher sugar content, from between 22 and 26 per cent, and a short contact period between husks and fermenting wine is allowed, so that more body and colour can be extracted from the husks.

Sweetening with sugar is not permitted under South African law and therefore, for sweetening purposes, the heavier brown sherries are sweetened with matured *Jeripegos* made from Stein grapes and are allowed to mature for three to four years.

To ensure that the quality of sherry blends remain constant, it is normal practice to make very large blends of sherries of various vintages and to constantly replace the wine which is drawn off for bottling with newly blended sherry. Prior to bottling, the wines are stabilised by refrigeration.

Table Wines

Dry Red Wines

The grape varieties used for the manufacture of dry red wines in South Africa are Cabernet, Hermitage and Shiraz for the lighter or Claret type, and for the heavier Burgundy type Shiraz, Hermitage, Cabernet, Gamay, Pontac, Pinot and Pinotage. The areas most suited to the light types of wines are those in the coastal regions, particularly around STELLENBOSCH.

A new red variety which is fast gaining popularity is the Pinotage, a cross between Hermitage and Pinot. This variety does extremely well and produces a wine which is fruity and full of colour and character, without being too heavy. It is a wine which matures very quickly, but appears at this stage to fall off rapidly after it has reached its peak, which seems to be the third year.

For the heavier Burgundy types of red wine, the areas of PAARL and STELLENBOSCH produce superb wines, especially those on the slopes of the majestic Simonsberg mountain. The soils producing the best wines are generally stony and poor and this area is ideal for the production of really superb red wines. Local demand is, however, comparatively small (probably less than 5 per cent of the total table wine consumption is red) and the incentive for the producer and wine merchant to produce quality red wines is therefore lacking.

488

Usually in South Africa climatic conditions are so constant that the quality of white wine varies little from year to year and it is therefore not common practice to give a vintage to South African wines. This, however, does not apply to the red wines where, as the grapes ripen very late compared to the white varieties, there can be considerable variation from year to year. The red grapes are picked at full ripeness with a sugar content of at least 22 per cent, and whereas it is possible to pick white grapes before they have fully ripened, this cannot be done with the red, as full colour is only developed on full ripeness.

As the South African red wines are normally a blend of more than one grape variety, wherever possible the different varieties are picked, crushed and fermented together to allow for better marrying of the wine. This is, however, not always possible, as some of the varieties ripen later than others.

The grapes are crushed and the stems removed, a pure yeast culture is added and the wines allowed to ferment in open *kuipe*. As in the case of Port, the cap is kept submerged or moist and the temperature of the fermenting wine is kept by cooling below 80°F. When the fermentation has proceeded to a point where there is approximately 4 to 6 per cent of sugar left, the wine is racked from the husks and the husks subjected to a light pressing with hydraulic presses. The wine resulting from the pressing of the husks, together with the free run juice, is transferred to closed vessels and fermentation is allowed to proceed until all the sugars have been converted into alcohol. When the fermentation is complete, the wine is racked two or three times and, after clarification by fining, is put into wood for further maturation.

Unfortunately the tendency in South Africa is to mature for too long a period in wood and not bottle-mature for any length of time. Experience has, however, shown that by far the best results have been obtained by maturing in wood for eighteen months to two years and then allowing for further bottle-maturation of two to three years. Too long a maturation in wood usually results in wines that are flat in flavour and brown in colour.

489

Yields for the grape varieties required for quality red wine are very low, roughly one-third to one-quarter of the yield obtained from white grape varieties. There is very little difference in the price paid for red and white wines, and economically the producer is therefore not encouraged to increase his production of red varieties. Most of the vineyards producing quality red wine are very old and not many new vines have been planted.

In recent years, however, there has been a gradual increase in dry red wine consumption and the wholesale merchants are taking a bigger interest in this type of wine. Additional bonuses are being offered and the required varieties are being planted again. In the STELLENBOSCH area there are a few wine growers who have the vineyards and soil, the knowledge and dedication, and who produce really superb red wines. Among these are the farms: UITKYK, KANON KOP, ALTO, SCHOONGEZICHT, as well as the Zonnebloem Estates in SIMONDIUM, DRIESPRONG, RUSTENBURG and MURATIE.

The South African climate is hot and is therefore not ideally suited to the consumption of red wine, as it is never very pleasant to drink a heavy type of Burgundy wine on a hot day. Traditionally, South African red wines have been heavy and this probably accounts for their lack of popularity. The future of the South African red wine industry therefore appears to be in the development of a lighter, fruitier, Claret type wine which is low in alcohol and light in body.

As in other parts of the world, *rosé* wines are fast growing in popularity and some excellent wines are now on the market. These wines are mainly produced in the STELLENBOSCH/PAARL area and the most popular method is to use the free run juice from the Cabernet vine. The *rosés* appeal to the feminine palate and most wines on the South African market are of the semi-sweet type. They are most palatable when consumed young and, by and large, do not mature or travel well.

White Wines   The grape varieties most commonly used for quality white wines

490

are Riesling, Stein, White French and Clairette Blanche. Very successful wines have also been produced by using Sauvignon Blanc and St. Émilion. The best vines are grown on well-drained, loamy soil which is cool, deep and fairly fertile.

The best areas for the production of South African white table wines are undoubtedly PAARL, STELLENBOSCH, DRAKENSTEIN and TULBAGH.

In the last ten years there has been a big improvement in the quality of South African white table wines. The soils have always been suitable for producing excellent grapes, but the high, ambient temperature during the vintage resulted in quick, hot fermentation and oxidation of the wines during fermentation. On the whole the wines were of indefinite or mediocre standard. Some years ago, a German immigrant with brewing connections, Mr. Graue, settled in the Paarl valley on the Nederburg Estates. Mr. Graue applied his knowledge of beer-making and beer-fermenting techniques to the making of wine and the results were unbelievably good.

Later, Mr. N. C. Krone of the Twee Jongegezellen Estates in the Tulbagh valley also modified his whole cellar to carry out the entire fermentation under refrigeration. The results were so outstanding that in the first year Mr. Krone, with his cold fermented wines, won practically every prize on the Cape Wine Show, where all producers exhibit their wines annually.

Although all the grape varieties used for South African white wines have been imported from France and Germany, the characteristics of these wines are different from those of Germany and France. The South African Stein wines are usually very well balanced, but lack the fruitiness of the European Steins. The South African Rieslings are fruity, but slightly mellower on the nose and have less acidity than European Rieslings.

METHODS OF PRODUCTION

Most South African white grape varieties will, if allowed, reach full maturity with a very high sugar content and relatively low acidity. It has therefore become standard practice to pick the white varieties before they reach full maturity, when the acidity is still fairly high. Grapes with a sugar content in excess of 22 per cent rarely make a good wine and producers normally pick at about 18 per cent.

After crushing and de-stemming, the juice is immediately removed from the husks, a pure yeast culture (usually imported from the Research Institute at Geisenheim on the Rhine) is added and the wines allowed to ferment.

It is now common practice among all producers who can afford the equipment, including the co-operative cellars, to have cooling plants installed. The usual method is to instal a plant for the production of cold water which is circulated through the fermenting tanks to keep the average temperature below 60°F. In some instances, as for instance on the Twee Jongegezellen Estates, the system is more elaborate, inasmuch as the fresh juice from the grapes is pre-cooled in a shell and tube cooler and thereafter transferred to fermenting cellars which are air conditioned to about 40°F.

When the fermentation is complete, the wines are racked from the lees as soon as possible and clarified by the addition of finings.

Another reason for the improvement in the quality of white wines is the fact that producers have realised the importance of oxidation. Many cellars are now equipped to cover the freshly picked grapes, as well as the fresh grape Must, with a layer of carbon dioxide to prevent oxidation before fermentation. This results in wines of a lighter and more delicate character and which live far longer in the bottle.

Semi-sweet wines have become extremely popular in South Africa as in other parts of the world, but the methods of production of these wines vary somewhat from the traditional methods practised in Europe. The basic wine is always allowed to ferment completely, leaving no residual sugar, but in addition producers

492

ferment a sweet blending wine, usually made from the Stein variety of grapes. This sweet blending wine is produced by allowing wine to ferment to approximately 6 to 8 per cent of residual sugar, when the fermentation is stopped by refrigeration and the addition of sulphur dioxide. These sweet blending wines are then fined and filtered and stored in refrigerated cellars at about 32°F. Just prior to bottling, the basic wine is then blended with the required amount of sweet blending wine. Prior to bottling, all the wines are stabilised by refrigeration.

Sparkling Wines

Sparkling wines are usually made with the same varieties as used for the manufacture of white table wines. Varieties such as Sauvignon Blanc and St. Émilion, which have a high natural acidity, have proved very successful.

Sparkling wines are produced in three different ways. The cheaper types are really sparkling Moselles, as they are made from good quality white table wines to which sugar has been added and which are then impregnated with CO_2 gas.

The second method, which is very widely practised, is the bulk fermentation method. A good quality white wine is sweetened with sugar and a yeast culture is added in a bulk pressure tank. The wines then re-ferment and build up the required pressure in about three weeks. These re-fermented wines are then filtered and bottled.

A few producers are now manufacturing sparkling wine in the traditional French method of bottle fermentation. Sweetened wines are inoculated with yeast cultures, usually from Epernay in France, and allowed to ferment in bottles. This fermentation generally takes a year or more and the bottles are shaken at frequent intervals. Degorging, as practised in France is, however, not carried out. As in Germany, the bottle fermented wine is chilled and then emptied under counter pressure into a pressure vessel. The sparkling wine is then filtered under pressure and re-bottled.

493

Of the three methods the last one produces by far the best re-sults as it allows a long contact period between yeast and wine to give the typical flavour of a good sparkling wine. The second method produces excellent results and a very fine carbonation, but there is insufficient time for contact between yeast and wine to give a truly good quality. South African law does not require the producer to state on the label what process is used in the manufacture of sparkling wines.

The following estate wines are available in the United Kingdom:

Bellingham Estates:

Late Vintage, Premier Grand Crus, Vintage Johannisberger Selected Stein, Riesling.
Rosé, Almeida Rosé.
Shiraz.

Nederburg Estates:

Nederburg Late Harvest, Nederburg Sylvane, Nederburg Stein, Nederburg Selected Riesling, Nederburg Riesling.
Nederburg Rosé, Nederburg Rosé Sec.
Nederburg Selected Cabernet, Nederburg Cabernet.
Nederburg Cuvée Sparkling Wine.

Twee Jongegezellen Estates:

Twee Jongegezellen Riesling, Twee Jongegezellen Stein.
Twee Jongegezellen Spätlese.
Twee Jongegezellen Rosé.

Kanon Kop and Zonnebloem Estates:

Zonnebloem Riesling, Tasheimer Goldtropfchen, La Gratitude.
Zonnebloem Cabernet, Lanzerac Cabernet, Château Libertas.
Lanzerac Rosé.
Grand Mousseux Sparkling Wine.

494

Schoongezicht and Rustenburg Estates:

Schoongezicht Riesling.
Rustenburg Cabernet.

Alto Estate:

Alto Rouge.

Brandy   Excellent brandies are produced in South Africa from the French, Green grape, Stein and Sauvignon Blanc varieties. The Little Karroo areas of WORCESTER, MONTAGU, BONNIEVALE, ROBERTSON and BARRYDALE produce the most suitable wines. Experience has shown that the best soils for brandy production are sweet, alluvial soils of decomposed Bokkeveld shale.

Brandy was first distilled in South Africa in 1672, but the first products were of very inferior quality. Little care was taken in the wines which were used for brandy production and producers very seldom allowed the product to mature for any length of time. At present, however, a very strict control is exercised on the production of brandy to ensure that the quality is kept up to a certain standard. Wines destined for brandy production have to be specially selected and fermented without any sulphur dioxide. These special young wines are then submitted to a Government Brandy Board for approval. If the wine is approved it must be distilled within fourteen days of approval being granted. The stills must also be of the same design as those traditionally used in Cognac in France, and no restrictions in the helm are permitted. The normal practice is to use the system of double distillation. The young wine is first distilled into a product called low wine, which is a straight distillation extracting all the alcohol. This low wine is then redistilled and at this stage the art of the distiller is very important. The "heads" and "tails" are kept separate and only the "heart" or middle run is used. This middle run brandy must again be submitted to the Government Brandy Board for approval. Once approval has been obtained, this brandy must be matured for a minimum of three years in wooden casks of a capacity not larger than seventy-five gallons. South African brandy producers have found that the type of wood used in brandy maturation plays a very big part in the quality of the finished article. The casks normally used are made from Limousin and Troncain oak, imported from France. To encourage local distillers to improve the quality of their product, the Government also grants a rebate of duty on brandies matured for longer than three years.

Most South African brandies are blended brandies as the South African is a beverage drinker and very seldom drinks the product neat. The brandies therefore mainly consist of blends of from 25 to 75 per cent matured brandy blended with rectified neutral grape spirit. South African law permits the addition of cane sugar for sweetening and caramel for colouring. Unblended liqueur brandies, varying in age from five to ten years, are also produced, mainly for the export market. The larger merchants all distil and mature their own brandy, but the small merchants purchase spirits and pot stilled brandy from the K.W.V. and blend them to suit their requirements.

AUSTRALIA

Speed of communication can be a mixed blessing. Today, an inflammatory political speech can be studied in the Chancelleries of all the world within an hour or even minutes of its delivery; reactions are apt to be too rapid if tempers are still inflamed.

Commercially, on the other hand, the quicker contact can be maintained, the better. Australia, in the Antipodes, is a case in point. In its earlier days, before the steamship, correspondence

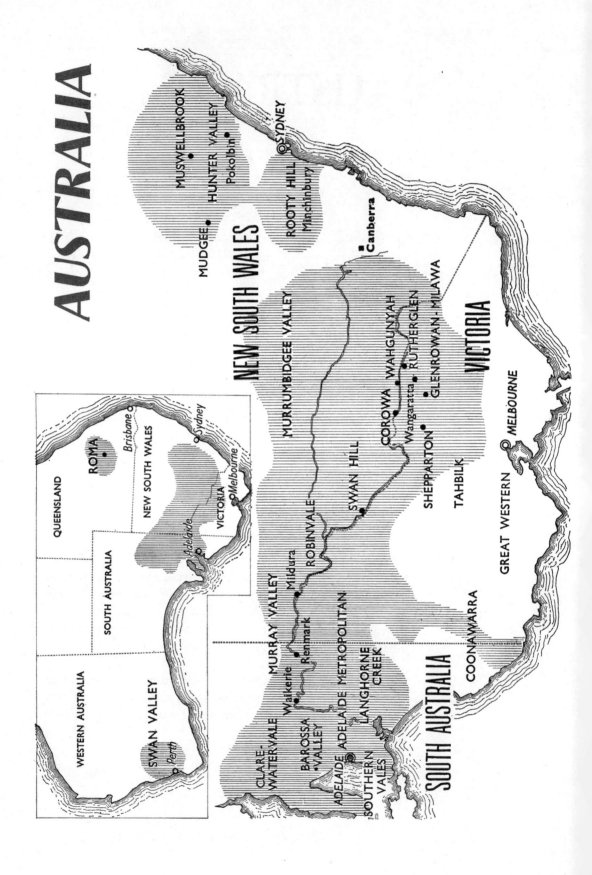

between England and that far-off land meant that twelve or more months could elapse before a reply might be received. Even forty years ago, it took nigh on three months to get an answer to one's letters. Today, airmail services have reduced the gap to a week or even less.

The fact remains that Australia is still 12,000 miles away and, despite the rapidity of modern communications, a chat across a table, proverbially worth a ream of correspondence, is still not so easily brought about as it can be with our wine-producing neighbours in Europe. In short, that altogether desirable state where the producer is completely in touch with his export market's problems and requirements—and vice versa—is not so simply achieved when the two are half the world apart.

Even so, Great Britain is, and has been for nigh on a century, Australia's biggest market for her wines outside her own shores.

HISTORY

As one of the youngest vineyard industries in the world, one must realise that Australia planted vines on the newly discovered continent in the very year it was first settled, practically two centuries ago.

It was in 1788 that a mixed fleet of naval and merchant ships, eleven in all, under Captain Arthur Phillip, R.N., sailed through the headlands enclosing one of the world's greatest natural harbours. Named Port Jackson for a while, the greatest city in the Southern Hemisphere, whose first foundations were then laid with such sound judgment, is today Sydney.

The origin of the many vines taken out with these first settlers is difficult to trace. It is said, however, that a vineyard was planted almost on the edge of Sydney Harbour. It was an ill-chosen site for climatic reasons, but that same area of land is now part of the Sydney Botanical Gardens. The first successful vineyard, possibly established with transplanted vines, was only twenty miles inland at Parramatta. It produced excellent crops and greatly encouraged further development.

James Busby, a Scot from Northumberland, can, with justice, be called the father of Australian viticulture. Arriving in Sydney in 1824, he took a post as the teacher in a Male Orphans' School nearby. He had two duties to perform for his salary of £100 a year: to educate the orphans and to tend the small vineyard attached to the school. Convinced of the future of wine-making in his new home in New South Wales, he later returned to England and spent four months during 1831 travelling through the wine lands of Europe, from Jerez northward. By dint of truly Scottish determination, he not only extracted gifts of many cuttings from each of 570 different varieties of grape from various sources on the Continent, but persuaded Lord Goderich, the Principal Secretary of State for the Colonies, to ship the vast collection, at Government expense, "on any of the convict ships about to sail, in order to secure their early and safe arrival in the Colony". The great majority did indeed arrive safely after the lengthy and trying journey across the Equator and round the Cape of Good Hope. By establishing, in one bold step, nurseries containing the pick of the varieties of wine grapes grown in Europe, Busby's remarkable enterprise may well have saved many years of experimental work in deciding which vines were most suited to the different climatic and soil conditions in the new land.

Not surprisingly, it was only after the influx of many new settlers to swell the population that any urge was felt to move very far afield. But, once the movement started, developments were rapid. In what is now the State of Victoria, the first township of any size to be established was on the site of Melbourne around the year 1830, and four years later the "new explorers" had built the first shacks of Adelaide in South Australia. This involved thrusting nearly a thousand miles over trackless, unknown country from Sydney. In each of these newly established States, the planting of vineyards was recorded within three or four years. Tempting as it is to delve further into the romantic past, one must come up to date and trace the many factors, economic and political, which have influenced the importation of Australian wines into Great Britain in recent decades.

Commercially, the wines started reaching London practically a century ago, in 1870; for the previous forty years, small, sporadic shipments had been made, mainly for experimental purposes and for showing at British and Continental exhibitions. For the first dozen years progress was comparatively slow, but from the middle 1880s sales increased rapidly and by the turn of the century Britain was drinking annually up to three-quarters of a million gallons of Australian wine. Certainly quite a range of different types were exported to this country in these early days, but there is no doubt that the British public rapidly came to favour the very full, robust Burgundies, which have ever since maintained considerable popularity as one of the most characteristic and distinctive types of wine to reach us from the Commonwealth of Australia.

NAMING OF WINES

Whereas in recent years there has grown an increasingly "purist" attitude over the naming of wines (in some quarters, the use of such widely used expressions as "Spanish Sauternes" or "Australian Burgundy" is deeply resented), the fact remains that eighty or ninety years ago little or no such feeling was evident. Even so, it is worth recording the reason for the origin of the distinctively shaped Australian burgundy "flagon" introduced in 1875. The writer's grandfather often related, before his death at a very ripe old age in 1929, that he evolved it for one main purpose. That was to avoid the possibility of any confusion of identity between French and Australian Burgundies when the latter were first coming into prominence on the British market. He clearly had the right ideas but, not being blessed with foresight, could not realise that the use of "type" names, long regarded as generic, would be questioned in the mid-twentieth century. This whole matter of the *appellation* of wines (to use the French expression) is far more involved than is usually recognised, but is outside the scope of this article.

For the first fifty years of Australian wine shipments to Great Britain, they received no preferential treatment of any sort. All credit is due to the merchants of those early days for having established a flourishing trade in so competitive a market when the products they dealt in had to be shipped half-way around the globe. It seems, however, more than possible that the onset of phylloxera, a minute beetle-like insect which reached Europe from America and proved to be a plague that spread like wild-fire, may well have brought a fortuitous advantage to the earlier importers of Australia's wines. During the latter third of the last century this root-attacking pest necessitated the replanting of the great majority of European vineyards on American "resistant" root stocks. For a time this naturally resulted in a period of short supplies and rising prices. The same pest has since swept through much of Australia, but it is interesting to note that the State of South Australia, where more than three-quarters of all the continent's wine is produced, still remains immune. It is today the largest vineyard area in the world to be in this fortunate position, and to maintain it involves the constant application of most stringent "quarantine" regulations.

In 1927 Mr. Winston Churchill, as he then was, introduced the Budget. One of its features was a very material increase in the preferential duty advantage given to dessert wines from Commonwealth sources. The results were dramatic. At that time and until the Second Great War, overwhelmingly the favourite wines in Great Britain were of Port character. Australian wine consumption climbed within a year or two to an average of three million gallons annually, a level which continued until 1939. The great bulk of the increase was in wines of port character and Australian sales amounted, roughly, to one-fifth of the total consumption of imported wine from all sources.

Certainly the World War of 1939 to 1945 has since brought about many vast changes in the social structure and today wine has become a part of "gracious living" for a greatly increased proportion of the population. This effect is very apparent in the official figures issued by H.M. Customs.

In 1938, the last complete year before the war broke out, the total consumption in Britain of imported wines was just under fifteen and a quarter million gallons. In 1964, it reached practically twenty-eight million gallons, and during recent years it has increased each year by at least 10 per cent. The present figures constitute an all-time record and, given the right economic circumstances, there is justification for the view that sales of all wines could reach the fifty million gallons figure a year in Great Britain within ten, or even five, years.

For the last five or six years the British as a nation have been drinking more low-strength wines than high. In other words, table wines claim more consumers (in terms of gallonage) than do high-duty types, meaning, in effect, Sherries and Ports and the equivalent Commonwealth wines. In 1938, by comparison, the fortified strong wines comprised 76 per cent of the total.

These figures help us to appreciate the underlying reasons for the varying popularity of wines of very different character which have reached the United Kingdom from the Commonwealth. As mentioned earlier, Australia is comparatively very young as a wine-making country. She has not yet settled down as a recognised source of wines of certain defined characteristics. With many centuries of tradition behind them, such countries as France, Germany, Spain and Portugal are mainly linked in one's mind with wines of certain limited types. But even the latter two countries mentioned, which used to remind British consumers almost alone of Sherry and Port respectively, have lately supplied ever greater quantities of table wines. Many more holidays abroad provide part of the explanation for this demand, but basically the reason is economic. In 1949, largely for political reasons, the duties on all imported table wines were, in round figures, halved. Dessert wine duties remained unchanged. As a result, during most of the 1950s, table wines were taxed little more than one-quarter the rate of dessert wines and, from the price aspect, provided the British public with the best value. This is, incidentally, a good example of how powerfully Government fiscal policy can influence the consumers' tastes.

GEOGRAPHY   When it comes to actual wine making, the hardy grape vine is very particular in its climatic requirements. A glance at an atlas of the world quickly establishes that, for this purpose, it will only flourish in two comparatively narrow bands of latitude north and south of the Equator.

The southern band, where the land masses are fewer than in the north, sweeps through the great wine-making countries of Chile and the Argentine, the Province of the Cape in South Africa and through the southern part of the continent of Australia. The Australian vineyards in general are about as far south of the Equator as are Spain and Algeria to the north.

CLIMATE These facts establish that, taking an overall view, the wine-making areas of Australia approximate in general climate to the warmer parts of Europe. There are, however, other factors involved, and to draw too close a comparison would be grossly misleading. There is on the one hand, for instance, nothing but sea between Southern Australia and the ice masses of Antarctica. Whereas, sweeping down from the north over 1,500 miles of sun-baked Continent, the winds can, in some parts, have an extremely dry and oven-like quality during the hotter months. Consequently along the southern strip of the continent, to which the vineyards are confined, the winters can be very chilly (although hard, damaging frosts are unusual), while the summers in general are hot and dry. Rainfall over so huge an area is very variable, but tends to be heavier, both in winter and summer, in the east. Thus Sydney has a much moister climate than the State capitals of Melbourne and Adelaide which are, progressively, 300 to 400 miles westward. Similarly, the further from the coast the less are the inches of rain normally recorded. It does not do, however, to generalise too much, since the effect of a range of low mountains near the coast can be virtually to double the rainfall in the area concerned.

NEW SOUTH WALES

The map of the Australian wine-making centres shows the more important areas under vines and is worth considering from the

504

climatic point of view. This has profound effects on methods of cultivation and upon the style of wines best produced. One of the earliest and, to this day, one of the most famous areas in Australia for the production of fine table wines, both red and white, is the HUNTER VALLEY, not one hundred miles north of Sydney. James Busby was given a grant of land in this area by a grateful Colonial Government and established the first vineyard soon after 1830. As is so often the case, outstanding wines are often produced in uncertain climates. The Hunter valley is no exception and, whereas the overall rainfall is ideal, too great a proportion is liable to fall in the summer and autumn months, which makes for a difficult ripening season and vintage in some years. In general, however, the majority of Australian vineyards are blessed with hot and, on the whole, dry ripening seasons and the main rainfall occurs during the six winter months.

The State of New South Wales today is comparatively small in terms of wine production, but certain areas are renowned for the production of distinguished wines. MINCHINBURY, not far west of Sydney, is noted for its sparkling white wines made by the traditional *méthode champenoise*. The most extensive but most recently established area is in the MURRUMBIDGEE VALLEY where the vineyards are perhaps more distant from the sea than any others in Australia. The natural rainfall is in consequence very low and is altogether insufficient to produce an economic grape crop. Vine planting has, nevertheless, followed in the train of a great irrigational scheme whereby the waters of the Murrumbidgee river can be used to water the vineyards when needed, at appropriate times of the year. It follows, therefore, that the bulk of them are on the "flats" near the river. Most of the resulting wines are on the thin side, but mature quickly, finding a ready market in nearby Sydney.

The largest river in the continent is the Murray, which over much of its length marks the border between New South Wales and Victoria, the smallest of the mainland States. Over some 450 miles of its length are concentrated many of the most productive vineyard areas of the Commonwealth. The tonnage of grapes on each acre is, on average, exceptionally heavy. Here again the majority of the vines can be irrigated. Only extensive experience has established that delicate balance in the use of irrigation which ensures the finest quality of wine combined with truly economic productive costs. It is a sad fact that rarely do great crops make great wines. Nevertheless, the very extensive vineyards centred round SWAN HILL, MILDURA, RENMARK, BERRI and WAIKERIE along the River Murray produce wines of excellent average quality. Traditionally the main production in these areas has been fortified wines of Port and Sherry character, and the majority of Australian brandies and fortifying spirits produced in the Commonwealth come from the Murray valley.

VICTORIA

In contrast to these irrigated vineyards, the RUTHERGLEN and surrounding area in Victoria, within a few miles of the river but not using its waters, was one of the chief centres of wine-making in Australia until the early years of this century. Hot and comparatively dry, crops were always fairly small but the wines were often of outstanding quality. The vineyards were famed for full, robust Burgundies and the richest dessert wines from the Frontignan and Brown Muscat grapes. Unfortunately economic stringency, particularly since the last war, has brought about a sad shrinkage in the acres under vines. The vast increase in wage-levels and production costs generally could no longer be covered by the small tonnage of grapes grown on each acre, and untold thousands of carefully tended vines have disappeared.

SOUTH AUSTRALIA

Now to move farther west into South Australia, which has evolved into the greatest State for wine production. Four gallons out of five emanate from there. The reasons for this concentration cannot be expressed in a sentence, being many and, possibly, subtle. Obviously climatic and soil conditions are very major factors, influencing as they do the final quality of the wine made and the cost of producing it. But, more indirectly, the makers of wine are a gregarious, friendly crowd and tend to stay among their own kind, while—who knows—Adelaide being so often the first main port of call for the new immigrants' ship may well have tempted many to try their fortune in the delightful surroundings of their first landfall. Certainly many of the families, now famed for the wines they produce, are descendants of settlers of up to or more than a century ago who arrived, with the tradition of wine in their blood, from many lands in Europe.

Much of the State's wine comes from the prolific vineyards of the valley of the River Murray, but the fact remains that a wide belt of land extending from the ocean in the south, through Adelaide, to the CLARE and WATERVALE districts in the north, is largely monopolised by vineyards. This extends over more than 150 miles and, in terms of English equivalents, is a distance reaching from London to well into Yorkshire. Undoubtedly one of the main favourable influences is climatic. Much of this part of South Australia is hilly, and to mention one area alone, where the rugged Barossa range lies to the east, the many vineyards in the higher foothills are blessed with about thirty inches of rain a year, falling at just those times when the *vigneron* most prays for it. Such is the influence of a low range of mountains to precipitate the water content of the damp winds sweeping in from the Southern Ocean. Many of the vineyards in this extensive belt are situated from 1,000 to 2,000 feet above sea level, and this fact alone ensures cool conditions at the crucial period of vintage. South of Adelaide itself the areas of MCLAREN VALE, MORPHETT VALE and REYNELLA are well worthy of note. They are mainly famed for red table wines, but also produce distinguished wines of Port character. Moving farther north, the BAROSSA VALLEY has long been noted for excellent fortified wines and brandies, while in the cooler, higher vineyards some very distinguished table wines, both red and white, have achieved expanding fame.

TYPES OF WINE   The actual places of origin of the wines of Australia do not, in general, convey much information to the British consumer.

Possibly unwisely, nearly a century ago the table wines in particular were introduced into England under brand names as opposed to the "regional" or "estate" labels under which so many of the French and German wines were known. It is, however, interesting that today, because of the rapidly widening British market and the galloping cost increases of the better European wines in limited supply, "branded" wines, long known on the Continent, are rapidly being accepted here. What does that phrase mean? In short, it indicates a wine, usually blended from supplies from various sources, which is almost unvarying in style and quality from year to year, and which can be supplied to the ever-growing public at an extremely reasonable price. This is in fact what Australia has been endeavouring to do for many years past on this market. It has, indeed, been easier for the Australian wine merchants in Britain than for those of European wines. Climatic conditions, again, are the answer, since the seasons in Australia are more consistently favourable than in Europe. There the ideal wine-making season is the exception, whereas in the Antipodes virtually every year is a vintage year.

Table Wines

Since we are referring at this stage mainly to table wines, it would not be out of place to trace, in slightly more detail, the great changes in consumers' habits during the last twenty years in Britain. In general our parents and grandparents were ultra-conservative. To them, all too often, the only sources of drinkable red wines, for instance, were the Côtes d'Or for Burgundies and the Bordeaux district for Clarets. No other red wines were, by tradition, really worthy of consideration. The younger generation, on the other hand, has different ideas. This is mainly because many of our new wine-drinkers are not imbued with parental traditions, for the simple reason that father and mother seldom, in their own youth, drank wine. So today the criteria among the young, for judging a wine, very largely are two. First, do we like it? and second, is the price right? Where it comes from is of lesser importance. As a result, we in Britain are consuming large quantities of table wines from countries that before the last war found little favour. Spain, Portugal,

Italy and such countries as Yugoslavia and others are now supplying Britain with a flood of light wines which meet with very general approval. On the whole they are comparatively inexpensive, and it is safe to say that almost all the increase in recent consumption has been confined to low-priced wines.

Where does Australia share in this rapidly growing market? Unfortunately, not as much as the wines merit. The reasons, however, are clear. The available wines are good—indeed, they are excellent. As just mentioned, the great increase in consumption has been in the inexpensive wines. Australia is at the other end of the world; freight charges are very heavy; Australian standards of life are exceptionally high. Certainly a year or two ago wages in the vineyards were anything up to four or five times those paid in many countries in Europe, where living costs were still comparatively low. Consequently the distinguished red and white table wines from Australia have to be searched for since they must be sold, in general, for a shilling or two more a bottle than their European counterparts. Without any doubt the finest selection available in this country is to be found in the Australian Wine Centre in Frith Street, Soho, London, where the Australian Wine Board offer a warm welcome to all interested members of the wine trade as well as the public.

Before leaving the subject of table wines as grown in Australia, a few points should be made clear. The varieties of grapes used are, certainly for the finer wines, very much the same as the predominating vines of Europe. Thus for red wines, large areas of the distinguished Cabernet Sauvignon provide the basic character for the lighter Clarets. Shiraz, Hermitage (known in Europe as Syrah), Malbec and, in lesser quantities, Pinot Noir are the backbone of the finer Burgundies; while for white wines the Riesling of Germany and Alsace, Sémillon and such varieties as Chasselas, Traminer and Pinot Blanc provide solid foundations for quality. It must, however, be borne in mind that every different country imparts its own particular charms to its own wines for reasons of differing soil and seasonal conditions. Thus it does not take a great connoisseur to distinguish between the general characteristics of, say, red wines made in France, Spain, Italy and Australia. Each has its own especial merits; each should be judged accordingly and not compared with its counterparts from other lands.

In a comparatively warm country the location of vineyards where the finer table wines are made is vital. Such wines, both red and white, need a relatively high proportion of acid in the ripened grapes. Many other more subtle requirements necessary to the production of fine, well-balanced wines are only met when the vines are grown under reasonably cool conditions, which can often mean in a somewhat uncertain climate. Thus, in Australia the right conditions are only to be found in certain areas. These are sometimes near the sea, sometimes under the shadow of a range of hills which precipitates ample cooling rains, and sometimes on mountainous slopes up to 2,000 feet high which are blessed with fresh breezes, particularly at night.

Fortified Wines
The other main categories of wines, those of fortified Sherry and Port character, are now more happily placed in that they receive a more realistic duty preference in Britain amounting to one shilling and eightpence a bottle (as against fourpence for light wines). They are likewise wines which are produced, as in Europe, from the warmer countries. It follows that since 1927, when material preferential duties were granted to Commonwealth strong wines, the greater part of Australian exports to this country has consisted of fortified wines. Up to 1939 the British were confirmed Port drinkers, but at the end of the war they transferred their main allegiance, for no very obvious reason, to Sherries. This switch in British tastes was no easy problem for the Australian producers to solve. They wished very naturally, as did the importers in Britain, to recover their pre-war trade. The wines they were organised to supply were no longer in great demand, while the export of Sherry-style wines had previously been fairly negligible. The potential market, nevertheless, was great—with demand ever increasing. Yet, owing to unbalanced duty structures, there was an unfilled gap

in the price range. At the lowest end of the price scale "British Wines" had a more than substantial sale. Many more shillings a bottle, however, had to be paid for imported high strength wines, so, by close co-operation between British importers and their Australian producers in the early 1950s, high and low strength wines of suitable characteristics were produced which, when blended, resulted in a most attractive finished article at an intermediate rate of duty. Thus the price gap was filled with wines retailing at 10s. to 11s. a bottle which clearly met an unsatisfied demand at the time, since their sales rose with astonishing rapidity.

The production of fine wines of Sherry character has been closely studied in Australia, particularly during the last twenty years. Most of the specialist producers now maintain selected strains of sherry-*flor* from year to year, and make and mature their wines according to long-established traditions. Many of the leading Houses, either with their own British establishments or with English agents, can supply a considerable range of such wines. Possibly the most outstanding are the pale, very dry, wines which are closely comparable to the Spanish finos.

Whereas the British demand for all wines of Port character has regrettably shrunk recently, such wines from Australia have many faithful adherents. It is widely considered that, of all Commonwealth sources, they excel in those qualities and characteristics most looked for in the United Kingdom. To provide a general summing up of the various factors involved in the export to this country of Australian wines there are several relevant aspects involved. On the favourable side, in such a young country there undoubtedly exists a fresh outlook: an outlook which in effect maintains that modern scientific practices are to be preferred to "rule-of-thumb" methods inherited from one's forbears. And it must be realised that in this modern, highly competitive world the application of science, even in so traditional a trade as that of wine, must come into its own. It will without doubt lead to improved quality of the resulting product. It is probably a fair statement that Australia produces a bigger proportion of good, well-made wines than most other countries.

As against this, distance itself adds greatly to exporting costs, while a further adverse factor is that, far from still being only an agricultural land mainly interested in "primary products", it has rapidly developed into a largely industrialised nation, manufacturing a great proportion of its own requirements, extending even to highly successful Australian designed and home-built cars. Still short of population, this has led to a very high standard of life and the wage paid on the land for, say, vineyard labour is exceptionally expensive. This, however, is a world-wide trend and there are many indications that the same problems of cost are increasingly facing the majority of wine-producing lands. The situation could, therefore, well balance itself to Australia's advantage before many more years have passed.

Finally, the British are still, by nature, traditionally minded, but in regard to wine a refreshing wind of change has swept through the younger generations. Now, perhaps, we should pray for an enlightened Government—one that realises the social benefits, the health-giving properties of one of Nature's own greatest gifts to mankind. In a word, one that will reduce the present penal and crushing taxation on wine.

MADEIRA

Madeira Wine is a unique product. It is made in a different way from every other European wine on a unique island. The Island of Madeira lies 200 miles to the west of the north-west coast of Africa in the middle of the Gulf Stream which ensures an even temperature all the year round. It is thirty-four miles long and seventeen miles wide, rising to peaks of 6,000 feet in the centre.

S

When the Island was discovered over 500 years ago it was covered with a dense forest of great trees. In the course of clearing a settlement these trees caught fire and burned for years, destroying nearly the whole forest but bequeathing to posterity an exceptionally rich soil. This island is of volcanic origin and extremely steep, so that areas of cultivation are small and confined to terraces.

The original vines were imported from Crete and the areas best suited to their cultivation are around the capital, Funchal, and the southern sea coast.

TYPES OF VINE

Four main types of vine were planted, Boal, Verdelho, Sercial and Malvazia. They all produce white wine of different styles and the wines are called by the name of the vines producing them. The first three have never altered, but the fourth, Malvazia, is sometimes called by its French version Malvoisie or, more usually, the English Malmsey.

The character of each is very distinct. BOAL, or Bual, is perhaps the most common type, being full-bodied, full-coloured and medium sweet; it is also the cheapest of the four. VERDELHO is a softer, lighter wine suitable for before or after meals; SERCIAL, dry or very dry and light in colour; MALMSEY, very sweet.

PRODUCTION

The usual method of production is to train the vines over trellis work so that the pickers stand underneath and pick the grapes above their heads.

The vintage takes place usually in September.

Owing to the steepness and inaccessibility of the terraces it is impossible to use carts or lorries, but there are a number of press houses dotted about the hills within easy reach of the vineyards and grapes are carried there in baskets for the pressing.

514

After the grapes have been pressed the juice is run into goatskin containers and is carried on men's backs to the nearest road where a lorry takes it to the shippers' cellars.

Fermentation takes place in wooden casks or vats and lasts about three weeks; it is then that the treatment of the young wine differs from that of other countries.

The strong volcanic soil gives the immature wine a certain astringency, and in order to eradicate this and soften the wine it is stacked in oak barrels in what is known as an *Estufa*. This is nothing else but a "hot house", a shed, under the floor of which are hot pipes, and the wine is subjected to quite a high temperature for several weeks.

After this treatment alcohol is added (as in the case of other strong wines) and the wine is left to mature in the Lodges.

SUMMARY

Many people are puzzled at the difference between the three great strong wines or dessert wines—Port, Sherry and Madeira. Port is a red wine, while the other two are white, and is essentially an after-dinner wine because, in its making, alcohol is added during the fermentation to stop it and keep sugar in the wine. It is therefore fundamentally a sweet wine.

Sherry can be both sweet and dry. It is fermented and fortified like Madeira but is not subjected to heat. It is usually considered a "before-meal" wine.

Where does Madeira come in? Here again, Madeira can be sweet and dry and therefore it competes directly with both Port and Sherry. It is a matter of taste, but as Madeira is subjected to considerable heat in its manufacture, it is far more stable than other strong wines in extremes of heat and cold.

The great markets for Madeira before the world wars were Russia and India, showing that it is an ideal wine in cold climates and in hot.

It was a custom years ago to send Madeira round the world in a sailing ship. There is no doubt that the heat to which the wine was subjected over so many months improved its quality because it was merely a continuation of the treatment it had received when young.

As a result of the loss of the Russian market and the almost total loss of the Indian market, the production of Madeira wine has fallen considerably. Its place has been taken by bananas and sugar cane, but there is room for a big increase in the production of Madeira wine if more people realise its possibilities.

Owing to the volcanic soil and the heating process, Madeira is almost indestructible and lives to an incredible age.

Madeira has always been the odd man out among the three strong wines. Combining as it does the attributes of Sherry and Port, the public has never been certain when it should be drunk. The short answer is that it can be served with great success as an *alternative* to both and occasionally it is preferable to either.

On either very cold or very hot days it is ideal. Out of doors on a picnic, perfect, and many people find that they can drink it with impunity after Champagne.

As the wine is matured, like Sherry, in the *Solera* system there are no vintages any more but only the date when the blend or *Solera* was begun.

Another curiosity about Madeira is the great improvement in flavour after several years in bottle, so the longer the age in bottle, the better the flavour.

The Island of Madeira itself is very beautiful. The rich soil and the warm, moist, equable climate produce abundance of European and tropical flowers and the scenery is magnificent. It is difficult to find fault with the Island of Madeira and certainly impossible to find fault with the wine.

VERMOUTH

When Burgundy or Claret, Hock or Champagne, Port or Sherry, to name but six wines, are mentioned in conversation everybody effortlessly and immediately thinks of them as wine; but how many automatically think of Vermouth as such. If you were to ask the next five people you met on the street: "What is Vermouth?" it is a fair bet that four of them would say: "I've no idea: something you put with Gin." So I beg forgiveness of the knowledgeable when I stress—Vermouth is wine; however surprising to many, it is just that, wine.

But of course it is a wine with a difference, in that it is flavoured with plants, herbs and spices which produce its aromatic property.

HISTORY   It is certainly no upstart, however. We can reasonably go back as far as Hippocrates (the father of medicine, incidentally) for our origin. He did not call his infusion of cinnamon in wine sweetened with honey by the name of Vermouth, of course. He called it *Hippocras*. But he started the idea. It should be remembered that in the old days the herbalist was the family doctor, and these wise old birds soon realised that some of their unpleasant tasting concoctions were more easily taken by their patients when given in wine.

So the Greeks and the Romans did a lot of infusing of various ingredients in wine. The Romans in particular used all kinds of things. The list is interesting and even horrifying to us: take bitumen, pepper, mastic, gum, boiled sea-water, asafoetida and spikewood, all of which sound horrible: while camomile, myrrh, hyssop, marjoram, myrtle and rosemary all sound delightful. These are only some of the things the ancient Romans infused in their wine, to the benefit (*sic*) of their patients.

517

The popularity of aromatic wine, the recipes for which underwent constant modification, continued through the Middle Ages. It is known to have been served at the Courts of Louis XIV and Louis XV of France.

In the sixteenth century the Germans infused the flowers of the wormwood shrub in Rhein wine, which they called Wermut wine, *wermut* being the German for wormwood. This is when the name first made its appearance. As the Germans pronounced their "W" as a "V" it was not long before the spelling was altered by the Latin countries to its present form.

But it was not made on a commercial basis for many more years. It was not until 1786 that Antonio Carpano introduced it as a commercial proposition, and since then both France and Italy have steadily increased its popularity throughout the world.

Until recently, the tendency was for Italy to produce "Sweet" and for France to produce "Dry", but today both countries produce both "Dry" and "Sweet". But it should not be forgotten that the words "French" and "Italian" have real meaning, and are not just synonyms for "Dry" and "Sweet".

It should not be necessary for a customer at a bar to ask for a Gin and French French, or Italian Italian. All labels bear the country of origin, and the product of the country asked for should always be served. Vermouths have been and still are made by other countries, both inside and outside Europe, but these cannot, of course, call themselves "French" or "Italian".

PRODUCTION   Coming now to the actual production of Vermouth today, let us start by clearing the decks.

    1. There are no vintages in Vermouth, nor yet a *Solera* system as with Sherry. Continuity is maintained by the careful selection and blending of the wines employed.

    2. There is no definite area from which a Vermouth comes,

as with Bordeaux, Chianti, Champagne, etc., so that there is no such thing as "Vermouth country".

3. There are no hard-and-fast rules about how a Vermouth *must* be made.

You may well wonder what there is left to say! I think that we can lay down quite a lot, which will make clear what Vermouth is. The *Encyclopedia Britannica* tells us that Vermouth is "A wine fortified with spirit up to about 15 per cent alcohol, then stored in casks exposed to the sun's rays for a year or two. Another portion of wine is fortified to 50 per cent and in this a mass of tonic and aromatic materials are macerated, which are exposed to the sun, the same way as the bulk wine. The two liquids are then mixed in such a proportion as to make the ultimate product about 17 per cent alcohol by volume." As a matter of interest, the strength of the first wine these days does not exceed 14° Gay Lussac, or 24·5 proof spirit, for the obvious reason that at greater strength it would be a high strength wine by our present standard, and the high strength wine does not exceed 42 per cent proof spirit, this being the maximum for fortified wines at normal duty.

FRENCH VERMOUTH

The quotation from the Encyclopedia is all very well, but so condensed that it wants some elucidation. But rather than hop backwards and forwards, let us start with French Vermouth and then go on to the differences in the production of Italian Vermouth.

Taking French to mean the dry form of Vermouth, it is true that it can be and is made from wines of more than one region of France, but the French professional archives have it that it is the particular feature of the region of Marseilles.

In the bulk of Vermouths, to wit, those made in the Marseilles region, wines of the *Midi* are largely used. The *Midi* is that large area of Southern France stretching roughly from the Spanish border to Marseilles and northward as far as Avignon.

This area produces more than 25 per cent of France's total production of wine. The red wine yield per acre in this part of the world is very large; the white wine yield is, however, very much smaller, and it is these wines that are used by most producers of French Vermouth. The soil is largely sandy, mixed with silex and clay, with a fair content of lime.

The white wines most generally used are Picpoul, Bourret and Clairette. The first two are mainly grown on the plains, while Clairette grows mainly on the slopes of the hills.

As you will appreciate, the area of vines to be picked in this part of the world is enormous. The pressing is largely done in co-operatives, which are built in different centres to handle large quantities, thus eliminating the need for every small grower to have all the necessary equipment himself. The most modern methods are thereby employed, ensuring a high average standard of quality. Maybe it is not as picturesque as treading, but it is certainly rapid and efficient.

Now, both Picpoul and Bourret are very dry, one might say somewhat astringent, and even the addition of Clairette, a much richer wine, would not be sufficient to offset this dryness. A further wine known as Mistelle is therefore employed. This is made of Muscat grapes, the fermenting of which is checked by the addition of Brandy, thus producing a sweet wine.

So our Mistelle is a wine whose sweetness is retained and the strength of which is high. In some cases grape juice is used instead of Mistelle to enrich the dry wines, in which case more spirit is needed to make up the alcoholic content.

Even when wines of other parts of France are used, they will still be of a very dry type, and Vermouth made in Bordeaux will often have up to 40 per cent of wine from the Midi. The Mistelle in a Bordeaux Vermouth will almost certainly be from the Graves, but there is no difference in principle.

But now we come to a major difference between the Midi

520

Vermouth and a Western France Vermouth. In Bordeaux the wines are almost never *maderisé*, as it is maintained that it doesn't suit them. And here we come back to our Encyclopedia with its mention of exposure to the sun. In the Midi, the wines of the world-famous houses are subjected to weathering for anything up to two years, before blending, which means that the casks full of wine are left in the open to bask in the considerable summer sun and to suffer the vagaries of the winter—a remarkably impressive and heartening sight it is to see rows and rows of casks symmetrically laid out to weather. The wines so treated are oxidised to a certain extent, which the French call *maderisé*, presumably having coined the word from *Madère*; as in *Madère*, or Madeira to us, the wine is subjected to heat either in the sun or in special chambers.

This long process of basking in the sun, which that famous scientist Pasteur considered admirable, is naturally a costly process, and is far from being employed by all Vermouth makers. A loss of 10 per cent is to be expected, which is no small matter after all!

The wines are now ready for blending. The actual quantity of any one wine in the blend will vary from year to year, according to how the wines turn out each vintage. And here the skill of the blender plays a most important part in the maintenance of continuity of quality. The blending is done in large vats where many casks can be married at one time.

So now we have reached the stage where we have a blend of wines at about 14° Gay Lussac, which may have had a little Brandy added to them to bring them to this strength, and a further blend of richer wines which will be considerably higher in strength. And now we come to the actual making of Vermouth.

Either one or both of these base wines can be *Vermouté*, the normal practice being to flavour the higher strength wine with the chosen herbs, plants and spices.

The actual ingredients employed, and the proportion of any one of them, is the prized secret of the individual firm; but a very large number of different herbs and plants are used, among which is certain to be found a fair proportion of camomile flowers. Present also, in different quantities for different Vermouths, are likely to be some of the following: hyssop, marjoram, linden tea, elder flowers, gentian, coriander seed, and others, not forgetting our old friend the *Wermut* flower. All of them, you will note, are recognised as healthful, and while no claim is made that Vermouth is a tonic wine, it is certainly an appetite promoter.

There are three methods of getting the required flavour into the wine.

Maceration: This consists of placing a given quantity of the mixed plants, herbs and spices, in the bottom of a large vat, on to which the suitably blended base wine is poured. This is left so that the herbs are steeped in the wine for a period of fifteen to twenty-one days, according to the rate of extraction. The wine is then drawn off into casks and from a special trap at the bottom of the vat the solid matter is withdrawn. This, you will appreciate, is sodden with wine, and it is put into special presses where it is squeezed into solid cakes, the wine which runs out being naturally highly aromatic. This latter is then portioned out in exact quantities among the casks filled from the vat.

Infusion: This is much the same process eventually as maceration, but the wine does not lie on the herbs but is continually passed through them in the same way as a coffee percolator works. Either of these methods, as you will realise, is extracting the flavour from the herbs by no other means than by bringing the wine into contact with them.

Distillation: This is the third method, which is that of obtaining an aromatic liqueur of the herbal ingredient by distillation which is then used to flavour the wine.

In isolated instances a combination of one and three and two and three is used; but whatever method is adopted, we have now got our *Vermouté* wine.

The wines will now have a further period of storage either in wood or glass tanks. For some countries the two wines will be blended and bottled before shipment; for others, it will be shipped separately for blending on arrival; and still again for others it will be blended and shipped in bulk. But in every case the result will be the same product finally. French law lays down that it shall not finally exceed 19° Gay Lussac, that is to say 33° Sykes.

The spirit used for the fortification of the high strength wine is of course not Cognac but locally distilled Brandy. The strength of this is very high indeed, so that no great quantity is required to lift the strength of the wine.

A top quality Vermouth will be an average minimum of four years old. That is, two years weathering and a year of after-keep, plus a year from the start of the Vermouth process to the time of bottling.

As with other white wines, a deposit is liable to form in the bottle. This takes the form of crystals, which are unsightly in the public eye. To avoid this, certain firms subject the wine to a refrigeration process which takes place in special large vats reduced to eight degrees below zero Centigrade, approximately sixteen degrees Fahrenheit, causing the formation and precipitation of these crystals. This is not an essential procedure and is an expensive plant to instal, but it does ensure that, except in absolute extremes of cold, this precipitation will not occur. As and when the wine is required for delivery, either in cask or bottle, it will be put through a filter to ensure that it is star bright. We now have our French Vermouth which, as one Frenchman so happily put it: "is in the plenitude of its quality, its generous vinosity deliciously married to its savoury and subtle perfume". Only a Frenchman could think that up!

ITALIAN VERMOUTH

Now to leave France and cross the Italian border to Turin.

Just as in France, there is good and bad wine in Italy; but Vermouth is made from good, sound wines selected specifically for this purpose.

Originally the wine used was the *Moscato d'Asti*, but the quantity now required for present sales makes it necessary even for the great Turin firms to buy wines from outside this area, from Sicily, Sardinia and elsewhere.

A large variety of aromatic ingredients are used, some grown locally in the Alps and some imported from the East. Among these are: coriander seed, orris root, cascarilla, angelica, cinnamon, dittany, sage, thyme, and our old friend the *Wermut* flower, all of which are considered beneficial. Thus Italian Vermouth too is salutary, as well as being a most enjoyable aperitif.

The normal method of production is for the herbs, plants and spices to be infused in a solution of 68 per cent spirit in smallish casks (around twenty-eight gallons), left for a fortnight or so, filtered, and put into the vat containing the wine to be *Vermouté*. It is then left for a month, racked, and then left again to mature together. Some makers do make a distillate of the aromatic herbs, but the usual method, as stated, is to infuse them in the spirit. Italian Vermouth is not subjected to weathering.

The wines from Sicily are almost always big wines, due to the amount of sun the grapes get. They are often around 15° Gay Lussac, natural strength, but additional Brandy may be used to increase the alcohol to the required strength. As with the French, high and low strength wines are blended to arrive at the final product around 30° proof Sykes.

There are nowadays three main types of Italian Vermouth produced.

DRY VERMOUTH has no colouring matter and no additional sugar. One might say this is the Italian production of the French type. It is light and dry and does not contain more than four per cent sugar.

THE BIANCO has had no caramel colour added, but has been considerably sweetened. This has a distinct flavour of its own.

The most popular of all Italian Vermouth is the, may we say, standard Vermouth—a heavier, dark wine, which has both sugar and caramel added to produce the typical ITALIAN we all have known for so long.

The sugar used for sweetening is the purest cane sugar, which can be quite an expensive item.

STORAGE

Bottles of Vermouth can be stored while still unopen for an almost indefinite period.

As with all wines—and let it be stressed once again that Vermouth is wine—this should be binned lying down.

A Vermouth is known as being one of the few wines that will remain good after having been opened, even for a matter of weeks. It is, however, unwise to keep even Vermouth when the bottle has got only two or three inches of wine left in it.

SUMMARY

It should be borne in mind that Vermouths, both dry and sweet, are produced in parts of the world other than Italy and France, not forgetting the United Kingdom.

The method of production may vary slightly, but in all cases the grape is the base from which they all stem, and I finish as I started by stressing this point.

It is to be hoped that the foregoing has made clear the fact that:

Vermouth is made only from sound white wines.

It is not just a liquid to make Gin go further. It is an aperitif in its own right, either neat or diluted with soda, and a pinch of lemon peel if you like, though no one wishes to decry its use with Gin or other things. Like most beverages, its uses differ in different countries. In France and Italy it has always had its largest sale as an aperitif, either neat or with aerated water. The French often add *cassis*, a luscious blackcurrant syrup, to their Dry Vermouth, along with soda water. In so far as the United States is concerned, French Vermouth is mainly used in Dry Martini cocktails, and Italian in Sweet Martini cocktails. But in this country it is as the "Gin and French" or the "Gin and It" that it has its biggest sales. Strictly speaking, these are not cocktails as no cocktail is possible without ice.

More and more people, following upon their holidays in France and Italy, are coming to drink Vermouth without the addition of spirits. But however it is taken, Vermouth is an honest *wine* whose presence in a well-stocked cellar is as necessary as that of any other item in it.

Finally, it is worth noting that the uses of French Vermouth in the kitchen are many, more particularly where white wine and herbs are suggested.

BRITISH WINES

The consumption of wine in the United Kingdom has increased very rapidly in recent years and, judging by current trends, the market is likely to continue expanding for some time to come. This rapid progress applies to nearly all sections of the trade, but in particular to the two main categories of the wine market: Table Wines and Dessert Wines.

TABLE WINES

Table wines have increased in popularity since the war and particularly during the last twelve years. There is no doubt that the increase in the number of people travelling abroad accounts to a large degree for the great progress made in Britain by this section of the wine trade. This growing knowledge and popularity of wine drinking among an ever-increasing public is also extending to the other main section of the trade, that of Dessert Wines.

DESSERT WINES

This is the field in which the British wine industry is predominantly engaged and it consists chiefly of wines of Sherry type, ruby wines and Fruit wines, all of alcoholic strength in excess of twenty-five per cent proof spirit. In this highly competitive section of the market, British wines hold an overall lead over Spanish, Portuguese, South African, Australian, Cyprus and Commonwealth wines, largely owing to their reasonable price and the excellent and reliable quality that goes with it. In fact, for thirty years of more, British wines have accounted for between twenty-five and thirty-five per cent of the total annual consumption of all wines in the United Kingdom, and around fifty per cent of the Dessert Wine market.

HISTORY

The history of wine making in Britain dates back for many centuries and there is evidence of its production and consumption in Roman times. It is interesting also to know that the Domesday Book specifically mentions that in the eleventh century there were thirty-eight vineyards in various parts of the United Kingdom. By the sixteenth century these were beginning to die out and this decline was accelerated in the middle of the century by the dissolution of the monasteries, under whose order wine-making had for so long flourished. It is evident that for centuries the people of Britain successfully made wine for home consumption, but with a gradual change in the climate and improved and cheaper transport facilities, foreign wines eventually ousted the home-made wines of Britain.

Many British wine-makers have, however, been established for a considerable period of time, and one such wine-maker, Francis Chamberleyne, made a petition to King Charles I that he be granted a licence to make wines from dried grapes or raisins. The wording of his petition, which is still in existence, was as follows:

"To the King's Most Excellent Majesty

The humble petition of Francis Chamberleyne Humbly showing

That ye petition by his travell into forraigne parts, hath observed the making of wynes of dryed grapes, or raisons which wynes have been approved of by all such as have tasted the same to be a most wholsome and good wyne, and will keep his naturall strength and force for Sea Voyages, yea although it be beyond the Lyne, without any decay, as well as any other wynes whatsoever; and ye petitioner having to his preat charges atteyned to the knowledge of the making thereof.

His most humble suite to Your Majesty is; that you wilbe graciously pleased to grant unto him or his assignees a Licence under Your Majesty's great seale of England for the sole making of the said wynes for twenty-one years to come. . . . "

This petition was granted in 1635, in what must be one of the earliest patents in existence, on payment of £2 per year. Francis

Chamberleyne is, therefore, the earliest known forerunner of present-day British wine production.

British wine-makers have therefore been established for several centuries, and over the years improvements in the quality of their wines have been made by more exact and scientific methods of fermentation and by substituting as the fermentable base imported grape juice for the imported raisins or indigenous fruits previously in use.

There has, therefore, been a considerable change over the years in the character of British wines, but it was not until the turn of the century that, with the introduction of concentrated grape juice as the basis for their production, British wines started to take the great strides which have brought about their success, and have made them an integral part of the wine trade of the country. In the last fifteen years alone the sales of British wines have almost doubled from five million gallons in 1954 to just over eleven million gallons in 1969.

A considerable export trade has also been built up in many countries throughout the world and today over five hundred and fifty one thousand gallons are exported to these countries, in competition with wines from all other parts of the world.

The methods used in the production of British wines are, however, not fully known and perhaps a greater understanding of this would help to dispel the misconceptions that persist. In practice the making of British wine varies little from the traditional methods used by all wine-making countries throughout the world and by our own forbears in Britain, many of whom had their own vineyards from which they made excellent wine.

Climatic conditions and the great expansion of the British wine industry obviously made it impossible for British vineyards to produce anything like the enormous quantity of grapes required, and today only a very small quantity of wine is made from grapes grown in this country by a small band of enthusiasts.

To grow sufficient grapes for the needs of the British wine industry, something like thirty square miles of vineyards would be needed.

It is therefore necessary to import grape juice from abroad and it comes from countries such as Spain, Greece, Cyprus, France, South Africa, etc. It is in these countries that the process of British wine making begins.

At the time of the vintage the grapes are gathered and the juice from them is extracted in the traditional winepress manner. The grape juice so produced would, of course, start to ferment immediately if allowed to stand. Fortunately, however, grape juice if it has an excess of sugar will not ferment, so if a percentage of the water is evaporated the resulting concentrated grape juice can be shipped to this country without danger of fermentation. The water is therefore evaporated in special vacuum pans at a very low temperature which does not in any way affect the quality of the grape juice. This not only ensures that fermentation will not take place in transit but also reduces transport costs considerably.

When the grape juice arrives at the winery, it is stored until such time as it is required for production. The water which has been evaporated is then replaced and, with the addition of special yeasts, the wine ferments as Nature ordained. Fermentation is simply the yeast feeding on the sugar in the juice, multiplying and at the same time turning the sugar into alcohol and carbon dioxide. Fermentation can take anything from three to four weeks to complete, after which the wine is allowed to settle. It is then transferred to secondary containers, known as maturing vessels. Next it is filtered, by the process of passing the wine through a series of filters and subsequently passing it back into maturing vessels for fining and thereby giving clarity and lustre to the wine. Final filtration, by means of stainless steel sterilising filters, then takes place, after which the wine is stored in bond until it is mature. Passing out of bond through Customs to duty-paid storage vessels, it is then ready for bottling.

530

British wines are all too often discredited and misjudged by members of the wine trade and the consuming public, due to a lack of knowledge about British wine and the methods and basic ingredients used to produce them. There is a predilection on the part of both to the misconception that the lower price of British wines is related to poor quality, whereas in truth British wines really represent excellent value. This misconception is unfair and unfortunate, as the unprejudiced who have tasted British wines know of their consistent high quality and the value for money they represent.

To many, however, the importance of British wines in the British market need not be emphasised, and it is greatly to the industry's credit that it can provide an excellent range of products which are enjoyed by a large proportion of the adult population throughout the country. Increasingly wide acceptance of British wines indicates that preferences are becoming less and less allied to wine snobbery and that British wines, whilst inexpensive, are judged on their own merits.

British wine receives its fair share of promotional and advertising support and relations with the wholesale and retail trade, which are long established, continue to flourish.

TYPES OF WINE

But let us take a closer look at the types of British wines available. They fall into three main types, British Sherries and Ruby wines being the most important with Fruit wines taking a lesser but increasingly popular part.

RUBY WINES for many years predominated in the British wine field (with British Sherries a good second). These wines, which are mainly of a Port character, command a very loyal and large market both for the red and white types. They are sweet and of a rich full body and character.

BRITISH SHERRIES. The market in British Sherry has expanded parallel with the market in Sherry. British Sherries are comparable in quality with Commonwealth and Spanish equivalents and a simple tasting can prove this point over and over again. The traditional *flor* process is used in the preparation of a growing proportion of British Sherries, these wines being matured in casks in large *bodegas* at carefully controlled temperatures.

FRUIT WINES, for many years regarded as simple home-produced country products, are now becoming increasingly popular in their new branded bottle form and their rapid success indicates that they are here to stay. They are also drunk with the addition of lemonade or soda and ice, which makes a refreshing summer drink.

BRITISH VERMOUTHS, which are perhaps the least known today of British wines, are of excellent quality, comparable with most of the Vermouth imported from abroad and considerably cheaper.

The quality of British wines is very carefully controlled by highly experienced œnologists. Quality is in no way impaired by the wine being kept for a long time, its consistency being absolutely reliable, and even when a bottle is opened the wine will retain its bouquet and flavour for a very long period.

British wines are drunk by people of all income groups, and research shows that men appreciate these wines as much as women. British wines represent outstanding value when compared in quality and price with foreign and Commonwealth imports.

Distribution of British wines is completely national and a wide range to choose from can be found in most off-licences, wine-merchants, licensed grocers, some chemists and supermarkets.

The Serving of Wine

All of us who spend our lives in the Wine Trade can never cease to be intrigued by the complexity and variety of wine, and the greater our experience the more we come to realise there is always something new to learn. Whether we be a shipper, a wholesaler, a restaurant proprietor, a sommelier, an off-licence manager or, perhaps the most important of all, a consumer, we are always coming across something new to delight our eye, our nose and our palate. If we are fortunate enough to have visited any of the wine districts and seen the labour, care and experience that contribute to the making of a fine wine, we must surely become filled with a determination to play our part in bringing wine to the table in the best possible condition for the pleasure and enjoyment of our customers.

STORAGE   The first important matter to be considered by all hotels and restaurants is the condition under which their wines are stored. The cellar or store should be kept at as near a constant temperatire as possible—between 50° and 60°F. There are far too many cases of wine being stored near the central heating boiler, or in a cold and draughty store. While the latter is probably preferable to the former, neither will assist the wine's maturation and, over a period of time, will result in positive harm. The wine required for day-to-day use is usually kept in a dispense bar to be quickly available, and this can cause difficulties. Such bars often tend to be rather warm, and while this may be satisfactory for the red wines, white wines, which must be chilled, should not be stored there. The most common method of chilling wines is in an ice bucket at the table, but in many cases wines are kept ready for serving in a refrigerator. This is all right if they only remain there for a day or so and the temperature is moderate, but slow selling wines should not be left in the refrigerator for days or even weeks. No wine can show to advantage after this kind of treatment. It will soon begin to lack bouquet and flavour and, if the treatment is prolonged, will certainly suffer permanent damage. Probably the most satisfactory method of storing white wines so as to be ready for serving is in cold shelf cabinets which are now being increasingly widely used in the restaurant trade. These enable the wine to be stored at between 40° and 45°F, which is the temperature of a good Champagne cellar and is not detrimental to a white wine. After being stored in such conditions, the wine can be served in a moderately cool ice bucket so that it preserves its freshness during the meal. If, on the other hand, a refrigerator is being used for the more ordinary wines, for which there is a steady day-to-day sale, a safe rule is to put them in the refrigerator for about two hours before they are required.

THE SOMMELIER

It is in the restaurant, where so much wine is drunk, that the sommelier has a vital role to play. If he is a master of his craft, all the care and attention that have gone before will be brought to fruition with a well-served wine. On the other hand, all this can be thrown away if the wine is carelessly and badly served. This applies not only to the fine wines; humbler wines also amply repay the proper attention which is meted out to their superiors.

To achieve the best results when a special meal has been ordered in advance, the wines should also be ordered to enable them to be brought to the table, decanted if necessary at the right temperature, but this of course does not normally happen. Usually the customer orders his wine when he is already at the table after having ordered his lunch or dinner. The sommelier should be on hand with his wine list, ready to help, advise and take the order as soon as the meal has been decided on. There is nothing more annoying than to be left waiting for a sight of the wine list until the meal is already on the table and sometimes, alas, even longer than that. For this there is no excuse. It may well lead to the loss of a sale and can scarcely enhance the reputation of the

534

restaurant. If the sommelier is unable to attend to a customer at once, then at least there should be a wine list on hand for him to linger over and consider his selection.

CHOICE OF WINES While many people like to be left to choose for themselves, others welcome tactful assistance, and here we can suggest some guiding principles. Wine is a beverage to be enjoyed, and if some like to drink a sweet white wine right through a meal, or if others prefer Claret or Burgundy with their fish or egg dish, we must presume that this is what they like! We must not be too dogmatic about what is the right wine with a particular dish, at least they are drinking wine and this will improve their enjoyment of the meal, their sense of well-being and, one hopes, their digestion!

Nevertheless, it is generally agreed some wines show to a better advantage with one dish rather than with another; for example, most people prefer white wine with a fish or egg course and red wine with meat or poultry. Champagne, on the other hand, can be drunk right through a meal and of course as an apéritif. If there is an occasion to be celebrated, what better greeting for the guests than a glass of Champagne? The success of your party is assured.

While, therefore, no hard-and-fast rules can be laid down to cover the serving of particular wines with suitable foods, the view of knowledgeable wine drinkers can be summarised thus:

WITH	SERVE	TEMPERATURE
Soup	Oloroso Sherry	Room temperature
	Madeira	„ „
Fish	Dry Sherry	Chilled
	Madeira	„
	Champagne	„
	A dry white wine	„

WITH	SERVE	TEMPERATURE
Poultry	Full white Burgundy	Chilled
	Hock	,,
	Claret	Room temperature
Red meat,	Claret	Room temperature
Game, etc.	Red Burgundy	,, ,,
	Red Rhône wine	,, ,,
Cheese	Full red wine from	
	Burgundy, Bordeaux	Room temperature
	or Rhône	
Dessert	Sweet Sauternes	Well chilled
	Beerenauslese Hock	,, ,,
	Champagne	,, ,,
	Port, Sweet Madeira,	Room temperature
	Sweet Sherry	

These are not hard-and-fast rules, but may form a useful guide.

DECANTING

If a red wine is selected it has to be decided whether it should be decanted or served from a cradle. It is natural for all red wines which have been in bottle for a period to throw a deposit, although the time this takes and the amount of the deposit vary considerably from vintage to vintage. If this deposit is allowed to cloud the wine while being served, this will spoil the flavour and can reduce a fine delicate wine into a coarse and ordinary one. If it is known that a particular wine has a deposit, then it should be stored in the cellar or dispense in a horizontal position so that the cork remains in contact with the wine and the deposit settles along the bottom of the bottle. Then, when the wine is required, it should be lifted from the bin as smoothly and gently as possible and put, still horizontal, into the cradle. There is no possible point in standing the wine upright, drawing the cork and then putting the wine in a cradle. Once in the cradle the wine should be first shown to the customer, so that he is satisfied it is the wine he has ordered. Ideally the operation which follows

536

should then be carried out in front of the customer. Decanting is a simple, straightforward operation, but it must be carried out carefully and methodically. First the capsule should be removed and the neck of the bottle and top of the cork carefully wiped with a clean cloth. Then the cork should be drawn as smoothly as possible. There are a number of good corkscrews available with a lever action which makes it quite simple to draw the cork while in the cradle, without shaking the bottle. A clean, dry white glass decanter should be ready at hand and the wine can then be slowly and carefully poured from the bottle to the decanter, taking care not to allow any deposit to go through with the wine. To ensure this it will be necessary to have a bright light behind the neck of the bottle so that it can be seen at once when the deposit begins to mingle with the wine.

The wine can now be presented to the customer and many like to see the empty bottle from which the wine has been decanted, together with the cork which can be put on the table in a small glass.

White wines and red wines with no deposit do not need decanting although, in fact, this nearly always improves a red wine, but, nevertheless, they should still be served with care and respect and, of course, always at the right temperature.

GLASSES

Suitable glasses can add considerably to the enjoyment of wine. The first essential is that the glass should be of a good size. No wine tastes well out of a small glass. It is far better to have a glass which is, if anything, a little too large and to fill it only about a third or half full. This leaves room for the wine to develop its bouquet. All wine glasses should be white, and it is no longer thought necessary to have completely different types of glasses for different table wines. The tradition of coloured glasses for the serving of German wines originates from the era when imperfect treatment of these delicate white wines in cask often resulted in their being cloudy, and the colour masked such imperfections. Today, when one hopes that the wine will arrive in perfect condition, it is better to be able to observe such imperfection rather than to veil it, although of course fine, old, coloured hock glasses are always a delight to the eye in their own right. A stemmed glass should be used and the bowl should be shaped gently curving into the lip. This is what is generally called a tulip shape and helps to concentrate the bouquet in the glass. Many restaurants have glasses of the same design in different sizes, using the largest size for Champagne and possibly Burgundy, the middle size for all other table wines, and the smallest size for Port, Sherry and Madeira. This small size can also be used for Brandy, although some prefer to have a special balloon-shaped glass for this purpose. There is an unfortunate tendency in some restaurants to use minute glasses, better suited to liqueurs than for the serving of Port or Sherry. This is an abomination and an insult to the wine. Port and Sherry should be served in decent-sized glasses like any other wine. Nothing more enhances the appearance of a table than to see attractive glasses, well polished, properly set out at the outset, and this may indeed serve as a suggestion that wine is the best drink to go with the meal

SERVING   Having chosen the wine and prepared it for serving, the sommelier should first pour a little into the bottom of the host's glass to enable him to smell it, taste it and satisfy himself that it is as it should be. He will then serve the other members of the party, never filling the glass more than about a third to a half, and finally the host. When pouring the wine, it is important to do so slowly and carefully and not as if it were a bottle of beer to be rushed into the glass to slake an urgent thirst. This is not to say ordinary table wines are not thirst quenchers—there is nothing better for the purpose on a warm day than a glass of chilled dry white wine—but wines served with a meal deserve and require greater consideration if they are to be enjoyed to the full. Finally the sommelier should not forget during the meal to replenish glasses from time to time, and also to ascertain whether a further bottle may be required, or perhaps even a further wine with a subsequent course.

538

All this may sound a little elementary but, taken together, the points mentioned ensure the proper choice and serving of wine, and add to the enjoyment of the meal and hence to the reputation of the restaurant. Even if a restaurant has only a very modest wine list, it can add greatly to its reputation if it is obvious that the sommelier is interested in the wine, and that his first consideration is the interest and enjoyment of his customer. Almost invariably people respond to good service, and what might have been a very ordinary meal can become one to be remembered and the restaurant which served it one to be recommended.

WINE IN THE HOME

Of late years there has been a great increase in wine drinking in the home. This is no longer confined to the special occasion or to the entertainment of friends. Foreign travel, no doubt, is partially responsible for this and many have come to realise how a bottle of quite ordinary local wine can add to the enjoyment of a meal. The Wine Trade in England has been quick to realise this and has indeed put a great deal of effort into educating the potential wine drinkers of this country. Equally important, it has searched the wine producing countries of the world for good sound beverage wines which can be sold at a price at which they can be enjoyed daily.

Many local wine shops offer such wines, and recently, in addition to the usual size bottle, they have become available in litres and half gallons. The use of these larger sizes reduces the cost of bottling and handling and makes it possible to offer a wine that can be enjoyed at the lowest possible price. To enjoy these wines to the full, all that is necessary is to serve it at the right temperature, remove the cork or plastic seal, which is now often used for this type of wine, carefully wipe the neck of the bottle, serve the wine, drink and enjoy it. These wines should not be despised and indeed they may well serve as an introduction to their more sophisticated cousins. Although England is not (if Sir Guy Salisbury-Jones will forgive me) a wine producing country, she is fortunate in having a Wine Trade with a great tradition, and many of the finest wines produced in Europe find their way to this country, and to the lists of the many merchants up and down the country.

These finer wines to be enjoyed to the full should be given all
the care and attention that can be lavished upon them. These
days we cannot all have wine cellars, but many a cupboard
under the stairs has been converted into a very reasonable wine
store. Your local wine shop can always obtain for you a small
wine rack to fit any space that may be available, and it is not an
expensive business to assemble, over a period of time, a small
assortment of interesting wines.

PANTHEON, OXFORD STRE̶

—o—

MENU 4th February 1870

—o—

AMONTILLADO	**POTAGES** Julienne Creci
MARKOBRUNNER AUSLESE '62	**POISSONS** Filet de Sole a la Montpensier Saumon Eperlans Frits
CHATEAU YQUEM '58 CHATEAU YQUEM '47	**ENTREES** Filet de Ris de Veau a la Dauphine Mauviettes à la Pompadour Vol au Vent des Huîtres
CHAMPAGNE '62	**RELEVES** Selle de Mouton Bœuf Rôti Chapons a la Toulouse Langue de Bœuf
CLARET, BARTONS' '54	**ROTS** Les Faisans Les Perdreaux Les Becassines
CHATEAU LAFITTE '51 PORT '40	**ENTREMETS** Beignots d'Abricot La Gelle de Fruits La Chalotte de Russe La Boudin Glace a la Macedoine Ramequins de Parmesan

DESSERT

PORT '34	CHATEAU LAFITTE '41
SHERRY '20	CHATEAU MARCAUX '48

540

Wine Tasting

In the last ten years the British public has shown a gratifyingly increased interest in wine, and, to a large extent, this must be attributed to holidays being spent abroad.

At the time of writing, wine drinking is increasing steadily by ten per cent per annum, and there seems no reason why this upward trend should not continue for some years to come.

To accelerate the British interest in wine drinking must be a major aim, and certainly "wine tasting" is a medium for so doing. However, a careful selection of wines for each occasion is necessary, thereby avoiding the haphazard approach to the customer which often does more harm than good.

For this reason, various tastings are set out in detail at the end of this article and it is hoped they will be useful as a general guide.

A tasting, therefore, should have a *raison d'être* if it is to stimulate the public curiosity in wine. At this point, may there be a plea for less of the pompous mystique, the hushed whisper and the tiresome snobbery which in the past has been inflicted on the unsuspecting layman. But there *are* common-sense rules of procedure which should be followed if the tasting is to be successful. The undermentioned points to be considered when organising a wine tasting are:

Cards These should be fairly stiff if possible, and on them should be printed the date of the tasting, the name of each wine, the year if it is a vintage wine, the shipper and the price. There should also be space on the card for the taster to make notes.

Glasses Provide one glass per guest. Glasses should be rinsed after the red wines are tasted preparatory to tasting the white wines. The clear 8-oz. Paris goblet is recommended for general use.

Amount of Wine The normal seventy-five centilitre bottle of wine should give a minimum of fifteen samples to the bottle. Hence if thirty people are invited to the tasting and six different wines being shown, the number of bottles required is twelve.

Food They say in Bordeaux that cheese flatters the wine. Rocquefort is generally considered the best, but never serve cream cheese. Other cheeses recommended are English Cheddar and Gruyère. Biscuits are frowned upon by the professionals.

Order of Wine Dry wines followed by sweet wines. Red before white (N.B. Claret before Burgundy). The extra acidity normal in white wines is inclined to spoil the palate for red wines, which should therefore be tasted first. If you are offering a wine with sediment, it should be decanted one/two hours before the start of the tasting.

TEMPERATURE
OF WINE

Sparkling Wines should be iced, preferably in an ice bucket.

White Wines—for example, Hocks, Moselles, Alsatian wines, White Burgundies, White Bordeaux—should be served chilled and not iced.

Rosé Wines should be chilled.

Burgundy should be served at the temperature at which they have been kept—that is, normal cellar temperature.

Claret The chill should be taken off the wine, but do not attempt to warm it too quickly.

It is not always feasible to provide boxes of sawdust to spit into, and it is not usually necessary except at large trade tastings. Empty bottles with funnels should be placed on the tables.

HOW TO TASTE

To put pen to paper on this subject invites a lengthy diatribe which may well confuse rather than clarify. The old cliché that "practice makes perfect" applies as much to wine tasting as to any other skill. One is also helped by having a good memory, and the really enthusiastic taster always makes notes. Be that as it may, the following routine is advisable:

1. Pour a small amount of the wine into the glass and inspect the colour of the wine for clarity against the light. The wine should be clear and free of sediment: if the wine looks dull or cloudy, it must be suspect.

2. To smell the wine and adjudge its bouquet is necessary before tasting. This gives you clues to its condition, age, and its district of origin. If the wine smells unpleasant it may be musty; the two main reasons for this being that it is corked or that the wine has been delivered in a faulty cask. Two other principal checks to be made are whether the wine smells too much of sulphur, which is used as a preservative in the cheaper range of white wines, or whether the wine has a smell of sourness, indicating an excess of acidity.

3. When tasting the wine, the tip of the tongue and then the palate (after a larger mouthful has been taken) will indicate (a) whether the wine is sweet or dry, (b) whether it is full-bodied or not, and (c) whether it is well balanced, that is, that there is neither a predominance of acidity nor tannin. Lastly it will indicate the flavour of the wine.

It is recognised that the professional taster and buyer of wine would go into far greater detail in the above paragraph and the information given sets out only the basic points to look for when tasting.

The undermentioned tastings are merely a guide, but they have been suggested for the reasons given.

The inexperienced As an excellent introduction to wine drinking a tasting of three cheap ordinary wines (*rouge*, *rosé* and *blanc*) is suggested to indicate a good quality range from the Bordeaux district.

For 20/25 age group The object of this tasting is to give a simple example of three white wines, a *rosé* and two red wines with comparisons and districts.

WHITE WINES

Pouilly Fuissé	Dry wine from Mâçonnais
Bernkasteler Riesling	Medium dry from the Moselle
Sauternes	Sweet wine from Bordeaux district

ROSÉ WINE

Anjou Rosé	A semi-sweet rosé from the Loire

RED WINES

Château Plaisance	A good cheap St. Émilion
St. Amour	Fine example of a growth Beaujolais

For 25/30 age group This is a slightly more sophisticated tasting whereby two red and two white wines from Bordeaux are shown and also two red and two white wines from Burgundy.

RED WINES

St. Émilion ⎫	Exemplifying two famous Claret
Margaux ⎬	districts
Nuits St. Georges	Burgundy from the Côte de Nuits
Pommard	Burgundy from the Côte de Beaune

Château Loudenne Blanc ⎫	One dry and one sweet wine
Château Suduiraut ⎬	from the Bordeaux district
⎭	—both château bottled
Pouilly Fuissé ⎫	Shows difference in "class"
Puligny-Montrachet ⎬	of two white Burgundies

For the 35 upwards age group Under this heading, here are four tastings of possible interest:

RED BORDEAUX (Wines from the seven main districts).

Château Beau Site	St. Estephe
Château Ducru Beaucaillou	St. Julien
Château Batailley	Pauillac
Château Rauzan Gassies	Margaux
Château Smith-Haut-Lafitte	Graves
Château Le Gay	Pomerol
Château La Clotte	St. Émilion

RHINE WINES A tasting to illustrate wines from the Rheingau, Rheinhessen, Nahe, Palatinate and Moselle districts.

Johannisberger Erntebringer	Rheingau
Niersteiner Rehbach	Rheinhessen
Schloss Böckelheimer	Nahe
Durkheimer Spielberg	Palatinate
Piesporter Goldtröpfchen	Moselle

ROSÉ WINES

Provence Rosé	Provence
Anjou Rosé	Loire
Tavel Rosé	Rhône
Vin rosé de Bordeaux	Bordeaux
Beaujolais Rosé	Beaujolais
Portuguese Pétillante Rosé	Portugal
Spanish Rosé	Spain

T

SHERRY These should be tasted in the order shown, that is, from dry ranging to sweet.

Dry	Sweet
Manzanilla	Amoroso
Fino	Oloroso
	Cream

Medium
Amontillado

Spirits and Beers

SPIRITS

ORIGIN   Who was the benefactor of the human race who discovered the
art of distillation? We do not know, but, while it is probable
that wine was first made by the accidental fermentation of
grape juice, it is likely that Spirits were the result of careful
experiment.

We do know that Liqueurs were first distilled by learned monks
who were the medicine men in the Middle Ages, and it is likely
that Spirits also had a medical origin, especially when one

547

considers that the names for Spirits—*Eau-de-Vie*, *Usquebagh* (Gaelic for Whisky), *Aquavit*, and *Vodka*—all mean "Water of Life".

As a corollary, Spirits may have been further developed for economy in transport, once it was found that the alcohol in a fermented liquor could be separated from the bulk liquid so that an equal amount of alcohol could be carried in a tenth of the bulk.

MANUFACTURE Spirits can be produced from any raw material containing starch or sugar, first fermented and then distilled.

The principle of distillation is simple: as alcohol boils before water, if a fermented liquor is heated the alcohol therein rises in the form of vapour. The vapour is then cooled and returns to a form of liquid, which is Spirit.

Whisky is distilled Ale, the fermented product of malted or unmalted grain; Brandy is distilled (or "burnt") wine; Rum is distilled Molasses, produced from sugar cane, etc.

Two kinds of Still are used for the production of potable Spirits, the Pot and the Patent (or Coffey) Still.

The Pot Still is not unlike a large kettle (and is sometimes so called) and its design has altered little over the centuries. The spout on top of the pot is tapered, and then coiled into a "worm" which passes through a condenser surrounded by cold water. The "wash" or fermented liquor is heated in the pot and the vapour, when cooled, falls as Spirit into a spirit receiver. Much depends on the shapes of the pot and the spout, as these, as well as the water used in the mash, do much to give to the Spirit from each distillery its own characteristic flavour

Technically, the Pot Still is comparatively inefficient, but the very fact of its chemical failure to extract all the impurities, such as esters, acids, higher alcohols and fusel oil, imparts the taste and bouquet so much prized in many agreeable Spirits, and its use is essential to impart the basic character of Whisky, Brandy and Rum.

Pot Still Spirits require a substantial period of maturation in cask, where they undergo a slow chemical change and merger of the various constituent parts. For this process there is no substitute for Father Time. While the actual distilling is an art, the final product can still be called a mystery.

The Patent Still was invented in 1830 by Aeneas Coffey, a Dublin Excise Officer, and produces a more neutral (or more lightly flavoured) Spirit at a higher degree of proof. It consists of two parallel columns each containing a series of perforated plates, called the Analyser and the Rectifier. Briefly, the cold wash is introduced to the top of the rectifying column in a pipe which zigzags down, being warmed by rising vapours. The hot wash empties into the top of the analyser, flows down through the compartments and is vaporised by steam. The vapours rise up through the Analyser Column and thence pass into the bottom of the rectifier and, as they rise through the plates, are condensed by the cold wash pipe and the heart of the resulting Spirit is caught on an unperforated plate and drawn off.

Thus the rising spirit vapours heat the wash and the cold wash condenses the vapours in a continuous process.

The Patent Still, by reason of its higher technical efficiency, produces Spirits which require a shorter time for maturing; some, if distilled at a very high proof, require no maturing, but it is impossible to get absolutely pure alcohol.

SHION IN SPIRITS   As in the case of wine, fashions in spirit drinking have varied over the years.

For a long time Brandy was the only spirit drunk by the wealthy, and throughout the Napoleonic wars there was an extensive smuggling trade with France. During the nineteenth century the consumption varied, but Mr. Pickwick was fond of Brandy and water, and towards the end of the century Brandy and Seltzer (or B and S) was the fashionable drink.

In the last fifty years of the nineteenth century Irish Whiskey enjoyed a tremendous vogue, and it was only at the very end of that century that Scotch Whisky, as we now know it, became popular in England and shows no sign of losing its appeal.

Rum was long associated with the Navy; in fact, it was the only alcohol carried for ships' companies. This was mainly for economy in space as high-strength Rum in cask took up little room in fighting ships. It has always been popular with deep-sea fishermen and the "tot" served in the trenches at "stand-to" in the 1914–18 war did much to alleviate the discomfort of life.

Gin, in its early days, was very cheap and consumed in large quantities by the masses, but, as it became more expensive, owing to high Excise duties, its status was raised and, with the introduction of cocktails and then Gin-and-Tonic, Gin-and-Vermouth and Gin-and-Bitters, its use has become universal.

Today there is a trend towards lighter-flavoured and less pungent Spirits. Scotch Whisky and Rum have tended to prove more popular when lighter in character, and now Vodka, the lightest of all, is increasing its hold on the public taste.

CONSUMPTION Around 1900 the consumption of Spirits in the United Kingdom was 48 million gallons per annum. Furthermore, the strength at which they were sold was much higher than today, varying from proof to 17 under proof, which was the popular strength for Gin. In 1886, Whiskey at 10 under proof was sold at 3s. 6d. per bottle, but then the duty was only ten shillings per proof gallon.

Immediately prior to 1914, the usual strength was 25 under proof, but during the war the strength became 30 under proof (and the duty 72s. 6d. per gallon), the strength at which most Spirits are sold today.

With the current Spirit Duty at £16·50 per proof gallon, it is hardly surprising that consumption has declined to seventeen million gallons.

"PROOF"   The official method of measuring alcoholic strength in Great Britain is by Sikes' formula, under which "proof" means 100° of Proof Spirit, and all strengths are measured from that. It used to be common to refer to spirits as so many degrees under proof (or u.p.), but the labelling orders since 1945 require Spirits to be labelled as degrees of proof, so that 30 u.p. became 70° proof.

It is unfortunate that there is no world standard of expressing strengths or capacities. There are several different systems in Europe, while in the U.S.A. a "proof gallon" is not the same as in Britain, either in strength or measurement.

The principal methods of measuring strengths of wines and spirits are Sikes (British), Gay Lussac (European) and American.

Gay Lussac is to all intents the same as alcohol by volume though it differs fractionally.

To convert Gay Lussac to Sikes, divide by two, then the result by two, then add the three figures together.

> *Example:* 20° Gay Lussac divided by 2 = 10
> divided by 2 = 5
> 20+10+5 = 35° Sikes
> (or multiply by 7 and divide by 4)

To convert Gay Lussac to American, multiply by 2.

To convert Sikes to Gay Lussac, multiply by 4, then divide by 7.

To convert Sikes to American, multiply by 8 and divide by 7.

The following table shows the principal comparative strengths.

GAY LUSSAC	SIKES	U.S.A.
7°	12·2°	14°
8	14	16

551

GAY LUSSAC	SIKES	U.S.A.
9	15·7	18
10	17·5	20
11	19·4	22
12	21	24
13	22·8	26
14	24·5	28
(a) 14·28	25	28·56
15	26·4	30
(b) 15·5	27	31
16	27·9	32
17	29·7	34
17·14	30	34·28
18	31·5	36
19	33·2	38
20	35	40
21	36·7	42
(c) 24	42	48
37·45	65·5	74·9
40	70	80
42·8	75	85·6
45·7	80	91·4
50	87·7	100 (proof)
57·14	100 (proof)	114·28
100	175	200

(a) Maximum strength of Table Wines
(b) Maximum strength of Table Wines (Commonwealth)
(c) Maximum strength of Dessert Wines

CONTROL   Spirits, taken in moderation, can be beneficial: in excess, disastrous. The U.S.A. tried the experiment of control by total prohibition, but self-discipline is preferable to compulsory abstinence by legislation. Most Governments, including our own, now control consumption by levying high rates of duty, but the distilling industry has managed to survive and retain its high standard of integrity mainly perhaps because people still believe that, in the words of the famous Miss Marie Lloyd, "a little of what you fancy does you good".

BRANDY

Just as wine is steeped in history, tradition and romance, so also is the story of Brandy. For Brandy is, after all, the very heart of wine.

Within these pages, however, the reader is looking rather for facts and for answers to the practical questions which so often confront those who are closely interested in the handling of wines and spirits.

Here perhaps are some of those questions which immediately spring to mind. From where did the word Brandy originate? Why Cognac, why Armagnac, and how, indeed, has the description "Champagne Brandy" crept in to confuse the issue? Why, perhaps more than with other spirits, is so much importance attached to the ageing of Brandy, and has the claim for medicinal qualities any foundation? Have the well-known symbols such as XXX and V.S.O.P. any common significance? What should one look for in choosing a Brandy—how should it be served? Why indeed is it so expensive?

Many of these questions cannot be answered and the story of Brandy cannot be truly told without delving into the historical background. But first of all, let us examine how it is made—how it is made today and how it has always been made.

COGNAC

Wine—a light white wine for preference—is placed in the copper receptacle of a still and slowly brought to the boil. Because alcohol boils at a lower temperature than water, the still can be controlled so that the alcohol vapours from the wine pass over the still first. When condensed, these fall as a pure white spirit. Thus the heart has been drawn from the wine and turned into what the French call *Eau-de-Vie* or Water of Life. Why then do we give to it the very un-French name of Brandy?

ORIGIN OF THE NAMES

It is here that COGNAC comes into the story; for Brandy can be made in any part of the world where grapes grow in sufficient quantity to warrant the making of wine. But COGNAC must be made within the confines of a limited area surrounding the ancient town of that name which lies near the Biscay coast some seventy miles north of Bordeaux.

Here it was that the word Brandy was conceived and here, briefly, is the story.

"BRANDY" AND "COGNAC"

Since the days of the Romans the town of Cognac was in existence, later to become famous as the birthplace and eventually the Court of King François I. Since the earliest times the farmers had made wine in the district and during the sixteenth and seventeenth centuries they started to develop an export trade through the nearby port of La Rochelle, which was particularly prosperous in those times. Their wine was not of a particularly high quality, being dry and harsh, and it stood up none too well on its travels. But, when it came, the reason for the sudden loss of this prosperous export trade stemmed rather from the wars and blockades which, in the early seventeenth century, gradually ruined the trade of the local ports. Over-production, lack of storage space and in fact ruin stared the wine-growers in the face.

HISTORY

It fell to a Dutch apothecary, who happened to be passing through Cognac at the time, to save the local farmers from their

ARMAGNAC

Villeneuve de Marsan

Gabarret

Cazaubon

Eauze

Nogaro

Riscle

Nérac

CONDOM

Lectoure

Vic-Fézensac

Aignan

AUCH

MIRANDE

COGNAC

plight. He solved the storage problem by teaching them the art of distillation—by drawing the heart out of the wine and storing it in one barrel where ten had been needed before. He called this product *Brandewijn* or BURNT WINE. Its ease of handling and storage, its resistance to climatic conditions and, above all, its beautiful perfume, soon earned for this new spirit a far-flung reputation and it was not long before the English gave to it their own pronunciation—"Brandy" it was, and Brandy it has remained.

Thus, the people of Cognac can justly claim this close association with the origin of Brandy. But the exclusive right to label their product "COGNAC" goes much much deeper than that. It must be mentioned that the Brandy of ARMAGNAC, coming from a district some hundred miles south-east of Cognac, enjoys a similar exclusivity to its name, though the method of distillation differs slightly.

This exclusivity—backed by French law—is based not merely on the geographical boundaries of the area, but also on the method of distillation. For the technician it will be sufficient to say that not only does the law require that the grapes should be grown, the wine made and distillation take place within the legally defined boundaries of these districts, but that the distillation must be carried out exclusively by the Pot Still method.

PRODUCTION OF COGNAC

An explanation of the difference between the Pot Still and the Patent Still can be as tedious as it is technical. Nevertheless, it is of significance, particularly where Brandy is concerned. The Patent Still is the modern and more efficient development of the Pot Still. If the distiller wishes to extract from his basic material (be it wine, grain, molasses, etc.) a pure spirit of high strength and little flavour, then the Patent Still will do the job admirably. If, on the other hand, his task is to produce a spirit with a strong flavour of the wine or other product from which it was made, it is the skilful use of the ancient Pot Still, with (as the French say) its "delicate nose", which will achieve this result. By the Cognac method, not only are the "tops and tails"

of the first distillation removed, but the low strength spirit is returned a second time for further distillation, producing a final result of around 70 per cent alcohol and 30 per cent of the finest elements from the wine.

It is from this precious 30 per cent—from these elements of the wine—that Cognac derives the rich "bouquet" which is its main characteristic. Here also is found the answer to our other questions—the importance of ageing and the claim to medicinal properties.

MATURING

First let us take the question of ageing. Pure straight alcohol will not alter appreciably however long it is kept. But the combination of, say, 70 per cent alcohol and 30 per cent of wine elements, having gone through the shock of distillation, require time to re-marry and develop the characteristics of each. This can only take place through contact with the air. Casks made from the finest matured oak are used and, through the pores of the wood, the spirit draws tannin to give it that rich golden colour.

Less often nowadays is the "fabulous" old bottle of Brandy, covered in crowns and cobwebs, discovered in the cellars of a deceased uncle and produced as the showpiece for a special occasion. Most people have learned that Brandy does not improve in bottle. Sad to tell, the "fabulous old brandy" may only have a few years of genuine cask age behind its venerable façade.

How long should Brandy be matured in wood? How long indeed! One might almost say, the longer the better, but this is not necessarily so. Just as the character of a man will mould and mature with the years, so will the character of Brandy. But the faults of youth may be accentuated rather than mellowed with age. Thirty to forty years is ideal, with perhaps another score for those of exceptional quality. After that, their life is more easily preserved in glass.

OTHER VARIETIES OF BRANDY

If too much emphasis would seem to have been laid on the straight Pot Still Brandies of Cognac, it is because. due to the soil, the climate, the method of distillation and the traditional skill of its inhabitants, Cognac is accepted universally as the most popular of Brandies. It is important to stress the word "universally" because in those countries which make their own, the local Brandy often enjoys wide popularity. Notable amongst these are Spain, South Africa, Australia, California and now Germany and Italy, not to mention others.

The difference in the case of these other Brandies, as also with the French "Pure Grape" variety, is that a blend of Pot Still and Patent Still spirit is permitted, provided it derives originally from the grape.

We have shown that, while Cognac is Brandy, Brandy is not necessarily Cognac. What, then, is "Champagne" Brandy? The Cognac district, covering roughly the area of the two counties of Charente and Charente Maritimes, is itself subdivided into seven districts of varying qualities, the first two being La Grande Champagne and La Petite Champagne. Whilst the use of the word on labels can be slightly confusing, the right to the *appellation* is authorised and controlled by the French Government.

BLENDING UNDER BRANDS AND SYMBOLS

It is from the varying qualities of these subdistricts, some giving more "finesse", some more body, that the skilful blender finally balances his House Brand.

This House Brand counts for more than the well-known symbols such as XXX, V.S.O.P., etc., which in themselves really represent no common standard of age or quality. The star symbol was chosen by chance some hundred years ago when the big shipping houses in Cognac took the decision to bottle their own blends in Cognac. At that time XXX was the superior of the three categories, the younger blends being XX and X. Later on V.S.O.P. crept in, taken from the simple phrase "Very Special Old Pale". Many other symbols have been added by individual Houses, but it is the shipper's name and price that counts, not the symbol.

559

VINTAGE BRANDIES

Old vintages are becoming more and more difficult to find. The French Government will no longer grant age certificates for old vintage Brandies, except in a few very special instances, and therefore the straight vintage lovers must seek the rarity of the "English-landed" vintage Brandies. Wine merchants in this country are still at liberty to pursue their age-old custom of shipping a few hogsheads of young Cognac and, themselves, holding these in bond until ready for bottling. These Brandies are usually pale in colour and lighter in flavour than the "Bottled in France" variety.

Finally, what to look for and how best to serve a fine Brandy? Look first for the clean, round taste which can only come from natural maturation—warm the glass in the palm of your hand and thus release the "bouquet" which is the charm of the Pot Still spirit. Heating the glass over a flame will shock the bouquet into rapid dispersal. This also takes place when water, soda or other minerals are added. This is not to say that Brandy as a long drink is sacrilege—quite the contrary. But do not leave it standing too long. For such a delightful beverage, this could be sacrilege indeed.

ARMAGNAC

This Brandy in France second only to Cognac, and without serious rival for quality elsewhere in the world, is produced chiefly in the Gers department and marginally in its neighbours. In this inland isolated region, lying broadly between Bordeaux and Toulouse, Brandy has been distilled for several hundred years. That it is less well known and drunk than it deserves arises from this geographical isolation, lacking the river and sea transport means available in the Charente. Also the absence of commercial development and substantial firms have curtailed its distribution and renown, particularly in the export field, which Cognac exploited so successfully from the start. But such shortcomings are no reflection on the quality of the Brandy itself.

As the map on p.556 shows, the Armagnac production area is divided into three: Haut Armagnac to the east, Ténarèze in the middle, and Bas Armagnac to the west, spilling over into the Landes department. Three-quarters of Brandy production comes from this last area, whose sandy, clay soil produces softer Brandies than the more robust Ténarèze and the coarser Haut Armagnac. Both red and white wines are made in the region, but only the white is used for distillation. The grapes most commonly grown are the Folle Blanche, well known also in the Charente and the Baco.

DISTILLATION Unlike Cognac, the Armagnac Brandy is only distilled once, and in a continuous still, the *alambic armagnacais*. The system is not unlike that used for producing Grain Whisky in Scotland. Armagnac is distilled at a lower strength than Cognac: at not more than 10 over proof compared with up to 25 for the latter. Average production per year is about 18,000 hl. of pure alcohol —about 8 per cent of the comparable production in the Charente.

The young spirit has to be kept for a minimum of three years in large casks made from the local oak, before being bottled in the special, flat-sided bottles, the *basquaisè*, peculiar to Armagnac but resembling the German *bocksbeutel*. The three-star quality (the Cognac ratings are often used) will average five years age, the V.S.O.P.s are about ten years old, and the X.O. or Hors d'Age go up fifteen to twenty-six years. Armagnac does not generally improve much over twenty-five years, but there are fine old exceptions.

Although sold under a number of brand names, nearly half the production is carried out in one or other of the eleven co-operatives which distil the local wine. The production centre is Éauze, where the Union of co-operatives has its headquarters, but the main commercial town is Condom, where several firms have their premises.

FLAVOUR Armagnac is usually more powerfully flavoured, though alcoholically no stronger, than Cognac; it often has a taste reminiscent of prunes. Generally less "commercial" and lower priced than its rival, Armagnac is a clean Brandy, to be recommended particularly to those who like plenty of flavour in their spirits. It can be very mellow and fine, although at the top end of the quality scale it must yield to fine old Cognac.

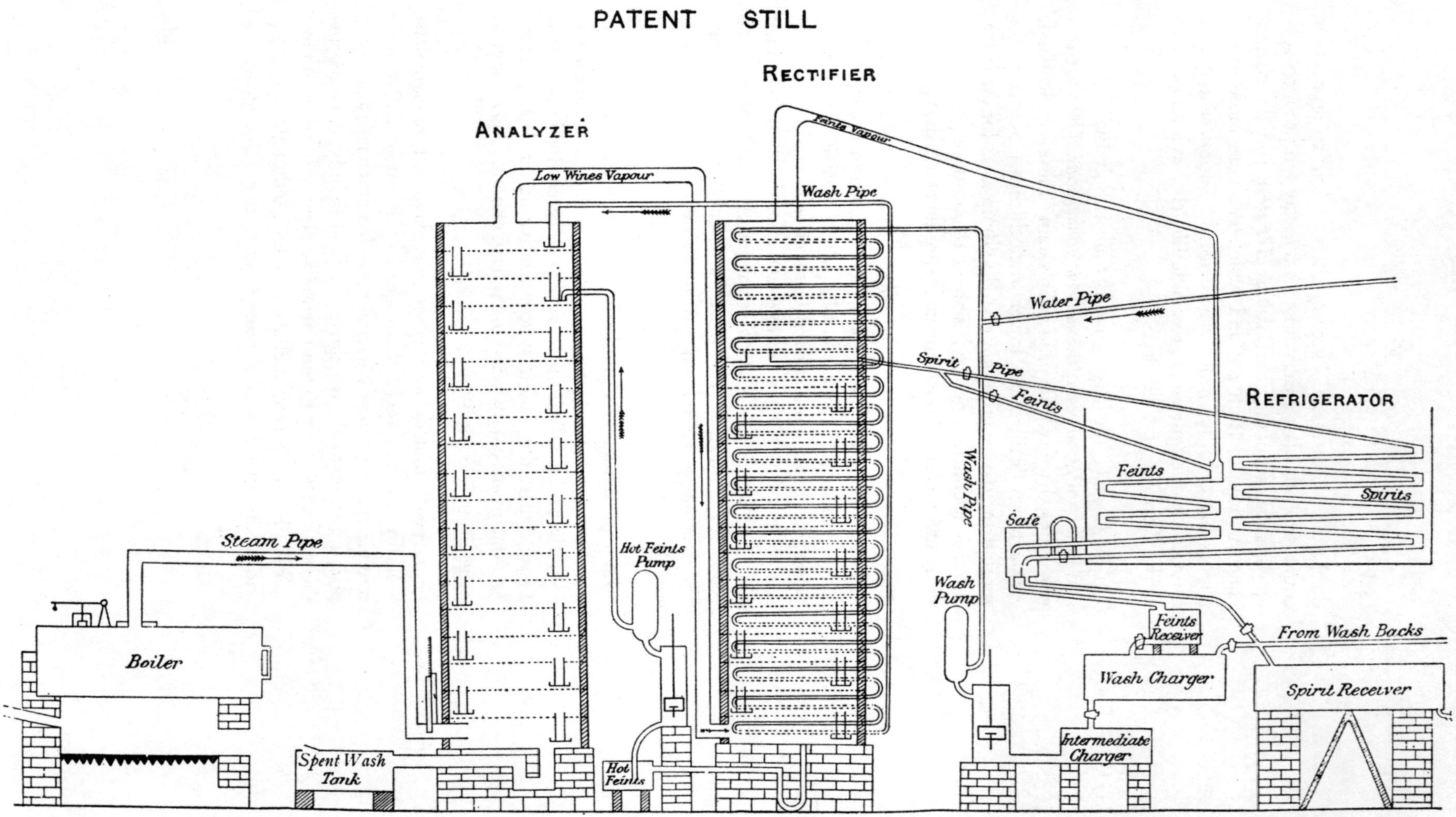

PATENT STILL

RECTIFIER

REFRIGERATOR

Spirits

Feints

Water Pipe

Spirit Pipe

Feints

Wash Pipe

Wash Pump

Feints Receiver

Wash Charger

From Wash Backs

Spirit Receiver

Intermediate Charger

Safe

Feints Vapour

Wash Pipe

ANALYZER

Low Wines Vapour

Hot Feints Pump

Hot Feints

Spent Wash Tank

Steam Pipe

Boiler

VERTICAL SECTION OF COFFEY'S DISTILLING APPARATUS

WHISKY

Whisky can be described as a spirit made from starch. The word whisky comes from the Gaelic *uisgue beatha* which means "Water of life". Scotland has for long been the chief centre of the whisky-distilling industry, though it is true that Whisky was first produced in Ireland. It is Scotch Whisky, however, that has become world famous as a beverage and stimulant.

Although "whisky" and "whiskey" are both used it is usual in Britain to find "whisky" for Scotch and "whiskey" for Irish. In America "whiskey" is more commonly used for both; in Canada and Australia it is "whisky".

Whisky is drunk throughout the Anglo-Saxon world and is now steadily increasing in popularity in Continental countries such as France, Sweden, Belgium and Germany.

Scotch Whisky

The story of Scotch Whisky is both romantic and remarkable. There is romance in its history, which stretches back through centuries and which has left its mark in Scotland's culture, in song and ballad, verse and prose. There is romance, too, in the legends that have survived the stormy years when Excise Duty was first introduced, bringing a feud between distillers and revenue men, when the Scot used all his ingenuity and his wit to fight what he believed to be a monstrous attack on his right to make whisky.

More recently, there has been the remarkable success story that has seen the national drink of a tiny country, which had its origins on highland farms, grow to international stature. Today, Scotch Whisky, exported to more than 160 countries throughout the world, can justly claim to be the best-known drink in the world, drunk and appreciated in every continent and every civilised country. For many years it was popular mainly in English-speaking countries; first in the Dominions of the British Empire which gave Scotch its first big overseas market, and later in America. Since the last war, however, Scotch Whisky has become a fashionable drink throughout the countries of the Common Market, in Scandinavia and Latin America. France, Belgium and Germany are now large consumers, ranking with, and in some cases outstripping, traditional markets like Canada, Australia and New Zealand. In the last year or two even the countries of Eastern Europe have shown growing interest in Scotland's greatest export and it is now being shipped behind the Iron Curtain.

THE SECRET OF SUCCESS

In countries like America, Scotch Whisky sells well against competition from locally produced whiskies. In others, like France, it has become popular in spite of stringent laws which prevent it being advertised. There can be no doubt that the main reason for this success is the distinctive flavour of Scotch. Many attempts have been made in different countries to imitate this flavour, but all have failed. The very fact that such attempts have been made—other whiskies have never been subjected to this particular form of flattery—is proof that the main appeal of Scotch lies in its unique flavour.

It has, of course, other properties as well which commend it to the drinker. It is a versatile drink suitable for all climates from the arctic to the tropical. Reputable brands of Scotch may also be relied on to maintain a consistent flavour and quality. Again, Scotch has the reputation of being a "clean" drink which, unless it is drunk to excess, has no unpleasant or injurious after-effects. Indeed, it is frequently prescribed by doctors for patients who may take no other form of alcohol and especially for those suffering from circulatory diseases.

TYPES OF SCOTCH WHISKY

Although it is now so widely drunk, surprisingly few people know anything about Scotch Whisky, except perhaps the name of their favourite brand. The nature of the processes by which it is made, the difference between whisky and other spirits, and the various types of Scotch produced, are not generally known. There are in Scotland 110 distilleries and 98 of these produce Malt Whisky by the traditional Pot Still method. The remainder make Grain Whisky by the Patent Still process, which was invented in 1831. Some of the different whiskies made by these distilleries are bottled and sold as "single" whiskies, but the vast majority of the branded whiskies on sale today are blends, in other words, they are a blend of malt and grain whiskies.

MALT WHISKY

Malt Whisky is made solely from malted barley by a process which has remained virtually unchanged since the first Scotch Whisky was made many hundreds of years ago. There are four recognised types:

HIGHLAND MALTS—made in the area north of the line from Dundee to Greenock.

LOWLAND MALTS—made in distilleries south of that line.

ISLAY MALTS—from the Isle of Islay.

CAMPBELTOWN MALTS—from the town of that name in the Mull of Kintyre.

The process of making malt whisky may be divided into three stages—germination, fermentation and distillation. Firstly, the barley is passed through cleaning machinery and then stored until it is needed. Next it is soaked in burn water, which must be at the correct temperature, for two or perhaps three days until it is soft. It is then spread on the malting floor where it begins to germinate.

This stage may take eight to twelve days and about three times every day the barley is turned to control the speed of germination and to prevent mould forming. Large wooden shovels known as shiels are used to turn the barley so that the grain will not be bruised. As the days pass, the grain starts to sprout and the starch in the barley begins to be converted to sugar ready to feed the shoots. But germination has to be halted before this process goes too far, and the malted barley or green malt as it is called is dried in a kiln and the growth stops.

PEAT REEK

The kiln is heated by a peat fire and the aroma of the burning peat, known as peat reek, is absorbed by the barley at this time and gives Scotch Whisky much of its characteristic flavour. The dried malt from the kiln is then placed in large bins, where it is left to rest for three or four weeks and allowed to cool.

When the time has come for it to be used, the malted barley goes to the mill where it is crushed and the resulting grist is then taken to the mash tun—a cast iron vessel some 20 feet wide—where it is mixed with hot water in order to extract the sugar. After some hours the sweet liquor, or wort, is drained off, but nothing is wasted, the draff, or residue, being taken away and used as cattle food.

FERMENTATION	The wort is then cooled and passes to the tun room for fermenting. The tuns are great wooden vessels about 18 feet high and 12 feet across made of larch or Oregon pine. Each tun may hold from 2,000 to 12,000 gallons. At this stage the fermenting agent, yeast, is added and, working on the sugary liquid, it converts all the sugar into raw spirit.

During fermentation the liquid bubbles and froths and wooden rotating arms, called switchers, are fitted near the top of each tun to prevent the liquid overflowing. These arms spin round and from time to time the liquid is agitated with a perforated board called a rouse which is fitted to the end of a long pole.

Fermentation takes about forty-eight hours and at the end of that time the liquid, or wash, contains about 10 per cent low-strength alcohol, some yeast and the by-products of fermentation. After each fermentation the tuns are cleaned, and small besoms made of heather from the nearby hills are fastened to long poles and used to scrub down the walls of the tuns.

DISTILLATION	Malt whisky is distilled twice, first in the Wash Still and then in the Spirit Still. The spirit, which has a lower boiling-point than water, is driven off as a vapour and then condensed back as a liquid.

The Wash Still and the Spirit Still stand side by side; large copper vessels, with the fires beneath them. In the Wash Still the crude whisky is separated and the yeast and other unfermentable matter is eliminated. The Wash Still is heated by a naked fire and inside the Still is what is called a rummager—four rotating arms carrying a copper chain mesh which is dragged round the bottom of the Still to prevent the solid particles of the wash from sticking and burning.

The alcohol from the Wash Still is known as low wines and when no more alcohol is left in the Still the process is stopped and the residue, called pot ale, is removed. The Wash Still is then recharged and distillation begins again.

The low wines from the Wash Still contain impurities and must be redistilled in the Spirit Still. It is here that the skill of the stillman comes to the fore. The first and last runs from the Spirit Still—the foreshots and feints—are not considered from the point of view of the high standard of the distiller to be suitable for drinking, and it is up to the stillman to decide when to switch the flow of spirit into the spirit receiver. The foreshots and feints are held back and returned for further distillation with the next batch of low wines from the Wash Still.

Although all malt whiskies are made by the Pot Still process, they differ considerably among themselves in flavour and character. No one has ever produced a satisfactory explanation for this. Obviously, geographical location, the quality of the water used, and the type of peat are contributory factors. And yet there are in one part of Scotland two malt distilleries separated only by a road which draw their water from the same sources, but the whiskies they produce are entirely different in character. This matter is enlarged upon later in this article.

GRAIN WHISKY

Grain whisky differs from malt whisky in two respects; it is made from a mixture of malted barley and unmalted cereals, usually barley and maize; a Patent Still is used for the third stage in the production process, distillation.

Whereas the Pot Still process is an intermittent method of distillation, the Patent Still works continuously and the alcohol in the wash is vaporised by steam. The process has also a rectifying element and the distillate therefore lacks some of the secondary constituents to be found in Malt Whisky. As a result Grain Whisky is milder in flavour than Malt Whisky, but it is, nevertheless, true Scotch Whisky and in no sense a neutral spirit.

MATURATION

After it has been distilled, all Scotch Whisky, malt as well as grain, is filled into wooden casks and stored in bonded warehouses to mature. This is usually done at the distillery where the whisky has been made and clusters of low buildings in which vast stocks of whisky are stored may be seen around most of Scotland's distilleries. Maturation is accepted as an essential process in the production of Scotch Whisky. After distillation the spirit contains certain undesirable secondary constituents and these may only be removed by slow evaporation. It follows that, while maturing, the whisky must be stored in casks made of a porous material. Long experience has shown that oak wood casks are the most suitable and casks which have previously contained Sherry have been found particularly good for this purpose. The temperature and humidity of the air where the whisky matures are also extremely important and the soft, mild climate of the Scottish highlands is known to give the best results.

New whisky kept in casks in this way becomes, after a sufficient period, a pleasant mellow spirit having lost all undesirable fiery characteristics. The time taken to achieve this varies for every different whisky. Malt whiskies are frequently left maturing for as long as fifteen years and some will continue to improve even after that. But there is a danger that after twenty years or so they may acquire traces of "woodiness". Grain whisky, being milder spirit, and because there has been an element of rectifying in its distillation, does not require so long to mature.

Since evaporation is essential to maturation, some whisky must be lost during the process. It has been estimated that on the average a cask will lose 15 per cent of its contents over the whole period that it is in the warehouse. As stocks of whisky now maturing in Scotland are over 460 million gallons, it follows that over 10 million gallons are lost each year by evaporation. The Scots are well known as a thrifty race with a great love of their whisky, and they would certainly not countenance such wastage if they did not know it was essential to the production of a really high quality whisky.

BLENDING   It was said earlier that the vast majority of branded Scotch Whiskies on sale today are "blends"; in other words, they are made of malt and grain whiskies blended together. For many centuries the traditional drink of the Scotsman was Malt Whisky made in a Pot Still, and a number of single Malt Whiskies are still bottled and marketed today. They are still popular in Scotland and in recent years there has been growing appreciation for them south of the border. It was only after blending started in about 1860, however, that "Scotch" began to be drunk outside Scotland, and it is blended whiskies that have built up the great reputation and world-wide markets of Scotland's national drink.

A blended whisky may contain between twenty and forty different single whiskies, and the art of the blender requires considerable skill and judgment which can only be acquired after long experience. A firm of whisky blenders will own large stocks of different whiskies purchased at the time the spirit was distilled and allowed to mature in warehouses at the distilleries. When any particular batch of whisky is mature and deemed ready to be called forward to the blending centre, it is sampled— a tenth of a gallon is drawn duty free and sent to the blender, who assembles a sample from each cask earmarked for his firm.

Blenders rarely taste whisky as they are able to judge the quality and characteristics of whisky by its smell alone. In the quiet of his sample room the blender "noses" each individual sample. If he is in doubt he may either taste or reject outright. What is this expert looking for? He looks for woodiness imparted by a faulty cask; hardness caused by the wrong type of wood; alien flavours caused by contamination. In the larger firms sometimes two or three experts are in daily attendance in the sample room, checking one another and making absolutely certain that the whisky is up to standard. Fortunately, rejects are few owing to the selected high quality of the wood used and the careful checks that are made at the distillery, both while the whisky is being distilled and while it is maturing in the warehouses.

Blending is not a haphazard mixture of any malts with any grains, but a great art. Each individual blender carefully follows a formula of his own with a definite standard of quality and character in mind. He decides the quantities of each whisky to be mixed and when a particular whisky is ready for blending. Every firm keeps secret the proportion of its blend.

The object of blending is to produce a whisky for sale to the public which is uniform year after year. Since single whiskies are not precisely uniform, the blender must work to a standard, and it is only his skill that enables him to produce whisky conforming to this standard consistently year after year. Moreover, experience has shown that Pot Still Malt Whisky is apt to be too strongly flavoured for most people in sedentary occupations, and the demand for something milder in flavour and more suited to conditions of life today can only be met by blending Malt Whisky with Grain Whisky, which has less pronounced characteristics.

Finally, blending is in no sense a dilution. On the contrary, the malts and grains combine to bring out the respective flavours of each in a harmonious whole.

BOTTLING

After blending, the whisky is put once again into casks where it is left to "marry", a process which may take several months and which allows the constituent whiskies in the blend to become intimately united. Some firms prefer to vat their malts and their grains separately, leaving them to marry before bringing the two together for bottling. There is no common formula and practice varies from firm to firm.

When the blended whisky is ready for bottling it is reduced in strength by the addition of a soft water. After distillation whisky is completely colourless, but it acquires a certain amount of colour if it is matured in a cask that has previously held Sherry. Blending firms try to maintain a consistent colour in their whiskies year after year, and to achieve this a very small amount of caramelised sugar is added at this stage. The whisky is then carefully filtered and poured by automatic or semi-automatic machines into bottles which are then sealed, labelled and packed. The type of seal may be a cork, a cap of the screw, lever or pilfer-proof type, or other patent closure.

Most Scotch Whiskies are marketed at home and abroad in branded bottles, and in recent years there has been an increasing tendency for these to be packed in fibreboard cases. For a number of overseas markets, however, the traditional wooden case is still sometimes used.

There are certain countries to which, in order to obtain benefits of a lower import tax, it has been found preferable to export in bulk. In these instances the blended whisky, either at original strength or suitably reduced, is exported in casks of varying size according to the market and the bottling is carried out by the distributors or agents of the blenders in the country concerned.

PROOF STRENGTH
Proof strength is a technical standard by which the strength of spirit is measured. Hundreds of years ago, spirit of this strength was proved when whisky and gunpowder were mixed and ignited. If the gunpowder flashed, then there was enough whisky in the mixture to permit ignition. Such whisky was held to have been proved. If the spirit was weaker than this proof strength, ignition did not take place. In the 1740s the Customs and Excise and the London distillers began to use Clark's hydrometer, an instrument devised to measure spirit strength. A more accurate version by Bartholomew Sikes was universally adopted under the Hydrometer Act, 1818, and is in standard use today.

The Customs and Excise Act of 1952 defined spirits of proof strength as follows:

"Spirits shall be deemed to be at proof if the volume of the ethyl alcohol contained therein made up to the volume of the spirits with distilled water has a weight equal to that of twelve-thirteenths of a volume of distilled water equal to the volume of the spirits, the volume of each liquid being computed as at fifty-one degrees Fahrenheit." (Clause 172(2).)

In other words, proof spirit means that the spirit at a temperature of 51°F weighs exactly twelve-thirteenths of a volume of distilled water equal to the volume of the spirit.

The strength at which whisky is usually sold on the U.K. market is 30° under proof and contains therefore 70 per cent of spirit of proof strength.

After distillation whisky is considerably stronger than 70° proof and so water has to be added after it is blended to bring it down to the right strength for bottling. Some whiskies, particularly single malts, are bottled at higher proof strength, either 75° or 85° proof, or in some cases 100° proof. The normal strength of 70° proof is dictated by economics and not by general desire, because the duty levied on a bottle of Scotch Whisky would be much higher if it were bottled at higher strength. Most whisky for export is, in fact, bottled at 75° proof.

AGE   The question of age sometimes causes confusion when Scotch Whisky is being talked about. By law, whisky may not be sold in Britain until it has matured for a minimum of three years. The blenders of reputable brands, however, are all aware that a longer period than this is necessary to maintain the highest standards of quality and most of the whiskies which they use in their blends are allowed to mature for a very much longer period than this minimum. Some brands, particularly the more expensive de-luxe brands, state on the bottle the age of the whisky it contains. By law, any age thus stated must be the age of the youngest whisky in the blend. It is not permissible to give an average. As we have said earlier, some whiskies, particularly grain whiskies, do not require a long period of maturation to reach their best and they may be quite ready for blending after as little as four or five years. Nevertheless, the malt whiskies with which they are blended will almost certainly be considerably older than this and, in general, one might say that the average age of the whiskies in a standard blend would probably be between six and seven years.

It should be remembered that the maturing of whisky is necessarily a costly process, since it involves having a large capital investment tied up for many years. There is also the loss of whisky by evaporation, which has already been mentioned. It follows that older whiskies must be more expensive and this is why de luxe brands in which the blend is made up of older whiskies are sold at a higher price than ordinary standard brands.

IMMATURE WHISKY Although whisky cannot be sold in the home market until it is at least three years old, there is no legislation to prevent immature spirit being exported. It may not be exported as Scotch Whisky, but must be described as Plain British Spirits. A small quantity of new Scotch Whisky does leave the country each year in this form. On arrival abroad it is often bottled and sold as Scotch, very often with the addition of large quantities of local spirits. Admixtures of this type are marketed in many countries abroad, usually with labels designed to mislead the public into believing that they are genuine Scotch Whiskies.

Although the quantity of immature whisky exported for this purpose is small—equalling only about 1 per cent of all exports, reputable blenders are aware that it could do great damage to the reputation of Scotch Whisky. This is particularly true in countries where Scotch is still a relatively new drink and where people are not able to distinguish between genuine Scotch and inferior imitations. The Scotch Whisky Association, aware of this danger, has been campaigning for several years to have legislation passed which would prevent this abuse by banning the export of immature whisky. So far the British Government has been deaf to this appeal, but fortunately the governments of several foreign countries have proved more foreseeing. Many of them have already passed domestic legislation preventing the import of whisky, unless it can be proved to be mature. The usual age requirement is three, four or sometimes five years.

The people who drink or serve Scotch Whisky in countries abroad should, however, always take great care to ensure that the Scotch Whisky they buy or sell is of a reputable brand that has been properly matured. As a general indication, it is fair to say that one should be suspicious of any whisky offered at a price well below that which the ordinary standard brands command in the market.

Once it has been bottled, Scotch Whisky does not improve with age, nor does it deteriorate. This must be stressed because many people are misled by popular fallacies on this point. Some people in the whisky trade believe that after about two years in bottle "Scotch" may acquire traces of "bottle character". This is a matter of opinion, but even if it is true, "bottle character" is imperceptible to the average consumer and in no way harms the whisky.

Unlike many drinks, "Scotch", once it has been bottled, does not need to be stored under any special conditions. Neither heat nor cold affects it, and although extreme cold may cause it to become cloudy, this cloudiness will disappear as soon as the whisky is brought back to normal temperature. There are no rigid conventions on how "Scotch" should be drunk. In Scotland the majority of people probably prefer to take their whisky with an equal amount of water, but many people drink it neat, or with soda, or ice, or sometimes both. Because of its distinctive flavour, "Scotch", unlike other spirits, has not made its reputation as a mixing drink, in other words, as a base for cocktails. Nevertheless, there are several cocktails in which Scotch whisky is one of the principal ingredients, for example, "Rob Roy" which is basically a mixture of "Scotch" and Italian Vermouth, and "Derby Fizz" in which "Scotch", Curaçao and lemon juice are combined with egg, sugar and soda. "Whisky Mac", a simple mixture of "Scotch" and Green Ginger Wine, is also very popular especially in cold climates. A famous drink, traditional in Scotland, is "Atholl Brose", and this is made of whisky, honey and oatmeal.

While dealing with the subject of serving "Scotch", the opportunity may be taken to debunk another fallacy which is still current. This is the notion that whisky should not be drunk with oysters or other shellfish. There is absolutely no foundation for this ancient superstition. Doubters can easily prove this for themselves by personal experiment.

The Scottish dish of *Haggis*, served with mashed potatoes and turnips, is not complete without Scotch Whisky taken either

U

at bottling strength from a liqueur glass or poured from a liqueur glass over the *Haggis*. Either way brings out the unique flavour of this traditional Scottish fare.

THE CHOICE
OF BLENDS

Well over 100 brands of Scotch Whisky are marketed in Great Britain and there are some 2,000 brands registered for export only. This is not surprising. Since the whisky produced at each distillery varies in flavour and character, and as there are over 100 distilleries, the blender has a virtually unlimited number of combinations of whisky at his disposal.

In the circumstances it is clearly impossible to advise anyone on which whisky he should drink. A choice of blend must always be entirely a matter of personal preference. Some people like their whisky to have more body, others less; some prefer it sweeter, others not so sweet. Indeed, there are connoisseurs of whisky who will ask for a different brand in different seasons, in different places or at different times of day. A whisky that one relishes after a day's fishing in the Highlands many not appeal so much on a hot summer's day in London. A man taking two or three drinks at a pre-lunch party may well choose a different brand later in the day for the drink he wishes to savour and enjoy at his leisure after dinner.

The only advice one can give to the man or woman who wishes to enjoy Scotch Whisky to the full is that they should learn by experiment and experience which brands suit them best. In passing, one should perhaps explain that the "de luxe" brands of Scotch, which cost slightly more, are sometimes known as liqueur whiskies, but this is a misnomer. They are in no sense liqueurs, but are produced by exactly the same process as all other whiskies.

THE FLAVOUR
OF SCOTCH
WHISKY

It has already been said that the reputation of Scotch Whisky and its growing popularity are based to a large extent on its flavour. Other countries, for example Ireland, America and

576

Canada, have their own whiskies which are drunk and appreciated at home, but none of these have had even a fraction of the success outside their borders as Scotch enjoys. At the present time, for instance, exports of all American whisky, Bourbon as well as Rye, are only equal to about 2½ per cent of Scotch Whisky exports, and almost half of that amount is shipped to neighbouring Canada.

As already mentioned earlier in this article, many people in many countries have tried to produce a spirit like Scotch Whisky. In some cases they have gone to fantastic lengths to imitate its flavour and characteristics—building distilleries identical to those in Scotland, photographing and reproducing Stills and other plant, seeking out sources of water as similar as possible to the Highland burns, even hiring men from Scottish distilleries to run their own. Elsewhere scientists have boasted openly that with modern techniques of water analysis and process control they would be able to produce good quality "Scotch" in their laboratories. These attempts have all ended in failure and often in expensive failure for the instigator.

The truth is that no one fully understands why Scotch Whisky has its distinctive and inimitable flavour. Even scientists have now recognised that there is an elusive quality in "Scotch" which defies analysis, an element of mystery which has long been accepted by poets and writers and indeed by all who know and love their whisky.

Of course many theories and partial explanations have been advanced. Water is probably the most important single factor in deciding character and flavour. The water best loved of distillers is soft and from red-granite streams. Certainly they guard their water supplies most jealously, and as the water supplies vary in the north of Scotland so do the whiskies with them. Adjoining distilleries with water supplies very close to each other are known to produce two quite different whiskies, and it is a commonplace of daily life that water from different areas can make all the difference in the world in even so simple a process as making tea.

The peat used in drying the malt certainly affects the character of the whisky. It is customary to remark the "peaty" or "smoky" bouquet and flavour of many Scotch Whiskies. The explanation given is that the peaty emanations with which the malt becomes impregnated during drying pass through the operations in a more or less chemically unchanged condition, thus imparting distinctive characters to the whiskies. This is especially so when the usual forms of Pot Stills are used for distillation.

The most likely explanation is that, besides the water and ethyl alcohol which are the main constituents of Scotch whisky, there are small but variable amounts of other constituents and it is these which impart the characteristic flavours and aroma to the spirit. These constituents are rarely more than one-half per cent of the ethyl alcohol and they are best described as secondary products.

When the wort is prepared, other substances besides the sugar are obtained in solution and from these the secondary constituents are derived, both directly and indirectly. The exact nature of these is not fully understood, but it is argued that they are some of the essential oils naturally existing in the malt and other cereals, together with the peaty bodies incorporated during the drying. The volatile secondary products pass over with the alcohol into the low wines receiver on the distillation of the wash, although a portion escapes with the spent lees. The extent to which the secondary constituents may be retained, thus affecting the character of the whisky, largely depends on the variety of Pot Still used and the manner of its operation.

The Scottish climate, too, plays its part in producing the flavour and bouquet of Scotch Whiskies, and achieves its greatest influence during the maturing process. Then the pure fresh air of the Highlands, permeating the casks in the warehouse, works on the whisky, helping to mature it, and bears off undesirable secondary constituents at just that rate which ensures the smooth mellow qualities expected in Scotch Whisky. The climate also is important during the earlier stages of manufacture, and even during the temperate Scottish summer distilling

578

stops, temperatures then being too high for successful operation of the plant. The period from autumn to late spring or early summer constitutes the distilling season, when climatic conditions are most suitable for distilling. Finally, in leading to differences between Scotch and other whiskies, must be mentioned the skill and experience of the men engaged in the manufacture of Scotch Whisky. The production of Scotch is much more an art than a manufacturing process, and an art which requires above all a certain quality of water found only in parts of Scotland.

Scotch Whisky Distilleries in Scotland

HIGHLAND MALT

Aberfeldy	Dalwhinnie
Aberlour-Glenlivet	Dufftown-Glenlivet
Ardmore	Edradoui
Aultmore	Fettercairn
Balblair	Glen Albyn
Balmenach-Glenlivet	Glenallachie
Blavenie	Glenburgie-Glenlivet
Banff	Glencadam
Ben Nevis*	Glendronach
Benriach-Glenlivet	Glendullan
Benrinnes	Glen Elgin
Benromach	Glenfarclas-Glenlivet
Ben Wyvis	Glenfiddich
Blair Athol	Glenglassaugh
Royal Brackla	Glengoyne
Caperdonich	Glen Grant – Glenlivet
Cardow	Glen Keith-Glenlivet
Clynelish	Glenlivet
Coleburn	Glenlochy
Convalmore	Glenlossie
Cragganmore	Glen Mhor
Craigellachie-Glenlivet	Glenmorangie
Dailuaire	Glenmoray-Glenlivet
Dallus Dhu	Glenrothes-Glenlivet
Dalmore	Glen Spey
Glentauchers	Mortlach

	Glenturret	North Port
	Glenugie	Oban
	Glenury-Royal	Ord
	Highland Park	Pulteney
	Hillside	Royal Lochnagar
	Imperial	Scapa
	Inchgower	Speyburn
	Isle of Jura	Speyside
	Knockando	Strathisla-Glenlivet
	Knockdhee	Strathmill
	Linkwood	Talisker
	Loch Lomond	Tamdhu
	Lochside*	Tamnavulin-Glenlivet
	Longmorn-Glenlivet	Teaninich
	Macallan	Tomatin
	MacDuff	Tomintout-Glenlivet
	Millburn	Tormore
	Miltonduff-Glenlivet	Tullibardine
LOWLAND MALT	Auchentoshan	Littlemill
	Bladnoch	Moffat*
	Glenkinchie	Rosebank
	Inverleven	St. Magdalene
	Kinclaith	
ISLAY MALT	Ardbeg	Caol Ila
	Bowmore	Lagavulin
	Bruichladdich	Laphroaig
	Bunnahabhain	Port Ellen
CAMPBELTOWN MALT	Glen Scotia	Springbank
GRAIN	Ben Nevis*	Lochside*
	Caledonian	Moffat*
	Cambus	North British
	Cameronbridge	Port Dundas
	Carsebridge	Strathclyde
	Dumbarton	Strathmore ("North of Scotland")
	Girvan Grain	
	Invergordon	

* The distillers thus marked produce both Highland Malt and Grain

Irish Whiskey

The word whiskey or whisky is an anglicisation and abbreviation of the Irish or Gaelic words *uisgue-beatha* (or *uisee baugh*)—pronounced *issge-baha* or *issge-baw*—meaning "water of life". It is generally accepted that the Irish first discovered this popular spirit. The art of distillation is, of course, based on the fact that alcohol boils at a lower temperature than water (to be exact, at 170°F as against 212° for water), so that if a fermented mixture is heated the earlier vapour given off and condensed is largely alcohol. It is probable that the Chinese were acquainted with this art and the Persians and Arabs used it for distilling perfume. The extant works of Aristotle, philosopher and tutor of Alexander the Great, who lived 500 years before Christ, contain a description of distilling, and it was known in the Mediterranean basin at an early date. It is not known how or when the knowledge came to Ireland, whether through the incursions of the Phoeniceans, the Milesians, the Firbolgs, or the Tuatha de Danaan, or whether it was discovered there.

An Irish legend states that St. Patrick, who went to Ireland 1,500 years ago, first taught the Irish the art of distillation. Certainly the manufacture of spirits from grain was known to the inhabitants 800 years ago, at the time of the invasion of Ireland during the reign of Henry II. Doubtless the spirit made from native grains was similar to the whiskey which is made today. Thus the art of whiskey-making has been practised for very many hundreds of years in Ireland, and there are authorities both there and in Scotland who consider it probable that Ireland is the birthplace of whiskey, and that whiskey first came to Scotland from Ireland.

People all over the world have always produced a native beverage based on materials available to them. Where vines grew, wine was evolved and afterwards its distillate, brandy; where apples were plentiful cider resulted and its distillate, calvados; rum from the sugar cane; koumis from goat's milk; saki from rice; arrack from the palm; the list is legion. In Ireland, where barley, one of the earliest cultivated cereals in Western Europe, flourished, the Irish made a strong beer and its distillate, whiskey. The history, then, of whiskey-making in Ireland goes back a long way. The Annals of the Four Masters has a reference to it under the date 1406. We find an Elizabethan chronicler, Richard Stanihurst, who was admitted to Oxford in 1563, describing its attributes in glowing phrases and recommending it as a panacea. John Marston's play *The Malcontent* produced in London in 1604 contains a stanza:

> "The Dutchman for a drunkard,
> The Dane for golden locks,
> The Irishman for *uisce baugh*,
> The Frenchman for the pox."

It is recorded that Sir Walter Raleigh, on his last voyage to the West Indies in 1617, called in to Youghal and was provisioned by John Boyle 1st Earl of Cork, the provisions including "a supreme present—a 32 gallon keg of his own *uisce baugh*".

Peter the Great of Russia declared: "Of all wines the Irish wine is the best."

Dr. Johnson's dictionary published in 1755 does not contain the word "whiskey" but lists "*usquebaugh*" as "a compounded distilled spirit . . . the Irish sort is particularly distinguished for its pleasant and mild flavour".

A Dublin wine and spirit merchant has records of correspondence with Charles Dickens, who bought his Irish Whiskey direct from Dublin, and Dr. W. G. Grace, the cricketer, prescribed an Irish Whiskey and soda for himself at the lunch interval and at close of play.

MANUFACTURE   The most important basic raw material for both Irish and Scottish whiskey is barley, which grows well in the moist climate of Ireland and Scotland, and provides distillers with an ingredient of the highest quality. It is therefore surprising that the flavours of Irish and Scotch whiskey are not more alike; and students and connoisseurs of whiskey (the Irish variety is usually spelt with an "e", whereas the Scotch is spelt without it) are interested in the cause of this difference.

The method of making Scotch is described on p. 565, and much interest will be found in comparing the Highland Pot Still Malt Distilleries with their counterparts in Ireland, since it is in the Pot Still that the distinctive flavours of both "Irish" and "Scotch" are born.

Barley is the principal ingredient of both Irish and Scotch whiskey, but it is the processing of this barley which contributes most perhaps to the difference in flavour of these two age-old whiskies. Malt for Scottish Pot Still Distilleries is kilned after germination by the application of peat smoke, whereas in Ireland it is dried by coal, which imparts virtually no flavour of its own. In addition to the use of highly flavoured malt the Highland Pot Still Distilleries use 100 per cent malt, whereas Irish Distilleries generally use in the mash only 25 to 50 per cent malted barley and 50 to 75 per cent of a mixed grist of unmalted cereals; barley, oats, wheat, and occasionally very small quantities of rye.

The fermenting process is similar in both countries, but the distillation processes vary considerably. Not only are Irish Pot Stills larger, the Stills holding up to 30,000 gallons, but there are more processes, as the Irish method is based on three distillations as against two for Scotch. The design of the still head, it is generally agreed, has considerable influence on the flavour of the distillate. Irish Pot Stills not only have unusually tall still heads, but often have a characteristic portion called the lyne arm between the head itself and the condenser or worm tub. The lyne arm (or lying-arm) is a long horizontal portion of the still head in which it lies submerged in a shallow trough filled with water. A return pipe, sometimes called the "foul-pipe", returns condensate from the lyne arm to the still and assists the distiller in the job of rectification and concentration of the weaker spirits.

Whereas Scottish Pot Still Distilleries have a Wash Still and a Low Wines Still, Irish distilleries have a second Low Wines Still, and three separate distillations are involved. The process is very complex. The distillate is divided into strong and weak fractions at each stage, and the strong fraction is sent forward whilst the weaker fraction is returned for further distillation. As a result a higher degree of rectification is achieved than might be expected in the Pot Still process.

Irish Whiskey is bonded both in casks which previously contained Sherry and in "plain" casks. The minimum age for removal from bond in Ireland for home consumption is three years, but the distillers generally mature it for considerably longer periods; there are several well-known brands with age guarantees of ten and twelve years' maturity.

Until recently it was traditional for most Irish Whiskey to be marketed as straight Pot Still whiskey. Blending with grain whiskey was uncommon, although blended Irish Whiskey has been sold ever since Aeneas Coffey, an Irishman, first invented the Column Still in 1830. Blends however are increasing in popularity, and today there is a range of Irish whiskies varying from the most full bodied to the very lighest blends.

EXCISE DUTY   In 1661 the Government of the day had the bright idea of imposing a duty on *usque baugh* and started with 4d. a proof gallon. They have progressed steadily since then! The licensing of distilling plant followed and by 1770 there were more than 1,000 licensed distillers in Ireland, "mostly men of little substance and no great honesty and well placed for defrauding the Revenue", in the words of a contemporary government report. Shortly after this, very small Stills were outlawed and the basis for raising Revenue was changed in order to encourage larger

584

production units. All the present Distillers in Ireland were established about this time, the late eighteenth or early nineteenth century, but the independent Irish were making whiskey or "poteen" in plenty, for in 1833 and 1834 no less than 10,000 illicit Stills were seized!

The legitimate industry was well established by the middle of the nineteenth century and the fame of Irish Whiskey was spreading all over the world. Revenue Duty was nominal, compared to present-day rates, so whiskey was cheap and plentiful. The twentieth century saw a rapid reduction in the number of Distilleries from twenty-seven in 1907 to four today, due mainly to fall in population and tremendous increase in duty. With the rapid fall in emigration figures and the possibility of increasing exports the present-day Distilleries, with up-to-date plant well capable of increasing production, look forward with confidence to the future, particularly if their Governments realise their economic importance to the farmers, the bottle and carton makers, coopers and other ancillary trades and to the country's balance of payments position.

While most Irishmen drink their Irish Whiskey diluted with water, there are many who prefer it with soda, and it is a mistake for a person tasting Irish Whiskey for the first time to take it with water rather than soda if *he is used to drinking other whiskies with soda*. The organoleptic qualities are probably better appreciated with water or indeed neat. The average Irish Pot Still whiskey, on general sale, is so smooth that it can be taken this way, and the fashion of serving an old Irish Whiskey neat as an after-dinner liqueur is growing with the connoisseur.

To those who appreciate good whiskey it is anathema to suggest a whiskey cocktail, and indeed there are few cocktails of real worth which one can make with whiskey. However, these can be honestly recommended:

Irish Whiskey Sour: Shake violently with chipped ice the juice of a lemon, a teaspoonful of sugar and little white of egg. Pour into glass, add 2 oz. of Irish whiskey and a little soda.

585

Irish Handshake: 2 parts Irish whiskey, 1 part Green Curaçao, 1 part fresh cream. Shake well with chipped ice and serve as cocktail.

The Leprechaun: 1 part Irish whiskey, 2 parts Tonic water. One twist of lemon peel. Serve over ice in a tall glass.

Now a word about *Irish Coffee* which is often so badly made. This is the correct method:

Preheat the stemmed glasses in which it should be served. Over 2 lumps of sugar and a jigger of Irish Pot Still whiskey pour *really hot* black coffee. Stir vigorously and top off with a layer of fresh cream poured gently over a spoon poised near the surface, or use slightly whipped cream. Do *not* stir or let the spoon into the glass. The charm of the drink is the hot punch-like coffee coming through the cool cream.

Canadian Whisky

HISTORY When the first settlers arrived in Canada they brought their own spirits along with them. To lessen the importation of wines and spirits, Jean Talon, the Intendant, established a brewery about the year 1668 in the infant colony of Ville Marie (later Montreal). There is evidence to support the contention that this brewery contained a Still, and it is therefore the earliest known distillery in Canada. As the years went by, the trade and shipping laws of the times, with the heavy duties on West Indian rums, were such that settlers on the East Coast and Inland Ports began distilling their own rum from molasses.

What might be termed the true birth of the Canadian distilling industry took place during the latter part of the eighteenth century when many grist mills situated throughout the grain farming areas adopted the practice of distilling spirits from the surplus grain. A few of these early grist mills produced whiskies of rare quality and their product became so popular that they abandoned the flour milling business and confined their efforts to producing whiskies. This whisky was of such subtle and distinctive character that the demand for it spread beyond the borders of Canada as early as 1861.

Although many changes have taken place since early times, some of our leading Canadian Distilleries of today had their beginning in the 1850s or earlier, and in the year 1965 there are twenty-nine Distilleries in Canada actively engaged in the production of distilled beverage products. From the modest beginnings of over 100 years ago the Distilleries in Canada have kept pace with the growth of the country. For the year ending 31st March, 1964, records show that over $90 million worth of potable spirits, practically all Canadian whisky, was exported and carried the name of "Canada" to over one hundred different countries throughout the world.

The Stills used by the early settlers were perforce of a crude design. Improvements in distilling were made as time and experience permitted, and as early as 1861 copper and brass Stills and other equipment were coming into use to replace the old wooden apparatus. The Stills in use in Canada today have benefited by research and are some of the most modern in existence. The current production figure of beverage spirits is now in excess of seventeen million proof gallons per year. Canadian Whisky, which comprises the greatest percentage of production, must by law be produced from grain, and matured in oak casks.

In conclusion, we feel that Canadian Whisky has for some time past taken its place as one of the four great types of whisky sold throughout the world. They are Scotch, Irish, American and Canadian.

Canadian Whisky is undoubtedly more widely distributed and sold in greater volume outside Canada than any type except Scotch.

It is a light, pleasant, well-made and mature spirit and its popularity throughout the world and especially in the United States of America is ever on the increase.

TYPES OF WHISKY

Canadian Whisky as produced and marketed today is manufactured from a mixture of cereal grains, normally corn (called maize in the United Kingdom), rye, and barley malt.

The general character of Canadian Whisky is obtained from the rye; consequently in Canada, Canadian Whisky is nearly always referred to by the public as Rye Whisky, although there is a recent trend to label the product "Canadian Whisky" rather than "Canadian Rye Whisky" or just plain "Rye Whisky".

Canadian Whisky is nearly always a blend of grain spirits generally produced from corn and barley malt—and a rye distillate obtained from the fermentation of a rye mash. The rye mash formula may be an extreme of 90 per cent rye grains and

588

10 per cent barley malt, through various formulae in which the rye content might be as low as 51 per cent, the remaining grains apart from barley malt being corn or perhaps part barley.

It is therefore apparent that Canadian Whisky can be compared with Scotch from the point of view that Scotch is normally a blend of grain whisky and malt whiskies of various types, and Canadian Whisky is a blend of grain spirits and rye type whisky, which has varying degrees of rye content, depending on the object of the distiller. In some cases the rye whisky content is very low. This is a modern trend, as Canadian Whisky has assumed an image of being a very light-bodied product. Canadian Whisky must by law be aged for a minimum of two years in small wood; in practice, none is sold under three years, the average age being about five years, and some as old as eight to ten years.

MANUFACTURE   It will be seen from our description of types of Canadian Whisky that a Canadian Whisky Distiller is mainly concerned with producing two types of spirits. Firstly grain spirits: these are produced in much the same way as Scotch grain whisky, normally from corn, that is, maize, and barley malt, the malt used being more akin to brewer's malt than the peat dried malt used in Scotland. The ground grain meal is normally pressure cooked to get the starch into solution, cooled and mixed with a small percentage of barley malt in order to convert the starch into sugar. The resultant sweet mash is pumped into fermenters complete, that is, the grain is not screened off in a mash tun as is common practice in Scotland.

In the fermenting vats a quantity of pure culture yeast is added, each distiller normally producing his own culture. The fermentation starts rapidly, and after approximately seventy-two hours the fermentation is completed, and the "beer," as it is called in Canada, is now ready for distillation. It contains (approximately) 12 per cent of proof spirits.

The "beer" is then passed through very elaborate continuous

distilling apparatus which purifies the spirit by removing undesirable products such as aldehydes and fusel oil. The resultant spirits are usually nearly neutral in character and of a very high strength up to 69° overproof. It is generally true to say that it is more neutral than Scotch Grain Whisky. These spirits, after being reduced in strength, may be blended with Rye whisky and barrelled off, or in some cases matured separately as straight spirits.

The rye distillate which is the other part of the final blend is treated in rather a different way: for technical reasons the rye meal is often not pressure cooked, otherwise the fermentation process is similar.

It is in the distillation that the process varies. We must realise here that it is largely from the whisky mash rather than the spirit mash that we expect to get the character of our whisky, therefore the whisky mash after being fermented into so-called "beer" is not normally exposed to anything like the degree of rectification in distillation as are spirits.

The Scotch distiller has the same object in mind when he passes his malt wash through various types of Pot Stills.

The Pot Still as such is no longer used in Canada for producing Canadian Whisky; however there are various types of modified rectifying stills of both the batch and continuous type used for the purpose. The design and method of operation are dictated by the individual distiller's requirements.

The spirits and whisky obtained from the above process are matured in small forty-gallon oak barrels charred on the inside; some distillers use a proportion of new wood. Spirits and whisky may be blended at the time of barrelling, or may be matured as single whiskies and blended and barrelled some months before they are required for bottling.

Taking a sample from Spirit safes in a Gin distillery.

facing p. 590

Cooperage at Denis Mounie, Cognac. In the foreground are traditional coopers' tools and the block is made from the hub of a carriage wheel of the Napoleonic period.

following p. 590

A Hennessy cooper having shaped the oak staves and ringed them together with iron hoops, then slaps the staves with water on the outside and places the skeleton barrel over a fire to bend the wood and form a spirit-tight container.

The Pot still in a Hennessy distillery. The distiller is awakened by his alarm clock at certain hours through the night to check the furnace temperature so as to ensure that every stage of the process is perfect.

following p. 590

The Mash Tun in a Highland distillery.

The Still House.

A Scotch Whisky bottling plant.

facing

American Whiskey

In earliest Colonial days in America, the most popular alcoholic beverage was Rum from Cuba and the West Indies. It wasn't until 1783 that whiskey distilling made its appearance. The Revolutionary War interrupted trade and cut off rum supplies, stimulating whiskey demand.

Farmers were the first distillers in the United States. Located in Ohio, Kentucky, Pennsylvania, Virginia and North Carolina, the farmer-distillers were isolated from the big Eastern cities by mountains and rugged, untravelled trails. Most of the country's founding fathers were farmers and distillers. Included among them were George Washington and Thomas Jefferson. Farmers used distilling as a method of conserving surplus grains. Lacking present-day methods of grain processing and storage, they had no way of preventing spoilage of surplus. By converting grain into whiskey, they solved the spoilage problem. What's more, a pack-horse travelling the rough trails east could carry the equivalent of more grain in the form of whiskey.

Highly desirable as a beverage, a medicine, and as a protection against the wintry wind, whiskey was accepted in many localities as a medium of exchange. Ironically, although frequently used as a medium of exchange, the Federal government refused to take it in payment of excise duty. This helped set off the spark which lighted the Whiskey Rebellion. On 3rd March 1791, the Federal Government levied a tax on spirits ranging from 7 to 30 cents a gallon, amounting to one-third the price of the article if paid in cash.

If the Government had taken whiskey in payment of excise, farmer-distillers would have accepted the tax. Instead, they resented being singled out for taxation which did not touch New England commercial interests. Farmer-distillers advocated a land tax, so as to put the burden on Eastern interests. Distillers in Western Pennsylvania refused to pay the tax. On 15th September, 1793, President George Washington ordered out troops to quell violence. This became known as the Whiskey Rebellion.

The Federal tax has risen from that original 7 cents a gallon to 10·50 dollars a gallon. With State and local taxes added, the total tax on spirits now represents more than half the price per bottle paid by the consumer.

BOURBON

While traditional American whiskies are Bourbon and Rye, Bourbon is by far the most popular product. Bourbon gets its name from Bourbon County, Kentucky. "Bourbon" was the name of the family which governed France, Spain, Sicily and Lucca around 1570. It is likely that Bourbon County got its name from this family.

Early American distillers chose the Blue Grass area of Kentucky as an ideal place to build distilleries. It abounded in limestone springs, the best water for making Bourbon. Dr. James Crow, a Scotsman, settled in Kentucky and built a distillery in 1835 at Frankfort. He was the first distiller using scientific methods to make Old Crow Bourbon. The Old Crow distillery is owned today by National Distillers, the oldest whiskey brand marketed today, and largest-selling straight whiskey in the country. Another great Bourbon is Old Grand-Dad, known as the "Head of the Bourbon Family". It came on the scene around 1880. Col. E. H. Taylor founded Old Taylor shortly after. It is one of the finest Kentucky Bourbons on the market today.

MANUFACTURE

There are five basic stages in the production of spirits: milling, mashing, fermentation, yeasting and distillation.

Milling: Quality of grain is important. Grain samples are taken and studied to make certain each shipment is of high standard.

592

The purpose of milling is to smash the grain kernel to release starch in cooking or mashing which follows.

Mashing: This is the next process. The ground meal is fed into mash tubs or pressure cookers. Here the meal is mixed with hot water and cooked to release the starch and render it more easily convertible into sugar. This cooked meal is now known as mash. It is cooled to receive the barley malt which is now added. Enzymes, microscopic miracle workers, convert the starch into fermentable sugar.

Fermentation: Now the malted mash is ready for fermentation. It is pumped through pipe coolers, cooled to approximately room temperature, and then fed into fermentors. A fermentor is a vessel in which fermentation takes place.

Yeasting: Now comes the important operation in fermentation—the addition to the mash of the pure culture of yeast. Purity of yeast is scrupulously guarded. It is prepared separately in equipment carefully protected by steam sterilisation from bacterial contamination. Through fermentation, yeast changes "sugar", previously created in the mash, into alcohol and other substances. When fermentation of the mash is complete the end result is called "beer".

Distillation: The purpose of distillation is to separate the alcohol from the other liquids and solids in the "beer". This is done by boiling the "beer" in a Still. The alcohol vaporises, rises and separates from the other materials. This vapour is then cooled. It condenses back into a liquid and is drawn off. The vapour leaving the top of the Still is cooled and condenses back into a liquid. It varies in proof from 90° to 130° proof and is fed into a kettle Still and re-distilled. This is called "doubling", further concentrated until the proof has been increased to that proof desired by the individual distillers within the range of 115° to 160° proof. Under government standards, if the proof is over 160° but below 190°, the product may not be designated as whiskey. If distilled at 190° proof or over, the product is "grain neutral spirits". It is from grain neutral spirits that gin and vodka are made.

Ageing: Whiskey which has come from the Still is now ready to be aged in warehouses until maturity. The time of maturity depends upon the taste result desired.

When the whiskey is "green" off the Still, it is colourless. The purpose of ageing is to allow time for the chemical elements in the whiskey to react upon the chemicals in the wood, giving the finished product the colour, taste, and aroma. Many distillers make whiskey to reach optimum quality after ageing, say, four, five or six years. In this case, ageing beyond the necessary period adds little or nothing to the product, and may even detract from its quality. To achieve quality ageing, two conditions must prevail: there must be perfectly charred new white oak barrels, and ideal warehousing conditions.

To increase stability, particularly against cold temperatures, all straight whiskey is refrigerated before bottling. Refrigeration with subsequent filtrations is designed to produce a uniform, stable whiskey of the highest quality.

Returning to what happens after the alcohol has been separated from the "beer": the remaining liquid, which contains the grain particles from which only the starch has been removed, is called "stillage". This "stillage", or grain residue, has all its original food value of proteins, minerals and vitamins without the starch. Nothing has been lost, but something gained. It has gained the additional food value of the added yeast. This residue is now recovered to produce feed for cattle, hogs, and poultry by removing the water from the "stillage".

Here is a brief glossary of types:

Whiskey is a beverage distilled from a fermented mash of grain at less than 190° proof. If it is four years old and 100° proof (50 per cent alcoholic content by volume) and made under government supervision, it is called "bottled-in-bond". Bourbon and Rye are the traditional American whiskies.

594

A straight Bourbon whiskey is one which has been distilled at not exceeding 160° proof from a mash of grain containing at least 51 per cent corn grain.

Rye whiskey is distilled from a fermented mash of grains containing at least 51 per cent rye grain.

Spirit blends or blended whiskies usually contains from 30 to 40 per cent aged whiskey, blended with 60 to 70 per cent. neutral spirits.

Grain neutral spirit is a fermented mash of grain distilled at 190° proof or over. It is "neutral" in taste, colour and aroma.

Australian Whisky

As with all other countries originally populated by emigrants from the United Kingdom, the distilling industry went hand-in-hand with the growth of the population.

Unlike Canada, which early on produced a distinctive type of whisky of its own, Australia was more inclined to follow the Scotch method, firstly producing Malt whisky and then a blend of malts and grains.

Although made on the Scotch pattern, Australian Whisky has a character of its own and, as mentioned in the article on Scotch Whisky, no country has ever succeeded in producing an exact imitation of Scotch.

Freight and duty virtually preclude importation of Australian Whisky into the United Kingdom.

GIN

Gin has had a remarkable success story. It has for over three centuries been immensely popular; it has given much happiness; induced great misery; been the cause of civil disorders; been attacked and denigrated; has achieved triumphant acceptance globally by prince and pleb, in pub and palace—and has contributed enormously to the Exchequer.

HISTORY   This drink, which was soon to become inextricably interwoven with English social history (its truly British national character is of more recent origin), started as a distillation from rye flavoured with juniper, perfected in the Low Countries at Leyden in the sixteenth century. From the French for juniper, *genièvre*, the new drink became known first as "Geneva" and thence was contracted by the English to "Gin".

Previously, the Dutch had been considerable distillers of raw and potent spirits with which the English soldiery were well acquainted and whose stimulating effects ("Dutch Courage") they much appreciated during damp, interminable campaigns in the Netherlands. The new drink, often known as "Hollands", was a great improvement and the infant English distilling industry began to make it.

Charles I brought the first measure of control into an unlicensed and disorganised business by founding the Worshipful Company of Distillers. Brewers were encouraged to distil from home-grown grain, but French brandy imports were also supported until the flight of James II to the Continent. One result of that was the cessation of legal brandy importation and an immense fillip to English distillers. Gin-drinking became patriotic; a form of spirituous patriotism to which Londoners in particular took with enthusiasm. From half a million gallons in 1690, by 1729 national consumption of Gin was approaching five million gallons. One in four Houses in the Cities of London and Westminster sold hard liquor; shops and hawkers retailed it; and there was a door-to-door delivery service.

Seeing the urban masses in that state of happy intoxication they considered their own prerogative, the ruling classes sought to reform the trade, and in 1729 imposed a tax on Gin and established licences for sellers. This put true Gin beyond the means of the great majority, but poor quality unflavoured spirit—called Parliamentary Brandy—was outside the scope of the regulations. So in 1733 an Act was passed that forbade the sale of spirits outside dwelling houses; the results were surely predictable.

Three years later Parliament introduced the only attempt in English history to impose "Prohibition". The new Gin Act banned the selling of Gin in lesser quantities than two gallons, with a duty of £1 per gallon plus a retail licence at a penal £50. This was the last straw and the London mob rioted. However, the law remained on the statute book for six years, during which time illicit distilling and sale were rife; numerous informers (the only way of enforcing the law) were murdered, and of the 12,000 convictions obtained few resulted in the collection of fines imposed. Revenue fell; drunkenness was widespread.

LONDON GIN   In 1743 came, at last, more sensible regulations, with the consequent encouragement for reputable distillers to produce pure

598

Gin. The only London firm in continuous business since then is Booth's (founded in 1740). But it is not to be thought that Gin suddenly became respectable. This was the era of Hogarth's "Gin Lane", of "Drunk for a penny, dead drunk for tuppence, clean straw for nothing" (a sign on a Shoreditch grog-shop), and of the scoundrel who ingeniously invented a primitive self-vendor in the shape of a cat's head—when two pennies were placed on the animal's tongue and it was asked to supply Gin, it obligingly shot a quantity of spirit into the applicant's receptacle. Gin was not the drink of the gentry (or only secretly by their ladies).

We do not know exactly what this London Gin was like. It was certainly more highly flavoured than the London Dry Gin of today, while probably less pungent than the aromatic Dutch Gin from which it had evolved and which has retained its high oil of juniper content. It was sold from bulk containers at a strength dictated by the trader's honesty and his customers' requirements, with brand-names in the modern sense playing little part in the commerce. The earliest illustration of brand-consciousness we retain is an original Rowlandson cartoon of 1808 called "Rum Characters in a Shrubbery" which depicts three blowzy females enjoying a noggin with a rascally-looking landlord, one of whose casks is marked "Booths Best Gin".

Indubitably the English were then great drinkers, the working classes with their Gin, their betters with their Port and Brandy, and it is for serious social historians rather than for me to probe into why this national obsession with strong drink coincided with Britain's expansion as the world's greatest industrial and imperial power.

Came a gradual improvement in urban conditions, though the workers' lot was pretty grim by our standards. The mid-nineteenth century saw the magnificent Gin Palaces—the apotheosis of the Victorian public houses—whose passing we regret to the extent of rebuilding them complete with electric "gas-lamps".

The Gin Palace, wonderful refuge from dark, dank homes,

roused the particular ire of the powerful Temperance Movement. In 1871 an Act was introduced which would have halved the number of pubs in the country. In more robust times, this illiberal measure would have caused riots, and the extent to which opinion was incensed is witnessed by an eminent bishop who, opposing the Bill, declared he would prefer to see "England free better than England sober". The Act was withdrawn, and, when defeated three years later, Gladstone stated he had "been borne down in a torrent of Gin . . ."

In the 1880s, an American inaugurated a Saloon near the Bank of England in the City of London and served a variety of novel concoctions which introduced staid and conservative businessmen to Gin. In the first decade of the century, London's first "American Bar", the Criterion, was opened. Mixed drinks, mainly founded on Gin, began to enjoy a certain vogue, but the British did not easily take to Cocktails, nor did the general non-availability of ice help to popularise them.

Legend apart, the word "Cocktail" in approximately its modern sense was first used in an American publication of 1806, and certainly the United States showed an interest in mixed drinks well ahead of Britain. In the 1860s, the American bartender Jerry Thomas had published his *Bon Vivant's Companion, or How to Mix Drinks*. Two years earlier he toured Europe seeking fresh ideas, accompanied by £1,000 worth of sterling silver bar equipment.

So, at the outbreak of World War I, Gin was certainly no longer a vulgar word. It was making its way into polite society in the form of "Gin-and It", in various mixed drinks such as "Gin Slings", and some people were aware of the virtues of Gin with Indian Quinine Water (Tonic).

PROHIBITION IN U.S.A.

Following the social and commercial upheavals of 1914-18, the Americans, ignoring all examples from the past, tried the great experiment of amending the Constitution of the United

States so that, throughout the land, the manufacture and sale of alcohol were prohibited. Anyone old enough to have seen an old gangster film on Television knows the chaos and mayhem that resulted and many people think that from Prohibition stems the American current problem of alcoholism.

There were two particular results of Prohibition which concern the subject of this article. Exports of Gin from London soared, with tiny barely-populated islands, within convenient distance of the eastern seaboard of the U.S.A., taking in weeks' consignments of Gin so large the inhabitants could not have drunk them in a century of celebration. Because prohibition inevitably increases demand, even the giant flow of illicit alcohol into the States could not assuage the national thirst. Thus there came "bath-tub" gin or "hooch" which ranged from adulterated real spirits to industrial alcohols and home-made distillations. Where these lurid intoxicants were not downright lethally poisonous, they were revolting to the taste. Thus grew up the habit of mixing "bath-tub" gin with anything that would render it palatable, possibly even pleasant. Great ingenuity was shown and folk rivalled each other in the complexity of their concoctions. What was a necessity with some became a virtue with others, so that those fortunate in obtaining real London Dry Gin fell into the habit of mixing exotic drinks.

COCKTAIL AGE

Thus came the Cocktail Age, adopted with alacrity by the Bright Young Things of Britain, which fitted well with the disillusioned mood of the times. Cocktail recipes proliferated to an absurd degree.

The Cocktail Age only touched a fringe of society—it could not interest millions concerned with very serious problems of employment or actual survival—but it did make London Dry Gin entirely acceptable at all levels. Women, too, achieving equal status, began to drink Gin on a much wider scale.

The Cocktail Age, as such, killed itself by its own inanity, while the antics of some of its protagonists were ill-attuned to the world-wide Depression. In the United States, sanity returned with the repeal of Prohibition in 1933, leaving the cocktail habit firmly entrenched but shorn of its less desirable features, while in Britain there was a fashion for drinking Gin-and-Tonic. The Dry Martini and a handful of other "classic" recipes for Gin cocktails remained, and remain, popular.

After the shortages of World War II and the immediate post-war period, it was found that Gin-and-Orange was the single most popular drink, closely followed by Gin-and-Tonic, and then Gin-and-Bitter-Lemon when that additive was invented. In Cocktails, the Dry Martini—increasingly dry—reigned supreme. It still does, yet I detect a steadily growing interest in other mixed drinks, not so much in bars but for home consumption. The Cocktail Party is certainly enjoying a vogue, and the growing sale of Home Bars (a considerable status symbol) makes for enhanced interest in mixing drinks. And, at last, one finds ice almost everywhere. In non-Anglo-Saxon cities overseas, whose inhabitants were resistant to Gin's attractions before the war, the wealthier people are showing much more interest in London Dry Gin. Exports increase all the time, and senior British Gin firms have found it useful to establish distilleries abroad. At the same time, there are few civilised countries which do not make some kind of "London" Gin.

PLYMOUTH GIN   While virtually the whole trade in Gin in the British Isles is concerned with a few major brands of London Dry Gin, there are some other varieties of Gin. The most important of these minority Gins is certainly Plymouth Gin, traditionally the Gin for "Pink Gin" (Gin with a touch of Angostura Bitters). This was much associated with the Royal Navy, and there is a theory that "Pink Gin" was invented as a tolerable means of taking those aromatic "bitters" which were at one time considered a prime specific against intestinal disorders induced by tropical conditions and the notorious deficiencies of naval diet, of which the worst ill-effects were reduced by the use of lime juice. To this we owe the word "Limey" as a description of an Englishman.

Plymouth Gin is today somewhat similar to London Gin but with a distinctive flavour of its own. The present exiguous Navy may be less addicted to it than previously, since Scotch Whisky and Dry Gin are now acceptable wardroom beverages, yet there are a number of people who like Plymouth and will drink nothing else.

Other Types

The demand for Orange and Lemon Gins, formerly considerable, has greatly fallen in recent years, though, together with Sloe Gin, they are made by leading firms. They can easily be made at home, using good Dry Gin as the base, and particularly when there is a good crop of sloes large quantities of Sloe Gin are thus produced.

Apple Gin and similar concoctions have virtually disappeared from normal commerce.

There is very little call nowadays in the United Kingdom for "Old Tom" Gin. This is sweetened Gin that once enjoyed enormous popularity. It is still exported from London, the place where it is most in demand being Lapland. The Finns, however, are now making an "Old Tom" themselves. Small quantities go to Japan and a few other very limited markets.

"Old Tom" may owe its origin to the famous "cat" vending machine already mentioned. It became more or less the popular word for Gin. Apart from the joke phrase "Mother's Ruin", there were numerous slang words for Gin, which have disappeared in modern times—Nig (back slang); Lap (chorus girls' word); Duke (servants' slang); Daffy's elixir (from a celebrated eighteenth-century patent medicine); Snaps (from Schnapps); Eye Water (printers' slang); and Brian O'Lynn (rhyming slang).

Dutch Gin had a considerable sale in Britain, and while this pungent spirit has its devotees, its popularity has greatly declined. In the Netherlands, though "Hollands" remains the national drink, London Dry Gin sales are increasing yearly.

Everywhere in the world, it is London Dry Gin—preferably bearing the name of famous British firms, and even more preferably imported from London—that dominates the Gin market.

MANUFACTURE

Whence springs the superiority of London Dry Gin—for that matter, what is it? London Dry Gin is rectified (that is, re-distilled) from pure potable spirit, and is lightly flavoured with juniper and coriander, together with certain other ingredients for which the formula varies according to the firm concerned.

It sounds an extremely simple process, but if it truly were, any-one could make good Gin anywhere—and that is certainly no more the case than it is with fine Whisky or Brandy. A vast amount of expertise and experience is needed, and these skills are concentrated in a handful of Gin distilling concerns, who alone also have the necessary knowledge to exercise effective quality control over distilleries abroad.

London Dry Gin, for so long the spirit of the English, is now more popular than ever throughout the British Isles, is a drink favoured without distinction of class, and is an item of inter-national commerce of the highest importance.

DUTCH GENEVA

The first complete description of alcohol distillation dates from the Middle Ages. The method, lengthy and primitive, was suddenly and by happy chance improved by one Edward Adams. Though knowing nothing of chemistry he designed an apparatus that was to revolutionise the whole practice of distilling. From that time the distilling industry rapidly advanced, eventually reaching a high degree of perfection.

It is the juniper berry that gives to Geneva part of its characteristic flavour, and its use in this way has been traced back to the perfecting of Juniper Wine by a son of the then King of France, Henry IV. It was the custom of that time to flavour with some aromatic substance (for example, Ginger) and so dispel the unpleasant taste of the crude spirits then being made.

Here, more than 300 years ago, the famous distilling names enter our story. This invention of Juniper Wine prompted them to try the juniper berry in aromatised spirits. And it was very successful. Not only did the combination produce a more than agreeable drink, which has always been prized by connoisseurs, but the addition of the berries gave to the spirits a medicinal quality. The Alpine Juniper berry has been all-important from that time on in the guarded recipe for Hollands Geneva.

The centre of Holland's distilling industry is the town of Schiedam. At Schiedam, in the shadow (geographically speaking) of Rotterdam, the distilleries produce the wonderful "magic potion" for which they have been famous since 1695. The establishment of the firms here in this particular town was no accident of planning—grain is the one indispensable raw material for Dutch Geneva, and Schiedam has an extensive grain trade. While this business has gradually declined in other erstwhile grain centres such as Rotterdam, Delft and Amsterdam, it has expanded and grown in importance in Schiedam, thanks to the progressive local administration policies. Here are the distilleries whence come the unique Geneva, variously called Hollands, Old Schiedam and Squareface (from the shape of the bottle).

MANUFACTURE

A modern plant ensures hygienic processing and improved production, yet the lay visitor is often surprised to see how the Geneva, paradoxically, is still distilled by a method reminiscent of the seventeenth century. The reason for this is that heating the big Pot Stills over coal fires still achieves the best results. Even in this twentieth century it proves the most satisfactory arrangement at this stage of the distilling process, despite any more modern methods yet invented.

In the language of the trade, the Schiedam distillers are "Rectifiers of Malt Liquor". This Malt Liquor—the all-important preparation which is the basis of Geneva—is distilled from barley grain. The barley goes to the malt house, where the maltster deposits the grain in a stone trough (or steep) and pours water over it, the temperature of which is carefully regulated, the water being renewed as often as necessary. In this way the barley is soaked in the water until it is sufficiently saturated, when the water is allowed to run off and the grain is spread over the malt-floor beside the trough in a rather thin layer, care being taken to maintain the proper temperature for the process of germination, the grain being constantly turned. Then commences a visible germination of the barley and there now begins the desired production of an activating agent in the grain, a sub-

606

The traditional method of producing Cognac brandy by double distillation in the old pot still has never been improved upon. Hennessy's distillery at Le Peu is one of the most modern in the region but it carries out exactly the same process as has been handed down for more than 300 years.

facing p. 606

The moment of creation in a bottle factory. A very accurate measure of glass ("the gob") is cut off a continuous flow of molten glass moving out from the furnace into moulding equipment which shapes the bottle. The picture shows bottles being made for Hennessy in Cognac.

following p. 606

At Jas. Hennessy & Co., the storehouses where they keep the very oldest Cognacs are called "Paradis". This one was once the chapel of an ancient monastery. Details of each brandy are lettered on the casks of Limousin oak dating back to 1800—to the cask from the Grande Champagne ("GC") area of Cognac, seen in the foreground here.

following p. 606

A bottling line at the House of Melini in the Chianti Classico district. The bottles in the foreground are of Chianti Classico Riserva Melini.

following p. 606

The great "chais", or above-ground "cellars", at Château Loudenne in the Médoc.

following p. 606

Vintage time at Château Loudenne in the Médoc. The families of the vineyard workers, helpers from the nearby village of St. Yzans, and students all come to pick the grapes.

following p. 606

Mr. Peter Brennan, President of the United Kingdom Bartenders' Guild, serving drinks at the Beachcomber Bar, Mayfair Hotel.

following p. 606

4th Hussar Bar at the Washington Hotel

stance termed diastase, which has the capacity of turning, at a certain temperature, the fecula of the barley grains into sugar. By fermentation and several distillations the sugar is transformed into what, in Holland, is called *Moutwijn* (Malt Wine). When the fermentation of the diastase has reached its highest point the malt is taken to the oast (kiln), where it is dried at a low temperature for the purpose of arresting the germination as quickly as possible without affecting the diastase. When dry, the malt is ground in the mill and delivered to the distillery. There, a mixture is made at a suitable temperature of different kinds of grain, to which is added the required quantity of malt for the purpose of turning the fecula of the grain into sugar. After this process the mixture is cooled down to the temperature required for good fermentation. In twelve or fourteen hours the vats become covered with a thick, creamy layer of froth, the renowned Dutch yeast, which is skimmed off, pressed dry and supplied to bakers. The mixture in the vats, now denuded of its top layer of yeast, is allowed to flow off into troughs, underground, and is then pumped up into the Pot Stills. The vapour produced by the heating of the Still is condensed by being conducted through the "worm", placed in the vat, into which a constant supply of cold water is pumped, while the heated water flows off on the top. This process, repeated twice more, produces the Malt Wine. After the third distillation the Malt Wine leaves the distillery and goes for "rectification" by the merchants of Schiedam who add juniper and other ingredients which must remain each individual firm's secret.

Outside of Holland, Geneva has retained its popularity most successfully in the colder countries of Scandinavia, and particularly in the State of Quebec in Canada, and New Zealand.

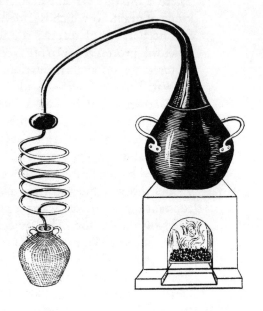

VODKA

Historically the national drink of Russia and Eastern Europe, Vodka has, until recently, been viewed with some alarm and suspicion elsewhere. During the last fifteen years consumption in many countries, particularly English-speaking ones, has increased dramatically. In these areas Vodka-drinking has proved not merely a fleeting fashion but an established alternative to the classic quartet—Whisky, Gin, Rum and Brandy.

Its name is derived from the Russian or Polish word *voda* or *woda*, meaning "water" and is an affectionate diminutive; thus "little water". The connection can be seen with *eau-de-vie*, from the Gaelic equivalent of which the word "whisky" itself comes.

Vodka is made from the purest spirit available. The raw material comes from a variety of vegetable products, chiefly grain, but molasses, grapes or potatoes have often been used. It is said that in Russia in the old days it depended on which had the largest annual surplus. Provided that the distillation and rectification after fermentation are scrupulous enough, the base is relatively unimportant.

However clean the resulting spirit, it is not yet Vodka. From then on the processes of re-purifying and treatment vary according

609

to national and individual commercial methods. It was a requirement that Vodka imported into this country be aged for three years, in contrast to those locally produced which were not aged; the age qualification was removed during 1966, although some would claim that ageing helps to smooth the product. Other processes include one of filtration through activated charcoal which helps to remove oils and congenerics which may have escaped the preceding purification. This method is used for a very large selling brand with historical Russian connections, but which is now produced in many other countries.

The neutral character of softness and purity of Vodka coming from the high degree of rectification, as opposed to Whisky and Brandy, and the lack of added flavouring agents, as in Gin, produce its greatest appeal. It is rare that a lack of positive features adds up to charm, but whether drunk straight with hors d'oeuvres à la Russe or as a mixer, Vodka accentuates the best features of the accompanying food or drink. Some research in the United States has evolved the theory that as a spirit it produces less painful "morning-after" effects. While personal tests of comparision would be difficult and unpleasant, the writer can vouch for a grain of truth here.

Many variations on the Vodka theme come out of Eastern Europe, particularly where infusions and mixtures with herbs, grasses, leaves, spices and seeds are common. Some of these Vodkas are coloured, as are Vodka-based liqueurs, sweetened and fruit-flavoured.

As already mentioned, Vodka is the national drink of Slavic countries such as Russia and Poland and has been for some hundreds of years. Other countries where there is quite a long tradition of Vodka-drinking are Turkey and Iran. After the Revolution in Russia, emigré members of Vodka-producing families set up production plants in other European countries between the wars, but the real consumption explosion awaited the Second World War, when the Paris company of St. Pierre Smirnoff Fils was bought by the American firm of Heublein.

Heublein started to produce Smirnoff Vodka after the war in Hartford, Connecticut, for the few dedicated Vodka drinkers on the American market. It is said that the fashion of Vodka as a "mixer" was really started by Jack Morgan of the Cock 'n Bull Tavern in Los Angeles, who mixed Vodka and ginger beer (itself an unusual product to Americans) and called it a Moscow Mule. From then on Vodka drinks multiplied and the Bloody Mary was born, to become the cocktail most uniquely identified with Vodka. Its basic ingredients of Vodka and tomato juice can be decorated with Worcester sauce, celery salt, pepper and lemon juice, according to taste.

In fifteen years Vodka consumption in the U.S.A. has grown to a point where it claims about 10 per cent of the Spirit market there and is expected to become (if it is not already) the second largest selling spirit after Bourbon whisky. During this time all other spirits have shown rising figures, some sensational, some moderate. It is impossible to tell how much from any one other spirit has been "taken away" by Vodka, but there are good grounds for believing that this interesting newcomer has helped to increase general consumption. It is a theory proved in marketing other products, particularly foodstuffs. Also, Vodka has possibly tapped a section of the public who like a drink but not the taste of it. Neutrality can have positive advantages.

In the United Kingdom, the market was largely pioneered by licensees of the same brand that captured and still dominates the American scene (although it now has literally hundreds of competitors). Slowly it became known to the drinking connoisseur in the West End of London and elsewhere, but the first evidence of mass market acceptance came suddenly and surprisingly from Scotland. Given that the Scots are habitually greater spirit drinkers than the English and that in a smaller community new habits can spread more easily, still the traditional image of the cautious Whisky-drinking Scotsman does not tally with the sudden adoption of the "in" drink of this "switched-on" age. There it is, however, and now it has been estimated that the *per capita* intake of Vodka in Scotland is at least as great as that of the U.S.A., the spirit-drinking centre of the Western world.

News travels fast and many companies started in the late 'fifties to take an interest in the production or importation of Vodka, so that under many brand names the publicity for Vodka-drinking as a concept increased rapidly. There is still no evidence that a Vodka consumer is abandoning any one other spirit in its favour, most types continuing to advance their yearly figures, despite successive increases in duty. It would seem that the pattern is likely to follow the American one; after all there are very few people who stick rigidly to one type of food or drink, except unwillingly. When they find an exciting and wholesome alternative to their diet, they are prepared to give it a try. Often it is a passing fad, but not so with Vodka.

The evidence is incontrovertible; the summing-up is favourable; the verdict is unanimous and the sentence is—"Vodka is here to stay".

RUM

The familiar picture of pirates and buried treasure conjured up by the word "Rum" would associate the drink with the West Indies and the seventeenth century. It can, however, be traced to more distant places and to far earlier times.

Sugar cane was cultivated in China in the second century A.D., and it can be assumed that a sugar cane spirit was produced, a spirit resembling Rum. In the third century sugar cane was being cultivated in Cyprus, Sicily, Madeira and Spain, and it was not until the end of the fifteenth century that we hear of its cultivation in the West Indies. Here, though, the climatic conditions were so favourable that the area became the largest sugar producer in the world. It is therefore not surprising that the West Indies is now also the largest Rum producing area in the world.

Up to the seventeenth century the spirit distilled from sugar cane may have been called many different names—complimentary and otherwise—but not until this country's interests in the West Indies were increasing did we hear of it being given definite names, some of them terrifying. In literature describing the islands, and in letters and dispatches received from that area, mentions of "kill-devil", "Rumbullion" and "Rumbustion" abound, the latter being defined by Chambers's dictionary as "a great tumult or a strong liquor . . .". At that time there would

613

seem to have been every justification for defining the spirit in such a way—a raw spirit drunk straight from the Still with no time to mature. However, with better distillation techniques and the realisation that such a spirit did need time to mature, Rum improved, and was, by the early eighteenth century, being exported to England. A reference to Rum in *History of Barbados* published in 1708 illustrates its enhanced reputation: "The famous spirit known as rum which by persons is preferred to brandy. It is said to be very wholesome and has therefore lately supplied the place of brandy in punch. It is much better than malt spirit and the sad liquor sold by our distillers."

DEFINITION

Rum thus had respectability, and a name, but it was not until 1909 that it gained legality by definition. "Rum is a spirit distilled direct from sugar cane products in sugar growing countries" was the definition submitted by Sir Algernon Aspinall to the Royal Commission on Whisky and other Potable Spirits in that year. It was accepted and the simple definition remains to this day, so that we in this country accept as Rum the spirit which comes not only from the West Indies, but also from the Argentine, Peru, Mauritius, Queensland, Brazil, South Africa (Natal), Java and India, providing the conditions of production are adhered to. Nevertheless, we have remained faithful to the West Indies and very little is imported from these other countries. Jamaica and British Guiana account for over 90 per cent of the bottlings we see, the remaining 10 per cent being almost all divided between Trinidad and Barbados, with a very small share coming from other Commonwealth countries.

COLOUR AND
CHARACTER

The Rums from the four areas in the West Indies vary greatly in colour and character. From British Guiana come Rums that are dark in colour, heavy in body, but relatively neutral in character. Those from Barbados are similar but not quite so dark in colour nor as heavy in body. Trinidad Rums are traditionally light in colour and body and neutral in character. Finally, from Jamaica come the Rums that have the full permutation of colour, body and character, ranging from light coloured, heavy, full charactered spirits to those of dark colour and light character.

PRODUCTION   In all countries where Rum is made the basic method of production is the same. The cane is cut in the fields, usually by hand, and stripped of side shoots to leave the main stem, which resembles a green bamboo. The stripped canes are then taken to the factory and fed into roller mills for crushing, the juice extracted flowing into large clarifying tanks. In the crushing process a great deal of unwanted water results and this is evaporated off, leaving a thick syrup.

This syrup is heated again at a low temperature until granulation takes place. When sufficient crystallisation has set in, the substance is transferred to large drums which have meshed or perforated walls (centrifugals). The centrifugals are rotated at high speed to separate the sugar from the "molasses" from which Rum is made.

At this stage the "molasses" is transferred to the distillery where it is mixed with water and fermenting agents in large tanks to form a solution, known as "wash", and left to ferment. The length of time that fermentation is allowed to continue, and the strain of yeast used as the fermenting agent, are two of the many factors which determine the eventual character of the Rum. In British Guiana fermentation lasts for about forty-eight hours and is caused almost entirely by natural yeasts in the "molasses". In Jamaica, depending on the type being produced, fermentation may be allowed to continue for ten to twelve days, and is initiated by adding the "wash" from the previous distillation in which the local micro-organisms have remained alive.

Two different methods of distillation are used: by Pot Still, where a large number of secondary products are allowed to pass over the Still, and the Continuous Still, where the process of distilling is carried out with a more intense heat and the secondary products are refined out: the second method gives a far more neutral and higher strength spirit.

615

The colour of Rum has been referred to as playing a part in the make-up of character, but as all distillates are colourless the colour in Rum is only produced by an additive. A certain amount may be added directly after distillation and colour will also be taken from the cask during time of maturation; it may further be added just prior to bottling.

Generally speaking caramel (burnt sugar) is the main additive, and this has the effect of subduing character and adding to the body of the Rum. In some parts of the country where the demand is for a very dark Rum, the quantity of caramel necessary to be added to obtain the depth of colour required would not remain in suspension in the liquid and so a tasteless, odourless dye is used, either in conjunction with the caramel or by itself.

The Rum industry in the producing markets has altered tremendously over the years. In 1800 there were over 1,000 estates in Jamaica growing sugar and producing Rum on the Still attached to the plantation. For the 1964 distillation there were only eight still producing.

Consolidation in Jamaica has taken place under a virtual co-operative system, the Sugar Manufacturers' Association of Jamaica having been evolved to give protection to the estate owners, and to ensure that a stable production and a stable price were maintained. But, as Rums from Jamaica or the other producing countries mentioned are supplied to importers on demand, the onus of retaining stability falls on the importers, who must correctly assess their market. During the past ten years stability has been maintained.

TYPES OF RUM   In this country the Rums traditionally consumed were, until recent years, the heavy Pot Still types. They are full-bodied, pungent, quality spirits which have the ability to tell everyone in the vicinity of the "drinker" that he is, or has been, drinking Rum! This type is still drunk very widely in the North of England and in the Midlands.

616

As the cold weather comes along, and colds and 'flu develop, sales of rums such as "Old Charlie" go roaring up. In an October broadcast the Radio Doctor recommended the method he uses to "break" a cold ... from a hot bath into a hot bed with additional blankets and in heavy pyjamas; take two aspirins and/or Dover powders with a treble tot of rum and hot water—he suggested that the treatment might be enjoyed to such an extent that people may even preconceive the arrival of a cold!

Rums drunk in the West Indies, however, have always been light in character and a production of the Continuous Still. As there is no requirement to keep and mature in wood, they are drunk virtually right off the Still, mixed with fruit juices and well iced —a most refreshing drink in hot weather.

The third type, known as "Continental Flavoured" Rum, is peculiar to the German market and produced only in Jamaica. In character it is very highly flavoured and aromatic, and is sometimes described as of "pineapple" flavour. The Germans blend this Rum with their own neutral spirit to produce *Rum Verschnitt*, and demand is so great that production is never sufficient. This has initiated a trend to pure Rums, but the difference in price to the public between the *Rum Verschnitt* and pure Rum is so great that it will be many years before the Germans drink the pure spirit to any degree.

Other than the specific markets outlined above, a Rum from the West Indies is exported direct, or re-exported from the United Kingdom, to markets all over the world, and all have their idiosyncrasies. In New Zealand and Eire, age requirement in small wood before bottling is five years. Conversely, in France, age requirement before bottling is two years, and does not stipulate that the Rum should be in small wood for that period of time. As a consequence, shipments from the West Indies are made mostly in metal containers and the Rum is pumped into very large wooden vats on arrival in France, where it is matured until bottling is due. Consumption of Rum in France is surprisingly high—about five times that of the United Kingdom—and most imports are from the French West Indies. With their large consumption, it would seem that there can be nothing wrong with the form maturation takes.

By tradition, Rum is imported into the United Kingdom from the West Indies in casks. These have three sizes: puncheons (contents approximately 110 liquid gallons), barrels (approximately forty liquid gallons) and hogsheads (approximately fifty-six liquid gallons). Importation in cask is not a requirement by law, but has always been the most economical means of importing—recently, however, casks have become so expensive that other means of shipment are being considered.

BOTTLING When the spirit is imported its strength varies from 130° to 145° (by *Sikes* hydrometer)—that is, approximately double the strength normally bottled for distribution to the public. But, whatever the strength, a law which became effective during 1917 demands that Rum should be matured for at least three years in wood before bottling. If the Rum entered the cask in the country of origin the three-year period would begin then; but if shipment were in other than wood, time for age would not begin until the Rum was "turned over" into small wood in this country. Despite the legislation for a three-year period some of the heavy Rums need at least six years before they become acceptable to marry into a blend, and this is where the art of the blender becomes important—his "nose" and palate can make or mar a whole bottling.

VARIETIES During recent years, companies concerned with marketing national brands of Rum have been trying to establish what the public require, and it has been realised that while there is a demand in parts of the country at certain times of the year for the traditional type of Rum, the majority of people would find a less pungent Rum with darker colour more acceptable. National brands marketed to fall in line with this belief have found ever-increasing success. It is certain that such Rums have been instrumental in increasing sales since 1960 by some 186,000 cases,

618

to a national consumption of 1,177,000 cases per year. But, while it would seem that in general terms Rum has become more acceptable as a drink, the addition of caramel colouring to darken it has made the product heavier in body and so restricted its consumption basically within the accepted period of the year when Rum is consumed—the winter months.

There are, therefore, pungent types of Rum for colds and 'flu which many may choose always to drink; and, of course, the more acceptable Rums for general winter drinking—but what of the rest of the year? Where better to start seeking the answer than the countries of origin, the sunny West Indies, where the population have always drunk the neutral charactered Rums.

BACARDI, which was originally a Cuban Rum, falls into this category of light character and light colour, and has long been marketed in this country. In the past three or four years our own national brand owners have produced TROPICANA, DAIQUIRI, WHITE DIAMOND, and others which are of similar character. These Rums open up a whole new vista and a different way of drinking, for their mixing ability has no equal.

In no other spirit is there such a span of variety as in Rum, but the person drinking it for the first time may damn it for ever if he is given the wrong type. Obviously, the introduction should be made with the lighter charactered Rums, and once the taste is accepted, Rum in whatever form or in whatever mix will be a friend for life.

LIQUEURS, BITTERS AND APERITIFS

Liqueurs

The word "liqueur" is derived from the Latin *liquefacere*—to melt, to make liquid, to dissolve—and a liqueur is a drink the essential elements of which must be dissolved and blended together.

At H.M. Customs House the technical definition of liqueur is "sweetened spirits".

The word "liqueuring" is used, particularly of Champagne, to denote the sweetening of wine. The degree of sweetness is measured according to a table invented by Monsieur Baumé.

The "aroma" of a liqueur is its natural fragrance, derived from the herbs and fruits that are used in its preparation.

HISTORY   Liqueurs are digestives, and in France they are often referred to simply as *digestives*.

According to Hippocrates, great doctor of antiquity (460 B.C.), the ancients were already practising the distillation of aromatic herbs and plants. About the year A.D. 30, Pliny, the famous Roman naturalist, practised such distillation. Before the discovery of liqueurs as such, the ancients made use of wine very strongly "perfumed" to which honey was added. Wine, by the way, is known to have been used much earlier in history than liqueurs. Noah, for example, "began to be an husbandman and he planted a vineyard".

Good liqueurs have always been both digestive and curative. The monks were the medical men of the Middle Ages: they lived near the earth, were industrious and learned. They knew the curative value of herbs and plants and found ways of distilling them and of making liqueurs. In every instance, the distinguishing secret of each sort of liqueur has been handed down—by word of mouth only—from generation to generation. Hardly ever has anything been written.

HERBS. Some famous liqueurs are known to be distilled from many herbs: for instance, CHARTREUSE contains 130 herbs; BENEDICTINE contains 30 herbs as well as Brandy, honey, sugar and (formerly) China tea. AIGUEBELLE has 50 herbs. MENTUCCIA, invented by Fra San Silvestro and now made by the Aurum Distillery in Italy, is also called CENTERBE, that is to say, "a hundred herbs". Among many liqueurs of the same herb type are SENANCOLE, VIEILLE CURE, LIQUEUR D'OR, TRAPPISTINE, VERVEINE DU VELAY, LIQUEUR DES MOINES and MILLEFIORI (a thousand flowers).

Certain ingredients of liqueurs such as aniseed, caraway seed (kümmel), and peppermint are specially good for the digestion. It is interesting that the best mint for making CRÈME DE MENTHE was at one time grown in Mitcham and sent to France. Aniseed is incorporated in many liqueurs and in a concentrated form in ABSINTHE and similar preparations, such as PERNOD.

METHODS OF MANUFACTURE

Roughly, there are two methods of manufacture. The first might be called the "hot" method. By this method, all the elements are distilled and the finished liqueur is water white. Generally, for psychological reasons, such liqueurs are coloured before being served—for example, Crème de Menthe is coloured green. All these liqueurs are sweetened.

The second method is the "cold" method. To the basic spirit (Brandy, Whisky, Gin, Vodka, etc.) are added infusions of steeped fruits or herbs (aromatic plants, roots, seeds and leaves) containing heavy essential oils and other attributes. By this method the freshness, colour, and fragrance of the fruits and herbs are preserved. The aroma must always be natural and never synthetic; the fruits and other elements used must be at their optimum stage of maturity and in perfect condition without any blemish.

RATAFIA. This was the name originally given to any liqueur drunk at the ratification of a treaty or agreement. Later the name was applied to any fresh fruit liqueur made by infusion (cold method) and particularly to liqueurs made from preparations containing the fresh kernels of stone fruits.

INGREDIENTS The names of the ingredients used in the making of liqueurs are legion. Among the best known are aloe, angelica root and seed, angostura bark, aniseed, caraway seed, cinchona bark, cinnamon, cloves, coriander seed, cumin (caraway), ginger root, liquorice wood, musk seed, nutmeg, orris, sandalwood, and tonka beans; the kernels of many nuts, sweet and bitter almonds, the kernel of the stones of apricots, peaches and other stone fruit; the outer rind or peel of lemons, oranges, grapefruit, tangerines; cocoa, coffee, vanilla, sugar, honey, tea; gentian, wormwood (Vermouth), rose petals, orange blossom, violets, hyssop, myrtle, thyme, rosemary, sage, mint, peppermint, peach leaves (dried), myrrh, balsamite, arnica flowers, fennel, sassafrass; the juice of cherries, apricots, peaches, pineapples, strawberries, raspberries, quinces, small wild strawberries, and gold.

The following are some of the principal Liqueurs on the British market. The alcoholic strength of each is as stated on the label.

BENEDICTINE. About the year 1510 the learned monk Dom Bernardo Vincelli, at Fécamp, is said to have discovered during his studies this "elixir" which the monks drank in modest quantities when they were tired out: it revived them. They may well often have been tired out, for the Benedictine Rule was a strict one which provided for many tasks throughout the day and only a few hours of sleep at night. Indeed, this verse about sleeping hours is said to be of Benedictine origin:

> Nature gives five;
> Custom takes seven;
> Laziness nine
> And wickedness eleven.

This Benedictine liqueur was also used to fight the malarial diseases which were prevalent in the country around, and the monks used it to treat the fishermen and peasants whom they visited as part of their duties.

In 1534, Francis I, King of France, visited the Abbey and praised the liqueur which, by this time, was called *Bénédictine, ad majorem Dei gloriam*—that is, "Benedictine, for the greater glory of God". During the French Revolution the Abbey of Fécamp was destroyed and the Order was dispersed; but the recipe for the liqueur was entrusted to the procurator fiscal of the Abbey and, some seventy years later, came into the hands of Monsieur Alexandre le Grand, a wine-merchant and a descendant of the original trustee. He experimented until he had successfully reconstructed the liqueur, and established a vast business. Every bottle of the liqueur bears the ecclesiastical intitials D.O.M. —*DEO OPTIMO MAXIMO*, that is, "To God most good, most great".

CHARTREUSE. The Carthusian Order (The Charterhouse) was founded by St. Bruno about 1084, at Chartreuse, near Grenoble. The monastery was destroyed eight times by fire and the present building—at Voiron—dates from 1676. In 1848 a group of thirty officers of the army of the Alps were quartered in the monastery and were offered the liqueur after dinner. They found it of such fine quality and so delicious that they said: "It needs only to be made known, and we will see that it gets the publicity it deserves." They kept their word, and by 1860 the demand for the Chartreuse liqueur had become so great that a big distillery was built at Fourvoirie, five miles away. In 1903 the Carthusian Order was expelled from France and took refuge in Tarragona in Spain. There, until 1931 when their manufacture was resumed in France, they made the green and yellow Chartreuse liqueurs.

LA VIEILLE CURE is another liqueur of high quality which has been made since medieval times by the monks of the Abbey of Cenon in the Gironde district. It is made from a secret formula now in the hands of the house of La Vieille Cure near Bordeaux. It is prepared by maceration from more than fifty tonic roots and aromatic plants on a base of Armagnac and Cognac brandies.

DANZIG GOLDWASSER was made from 1598 onwards, in Danzig, by the firm of Der Lachs. Originally the liqueur was made without the gold flakes. It was water white and flavoured with aniseed and caraway. When the value of gold in the treatment of certain dread diseases became known, gold flakes were added to the liqueur.

STREGA is a very popular herb liqueur made in Italy. It is pale yellow in colour and of attractive flavour.

KÜMMEL, being translated, is caraway. We begin to drink caraway—as gripe water—when we are no more than a week old. Later we eat it as seeds in cake and eventually drink it in liqueurs called Kümmel. Caraway seeds are an excellent aid to digestion, and are borne by a wild plant with big heads of tiny flowers. Caraway has been used by mankind for the past two thousand years. The Dutch have always had a predisposition to use caraway, and in the Middle Ages the plant was cultivated in Holland in great profusion. On the Continent, caraway seeds were served in little dishes with the cheese course—particularly when the cheese was a soft one. The cheese was spread on the bread and the caraway seeds then sprinkled over it. Until 1914 there was a restaurant in the East End of London where cheese was served in this way, and caraway seeds are still used in rye bread, and in certain kinds of soft cheese.

MINT or peppermint is well known as a digestive herb and belongs to the same sweet herb family (*Labiatae*) as "garden mint". CRÈME DE MENTHE may be either green or water white.

ANISEED. The aromatic seeds of the anise plant are used to flavour the liqueur ANISETTE, in a concentrated form in ABSINTHE and PERNOD.

CITRUS FRUIT LIQUEURS

CURAÇAO. Originally made by infusing Curaçao orange peel in spirit; more finesse was achieved by distilling an essence of Curaçao from this. A higher proportion of distilled Curaçao gave, progressively, double Curaçao, fine Orange and triple Curaçao. The last was presumably too sweet, so a recipe with a high concentration of flavour, but less sugar, was marketed as Triple *Sec* Curaçao. The best-known of these is made by Cointreau in France.

Equally well known amongst the Curaçaos is GRAND MARNIER, made in France. This liqueur is distinguished by the fact that it has always been prepared exclusively on a base of Cognac. The extract used in the manufacture is produced by distillation and not by maceration of the peel of bitter oranges. The bouquet is subtle and closely blended and the liqueur can be exactly defined as an orange-flavoured Cognac.

VAN DER HUM is a South African liqueur made from a small orange-like fruit called the *Naartje* (Cape orange) which grows in South Africa.

FORBIDDEN FRUIT is an old American liqueur, originally from a citrus fruit called the Shaddock, a kind of bitter-sweet grapefruit, said to be a cross between a tangerine and a grapefruit and shaped rather like a pear. It is now made mainly from oranges.

626

FRUIT LIQUEURS

CHERRY, CHERRY BRANDY and CHERRY HEERING are of a red colour, made by infusing cherries in Brandy and sweetening the liqueur.

MARASCHINO is a water white, sweet liqueur of highly concentrated flavour; it is made from the distillation of fresh green cherry kernels.

APRICOT. Apricotine—Apry—Apricot Brandy.

ALMOND AND OTHER KERNELS. Noyau.

PEACH. Peach Liqueur—Peach Brandy.

SLOE. Sloe Gin Liqueur.

BLACKCURRANT. Cassis—Crème de Cassis.

FRUIT SPIRITS

APPLE. CALVADOS—Apple Brandy from Normandy. In the eleventh century the Normans discovered that the drinking of a glass of Apple Brandy greatly facilitated digestion and sharpened the appetite for further dishes. Hence the spirit became known as *Trou Normand* (a Norman hole), its object being to make a hole or space for further food.

PLUM. SLIVOVITZ is Hungarian Plum Brandy also imported from Yugoslavia.

CHERRY. KIRSCH or KIRSCHWASSER made from the kernels of cherries.

RASPBERRY. EAU-DE-VIE DE FRAMBOISE—an unsweetened distillation of raspberries.

PEAR. EAU-DE-VIE DE POIRES is made from the distillation of pears.

WHISKY LIQUEURS

DRAMBUIE. A Scottish liqueur made on a basis of Whisky, made originally from a private recipe of Prince Charles Edward Stuart (known as "Bonnie Prince Charlie").

GLEN MIST. A more modern Scotch Whisky liqueur. Glen Mist Red Seal 70° proof dry, Gold Seal 45° proof sweet.

GLAYVA. Another modern liqueur made in Scotland.

IRISH MIST. An Irish liqueur with an Irish Whiskey base.

CHOCOLATE AND COFFEE LIQUEURS	CRÈME DE CACAO—CRÈME DE CAFÉ—CRÈME DE MOKA—TIA MARIA (a Jamaican coffee liqueur)—KAHLUA.

CHOCOLATE AND COFFEE LIQUEURS

CRÈME DE CACAO—CRÈME DE CAFÉ—CRÈME DE MOKA—TIA MARIA (a Jamaican coffee liqueur)—KAHLUA.

ROYAL MINT-CHOCOLATE. The first in Peter Hallgarten's series of four, reproducing perfectly the flavour of after-dinner chocolate mints.

ROYAL ORANGE-CHOCOLATE. The smooth combination of orange and chocolate.

ROYAL CHERRY-CHOCOLATE. A new sensation, rich and smooth, dual flavoured.

ROYAL GINGER-CHOCOLATE. An original liqueur, smooth and delicate, yet retaining a tang of ginger.

SABRA. A dryish chocolate-flavoured liqueur.

SUNDRY

ADVOCAAT, which looks like custard, should be made from the raw yolks of new laid eggs and Brandy. It is not strictly a liqueur since the alcoholic strength is too low.

UNSWEETENED SPIRITS

AQUAVIT. A dry spirit made in Scandinavia.

OUZO. An aniseed aperitif made in Greece called RAKI in Turkey.

SCHNAPPS. A strong, dry, white spirit from Holland, Denmark, Norway and Sweden.

Bitters

Bitters are used to give a finishing touch to dry drinks (Aquavit, Gin and so on) and nowadays to cocktails. They are digestives and stimulate the secretion of the various digestive juices in the body. In the Black Forest there was an old saying that "out of bitter comes sweetness", and, in addition to being a good preparation for food, bitters act as a corrective if food or alcohol has been unwisely taken.

ANGOSTURA AROMATIC BITTERS are world-famous. They were first made by Dr. Siegert who, after having fought in the Napoleonic wars, left France with two or three friends for "adventure". This they found with the army of General Bolivar, leader of the South American revolutionary armies which eventually freed the South American Republics from the domination of Spain. Dr. Siegert was appointed Surgeon-General to one of the military hospitals and soon began research which led him to produce, from tropical herbs and plants, an antidote to the enervating influence of the climate. He made Aromatic Bitters which found so much favour that he devoted himself almost entirely to their preparation. The demand increased and in 1830 exports were made to both Trinidad and England.

About this time, the bitters were first called ANGOSTURA AROMATIC BITTERS, a tribute to the town of Angostura (now Ciudad Bolivar) in Venezuela, then the centre of distribution. They can be used for immediate tonic effect, as an appetiser, as a flavouring for drinks, and to give flavour to a wide range of food dishes. The ingredients used in the manufacture of the bitters are still the secret of the Siegert family.

AMER PICON are French orange bitters of very pleasant and delicate flavour.

CAMPARI BITTERS are made, and have been made for over fifty years, by Fratelli Campari of Milan. Derived from an infusion of aromatic and bitter herbs with orange peel, they are a stimulating appetiser and can be served plain with soda water or added to cocktails and other drinks. Their colour is light ruby.

PEACH BITTERS
ORANGE BITTERS
FERNET BRANCA—from Italy
UNDERBERG GERMAN BITTERS.

Aperitifs

The word aperitif means an "appetiser", so an aperitif is almost any drink taken before a meal as an appetiser. Sherry, champagne or white wine can be taken as appetisers. Vermouth sweet or dry is another popular aperitif, and then there are a number of fortified and flavoured wines with brand names—Dubonnet, Byrrh, St. Raphael and so on. Many people still think that Champagne, dry Sherry and Sercial Madeira are the best aperitifs.

DUBONNET is a tonic aperitif made by the maceration of cinchona bark (quinine) in carefully chosen sweet red French wine. It is of claret or pale colour and of neutral pleasant flavour. There is now a *blonde* variant based on sweet white wine.

LILLET is made with white wine grown in the Sauternes district and is fortified with cognac. Its formula is a secret.

BYRRH is a dark, rather dry and slightly bitter aperitif wine to which quinine, Peruvian bark and certain other herbs are added.

ST. RAPHAEL is highly esteemed in France and is well known all over the world. It is of deep pinkish colour, with a very pleasant mild bitter-sweet taste, with a delicate peach flavour. It can be served alone, iced with lemon, with gin, or as an ingredient in cocktails. It is of high wine strength.

VERMOUTHS. See pp.517–526.

U.S.A.

The grape-vine is native to North America. Such fact is recorded by the Vikings who landed on the East Coast a thousand years ago and apparently were so impressed by the abundance of vines that they called the continent "Vineland".

The viticultural natural resources of the United States are among the richest in the world. It is interesting to note that more than half the known grape varieties on earth are indigenous to the North American Continent. The new found land was indeed a natural vineyard.

The earliest colonisers on the East Coast made wine from the native grapes *vitis labrusca*. The taste was different from that of European wines and the recently arrived consumers preferred the flavour of the imported European types with which they were familiar. It is thus that imported varieties, *vitis vinifera*, were planted. Although the missionaries in California were successful, the eastern plantings failed. The eastern land, rich in sturdy native vines, was hostile to the delicate European varieties. Worse still, the soil and climate, unfriendly to the imports, also had a dread disease-producing plant louse called phylloxera that attacked the gentle foreign root stock.

Phylloxera is a native American plant pest that lives on the roots of the grape-vine. In the early 1860s many American vines were exported to Europe for botanical experiments. Phylloxera was transported on the American root stocks and within a few short years became the scourge of Europe's vineyards, wreaking continuous devastation between 1870 and 1890. All countries of Europe were affected, even Russia. The pest then turned up in Australia and later became a problem in California where it had not been seen before.

All known methods of combating diseases of the vine were tried without success. Finally, viticulturists in Europe discovered that the vine stocks of the European varieties could be grafted on to American roots. Thus did the United States dramatically and vitally affect the viticulture and viniculture of the world. After phylloxera was conquered and the American wine industry was progressing toward a world reputation, still another and even more devastating blow came to the vineyards in 1919. This was national Prohibition. Tragically, many vineyards were uprooted or left fallow and in some cases replanted with table grapes or even other fruits. Only a few thousand acres remained under cultivation during Prohibition to produce sacramental and medicinal wines. The perfection of quality wines in America was retarded by a generation. At the time of Repeal in 1933 the industry virtually had to start from scratch. Although some fine wine grapes were growing in California vineyards, there was not nearly enough for a national market. Immediate demand was supplied from volume-producing low-quality grapes. It was only by the 1960s, and primarily in California, that quality wines were finally produced in commercial quantities.

Wine drinking in the United States came of age during the 1960s and promises progressive sophistication and demand for quality in the '70s. It is significant that American production of table wines surpassed fortified wines only in the past decade, the best coming from California counties north of San Francisco, Napa being the most notable. Here the finest varieties of *vitis vinifera* flourish and deliver wines now often equal to the great *appellations* of Europe.

Grapes are grown also in the states of New York, Ohio, Michigan, Maryland, Oregon and Washington. The extremes of climate, however, especially in the north-east, practically forbid cultivation of varieties other than indigenous *vitis labrusca* (Catawba, Concord, Delaware, Elvira, etc.) and hybrids that produce "foxy" non-traditional wine-tasting juices best suited to sweet, fortified and sparkling wines. A rare exception is an experimental vineyard in the Finger Lakes region of New York where a hardy German is challenging nature with his attempts to make the Riesling survive bitter winters and torrid summers. Total wine consumption in the U.S.A. is approximately 220,000,000 imperial gallons per year, 90 per cent domestically produced and 10 per cent imported. It is interesting to note a strong consumer movement in the direction of wines as the rate of gain for wines surpasses that of distilled spirits. Table wines account for 45 per cent of consumption, fortified wines 43 per cent, sparkling wines 7 per cent, and vermouth 5 per cent. Table wines have been increasing nearly 20 per cent per year, while fortified wines and vermouth have in fact declined. Sparkling wines, although small in terms of market share at 15,000,000 imperial gallons, have been gaining steadily at 20 per cent to 25 per cent per year.

About 75 per cent of American wine is produced in California, another 15 per cent in New York State, and 10 per cent in other States.

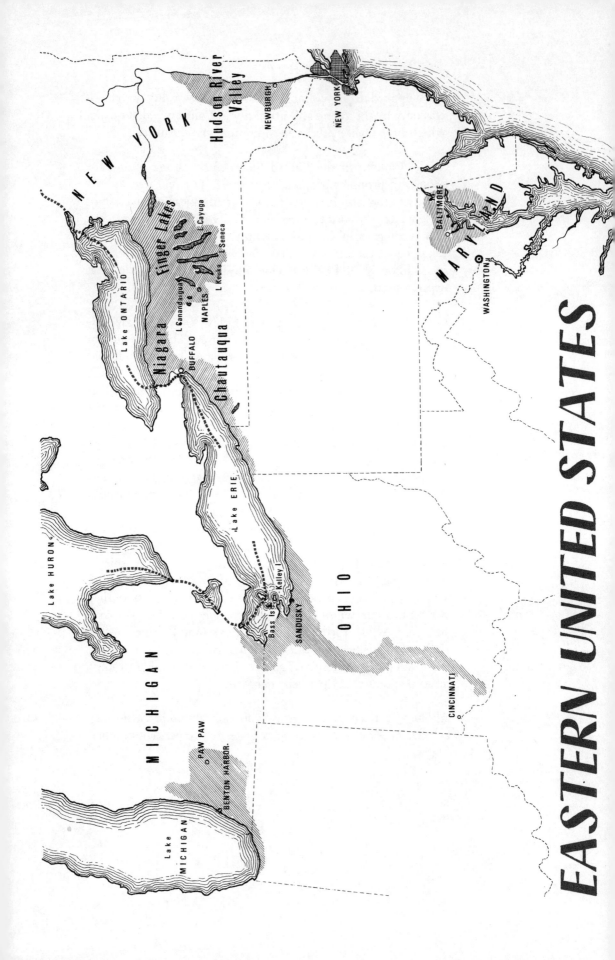

EASTERN UNITED STATES

Before recounting a short history of the vine in the Eastern United States, it is important to acknowledge the distinct difference between the wines of California and those produced elsewhere, especially in the eastern states. In California the vines are almost exclusively European grape varieties. The others, such as those in New York and Ohio, come either from native North American grapes or from hybrids. Accordingly, Eastern American wines do not very much resemble what is made in Europe.

When the Vikings named the East Coast of the New World "Vineland" it presumably was for what they saw: native American vines. When settlers arrived centuries later only cursory attempts were made to produce from wild grapes.

For some two hundred years throughout the period of colonisation, many experiments were made in all parts of the Eastern United States to grow varieties of European *vitis vinifera*. The native parasite, phylloxera, to which the wild vines growing in the woods were comparatively immune, took hold of the foreign vines, however, and eventually destroyed them. If the early settlers and later the colonisers could have foreseen the value of the wild native grapes, viticulture could have been advanced by almost two centuries.

In the early 1600s the first governor of Virginia sent to France not only for wine-makers but also the greatest botanists known at the time. The legislature of Virginia promoted and encouraged grape growing by enacting laws and by issuing grants and bestowing rich rewards for attempts to cultivate the vine.

To understand fully the vital concern of the early colonisers with viticulture it must be remembered that England had just taken a great interest in the development of Sherry in Spain after Sir Francis Drake had defeated the Spanish Armada and brought back the Sherries stored in Cadiz. Treaties were being made with Portugal for the exchange of British woollens for Port. Bordeaux had been occupied by the British for some three hundred years. In short, the British had developed a taste for wine that they brought to the New World.

The French Huguenots, mostly farmers and skilled horticulturists, settled in the Carolinas and Georgia and proceeded to plant European vines in that part of the country. Louisiana, at the time a French possession, was literally covered with plantings of *vitis vinifera* by the Jesuit fathers. King Charles II, in granting the charter of Rhode Island, specified the culture of the vine. The complete disaster of these extensive experiments was certainly not due to lack of skill, money or efforts, but because of phylloxera.

The first vine to produce anything at all recognisable as wine is named "Alexander" for its discoverer, John Alexander, William Penn's gardener.

The first great American to realise the long-term value of the wild native grape, *vitis labrusca*, was Thomas Jefferson. He advised his farmers that the future of viticulture in this new land lay in its cultivation. With his friend John Adlum, a well-known botanist of the period, he planted a vineyard in Georgetown, Virginia. There the first successful native variety, Catawba, was

636

developed. At about the same time Isabella was introduced by William Prince, of Flushing, Long Island, New York. For several decades these two became the leading native pure-bred varieties. Nicholas Longworth, an Ohio banker with a consuming interest in the vine, propagated the culture of these two varieties to such an extent that he became known as the father of Eastern viticulture. At that time, only a few scattered vineyards existed in New York State, mostly on Long Island, and production was used almost exclusively for table grapes.

THE CONCORD GRAPE

In 1853 two events gave Eastern American viticulture its greatest impetus: discovery of hybridisation and introduction of the Concord grape. Hybridisation made it possible to cross-breed varieties and obtain the best qualities of each. Many thousands of hybrids were developed by horticulturists and amateur gardeners. Out of these experiments came the names of today, such as Delaware, by whose standard all others were measured. A number of other native varieties evolved and some continue: Elvira, Diana, Duchess, Noah, and a few more.

The Concord grape, however, remains the dominant variety of Eastern American species because it adapts to almost any soil and can withstand the ravages of disease and harsh climates better than any other. It blossoms and leafs out rather late in the spring, avoiding the damages of late frosts; and it ripens rather early, again escaping the early frosts of fall. Unfortunately, its quality is questionable. It requires a great deal of sugar to make wine characterised by a pronounced grapy taste. Concord grape juice, on the other hand, is a pleasant, standard household staple. Also, many thousands of carloads of Concord are shipped to markets everywhere for use as table grapes. Recently, Concord has been used as a flavour for some specialty sparkling wines such as the popular "Cold Duck". At the time the Concord grape first came into prominence, fewer than 6,000 acres of grapes of all native varieties were in production. Due to the efforts of Cincinnati banker Nicholas Longworth half of those were in Ohio.

With the advent of new hybrids and the phenomenal success of

637

the Concord, some 400,000 acres were planted within a few years toward the end of the nineteenth century. Eastern viticulture had come into its own.

By this time California had firmly established its own viticulture and began to compete for table grapes and wine with the booming East. Toward the end of the nineteenth century, grape culture began to become more and more localised. By trial and error, as had happened in the Old World, it was discovered that ideal conditions for the production of good wines are found in certain limited areas only, and for that reason the output of the finest wines is restricted by nature. The Finger Lakes region of New York State was found to be best for the native American grape varieties.

SOIL The soil of the Finger Lakes region is of volcanic origin, rich in minerals responsible for the high degree of acidity in the wines. The volcanic soil, being porous, permits the roots of the vines to penetrate deeply and seek their own water level. This protects the roots in extremely cold weather and also makes the vine fairly independent of rainfalls during hot summer days.

In winter, heavy snowfalls protect the roots during severe weather and leave moisture in the soil necessary in the spring. Summer days are hot and dry and cool nights produce heavy dewfalls.

TEMPERATURE The gently sloping hills of the Finger Lakes valley provide many exposures to the south-east, giving the vineyards the earliest rays of the sun. The deep surrounding water of the lakes acts as a moderator of temperature in spring and fall. Large bodies of water temper cold winter weather, retard vegetation in the spring, equalise night and day temperature in summer, lengthen the growing season, and ward off autumn frost. In the spring the cold water of the lake cools the surrounding atmosphere; the blossoms of the grape are delayed and thus escape the late frosts of their temperate zone. The opposite takes place in the fall, when the warm air waves from the deep waters prevent the early fall frosts from damaging the ripening grapes. These

638

"Nose" is the wine-taster's term for bouquet or aroma. Here, Maurice Fillioux is seen "nosing" the Cognac at Jas Hennessy & Co's 200-year-old firm. M. Fillioux is the sixth generation of his family to hold the exacting and highly-skilled post of Chief Taster and Blender for the firm.

A pipette is used to draw Cognac from the demijohns in the cellars of Maison Otard.

A wine press is overhauled in preparation for the vintage on a Hennessy vineyard in the Cognac region.

The traditional tools of the cooper's craft.

following p. 638

An Exciseman, in deerstalker cap, is taking the specific gravity of the Spirit while the workman keeps the liquid mixed with a long-handled "rouser".

The Low Wines, Feints and Spirits Receiver in a Highland distillery. The safe is fitted with a Customs Lock to which only the Exciseman and the distillery Manager have the key. As it passes through the safe the strength and purity of the Spirit is tested without handling.

following p. 638

Men using sharp knives known as machettes, cutting sugar cane from which Rum is made. The crop in Jamaica is gathered once a year and a great deal of temporary labour is employed.

following p. 638

A pestle being used to pulverise the ingredients for a liqueur. The ingredients and proportions are a family secret.

A sample tray showing some of the ingredients used in the making of a well-known liqueur.

following p. 638

A laboratory assistant prepares the wort to be used for experimental fermentation in a modern brewery.

Brewery workers mixing the yeast in buckets before it goes to the fermenting tanks.

following p. 63

Modern Swedish Crystal glasses.

A very widely used, basic traditional shape seen in many catering establishments. The ones shown here, the "Club Optic", are hand made at the Nazeing glass works.

"Titan" fine-stemmed glasses by Ravenshead Glass, shatter and scratch resistant, and available in six sizes. Equally suitable for top hotels or for the modern home.

following p. 638

An elegant and delicate hand-made wine service with thinly blown body. Based on the copita shape it is made in full lead crystal by Whitefriars Glass Ltd.

Elegant, long-stemmed "Paris" suite of glasses suitable for any party when a wide range of glassware is needed.

Hand-made wine service based on the traditional Georgian design. In production by Whitefriars Glass Ltd., almost continuously since that period but slightly amended to contemporary requirements.

A modern adaptation of the "Paris" suite—the "Paris Pullman" specifically designed for use on Pullman rail cars.

natural safeguards allow a long growing season in a rather hazardous temperature zone.

THE VINES   The grape-vine will do its best only in its proper setting. Pinot Noir is responsible for the great Burgundies of France, Cabernet for the famous wines of Bordeaux. The same grape varieties planted elsewhere in Europe, however, produce wines of indifferent quality. By the same token, Delaware, Elvira, Niagara are grown all over the eastern part of the United States, but only in the Finger Lakes section of New York do they find a harmonious combination of the conditions that make for quality.

Although each of these vines is a crossing of different native American types (hybrids) there is no European *vinifera* ancestry. Recently viticulturists have been hybridising *vinifera* and American vines with the goal of combining the quality of European grapes with the hardiness of native vine stock. Progress is being made and it is now generally acknowledged that such European and American crossings are the only solution to successful wine grape cultivation in states other than California.

Nevertheless, even a hint of the native grape variety imparts to the wine a characteristic "foxiness" or pronounced wild taste and pungent bouquet. Wine drinkers who are not disturbed by the wild taste consider it an individual and desirable flavour for American wines.

The regions where American vines are grown, with the exception of the states of Oregon and Washington, are all located east of the Mississippi river. New York State and Ohio are the most important, with some wineries also in Maryland, Michigan, New Jersey, as well as Arkansas, Georgia and Illinois.

New York State is a large producer of sparkling wines, red, white and pink "champagne" as they are called in the United States. Some 10,000,000 imperial gallons of still table wine are also made per year. Principal regions are the valley of the Hudson river, the Finger Lakes district, Chautauqua and Niagara.

HUDSON RIVER VALLEY

The Hudson River Valley region runs north along the Hudson river about 15 miles from the town of Newburgh, New York, which is a little more than 70 miles above New York City. Mostly Concord grapes are grown for table use or sweet wine. Hybrids, Delaware and Catawba grapes are also used for dry red and *rosé* wines.

FINGER LAKES

The Finger Lakes district is the most important of New York and the best vineyards lie along the banks of Lakes Keuka, Canandaigua, Seneca and Cayuga, all Indian names. The Finger Lakes are glacial formations that extend in parallel lines like the fingers of a hand reaching into the rolling land. Both sparkling and still wines are produced.

At the southern end of Lake Keuka are such firms as the Pleasant Valley Wine Company and Taylor Wine Company. Other brands are Gold Seal and Charles Fournier. The Pleasant Valley Wine Company produces the well-known Great Western New York State "champagne" from both native American and hybrid grapes.

On Lake Canandaigua at Naples are the Widmer's Wine Cellars. Traditional native American vines are maintained here, and the wines, as a result, have a rather distinctive pungent taste and bouquet of the Catawba, Delaware, Diana, Duchess and Elvira grape varieties that make up the vineyards. Widmer wines are generally light and palatable. They are probably the best that can be made from indigenous American grape varieties.

CHAUTAUQUA

The Chautauqua region is a strip that extends from the city of

Buffalo toward the west along the south bank of Lake Erie. The district continues as far as Ohio. Most vineyards grow exclusively Concord grapes for table wines.

NIAGARA

The Niagara vineyards run along both sides of the Niagara river between Lakes Erie and Ontario. There are also vineyards on the Canadian side of the river. Quantity table wines are produced from both hybrid and native American grapes.

OHIO

The main wine-growing region of the State of Ohio is on the banks of Lake Erie centred on the town of Sandusky and extending east and west. The principal plantations are on Middle Bass Island, Kelley, and North and South Bass. Catawba is the most prevalent vine, making primarily still white wines and some sparkling wines. Many wines are blended with neutral Californian production which reduces the pungent, wild character of the native grape.

The best known winery is Meier Wine Cellars at Sandusky and Cincinnati.

MARYLAND

The climate of the State of Maryland is milder and suitable for viticulture although there are few vineyards of note. The best known is Boordy Vineyard at Ryderwood. Most of its production, however, is consumed locally in Baltimore. The owners of the Boordy Vineyard have in recent years also planted a New York State vineyard by the same name on the south shore of Lake Erie.

MICHIGAN

Michigan produces wines in the southern part of the state at the edge of Lake Michigan. Vineyards abound at Benton Harbor and Paw Paw, Concord being the most prevalent grape variety, plus Catawba and Delaware. Dry, sweet and sparkling wines are made. The most significant development of the Michigan vineyards, however, is the red sparkling product called "Cold Duck" that has spread across the United States much as Coca Cola. Sweet and effervescent, it has enjoyed considerable growth in recent years.

PRINCIPAL
GRAPE
VARIETIES

Red Grapes

Delaware   Small, light-red, sweet grape, best of the wine grapes produced in the East. Used for both red and white wines as well as "champagne" and sparkling wines. The variety is believed to have been originated in 1848 at Delaware, Ohio, by A. Thompson.

Catawba   Large red grape with high sugar content, producing some of the best sweet white and sparkling wines of the Eastern United States. The variety was introduced by John Adams, who discovered it growing along the banks of the Catawba River in North Carolina in 1823.

Diana   Large red grape, full of juice, used primarily for white wines. The variety is a seedling of the Catawba originated by Mrs. Diana Crehore of Massachusetts in 1844.

Concord   Most widely used Eastern American grape variety, producing primarily grapy-sweet, wild-flavoured wines. The variety was introduced in the late 1840s by S. W. Bull.

Duchess   A light green, thick-skinned grape used often for sweet white wines. The variety is said to have been developed by A. J. Kaywood from white Concord and Delaware grapes.

Elvira   A late-harvested white grape producing white wines of rich bouquet and flavour because of the "noble mould" that develops similar to Sauternes. The variety was introduced by Jacob Rommel of Missouri in 1863.

Niagara   White grape, producing dry and sweet white wines, believed to have resulted from the crossing of a Concord with another native variety. The type was developed by Hoagland Clarke of New York in 1872.

Other varieties are new hybrids introduced within the last twenty-five years. The leading developments have been those of the French hybridiser, Louis Seibel. Varieties have been developed for red wines, *rosés* and "champagne." Other good red wine hybrids are Baco ♯1 and Foch. Most of these new varieties are grown in the Finger Lakes region of New York State.

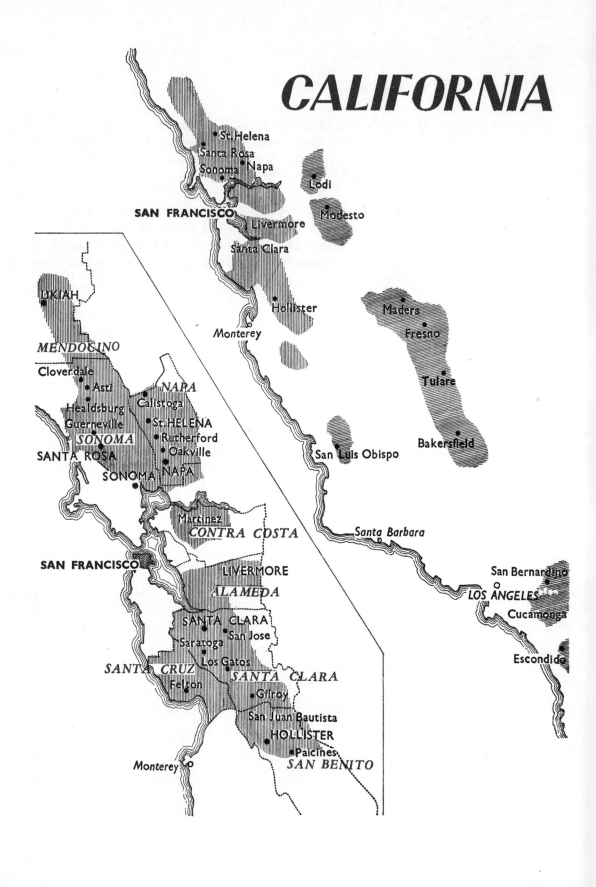

CALIFORNIA

CALIFORNIA

Soil, climate and other growing conditions necessary in the making of quality wine are equal in California to the best *vitis vinifera* areas of the world.

Ordinary wines are produced in volume from red grapes such as Carignan, Grenache and Alicante-Bouschet, and white grapes such as Thompson Seedless, French Colombard and Sauvignon Vert. Zinfandel is a special exception in that, depending on where it is grown, it makes both quantity and quality wines. In the cool northern regions of the counties surrounding San Francisco (Napa, Sonoma, Mendocino, Livermore, Santa Cruz and Santa Clara) Zinfandel yields outstanding wines of distinction and character.

It should be noted that it is exclusively the imported European *vitis vinifera* grape variety that produces the quality wines of California.

Wine-making came to the west of the New World via Cortez, who, after his conquest of Mexico, made the growing of grapes an industry. He brought European cuttings to Mexico and established such successful wine production that Spain ordered its colony to cease and desist the competition. The vintners went underground and moved gradually north with the missionaries.

The vine was first planted in California by Franciscan fathers in the late 1690s. Fine table wine, however, was the vision of a Hungarian count named Haraszthy in the 1850s. He brought some 100,000 cuttings of 1,400 varieties from the great vineyards of Europe. These began what have since become the great American vineyards.

At the same time that Haraszthy was planting cuttings, Pasteur was discovering the government of fermentation by yeasts. Since then world wine-making has progressed more than in the previous two thousand years.

Much of new learning has been put to use, first in California— a most important discovery being that temperatures during fermentation should be regulated. The process was perfected in the 1960s in California and is now exported world-wide—a hopeful reparation for the ravaging phylloxera disease sent forth a century earlier in the vine cutting exchanges with Europe.

Vinification has reached a peak of advanced technology in California, thanks to the tireless and objective research of the doctors at the University of California at Davis. This now famous oenological station has become a world wine centre for experiment and consultation. As a result, the development of fine wine growing, in the generation since repeal of Prohibition in 1933, matches that of centuries in France and Germany.

Time and advance in American viticulture appear in geometric progression: 1,000 years since Vikings called the continent "Vineland"; 200 years since Spanish missionaries planted grapes in California; 100 years since Haraszthy's cuttings arrived; 25 years since the action of fermentation was fully understood; 10 years since vine growing techniques were perfected and practised.

646

Only in the 1970s are the best wines being made in quantities large enough for exportation. Names hardly known a few years ago will be famous by 1980. California wines have come of age. Their ancestors should be proud.

The major wine-growing areas are the North Coast Counties, Sacramento, the Central Valley, the San Joaquin Valley, and the South Coast.

NORTH COAST COUNTIES

This area is made up of the valleys lying parallel to coastal mountain ranges north and south of San Francisco Bay. Fine red and white dry table wines are grown here.

SONOMA AND MENDOCINO COUNTIES

This region runs north of San Francisco and produces a number of excellent table and sparkling wines known among the best in the State. Sonoma County, with some 14,000 acres in cultivation, is one of the three most important quality wine-producing regions in California.

The Sonoma Valley is a relatively narrow strip that runs parallel with the Napa Valley, separated from it by the Mayacamas mountains. The Italian Swiss Colony at Asti and Buena Vista are the most important vineyards of the area. In the Russian River Valley are most of the district's vineyards, one of the best known being Korbel. Mendocino County produces primarily dry red table wines from the better varieties of *vitis vinifera*.

NAPA VALLEY

The finest American vineyards are in the Napa Valley. Seventy-five per cent of production is red wine coming from some 15,000 planted acres. Cabernet Sauvignon is the greatest fine wine grape, producing slow maturing wines that age in cask often up to four years and resulting in rich bottles of great longevity equal to the classified Chateaux of Bordeaux.

647

Planting of the Merlot vine has been extended recently and its produce, blended with the Cabernet Sauvignon as in the Medoc of Bordeaux, is producing good results. Excellent white wines are also made in the Napa Valley, from the Pinot Chardonnay grape of Burgundy, the Riesling of Germany, Sauvignon and Semillon of Graves and Traminer of Alsace.

The valley is divided into upper and lower parts, the centre and best Cabernet growing area being Rutherford.

The best-known vineyards are Beaulieu, Beringer, the Christian Brothers, Inglenook, Charles Krug and Louis Martini.

LIVERMORE

Primarily white wines are produced in this region. The soil is mostly gravel not unlike that found in the Rhône Valley or the Graves and Medoc of Bordeaux. The soil seems well suited to the production of both dry and sweet rather full-bodied white wines. Among the better-known vineyards are Concannon and Wente Brothers.

SANTA CLARA AND SANTA CRUZ

Three vineyard areas make up this region: Los Gatos, Santa Clara east of San Jose, and the southern part of Santa Clara County around Madrone, San Martin and Gilroy.

The Lost Gatos area produces excellent table wines and "champagne". The best-known vineyard is Almaden.

SACRAMENTO

This is the northern part of the great inland valley of California. Being closer to the San Francisco Bay the climate is somewhat more temperate than to the south. Volume production of ordinary table and dessert wines comes from around Lodi, which is the centre of the better part of the district's wine-growing area.

CENTRAL VALLEY

Some of the largest volume wineries are located in the Escalon-Modesto area. Much Thompson Seedless is planted here and used for making neutral wines.

SAN JOAQUIN VALLEY

This is the warmest area in California with summer temperatures averaging over 80 degrees Fahrenheit. Good quality sweet fortified wines are made here. The centre of the region is Fresno.

SOUTH COAST

Extending from Los Angeles south, this area is desert-like with summers similar to those of the San Joaquin Valley. Some good sweet table wines are produced here.

WINE NAMES California wines are sold under grape names, European place names ("Burgundy" or "Sauterne"), or types identified by brand and description ("Bali Hai" tropical fruit flavoured).

Grape named wines, the first and premium class, are called "varietals", contrary to French wines whose names derive from the geographic region or vineyard of origin. Examples are "Cabernet Sauvignon", "Chardonnay" and "Riesling".

The second group is termed "generic" or district wines, named for regions of Europe originally producing wines of similar characteristics, such as "Burgundy", "Beaujolais", "Chablis" or "Rhine".

Hybrid types and branded or flavoured wines make up a third category and include the "mountain" red, white and *rosés*, and specialty flavoured wines like "Key Largo" with citrus and tropical fruit overtones.

Sherry, port, champagne and brandy are also made. Some sherry-types closely resemble the Fino and Oloroso styles of Spain, as do the ruby and tawny ports resemble Portuguese prototypes. "Champagne" is a fast-growing category, partly because of reasonably priced quality bottles produced by the

Charmat bulk process. Recognised names to look for are Jacques Bonet and Lejon.

Vintages in California are important as an indication of age and maturity and have become recognised in recent years as flags to point up peaks of quality, like outstanding 1968 in the Napa Valley and rare 1970 when half a crop of fit survivors came through the severest spring frost of forty years to make extraordinary wines.

<table>
<tr><td>PRINCIPAL GRAPE VARIETY</td><td colspan="2">*Red Wines*</td></tr>
<tr><td></td><td>Cabernet Sauvignon</td><td>5,000 acres in California
Best ages four years in wood, peak fifteen years in bottle.</td></tr>
<tr><td></td><td>Pinot Noir</td><td>3,000 acres in California.
Classical lightness of unchaptalised must, a rarely found practice in France's Burgundy. It is illegal to chaptalise in California.</td></tr>
<tr><td></td><td>Zinfandel</td><td>20,000 acres in California.
Orphan grape probably of Hungarian origin, full flowery taste of berries, fresh as Beaujolais when young, elegant as fine claret with ten years' age but richer in body, uniquely rewarding for drinking young or, best, old.</td></tr>
<tr><td></td><td>Gamay</td><td>2,000 acres in California.
Fuller than Beaujolais, fruity but different, liking bottle age, distinctive and probably best young.</td></tr>
<tr><td></td><td colspan="2">*White Wines*</td></tr>
<tr><td></td><td>Chardonnay</td><td>2,000 acres in California.
Some also planted in New York and Niagara peninsula of Ontario.</td></tr>
</table>

	Graceful, rounded, fragrant wine closest to Chassagne-Montrachet of any white, considered greatest and rarest companion to Cabernet.
Riesling	1,800 acres in California. Light, dry, flowery wine, but less sharp acidity than Rhine and Moselle, some resemblance to the best production of the Wachau of Austria.
Sauvignon Blanc and Semillon	1,200 acres in California. Dry flowery wines, relatively soft, best drunk young.
Chenin Blanc or White Pinot	3,000 acres in California. Fruity, flowery wines like Vouvray and Anjou of the Loire Valley, often marketed in U.S.A. as "Chablis".

Rosés

| Grenache | 14,000 acres in California. Light, fresh, fragrant, dry like Tavel. |
| Gamay | 2,000 acres in California. Fuller than the rare Beaujolais *Rosé*, known primarily because of Inglenook's precedent-setting Navalle *Rosé*, the first California *rosé*, made in 1937. |

Summary of Some Leading American Winemakers

Leading producers of sherry and port-type fortified wines, vermouth and popular priced table wines are Gallo, Italian Swiss Colony, Petri and Lejon. The classical varietal vines such as Cabernet Sauvignon, Pinot Noir, Chardonnay, Chenin Blanc, Riesling, Traminer, Gamay, and types unique to California-Zinfandel and Charbono-are grown and estate bottled by château-style vineyards like Beaulieu and Inglenook at Rutherford in the Napa Valley.

651

CALIFORNIA

Napa Valley   Beaulieu Vineyard
15,000 acres.   Inglenook Vineyards
Best dry table   Louis Martini
wines, red and   Charles Krug
white.   Christian Brothers

Sonoma and
Mendocino   Buena Vista
14,000 acres.   Italian Swiss Colony
Excellent dry   Korbel
table and
sparkling wines.

San Joaquin Valley Gallo
100,000 acres.   Lejon
Volume table   Petri
and fortified
wines.

MARYLAND

Ryderwood   Boordy Vineyard
600 acres.
Hybrid table
wines.

NEW YORK

Finger Lakes   Taylor
6,000 acres.   Vinifera
Sparkling and   Widmer
still wines.

OHIO

Middle Bass Island Meier's
3,000 acres.
Catawba and
sweet table
wines.

COCKTAILS—
PUNCHES—CUPS

THE
BEGINNING How the word Cocktail was derived is pure conjecture, but it is a fact that wherever in the world a bartender mixes a drink, it is known as a Cocktail. The following is an interesting extract from the U.K.B.G. "International Guide to Drinks":

"Although the evidence proves that the idea of making mixed drinks existed centuries before the United States of America was discovered, it is pretty well certain that the Cocktail first became popular in America."

Dictionaries at the end of the eighteenth century give the meaning of the word "Cocktail" as appertaining to horses of mixed breeding, and in a Yorkshire dialect as being beer that was fresh and foaming. Although it is impossible to trace the origin of the drink called "The Cocktail", it seems that from earlier times the cock, the sacrificial bird, has been associated with both strong and delicate drinks which gives rise to the story sent to Harry Cradock from Lucas de Palacio, which was published in the *Bartender* in January 1936 as follows:

"In a picturesque bay of the Peninsula of Yucatan washed by the waters of the Gulf of Mexico, lies the historical port of Campeche. In its time Campeche saw the birth of America's most daring sailors and brilliant shipbuilders.

"Many years ago noble English sailing vessels arrived at the tropical port to take in cargoes of mahogany and other precious woods and other products. The English officers went ashore to visit the port and contemplate the ruins and fortifications that in former times had defended the town against pirates, some of whom reached the high rank of Admiral in the Armada of Her Majesty the Virgin Queen.

"They quenched their thirsts at the doors of the taverns in the narrow streets of the city or under the deep arches of the main square. In those times wine, liqueurs and strong alcoholic drinks were drunk without mixing, but in this particular part of the world, drinks were sometimes ordered which were called 'dracs' either of brandy, rum or some other alcoholic ingredient. These were mixed drinks prepared in a thick coarse glass, slowly stirred with a spoon. Metal spoons were not always used as they often lent an unpleasant flavour to the drink. Wooden spoons or even sticks were often employed. The word 'drac' was probably a corruption of 'Drake' the British hero adventurer of the seas.

"In one of these taverns in this picturesque Mexican port, shaded by graceful palms and perfumed by both the sea breeze and the scent of the sandalwood from the forests, the boy who served the drinks, instead of a spoon used the fine, slender and smooth root of a plant which owing to its peculiar shape was called a 'Cola de Gallo'. Translated into English this means 'cock's tail' The English sailors accustomed to drinking dracs, upon seeing the boy mix their drinks with this root, asked what it was and of course the reply was 'Cola de Gallo' or 'cock's tail'. Soon the word with which they had baptised the drinks of that port mixed with the famous root became famous amongst the sailors landing in Campeche. Hence, the sailors no longer ordered 'dracs' but 'cock tails'.

"The English sailor soon made the new name very popular in the taverns in the ports of the British Isles. From here it passed to the bars on the piers of American ports. The cocktails became numerous and the cocktail shaker was born."

654

That is one story. Others, probably better known, include that of Xoc-tl, daughter of a Mexican king, who served drinks to visiting American officers during a conference with her father. The Americans, approving of the drink and later introducing it at home, named it "Cocktail" after the king's daughter, it was the closest translation they could find in English.

Also there is the story of Betsy Flanagan, tavern-keeper in America during the days before the American Civil War who was said to have mixed drinks to her own recipe. These drinks became known as "Cocktails" due to an escapade in which she and others were involved.

The Guild is of the opinion that it will always be a matter of conjecture as to the origin of the Cocktail as we know it. One claim appears to be as fantastic as another where drinks are mixed.

It is said that the great Cocktail era was the ten-year period between 1925 and 1935. This may or may not be true but since then much has been written and much has been said on the art of mixing drinks or rather the mixing and shaking of Cocktails. From time to time over the past fifty years, many famous bartenders have published recipes which have stood the test of time and are still being drunk in bars, restaurants and hotels throughout the world. It is also true to say that many of these recipes were conflicting to both public and bartender alike and so the huge task of collecting, exploring, checking and filing these recipes was undertaken by a handful of members of the United Kingdom Bartenders' Guild.

The United Kingdom Bartenders' Guild is an influential and exclusive professional association. It was formed in 1933 when the first United Kingdom Cocktail Competition was held at the Wine Spirit and Catering Trades Exhibition in London. It was as a result of this competition that bartenders from the whole of Britain came to know one another and decided that the time had come when the formation of a Guild of Bartenders was to their advantage. The Guild would protect their professional standing and would encourage aspiring bartenders to become efficiently trained, thus establishing high standards of bar-keeping.

In addition to encouraging a high standard of conduct and competence, to assisting in finding employment for members and arranging social activities, the U.K.B.G.'s educational policy has been of great importance. Young members are expected to take the Guild's Educational Course which gives them an opportunity to better their position.

VARIETIES

By 1968 they had compiled the astronomical number of 9,000 various Cocktails. There were even twenty-two different ways of mixing a Martini. At this point the committee of helpers was given the job of sifting out the dead Cocktails and re-filing the numbers down to a more manageable 5,000. I should enlighten you, of course, to the word "dead" Cocktail. This is a drink where one or more of its ingredients has gone out of production.

This file is now recognised by the International Bartenders Association of which there are twenty-five member countries. So you can see that the job of a Standard International Guide to the popular mixtures is now nearly world wide, and I see no reason why a person ordering his favourite drink in Rome, Paris, Cape Town or Wellington should not expect the same as he would receive in London or New York. This is a far cry from a few years ago, when his "Daiquiri" or "Whisky sour" that he enjoyed in the bars of his home-town, bore no resemblance whatsoever to the same ordered in a foreign city.

It has been said and repeated many times that the Cocktail trade in Great Britain and Ireland is dead or dying. How wrong this statement is! In thousands of homes throughout our islands, people are mixing and shaking their various recipes or copying standard Cocktails when entertaining guests at home, and woe betide the professional bartender who cannot pit his skills against the enthusiastic amateur when asked for the ingredients of a certain concoction.

656

It is also said that Cocktails are only consumed in the very *élite* establishments of hotels and restaurants throughout the country. This statement is also wrong. Good, modern public houses everywhere recognise the fact that young people today can be as discerning as anyone when consuming their mixed drinks. The good publican will widen his clientele's tastes still more by the introduction of "House Specialities", "Mixed Drinks" or "Cocktails". Six or more of the well-known popular Cocktails listed on a small tariff is a good start. As mine host widens his own knowledge so he can extend his repertoire. He is wrong if he feels that too much time is wasted in making these types of drinks.

ESSENTIAL
UTENSILS

1. Two cocktail shakers (one for blends which include highly flavoured ingredients and one for lighter types).
2. Ice, ice cutter, shaver, pick, scoop, ice bucket and tongs.
3. Mixing glass, Hawthorn strainers and bar spoons.
4. Small decanter bottles for such ingredients as Angostura, Orange and Peach Bitters, also Pernod.
5. Corkscrew and crown opener.
6. Spirit measure as nominated by the management under the Weights and Measures Act.
7. A fruit knife, fruit squeezer and cutting board.
8. Drinking straws, swizzle, cherry and olive sticks.
9. A strainer and funnel.
10. Champagne cooler and stopper.
11. A selection of good glasses.
12. A supply of clean glass-cloths and serviettes.
13. Egg, cream, milk, lemons, oranges, cherries, cucumber rind, olives, pearl onions, cloves, nutmeg, ginger and cinnamon.
14. Lump, castor and demerera sugar.
15. Tomato and Worcestershire Sauce, vinegar, salt, pepper and celery salt.

Naturally, an establishment starting their own mixed drinks on a limited scale would choose from the items mentioned the barest essentials required. The following points will greatly assist in the better mixing of Cocktails:

657

To obtain the perfect blending of Cocktails, accurate mixing is essential. Whilst the professional bartender can judge simply by "eye", it is suggested that the beginner uses a measure. One of the most common faults of a learner is to over-measure therefore wasting a proportion of his drink.

Always leave enough room in the shaker for shaking, never fill more than four-fifths.

Do not rock the drink. A short sharp action is sufficient.

Make the drink look as attractive as possible, as when the eye is attracted so is the palate.

Never shake a drink of the effervescent variety. If you do, the shaker will fly apart in your face.

You will extract more juice from oranges and lemons if they are warmed in hot water first.

Make sure that only clean, clear ice is used.

Always handle a glass by its stem or base.

Abbreviations: After most recipes are the words "Mixing glass" or "Shaker". The procedure is as follows:

Mixing glass
Put ice into mixing glass, pour in necessary ingredients, stir until cold, then strain into glass.

Shaker
Put ice into cocktail shaker, pour in necessary ingredients, shake shortly and sharply and strain into cocktail glass.

Glasses

Unless stated otherwise, the normal two or three-ounce cocktail glass should be used.

Where a twist of orange or lemon peel is stipulated, the oil from the peel should be squeezed on the top of the Cocktail and then the peel should be dropped into the drink.

Whereas to put ice into a drink is self-explanatory, the expression "on the rocks" means to fill the glass completely to the top with ice and then pour the drink on to the ice.

A great number of bartenders use a small amount of egg white when shaking certain drinks. Their claim is that it gives more eye appeal and a more creamy texture to the finished article.

The following is a list of mixed drinks that may prove useful either at home or at business.

Mixed Drinks

A.I.: $\frac{2}{3}$ Dry Gin, $\frac{1}{3}$ Grand Marnier, 1 dash Lemon juice, 1 dash Grenadine. Shaker.

AFFINITY: $\frac{2}{3}$ Scotch Wisky, $\frac{1}{3}$ Sweet Vermouth, 1 dash Angostura Bitters. Mixing glass. (For ROB BOY add cherry.)

BACARDI: $\frac{3}{4}$ Bacardi Rum, $\frac{1}{4}$ Lemon Juice, 1 Teaspoon Grenadine. Shaker.

ALASKA: $\frac{3}{4}$ Dry Gin, $\frac{1}{4}$ Yellow Chartreuse. Shaker.

ALEXANDER: $\frac{1}{3}$ Brandy ***, $\frac{1}{3}$ Crème de Cacao, $\frac{1}{3}$ fresh cream. Shaker.

BALALAIKA: $\frac{1}{3}$ Vodka, $\frac{1}{3}$ Cointreau, $\frac{1}{3}$ lemon juice. Shaker.

BANANA BLISS: $\frac{1}{2}$ Brandy, $\frac{1}{2}$ Creme de Banane. Mixing glass.

BETWEEN THE SHEETS: $\frac{1}{3}$ Brandy, $\frac{1}{3}$ White Rum, $\frac{1}{3}$ Cointreau, 1 dash lemon juice. Shaker.

BLACK RUSSIAN: ½ Vodka, ½ Kahlua, on the rocks. 5 oz. goblet.

BOBBY BURNS: ½ Scotch Whisky, ½ Sweet Vermouth, 3 dashes Benedictine. Mixing glass.

BOSOM CARRESSER: ⅔ Brandy ***, ⅓ Orange Curaçao, yolk of one egg, 1 teaspoon Grenadine. Shaker. (Into double cocktail glass.)

BLUE LADY: ½ Blue Curaçao, ¼ Dry Gin, ¼ lemon juice, 1 dash of egg white. Shaker.

BENTLEY: ½ Dubonnet, ½ Calvados Brandy. Mixing glass.

BRONX: ½ Dry Gin. ⅙ Dry Vermouth, ⅙ Sweet Vermouth, ⅙ orange juice. Shaker.

BRANDY (1): 1 measure Brandy, 2 dashes Sweet Vermouth, 1 dash Angostura. Mixing glass.

BRONX TERRACE: ⅔ Dry Gin, ⅓ Dry Vermouth, 1 dash lime cordial, Add cherry. Mixing glass.

BRANDY (2): 1 measure Brandy, 1 dash Orange Curaçao, 1 dash Angostura. Mixing glass.

DAIQUIRI: ¾ White Rum, ¼ lemon juice, 3 dashes Gomme Syrup. Shaker.

BRANDY GUMP: ½ Brandy, ½ lemon juice, ½ tablespoon Grenadine. Shaker.

DAIQUIRI BLOSSOM: ½ White Rum, ½ orange juice, 1 dash Maraschino, Shaker.

BLUSHING BRIDE: ¼ Vodka, ¼ Cherry Brandy, ¼ Orange Curaçao, ¼ lime cordial, 1 dash Orange Bitters, 1 dash egg white. Shaker.

660

COFFEE: $\frac{2}{3}$ Port Wine, $\frac{1}{3}$ Brandy***, 2 dashes Orange Curaçao, yolk of egg. Shaker. (Into double Cocktail glass.)

CORONATION: $\frac{1}{2}$ Dry Vermouth, $\frac{1}{2}$ Med Sherry, 1 dash Maraschino. 2 dashes Orange Bitters. Mixing glass.

FALLEN ANGEL: $\frac{3}{4}$ Dry Gin, $\frac{1}{4}$ lemon juice, 2 dashes Green Crême de Menthe, 1 Dash Angostura. Shaker.

DEANSGATE: $\frac{1}{2}$ White Rum, $\frac{1}{4}$ lime cordial, $\frac{1}{4}$ Drambuie, twist of orange peel. Mixing glass.

GIBSON: $\frac{5}{6}$ Dry Gin, $\frac{1}{6}$ Dry Vermouth, 1 pearl onion. Mixing glass.

DUBONNET: $\frac{1}{2}$ Dubonnet, $\frac{1}{2}$ Dry Gin, twist of lemon peel. Mixing glass.

GIMLET: $\frac{2}{3}$ Dry Gin, $\frac{1}{3}$ lime cordial. Mixing glass. Add splash of soda.

DUCHESS: $\frac{1}{3}$ Sweet Vermouth, $\frac{1}{3}$ Dry Vermouth, $\frac{1}{3}$ Absinthe or Pernod. Mixing glass.

GRAPEFRUIT: $\frac{1}{2}$ Dry Gin, $\frac{1}{2}$ grapefruit juice, 1 dash Gomme Syrup. Shaker.

EAST INDIA: $\frac{3}{4}$ Brandy, $\frac{1}{8}$ Orange Curacao, $\frac{1}{8}$ Pineapple juice, 1 dash Angostura, lemon twist and cherry. Shaker.

GRASSHOPPER: $\frac{1}{3}$ White Creme de Cacao, $\frac{1}{3}$ Green Creme de Menthe, $\frac{1}{3}$ fresh cream. Shaker.

HAWAIIAN: $\frac{1}{2}$ Dry Gin, $\frac{1}{2}$ orange juice, 1 dash Orange Curaçao. Shaker.

MAGIC TRACE: $\frac{4}{10}$ Bourbon, $\frac{3}{10}$ Drambuie, $\frac{1}{10}$ Dry Vermouth, $\frac{1}{10}$ orange juice, $\frac{1}{10}$ lemon juice. Shaker.

HOOTS MON: $\frac{1}{2}$ Scotch Whisky, $\frac{1}{4}$ Sweet Vermouth, $\frac{1}{4}$ Lillet. Mixing glass.

MANHATTAN: $\frac{2}{3}$ Rye Whisky, $\frac{1}{3}$ Sweet Vermouth, 1 dash Angostura. Mixing glass. Add cherry.

HUNTER: $\frac{2}{3}$ Rye Whisky, $\frac{1}{3}$ Cherry, Brandy. Mixing glass.

MANHATTAN DRY: Use Dry Vermouth instead of Sweet and add a twist of lemon.

INK STREET: $\frac{1}{3}$ Rye Whisky, $\frac{1}{3}$ orange juice, $\frac{1}{3}$ lemon juice. Shaker.

MANHATTAN PERFECT: $\frac{1}{3}$ Rye Whisky. $\frac{1}{3}$ Dry Vermouth, $\frac{1}{3}$ Sweet Vermouth. Mixing glass.

LITTLE PRINCESS: $\frac{1}{2}$ White Rum, $\frac{1}{2}$ Sweet Vermouth. Mixing glass.

MARGARET ROSE: $\frac{1}{2}$ Dry Gin, $\frac{1}{6}$ Calvados, $\frac{1}{6}$ Cointreau, $\frac{1}{6}$ lemon juice, 1 Dash Grenadine. Shaker.

MAINBRACE: $\frac{1}{3}$ Dry Gin, $\frac{1}{3}$ Cointreau, $\frac{1}{3}$ grapefruit juice. Shaker.

MARTINI: $\frac{2}{3}$ Dry Gin, $\frac{1}{3}$ Dry Vermouth, twist of lemon peel. Mixing glass.

OLYMPIC: $\frac{1}{3}$ Brandy, $\frac{1}{3}$ orange juice, $\frac{1}{3}$ orange Curaçao. Shaker.

MARTINI MEDIUM: $\frac{2}{3}$ Dry Gin, $\frac{1}{6}$ Sweet Vermouth, $\frac{1}{6}$ Dry Vermouth. Mixing glass.

ORANGE BLOSSOM: $\frac{1}{2}$ Dry Gin, $\frac{1}{2}$ orange juice, 1 dash of egg white optional. Shaker.

MARTINI SWEET: $\frac{2}{3}$ Dry Gin, $\frac{1}{3}$ Sweet Vermouth, add cherry. Mixing glass.

PERFECT LADY: $\frac{1}{2}$ Dry Gin, $\frac{1}{4}$ Peach Brandy, $\frac{1}{4}$ lemon juice, 1 dash of egg white. Shaker.

MONKEY GLAND: $\frac{3}{4}$ Dry Gin, $\frac{2}{5}$ orange juice, 2 dashes Pernod, 2 dashes Grenadine. Shaker.

PICCADILLY: $\frac{2}{3}$ Dry Gin, $\frac{1}{3}$ Dry Vermouth, 1 dash Absinthe or Pernod, 1 dash Grenadine. Mixing glass.

NEGRONI: $\frac{1}{3}$ Dry Gin, $\frac{1}{3}$ Sweet Vermouth, $\frac{1}{3}$ Campari. Prepare in 'old-fashioned' glass, add cubes or ice and slice of orange.

PARADISE: $\frac{1}{2}$ Dry Gin, $\frac{1}{4}$ Apricot Brandy, $\frac{1}{4}$ orange juice. Shaker.

PORT WINE: $\frac{4}{5}$ Port Wine, $\frac{1}{5}$ Brandy***, twist orange peel. Mixing glass.

VODKATINI: $\frac{2}{3}$ Vodka, $\frac{1}{3}$ Dry Vermouth, add twist of lemon peel. Mixing glass.

RUSTY NAIL: $\frac{2}{3}$ Scotch Whisky, $\frac{1}{3}$ Drambuie, Serve "on the rocks" in "old-fashioned" glass, add twist of lemon peel.

WHITE LADY: $\frac{1}{2}$ Dry Gin, $\frac{1}{4}$ Cointreau, $\frac{1}{4}$ lemon juice. Shaker.

SILENT THIRD: $\frac{1}{3}$ Scotch Whisky, $\frac{1}{3}$ Cointreau, $\frac{1}{3}$ Lemon juice. Shaker.

WHITE LILY: $\frac{1}{3}$ Dry Gin, $\frac{1}{3}$ White Rum, $\frac{1}{3}$ Cointreau, 1 dash of Pernod. Mixing glass.

SIDECAR: $\frac{1}{3}$ Brandy ***, $\frac{1}{3}$ Cointreau, $\frac{1}{3}$ Lemon juice. Shaker.

STINGER: $\frac{2}{3}$ Brandy ***, $\frac{1}{3}$ White Creme de Menthe. Mixing glass.

663

Champagne Cocktails

ALFONSO: Into a 5 oz. wine-glass put 1 lump of sugar and 2 dashes of angostura Bitters and 1 oz. of Dubonnet. Fill up with iced Champagne. Squeeze lemon peel on top and stir slightly.

BUCK'S FIZZ: Put 1 ice cube into a highball glass. Add 1 oz. of fresh orange juice and fill up with iced Champagne.

CHAMPAGNE COCKTAIL: Into a Champagne cocktail glass, put 1 lump of sugar and 3 dashes of Angostura Bitters. Pour on a little Brandy and fill up with iced Champagne. Add a slice of orange.

FRENCH 75: Into a highball glass put the juice of $\frac{1}{2}$ lemon, 1 teaspoon of castor sugar and 1 measure of dry Gin. Stir, add piece of ice and fill up with iced Champagne.

HAPPY YOUTH: Into a 6 oz. goblet put 1 measure of Cherry Brandy, the juice of 1 orange, 1 lump of sugar and fill up with iced Champagne.

VALENCIA SMILE: $\frac{2}{3}$ Apricot Brandy, $\frac{1}{3}$ fresh orange juice, 4 dashes orange Bitters. Shake and strain into 6 oz. glass; then fill up with iced Champagne.

Collins

Before the 1930s a John Collins was made with Dutch Gin, and Tom Collins with "Old Tom" Gin. The modern trend is to use a London Dry Gin for both these drinks.

JOHN OR TOM COLLINS: Into a tall tumbler put cracked ice, the juice from 1 lemon, 1 teaspoon castor sugar, 1 measure Dry Gin Fill up with soda water. Stir and serve with slice of lemon and drinking straws.

Some people also like a dash of Angostura Bitters. Brandy,

Rum, Vodka, Scotch, Rye or Bourbon Collins are made as above simply by substituting the Gin.

CRUSTAS: Use a 5 oz. wine-glass: Rub rim of glass with a slice of lemon. Dip edge of glass into powdered sugar and spiral the rind of half an orange into glass. Put into mixing glass, 1 measure Brandy, $\frac{1}{4}$ measure Maraschino, 1 dash Angostura Bitters. Stir and strain into prepared glass. Add ice and cherry. As in the Collins, alternative spirits can be used.

Fizzes

GIN FIZZ: 2 oz. lemon juice, 1 tablespoon sugar, $1\frac{1}{2}$ oz. Gin. Shake and strain into highball glass. Add large cube of ice and fill with soda water.

SILVER FIZZ: The same as above, but add a little egg white before shaking.

GOLDEN FIZZ: The same as above, but use the yolk of an egg instead of the white.

ROYAL FIZZ: The same as above, using the whole egg.

RUM AND BRANDY FIZZES: The same as Gin Fizz, but substitute the required spirit.

FLIPS: Use a 5 oz. wine-glass and any of the following "bases": Brandy, Rum, Whisky, Claret, Port or Sherry. 1 teaspoon sugar, 1 whole egg, 1 oz. of the required base. Shake with ice and strain. Add grated nutmeg on top.

FRAPPES: Any liqueur can be used in this drink. Fill a 5 oz. wine-glass with crushed ice and pour a measure of your chosen liqueur into it. Serve the drink with two short straws.

HIGHBALLS: Using a 10 oz. highball glass, add 2 pieces of ice and a large measure of the chosen spirit. Fill with ginger ale or soda water, whichever is preferred. Squeeze a piece of lemon peel on top.

Punches

PLANTER'S PUNCH: Using a highball glass with plenty of ice, add 1 large measure of Jamaica Rum, the juice of 1 lemon or lime, 1 teaspoon of Grenadine. 1 dash of Angostura Bitters. Fill up with soda water. Stir and add slice of orange and lemon Serve with straws.

CLARET PUNCH: Fill a 9 oz. goblet with fine ice. Add 3 oz. Claret, juice of 1 lemon, 1 teaspoon sugar, 2 dashes of Curaçao. Fill up with ginger ale and top with a slice of orange and lemon.

ST. CHARLES'S PUNCH: ½ oz. Brandy ***, ½ oz. Port wine, 4 dashes Curaçao, juice of ½ lemon, shake and strain into a tumbler into which fine ice had been placed. Add a slice of orange and lemon. Serve with straws.

BRANDY PUNCH: Fill a 9 oz. goblet with fine ice, 1 large measure of Brandy, 4 dashes of Curaçao. Stir and fill up with ginger ale. Add mint and any fresh fruit.

SOURS: Practically any spirit can be used in this drink. 1 oz. of lemon juice 1 teaspoon sugar, 2 oz. of desired spirit. Shake and strain into 5 oz. wine-glass (dash of egg white into your shaker before shaking is optional).

HORSE'S NECK: Peel the rind of a whole lemon in one piece. Place one end of the peel over the edge of a highball glass allowing the remainder to curl inside and anchor at the bottom with 2 lumps of ice. Add a large measure of Brandy and fill with ginger ale. A dash of Angostura Bitters is optional.

Hot Drinks

GROG: Using a 10 oz. tumbler take a large measure of Jamaica Rum, 1 teaspoon of sugar, 2 cloves, the juice from ½ lemon. Add piece of cinnamon stick. Top up with boiling water.

BUTTERED RUM: Using an 'old-fashioned" glass, take 1 large measure of Jamaica Rum, 1 teaspoon of sugar, small knob of butter, 2 cloves, Fill up with boiling water and stir.

TODDIES: Using an "old-fashioned" glass take a large measure of desired spirit, 1 teaspoon of sugar, 2 cloves, slice of lemon, a small stick of cinnamon. Fill up with boiling water.

Pick-me-ups

PRAIRIE OYSTER: Into a small wine-glass drop an unbroken egg yolk, 1 teaspoon Worcester Sauce, 1 teaspoon tomato sauce, 2 dashes vinegar, 1 dash pepper.

PICK-ME-UP-COCKTAIL: ⅓ Brandy***, ⅓ Dry Vermouth, ⅓ Pernod. Stir and strain into cocktail glass.

Cups

I suspect that over the centuries countless recipes have been compiled, both alcoholic and non-alcoholic, and most professional bartenders have a preference for one, or a recipe of their own. One has to face the fact that today a good Cup can be an expensive form of drink and, therefore, I am not going to offer any suggestions.

However, one famous company has been producing Cups for many years and has now numbered them in the following order: No. 1 Gin, No. 2 Whisky, No. 3 Brandy, No. 4 Rum, No. 5 Rye, No. 6 Vodka. With the addition of lemonade, ice, a slice of lemon and a little cucumber rind, these make excellent drinks.

A word of warning, you only make a rod for your own back if you start putting pieces of fruit into the drink thinking you are enhancing the taste. You are wasting time, and other people are waiting for a drink.

EGG NOGG: 1 whole egg: 2 teaspoons sugar, 1 oz. Brandy ***, 1 oz. Dark Rum. Shake and strain into a tumbler. Fill with milk and add grated nutmeg on top. This can be made into a hot drink by adding hot milk instead of shaking with ice.

BREAKFAST NOGG: 1 whole egg, ½ oz. Curaçao, 1 oz. Brandy ***. Shake and strain into tumbler. Fill with milk and add grated nutmeg on top.

Miscellaneous Drinks

AMERICANO: Us a 6 oz. goblet with 2 pieces of ice, 1 oz. of Campari Bitters, 2 oz. of sweet Vermouth. Fill up with soda water and slice of lemon.

ANGEL'S TIP: Into a cocktail glass pour 1 measure of Crême de Cacao. Float a ¼ inch of fresh cream on top.

BLACK VELVET: Into a large tumbler pour chilled Guinness and iced Champagne simultaneously.

BLOODY MARY: Into a 6 oz. goblet put ice and 1 measure of Vodka, a touch of lemon juice. Fill up with tomato juice add Worcester Sauce to taste and stir.

CUBA LIBRE: Half fill a 10 oz. tumbler with ice, the juice of ½ lemon or lime. 1 measure of white Rum. Fill up with Cola. Add a slice of lemon or lime. Serve with straws and a swizzle stick.

MOSCOW MULE: Half fill a 10 oz. tumbler with ice. Add 1 oz. of lime juice, 1 measure of White Rum. Fill up with ginger beer. Add a sprig of mint. Serve with straws.

668

BEERS AND CIDERS

Beer

Beer, like bread, contains the staff of life. Bread is made by "raising" flour with yeast; beer is brewed by fermenting with yeast, a water extract of ground malt which is germinated barley. Hops are always used and also help to preserve the beer. Less is used in mild beer than in bitter, and even less in lager beers.

HISTORY   Whether it be true or not that barley was man's first cultivated grain, beer was certainly brewed from it in ancient Egypt and by the tribes who thousands of years ago came out of the East to invade Europe. The Norsemen who won a foothold in Britain cultivated yeast and brewed ale; the brewhouse was essential to every medieval monastery; with the growth of travel, inns became a notable feature of Britain; by 1437 the Brewers' Company had its charter and in Victorian England Mr. Gladstone recognised the respectability of beer by taxing it.

In fact, beer has been the national drink of Englishmen for nearly a thousand years, and when in William Cobbett's day tea and white bread threatened to replace beer and brown bread as the basis of the national diet, he predicted disaster.

However, Britain and beer survived, and although we no longer drink it at breakfast—as, we are told, the first Elizabeth did— and our womenfolk no longer quaff two gallons a day—which was the beer allowance for maids of honour in Anne Boleyn's day—beer is still the national beverage, a rich source of energy, health and pleasure and an essential part of the good life.

MANUFACTURE   To brew beer you require malted barley, water, sugar, hops and yeast.

The malt is made from the best barley in Britain. The hops are specially selected and the yeast is constantly examined by scientists to see that there is no impurity in it, and no change in its nature. The water is absolutely pure and the sugar is the finest refined sugar available. The malt and yeast contribute valuable vitamins.

For the malting process, specially chosen barley is steeped in water and then allowed to germinate under controlled conditions of temperature and humidity. After the required period of germination the growth is stopped (the rootlets having grown to about $\frac{3}{4}$ in. in length) by drying in a kiln. This has a perforated floor on which the malt is spread, and air, heated by smokeless anthracite fires, by oil burners or by steam, is passed through. On completion the temperature is raised to "cure" or cook the malt until it has the required flavour.

In the milling room the malt is coarsely crushed and stored in the grist case to await "mashing". This crushing separates the surrounding husk and enables the water used in the mashing to reach the soluble portion.

As the crushed malt falls into the mash tun it is mixed with hot brewing water (known as brewing liquor), to form an infusion, much as you brew tea in a teapot. The water extracts the soluble malt sugars from the ground malt and a malt extract, or "wort", is drawn off through the slotted bottom of the mash tun, leaving the insoluble grains and husks behind. These grains are further

670

sprinkled or "sparged" with more brewing water to ensure that none of the valuable extract is wasted. The sweet taste of this malt extract is due to the presence of the malt sugars which include glucose—the "energy" sugar.

In the coppers, liquid sugar is added to the wort. This gives extra body and flavour to the beer. Then hops are added, and the whole is boiled to extract the hop flavour. After boiling, the hops are strained off from the hopped wort.

This hot wort is cooled in a paraflow cooler where the cooling water and wort are kept separate by very thin plates of stainless steel (or copper) which allows a rapid transfer of heat, and at a set temperature the wort flows to the fermenting vessels where the yeast is pitched into the wort. Here the yeast converts the various sugars of the wort into alcohol and carbon dioxide gas which gives the beer its sparkle and head and also plays an important part by giving a distinctive flavour.

Until recent times it was not possible to ensure consistent quality right through to the consumer, and even now most draught beers and some bottled beers depend on the landlord's ability for their condition.

To ensure the consistent condition and stability of beer all brewers use elaborate equipment. Beer brewed for draught is cooled and drawn off into casks which bear the traditional names—hogsheads (fifty-four gallons), barrels (thirty-six gallons), kilderkins (eighteen gallons), firkins (nine gallons) and pins (four and a half gallons).

Beers for bottling and canister are conditioned in glass-lined tanks which allow the beer to mature naturally at carefully controlled temperatures and pressures, and at the same time develop its natural gas. It is then passed to the cold room where it is brought to full maturity at near freezing temperature.

Finally, beers in canister and in bottle are pasteurised to ensure that the condition remains unchanged until it reaches your glass.

STOUT
The process of brewing stouts is essentially the same as brewing beer. Roasted barley is used to give stout its distinctive colour.

DRAUGHT BEER
One of the greatest advances in brewing has been the development of draught beers served under full pressure.

Traditional draught beers served through the pumps when well cared for by the experienced licensee are very hard to beat, but with the introduction of fully pressurised beer, it is easier for everyone to serve a perfect pint. In fact, the last pint drawn from the pressurised system is as good as the first and every pint has an extra sparkle.

What happens is that after the cask or canister has been filled with beer at the brewery it is dispensed using a carbon dioxide gas at top pressure to supply the pumps. This keeps the natural condition of the beer in and, in the case of traditional beers, the cellar air out. As the beer is being drawn off, this will always ensure ideal conditions and it also helps to prolong the life of the beer.

LAGER
Recently there has been an increasing demand in Britain for Lager —and nearly ten times more Lager is drunk in Britain than in 1939.

Literally translated from the German, the word lager means "Store"—because the process of brewing Lager is essentially one of storage and of conditioning it at near freezing temperature for lengthy periods after initial fermentation.

There are two main types of Lager—the pale, delicately flavoured Pilsner, like SKOL International, and the dark Munich type.

The taste for Lager spread from Munich throughout Europe. A Bavarian monk smuggled lager yeast to Pilsen and it was

672

brewed there for the first time in 1842, but whereas in Munich they preferred dark beer, in Pilsen the paler beer was more popular.

About this time Lager brewers co-operated with Louis Pasteur, who showed that the souring of beer was due to the presence of bacteria, and not only to contact with the air as had been thought. The discovery was used to brew beer of a higher and more consistent quality.

The basic ingredients of Lager are much the same as those used in ale brewing—malt, water, hops and yeast—but they are treated somewhat differently. In lager brewing a decoction mash takes place at a lower temperature than in the case of ale brewing. A short time after mashing, the lager brewer pumps a quantity of this mash from the mash tun to another vessel, the mash copper, where it is boiled. When this part of the mash is returned to the mash vessel it raises the temperature of the remainder. This may be done twice; the mash is then transferred to the *lauter* (mash) tun and the resultant wort is then drained off into a copper and boiled for two hours with the addition of sugars and continental hops.

The Lager fermenting process is in two stages. Initially fermentation takes place at a much lower temperature than used in ale brewing—46° to 47°F being the usual starting-point. As a result fermentation is slower and generally extends to nine or ten days, at the end of which time the yeast has settled to the bottom of the vessel. This is what we call "deep fermentation". It differs from the ale process in which yeast rises to the top of the vessel after fermentation. The beer is then run off into storage tanks where it is kept for maturing for anything between six weeks to three months before it is filtered, bottled and sent out for sale. During this conditioning period a secondary fermentation takes place.

To enjoy the flavour of Lager at its best, drink it cool, but not too cold as to dull the palate.

673

Recently there has been a substantial increase in the popularity of canned beer, and though in fact there is only one beer in Britain that is brewed specially for canning, canned beer has come into its own because beer has become a home drink on a scale greater than ever before. Cans are easy to carry, easy to store; there are no empties to return and the beer keeps better and longer.

STORAGE AND HANDLING OF BEER

Keeping and serving beer is an art in itself. Beer is not a simple, manufactured product which will keep on a shelf or in a store room until it is required. It is a living thing, coming to maturity and declining from it. The care and constant attention of cellarman and barman are essential if beer is to be sampled at its best.

There are three main types of beer: Fined Draught Beer, Canister Beer and Bottled/Canned Beer. Each beer is distinguished by the way in which it is presented to the customer and it is specially brewed to meet his requirements.

FINED DRAUGHT BEER. The handling of fined draught beer in the "pub" is a continuation of the brewing process. In all breweries great care is taken to produce beers of a consistent quality and they are brewed under the most hygienic conditions.

Similar conditions should exist in the cellar of any public house. All utensils and equipment for the handling of beer must be scrupulously clean and the atmosphere of the cellar as fresh as possible.

Fined draught beer is delivered when partially fermented. The last and final fermentation takes place in the cellar of the public house, and because fermentation is affected by temperature, beer should be stored between 55° and 58°F. A careful check should be kept by thermometer, which should hang away from the wall at cask level.

The "condition" or CO_2 content of draught beer is produced by the natural fermentation of yeast within the cask. Surplus

674

CO_2 is allowed to escape through a porous peg, and the yeast is carried to the bottom of the cask with the aid of fining. Finings are added before the beer is despatched from the brewery. Casks must always be considered and treated individually. The amount of condition in the beer is determined by the careful use of vent pegs.

The fermentation in the cask eventually slows down and as the beer is drawn off, air starts coming into contact with the beer remaining in the cask. It is at this point that deterioration of quality in the beer can start. It is therefore important to keep air away from beer as much as possible; to this end casks must be tight pegged when not being drawn on, and the casks should be on storage for as short a time as possible.

One of the main causes of unsatisfactory beer is the return of beer to cask. No matter what care is taken or how small the quantity, if the beer is returned there is a very serious risk of upsetting the whole cask.

CANISTER BEER is a bright filtered beer with a predetermined CO_2 content. It is rendered biologically stable by pasteurisation and is dispensed from a metal container by CO_2 pressure.

CO_2 is soluble and the dissolved CO_2 is kept in solution by applying a specific pressure for a given temperature. This equilibrium is known as balanced pressure. All reducing valves are set to the correct pressure at the time of installation and it should never be necessary to interfere with them.

The successful dispensing of canister beers with a high CO_2 content depends almost entirely on the dispense tap. There are specially designed taps with a flow regulator, which can be adjusted, to dispense this type of beer.

BOTTLED AND CANNED BEERS are bright filtered beers with a predetermined CO_2 content. Beer will stay bright in bottle only for a limited time and so it is important not to carry unnecessary stock and that stocks are properly rotated.

Cider

Good cider can be made only from a special form of cider apple. There are many varieties, the best known being the "Foxwhelp" and "Kingston Black". These apples are very sweet and have little acidity. They have a quality which gives the cider made from them both character and body.

Ciders produced in the various cider-making counties differ considerably in style and flavour and potency, the choice being one of individual taste. But, generally, cider has many claims to favour for general household use with its delightfully refreshing character. Like beer, it will stay bright in bottle only for a limited period.

APPENDICES

British Drinking Glasses

HISTORY Of all the materials from which, for over two thousand years, drinking vessels have been made—and these include horn, silver, wood, pewter, pottery and glass—the only survivor in our country for the consumption of wines and spirits, apart from use on ceremonial occasions, is glass.

This is remarkable if only by virtue of the fact that of all these materials glass is by far the most fragile. To understand the universal appeal of glass today it may be helpful to examine very briefly the growth of the industry and how it took root in our country.

All glassware for the purpose of drinking, and, incidentally, for many other uses, owes its origin to a device of the simplest character. Some 2,000 years ago, in Syria, the blow-pipe—a hollow rod—replaced the original solid iron rod round which threads of molten glass were wound.

From that moment onwards the story of the glass vessel was one of rapid progress in the Roman-occupied world, with the Syrians and Egyptians as the pioneers in the craft.

It has always been assumed, from the discovery of a Roman glass furnace at Caistor near Norwich, that glass-making was brought to Britain by the Romans. Certainly we know, from the relics that remain from the Roman occupation, that much glass was imported into Britain from Egypt, Syria, and from the neighbouring province of Gaul, and it is reasonable to suppose that foreign glass-makers may have been brought over by the Romans.

The records show that by the thirteenth century glass-makers from Normandy had settled in the forest districts of Kent, Surrey and Sussex, where their principal product was coloured window-glass. One of these was Laurence Vitrearius (that is, Laurence the glass-maker), a Norman who settled at Chiddingfold in 1226 and was soon busy making glass for the windows of Westminster Abbey.

The essential requirement for the early glass-makers, as indeed it is today, was fuel. By settling in forests they were assured of an abundant supply of cheap fuel and also of an essential ingredient, the potash that comes as a by-product from burning bracken. When the forests could yield no more fuel the early glass-makers moved elsewhere, and by the sixteenth century their successors had established small glass works in Hampshire, Gloucestershire, Worcestershire, Shropshire, and finally in areas where coal was abundant, such as Newcastle-upon-Tyne, and at Stourbridge where pot-clay was also available.

In the fifteenth and sixteenth centuries the finest glass in the world came from Venice and in 1575 an Italian glass-maker, Verzelini, was granted by Queen Elizabeth a twenty-one-year exclusive licence to make Venetian glassware in London and to teach the craft to the English. Verzelini set up his glass-house in Broad Street in the City of London, but it is to a French Huguenot, Carré, and his glass-makers from Lorraine to whom may be ascribed the chief credit for establishing glass-making in England. Later, Verzelini's licence was taken over by a retired soldier and financier, Sir Jerome Bowes, who, pursuing a policy of monopoly, combined the twin practices of importing glassware from Venice and of employing Italians to make it at Broad Street.

In 1615 a retired admiral, Sir Robert Mansell, set out to bring the industry under single ownership, and with such success that three years later he had bought out all his competitors. To Mansell rather than to any other may be assigned the retrospective title of "father" to the British glass industry, for it was under his control of the trade that the first steps were taken to create an individual art of British glass. Like Bowes, Mansell lacked knowledge of glass itself and was therefore largely at the mercy of his workmen. But he knew where to get the craftsmen he needed and these came to him from Murano and Mantua. Coal supplies for the Broad Street furnaces came by sea from Scotland until the cost became prohibitive, when Tyneside coal was used. Irritated by Scottish glass-makers who lured his workmen away, he bought the Fifeshire glass industry and moved its employees to London.

In 1664 an event with consequences of far-reaching value for British glass took place when the London Glass-Sellers Company was incorporated by Royal Charter. Inspired, as was the Royal Society founded two years earlier, by the spirit of scientific enquiry and possibly by a determination to be rid of temperamental foreigners, the Glass-Sellers Company engaged an amateur chemist, George Ravenscroft, to undertake glass research, granting him a patent for seven years for the invention of an English glass resembling rock-crystal. The Company built two glass-works, one in London, and the other, chiefly for experiment, at Henley-on-Thames. It was mainly at Henley that Ravenscroft worked until his death in 1681 and where he made the discovery which had consequences as dramatic as the Syrian invention of the blow-pipe some 1,700 years before.

Ravenscroft's quest was for a metal combining the strength and clarity of rock crystal with the tractability of glass. It is probable that for his source of silica Ravenscroft used English flints in place of Venetian pebbles and for the alkali, potash in place of soda. But the reluctance to melting of the flints required a fluxing agent and, for this purpose, Ravenscroft introduced oxide of lead (that is, red lead or litharge). In 1676 the Company was able to report that the characteristic defect (decay) in flint glass had been remedied and in the same year Ravenscroft was allowed to use a raven's head as a seal on the Company's glasses. This was indeed the beginning of what Mr. W. B. Honey (late Keeper of the Department of Ceramics of the Victoria and Albert Museum) has called "a truly English art of glass".

Ravenscroft's glass was the forerunner of all of what has come to be known since as lead crystal glass. It was much heavier, softer and more fusible at lower temperatures than the Venetian glass. It is recognisable by its great brilliance, by a characteristic darkness in the shadows and by its light-dispersing properties. Its acceptance was so rapid that, within a few years, nearly a hundred glass houses, substituting sand for flints, were making it. The period from about 1690 onwards represents, according to several authorities, a period in English table-glass making which has not been surpassed until recent years.

We may now consider the composition of glass and the basic method by which lead crystal was and still is made.

COMPOSITION AND MANUFACTURE

In its simplest form, glass is a mixture of silica (sand or flint), alkali (soda or potash) and limestone which, melted by heat to a temperature of about 1300 to 1400°C, is transformed into a smooth semi-translucent material. The resultant material on cooling would be unusable without the addition of other ingredients, and many of these were known to, and used by, the medieval glass-makers. They even knew, long before Ravenscroft's discovery, that lead oxide increased the brilliance of coloured glass and that it assisted the fusing process, that manganese oxide neutralised the residual green from the iron inherent in sand, and that oxides of iron, copper, cobalt, manganese and tin produced a range of bright colours.

Nowadays, many other materials are added to the basic mixture to produce the type of glass needed, the range of colours and tints available is endless (in the 1930s one firm alone was offering some 1,200 tints), and there is no problem, as there was in olden times, in producing a glass entirely free from colour.

682

To facilitate the melting process and for reasons of economy every mixture contains a proportion of broken glass ("cullet") of known composition.

The basic principles used in the production of hand-made lead crystal glassware have changed little since Ravenscroft's day, but methods and equipment, particularly furnaces, are, of course, greatly improved. Melting takes place in a dome-shaped pot of fire-clay made by hand. The pot usually has a hood with an aperture two feet above ground level. Heat, formerly from burning wood and coal, is now generated from town's gas, oil or electricity.

In many glass-works, pots, each containing its own mixture, are placed in a ring in the furnace, each with its own aperture facing outwards. The molten glass, sticky and ductile, is collected in an iron tube by the "gatherer" and formed into a cylindrical or globular shape by rolling on a cast iron slab ("marvering"). Several gatherings of molten glass may be needed before a sufficient volume has been collected, "marvered" and blown into a bubble. This bubble is then converted into a shape akin to its final form by swinging it and rolling it. In the case of pressed glassware, the white-hot glass is dropped straight into the metal mould without preliminary manipulation. Alternatively, the free part may be transferred to an iron rod ("punty") for further working. During these processes heat is lost and frequent visits to the "glory hole" are made to restore the glass to its original ductility and finally to impart to the surfaces the brilliant fire polish characteristic of all hand-made glassware. Symmetry of shape is preserved by a constant rotation of the tube or rod. When the final shape has been achieved and while the glass is still hot, such embellishments as handles for jugs or beakers, stems and feet for wine glasses, and other decoration, are applied to the basic article, which is then removed from the rod or pipe and placed in an annealing tunnel kiln ("lehr"). All glass from the hands of its maker, whether it be worked by machine or by man, contains strains and stresses which, on cooling, will inevitably cause it to disintegrate. These strains are removed by controlled cooling in the "lehr".

Superfluous portions of the glassware are then removed by grinding and the piece, if it is to be decorated, will pass to the decorating shop for cutting, engraving or etching, or applied colouring, as the case may be.

For cutting a pattern or design on the external surfaces, by far the most usual form of decoration, a rotating wheel of copper with an edge shaped according to the design is used. The wheel is fed with an abrasive, usually emery in oil, and the glass surface to be decorated is presented to the cutting edge and held firmly against it. Engraving by diamond point has been carried out by artists for hundreds of years. It can be seen nowadays on a commemorative goblet decorated by Lawrence Whistler, to mention one of our most celebrated glass engravers, but being a costly process is unsuitable for glassware in general use.

In etching, the article is coated with wax. The design is drawn through the wax to the glass surface. The article is then immersed in a mixture of hydrofluoric and sulphuric acids which eat away the exposed portions of the glass. The design can also be applied by means of a wax transfer and the glass surface etched with a paste of ammonium fluoride. Another method is by sand blasting in which very fine sand is projected by compressed air through a stencil in such a way as to remove the glass and to leave behind a matt surface.

Painting of drinking glasses by hand has now become a rarity and has largely been replaced by the transfer and silk-screen processes. Transfers for use on glass are available in a prolific variety of designs and tints. They are relatively simple to apply and after firing-in become a permanent part of the glass.

In a post-war development which reached England from Scandinavia, decoration can be applied by means of an offset printing plate. This again requires firing-in to render it permanent.

In the space available it has been possible to deal only with the basic processes used in making lead crystal glassware. There is no real substitute for seeing it made oneself, a fact which is

684

appreciated by the manufacturers, many of whom are notable for their willingness to allow conducted parties to visit their works.

EIGHTEENTH AND NINETEENTH CENTURIES

The design of British glassware under the Hanoverian dynasty was affected by two influences. First, by the influence of German taste imparted by Britain's monarchy, a general aversion to French drinking habits, and the importation of Bohemian glass under the Treaty of Utrecht (1713); and secondly by an excise duty on glass, imposed in 1745, which levied a tax by weight of article.

In those days drinking glasses tended to be much larger than anything we use today, but they were gradually supplemented by a great variety of smaller glasses, some with short stems for ale, others with tall stems and wide bowls. Bases of wine glasses were thick and solid and edges and feet were often folded over to give added strength. The excise duty was to exert a profound effect on design and decoration until it was repealed a century later. Inevitably, it encouraged manufacture of vessels of lighter weight and with more surface decoration, which by removing glass reduced the weight of the piece. It encouraged the manufacture of glass the value of which was represented more in applied decoration than in its weight. It also caused the lead content to be reduced, which in its turn gradually changed the appearance of the material.

Wine glasses devolved into a few basic shapes and it is for its decorative effects that this period is mainly notable. The great balusters of earlier periods gave place to smaller glasses more suited to spirits and fortified wines fashionable in the eighteenth century. These smaller designs were helpful to the glassmaker who, being taxed by weight, was able to make more glasses from the same volume of molten glass. They were decorated on bowl, stem and foot, either, as we have noted earlier, in the blowing or in the cold state by engraving and painting. Polished cutting became popular at the end of the century.

Another effect of the ever-increasing excise duty was the removal of English glass-makers to Ireland, where no duty existed, and in 1783 a glass house was established at Waterford with the help of a Stourbridge craftsman. Others were founded elsewhere by West Country and Midland manufacturers as an extension of their activities. Both in Ireland and in England the nineteenth century inaugurated a reaction against the glass fashions of the previous era. Deep cut patterns to a formal motif became the vogue and often covered the whole surface. But the Irish Excise Act of 1825 virtually brought Irish production to an end.

A further development was the trend towards a strict codification of drinking glasses and the production of vast sets of matching glassware for every social drinking occasion.

As capacities and numbers of glasses became more standardised so design and decoration increased in variety. In the second half of the century, drinking glasses were decorated by cutting, engraving, etching and enamelling or by a combination of several of these, and coloured glasses become popular.

English cut glass was by now much esteemed on the Continent, where the brilliance imparted by its lead content made it generally preferred to its Bohemian counterpart.

With the repeal of the Excise duty on glass in 1845 came a surge of activity in glass-making and a revival of past styles. It was also the beginning of a great advance in glass technology led by Robert Lucas Chance at Smethwick. The Great Exhibition of 1851, housed in a building constructed largely of glass, provided the focal point for the display of a great deal of elaborate glassware in, by the standards of today, execrable taste. Moulded glass to simulate cut glass made its first appearance and, owing to its relative cheapness, achieved a popularity which has lasted right up to our time.

The Exhibition was followed by a period of reform with William Morris expounding his theory of "fitness for purpose" and his emphasis on simplicity in design and rejection of elaborate decoration.

<table>
<tr><td>GLASS OF OUR
TIME</td><td>

The early part of this century will perhaps be recognised by glass historians as a period in which two developments of profound significance for table glassware took place. William Morris was to be followed over the years by a succession of eminent designers who have all made an impact on the design of British drinking glasses. It may be regarded as a period when copying of previous styles gave place to a serious effort in creative design and decoration.

</td></tr>
</table>

GLASS OF OUR
TIME

The early part of this century will perhaps be recognised by glass historians as a period in which two developments of profound significance for table glassware took place. William Morris was to be followed over the years by a succession of eminent designers who have all made an impact on the design of British drinking glasses. It may be regarded as a period when copying of previous styles gave place to a serious effort in creative design and decoration.

The second development really began in the 1920s with the importation from America of the first semi-automatic machines for the production of glass bottles and containers and the subsequent application of automatic methods to the manufacture of glass tableware.

But first let us examine some of the designers and their achievements. Even before the turn of the century, James Powell and Sons' glass factory at Whitefriars was making tumblers and wine glasses of pure shape and simple design for William Morris. From then onwards, the tradition was maintained by members of the Powell family and others in the firm for glass of fine quality and, by the standards of those days, of austere decoration. These designers, having been brought up in the glass trade, combined technical knowledge of their material with a flair for shape and colour. At the same time, some of the Stourbridge manufacturers made a break with tradition and took into their employment a number of independent designers with originality and talent. Amongst these was the architect Keith Murray who, in working for Stevens and Williams, was able to reveal in his designs for engraving a rare appreciation of the light-refracting properties of lead crystal glass. Other established artists who designed for the glass trade include Paul Nash, Dame Laura Knight, Graham Sutherland and Eric Ravilious. But this experiment, although salutary in its intention, has not had a lasting effect and most of the successful designs have come from designers who, trained at the Stourbridge School of Art or at the Royal College of Art in London or at the Edinburgh College of Art, have entered the glass industry.

Meanwhile, an entirely new approach to manufacturing methods was taking place elsewhere and the age of automation in glass had started.

So far in this chapter we have considered exclusively the hand-wrought production of lead crystal glass, glass which by virtue of its intrinsic quality was mainly destined for the tables of the well-to-do. Now we must turn to the mass market and to another group of manufacturers operating mainly in the North of England who, by intensive use of machines, were to bring to a successful conclusion their attempts to sell low-cost glass-ware of fine design to the general public and to licensed victuallers.

It is not possible, within the confines of this article, to examine the achievements of every manufacturer in this sphere. One of the early pioneers in the automatic field, however, was United Glass Works (now United Glass Ltd.) with their range of Sherdley pressed ware and of Ravenhead stemware. They had the misfortune to enter the field for automatic glass table-ware at a time of the worst national economic crisis in living memory, the crisis of 1931, and at a time when foreign imports were at their peak. They were also handicapped by lack of experience of their American machines and by the fact that there was no designer at hand with knowledge of designing for automatic machinery. Credit for the courageous decision to embark on this unfamiliar territory must be shared with the firm's sole distributors, Johnsen and Jorgensen Ltd., for the British public had been for long prejudiced in favour of patterns which simulated cut-crystal and there was no certainty about its acceptance of an unfamiliar range of table glassware. But by the end of 1932, after endless experiments and setbacks, the Sherdley range of forty articles had become established on the British market. The introduction of the Ravenhead stemware was interrupted by the war, but in 1945 the project was resuscitated.

Happily the Board of Trade endorsed it and made available the necessary licence for the American machines and for the currency with which to buy them.

As designer for the new range of stemware the firm appointed Mr. A. H. Williamson, A.R.C.A., and he has been their chief designer ever since. In 1949 Ravenhead ware came into being with a port and sherry glass. Today it has truly permeated the life of the nation and one finds it in every place where refreshment is served, from the humblest inn to the four-star hotel. Simplicity and uniformity of shape, the brilliance of its fire polished surfaces, and continuity of supply, all have contributed to a story in which manufacturer and designer, combining in a happy relationship, have achieved an outstanding success.

We may therefore bless the advent of automation in glass tableware manufacture, as practised by two of its principal exponents, United Glass and Dema, for what they have done to bring glass of excellent design within reach of the public. A portion of the drinking glass output goes to the factory of Clayton Mayers and Co. Ltd., where it is decorated by mechanical cutting to designs of exceptional distinction.

A section of the industry important to the public and to the catering trade produces a wide variety of drinking glasses from semi-automatic machines and from handpressing. Some of the glassware is decorated by transfers and by silk-screen and sold under the name of "Fiesta".

The British have always been fortunate in the variety of available wines and nowadays wine lists increase year by year. Our glass industry has kept itself in step with this trend and produces well-designed, quality-controlled drinking glasses for every occasion. All drinking needs are satisfied by a few basic shapes in different sizes. Although their use is not obligatory and capacities may vary, certain shapes have been evolved as being most

OLD FASHIONED

HOCK

TUMBLER

CHAMPAGNE

PORT

SHERRY

TABLE WINE

LIQUEUR

BRANDY

COCKTAIL

suitable for various types of wine and spirits. These are:

> Tumbler (for spirits with aerated additives)
> Hock
> Sherry
> Champagne
> Port
> Table Wine
> Liqueur
> Brandy
> Cocktail

Some of the forms in general use are shown in the accompanying illustration.

All the manufacturers employ designers who are either members of the staff or who are engaged for special commissions. There has been a welcome revival of the eighteenth-century practice of engaging artists to design suites for special purposes. B.O.A.C. aeroplanes, the *Canberra* liner, and the Hunting Lodge Restaurant in Regent Street, to choose three at random, all serve refreshments in glass specially commissioned.

For much historical material used in this chapter I am indebted to *Glass through the Ages* by E. Barrington Haynes, to *English Glass* by W. B. Honey, to Mr W. E. C. Stuart of Stuart's Crystal, and to the Glass Manufacturers' Federation. The Federation maintains a permanent display of glass at 19 Portland Place, London, W.1, where much of what has been described in this chapter may be seen.

A Cellar of One's Own

Every wine lover dreams of a cellar of his own. Although modern houses and flats pose formidable problems for the correct storage of wine, there is no reason why he should not accumulate a stock of wines to suit his individual requirements. It is surprising what enthusiasm and enterprise can accomplish in the most unpromising settings. If all else fails, much of the actual stock will have to remain in the cellars of some benevolent wine merchant, who will store his wine for a modest fee.

If he is fortunate enough to possess somewhere to store his wines at home, the points to remember are simple. It should not be exposed to light of any kind, for this is one of the great enemies of wine. The temperature should be as constant as possible. The range between 50°F and 60°F is ideal. Because fluctuations are so damaging, an unvarying temperature of even 65°F summer and winter would be preferable to day temperatures of 60° followed by night temperatures of 40°.

All wines, of course, must be stored lying down so that the wines come in contact with the cork. Unless this is done, the cork will dry out, contract, and so lose its effectiveness as a seal, for air is the third great enemy of wine. Oxidisation destroys the wine. On the other hand, a hermetic seal would prevent natural development. In contrast, spirits must be kept standing up, otherwise the action of the alcohol on the cork will in time make the spirit taste corky.

Wine racks of standard sizes or made to fit a particular space are nowadays freely obtainable through any good wine merchant. The honeycomb type with individual spaces for each bottle is the best and most durable, and this can be made to measure.

It is, of course, hardly possible in a chapter of this sort to give precise advice as to what a cellar should consist of. For one thing, any particular cellar must reflect the tastes as well as the pocket of its owner. On the other hand, there is a certain amount of general advice which can be given.

RED BORDEAUX

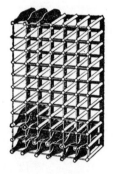

This usually forms one of the stable foundations of any good cellar. The best advice is to buy Red Bordeaux when it first becomes available. This is likely to be when the wine is about three years old. From a money-saving point of view, this is one of the best wines to buy, because Claret requires longer ageing than almost any other natural wine, and in these days wine merchants cannot afford to keep their stock for maturing for nothing as so many did in former days, therefore the sooner one can purchase the better. The inexperienced in the tasting and judgment of very young wines must to some extent rely on the advice of the wine merchant.

Good Clarets, whether from the better *Bourgeois* growths or from the *Cru Classé*, usually become mature enough to begin drinking when between six and eight years old, and are likely to be at their best when somewhere between seven and twenty years old, depending on the vintage and the district. Wines from St. Émilion and Pomerol usually mature more quickly than those from the Médoc and Graves.

WHITE BORDEAUX (DRY)

For the purpose of laying down, we must really confine ourselves to the Graves district. Wines may be bought when between two and three years old. They will be mature when between three and five years old and will be at their best when between four and ten years old. It is, however, only a few of the finest and fuller-bodied wines, such as Haut-Brion Blanc, Laville Haut-Brion and Malartic Lagravière, which really repay keeping for as long as ten years. On the other hand, a relatively light but extremely fine wine like Domaine de Chevalier often requires five or six years' ageing to be at its best.

WHITE BORDEAUX (SWEET)

These can first be bought when three or four years old. Mostly one can begin to drink them at five years, but they will remain at their best certainly up to twenty years.

RED BURGUNDY

This is the other great pillar for any comprehensive cellar. Some will find a more important place for these wines than Clarets, depending, of course, on taste. The wines should be bought when two to three years old. They mature more quickly than Bordeaux wines and are usually ready to drink when between four and seven years old, being at their best between five and twenty years old. Much depends here on the classification of the wine. There is a much greater difference in Burgundy between an ordinary Commune wine such as Nuits St. Georges or Beaune and a vineyard wine such as Nuits St. Georges Les Vaucrins or Pommard Rugiens, than is to be found in Bordeaux between *Bourgeois* growths and *Cru Classé*. In Burgundy few of the commune wines will repay keeping for more than seven or eight years. If one wants to drink older Burgundy than this, one must lay down single vineyard wines.

WHITE BURGUNDY

These can be bought when two to three years old, will be mature enough to drink when between three and four years old, and are likely to be at their best at between four and ten years old. With changes in vinification and in taste, White Burgundies on the whole are lighter and fresher than they were but, on the other hand, do not last so long. It is only the very best single vineyard wines from Puligny, such as Le Montrachet,

Chevalier Montrachet and Bâtard Montrachet, which will repay keeping for ten years, and even then much depends on the individual grower. The wine must have a certain amount of body and fatness to repay keeping for more than six or seven years.

MOSELLE | Because these wines are bottled very young these days, they are best bought when only one or two years old. They will be mature at between two and four years old, and at their best between three and ten years old. It is necessary, of course, to except from this generalisation a handful of very exceptional Beerenausleses, which may take six or seven years to reach maturity and then last for many years longer. On the whole, however, most Mosel wines are best drunk young, say within four to five years. This even applies to Spätlese wines. Good Auslese wines of years such as '59 or '64 will, however, benefit from longer keeping.

RHINE WINE | Again due to early bottling, these can now be bought when about two years old. They will be mature enough to be drunk between two and five years, and at their best between three and fifteen years. Again there are big differences according to vintage and style. On the whole it is best to suggest laying down only German wines of the best years such as '64, '59 and '53. There are, of course, important exceptions, particularly amongst the Eiswein. Both '61 and '62 produced quite an important crop of these. Most of the lighter wines, even of good vintage, are often enjoyable when three to four years old, but the heavier Ausleses, Beerenausleses and Trockenbeerenausleses require rather longer keeping. Well-kept '49s and '53s are still extremely enjoyable in this category.

VINTAGE CHAMPAGNE | Some people like to keep a small stock of vintage Champagne as they prefer not to drink the youngest wines. In 1967, for instance, the vintage generally available is the '61 vintage. The

696

'59 vintage, which is rapidly disappearing, has in most cases proved a rather bad bet for keeping. Most of its wines are ageing rapidly. Good '55s, however, are at their best. Many '52s and '53s are also still excellent. As a general rule, it would probably be true to say that vintage Champagne is at its best between six and fifteen years old, depending very much on one's taste. What is absolutely essential, however, for the preservation of Champagne in good condition is a really good cellar. It is no good laying down vintage Champagne for five years in a warm cellar and expecting to obtain a good result.

VINTAGE PORT

Vintage Port is bottled when two years old, and it is best to suggest buying this wine as soon as it is first offered. From then on it steadily appreciates in price. Most vintage Ports come to maturity when between twelve and fifteen years old and are at their best at between fifteen and thirty years old. Because of the way vintage Ports are made, these dates are very much more firm and sure than any other dates for wine maturation.

Other Fortified Wines

Most people probably do not think it worth while to lay down other fortified wines, but this depends very much on taste. Fine Amontillados, Olorosos and Cream Sherries can gain considerably in character if kept in bottle for three years and upwards. They would then, of course, need to be decanted. Light, dry Sherries of the Fino and Manzanilla types should only be bought as required. They lose their character in bottle.

Madeira is one of the most long-lived of all wines. Very few actual vintage wines are available, the finest wines often being sold as "Solera" followed by the date when this was begun. Like Sherry, Madeira essentially improves in cask, but a few bottles of a fine old Madeira are well worth putting away, if taste runs to this type of dessert wine.

The wines which have been mentioned so far all merit laying down for some reasonable period of time, but in a good cellar room must also be found for wines which justify only short-term cellaring but are none the less well worth a place. A few observations may be useful.

Beaujolais

These delicious wines deserve a place in every wine lover's cellar. The essential quality to be enjoyed, however, is one of youth and freshness, and Beaujolais should mostly be consumed when between one and five years old. A good Beaujolais, Beaujolais Supérieur or Beaujolais Villages, is an ideal everyday drink and should be consumed within the first year of its life. That is to say, one should suggest a wine bottled in the March after the vintage, to be consumed for the following twelve months until the next vintage is available. Good growth Beaujolais such as Fleurie, Julienas, St. Amour and Morgon are usually bottled when they are about a year old and make ideal drinking for two to three years after this. If a Beaujolais is to be kept for a longer period, the safest bet is Moulin à Vent.

Muscadet

This delicious light, dry wine is becoming more appreciated in this country and is now available both English bottled and Domaine bottled. The most recent vintage should always be purchased and it is a mistake to keep the wine for more than a couple of years if its essential qualities are to be enjoyed.

Sancerre and Pouilly Fumé

These two wines are probably the finest dry white wines made in the Loire. From the point of view of delicacy and breed they are often superior to many White Burgundies sold at a similar price. These wines are best bought French bottled. The bottling takes place in the spring following the vintage. The wines are usually at their best after about six months in bottle. It is unwise to keep them for more than four or five years.

Alsace

These attractive natural wines deserve a place in the cellar of any

698

lover of white wines. They are usually at their best when two to three years old, but the fuller Gewurztraminer and Tokay d'Alsace (or Pinot Gris as it is alternatively known) often repay keeping for six to seven years. The higher quality Riesling wines which are often followed by the word "Reserve", or sometimes indeed that of "Auslese", frequently do not develop their full character for four or five years.

Rhône Wine
There are three classic wines from this region which deserve the attention of anyone who enjoys full-bodied red wines— Côte Rotie, Hermitage and Châteauneuf-du-Pape. A good Châteauneuf-du-Pape or Hermitage should be drunk when between four and eight years old. The best Côte Rotie deserves to be kept rather longer, for ten or twelve years.

New German Wine Law

The new German wine law has now come into full effect with the 1971 vintage, although some bye-laws and area regulations have not yet been published. The laws are complicated, and this article is intended to explain the broad outlines as they will affect the trade and consumer.

The most important consideration in framing the new law was consumer protection, and the Germans have gone a long way in their endeavours on this score, in five basic points:

(1) Reduction in number of vineyard names.

(2) Definitive area names for "mass-wines".

(3) Minimum qualities are laid down for all types of wine and specially for predicate wines. The latter are based on original qualities of the grapes—determined analytically in the wine and registered with the reference number on the label. Even "Tafelweine" have official minimum standards.

(4) Vines may only be grown on land scheduled for vineyards.

(5) Only officially permitted or recommended grape varieties may be planted.

Need for new wine law

Until 1969 the wine law of 1930 was ruling. In the last 40 years the changes in the wine industry have been enormous; viticulture, grape varieties, quality of production, cellar techniques and bottling methods have improved, and it was obvious that a new law was necessary to accommodate them.

Unfortunately the various sectors of the trade (small growers, co-operatives, large estates) have always held their own views and agreement between them was only possible in 1969 after lengthy negotiation, when it was realised that the EEC wine laws were due for publication, and it was hoped that existent national laws could continue. As the EEC laws take precedence, much to the annoyance of the Germans, their "new" law was outdated even before introduction, and a new law was finally produced and passed in July 1971.

| Main points | (1) The definition of qualities (minima qualifications). |
| | (2) The definition of production areas. |

Main points

(1) The definition of qualities (minima qualifications).

(2) The definition of production areas.

(3) The creation of new vineyard sites and site names for larger sites (Grosslagen. Bereich) and the setting up of a vineyard register.

(4) The protection of quality by limiting vine varieties and quantities of production.

(5) The legal introduction of modern scientific methods, and the abolition of some old techniques of treatment.

(6) The EEC law classifies wine production as Table wine and Quality wine. For German wines with their traditional selective harvesting methods, it was necessary to divide the quality wines into two divisions under: (a) Quality wine from defined area (Qualitätswein bestimmter anbaugebiete) i.e. ObA and (b) Quality wines with predicate (Qualitätswein mit prädikat).

It must be remembered that the old term "natur" which referred to unchaptalised wines, is not permissible, and that it is the "Qualitätswein mit prädikat" which are the unchaptalised wines, that the QbA are the chaptalised wines. Qualitätswein may be natural, if the committee of examination refuses the applied for predicate. France, of course, has never differentiated between the natural and the sugar enriched wine.

Classification

Tafelweine and Quality wines, can be made in all German vineyards. but the Tafelweine can be offered only under the name of four main regions (Weinbaugebeite), whereas for quality wines the same area is divided in 11 regions (Anbaugebiete).

Tafelweine (see below for individual areas)
A. Rhine and Moselle (Areas 1–8 incl.)
B. Main (Area 9)
C. Neckar (Area 10)
D. Oberrhein [(a) Romertor, (b) Burgengau (both Baden) (Area 11).

The wines, as *all* German wines, must be made: (a) from permitted, recommended or temporarily admitted vines; (b) in accordance with the technical section of the law.

702

If only German wines have been used, the wine must be called "Deutscher Tafelwein". At the time of sale, a Tafelwein must have 8·5° alcohol and the label must state the type of wine (white or red) if it does not give another geographical designation, and the name of the bottler.

Qualitätswein bA

The eleven defined areas are: (1) Ahr; (2) Hessische Bergstrasse: (3) Mittelrhein; (4) Mosel-Saar-Ruwer; (5) Nahe; (6) Rheingau; (7) Rheinhessen; (8) Rheinpfalz; (9) Franken; (10) Württenburg; and (11) Baden.
The wines must be produced from grapes permitted per quality wines and must have been given a Prüfungsnummer (the official examination or analytical control number).

Qualitätswein mit Prädikat

The following predicates are allowed: Kabinett, Spätlese, Auslese, Beerenauslese, Trockenbeerenauslese, and Eiswin, and can only be used with their Prüfungesnummer. Eiswein is not permitted on its own, but with another predicate, e.g. Eiswein Spätlese or Eiswein Kabinett, etc.
The regulations for Qualitatswein mit Prädikat are:
(1) No addition of sugar is allowed (for enrichment).
(2) For Kabinett, Spätlese and Auslese. there are minima of natural alcohol laid down, which vary from district to district. and also in some instances between grape varieties (see chart).
(3) **Spätlese** must, apart from the minimum alcohol, be made from late gathered grapes which are fully ripe.
(4) **Auslese** can only be made from fully ripe grapes with the exclusion of unripe or sick grapes.
(5) **Beerenaulese** can only be made from "edelfaul" berries (those affected by botrytis) or "overripe" grapes.
(6) **Trockenbeerenauslese** can only be made from shrivelled "edelfaul" grapes, although under certain circumstances of weather when edelfaule is not present. TbA can be made from overripe shrivelled grapes.
(7) **Eiswein** can only be made from grapes which were frozen at the time of harvesting.

(8) The minimum alcohol for "prädikatsweine" are:
Kabinett, Spätlese, Auslese, Eiswein—7° alcohol.
Beerenauslese and Trockenbeerenauslese—5·5° alcohol.
(9) "Prädikatsweine" cannot be bottled until after January 1 following the harvest.
(10) Grapes for making Qualitätswein mit prädikat may only be harvested after informing the relevant authorities.
(11) A Prädikatswein may only originate from a single Bereich.

Qualitätswein and Appellation Contrôlée

There are similarities between the Qualitätswein regulations and the French system of Appellation Contrôlée, but the German law goes further than the French, and protects quality with compulsory analysis with this official reference number shown on the label. For the first time. German wine law mentions permitted production per hectare (rendement) as a principle, but this has not yet been detailed by the various authorities. However, it is said that if the production exceeds the limit, it may still retain its nomenclature rights if the analysis is satisfactory.

Production areas

The production areas have been shown as four main areas (Weinbaugebiete) for Tafelweine and the eleven areas for Qualitätswein. Labelling regulations must be strictly observed, and these must be explained in detail.

Weinbaugebiet—Large areas of production.

Ambaugebiet—Areas of production for qualitätswein, e.g. Rheinhessen, Mosel-Saar-Ruwer, Rheingau, exactly defined areas.

Bereiche—A district within an anbaugebiet, spanning many parishes and vineyards, all of which produce wines of similar character.

Grosslage—(transl. large site). A new name for a collection of Lagen (vineyard sites); replaces the old "generic" site names.

Lage—the site (vineyard). These have been reduced in number, and can only be used for Qualitätswein. In general, the minimum size for a site to be included in the Weinbergsrolle (vineyard register) is five hectares, but there are exceptions.

Naming of wines	"Tafelwein" is a denomination for "vin ordinaire" grown within the EEC, others are called "Tischwein".

"Tafelwein" is a denomination for "vin ordinaire" grown within the EEC, others are called "Tischwein".

(1) A Tafelwein—"Deutscher Tafelwein" is not entitled to use any name smaller than a Bereich. The Deutscher Tafelwein will therefore be labelled with its production area and *Bereich name*. only. It is expected that others will be replaced by Brand Names. *Tafelwein* must appear on the label.

The following may therefore be used:
Name of Weinbaugebiet;
Name (if any) of the sectional area;
The Bereich name;
The village name or Bereich;
The Vintage;

(2) The QbA wines are entitled to use lagen, but they must show qualitätswein and actual Anbaugebiet on the label, together with the prüfungsnummer, and may show the following:
The Bereich name;
The village name;
The lage or grosslage;
The vintage;

(3) Qualitätswein mit prädikat are named as with QbA but with the additional predicate Spätlese, Auslese, etc., etc.

Labelling

A vintage for German wine means that at least 75 per cent was produced from grapes grown in that year.

For a grape variety to be mentioned on a label, the wine must have been made from grapes, 75 per cent of which were that particular variety. If many varieties have been used and none to 75 per cent, then *all* names must be given in descending quantity order.

Exception: Trockenbeerenauslesen. The name of the vineyard is given from which more than 50 per cent of the wine originates.

Estate labels

Now that "original abfüllung" has been deleted, we must accustom ourselves to new terminology. The new wordings are: Auséigenem lesegut and Erzeugerabfüllung, both of which can be used for Tafelwein and Qualitätswein.

In my opinion the words "Estate Bottling" still apply to any wine made from grapes grown, vinified, cellared and bottled by one producer in his own cellars, so that for English-speaking countries, the "sales name" will not change, although the wording of the label will alter.

Other labelling terms

In general, the name of bottler must be given on the wine label. Therefore we may see some of the following:

Eigene abfüllung—own bottling

Abfüllung Weingut A—bottling by Weingut A

Abfüllung Weinkellerei A—bottling by Merchant A

Ausdem Lesegut Weingut A; Abfüllung B: Growth A. bottled by Merchant B and many other variations. Please note when the wine has been bottled by the shipper, the name of the grower can only be stated with his permission.

Deletions of terms used previously

There are many deletions, in particular "natur" and "originalabfüllung". Also descriptive terms, without a comparative standard have been deleted such as "feine", "feinste", "hochfeine, and "edel".

The use of special names for harvesting dates, such as "St. Nikolauswein", "St Barbarawein" are also forbidden as is "Strohwein", "Goldbeerenauslese" and "Edelbeerenauslese".

Liebfraumilch changes

New limitations have been placed on the use of Liebfraumilch as follows:

(1) Liebfraumilch cannot be a Tafelwein. It must be a QbA.

(2) Liebfraumilch can only be used for QbA from Rheinpfalz. Rheinhessen and the Nahe. It is *not* now permissible to use a Rheingau wine or a wine from the Mittelrhein for Liebfraumilch.

(3) The must for a Liebfraumilch must be over 60° oechsle.

(4) The wine must be of pleasant character, and its major part must be produced from Riesling. Sylvaner or Müller-Thurgau. and must possess the taste characteristics of one of these types.

(5) The names of vines may *not* be used with Liebfraumilch (e.g. no more Liebfraumilch, Riesling or Scheurebe)

(6) Liebfraumulch must not be sold with a Prädikat (e.g. no more Liebfraumilch Spätlese, or Auslese).

In my opinion, however, a possible method of overcoming this is to state *all* the normal Prädikat terms: as example.

Changes in taste of German wines

There will be changes as many growers who produced "natur" exclusively in the past are now producing QbA with excellent results. The consumer can buy chaptalised Estate Bottled unblended Quality wines of guaranteed origin at reasonable prices. A more important factor is the permitted "remnant sugar" proportion to the alcohol, which is an adjustable factor where the producer uses süss-reserve (partially fermented must, which is rich in sugar and low in alcohol), to produce the desired effect, by blending a small amount of this with a larger amount of fully fermented (dry) wine of the same vineyard.

Due to the strict regulations, where SO_2 limitations were too small for medium/medium sweet wines, the above blending methods are of necessity standard practice throughout Germany.

In the new law, notice is taken that some wine varieties with more than average acidity such as the Riesling (in most but the best years) require more sugar/alcohol than other types, and whereas the normal ration of alcohol remnant is 3:1, for the Riesling it is 2·5:1 or even 2:1.

In principle, the new law does not limit the remnant sugar proportion for Qualitätswein mit Prädikat, but in all cases the natural characteristics of the wine must be retained. In future, even more than in the past, the born taster with his inborn feeling for harmony and balance will come to the fore. The shipper's name will in future be most important as a guarantee of quality and selection.

A most interesting change will be introduced by the cost of the statutory analysis and printing of labels with the Prüfungs-nummer. We are bound to find growers producing large cuvées, with one analysis and one label printing with the prüfungsnummer, rather than the traditional production with individual casks, each one of which, would require its own analysis and specific labels. Although this is an obvious policy for good marketing it is a sad change for the enthusiast.

The day could be forecast when individual growers will follow the examples of estates such as Schloss Johannisberg and produce only one cuvée in each predicate class. Specialist shippers will of course continue to be highly selective and purchase individual casks for their connoisseur markets.

Specialist items

There are three specialist items of interest.

(a) *Diabetic wine* is a permitted designation when it fulfills three qualifications:

Less than 4 gm sugar per litre:
Less than 25 mg free and 200 mg/l total SO_2.
Less than 12° alcohol.

(This is not a permitted sugar level for a diabetic wine in the UK.)

(b) *Alcohol-free wine* is one which contains less than $\frac{1}{2}$° alcohol and for the sparkling version this is 2°. Labels on both must clearly be marked *alcoholfreier Wein* (alcohol-free wine).

(c) A wine may only be described as *dry* if it contains a maximum of 4 gm/litre unfermented sugar.

New developments

The new law has taken consumer protection as one of its main directives, and the permitted treatments are based on the following premises:

The treatment given, must: (a) protect the quality of the wine; (b) protect the health of the consumer; (c) ensure correct control of all procedures.

There have been changes in permitted treatments, the limit of sulphur dioxide and enrichment (chaptalisation, zuckerung).

The German Wine Law allows only treatments and additions which have been expressly included in the law and all others are strictly forbidden.

(1) Treatments which are forbidden but were previously allowed include the use of Agar-agar, Aferrin, Albumin, Spanish Earth, and Oxygen.

The permitted list now reads as follows (numbers 18–22 are newly permitted substances):

1 Pure Yeast; 2 Carbon dioxide (gas or solid); 3. Sulphur; 4. *Pure gaseous sulphurous acid (SO_2).

5 *Pure potassium sulphate; 6. *Pure L(+) Ascorbic acid (Vitamin C); 7. *Diethylpyrocarbonate (Baycovin); 8. Isinglass; 9. Gelatine; 10. Egg-white (chicken's egg.)

11. *Powdered tannin; 12. Silica gel; 13. Bentonite; 14. *Potassium ferrocyanide (blue fining); 15. Inert filter-material (asbestos, kieselgur and cellulose).

16. Activated charcoal; 17. Polyvinyl polypyorolidone; 18. Pure colloidal silver chloride on aminert carrier; 19. *Pure sorbic acid or potassium sorbate.

20. Pectolytic enzymes; 21. Pure nitrogen gas; 22. *Meta-tartaric acid *within certain strict limits (treatment not allowed in UK (nos. 7 & 19)).

(2) Sulphur dioxide limits

	free SO_2	total SO_2
Tafel and Qualitätsweine	50	300
Auslesen Eiswein and any wines over 14° GL	60	350
Beeren—Trockenbeerenauslesen (in mg/litres)	75	400

Sulphur dioxide is the only preservative/antoxidant permitted in all countries for wines. Many countries allow additional additives to preserve the wine, such as sorbic acid (and its salts) and Baycovin. In the UK only SO_2 is permitted as yet, but it is hoped that the above two products will also be allowed in the not too distant future. The new limits set in the wine-law reflect the necessity to keep the quantity of preservative as low as possible yet varying the dosage for different wine types. Growers and bottlers of German wines should not have any difficulty in adhering to the new limits.

(3) Alcohol

The minimum permitted is: Zone A (all German districts except Baden)—6°, Zone B (Baden)—7°. Special Definitions apply to "alcohol".

(i) *Actual* percentage alcohol of the wine is that actually in the wine.

(ii) *Potential Alcohol* is the percentage of alcohol produced in the wine by all the sugar fermenting.

(iii) *Total Alcohol* is the total of actual and potential alcohol.

(iv) *Natural Alcohol Content* is the total alcohol content (iii) before enrichment (if this takes place).

(4) Chaptalisation

Qualitätswein BA: Only the use of saccharose is permitted. Sugar in solution (wet sweetening) is principally forbidden, but is allowed for a transitional period to 1979 to a maximum of 15 per cent in Zone A for Tafelwein but only 10 per cent for qualitätswein if they have more than 12 gm acidity. Chaptalisation is forbidden for all "Predicate" wines.

Tafelwein: Enrichment is permitted with saccharose, with concentrated must, or concentration by partial freezing.

(a) *Limits of enrichment*

	QbA	Tafelwein
Blue Portugieser	4.0°G.L.	4.0°G.L.
All other types	3.5°G.L.	3.5°G.L.

(b) *Maximum total alcohol permitted*

	QbA	Tafelwein
White wines	12°G.L.	11·5°G.L.
Red wines	12·5°G.L.	12°G.L.

(c) *Enrichment* must be carried out in Zone A before March 16 of the year following the vintage of the wine to be treated.

(d) *Süssung* (sweetening)

Permitted with süssreserve "SR" of equivalent type (EG QbA with QbA "SR", Spätlese with Spätlese "SR") for Tafelwein, Qualitätswein and Qualitätswein with predicate. This is only permitted for the grower or wholesaler (and not for the retailer). The same rules apply as for other blends of wines.

With qualitätswein bA *must* may also be added but limited to an increase of 2 per cent alcohol.

Deacidification: This must be undertaken before 15th March following the harvest, and applies to fresh grapes, must, partially fermented must and wine.

Pure calcium carbonate and acidex are permitted treatments. For tafelwein the use of potassium tartrate is also a permitted treatment.

Further Treatment: it is interesting to note that after rackings, etc., that "fullwein" (topping-up wine) must be an identical classification to the bulk. The topping-up operation is classified as "blending" and an error here may lead to declassification and consequent loss of value.

Qualitätswein mit Prädikat

The minimum ochsle permitted for various grape varieties.

	Ahr	Hessische Bergshasse	Mittel-Rhein	Mosel Saar Ruwer	Nahe	Rheingau	Rhein-Hessen	Rhein-Pfalz	Franken	Würtemberg	Baden
Kabinett	1	2	3	4	5	6	7	8	9	10	11
Riesling	70	73	70	70	70	73	73	73	76	72	72
Müller-Thurgau & Sylvaner		80				80			76		72
All others	73		73	73			76	76	76	75	75/81
All Red grapes		78				78			80		72/75
Weissherbst											
Elbling			70	70	73		73	73			
Spätlese											
Riesling	76	85	76	76	78	85	85	90		85	85
Ruländer Traminer							90	90	90		
Scheurebe Rieslaner										88	
All other White	80		80	80	82		90	90	85	85/88	85/91
All Red	85	90				90	90	90	90		85/88
Auslese											
Riesling	83	95	83	83	85	95	92	92	100	95	98
All other White	88	100	88	88	92	100	95	95	100	95	101
All Red							100	100	100		101
Weissherbst		105				105	105				
Beerenauslese All	110	125	110	110	120	125	120	120	125	124	124
Trockenbeerenauslese All	150	150	150	150	150	150	150	150	150	150	150

GLOSSARY

ABBOCCATO A word used to describe certain Italian wines. It means "sweet" or "semi-sweet".

ACID, ACIDITY All wine has some acid but a wine described as "acid" has too much. Acidity in young wine gives it freshness. Without acidity the wine would be flat and insipid.

AGRAFFE The steel clamp which holds the pressure of the second fermentation in a Champagne bottle.

ALIGOTÉ Prolific white wine grape, grown in Burgundy. The wine is less fine than the Chardonnay and can only be called Bourgogne Aligoté.

APERITIF Any drink taken before a meal as an appetizer to whet the appetite—a Cocktail, a Sherry, etc.

APPELLATION CONTRÔLÉE French Law to protect names and limit production of Wine Districts (see under Bordeaux p. 19).

AROMA A distinctive fresh fragrance which is given off by the wine after being exposed to the air.

ASTRINGENT Term used by a wine taster and applied to wines with an excess of tannin. Many red wines are astringent when young but they mellow and soften with age.

AUSLESE The name given to German wines which are specially superior, are produced from especially ripe grapes, from perfect bunches. Those most affected by the Noble Rot—Botrytis —(in German: *Edelfäule*) are pressed separately and the wine that results is Auslese which is much sweeter than wine of the same year by the same producer. It is also more expensive.

BALANCE Term used to describe a wine which has all the good qualities combined. It has no deficiencies in its bouquet, flavour or character. A well-balanced wine is always a *good* wine— often it is a *great* one.

BARBERA A red wine grape grown principally in Piedmont, also to a small extent in California. The wine is deep-coloured, full-bodied and full-flavoured.

BAUMÉ Scale for measuring degrees of sweetness in wine.

BEERENAUSLESE The name given to rare, very special and expensive German wines made from single grapes which are affected by *Edelfäule*.

BIANCO Italian for white. Any white wine can be termed *Vino Bianco*.

BLANC French for white. Any white wine can be termed *Vin Blanc*.

BLANCO Spanish for white. Any white wine can be termed *Vino Blanco*.

BODEGA The name given in Spain to a warehouse for wine storage, usually above ground.

BODY Wine which is full-bodied is "winy" with an impression of weight which is caused by a fairly high degree of alcohol, say 12° or over. Wine which is light in body may taste watery. A great red Burgundy must have body but a full-bodied Mosel or Chablis would be lacking in balance.

BOTRYTIS CINEREA "Noble Rot". It is called *Edelfäule* in German and *Pourriture Noble* in French. The mould which in certain districts (such as on the Rhine and in the Sauternes district) forms on the skins of grapes which are ripening and gives a concentration of flavour and sugar to the shrivelled grapes. The wine that results is greatly improved in quality.

BOUQUET When young wine which is fresh and fruity has been in contact with the air for some time the oxidisation of the elements in the wine develops esters from which come varying smells. This collection of smells is called a *bouquet*. While the wine is in the cask this *original bouquet* develops with the wine. Then when the wine is bottled, changes take place in the bouquet and the result is more subtle smells called *acquired bouquet*. *Acquired bouquet* is characteristic of fine wines which have taken years to develop in which the balance of the elements which make up a wine make long life possible. Many experts can, on *bouquet* alone, tell the origin, the grape, and near enough the exact age and class of the wine.

BOURGEOIS GROWTH or "**CRU BOURGEOIS**" A category of Bordeaux wine second only in quality to the "classed growths"—the aristocrats. Not so famous as the "classed growths", these wines are of fine quality and worth looking for in a good vintage.

BRANCO Portuguese for white. Any white wine can be termed *Vinho Branco*.

BREED A term used to describe a wine of fine quality, distinguished of its kind.

BRILLIANT A term used for an absolutely clear wine.

BRUT A French term used to describe the driest Champagnes and other sparkling wines. It is drier than "Extra Dry".

BULK PROCESS The fermenting of sparkling wines in large sealed tanks instead of by the Methode Champenoise. No wine can be called Champagne if made by this process.

BUTT A Sherry cask with a capacity of 108 gallons which is equal to 54 dozen bottles.

CABERNET The famous superb wine grape which produces the finest red wines of Bordeaux.

CABINET This is often spelt Kabinett. Used particularly in the Rheingau it means a special reserve natural wine which has no sugar added and which is Estate Bottled. Originally it was the wine which the producer put aside for his own use. Now the term is used more loosely for wines which bring a certain minimum price.

CARAFE A clear glass decanter used for serving wine at table. Inexpensive wines are served "*en carafe*".

CAVE The French word for cellar.

CÉPAGES Vine variety—for example, one of the leading *cépages* of Burgundy is the Pinot Noir.

CHAIS Buildings used to store wine in France; usually above ground but similar to a *cave* or cellar.

CHAMBRER From the French *chambre* (room). The term used for the warming of red wine from cellar to room temperature.

CHAPTALISATION The process of adding sugar to the Must before fermentation. This is done in order to increase the alcoholic content of the wine.

CHARACTER Term used by wine tasters to denote wine with a definite and unmistakable, though not necessarily outstanding, quality.

CHARDONNAY One of the fine white wine grapes. It produces Chablis, Montrachet, etc., the great white Burgundies. It is also the white grape of the Champagne district.

CHASSELAS   White wine grape known as Fendant in Switzerland. Found also in Alsace and in Baden, where it is known as the Gutedel.

CHÂTEAU   The literal translation can be a castle, a manor house, a lodge, etc. In the wine country it can be a large or small country house or even a farmhouse attached to the vineyard where the owner cultivates his own vines and makes his own wine. French law does not allow the word Château to appear on a wine label unless the vineyard really exists, has produced the wine, and has a traditional right to use the name.

CHÂTEAU-BOTTLED   The words château-bottled on a label guarantee the authenticity of the wine—that it is bottled on the estate which has produced it. Not necessarily a guarantee of quality. It is used especially in Bordeaux and is the same as "estate-bottled" which is used in other districts.

CHENIN BLANC   Known also as Pinot de la Loire—a grape that produces white wines of the Loire.

CLAIRETTE   A good white wine grape, grown in southern France and to a lesser extent in California.

CLARET   Originally *Clairet* (clear wine). In England, by tradition, Claret means a red Bordeaux. In other countries the word is loosely used for a light red wine.

CLARETE   A term used in Spain to describe a light red wine of the Rioja district.

CLASSED GROWTHS   Wines of a specific vineyard or estate, officially classified. See *Bordeaux Classification*, p. 29.

CLAVELIN   A special bottle, squat in shape, used for wines of the Jura district of France. Certain *vins jaunes* come in this type of bottle which holds 20½ oz.

CLIMAT   A specific individual vineyard is called a *climat* in Burgundy.

COMMUNE   A township or the administrative council or parish in France.

CO-OPERATIVE   A cellar belonging jointly to a number of small producers.

CORKAGE   A fee paid to a restaurant when bringing one's own wine and having it served in the restaurant.

CRADLE   A wicker, straw or metal basket used for bringing wine to the table in the same horizontal position as in the cellar, so that the sediment is not disturbed—usually in old red wines.

CRIADERAS   Spanish for nursery. Applied to Sherry it means the second, third, fourth, etc., scale or tier where wines are selected and graded before reaching the Solera proper.

CRUS   When applied to vineyards it means the growths or production of the vineyard. The wines produced are usually classified into Crus—Grand Cru, Premier Cru, Deuxième Cru, Cru Classé, etc.

CUVÉE   French—literally meaning cask or vatful. A specific blend of wine different from others that may have the same or similar label. *Première Cuvée* means one of the best wines of a *commune*. *Tête de Cuvée* of a certain château will be the best batch of that vintage.

DEBOURBAGE   A term used in the making of white wine. It means the delaying for twenty-four hours of the fermentation of the grape juice after pressing. This allows time for the juice to clear so that it can be drawn off leaving the coarse sediment.

DECANT   The transferring of wine from its original bottle to a carafe or decanter for serving. This is to separate the clear wine from the sediment which may have formed. It is usually only necessary with old red wines, hardly ever with white wines. Usually two hours before serving is a happy mean for decanting but many wines should be decanted for a shorter period. Very few unfortified wines need decanting more than two hours before serving. The bottle should be placed gently in the cradle, the cork drawn and the wine poured slowly into the decanter until the first sediment appears.

DECANTER   A glass carafe into which wines are decanted. Decanting Sherries, Madeiras, etc., and leaving them on a sideboard causes the wine to deteriorate if left for more than a very few days. Originally, sideboard decanters were used for Spirits and this should still be their proper role.

DEGORGEUR   A skilled worker who releases the crown cork or unclips the first cork of a Champagne bottle to remove the plug with the deposit on it.

DELICATE   A wine-taster's term for a light rather than full wine, not great, but fine and elegant.

DEMI-SEC   Literally—half-dry. It is applied to Champagne and also to other sparkling wines and to some still wines such as Anjou Rosé.

DEPOSIT   The sediment which many red and some white wines throw while in bottle. In white wines this is tasteless and harmless but red wine deposit contains tannin and can be very bitter and unpleasant. It should be left in the bottle when decanting.

DESSERT WINES   Usually applied to fortified sweet wines such as Port or Sweet Sherry as opposed to table or light wines. Can also refer to Sauternes and some Rhine wines which could properly be served with sweet dishes.

DISTINGUISHED   A term used by the wine expert to describe the most distinguished wine. Used only for the finest wines of superb quality.

DOMAINE   In Burgundy a domaine is a single estate made up of vineyards which may not be close together or have the same names. The wines will be kept separate and sold under their vineyard appellations with the name of the Domaine as the producer, on the bottle. Domaine wines, which are estate-bottled have the words *Mise du Domaine* or *Mis en Bouteilles au Domaine* on the label. In the Bordeaux district and in Provence it has practically the same meaning as a Château.

DOSAGE   Before Champagne is disgorged it is quite dry. Then the *dosage* which consists of a varying amount of syrup is added. The amount of *dosage* added will decide whether the Champagne will be *Brut*, Extra Dry, etc.

DOUX   French, meaning sweet. When applied to wine, namely, *vin doux*, it means a wine not quite normal—usually it is not completely fermented. It is hardly ever applied to fine table wines.

DRY   When applied to wine it means one which has been fermented out, that is, a wine without any unfermented sugar remaining in it.

EARTHY   A term applied to wine which has a special flavour due to the kind of soil on which the vines grow. It can be applied to fine wines such as Red Graves.

EDELFÄULE   See Botrytis cinerea.

ÉGRAPPAGE   The process of removing the stalks from the grapes before fermentation.

ELEGANT   A term used by a wine taster to describe a wine of breed but it is not such high praise as "distinguished".

ESTUFA   A Portuguese name for the room where Madeira is held at a high temperature when it is first made, to give it its special flavour.

FINESSE A wine taster's term for a wine which has breed or class—that is, wine more than ordinary in quality.

FINING Clarifying wine by adding certain substances while the wine is in cask. These carry down, in the form of sediment, the particles suspended in the wine, leaving the wine clear.

FLINTY A term describing a dry, clean white wine which has a special bouquet, and a particular finish on the palate.

FLOR Spanish for "flower". In wine making it is the special yeast which develops in Sherry. *Flor* yeast forms a film over the whole surface of the wine and it can live in a higher concentration of alcohol than other yeasts. It introduces a special flavour into the wine and absorbs any sugar remaining in the wine after fermentation, thus making it completely dry. A perfect growth of *flor* is essential for a fine bouquet and flavour of Finos.

FLOWERY This is a term used to describe the bouquet of certain wines. It is likened to the scent of flowers. Fine Mosels have this particular quality as also do some Rieslings.

FOLLE BLANCHE A white grape which gives a pale wine, high in acid and low in alcohol. It is grown in France under various names. A variety found in Armagnac and Cognac (see Picpoul) gives outstanding Brandy.

FORTIFIED Fortified wines are those which have been strengthened by the addition of wine Spirit during or after fermentation. The wines include Sherry, Port, Madeira and Marsala. Their alcohol content is about 20 per cent by volume.

FRAGRANT A wine term which suggests a very pronounced and pleasant aroma.

FRAIS French for fresh or cool. When applied to wines as on a label *servir très frais* it means "Serve well chilled".

FRAPPÉ Used of a wine it means very cold. A liqueur which is served *frappé* is poured over crushed ice.

FREISA A quality Italian red wine grape of the Piedmont. The wine produced from it is also called Freisa.

FRESH This describes a young wine which has not lost its charm.

FRIZZANTE Italian word for a slightly sparkling wine.

FRUITY Wine which has a definite flavour and aroma of fresh fruit is called "fruity". Most fine young wines are "fruity".

FUDER This is a cask used in the Mosel and contains approximately 960 litres. It is used for storage purposes and as a measure rather than for shipping.

FULL A term used for a wine that is big in taste and not light or watery.

FURMINT The famous white wine grape of Hungary and the most important grape used in making Tokay. There are other Hungarian wines made from the Furmint grape and it usually appears on the label following the name of the district.

GAMAY The Beaujolais district produces almost exclusively this excellent red wine grape, for on the clay and granite soil it produces fine wines, but in the Côte D'Or it produces Ordinary wines, which when mixed with Pinot can be called Bourgogne Passe Tout Grains.

GAY LUSSAC French method of measuring volume of alcohol in wines or spirits.

GENERIC Wine name which is not related to the wine's origin; for example, *vin rosé*, sparkling wine. This is also used to denote a district wine such as St. Émilion or Médoc.

GRAPEY Certain grapes give their flavour to wines made from them. If the flavour is too pronounced the wines lack subtlety.

GREAT A term used to describe a wine which has no flaws and has real distinction.

GRENACHE A good quality wine grape produced in the South of France and in the Rioja district of Northern Spain. It is also grown in the Côte du Rhône, in North African vineyards and in California.

GRIGNOLINO An Italian wine grape of excellent quality grown in the Piedmont district and producing a red wine of unmistakable bouquet. Grignolino is an interesting and unusual wine.

GROS PLANT Grape grown near the mouth of the Loire and producing a fresh, light white wine. This is a similar but not so distinguished a wine as Muscadet and is grown in adjoining vineyards.

HARD A term used by wine-tasters for a wine without much charm. Many wines which are "hard" when young develop suppleness in time. The hardness is due to the tannin in the wine.

HARSH This is an extreme hardness in the wine and sometimes it is very astringent. Some wines lose this quality in time.

HEAVY This term applies to a full-bodied wine without much distinction. The heaviness is usually due to an excess of alcohol.

HECTARE Many vineyard areas are expressed in hectares; a hectare is 2·471 acres.

HOCK The English generic term for a Rhine wine—supposed to have derived from Hochheimer.

HOGSHEAD One half of a Butt or Pipe, about 56 gallons. A Claret hogshead is 48 gallons.

HYBRID This term is more usually used in viticultural circles in a derogatory sense to indicate a European vine which has been crossed with an American vine. This has been attempted as a substitute for grafting ever since the Phylloxera, but has never been wholly satisfactory. A cross of two European vines such as Riesling and Sylvaner is usually simply described as "a cross".

JEROBOAM A large-sized wine bottle holding as much as six ordinary wine bottles. For Champagne it is equal to a double magnum or four bottles.

KABINETT See Cabinet.

KNIPPERLE An Alsatian grape which produces a white wine of fair quality.

LAGE German for a specific, named vineyard.

LEES Heavy sediment which is thrown by young wines in cask after fining or racking.

LIQUEUR D'EXPÉDITION The final dosage of cane sugar given to Champagne and other Sparkling wines.

LIQUOREUX French word used to describe a sweet white wine which has retained much of the natural grape sugar. Such a wine would usually have about 3° Baumé or more.

MADERISÉ French term for a wine—white or rosé—which has begun to be spoiled. It is caused by the wine's contact with heat and air or oxygen. Maderisation makes the wine taste unpleasant, flat and musty.

MAGNUM A bottle which is twice the size of a normal bottle.

MALBEC Red wine grape of Bordeaux. A small percentage planted in a vineyard has been found beneficial blended with the Cabernet and Merlot.

MALVASIA (French: *Malvoisie*) Famous ancient white wine grape originally from Greece, now grown in most other Mediterranean countries, in Madeira, South Africa and California. The most famous wine from this grape is perhaps Madeira and the sweet, amber, fortified wines of the district of the Pyrenees.

MARC The lees and stalks remaining after fermentation of the grapes. Often distilled into *Eau-de-Vie-de-Marc* popular with vineyard workers.

MERLOT Prolific, early-ripening wine grape of Bordeaux, next in importance to the Cabernet.

MORIO-MUSCAT A German wine grape; a cross between the Sylvaner and Pinot Blanc.

MÜLLER-THURGAU A German wine grape—a cross of Riesling and Sylvaner—particularly popular in Rhinehessia, Franconia, Baden and Wurttemberg. It produces a wine which is mild, aromatic and pleasant with a slight Muscatel flavour.

MUSCADELLE White wine grape of the Bordeaux country cultivated in small proportions with the Semillon and Sauvignon Blanc, and giving a faint Muscat flavour to the wine.

MUSCADET White wine grape grown in the lower Loire valley around Nantes. The grape came from Burgundy where it was known as the Melon de Bourgogne. It yields a wine with a fresh aroma and a hint of Musk.

MUSCAT Wine and table grape with many varieties ranging from pale yellow to blue-black. In wine it produces a very distinctive bouquet and flavour.

MUST Grape juice in process of becoming wine.

NATURWEIN One of a number of terms appearing on German wine labels. It guarantees that the wine has had no sugar added before or during fermentation. All the finer German wines are thus labelled.

NEBBIOLO An Italian red wine grape of outstanding quality. At its best in Piedmont and Lombardy, where it produces full-bodied wines of high alcoholic content.

NEGRARA Red wine grape which produces Italy's Valpolicella and Bardolino.

NOBLE Term used for certain grape varieties, certain vineyards and certain wines which are inherently superior to other grapes, vineyards and wines.

NOBLE ROT See Botrytis cinerea.

NUTTY Usually applied to Sherries to describe a flavour reminiscent of walnuts or hazel nuts.

OCTAVE A cask—one-eighth of a Pipe or Butt.

ORDINAIRE French word applied to beverage wine of no stated orgin. Sold in France simply as *vin rouge, vin blanc* or *vin rosé*.

ORIGINAL-ABFÜLLUNG Term used in Germany to indicate that the wine is Estate Bottled. It guarantees that the wine is Estate Bottled by the producer whose name follows.

OXIDISED Term often used interchangeably with *maderisé* to describe a wine, especially a white wine, which has lost its freshness and has acquired a brownish colour by too much contact with the air. An oxidised wine is well on the way to being spoiled.

PEDRO XIMENEZ A Spanish wine grape grown in Montilla where it gives both a fine dry and a very sweet wine. Most of the Pedro Ximenez sweet wine used in the Sherry district of Jerez comes from the Montilla district. This is the only exception which is allowed to the general regulations delimiting the Sherry zone.

PERLANT French term for *very* slightly sparkling wine.

PERLWEIN German term for slightly sparkling wine.

PÉTILLANT   French term for slightly sparkling wine.

PHYLLOXERA   An insect or plant louse which destroys vines. Accidentally brought into Europe from America in the middle of the nineteenth century on vine cuttings, within twenty years it had destroyed over two million acres of vineyard in France alone. Every possible remedy was tried without any lasting success until vines with resistant roots were brought over from America and the European vine grafted on these.

PICPOUL   The name given to the Folle Blanche grape grown in Cognac and Armagnac. It gives thin, acid wine but an outstanding Brandy.

PINOT   One of the most distinguished of wine grape families.

PINOT CHARDONNAY   See Chardonnay.

PINOT GRIS   A member of the Pinot family, sometimes called Ruländer in Germany. It can produce wines of distinction in Alsace (Tokay d'Alsace), in Baden and in North Italy.

PINOT NOIR   One of the greatest red wine grapes. From it come the great red Burgundies. It is also the black grape used in the making of Champagne. The Pinot Blanc is found in the lesser Burgundy vineyards and also in Piedmont where it produces a dry white wine.

PIPE   A large cask found in Portugal for storing Port. A Port pipe contains 115 gallons or approximately 58 dozen. It is also used for Madeira and Marsala. A Madeira pipe contains 92 gallons and a Marsala pipe is 93 gallons.

POINTE   French word for "punt", the depression in the bottom of most wine bottles—the Champagne bottle especially. When Champagne is stacked before disgorging the phrase *mise sur pointe* means that the bottles are placed vertically with the cork of each bottle in the *pointe* or punt of the bottle below.

POT   A specially shaped bottle containing about 20 fluid ounces. Peculiar to Burgundy, especially Beaujolais.

POURRITURE NOBLE   See Botrytis cinerea.

PROOF   British system of measuring alcoholic content. Proof Spirit contains 57·1 per cent alcohol. A liquid containing a lower percentage is said to be "under proof" and one containing more "over proof".

PUNT   English for *pointe*.

PUPITRES   Racks in which Champagne bottles are placed for turning and shaking before disgorging.

QUINTA   Portuguese for a vineyard estate. It includes the actual vineyards and the buildings.

RACKING   The drawing off of young wine from one vat to another leaving the lees behind. Red wines are usually racked two to four times before bottling, as are many, but by no means all, white wines.

RANCIO   The special flavour that some wines, especially fortified wines, acquire as they are aged in wood; for example, Madeira, Tawny Port and Marsala.

RÂPÉ   Refuse of wine used for vinegar.

REFLETS   Union of Proprietors.

REGIONAL   Wine which takes its name from a district or region not from a specific town or vineyard. Usually regional wines are a blend.

REMUAGE   An operation essential in making Champagne. It is the turning and shaking of the bottles in their racks or *pupitres* so that the sediment settles on the cork before disgorging.

RIESLING   One of the greatest of white wine grapes grown principally in Germany, Alsace, Hungary and Yugoslavia. It produces superior quality white wines of the same name.

ROBUST   Term used by the wine taster to describe a sturdy, full-bodied wine.

ROSÉ   French for Pink or Rose-colour—*Vin Rosé*.

ROUGE   French for red—*Vin rouge*.

RULÄNDER   A German wine grape to be found mainly in Baden and Franconia. Sometimes called Grey Burgundy, it has a delicate aromatic taste. The wine is mellow and the acid content is usually low. It is the same grape as the French Pinot Gris.

SACCHAROMETER   An instrument for measuring sweetness in wine.

SAUVIGNON   An excellent white wine grape used for Graves and for Sauternes usually with Semillon. In the Loire it is used exclusively for making Pouilly Fumé and Sancerre.

SCHISTUS SOIL   This is composed of thin plates formed from the splitting of foliated rock consisting of layers of different minerals.

SCHLOSS   German for castle. When used of vineyards and on wine labels it is equivalent to the French *château*.

SEC   (French) means dry, when applied to still wines. When applied to sparkling wines such as Champagne, *sec* is not dry in the same sense but might be said to be dry but less dry than *Brut*.

SEDIMENT   The deposit thrown by most wines, particularly fine red wines, when they age in bottle. It is not a fault but is the sign that the wine is aged. If a fine red wine which claims to be old has no sediment then one should be suspicious. Some very fine, full-bodied red wines throw a heavy sediment and need decanting. With modern methods of vinification white wines now seldom throw a deposit.

SEKT   A general term for sparkling German wines.

SÉMILLON   An excellent white wine grape. In Sauternes and Graves it is vinified with Sauvignon Blanc.

SERCIAL   An excellent white wine grape producing the famous dry wine of Madeira.

SIEGERREBE   A German white wine grape which produces a mild wine with a fine Traminer flavour.

SIKES   British inventor of the hydrometer used in ascertaining proof strength.

SOLERA   The system by which fortified wines, Spanish Sherries in particular, are matured and blended, in order to provide continuity of style.

SOMMELIER   French name for wine waiter.

SOUND   A wine-taster's term for a wine which has no defects and shows no abnormal qualities.

SOUR   Describes a wine which is spoiled and is unfit to drink.

SPÄTBURGUNDER   German red wine grape flourishing on the Rhine and the Ahr and above all in Baden. It produces a dark, strong and finely spiced wine.

SPÄTLESE   German for "late harvest". When on a wine label it means that the grapes used were picked after the main harvest so the wine produced is fuller-bodied though unsugared. Usually a little sweeter than another wine from the same vineyard and costs more.

SPUMANTE   Italian for "sparkling". It is applied to a wine which is truly sparkling. *Gran Spumante* is made by the French Champagne method—fermentation in bottle. Others are fermented in bulk by the "cuve close" or tank method.

STEELY   A wine term for a hard though not harsh white wine.

STILL   Still wine is a non-sparkling wine.

SULPHUR   The principal use of sulphur in wine producing is as a general preservative and safeguard against oxidisation, especially for white wines, but to a lesser extent for red wines.

SWEET   Fine wines get their sweetness naturally from the grapes when they have been allowed to become over-ripe on the vines, for example in fine Sauternes and Beerenauslese. The natural sweetness may, in some wines, have sulphur added to keep the sweetness of the grape. In Port, Brandy is added. Sherry and Marsala have sweet wine or grape syrup added.

SYLVANER   Superior white wine grape grown extensively in Germany and also in Alsace. It is found also in Austria, Switzerland and California. The wine is fresh and fruity.

SYRAH   The excellent red wine grape which gives a deep coloured wine high in tannin with a distinctive bouquet. It is used in Chateauneuf-du-Pape and in Red Hermitage and is very important in the Côte Rotie.

TANNIN   Organic compounds found in the roots and stems of many plants. Tannin is found in wine—especially red wine—and gives an astringency to the young red wines of Bordeaux, especially pronounced if the stalks have been left too long in contact with the Must.

TINTO   Portuguese or Spanish for red. Vino Tinto—Red wine.

TINTOMETER   An instrument for measuring the colour of wine.

TONNEAU   Bordeaux wines are bought by the tonneau—equal to four hogsheads.

TRALLES   Scale used in Italy, Austria, etc., for measuring strengths—similar to Gay Lussac.

TRAMINER   A white wine grape grown in Alsace. Traminer wines are low in acid. The best are the Gewürztraminer. Also grown in Germany, principally in the Palatinate, and in Yugo-slavia.

TREBBIANO   Italian white wine grape which produces White Chianti and is one of the two principal grapes which produce Soave.

TROCKENBEERENAUSLESE   The name given to the sweetest and most expensive German wine. The grapes used have been left on the vine until raisinised. The yield is very small and happens only in great years.

ULLAGE   The space above the liquid in a wine cask when incompletely filled.

V.D.Q.S.   *Vins délimités de Qualité Supérieur*—French wines which are not legally entitled to an Appellation Contrôlée but include many of high quality. They are strictly controlled by the French Government and on their labels is a special stamp with V.D.Q.S. and the words *Label de Garantie*.

VENDAGE   French for grape harvest.

VENENCIA   An instrument used in the Sherry and Manzanilla districts to take samples of wine through the bung-hole of a cask. It usually consists of a whalebone rod with a silver hook forming a handle at its upper end and with a silver cup at the other end.

VERDELHO   Wine grape of Madeira producing a fortified wine generally sold under this name.

VERDE   Portuguese—literally: green. Vinho Verde is a wine coming only from the delimited area of the Minho, of Nothern Portugal. The wines are low in alcohol and are characterised by a slight prickle caused by the presence of malic acid.

VIGNERON   Vine-grower who may be working for himself or not.

VIN   French for wine.

VIN DE TÊTE Abbreviated form of Tête de Cuvée, meaning the best cuvée.

VINHO Portuguese for wine.

VINICULTURE The whole science and business of growing grapes for wine making; the making of the wine and its preparation for marketing.

VINIFICATION The making of the wine at all stages—fermentation, ageing, etc., excluding vineyard work.

VINO Spanish and Italian for wine.

VINTAGE The annual grape harvest and the wine made from these grapes. In this way every year is a "vintage" year and unless blended, wines are vintage wines—the vintage year being the year they were produced. There is, however, a great difference in quality between wines of one year and another in Northern temperate climates where the vintage year to be found on a wine is important. In warm, Southern climates where there is little variation from year to year, vintages are of little significance and seldom used.

VIOGNIER A white grape of the Rhône Valley.

VITICULTURE The science and art of grape-growing.

WEISSBURGUNDER One of the varieties of the Pinot grape grown in Alsace. It produces quality wines.

INDEX

A

Abbé-Gorsse, L', 39
Abruzzi e Molise, 355
Absinthe, 622, 626
Abymes, Les, 220
Achkarren, 313
Advocaat, 628
Affenthaler, 281, 314
Affenthaler Klosterreberg, 284
Agassac, Ch., 45
Agueda, 419
Ahn, 335
Aigrots, Les, 102
Aiguebelle, 622
Albana, 350
Alcamo, 358
Alcobaça, 419
Aleatico grape, 351
Aleatico di Portoferraio, 351
Alella, 385
Alessano grape, 356
Alicante, 386
Aligate, 466
Aligoté grape, 83, 166
Aloxe-Corton, 80, 99
Alsace, 195–210, Map 196
    Appellation Contrôlée, 210
    Climate, 199
    Geography, 197
    Grape Varieties, 201
    Types of wine, 205
    Vineyards, 199
    Vintages, 209
    Wines for laying down, 666
Alsheim, 258
Altenbamberg, 268
Alvarelhão grape, 415

Alzey, 261
Ambonnay, 118
Amer Picon, 629
Americano, 668
Amontillado, 369
Amoureuses, Les, 95
Anapa Riesling, 467
Ancenis, Coteaux d', 172, 191
Andron-Blanquet, Ch., 44
Angelus, Ch. L', 33, 56
Angles, Les, 104
Anglianico grape, 355
Angludet, Ch., 33, 39
Angostura Aromatic Bitters, 629
Anisette, 626
Anjou, 173, 175, 191, Map 168
Anjou-Coteaux de la Loire, 174, 191
Anjou Coteaux de la Loire Rosé
    de Cabernet, 191
Anjou Coteaux de Saumur, 191
Anjou Coteaux du Loir, 191
Anjou Mousseaux, 191
Anjou Rosé, 191, 192
Anjou Rosé de Cabernet, 173, 191
Anjou-Saumur, 174, 191
Anjou Saumur Rosé de Cabernet, 191
Antika, 451
Aperitifs, 629
Appellation Contrôlée
    Bordeaux, 19
    Burgundy, 82
    Alsace, 210
Apremont, 220
Apricot Brandy, 627
Aquavit, 628
Aragon, 384
Arbois, 217
Arche, Ch. d', 69

Arche Lafaurie, 69, 70
Arche-Pugneau, 70
Arlot, Clos, 98
Armagnac, 557, *Map* 556
Arvelets, Les, 103
Assmannshausen, 282
Assmannshauser Höllenberg, 284
Asti Spumante, 344, 345
Aubance, Coteaux de l', 191
Aubance-Rosé de Cabernet
        Coteaux de l', 191
Auerbach, 314
Auggener Letten, 313
Auslese, 226, 230, 276, 320, 429
Ausone, Ch., 30, 55, 58
Australia, 497–512, *Map* 498
   Geography, 503
   Grape varieties, 506, 509
   Naming of wines, 501
   Sherry and Port types, 510
   Table wines, 508
   Types of wine, 507
   Whisky, 595
Austria, 427–429, *Map* 426
Auvernier, 424
Auxerrois grape, 206, 306, 335, 337
Auxey-Duresses, 104
Avaux, Clos des, 101
Avaux, Les, 102
Avelsbach, 305
Avenay, 118
Avize, 118
Ay, 118
Ayios Georghios, 459
Ayias Mamas, 459
Ayl, 308, 324
Azay-le-Rideau, 177

B

Bacardi, 659
Bacharach, 286

Bad Durkheim, 253, 255
Bad Kreuznach, 325
Bad Munster am Stein, 268
Badacsonyi Szurkebarat, 434, 436
Baden, 311, 313, *Map* 316
Bahèzre de Lanlay, 102
Bahlingen, 313
Bairrada, 419
Baixo Corgo, 393
Balatoni Furmint, 434, 436
Balatoni Riesling, 434, 436
Balestard-la-Tonnelle, Ch., 34, 56
Bandol, 218
Banyuls, 219
Barbaresco, 344, 345, 347
Barbe, Ch. de, 66
Barbera grape, 344, 345, 347, 350
    wine, 344, 345
Barcelona, 385
Bardolino, 348, 349
Baret, Ch., 51, 52
Barolo, 344, 345
Barossa Valley, 507
Barrydale, 485, 495
Barsac, 70–71, *Map* 48
Bas-Medoc, 46
Bastardo grape, 415
Bastienne, La, 61
Basto, 419
Bastor-la-Montagne, 70
Batailley, Ch., 27, 28, 32, 43
Bâtard-Montrachet, 106
Baudot, 102
Béarnais, 215
Beaujolais, 79, 85, 110–114, 698, *Map* 108
   Growths, 111
Beaujolais Villages, 111, 113
Beaujolais Supérieur, 111, 114
Beaumes-de-Venise, 140, 163
Beaumonts, Les, 98
Beaune, 80, 101
   Hospices de, 101

Beaune (cont.)
    Red wines of, 101
    White wines of, 102
Beaune, Côte de, 99–107, *Map* 100
Beaune Cuvée Nicolas Rollin, 101
Beauregard, Ch., 33, 64
Beauroy, 89
Beausejour, Ch. (St. Estèphe), 33, 44
Beausejour, Ch. (St. Émilion), 55
Beausite, Ch., 44
Beausite-Haut-Vignoble, Ch., 44
Bech-Kleinmacher, 334
Bechtheim, 258
Beer, 669–675
    Manufacture of, 670
    Storage and handling of, 674
    Types of, 672–675
Beerenauslese, 226, 231, 251, 276, 320, 429
Bégadan, 46
Begorce, Ch. la, 29, 39
Bel-Orme-Tronquoy-de-Lalande, Ch., 46
Belair, Ch. (St. Émilion), 55, 58
Bel-Air, Ch, (Pomerol), 64
Bel-Air, Ch. de (Lalande de Pomerol), 65
Bel-Air-Marquis d'Aligre, Ch., 28, 34, 39
Belcier, Ch., 66
Beldi grape, 478
Belgrave, Ch., 27, 34, 45
Bellegrave, Ch., 43
Belles-Graves, Ch., 64
Belles-Graves, Ch. des, 46
Bellevue, Ch. (St. Émilion), 56, 61
Bellevue, Ch. de (Beaujolais), 113
Bellevue-St. Lambert, Ch., 43
Benedictine, 622, 624
Bensheim, 314
Bergerac, 214
Bergot, Ch., 56
Bergstrasse, 311
Bernkastel, 295, 300
Bernkasteler Doktor, 294, 301, 324
Bernkasteler Kurfurst, 239

Berri, 506
Berry, 179
Bétault, Hugues et Louis, 101
Beugnon, 89
Beychevelle, Ch., 27, 30, 40
Beynat, 66
Bianchello del Metauro, 353
Bianchetta grape, 351
Biancolella grape, 355
Bickensohl, 313
Bienvenue-Bâtard-Montrachet, 106
Billards, Clos de, 111
Billardet, 102
Bingen, 261
Bingen-Kempten, 262
Bingen-Stadt, 262
Bischoffingen, 313
Bitters, 628
Black Velvet, 668
Blagny, 105
Blanc de Blancs, 128
Blanc de Savoie grape, 220
Blanchots, Les, 89
Blancs, Côte de, 118
Blaye, 66
Blondeau, 102
Bloody Mary, 668
Boal grape, 514
    wine, 514
Böckenheim, 254
Böcksbeutel, 229, 313, 317
Bodegas, 364
Bodenheim, 260
Bodensee (Lake Constance), 311, 312
Boillot, 102
Bolsena, 354
Bonarda grape, 350
Bonnes-Mares, 94
Bonnezeaux, 174, 191
Bonnievale, 495
Bonvillars, 423
Boppard, 287

Bordeaux, 13–76, *Map* 12
    Appellation Contrôlée, 19
    Classification, 29–35
    Decanting of, 21
    Districts of:
        Graves, 47–53
        Médoc, 24–47
    Districts of:
        Pomerol, 62-66
        St. Émilion, 53-62
        Sauternes and Barsac, 66–72
        Other wine districts, 72–75
    Food to accompany, 22
    Geography of, 13
    Grape varieties, 16
    Maturing of, 18
    Negociants and Shippers, 14, 15
    Reference books, 74
    Serving of, 20, 535
    Vintage, 17
    Vintages, evaluation of, 22–24
    Wines for laying down, 694
Bordeaux, Premières Côtes de, 73
Boscq, Ch. le, 44
Botrytis Cinerea, 67, 226, 328
Boudriotte, Clos de la, 107
Bougros, 89
Bouqueyran, Ch., 41
Bourbon Whisky, 592, 595
Bourboulenc grape, 153, 154
Bourg, 65, 66
Bourg, Côtes de, 66
Bourgeais, 66
Bourgneuf, de Sales, 64
Bourgogne, see Burgundy
Bourgogne Passe Tout Grains, 83
Bourgueil, 176, 191
Bourret grape, 520
        wine, 520
Bourseau, Ch., 65
Bouscaut, Ch., 49, 51, 52
Bouschet Alicante grape, 464, 478

Bousquet, Ch. du, 66
Bouzy, 118, 216
Boyd-Cantenac, Ch., 26, 28, 34
Bozwin, 464
Brachetto, 334, 346
Brackenheim, 284
Braga, 419
Branaire Ducru, Ch., 27, 28, 31, 40
Brandy, 553–561
    Ageing of, 558
    Armagnac, 557, 560, *Map* 556
    Brandies, Vintage, 560
    Brands and Symbols, 560
    Cognac, 555, 560, *Map*, 554
    Greek, 452
    History of, 555
    Production of, 557
    South African, 495
    V.S.O.P., 553
Brane-Cantenac, Ch., 26, 28, 30, 38
Breganze Bianco, 348
            Rosso, 348
Bressandes, Les, 102
Bresses, Les, 112
Breuil, Ch. du, 46
Brillette, Ch., 41
British Columbia, 470
British Wines, 527–532
Bronx, 660
Brouilly and Côte de Brouilly, 113
Broustet, Ch., 69
Brune et Blonde, 142
Brunello grape, 351
Brunello di Montefalcino, 351, 352
Brunet, 101
Bucelas, 415, 419
Budesheim, 265
Bühl, 313
Bühlertaler, 314
Bulgaria, 445–447
Bull's Blood of Eger, 435, 436
Burgenland, 429

Burger Elbling grape, 202
Burger, Le, 206
Burgundy, 77–115, *Map* 78
  Ageing of, 86
  Appellation Contrôlée, 82
  Beaujolais, 110
  Chablis, 89
  Climate, 83
  Commune wines, 80
  Côte de Beaune, 99
  Côte Chalonnaise, 107
  Côte de Nuits, 91
  Fine wines of, 81
  Geography of, 77
  Grape varieties, 83
  Mâconnais, 109
  Negociants, 81
  Reference books, 114
  Serving of, 85, 535
  Shippers of, 80
  Vinification of, 84
  Vintages, 86
  Wines for laying down, 695
Bürkheim, 313
Burrweiler, 250
Butteaux, Les, 91
Byrrh, 630

C

Cabernet grape, 16, 172, 347, 348, 447, 466, 474,
  488
Cabernet Sauvignon grape, 16, 17, 447, 509,
  648, 650
Cabernet Sauvignon wine, 471, 472
Cadaujac, 49, 51, 52
Cadet-Bon, Ch., 56
Cadet Piola, Ch., 56
Cahors, 214
Cailleret (Chassagne), 107

Cailleret, Le (Puligny), 106
Caillerets, Les (Volnay), 104
Cailles, Les, 98
Caillou, Ch., 69, 71
Cairanne, 162
Calabria, 358
Californian Champagne, 472
         Wines, 645–652, *Map* 644
Calitor grape, 153
Calmont, 294
Calon Ségur, Ch., 26, 28, 30, 44
Calvados, 627
Cambus, 452
Camel, 464
Camensac, Ch., 27, 45
Cammarèse grape, 153
Campania, 355
Campari Bitters, 629
Canada, 469–472
Canaiolo grape, 353
Canon, Ch., 31, 55, 59, 65
Canon Bouché, Ch., 65
Canon la Gaffelière, Ch., 33, 56, 59
Canon Lange, Ch., 65
Canteloup, Ch., 44
Cantemerle, Ch., 27, 28, 30, 45
Cantenac-Brown, Ch., 26, 28
Cap Bon, 479
Cap-de-Mourlin, Ch., 34, 56
Capbern, Ch., 34, 44
Capitans, Les, 112
Capri, 355,
Carbonnieux, Ch., 33, 49, 50, 52, 187
Carcavelos, 417, 419
Cardinal Villemaurine, 60
Carema, 344
Carignan grape, 153, 165, 218, 219, 464, 478,
  645
Carinena, 384
Carles, Ch. de, 71
Carmel, 463, 464
Carmignano, 350

Carricante grape, 358
Carte, Ch. la, 56
Casa do Douro, 410
Casale Monferrato, 346
Cassis, 218
Castegenes, Ch., 66
Castel del Monte, 356
Castelli di Jesi, 353
Castelot, Clos, 60
Castera, Ch. du, 46
Castile, 383
Castillon, 66
Catalonia, 384
Catarrato grape, 358
Catawba grape, 636, 640, 641, 642
Cent-Vignes, Les, 102
Centerbe, 622
Central Valley, 649
Cerasuolo, 355
Cerons, 73
Certan-Demay, Ch., 32, 64
Certain-Giraud, Ch., 33, 64
César grape, 216
Chablis, 85, 86, 89–91, Map 90
Chablis Cup, 634
Chablais Vaudois, 423
Chaintré, 110
Chaise, Ch. de la, 113
Chalonnaise, Côte, 107–109, Map 100
Chambertin, 93
Chambertin, Clos de Beze, 93
Chambolle-Musigny, 80, 95
Champagne, 117–137, Map 116
    Blanc de blancs, 128
    Bottle sizes, 136
    Bottles, 124–126
    Classification of, 119
    Corks, 126, 127
    For laying down, 696
    Geography, 117
    Houses, 121–122
    Labels, 123

Principal vineyards, 118
Production of, 127–134
Serving of, 535
When and how to drink, 134
Champagne Cocktail, 664
Champagne Sparkler, 635
Champans, Les, 104
Champanski, 468
Champ-canet, 106
Chapelle Chambertin, 94
Chapelle des Bois, La, 112
Chapelle Madeleine, Ch., 56
Chapelot, 91
Chapitre, Clos du, 91
Chardonnay grape, 83, 109, 127, 166,
    447, 471, 472, 648, 650
Chardonnay wine, 471, 447
Charité, La, 188, 189
Charmes, Les, 95, 105
Charmes-Chambertin, 93, 94
Chartreuse, 622, 624
Chassagne-Montrachet, 80, 85, 106
Chasse-Spleen, Ch., 28, 32, 40
Chasselas grape, 180, 190, 202, 423, 424, 509
Chasselas, Ch. de, 113
Châtain, 91
Chautauqua, 640
Château-Chalon, 217
Châteaugay, 217
Châteaumeillant, 191
Châteunaeuf-du-Pape, 148, 167
    Reflets de, 152
    Soil and Climate of, 155
    Vines of, 153
Chatelard, Ch. du, 113
Chatelet, Ch. le, 57
Châtillon-en-Diois, 166
Chaume, Clos de, 174
Chaume, Quarts de, 174
Chaumiennes, Clos de, 190
Chauvin, Ch., 56
Chénas, 112

Chênes, Clos de,   104
Chenin grape,   172, 174, 178, 472, 651
Chenonceau, Ch.,   177
Cherry Brandy,   627
Cheval Blanc, Ch.,   30, 55, 60
Chevalier, Domaine de Ch.,   31, 49, 50, 52
Chevalier-Montrachet,   106
Chevret,   104
Chianti,   351, 352
Chiavennasca grape,   347
Chile,   473–475
Chinon,   176, 191
Chiroubles,   112
Chusclan,   160
Ciders,   644
Cima Corgo,   393
Cinque Terre,   351
Cinsault grape,   153, 154, 165, 218, 478
Cirò,   358
Cissac,   46
Cissac, Ch.,   46
Clairette grape,   148, 153, 154, 155,
        218, 220, 464, 478, 491, 520
Clairette wine,   148, 520
Clairette de Bellegarde,   148
Clairette de Die,   148, 220
Clare,   507
Claret,   3–6, 24, 535
Clavoillons,   106
Clerc-Milon-Mondon, Ch.,   27, 43
Climens, Ch.,   68, 71
Clinet, Ch.,   64
Clos, Les,   89
Clos-Blanc, Le,   96
Closerie-Grand-Poujeaux,   41
Clotte, Ch. la,   56, 59
Clusière, Ch. la,   56
Cochem,   293
Cocktails,   653–668
Cognac,   555, Map 554
    Origin of name,   555
Cointreau,   626

Colares,   416, 419
Cold Duck,   642
Colli Albani,   354
Colli dell' Oltrepo Pavese,   347
Colli Euganei,   348
Colombier-Monpelou, Ch.,   43
Combe-au-Moine,   94
Combettes, Les,   106
Commandaria,   454, 459
Commanderie, Ch. la,   64, 65
Commaraine, Clos de la,   103
Concord grape,   470, 637, 638, 640, 641, 642
Cond,   293
Condrieu,   143
Conseillante, Ch. la,   31, 63
Constantia,   485
Corbin, Ch. (St. Émilion),   56, 61
Corbin-Despagne, Ch.,   60
Corent,   218
Cormey-Figeac,   61
Cornas,   147, 167
Cotaillod,   423
Cortese grape,   344
        wine,   344, 346
Corton,   85, 99
Corton-Bressandes,   99
Corton-Clos du Roi,   99
Corton-Charlemagne, Ch.,   99, 105
Corton Château Grancey,   99
Corton-Les-Maréchaudes,   99
Corvées-Pagets, Les,   98
Corvina grape,   348, 349
Cos d'Estournel, Ch.,   26, 28, 30, 44
Cos-Labory, Ch.,   27, 28
Costières du Gard,   219
Côte Blonde,   141
Côte Brune,   141
Côtes-Canon-Fronsac,   65
Côte de Fronsac,   65
Côte d'Or,   77–82
Côte Rotie,   140, 141, 142, 167
Coteaux,   see Layon, etc.

Côtes, see Beaune, Nuits, Rhone, etc.
Coufran, Ch., 46
Couhins, Ch., 51
Coulée du Serrant, 175
Counoise grape, 153, 154
Couronne, Ch. la, 43
Couspaude, Ch. la, 56
Coustet, 71
Coutet, Ch., 34, 56, 68, 71
Couvent, Ch. le, 57, 61
Cramant, 118
Cras, Les, 96, 98
Crème de Cacao, 628
Crème de Café, 628
Crème de Cassis, 627
Crème de Menthe, 622, 626
Crépy, 220
Cressier, 424
Crimea, 467
Criots-Bâtard-Montrachet, 106
Croatina grape, 347
Croix, Ch. la, 64
Croix de Gay, Ch. la, 64
Croix St. Georges, Ch. la, 64
Croizet-Bages, Ch., 27, 43
Croque-Michotte, Ch., 33, 56
Croûte-Charlus, Ch., 66
Crozes-Hermitage, 145, 167
Cubzac, 66
Cuers, 219
Cully, 423
Cumières, 118
Curaçao, 626
Cure Bon, Ch., 56
Cure-Bon-la-Madeleine, Ch., 33
Cussac, 45
Cuvée Boillet, 104
Cyprus, 453-459
    Dessert wines, 459
    Sherry types, 457
    Table wines, 455
    Vineyards, 454

D

Dackenheim, 254
Daiquiri, 660
Dames de la Charité, 101
Dames Hospitalières, 101
Danzig Goldwasser, 625
Dão wines, 414, 419
Dauzac, Ch., 27
Debrö, 435
Debröi Harslevelu, 435, 436
Decanting of wine, 21, 536
Deidesheim, 252, 255, 324
Delaware grape, 470, 640, 642
Demestica, 451
Desmirail, Ch., 26
Deutscherrenberg, 299
Dézaley, Le, 423
Dhoros, 459
Dhron, 295, 304
Diamiat, 447
Diana grape, 640, 642
Didiers, Les, 98
Dienheim, 259
Dîmes, Domaine des, 113
Dirmstein, 254
Dizy, 118
D.O.C., 343
Doctor Peste, 102
Doisy-Daëne, Ch., 69, 71, 72
Doisy-Dubroca, Ch., 69
Doisy-Védrines, Ch., 69
Dolcetto grape, 344, 351
Dôle, 424
Dominique, Ch. la, 34, 56, 60
Dordogne wine, 214
Douro, 392, *Map* 390
Drakenstein, 491
Drambuie, 628
Drouhin, Maurice, 102
Dubonnet, 630
Duchess grape, 640, 643

Ducru-Beaucaillou, Ch., 26, 28, 30, 40
Ducs, Clos des, 104
Dudon, Ch., 71
Duhart-Milon, Ch., 27, 28, 31, 42
Dumay, Charlotte, 102
Duplessis, Ch., 41
Durbach, 313
Durchgegoren, 230
Durfort, Ch., 31
Durfort-Vivens, Ch., 26, 38
Dürkheim, 255
Duroc-Milon, Ch., 43
Dutch Geneva, 605
Dutruch-Grand-Poujeaux, Ch., 28, 41

E

Eastern United States, 635–643, *Map* 634
Ebernberg, 268
Eberstadt, 312
Ebringener Sommerberg, 313
Echézeaux, 97
Echt, 230
Edelauslese, 230
Edelbeerenauslese, 231
Edelfäule, 292, 328
Edelfraulein, 428
Edelwein, 230
Edelzwicker, 209
Edenkoben, 250
Efringe-Kirchener Weingarten, 313
Eger, 435
Église, Clos l', 33, 64
Église, Domaine de l', 64
Église-Clinet, Clos de l', 33, 64
Egri Bikavér, 435, 436
Ehnen, 335
Ehrenstettener Ölverg, 313
Eichstetten, 313
Eiswein, see Ice Wine
Eitelsbach, 310, 324
Elbing grape, 245, 306, 310, 335, 337

Elias, 463, 464
Elster, 253
Eltville, 273
    Classification, 322
Elvira grape, 640, 643
Emilia—Romagna, 350
Enclos, Ch. l', 64
Enkirch, 295, 296
Entre-deux-Mers, 73, *Map* 74
Envaux, Ch, d', 112
Enz Valley, 311
Épenots, Les (Épeneaux), 103
Épernay, 118
Erbach, 275, 324
Erden, 295, 298, 324
Eschendorfer, 317
Est! Est! Est!, 354
Estienne, 101
Estoril, 417
Etna, 358, 359
Etoile, 217
Evangile, Ch. l', 31, 63
Eyquem, Ch., 66
Ezerjó grape, 434

F

Famagusta, 457
Fargues, Ch. de, 70
Faro, 358
Fechy, 423
Fellbach, 312
Fendant, 424
    Grape, 424
Fernet Branca, 629
Ferrand, Ch. de, 61
Ferrière, Ch., 26, 32, 38
Fessenbach, 313
Fetiaska, 466
Fèves, Les, 102
Ficulle, 352
Fierte, La, 112

Fieuzal,·Ch., 49, 50, 52
Figeac, Ch., 31, 55, 60
Figeac, Clos la, 60
Figeac-Moueix, La Tour du Pin, 60
Filhot, Ch., 69, 71
Fiano grape, 355
Finger Lakes, 638, 640
Finos, 366, 368, 370
Fitou, 219
Fixin, 91
Fizz, 665
Flagey-Echézeaux, 96, 97
Fleckinger, 253
Fleur-Petrus, Ch. la, 64
Fleur-Pourret, La, 34
Fleurie, 112
Flip, 665
Flor, 365, 458, 487, 511, 532
Folatières, Les, 106
Fonbadet, Ch., 43
Fonplégade, Ch., 56, 59
Fonreaud, Ch., 41
Fonroque, Ch., 34, 56, 59
Fontenay, Côte de, 91
Foraste1a grape, 355
Forbidden Fruit, 626
Forêts, Clos des, 98
Forêts, Les, 91
Forneret, 102
Forst, 252, 255, 324
Forster Kirchenstück, 253, 324
Forster Neuberg, 284
Forster Ungeheuer, 234, 253, 324
Fortia, Ch. la, 150
Fouquerand, 102
Fourcas-Dupré, Ch., 34, 41
Fourcas-Hostein, Ch., 41
Fourchaume, 91
Fourtet, Clos, 55, 59
France, 9–220, Map 10
    Alsace, 195–210
        Bordeaux, 13–76

Burgundy, 77–115
Champagne, 117–137
Lesser wines of, 211–220
Loire, 169–193
Rhone, 139–167
Franc Mayne, Ch., 56
Franc-Maillet, Ch., 64
Franciacorta Rosso, 347
Francois de Salins, 102
Franconia, 315–318, Map 316
Frascati, 354
Freisa, 344
Fremiets, Les, 104
Freundstück, 253, 324
Fronsac, 65, Map 54
    Côte de, 65
Frontignan, 219
    Muscat de, 220
Fruit wines, 532
Fuissé, 110
Furmint grape, 432, 434, 442

G

Gaffelière-Naudes, Ch. la, 31, 55, 59
Gaillac, 215
Galego Dourado grape, 417
Gallais-Bellevue, Ch., 46
Gamay grape, 83, 110, 153, 166, 172,
        215, 217, 218, 220, 424, 488, 650, 651
Gamay de Savoie, 220
Gambellara, 348
Gamza grape, 447
        wine, 447
Garde, Ch. la, 51
Garganega, 348
Gattinara, 344, 346
Gauvain, 102
Gay, Ch. le, 64
Gay Lussac, 551
Gazin, Ch., 63

Geisenheim, 279
Général Muteau, 102
Geneva, 605–607
Genevrières, Les, 105
Georgia, 467
Germany, 221–332, *Map 222*
    Classification of wines, 318
    Favoured sites, 324
    Franconia, 315, *Map 316*
    Grape varieties, 242–246
    Mittelrhein, 285
    Mosel, 289
    Nahe, 263–269, *Map 264*
    Naming of wines, 229
    New Wine Law, page 701
    Palatinate, 247–255, *Map 248*
    Place names, 231–237
    Red Hocks, 280–284
    Red wines of, 284
    Rheingau, 271–280, *Map 270*
    Rheinhessen, 257–262, *Map 256*
    Ruwer, 309
    Saar, 307
    Southern Germany, Viticulture in, 310–314
    Vintages, 326–330
    Wine growing centres, 237
Gevrey-Chambertin, 80, 93
Gevrey-Chambertin Clos St. Jacques, 93
Gewächs Eigengewächs, 230
Gewürztraminer grape, 202, 208, 244, 251
    wine, 208, 244
Ghemme, 344, 346
Giennois, Coteaux du, 178, 192
Gien, Côtes de, 178, 192
Gigondas, 164
Gilette, Ch., 70
Gimlet, 661
Gimmeldingen, 255
Gin, 597–607
    Cocktails, 600, 601
    Dutch Geneva, 605
    Fizz, 665

London Gin, 598
    Manufacture of, 604
    Other types of, 603
    Pink Gin, 602
    Plymouth Gin, 602
Girard, Arthur, 102
Giscours, Ch., 26, 28, 31, 38
Givry, 109
Glacier Wines, 424
Glana, Ch. du, 40
Glasses, 679–691
    Types of glasses, 690, 691
Glayva, 628
Glen Mist, 628
Gloria, Ch., 28, 32, 40
Glun, 146
Goldbeerenauslese, 231
Goldriesling grape, 202, 206
    wine, 206
Goorjuani, 467
Goureau, 102
Goutte d'Or, La, 105
Graach, 295, 300, 324
Grace Dieu, La, 60
Gragnano, 355
Grain Whisky, 568, 580
Grand-Barrail-Lamarzelle, Ch., 56
Grand-Corbin-Despagne, Ch., 56
Grand-Corbin-Figeac, Ch., 56
Grand Marnier, 626
Grand Mayne, Ch., 56
Grand Murailles, Ch., 56
Grand Ormeau, Ch., 65
Grand Ormeau, Domaine du, 65
Grand Pontet, Ch., 56
Grand Puy Ducasse, Ch., 27, 28, 32, 43
Grand Puy Lacoste, Ch., 27, 28, 31, 43
Grande Rue, La, 98
Grandes-Ruchottes, Ch. les, 107
Grands-Echézeaux, Les. 97
Grandson, 423
Grandvaux, 423

Grape Varieties of:
  Alsace, 201
  Australia, 506, 509
  Austria, 428
  Bordeaux, 16
  Bulgaria, 447
  Canada, 470
  Burgundy, 83
  Champagne, 127
  Chile, 474
  Cyprus, 456, 457
  Germany, 242–246
  Hungary, 432–435
  Israel, 464
  Italy, 344–359
  Lesser Wines of France, 214–218, 220
  Loire, 170–174, 178–182, 186, 190
  Luxembourg, 337
  Madeira, 514
  Portugal, 397, 415, 417, 418
  Rhône, 153
  Rumania, 442
  South Africa, 485, 486, 488, 491
  Spain, 363, 383
  Switzerland, 423, 424
  Tunisia, 478
  U.S.A., 642–643, 650–651
  U.S.S.R., 466
  Yugoslavia, 439, 440
Gravains, Les, 103
Grave Trigant de Boisset, Ch. la, 64
Graves-St. Émilion, 60
Graves, 47–53, Map 48
  Classification (A. Lichine), 31–33, 35
  Grape varieties of, 47
  Red wines, 49
  White wines, 51
Graves Supérieur, 49
Graves de Vayres, 75
Gravières, Les, 107
Grechetto grape, 353
Greco di Gerace, 358

Greco di Tufo, 355
Greco grape, 354, 355
Greece, 449–452
Greiveldange, 335
Gremio, 410
Grenache grape, 153, 154, 155, 163,
    165, 218, 219, 464, 478, 645, 651
Grenouilles, Les, 89
Gressier-Grand Poujeaux, Ch., 28, 41
Grevenmacher, 335
Grèves, Les, 102
Grignolino grape, 344
           wine, 344
Grillet, Ch., 143, 167
Grillo grape, 358
Grimsbach, 312
Griotte-Chambertin, 94
Gris, Ch., 98
Grivault, Albert, 102
Grosplant du Pays Nantais, 172, 192
Grosplant grape, 171, 172
Gros-Caillou, Ch., 61
Grossa grape, 348
Gruad-Larose, Ch., 26, 28, 30, 40
Grumello, 347,
Gruner Veltliner, 429
Grunstadt, 254
Guadet-Saint-Julien, Ch., 56
Guarnaccia grape, 355
Guibeau-Lafourvielle, 61
Guigone de Salins, 101
Guiraud, Ch., 68, 69
Gumpoldskirchen, 429
Gumpoldskirchner, 429
Guntersblum, 258
Gutedel grape, 202, 245, 310
Gutenberg, 268
Gutes Domtal, 239
Gutturnio, 350

H

Haardt, 255

Hallgarten, 276
Haltinger Stiege, 312
Hambach, 250
Hamilton, 470
Hamm, 287
Hanepoot grape, 485
Hargesheim, 267
Hárslevelü grape, 432
Hattenheim, 275
Haut-Bages-Avérous, Ch., 43
Haut-Bages-Liberal, Ch., 27
Haut-Bages-Monpelou, Ch., 43
Haut Bailly, Ch., 32, 49, 50
Haut Batailley, Ch., 27, 28, 32, 43
Haut-Bommes, Ch., 70
Haut-Brion, Ch., 25, 30, 49, 50, 52
Haut Comtat, 165
Haut-Lavallade, Ch., 61
Haut Médoc, 37
Haut-Peraguey, Clos, 68, 70
Hautvillers, 118
Heddesheim, 265
Heilbronn, 312
Heppenheimer Steinkopf, 314
Hermitage, 144, 145, 146, 167
Herxheim, 284
Himmelreich, 299
Hochheim, 272
Hochheimer Hölle, 273
Hocks, 330
    Red, 280
    Serving of, 536
Hörsteiner, 317
Hörsteiner Abtsberg, 324
Hospices de Beaune, 101, 105
Houissant, Ch., 44
Hudson River Valley, 640
Hüffelsheim, 267
Humblot, Jehan, 102
Hungaria Sparkling Wine, 435, 436
Hungary, 431–436
Hunter Valley, 505

I

Ice Wine (Eiswein), 329, 330, 664
Ihrengen, 313
Inferno, 347,
Ingelheimer, 284
Irancy, 216
Irish Mist, 628
Irouléguy, 215
Ischia Bianco, 355
Israel, 461–464
Issan, Ch. d', 26, 29, 31, 38
Italy, 341–359, *Map* 342

J

Jacobins, Clos de, 56
Jacques, Ch. des, 112
Jagst Valley, 312
Jasnières, 192, 215
Jean Faure, Ch., 56
Jeandenam, Ch., 65
Jerez, 362
Jeripego, 486, 488
Jerusalem, 439
Jesuitengarten, 253, 324
Johannisberg, Schloss, 278, 319, 321, 324
    Classification, 322
Johannisberg (Swiss), 424
John Collins, 664
Journets, Domaine des, 112
Julienas, 111
    Château de, 112
Junayme, Ch., 65
Jura, Côtes du, 216
Jurançon, 215

K

Kaberne, 466
Kadarka grape, 435
    wine, 443, 447

Kahlua, 628
Kallmuth, 317
Kallstadt, 254, 255, 284
Kalokhorio, 459
Kalopanayotis, 456
Kanzem, 308
Kappelrodecker Dasenstein, 313
Karthäuserhofberg, 310
Kasel, 309, 324
Kaub, 287
Kellerabfüllung, 230
Kiedrich, 274
King Solomon, 463, 464
Kirchenstück, 253, 324
Kirchheim, 254
Kirchhofener Kirchberg, 313
Kirchpfad, 299
Kirsch, 627
Kirwan, Ch., 26, 29, 32
Kitzingen, 317
Klingelberger grape, 313
Klingenberg am Main, 284
Kloster Eberbach, 275, 287
Klosterpförtchen (Johannisberg), 239
Knipperle grape, 202, 206
Ko-operatieve Wijnbouwers Vereniging
    (K.W.V.), 482, 483, 496
Kocher Valley, 311
Kokkineli, 456
Königsbach, 252, 255
Königschaffhausen, 313
Königswinter, 287
Krasnodar, 468
Kröv, 295, 297
Kues, 295, 300, 302
Kümmel, 625

L

Labouronnes, Ch. des, 112
Labrusca grape, 470
Lacrima Christi, 355, 356

Ladismith-Oudtshoorn, 485
Ladoix-Serrigny, 99
Lafaurie-Peraguey, Ch., 68, 70, 72
Laffitte-Carcasset, Ch., 44
Lafite, Ch., 42
Lafite-Rothschild, Ch., 25, 27, 29
Lafleur, Ch., 32, 63
Lafleur-Petrus, Ch., 32, 64
Lage, 232
Lago di Caldaro, 348
Lager, 640
Lagoa, 419
Lagrange, Ch., 26, 40 (St. Julien),
    33, 64 (Pomerol)
Lagrima, 386
Lagune, Ch. la, 26, 29, 31, 44, 45
Lake Balaton, 434
Lake Constance (Bodensee), 311, 312
Lalande de Pomerol, 65
Lamarzelle, Ch., 56
Lambrays, Clos des, 95
Lambrusco grape, 350
              wine, 350
Lamego, 419
Lamothe, Ch., 46
Lamothe-Bergey, Ch., 69
Lamothe-Espagnet, Ch., 69
Landon, Ch., 46
Lanessan, Ch., 29, 45
Langenlonsheim, 265
Langenmorgen, 253
Langoa-Barton, Ch., 26, 29, 32. 40
Languedoc, 219
Lania, 459
Larcis-Ducasse, Ch., 33, 56, 59, 61
Larmande, Ch., 56
Larnaca, 457
Laroze, Ch., 56, 59
Larrivet Haut-Brion, Ch., 51
Lascombes, Ch., 26, 28, 30, 38
Lasserre, Ch., 57
Latour, Ch., 25, 27, 29, 42, 49

Latour Haut-Brion, Ch., 49, 51
Latour-Martillac, Ch., 51, 52
Latour-Pomerol, Ch., 33, 64
Latricières-Chambertin, 94
Laubenheim, 261, 265
Laudun, 162
Laufener Altenberg, 313
Laujac, Ch., 46
Laurets, Ch. des, 61
Lavières, Les, 103
Laville Haut-Brion, Ch., 52
Lay, 235
Layon-Chaume, Coteaux du, 192
Layon, Coteaux du, 174, 175, 192
Layon-Rosé de Cabernet, Coteaux du, 192
Layon St. Aubin, Coteaux du, 174
Lazio, 354
Lebelin, Jacques, 102
Léchet, Côte de, 91
Leisten, 315
Leiwen, 295, 305
Lemps, 146
Léognan, 49, 50, 52
Leoville-Barton, Ch., 26, 28, 30, 39
Leoville-las-Cases, Ch., 26, 28, 30, 39
Leoville Poyferré, 26, 28, 30, 39
Lesser known wines of France, 211–220
Lessona, 344
Lestage, Ch. (Listrac), 41
Lestage Ch. (St.-Seurin-de-Cadourne), 46
Levante, 385
Leyssac, Ch., 44
Lichine, Alexis, Classifications, 29–35
Liebeskummer (Traben), 239
Liebfraumilch, 240, 250
Lieser, 295, 302
Liguria, 351
Lillet, 630
Lima Amarante, 419
Limassol, 454
Limoux, 215

Linz, 287
Liot, Ch., 71
Liqueur de Tirage, 131
Liqueur des Moines, 622
Liqueur d'Or, 622
Liqueurs, 621–628
    Fruit, 626, 627
    Ingredients in, 622, 623
Lirac, 160, 161
Listrac, 41
Little Karoo, 485, 487
Livermore Valley, 648
Liversan, Ch., 46
Livran, Ch., 46
Locorotondo, 356
Loge aux Moines, La, 187, 188
Loir, Coteaux du, 192
Loire, 169–193, *Map* 168
    Wines of the, 191–193
Loire, Coteaux de la, 170, 175
Loire-Rosé de Cabernet,
        Coteaux de la, 191
Loiret, Coteaux du, 192
Lombardy, 347
Longuich, 305
Loppin, 102
Lorch, 285
Lorchhausen, 285
Lot, 214
Loudenne, Ch., 46
Loupiac, 72
Louvière, Ch. la, 51
Lower Haardt (Unterhaardt), 254
Lower Main, 317
Loyse, Ch. de, 113
Lubéron, Côtes du, 165
Ludes, 118
Ludon, 45
Lugana, 348
Luins, 423
Lunel, 219
Lussac-St. Émilion, 61

Lutomer, 439
Lutry, 423
Luxembourg, 333–340
    Grape varieties, 337
    Sparkling wines of, 337
    Vintage chart, 340
    Wine-growing communities, 334
Lynch Bages, Ch., 27, 28, 30, 42
Lynch Moussas, Ch., 27, 43
Lyonnat, Ch., 61
Lys, Les, 91

M

Macau, 45
Macay, 66
MacCarthy, Ch., 44
Machtum, 335
McLaren Vale, 507
Mâcon, 110
Mâcon Viré, 110
Mâcon-Villages, 110
Mâconnais, 79, 109–110, *Map* 108
Madeira, 513–516
    Serving of, 535
Madeleine, Clos la, 56
Madiran, 215
Magdelaine, Ch., 55, 59
Magyar Rosé, 435, 436
Maikammer, 250
Mailly-Champagne, 118
Maladière, La, 107
Malaga, 386
Malartic-Lagravière, Ch., 33, 49, 50, 52
Malbec grape, 16, 214, 464, 474, 509
Malconsorts, Les, 98
Malescot-St.-Exupéry, Ch., 26, 28, 31, 38
Malle, Ch. de, 69
Malmsey, 514
Malt Whisky, 565, 568, 579, 580
    Campbeltown, 566, 580
    Highland, 566, 579

Islay, 566, 580
    Lowland, 566, 580
Maltroie (Maltroye), La, 107
Malvasia grape, 351, 353
Malvasia Preta grape, 397
Malvasia Branca grape, 397
Malvazia grape (Malvoisie, Malmsey), 172,
    353, 424, 514
Malvazia wine, 514
Malvoisie wine, 424
Mamertino, 358
Mancha, La, 387
Mandel, 267
Manhattan, 662
Manseng grape, 215
Manzanillas, 368
Maraschino, 627
Maratheftika grape, 456
Marbuzet, Ch., 44
Marche, 353
Marcobrunn, 275
Marconnets, Les, 102, 103
Maréchale, Clos de la, 98
Mareuil, 118
Margaux, 37
Margaux, Ch., 25, 27, 30, 37
Marino Bianco, 354
Maritsa Valley, 446
Markgrafschaft, 312
Marquis d'Alesme-Becker, 26, 32
Marquis de St. Estephe, 44
Marquis-de-Term, Ch., 27, 29, 32, 39
Marsala, 358, 359
Marsanne grape, 145, 147, 220
Martillac, 49, 51
Martina Franca, 357
Martinens, Ch., 39
Martini, 662
Martinstein, 269
Martinsthal, 274
Maryland, 641
Marzemino, 348

Massandra Muscatel, 467
Massol, Jehan de, 102
Maucaillou, Ch., 41
Maucamps, Ch., 45
Mauerweines, 313, 317
Maury, 219
Mauves, 146
Mauvezin, Ch., 57
Mauzac grape, 153
Mavrodaphne, 451
Mavron grape, 456
Mavrud, 446
Maximin-Grünhauser, 310, 324
Maximin Herrenberg, 324
Mayerling, 429
Mazeyres, Ch., 64
Mazis-Chambertin, 94
Mazoyères-Chambertin, 94
Médoc, 24–47, Map 36
    Bas-Médoc, 46
    Haut-Médoc, 37
    Characteristics, 35
    Classification, 1855, 25–27
                    1961, 27–29
                    Lichine, 29–35
Melinots, Les, 91
Melon grape, 166, 170
Mendoce, 66
Mendocino County, 647
Menetou-Salon, 192
Mentuccia, 622
Mercurey, 109
Merlot grape, 16, 17, 348, 474, 648
Mertesdorf, 310
Mesnil, Le, 118
Methode Champenoise, 109
Meursault, 80, 85, 104
Meursault Genevrières Cuvée Baudot, 101
Meyney, Ch., 29, 44
Michigan, 642
Mildura, 506
Millefiori, 622

Minchinbury, 505
Misket, 447
Mission Haut-Brion, Ch. la, 31, 49, 50
Mistelle, 520
Mittelhaardt, 251
Mittelheim, 278
Mittelrhein, 285–287, Map 264
Moldavia, 466
Molinara grape, 350
Monagri, 459
Monbazillac, 214
Moncão, 419
Moncontour, Ch. de, 177
Monferrato, 344
Mont de Milieu, 91
Mont près Chambord
        Cour-Cheverny, 178, 192
Mont-sur-Molle, 423
Montagne de Reims, 118
Montagne St. Émilion, 61
Montagny, 109
Montagu, 485, 495
Montée de Tonnerre, 91
Montefiascone, 354
Montepulciano, 355, 356
Monthélie, 104
Montilla, 386
Montlouis, 177, 192
    Mousseux, 192
    Pétillant, 192
Montmain, 91
Montperay, 112
Montrachet, 85, 105
Montravel, 214
Montrose, Ch., 26, 28, 30, 44
Mor, 434
Morey-St. Denis, 80, 94
Morgeot, Abbaye de, 106, 107
Morgeot, Clos, 106, 107
Morgon, 113
Mori Ezerjó, 434, 436
Morio-Muscat grape, 246

Morphett Vale, 507
Morscheid, 310
Moscato d'Asti, 344, 524
Moscow Mule, 668
Mosel, 289–306, 664, *Map* 288
    Lower, 293
    Middle, 294
    Upper, 305
Moselblümchen, 241
Mouches, Clos des, 102
Mouilles, Les, 112
Moulin à Vent, 41, 112
Moulin à Vent, Clos du, 112
Moulin à Vent, Ch. de, 112
Moulin Bellegrave, Ch., 61
Moulin-du-Cadet, Ch., 57
Moulinet, Ch., 64
Moulis, 40, 41
Mountain, 386
Mourisco de Semente grape, 397
Mourvèdre grape, 153, 154, 165, 218
Mousse, Clos de la, 102
Mouton Baron Philippe, Ch., 29, 31, 43
Mouton Cadet, 42
Mouton d'Armailhacq, 27
Mouton Rothschild, Ch., 26, 27, 30, 42
Mukuzani, 467
Mülheim, 295
Müller-Thurgau grape, 206, 243, 244, 318, 335, 337
Müller-Thurgau wine, 206, 244, 310
Münster (nr. Bingerbrück), 265
Murcia, 385
Murrumbidgee Valley, 505
Muscadet, 169–173, 192, 698
    de la Loire, 170
    de Sèvre et Maine, 170, 192
    des Coteaux de la Loire, 170, 192
Muscadin grape, 153, 154
Muscat grape, 16, 148, 163, 202, 207, 220,
    345, 368, 372, 432, 485, 506, 520
Muscat wine, 207, 439
Muscat d'Alexandrie grape, 464

Muscat Ottonel grape, 428
                    wine, 429, 442
Muscat de Beaumes de Venise, 220
Muscat de Frontignan, 220
Muscatel, 310
Muscatel de Setubal, 418, 419
Musenhang, 253
Musigny, 95
Mussbach, 255
Myrat, Ch., 69

N

Nackenheim, 259, 324
Nacktarsch, 297
Nahe, 263–269, *Map* 264
Nairac, Ch., 69
Napa Valley, 647
Naturrein, 230
Naturwein, 230
Néac, 64
Nebbiolo grape, 344, 345, 346, 347
            wine, 344
Neckarulm, 312
Negramaro grape, 357,
Negrara grape, 348, 349, 350
Negri di Purkar, 466
Nemes Kadar, 435, 436
Nenin, Ch., 33, 64
Nerello grape, 358
Nertert, 335
Nerthe, Ch. de la, 150
Neuchâtel, 423
Neumagen, 295, 303
Neustadt, 251
Neuweier, 317
Neuweierer Altenberg, 314
New Castile, 387
New South Wales, 504–506
Nexon-Lemoyne, Ch., 45
Niagara, 470, 641
Niagara grape, 470, 643

Nicolas Rollin, 101
Nicosia, 454
Niederemmel, 304
Niederhausen on Nahe, 266, 325
Niederkirchen, 255
Nierstein, 259, 324
Niersteiner Rehbach, 545
Nivernaise, 179
Noble Rot, see Botrytis cinerea, Edelfaule, Pourriture Noble
Norheim, 267
Nufriello grape, 355
Nuits, Côte de, 91–99, *Map 92*
Nuits-St.-Georges, 80, 98

O

Oberbergen, 313
Oberdiebach, 286
Oberemmel, 308
Oberhaardt (Upper Haardt), 250
Oberrotweil, 313
Oberrotweiler Kirchberg, 284
Obidos, 419
Ockfen, 308, 324
Oeil de Perdrix, 424
Oeiras, 417
Offenberg, 313
Oger, 118
Olivier, Ch., 49, 52
Olorosos, 366, 370, 371
Ontario, 470
Oppenheim, 258, 324
Opthalma grape, 456
Orange Bitters, 629
Orbe, 423
Ordonnac-et-Potensac, 46
Originalabfüllung, 230, 239
Originalwein, 230
Orlèanais, Vins de l', 178, 193
Ormeau, Domaine du Grand, 65
Ormes de Pez, Ch. les, 44

Ormoz, 439
Ortenau, 313
Ortenberg, 313
Orvieto, 353
Osthofen, 258
Ostrich, 277
Otlinger Pflanzer, 312
Ouzo, 452, 628

P

Paarl, 485, 486, 487, 488, 490, 491
Palatinate (Rheinpfalz), 247–255, *Map 248*
Palette, 218
Palmer, Ch., 26, 28, 30, 38
Palo Cortados, 370
Palomino grape, 363, 364, 486
Palwin, 464
Pape, Ch. le, 51
Pape Clément, Ch., 32, 49, 50
Paphos, 454, 457
Paradis, 61
Parsac-St. Émilion, 61
Pascal Blanc grape, 153
Pasteur, Le Bon, 60
Patache d'Aux, Domaine de, 46
Patent Still, 549, 562 (*illus.*), 565, 568, 584
Pauillac, 41
Paveil de Luze, 39
Pavie, Ch., 32, 55, 59
Pavie-Decesse, Ch., 57
Pavie-Macquin, Ch., 57
Pavillon-Cadet, Ch., 57
Peach Brandy, 627
Peat Reek, 566
Pécharmant, 214
Pechstein, 253
Pécs Riesling, 435, 436
Pécs-Villány, 435
Pedesclaux, Ch., 27
Pedhoullas, 456

Pedro Ximenez grape, 363, 368, 372, 478
Penafiel, 419
Pepieux, 219
Perdrix, Les, 98
Periquita grape, 418
Perlwein, 331, 338
Pernand-Vergelesses, 99
Pernod, 622, 626
Perrière, Clos de la (Fixin), 91
Perrière, Clos de la (Vougeot), 96
Perrières, Clos des, 105
Perrières, Les, 105
Pessac, 49, 52
Petit-Faurie-de-Souchard, Ch., 57, 59
Petit-Faurie-de-Soutard, Ch., 57
Petit Verdot grape, 16
Petit-Village, Ch., 32, 63
Petits-Épenots, Les, 103
Petrus, Ch., 30, 63
Pez, Ch. de, 29, 44
Pez, Le, 113
Phélan-Ségur, Ch., 29, 44
Philippe-de-Bon, 102
Phylloxera, 7, 154, 185, 199, 635, 636, 646
Piada, Ch., 71
Pibran, Ch., 43
Picardin grape, 153
Pichon-Longueville, Ch., 26, 28, 30, 42
Pichon-Longueville, Ch. (Comtesse
        de Lalande), 26, 28, 30
Picpoul grape, 153, 154, 520
Pied d'Aloup, 91
Piediroso grape, 355
Piedmont, 344
Pierre Bibian, Ch., 41
Pierre Virely, 101
Pierrefeu, 219
Pierreux, Ch. de, 113
Piesport, 295, 303, 324
Pinhel, 419
Pinot Auxerrois grape, 206
Pinot Beurot grape, 172

Pinot Blanc grape, 202, 215, 471, 472, 509
        wine, 207, 471, 472
Pinot del Collio, 349
Pinot Fin de Bourgogne grape, 153
Pinot Gris grape, 424, 434, 442
Pinot Gris-Tokay d'Alsace, (Le Pinot Gris), 202
Pinot Noir grape, 83, 110, 127, 202, 215, 216,
        349, 424, 435, 471, 509, 650
Pinot wine, 216
Pizay, Ch. de, 113
Plaisance, 61
Planter's Punch, 666
Platres, 456
Plince, Ch., 64
Pointe, Ch. la, 33, 64
Pomerol, 62–66, Map 54
    Classification, Lichine, 31–35
Pomeys, Ch., 41
Pommard, 80, 103
Pommern, 293
Pomys, Ch., 44
Pontac-Lynch, Ch., 39
Pontac Monplaisir, Ch., 51, 52
Pontet-Canet, Ch., 27, 28, 31, 42
Porrets, Les, 98
Port Type Wine, 486, 510
Port Wine, 3–6, 391–411, Map 390
    Associations, 409–410
    Blending of, 402
    Lodge work, 401
    Tasting of, 404
    Types of, 406–408
    Vintages, 411
    For laying down, 665
Portets, 51
Portugal, 389–420, Map 412
    Bucelas, 415
    Carcavelos, 417
    Colares, 416
    Dão, 414
    Douro Valley, 391–411, Map 390
    Port Wine, 391–411

Setubal, 418
 Table wines, 413–420
 Vinhos Verdes, 413
Poruzot, Le, 105
Pot Still, 548, 565, 568, 583, 584, 616
Potensac, Ch., 46
Pouget, Ch., 27
Pouilly, 110
Pouilly Fumé, 180, 181, 182, 187, 192
 For laying down, 698
Pouilly, Blanc Fumé de, 180, 186, 187, 191
Pouilly Fuissé, 85, 109
Pouilly-Loché, 110
Pouilly-sur-Loire, 180, 192
 Local recipes, 190
Pouilly-Vinzelles, 110
Poujeaux, Ch., 29
Poujeaux-Theil, Ch., 34, 40
Poulettes, Clos de, 112
Poulsard grape, 217
Pourret, La Fleur, 60
Pourret, La Rose, 60
Pourriture Noble, 67, 174, 181, 203
Prémeaux, 98
Premières Côtes, 73
Pressac, Clos, 61
Preuses, Les, 89
Priban, Ch., 45
Pride of Oporto, 634
Prieure Lichine, Ch. le, 27, 29, 32, 38
Priorato, 384
Prodromos, 456
Prosecco grape, 349
Prosecco Spumante di Conegliano, 349, 350
Pruliers, Les, 98
Pucelles, Les, 106
Puglia, 356
Puisseguin-St. Émilion, 61
Puligny-Montrachet, 80, 85, 105
Punches, 666
Puyblanquet, La Tour, 61
Pyrenees, 215

Q

Quarts de Chaume, 192
Queen Victoria Vineyard, 273
Quincy, 179, 192, 215
Quincy Vin Noble, 186
Quinta da Roeda, 396, 397

R

Rabaud-Promis, Ch., 69, 70
Rabaud-Sigalas, Ch., 68, 70
Radda, 352
Radgona, 439
Randersackerer, 324
Ranina, 439
Rara-Njagra grape, 466
Rasteau, 140, 162
Ratafia, 623
Rauenthal, 274, 324
Rausan-Ségla, 26, 28, 30, 38
Rauzan-Gassies, 26, 28, 32, 38
Raya, 370
Rayne-Vigneau, Ch., 68, 70
Recioto, 349
Referts, Les, 106
Reflets de Châteauneuf-du-Pape, 152
Reil, 296
Reims, 117
Rein, 230
Remerschen, 334
Remich, 334
Rems Valley, 311
René, Clos, 64
Renmark, 506
Retsina, 450
Reuilly, 179
Reuilly wine, 192
Reus, 384
Reutlingen, 312
Reynella, 507
Rheingau, 271–284, Map 270
Rheinhessen, 257–262, Map 256

Rheinpfalz (Palatinate), 247–255, *Map* 248
Rhine Maiden, 634
Rhine Wines, see Germany
  For laying down, 696
Rhône, 139–167, *Map* 138
  Geography of, 139
  Grape varieties, 153
  Red wines of the, 158
  Rosé wines of the, 160
  White wines of the, 157
  Wines, for laying down, 699
      serving of, 536
      vinification of, 157
  Vineyards, 150
Rhône, Côtes du, 163, 166
Ribatejo, 419
Richebourg, 97
Richemonnes, Les, 98
Rieslaner grape, 318
Riesling grape, 202, 207, 243, 250, 251,
      260, 281, 292, 313, 318, 335, 337, 348, 429,
      442, 447, 464, 471, 491, 509, 648, 651
Riesling wine, 208, 243, 310, 428, 434,
      439, 442, 447, 467, 471
Rieussec, Ch., 68, 70
Rila, 447
Rilly, 118
Rioja, 381
Ripeau, Ch., 33, 57, 60
Rivaner grape, 335, 337
Rivesaltes, 219
Robert, 66
Robertson, 485, 495
Roche, Clos de la, 94
Rochefort, 174
Rochet, Ch., 27
Roi, Clos du, 102, 109
Roilette, Clos de la, 112
Rolland, Ch., 43
Romanée, La, 97
Romanée-Conti, 97
Romanée-St. Vivant, 97

Romer-Lafon, Ch., 69
Romorantin grape, 178
Roquemaure, 160, 162
Rosato del Salento, 357
Rosé de Béarn, 215
Rosé d'Anjou, 192
Rosé de Cabernet Anjou, 192
Rose Pauillac, La, 43
Rosette, 214
Rossara grape, 348, 350
Rossese grape, 351
Rosso Conero, 353
Rosso Piceno, 353
Rotclevner grape, 202
Rougemonts, Les, 112
Rouget, Ch., 64
Roumieux-Bernadet, Ch., 71
Roumieux-Goyaud, Ch., 71
Roumieux-Lacoste, Ch., 71
Rousanne grape, 145, 147, 153
Rousseau-Deslandes, 101
Rousette grape, 220
Rousset, 66
Roxheim, 268
Ruby wines, 531
Ruchottes-Chambertin, 94
Rudesheim (Nahe), 267
  (Rheingau), 279, 324
Rufete grape, 397
Rufina, 351
Rugiens, Les, 103
Ruländer grape, 202, 245, 306, 313, 337
      wine, 245, 306, 310, 313, 443
Rully, 109
Rum, 613–619
  Types of, 616
Rumania, 441–443
Ruppertsberg, 252, 255
Rutherglen, 506
Ruwer, 309–314, *Map* 288
Rye Whiskey (American), 595
Rye Whisky (Canadian), 588

S

Saale, 317
Saar, 307–308, *Map* 288
Sables-St. Émilion, 62
Sack, 374
Sacramento, 648
Sacy grape, 216
St. Amour, 111
St. Amour, Ch. de, 111
St. Blaise, 424
St. Christoly-de-Médoc, 46
St. Denis, Clos, 94
St. Émilion, 53–62, *Map* 54
   Classification, 55
         Lichine, 30–3,
   Côtes St. Émilion, 58
   Graves-St. Émilion, 60
St. Estèphe, 43
St. Genies-de-Comolas, 162
St. Georges, Les, 98
St. Georges-Côte-Pavie, Ch., 34, 57
St. Georges d'Orcq, 219
St. Germain d'Esteuil, 46
St. Jacques, Les Clos, 94
St. Jean, Clos, 107
St. Jean-de-Muzels, 146
St. Joseph, 146, 167
St. Julien, 39
St. Lambert du Lattay, 174
St. Laurent, 45
St. Laurent (Rhinehessia), 261
St. Laurent-des-Arbres, 162
St. Martin (Upper Haardt), 250
St. Martin, Clos, 57
St. Nicholas-de-Bourgheuil, 176, 192
St. Péray, 147, 167
St. Pierre, 34
St. Pierre, La Tour, 60
St. Pierre-Bontemps, 26
St. Pierre-Sevaistre, 26
St. Pourçain, 217

St. Raphael, 630
St. Saphorin, 423
St. Saturnin, 219
St. Sauveur, 46
St. Seurin-de-Cadourne, 46
St. Victoire La-Coste, 162
St. Yzans, 46
Ste. Croix-du-Mont, 72, *Map* 74
Samling 88 (Scheurebe) grape, 246, 318
Samos Muscatel, 451
San Domingos de Rana, 417
San Joaquin Valley, 649
San Sadurni, 385
Sancerre, 179
Sancerre wine, 192, 698
Sangiovese grape, 350, 351, 353, 354, 356
         wine, 350
Sankt Katharina, 268
Sanlucar de Barrameda, 368
Sansevero, 357
Sansonnet, Ch., 57
Santa Clara, 648
Santa Helena, 451
Santa Maddalena, 348
Santenay, 80, 86, 107
Saparvi grape, 466
Saperavi, 467
Sarnsheim, 265
Sassella, 347
Sauman, 66
Saumur, 175, 192
Saumur-Champigny, 192
Saumur, Coteaux de, 192
Saumur-Mousseux, 192
Saumur Rosé de Cabernet, 192
Saumur-Rosé de Cabernet, Coteaux de, 192
Sausenheim, 254
Sauternes and Barsac, 66–72, *Map* 48
   Classification, 68
   Serving of, 536
"Sauternes", Dry, 71
Sauvignon grape, 178, 180, 186, 216, 474, 645,

Sauvignon grape (cont.)
648, 651
wines, 186
Savagnin grape, 217
Savennières, 175, 192
Savigny-les-Beaune, 80, 103
Savoie, 66
Savuto, 358
Schallstadter Batzenberg, 313
Scharzhofberg, 308, 324
Schengen, 334
Scheurebe grape, see Samling 88
Schiava grape, 348
Schiller wine, 283
Schliengener Sonnenstück, 313
Schloss Böckelheim, 267, 325
Schloss Grafenegg, 429
Schlossabzug, 230
Schlossberg, 299
Schnapps, 628
Schwarzer Herrgott, 255
Schwebsingen, 334
Scotch Whisky, 564–580
    Blending of, 569
    Distillation of, 567
    Distilleries, 579
    Grain, 568
    Keeping and serving, 575
    Malt, 565
    Peat Reek, 566
    Proof Strength of, 572
Séchet, 91
Segacea Cabernet, 442
Sekt, 330
Semeillan, Cru, 41
Semillon grape, 16, 464, 472, 474, 509, 648, 651
Senancole, 622
Sercial grape, 514
        wine, 514
Serrig, 308
Serving of Wine, 533–540
Setubal, 418

Setubal with Periquita, 419
Sèvre et Maine, 170
Seyssel, 220
Sherry, 3–6, 361–378, Map 360
    Australian, 510
    Bottled, 375
    British, 531
    Canadian, 471
    Casks, 375
    Cyprus, 457
    Exports, 372
    Grape varieties, 363
    Serving of, 535
    Solera system, 365
    South African, 486
    Varieties of, 368
    Vineyards, 362
    Vintage of, 363
Sherry Cobbler, 634
Siaurac, 64
Sicily, 358
Sidecar, 663
Siegerrebe grape, 246
Sierre, 424
Sikes, 551
Sillery, 118
Silvaner grape, 348
        wine, 348
Simmern, Freiherr von, 322
Simone, Ch., 218
Siran, Ch., 29, 34, 39
"Sleepiness" in grapes, 226
Slivovitz, 627
Sloe Gin Liqueur, 627
Smith-Haut-Lafitte, Ch., 33, 49, 51
Soave, 349
Solera system, 365, 516
Solutré, 110
Sommelier, 534
Sonnenuhr, 300
Sonoma County, 647
Soutard, Ch., 34, 57, 59

South Africa, 481–496, *Map* 480
  Brandy, 495
  Dessert wines, 485
  Geography, 484
  Port types, 486
  Red wines, 488
  Sherry types, 486
  Sparkling wines, 493
  Table wines, 488
  White wines, 490
  Wines available in U.K., 494
South Australia, 506
Spain, 361–388, *Map* 382
  Sherry (Jerez), 361–378
  Table wines, 379–388
Sparkling Hock, 331
Sparkling Mosel, 331
Sparkling wines, 331, 337, 345,
    435, 446, 472, 493
Spätburgunder grape, 281, 318
Spätlese, 226, 230, 231, 276, 429
Spirit Still, 567
Spirits, 547–634
  Fashion in, 549
  Manufacture of, 548
  Origin of, 547
  Proof, 551
  Stills, 548, 549, 567
Squinzano, 357
Stadtbredimus, 335
Steeg, 286
Steigerwälder, 317
Stein grape, 485, 486, 488, 49
    wines, 315, 317
Steinbach, 317
Steinberger, 228, 276, 320
Steiner Hund, 428
Steinkopfer, 314
Stellenbosch, 485, 486, 487, 488, 49C. 4ː I
Stinger, 663
Storage of wine, 533
Stout, 672

Strega, 625
Stuttgart, 312
Styria, 429
Suau, Ch., 69
Suchots, Les, 98
Suduiraut, Ch., 68, 70
Swan Hill, 506
Switzerland, 421–425, *Map* 422
Sylikou, 459
Sylvaner grape, 202, 206, 242, 250, 260,
    306, 310, 315, 318, 424, 428, 471
Sylvaner wine, 206, 439, 471
Syrah (Shiraz) grape, 142, 145, 147, 153,
    154, 165, 166, 220, 488, 509
Szamorodni, 433

T

Tâche, La, 97
Taillefer, Ch., 64
Talbot, Ch., 26, 28, 32, 40
Talence, 49, 51, 52
Tarragona, 384
Tart, Clos de, 94
Tauber, 317
Taurasi, 355
Tauzinat-l'Hermitage, Ch., 60
Tavannes, Clos de, 107
Tavel, 160, 167
Tayac, Ch., 66
Terlano, 348
Teroldego, 348
Terrefort, Ch. de, 66
Terret Noir grape, 153
Terte, Ch., 27, 39
Terte-Daugay, Ch., 57, 61
Testeron, Ch. du, 41
Teurons, Les, 102
Teyssier, Ch., 61
Teysson, 64
Theurons, Les, 102
Thivin, Ch., 113
Thompson Seedless, 645

Thorey, Les, 98
Tia Maria, 628
Tiger Milk, 439
Tinta Carvalha grape, 415
Tinta Francesa grape, 397
Tinta Francisca grape, 397
Tinta Pinheira grape, 415
Tirnave, 442
Tirnave Perla, 442
Tirnave Riesling, 442
Tocai del Collio, 349
Tocai di S. Martino, 347
Tokaj-Hegyalja, 432
Tokay Aszu, 432, 436
    d'Alsace (Le Pinot Gris), 207
    Essence, 433
    Furmint, 434, 436
    Szamorodni, 433, 436
Torgiano, 353
Torres Vedras, 419
Toscano grape, 354
Tour Blanche, Ch. la, 68, 70
Tour Carnet, Ch. la, 27, 45
Tour-de-By, Ch. la, 46
Tour-de-Mons, Ch. la, 29, 32, 39
Tour-du-Breuil, Ch. la, 46
Tour du Mirail, Ch. la, 46
Tour-du-Pin-Figeac, Ch. la, 57
Tour-Figeac, Ch. la, 57
Tour-Gilet, Ch. la, 61
Tour-Haut-Brion, Ch. la, 33
Tour Marbuzet, La, 44
Tour-Martillac, Ch. la, 33
Tour Milon, Ch. la, 43
Tour-St.-Bonnet, Ch. la, 46
Touraine, 175–178, *Map* 168
Touraine, 192
  Amboise, 192
  Azay-le-Rideau, 193
  Coteaux de, 192
  Coteaux Mousseux, 192
  Croix de, 192 .

Croix de Mousseux, 192
  Mesland, 193
  Mousseux, 193
  Pétillant, 193
Tourigo-do-Dão grape, 415
Traben, 295, 300
Tracy, Ch. de, 187
Traisen am Rotonfels, 267
Traminer grape, 202, 208, 244, 310,
    313, 335, 337, 442, 509, 648
Traminer wine, 208, 244
  Austrian, 429
  Calif., 471
  Italian, 349
Trappistine, 622
Trarbach, 295, 300
Trebbiano grape, 347, 348, 349, 353, 354, 355,
    357
Trentino-Alto Adige, 348
Tresques, 162
Tressalier grape (Sacy), 217
Trifalter, 428
Trimoulet, Ch., 57
Trittenheim, 295, 304
Trnovo, 446
Trockenbeerenauslese, 226, 231, 243,
    251, 276, 320
Troeme, 91
Trois Moulins, Ch., 57
Trois Moulins Ch. des, 45
Tronquoy-Lalande, Ch., 44
Tropicana, 619
Troplong-Mondot, Ch., 34, 57, 59
Trotanoy, Ch., 32, 63
Trottevieille, Ch., 33, 55, 59
Trousseau grape, 217
Tsinandali, 467
Tuillac, 66
Tulbagh Valley, 485, 487
Tunisia, 477–479
Tuscnay, 351
Tzuica, 443

U

Ughetta grape, 347
Ugni Blanc grape, 153, 218, 464
Uisgue Beatha, 563, 581
Umbria, 353
Umweg, 317
Underberg German Bitters, 629
Ungezuckerter Wein, 230
Ungstein, 254, 255
United Kingdom Bartenders Guild, 655
Unterhaardt (Lower Haardt), 254
Unterturkheim, 312
Upper Haardt (Oberhaardt), 250
Urzig, 295, 297
U.S.A., 631–652
U.S.S.R., 465–468

V

Vaccarèse grape, 153, 154
Vacqueyras, 164
Vaillon, 91
Valais, 424
Valea Calugaresca, 442
Valencia, 385
Valgella, 347
Vallée de la Marne, 118
Valls, 384
Valmur, 89
Valpolicella, 349, 350
Valtellina Bianco, 347
Valwig, 294
Van der Hum, 626
Varnhalt, 317
Varnhalter Klingelberg, 314
          Klosterberg, 314
Vaucoupin, 91
Vaucrains, Les, 98
Vaud, 423
Vaudésir, 89
Vaulorent, 91

Vaupinent, 91
Velletri, 354
Venencia, 365
Veneto, 348
Ventoux, Côtes du, 163, 165
Verdelho grape, 514
          wine, 514
Verdello grape, 353
Verdicchio grape, 353
          wine, 353
Verdignan, Ch., 46
Vergisson, 110
Vermentino, 351
Vermouth, 517–526
    British, 532
    French, 519
    Italian, 524
    Storage of, 525
Vernaccia grape, 352
Vernaccia di San Gimignano, 352
Veroilles, Les, 94
Vertus, 118
Verveine du Velay, 622
Verzenay, 118
Verzey, 118
Veyrin, 41
Victoria, 506
Vieille Cure, La, 622, 625
Vienna, 429
Vieux-Castel-Robin, Ch., 61
Vieux Chateau Certan, 31, 63
Vignes-Franches, Les, 102
Vila Nova de Gaia, 400
Villafranca de Panades, 384
Villegeorges, Ch., 41
Villemaurine, Ch., 33, 57
Villenave d'Ornan, 51, 52
Vin Jaune, 217
Vin Nobile di Montepulciano, 352
Vinhos Verdes, 413, 419
Vino de la Tierra, 387
Vins de l'Orléanais, 193

Vins Délimités de Qualité Supérieur
    (VDQS),   165, 172, 178
Vins Gris,   173, 217
Vinsobres,   164
Vinzel,   423
Viognier grape,   142, 143, 153, 220
Vion,   146
Virgin,   386
Vodka,   609–612
Vodkatini,   663
Vollrads, Schloss,   278, 319, 324
    Classification,   322
Volnay,   80, 86, 104
Volnay Santenots,   104
Vosgros and Vogiras,   91
Vosne-Romanée,   80, 96
Vougeot Château de la Tour, Clos de,   96
Vougeot, Clos de,   80, 96
Vouvray,   177, 193
    Cremant,   177
    Mousseux,   177, 193
    Perlant,   177
    Pétillant,   177, 193
Vully,   423

                    W

Wachau,   428
Wachauer Schluck,   428
Wachenheim,   253, 255, 324
Wachstum,   230
Waikerie,   506
Waldböckelheim,   269
Waldhilbersheim,   265
Waldrach,   310
Waldulm,   313
Waldulmer Russhalte,   313
Walheim,   312
Walperzheimer,   282
Wasenweiler,   313
Wash Still,   567
Wasserbilling,   335

Watervale,   507
Wawern,   308
Wehlen,   295, 299, 324
Wehlener Sonnenuhr,   294, 324
Weiler,   269
Weinsberg,   312
Weinsheim,   267
Weisenheim,   254
Weiss-Clevner (Weissburgunder) grape,   202,
    335
Welland,   470
Wellenstein,   334
Welschriesling,   429
Weyher,   250
Whisky,   563–595
    American Whiskey,   591–595
        Manufacture of,   592
        Types of,   594
    Australian Whisky,   595
    Canadian Whisky,   587–590
        History of,   587
        Manufacture of,   589
        Types of,   588
    Irish Whiskey,   581–586
        Manufacture of,   582
        Whiskey Sour,   585
        Handshake,   586
        Leprechaun,   586
        Coffee,   586
    Scotch Whisky,   564–580
        Age,   573
        Blending,   569
        Bottling,   571
        Distillation,   567
        Distilleries,   579, 580
        Fermentation,   567
        Flavour,   576
        Grain Whisky,   568
        Immature,   574
        Keeping and Serving of,   575
        Malt Whisky,   565, 566, 579, 580
        Maturation,   568

Peat Reek, 566
Proof Strength, 572
Types of, 565
Whisky Mac, 633
White Diamond, 619
White Lady, 662
White Pinot wine, 472
Wiltingen, 308, 324
Windesheim, 265
Wine, 1–7
Cellar of One's Own, 693–699
Choice of, 535
Decanting, 536
Enjoyment of, 5
Fashions in, 4
Glasses, 537
In the U.K., 3
Names, 6
Proper use of, 7
Serving, 533–540
Storage, 533
Tasting, 541–546
Wine Cups, 667
Winingen, 293
Winkel, 278, 324
Wintrange, 334
Winzenheim, 265
Winzingen, 255
Worcester, 485, 495
Wormeldange, 335
Württemberg, 311, *Map* 316

Würzburg, 315, 317, 324
Würzburger Perle grape, 246
Würzburger Stein Sylvaner Trocken-
beerenauslese, 243

X

Xynisteri grape, 457

Y

Yalta, 467
Yecla, 386
Yeradjes, 456
Yerassa, 459
Ygreg, Ch., 71
Yon-Figeac, Ch., 57, 60
Yquem, Ch. d', 68, 69
Yugoslavia, 437–440, *Map* 438

Z

Zell (Mosel), 295, 296
Zell-Weierbach, 313
Zeller Schwarze Katz, 296
Zeltingen, 295, 298, 324
Ziegler, 253
Zinfandel, 645, 650
Zoopiyi, 459
Zwicker d'Alsace, 207
Zwingenberg, 314